INDEX OF "RELATED RESEARCH"

Financial Markets
and Institutions

FINANCIAL MARKETS AND INSTITUTIONS

Jeff Madura

Florida Atlantic University

West Publishing Company

Saint Paul   New York   Los Angeles   San Francisco

Artwork: Accurate Art
Composition: Parkwood Composition Service
Copyediting: Margaret Jarpey
Cover design: Peter Thiel
Cover photo: Koji Kitagawa, Four by Five

COPYRIGHT © 1989   By WEST PUBLISHING COMPANY
                     50 W. Kellogg Boulevard
                     P.O. Box 64526
                     St. Paul, MN 55164-1003

Printed in the United States of America
96 95 94 93 92 91 90 89   876543210
Library of Congress Cataloging-in-Publication Data

Madura, Jeff.
    Financial markets and institutions.

    Bibliography: p.
    Includes index.
    1. Financial institutions.   2. Capital market.
3. Money market.   I. Title.
HG173.M26 1989   332   88-26180
ISBN 0-314-46972-9

To My Parents

Contents

PART FOUR

Contents

xv

PART SIX

Contents

Contents

xxiii

Preface

Business news is increasingly dominated by events relating to financial markets and institutions. In the late 1980s, several related events occurred which have significantly changed the financial environment. These include:

■ the stock market crash of October 1987
■ the failure of several savings institutions
■ interstate expansion of all types of financial services
■ the expansion of financial services offered by financial institutions
■ increasing evidence of insider trading
■ the use of special techniques to hedge a security portfolio's risk (such as financial futures contracts)
■ the increasing international integration of financial markets
■ the popularity of leveraged buyouts and the use of junk bonds to finance them

This text provides a framework that can be used to understand how recent events have affected the financial environment. Each type of financial market is described with a focus on its utilization by financial institutions, its internationalization, and recent events that have affected it. Each type of financial institution is described with a focus on its regulatory aspects, management, use of financial markets, and performance.

This text presumes an understanding of basic corporate finance. It is suitable for both undergraduate and masters level courses in financial markets, financial institutions, or the combination of markets and institutions. Some masters level courses may attempt to maximize the comprehension level by assigning the more difficult questions and problems, as well as the projects in every chapter. In addition, selected articles summarized in the "Research" boxes (discussed shortly) and in the references could be assigned as required reading, as they help reinforce the concepts presented.

ORGANIZATION OF THE TEXT

This text is organized as follows. Part One (chapters 1 to 4) introduces the key financial markets and financial institutions, explains interest rate movements in the financial markets, and describes the impact that interest rates (and other factors) can have on security prices. Part Two (chapters 5 to 7) and Part Three (chapters 8 to 11) cover all the major financial markets, with each chapter focusing on a particular market. The integration of each market with other markets is stressed throughout these chapters. Part Four (chapters 12 to 14) describes the influence of government policies, and how financial markets react to expectations about these policies. Part Five (chapters 15 to 20) concentrates on commercial banking, while Part Six (chapters 21 to 27) covers all other types of financial institutions.

Numerous concepts relating to recent events and current trends in financial markets are discussed throughout the chapters, including:

- the impact of the stock market crash on financial institutions, default risk premiums, and the term structure of interest rates
- the measurement and use of duration
- the use of interest rate swaps and currency swaps by bond portfolio managers
- the impact of the monthly balance of trade deficit on exchange rate expectations and bond market reaction to the announcement
- the use of collateralized mortgage obligations (CMOs) and real estate mortgage investment conduits (REMICs) in the mortgage markets
- a methodology for testing market efficiency
- the use of portfolio insurance strategies to reduce risk
- empirical evidence on the relationship between the budget deficit and interest rates
- the integration between monetary and fiscal policies, and financial market reaction to policy announcements
- commercial bank issues, such as FDIC insurance pricing and government rescues of failing banks
- bank strategies for reducing exposure to the debt of less developed countries
- performance evaluation of savings institutions
- recent dilemmas confronting insurance companies, pension funds, and securities firms

Each chapter is self-contained so professors can use classroom time to focus on the more complex concepts and rely on the text to cover the other concepts. Chapters can be rearranged without a loss in continuity.

KEY FEATURES

The following features are contained in the text:

- Part openers introduce the chapters contained in each part and explain how they are integrated.
- "Point of Interest" inserts discuss how various techniques are used by practitioners and how specific events relate to financial theory.

- "Related Research" inserts summarize recent research conducted on the theories and concepts presented.
- Several comprehensive questions and/or problems are provided in all chapters.
- Projects are recommended to reinforce concepts and theories covered in each chapter.
- An Instructor's Manual/Test Bank and a set of transparency masters are also available.

ACKNOWLEDGMENTS

The motivation to write this textbook was primarily due to encouragement by E. Joe Nosari (Florida State University). Mark Thornton (Barnett Bank), Lynn Thornton (independent appraisal analyst), and Don Toland (Westinghouse Corporation) made my task easier. Michael Suerth (Interstate National Corporation), John M. Cheney (University of Central Florida), Robert Eisenbeis (University of North Carolina), Richard Fosberg (Florida Atlantic University), Thomas J. O'Brien (University of Connecticut), David F. Scott (University of Central Florida), and E. Theodore Veit (Rollins College) offered valuable suggestions on the text theme. Several professors helped to develop the text outline and offered suggestions on the coverage of concepts. They are acknowledged as follows in alphabetical order:

Henry C. F. Arnold
Seton Hall University

James C. Baker
Kent State University

Gerald Bierwag
University of Arizona—Tucson

Carol Billingham
Central Michigan University

Randy Billingsley
Virginia Polytechnic Institute and State University

Paul J. Bolster
Northeastern University

William Carner
University of Missouri—Columbia

Steven Dobson
University of Houston

Richard J. Dowen
Northern Illinois University

James Felton
University of Arkansas

Thomas A. Fetherston
Appalachian State University

Clifford L. Fry
University of Houston

Edward K. Gill
Boise State University

Owen Gregory
University of Illinois—Chicago

John Halloran
University of Notre Dame

Gerald A. Hanweck
George Mason University

Hildegard Hendrickson
Seattle University

Paul Hsueh
North Texas State University

John S. Jahera, Jr.
Auburn University

Mel Jameson
Louisiana State University

James B. Kehr
Miami University of Ohio

George Kutner
Marquette University

Robert Lamy
Virginia Polytechnic Institute and
State University

David J. Leahigh
Lehigh University

Morgan Lynge, Jr.
University of Illinois

Robert W. McLeod
University of Alabama

Charles Meiburg
University of Virginia

Neil Murphy
University of Connecticut

Dale Osborne
University of Texas—Dallas

Coleen Pantalone
Northeastern University

D. Anthony Plath
University of North Carolina—
Charlotte

Rose Prasad
Central Michigan University

Alan Reichert
Illinois State University

Lawrence C. Rose
San Jose State University

Jack Rubens
Cleveland State University

Robert Schweitzer
University of Delaware

Ahmad Sorhabian
California State Polytechnic
University—Pomona

S. R. Stansell
University of Mississippi

Geraldo M. Vasconcellos
Lehigh University

Colin Young
Bentley College

This text also benefited from the research departments of several Federal Reserve district banks, the Federal National Mortgage Association, the National Credit Union Administration, the U.S. League of Savings Institutions, the American Council of Life Insurance, and the Investment Company Institute. I especially wish to thank the Chicago Mercantile Exchange for their research reports on financial market instruments.

I also wish to thank Raymonde Toland for her typing assistance. In addition, the assistance of Gilda Mann, Judy Ryder, and Lillian Schacter on various tasks is also greatly appreciated.

Editors Esther Craig and Richard Fenton at West Publishing Company were helpful in all stages of the book writing process. A special thanks is due to the assistant production editor, Laura Mezner Nelson, for her efforts to assure a quality final product.

Finally, I wish to thank my parents, Arthur and Irene Madura, and my wife, Mary, for their moral support. Without their influence, this textbook would not exist.

Overview of the Financial Environment

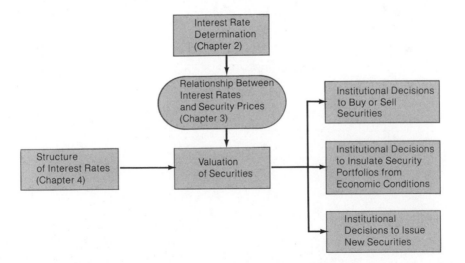

The chapters in Part One focus on the flow of funds across financial markets, interest rates, and security prices. Chapter 1 introduces the key financial markets and the financial institutions that participate in those markets. Chapter 2 explains how changes in the flow of funds affects interest rates. Chapter 3 explains how interest rate movements influence security prices. Chapter 4 identifies factors other than interest rates that influence security prices. Participants in financial markets use this information to value securities and make investment decisions.

Role of Financial Institutions and Markets

FINANCIAL MARKETS AND INSTITUTIONS IN PERSPECTIVE

In recent years, the following events have occurred within financial markets:

■ In 1982, less developed countries claimed that they were unable to repay their existing loans. Large banks were devastated by this so-called international debt crisis and continue to feel the impact to this day.

■ Continental Illinois Bank and several large Texas banks experienced severe financial problems in the 1980s and had to be rescued by regulators to avoid failure.

■ Regulatory provisions allowed commercial banks more freedom regarding interest rates offered on deposits, types of deposits offered, and types of services offered. In addition, banks were able to enter new geographical areas that were previously off limits.

■ On October 19, 1987, a stock market crash occurred, in which stock prices declined on average by a greater percentage than any other day in history (including the 1929 crash). Many stocks declined by more than 20 percent, causing the market value of stock portfolios at financial institutions to decline by a similar amount.

■ The investment environment was plagued with high volatility of security prices and evidence of the illegal use of insider information.

■ How would the performance of financial institutions be affected by the events cited above?

■ How have regulations changed in financial markets?

■ How have managerial techniques changed to deal with the increased volatility of stocks, bonds, and other instruments in the financial markets?

These broad issues are addressed throughout the text. This chapter introduces the key financial markets and the financial institutions that participate in them.

OUTLINE

Financial markets allow for the exchange of financial assets such as stocks and bonds. Financial institutions serve as financial intermediaries in financial markets by facilitating the flow of funds from individuals, corporations, or governments with excess funds to those with deficient funds. A variety of such institutions has been created to satisfy the types of financial intermediation desired. In recent years, their products and services offered have changed dramatically, affecting not only those who utilize the financial system, but also those that service it.

This chapter first provides a background on financial markets and then describes the most important financial institutions participating in them. Finally, it offers a brief preview of all chapters in this text.

FINANCIAL MARKET CHARACTERISTICS

Some of the key characteristics of financial markets are

- Participation of surplus and deficit units
- Role of primary and secondary markets
- Role of money and capital markets
- Role of organized and over-the-counter markets

Participation of Surplus and Deficit Units

The main participants in financial market transactions are households, businesses (including financial institutions), and governments that purchase or sell financial assets. Those participants that provide funds are called **surplus units,** while participants that enter financial markets to obtain funds are called **deficit units.** Some households, businesses, and state and local governments act as surplus units while others act as deficit units. The federal government commonly acts as a deficit unit. The amount of funds raised by various nonfinancial sectors is illustrated in Exhibit 1.1. The amount of

EXHIBIT 1.1   Net Funds Raised Annually by Nonfinancial Sectors

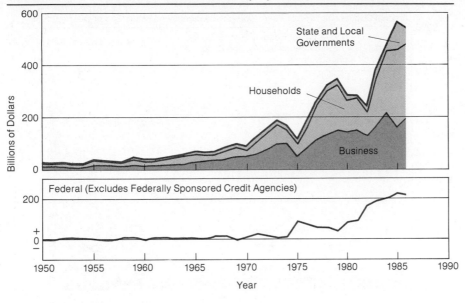

SOURCE: *1987 Federal Reserve Chart Book.*

funds raised by all sectors has increased over time, especially for households. Notice that household and business borrowing declined during the 1973–74 and 1982 recessions.

Exhibit 1.1 also shows a large increase in net funds raised by the U.S. federal government from the mid 1970s throughout the 1980s. The U.S. Treasury finances the budget deficit by issuing government ("Treasury") securities. Exhibit 1.2 identifies surplus units that provide financing to the U.S. government by purchasing Treasury securities. The main providers of funds are private domestic nonfinancial sectors (households and nonfinancial businesses) as well as commercial banks and other financial institutions. Foreign investors also commonly invest in U.S. Treasury securities, and so does the Federal Reserve System. The Fed plays a major role in the financial markets because it controls the U.S. money supply and participates in the regulation of depository institutions.

Many participants in the financial markets simultaneously act as surplus and deficit units. For example, a business may sell new securities and use some of the proceeds to establish a checking account. Thus, funds are obtained from one type of financial market and used in another.

Role of Primary and Secondary Markets

New securities are issued in the **primary markets,** while existing securities are resold in the **secondary markets.** Primary market transactions provide funds to the initial issuer of securities; secondary market transactions do not. Some securities have a more active secondary market and are therefore more marketable than others. This is an important feature for financial market participants to know about if they plan to sell their security holdings

EXHIBIT 1.2 Ownership of U.S. Government Securities

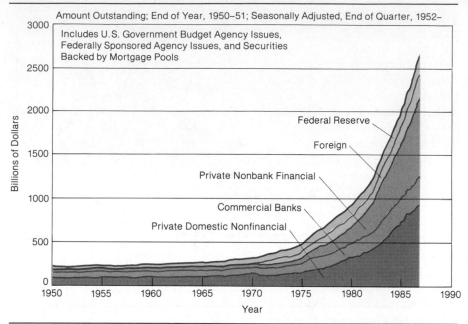

Amount Outstanding; End of Year, 1950–51; Seasonally Adjusted, End of Quarter, 1952–

Includes U.S. Government Budget Agency Issues, Federally Sponsored Agency Issues, and Securities Backed by Mortgage Pools

Federal Reserve
Foreign
Private Nonbank Financial
Commercial Banks
Private Domestic Nonfinancial

SOURCE: *1987 Federal Reserve Chart Book.*

prior to maturity. The issuance of new corporate stock or new Treasury securities represents a primary market transaction, while the sale of existing corporate stock or Treasury security holdings by any businesses or individuals represents a secondary market transaction.

Role of Money and Capital Markets

Financial markets can also be distinguished by the maturity of the securities traded. Securities with a maturity of one year or less are called **money market securities** and are traded in **money markets.** Securities with a maturity of more than one year are called **capital market securities** and are traded in **capital markets.** Common stocks are classified as capital market securities, since they have no defined maturity. Money market securities generally have a higher degree of **liquidity** (can be liquidated easily without a loss of value). However, capital market securities are typically expected to generate a higher annualized return to investors.

Role of Organized and Over-the-Counter Markets

Some secondary market transactions occur at an **organized exchange,** which is a visible marketplace for secondary market transactions. The New York Stock Exchange and American Stock Exchange are organized exchanges for secondary stock market transactions. Other financial market transactions occur in the *over-the-counter (OTC) market,* which is a telecommunications network.

FINANCIAL MARKET EFFICIENCY

When particular securities are perceived to be undervalued by the market, their prices increase in response to demand. Overvalued securities are sold by investors, and their prices decrease. Because securities have market-determined prices, their favorable or unfavorable characteristics as perceived by the market are reflected in their prices. When security prices fully reflect all available information, the markets for these securities are said to be *efficient*. When markets are *inefficient*, investors can use available information ignored by the market in order to earn abnormally high returns on their investments.

Even if markets are efficient, this does not imply that individual or institutional investors should ignore the various investment instruments available. Investors differ with respect to the default risk they are willing to incur, their desired liquidity, and their tax status, making some types of securities preferable to some investors but not to others.

Some securities that are not as safe and liquid as desired may still be considered if the potential return is sufficiently high. Investors normally attempt to balance the objective of high return with their particular preference for low default risk and adequate liquidity. As mentioned, when financial markets are efficient, any relevant information pertaining to risk will be reflected in the prices of securities.

SECURITIES TRADED IN FINANCIAL MARKETS

A wide variety of securities is traded in financial markets, but all can be classified as either equity or debt securities. **Equity securities** (common stock and preferred stock) represent ownership in a business. **Debt securities** represent IOUs, so investors who purchase these securities are creditors. While equity securities typically have no maturity, debt securities have maturities ranging from one day to twenty years or longer. Exhibit 1.3 identifies some of the more commonly traded securities. They will be discussed in more detail in later chapters.

FINANCIAL MARKET REGULATION

Securities markets are regulated in various ways. Many regulations were enacted in response to fraudulent practices prior to the Great Depression. The Securities Act of 1933, for example, was intended to assure complete disclosure of relevant financial information on publicly offered securities and prevent fraudulent practices in selling these securities. The Securities Exchange Act of 1934 extended the disclosure requirements to secondary market issues. It also declared a variety of deceptive practices illegal, such as misleading financial statements and trading strategies designed to manipulate the market price. In addition, it established the Securities and Exchange Commission (SEC) to oversee the securities markets, and the SEC has implemented additional laws over time. Securities laws do not prevent investors from making poor investment decisions but only attempt to assure full disclosure of information and thus protect against fraud.

EXHIBIT 1.3   Summary of Popular Securities

Money Market Securities	Issued by	Common Investors	Common Maturities	Secondary Market Activity
Treasury bills	Federal government	Households and firms	13 weeks, 26 weeks, 1 year	High
Retail CDs	Banks and savings institutions	Households	7 days to 5 years	Nonexistent
NCDs	Large banks and savings institutions	Firms	2 weeks to 1 year	Low
Commercial paper	Bank holding companies, finance companies, and other companies	Firms	1 day to 270 days	Low
Eurodollar deposits	Banks located outside the U.S.	Firms and governments	1 day to 1 year	Nonexistent
Banker's acceptances	Banks (exporting firms can sell the acceptances at a discount in order to obtain funds)	Firms	30 days to 270 days	High
Federal funds	Depository institutions	Depository institutions	1 day to 7 days	Nonexistent
Repurchase agreements	Nonfinancial firms and financial institutions	Nonfinancial firms and financial institutions	1 day to 15 days	Nonexistent
Capital Market Securities				
Treasury notes and bonds	Federal government	Households and firms	3 to 30 years	High
Municipal bonds	State and local governments	Households and firms	10 to 30 years	Moderate
Corporate bonds	Firms	Households and firms	10 to 30 years	Moderate
Equity securities	Firms	Households and firms	No maturity	High (for stocks of large firms)

In addition to the markets themselves, financial institutions participating in these markets are also regulated. Some regulations apply to all financial institutions while others are applicable only to a specific type. Details on regulations are provided throughout the text.

INTERNATIONAL

ASPECTS

INTERNATIONAL INTEGRATION OF FINANCIAL MARKETS

Until recently, certain barriers in foreign securities markets have historically limited international security transactions. One barrier was a lack of information about the foreign companies represented by the securities and the tax liability applicable to income earned from these transactions. Another was the excessive cost of executing international transactions. Information on foreign companies is now more accessible, and some financial institutions have created various opportunities for investors to invest in foreign securities without incurring excessive transaction costs. Consequently, the volume of international security transactions has greatly increased, causing these markets to become highly integrated.

Because of these more integrated markets, U.S. market movements may have a greater impact on foreign market movements, and vice versa. Since interest rates are influenced by the supply and demand for available funds, they are now more susceptible to foreign lending or borrowing activities. As an example, the U.S. financial markets have become a popular choice for foreign investment. U.S. interest rates would likely have been higher during the mid and late 1980s without this foreign inflow of funds. Yet now they are more susceptible to potential withdrawal of foreign funds.

ROLE OF FINANCIAL INSTITUTIONS IN FINANCIAL MARKETS

If financial markets were *perfect*, all information about any securities for sale in primary and secondary markets would be continuously and freely available to investors (including the creditworthiness of the security issuer). In addition, all information identifying investors interested in purchasing securities as well as investors planning to sell securities would be freely available. Furthermore, all securities for sale could be broken down (or *unbundled)* into any size desired by investors, and security transaction costs would be nonexistent. Under these conditions, financial intermediaries would not be necessary.

Because markets are *imperfect*, security buyers and sellers do not have full access to information and cannot always break down securities to the precise size they desire. Financial intermediaries are needed to resolve the problems caused by market imperfections. They receive requests from surplus and deficit units on what securities are to be purchased or sold, and they use this information to match up buyers and sellers of securities. Because the amount of a specific security to be sold will not always equal the amount desired by investors, financial intermediaries sometimes unbundle the securities by spreading them across several investors until the entire amount is sold. Without financial intermediaries, the information and transaction costs of financial market transactions would be excessive.

Functions of Depository Institutions

A major type of financial intermediary is the depository institution, which accepts deposits from surplus units and provides credit to deficit units through loans and purchases of securities. Depository institutions are popular financial institutions for the following reasons. First, they offer deposit accounts that can accommodate the amount and liquidity characteristics desired by most surplus units. Second, they repackage funds received from deposits to provide loans of the size and maturity desired by deficit units. Third, depository institutions accept the risk on loans provided. They have more expertise than individual surplus units to evaluate the credit-worthiness of deficit units. In addition, they diversify their loans among numerous deficit units and can absorb defaulted loans better than individual surplus units could.

To appreciate these advantages, consider the flow of funds from surplus units to deficit units if depository institutions did not exist. Each surplus unit would have to identify a deficit unit desiring to borrow the precise amount of funds available, for the precise time period in which funds would be available. Furthermore, each surplus unit would have to perform the credit evaluation and incur the risk of default. Under these conditions, many surplus units would likely hold their funds rather than channel them to deficit units. Thus, the flow of funds from surplus units to deficit units would be disrupted.

When a depository institution offers a loan, it is acting as a creditor, just as if it had purchased a security. Yet, the more personalized loan agreement is less marketable in the secondary market than a security, because detailed loan provisions on a loan can differ significantly among loans. Any potential investors would need to review all provisions before purchasing loans in the secondary market.

A more specific description of each depository institution's role in the financial markets follows.

COMMERCIAL BANKS. In aggregate, commercial banks are the most dominant financial institution. They serve surplus units by offering a wide variety of deposit accounts, and they transfer deposited funds to deficit units by providing direct loans or purchasing securities. Commercial banks serve both the private and public sectors, as their deposit and lending services are utilized by households, businesses, and government agencies.

SAVINGS INSTITUTIONS. Like commercial banks, savings and loan associations (S&Ls) offer deposit accounts to surplus units and then channel these deposits to deficit units. However, S&Ls have concentrated on residential mortgage loans, while commercial banks have concentrated on commercial loans. This difference in the allocation of funds has caused the performance of commercial banks and S&Ls to differ significantly over time. Recent deregulatory provisions, though, have permitted S&Ls more flexibility as to how they allocate their funds, causing their functions to become more similar to those of commercial banks. While S&Ls can be stock-owned, most are mutual (depositor-owned).

Savings banks are similar to savings and loan associations, except that they have more diversified uses of funds. However, the difference in uses of funds has narrowed over time. Like S&Ls, most savings banks are mutual.

CREDIT UNIONS. Credit unions differ from commercial banks and savings institutions in that (1) they are nonprofit, and (2) they restrict their business to the credit union members, who share a common bond (such as a common employer or union). Because of the common bond characteristic, credit unions tend to be much smaller than other depository institutions.

Functions of Nondepository Financial Institutions

Some financial institutions generate funds from sources other than deposits but also play a major role in financial intermediation. These institutions are briefly described here.

FINANCE COMPANIES. Most finance companies obtain funds by issuing securities, then lend the funds to consumers and small businesses. The functions of finance companies overlap the functions of depository institutions. Yet, each type of institution concentrates on a particular segment of the financial markets, as explained in the chapters devoted to these institutions.

MUTUAL FUNDS. Mutual funds sell shares to surplus units and use the funds received to purchase a portfolio of securities. Some mutual funds concentrate their investment in capital market securities such as stocks or bonds. Others known as *money market mutual funds*, concentrate in money market securities. The minimum denomination of the types of securities purchased by mutual funds is typically greater than the savings of an individual surplus unit. By purchasing shares of mutual funds and money market mutual funds, small savers are able to invest in a diversified portfolio of securities with a relatively small amount of funds.

SECURITIES FIRMS. Securities firms provide a wide variety of functions in financial markets. Some securities firms use their information resources to act as a *broker*, executing securities transactions between two parties. Many financial transactions are standardized to a degree. For example, stock transactions are normally in multiples of 100 shares. The delivery procedure for each security transaction is also somewhat standard, in order to expedite the securities trading process.

Brokers charge a fee for their services that is normally reflected in the difference (or *spread*) between their **bid** and **ask** quotes. The mark-up as a percentage of the transaction amount will likely be greater for less common transactions, as more time is needed to match up buyers and sellers. It will also likely be greater for transactions of relatively small amounts in order to provide adequate compensation for the time involved in executing the transaction.

Some securities firms place newly issued securities for corporations—a task that differs from traditional brokerage activities because it involves the primary market. Securities firms commonly **underwrite** the securities, meaning they guarantee the issuer a specific price for the securities to be placed.

Furthermore, securities firms often act as **dealers,** making a market in specific securities by adjusting their inventory of securities. While a broker's income is mostly based on the mark-up, the dealer's income is influenced by the performance of the security portfolio maintained. Some dealers also provide brokerage services and therefore earn income from both types of activities.

Certain financial institutions represent both securities firms and mutual funds. For example, Merrill Lynch provides brokerage services, underwrites securities, acts as a dealer for securities, and manages various mutual funds.

PENSION FUNDS. Many corporations and government agencies offer pension plans to their employees in which funds are periodically contributed by the employees, their employers, or both. The funds contributed are invested in securities until they are withdrawn (upon retirement) by the employees. Investments by pension funds provide financing for deficit units.

INSURANCE COMPANIES. Insurance companies receive premiums in exchange for insurance policies payable upon death, illness, or accidents and use the funds to purchase a variety of securities. In this way, they finance the needs of deficit units.

COMPARISON OF FINANCIAL INSTITUTION SIZE AND BALANCE SHEET COMPOSITION

Exhibit 1.4 shows the total assets of each type of financial institution as of 1970 and 1987. Note the dominance of commercial banks in 1970 and in 1987. The relative importance of various financial institutions has changed considerably over time. However, while their aggregate assets as a proportion of total financial institution assets have decreased, commercial banks are still much larger than other types of financial institutions.

Exhibit 1.5 summarizes the main sources and uses of funds for each type of financial institution. Households with savings are served by the depository institutions. Households with deficient funds are served by depository institutions and finance companies. Large corporations and governments that issue securities obtain financing from all types of financial institutions.

EXHIBIT 1.4 Total Assets of Financial Institutions

	1970		1987[a]	
	Amount (in Billions of Dollars)	Percent of Total[b]	Amount (in Billions of Dollars)	Percent of Total[b]
Commercial banks	$ 576.2	43.0%	$2,730.4	35.0%
Savings and loan associations	176.2	13.1	949.1	12.2
Savings banks	79.0	5.9	244.8	3.1
Life insurance companies	207.3	15.5	995.6	12.8
Private pension funds	110.4	8.2	1,295.1	16.6
State & local pension funds	60.3	4.5	397.2	5.1
Finance companies	64.0	4.8	371.5	4.8
Investment companies (excl. money market funds)	47.6	3.6	424.2	5.4
Money market funds			228.3	2.9
Credit unions	18.0	1.3	160.6	2.1
	$1,339.0	100.0	$7,796.8	100.0

a Preliminary estimates

b Because the estimated assets are drawn from a variety of sources with different dates, the percentages shown here are not perfectly accurate.

SOURCE: *Mutual Fund Fact Book*, 1987; *Federal Reserve Bulletin*, 1988; and *New England Economic Review*, Federal Reserve Bank of Boston, (November–December 1987), 4.

Impact of the Stock Market Crash of October 1987 on Financial Institutions

Due to their different characteristics, financial institutions react differently to any given economic event. However, all were adversely affected by the stock market crash of October 1987. The market value of stock portfolios managed by insurance companies and pension funds declined substantially as a result of the crash. The value of most stock mutual funds declined. However, some of the securities firms that manage these funds were not as severely affected because the investors shifted funds from stocks into bonds and money market securities. Nevertheless, investment banking activity declined overall because the low market prices of stock discouraged corporations from issuing new stock. The stock market crash even affected those depository institutions that did not maintain stock portfolios. It generated a pessimistic outlook on the economy that led to a decline in the demand for loans and a higher percentage of loan defaults, causing a consequent decline in stock prices of depository institutions.

Until recently, the business activities of the various types of financial institutions were for the most part clearly delineated. Today, however, many are offering a greater variety of products and services to diversify their business. As a consequence, their services overlap more. Since there are different regulatory agencies for different types of financial institutions, coordination among these regulators is important, but it is difficult to maintain. While they are considering requests by some financial institutions to offer various services, other financial institutions are exploiting regulatory loopholes and challenging the regulators to stop them. Meanwhile, still other financial institutions are attempting to enter geographic areas that were previously off limits.

Ideally, regulatory provisions would

■ Provide equitable laws for all types of financial institutions
■ Preserve the safety and soundness of the financial system
■ Allow for efficiency in the marketplace so that consumers are provided with low-cost services.

There may not be an ideal set of regulations that simultaneously satisfies all three objectives.

PREVIEW OF CHAPTERS

This textbook focuses on the flow of funds within the financial markets and the participation of financial institutions in these markets. Part One (Chapters 1 through 4) provides an overview of the financial environment, with a focus on how the flow of funds among markets can affect interest rates and securities prices. Part Two (Chapters 5 through 7) focuses on credit

Chapter 1

Role of Financial
Institutions and Markets

13

EXHIBIT 1.5 Summary of Institutional Sources and Uses of Funds

Financial Institutions	Main Sources of Funds	Main Uses of Funds
Commercial banks	Deposits from consumers, businesses, and government agencies	Purchases of government and corporate securities; loans to businesses and consumers
Savings institutions	Deposits from consumers, businesses, and government agencies	Purchases of government and corporate securities; mortgages and other loans to consumers; some loans to businesses
Credit unions	Deposits from credit union members	Loans to credit union members
Finance companies	Securities sold to consumers and businesses	Loans to consumers and businesses
Mutual funds	Shares sold to consumers, businesses, and government agencies	Purchases of long-term government and corporate securities
Money market funds	Shares sold to consumers, businesses, and government agencies	Purchases of short-term government and corporate securities
Pension funds	Employer/employee contributions	Purchases of long-term government and corporate securities
Insurance companies	Insurance premiums and earnings from investments	Purchases of long-term government and corporate securities

markets, with separate chapters devoted to money markets, bond markets, and mortgage markets. Part Three (Chapters 8 through 11) focuses on other financial markets, with separate chapters devoted to stock, futures, options, and foreign exchange markets. Part Four (Chapters 12 through 14) covers the federal government's influence on financial markets. This section explains how federal government policies can affect economic conditions and how financial market participants develop investment strategies in response to those policies.

Part Five (Chapters 15 through 20) focuses on the commercial banking industry, with special emphasis on sources and uses of funds, regulatory issues, risk management, and performance. Part Six (Chapters 21 through 27) devotes a chapter to each type of non-bank financial institution, focusing on their common sources and uses of funds, unique regulatory aspects, recent performance, and managerial strategies. Recent changes in regulations are also summarized along with their potential impact on future performance.

SUMMARY

Financial institutions allow funds to flow efficiently between surplus and deficit units. Depository institutions are especially valuable for this service. They make the flow of funds more efficient in the following ways:

1. They have greater access to information on possible sources and uses of funds.
2. They are more capable of assessing creditworthiness for loans provided.
3. They can repackage the deposited funds received in sizes and maturities desired by borrowers.
4. They are sufficiently large to diversify their loans and thus reduce the impact of loan defaults.

Because of regulatory provisions, each type of financial institution offers its own set of services. Consequently, various types of financial institutions are necessary to accommodate the diverse needs of surplus and deficit units. While all types of financial institutions have been given more flexibility to offer new services lately, some regulations continue to prohibit each type of financial institution from particular product markets. Therefore, it is important to recognize differences in the sources and uses of funds, management, and regulatory aspects of each type of financial institution.

KEY TERMS

bid

capital markets

capital market securities

dealers

debt securities

deficit units

equity securities

liquidity

money markets

money market securities

organized exchange

primary markets

secondary markets

surplus units

underwrite

QUESTIONS

1.1. Explain the meaning of surplus units and deficits units. Provide an example of each.

1.2. Distinguish between primary and secondary markets.

1.3. Distinguish between money and capital markets.

1.4. Distinguish between perfect and imperfect security markets.

1.5. Explain why the existence of imperfect markets creates a need for financial institutions.

1.6. Explain the meaning of efficient markets. Why might we expect markets to be efficient most of the time?

1.7. In recent years, several securities firms have been guilty of using inside information when purchasing securities, thereby achieving returns well above the norm (even when accounting for risk). Does this suggest that the security markets are not efficient? Explain.

1.8. What was the purpose of the Securities Act of 1933? What was the purpose of the Securities Exchange Act of 1934? Do these laws prevent investors from making poor investment decisions? Explain.

1.9. If barriers to international securities markets are reduced, will a country's interest rate be more or less susceptible to foreign lending or borrowing activities? Explain.

1.10. In what way is the international flow of funds used to explain the declining interest rates in the United States during the mid 1980s?

1.11. Distinguish between the functions of a broker and a dealer, and explain how each is compensated.

1.12. Why is it necessary for securities to be somewhat standardized?

1.13. What are the functions of securities firms?

1.14. Explain why some financial flows of funds cannot occur through the sale of standardized securities.

1.15. If securities were not standardized, how would this affect the volume of financial transactions conducted by brokers?

1.16. Commercial banks use some funds to purchase securities and other funds to make loans. Why are the securities more marketable in the secondary market than loans?

1.17. How have the asset compositions of savings and loan associations differed from commercial banks? Explain why and how this distinction may change over time.

1.18. With regard to the profit motive, how are credit unions different from other financial institutions?

1.19. Compare the main sources and uses of funds for finance companies, insurance companies, and pension funds.

1.20. What is the function of a mutual fund? Why are mutual funds popular among investors?

1.21. How does a money market mutual fund differ from a stock or bond mutual fund?

1.22. Classify the types of financial institutions mentioned in this chapter as either depository or nondepository. Explain the general difference between depository and nondepository institution sources of funds.

1.23. It is often stated that all types of financial institutions have begun to offer services that were previously offered only by certain types. Consequently, many financial institutions are becoming more similar in terms of their operations. Yet, the performance levels still differ significantly among types of financial institutions. Why?

1.24. Look in a recent business periodical for news about a recent financial transaction that involves two financial institutions. For this transaction, determine

    a. How each institution's balance sheet will be affected

    b. Whether either institution will receive immediate income from the transaction

    c. Who is the ultimate user of funds

    d. Who is the ultimate source of funds

1.25. Which types of financial institutions do you deal with? Explain whether you are acting as a surplus unit or a deficit unit in your relationship with each financial institution.

PROJECTS

1. OBTAINING INFORMATION ON FINANCIAL INSTITUTIONS

a. Throughout the semester various financial institutions will be discussed. Order an annual report from a (1) commercial bank, (2) savings and loan association, (3) finance company, and (4) life insurance company. These annual reports will allow you to relate the theory provided in related chapters to the particular financial institution of concern. In addition, your professor may assign projects on financial institutions (listed at the end of each chapter) that require an annual report. You should request the annual reports immediately so that they will arrive by the time you need them.

b. Order a prospectus for a stock mutual fund, a bond mutual fund, a money market mutual fund, and an international mutual fund. This information will reinforce the discussion on these types of funds.

2. TAKING POSITIONS IN INVESTMENT INSTRUMENTS

Throughout the semester a variety of investment instruments will be explained. By following the price of various investment instruments, you will more fully understand how prices respond to events that occur throughout the semester. Use the most recent issue of *The Wall Street Journal* to make the following investment decisions. (Near the end of the semester, you will be asked to close out your investment positions in order to determine your return or yield on each investment.) Write your decisions in your notebook. Exhibit A provides an outline you can use to fill in your notebook.

a. Look up the section, "New York Stock Exchange (NYSE) Stocks" (listed in the index on the front page of *The Wall Street Journal)*. Choose one stock that you would like to invest in. Write down the dividend and the closing stock price.

b. Look up the section, "American Stock Exchange (AMEX) Stocks" (listed in the index on the front page). Choose one stock that you would like to invest in. Write down the dividend and the closing price.

c. Look up the section, "NASDAQ National Market Issues" (listed as "NASDAQ OTC" in the index on the front page). Choose one stock that you would like to invest in. Write down the dividend and the closing price.

d. Look up the section, "Mutual Fund Quotations" (listed as "Mutual Funds" in the index on the front page). Choose one bond mutual fund (usually designated with the word "Bond" in the name of the fund). Write down the name of the fund. Write down the offer price (your purchase price) and the name of the company offering the fund (shown in bold letters).

e. Using the "Mutual Fund Quotations," choose one stock fund (often referred to as "Growth" or "Equity"). Write down the offer price and the name of the company offering the fund.

f. Using the "Mutual Fund Quotations," choose one international mutual fund (usually designated with "intl" or "foreign" within the name of the fund). Write down the offer price along with the name of the company offering the fund.

EXHIBIT A   Outline to follow for your notebook

a. NYSE Stock:

name of stock _____

purchase price of stock _____

dividend _____

b. AMEX Stock:

name of stock _____

purchase price of stock _____

dividend _____

c. NASDAQ Stock:

name of stock _____

purchase price of stock _____

dividend _____

d. BOND MUTUAL FUND:

name of company _____

name of specific mutual fund _____

offer (purchase) price _____

e. STOCK MUTUAL FUND:

name of company _____

name of specific mutual fund _____

offer (purchase) price _____

f. INTERNATIONAL FUND:

name of company _____

name of specific mutual fund _____

offer (purchase) price _____

g. CALL OPTION:

name of stock for call option purchased _____

strike price _____

expiration date (month) _____

premium paid per share _____

h. PUT OPTION:

name of stock for put option purchased _____

strike price _____

expiration date (month) _____

premium paid per share _____

i. FUTURES CONTRACTS:

financial futures contract purchased _____

settle (closing) price _____

expiration date (month) _____

g. Look up the section, "Listed Options," and choose a call option for a stock whose price you expect to rise, with an expiration date that is slightly beyond the end of your semester. The call option expiration dates for a given stock are in the third, fourth, and fifth columns. For a given expiration date, there may be more than one option, with each option specifying a particular strike price (see Column 2). Pick a strike price and write down the corresponding option premium quoted along with the expiration date and strike price, and stock of concern. Your professor may elaborate on this part in class.

h. Using the section, "Listed Options," choose a put option for a stock whose price you expect to decline, with the expiration date that is slightly beyond the end of your semester. The put option expiration dates for a given stock are in the sixth, seventh, and eighth columns. For a given expiration date, there may be more than one put option, with each option specifying a particular strike price (see Column 2). Pick a strike price and write down the corresponding option premium quoted, along with the expiration date, strike price, and stock of concern. Your professor may elaborate on this part in class.

i. Look up the section, "Futures Prices," which is on the same page as "Commodities" in *The Wall Street Journal*. Find the futures quotes on "Treasury Bonds, (CBT)," and on the "S&P 500 Index (CME)." If you believe that Treasury bond prices will rise by a greater percentage than stock prices in general over your investment horizon, you should purchase the Treasury Bond futures. Use a settlement month (in the first column under the heading) that is slightly beyond the end of your semester. Write down the "settle" price (in the fifth column) that corresponds with that month.

If you believe that stock prices will generally rise by a greater percentage than Treasury bond prices over your investment horizon, you should purchase the S&P 500 Index futures. Use a settlement month that is slightly beyond the end of your semester. Write down the "settle" price (in the fifth column) that corresponds with that month.

3. MEASURING YOUR INVESTMENT PERFORMANCE

Near the end of the semester (on a date specified by your professor), you will close out your investment positions. On the date you close out your positions, determine the existing prices of all the instruments you invested in. Using this information along with your purchase price, determine the return on each investment instrument. Use the following guidelines for calculating the returns on your investments.

a. The return on the stock can be determined as:

$$\frac{(\text{selling price} - \text{purchase price}) + (\text{dividend}/4)}{\text{purchase price}}$$

It is assumed here that one quarterly dividend is paid.

b. See Part a.

c. See Part a.

d. The return on the mutual fund can be determined as

$$\frac{\text{NAV} - \text{purchase price}}{\text{purchase price}}$$

where NAV represents net asset value. Some funds may offer shares as dividends, which would not be accounted for in this estimation of return. Yet, this computation can at least be used to assess the general performance of the fund over the semester. If the NAV is quoted as "N.L.," this means that the fund has no load fee, implying that the offer (purchase) price is the same as the net asset value.

If your fund does have a load fee, you may wish to calculate the return ignoring the fee, just to determine how the fund itself performed. Of course, the result would overstate your actual return on load funds because it ignores the load fee you would have paid.

e. See Part d.

f. See Part d.

g. If the existing price of the stock is above the strike price, the return on your options position can be determined as

$$\frac{\text{existing stock price} - \text{call option strike price} - \text{call option premium}}{\text{call option premium}}$$

If the existing price of the stock is below the strike price so that the option expires without being exercised, the return on the options position is −100 percent.

h. If the existing price of the stock is below the strike price, the return can be determined as

$$\frac{\text{put option strike price} - \text{existing stock price} - \text{put option premium}}{\text{put option premium}}$$

If the existing price of the stock is above the strike price so that the option is not exercised by the expiration date, the return on the put option position would be −100 percent.

i. Assuming that you sell the identical futures contract as the one you purchased at the beginning of the semester, the difference between the selling price and buying price represents the profit (or loss) per unit that will occur on the settlement date. The return could be determined as the profit (or loss) per unit as a percentage of the initial investment, where the initial investment represents a margin deposit. Assume your margin deposit is 50 percent of the buying price. Using this assumption, it is possible to lose more than 100 percent of your initial investment.

REFERENCES

Benston, George J., and Clifford W. Smith, Jr. "A Transaction Cost Approach to the Theory of Financial Intermediation." *Journal of Finance* (May 1976): 215–232.

Bryan, Lowell. "The Credit Bomb in Our Financial System." *Harvard Business Review* (January–February 1987): 45–51.

Davidson, Lawrence S., and Richard T. Froyen. "Monetary Policy and Stock Returns: Are Stock Markets Efficient?" *Review*, Federal Reserve Bank of St. Louis (March 1982): 3–12.

Fama, Eugene F., and Merton H. Miller. *The Theory of Finance*. New York: Holt, Rinehart & Winston, 1972.

Franke, Gunter. "Costless Signalling in Financial Markets." *Journal of Finance* (September 1987): 809–822.

Garbade, Kenneth. *Securities Markets*. New York: McGraw-Hill, 1982.

Gordon, Lawrence A., David F. Larcker, George E. Pinches. "Testing, for Market Efficiency." *Journal of Financial and Quantitative Analysis* (June 1980): 267–287.

Herring, Richard and Prashant Vankudre. "Growth Opportunities and Risk-Taking by Financial Intermediaries." *Journal of Finance* (July 1987): 583–600.

Hoskins, Lee. "Financial Reform at a Crossroads." *Economic Commentary*, Federal Reserve Bank of Cleveland, December 15, 1987.

Mullineaux, Donald J. "Efficient Markets, Interest Rates, and Monetary Policy." *Business Review*, Federal Reserve Bank of Philadelphia (May–June 1981): 3–10.

Pardee, Scott. "Internationalization of Financial Markets." *Economic Review*, Federal Reserve Bank of Kansas City (February 1987): 3–7.

Pyle, David H. "On the Theory of Financial Intermediation." *Journal of Finance* (June 1971): 737–747.

Van Horne, James C. *Financial Market Rates and Flows*. 2d ed. Englewood Cliffs, N.J.: Prentice-Hall, 1984.

Williamson, Stephen D. "Recent Developments in Modeling Financial Intermediation." *Quarterly Review*, Federal Reserve Bank of Minneapolis (Summer 1987): 19–29.

Determination of Interest Rates

INTEREST RATE DETERMINATION IN PERSPECTIVE

Two weeks after the stock market crash of October 19, 1987, *The Wall Street Journal* reported revised economic projections by several economists and analysts. Many of the economists and analysts reduced their forecast of interest rates. Some of the more commonly cited reasons were related to the potential impact of the crash on factors that affect interest rates:

■ the crash could reduce economic growth and even cause a recession
■ the dampening effect of the crash on the economy would also dampen inflationary pressures
■ the Federal Reserve would be more willing to use a loose credit policy to prevent a recession

On June 20, 1988, *The Wall Street Journal* reported fears in the financial markets that U.S. interest rates would rise in the near future. One reason for this fear was the consideration of Congress to impose a 5 percent withholding tax on interest paid to foreign investors. Expectations of higher inflation was also mentioned as a reason. Three days later, *The Wall Street Journal* reported that the dollar's value increased substantially against foreign currencies, which caused expectations of lower interest rates by financial market participants.

New information is constantly received by financial market participants which will affect their expectations about economic variables that influence interest rates. Because financial market participants make decisions based on interest rate expectations, they often rely on forecasts of economic conditions to develop interest rate projections.

■ How do the various factors just stated affect interest rates?
■ What other information could affect interest rate expectations on a daily basis?
■ Why are interest rate projections by experts sometimes inaccurate?

These and other related questions are addressed in this chapter.

OUTLINE

Interest rate movements affect the policies and performance of all types of financial institutions. For this reason, it is critical for managers of financial institutions to understand why interest rates change, how their movements affect performance, and how to manage according to anticipated movements.

While it is impossible to consistently and precisely forecast future interest rates, an attempt should be made to at least predict their general direction. To do this, one must understand what causes interest rate movements. This chapter explains the theory behind interest rate determination and identifies some of the more common factors affecting interest rate movements.

LOANABLE FUNDS THEORY

The **loanable funds theory,** commonly used to explain interest rate movements, suggests that the market interest rate is determined by the factors that control the supply of and demand for loanable funds.[1] The "demand for loanable funds" is a widely used phrase in financial markets pertaining to the borrowing activities of households, businesses, and governments. The common sectors that demand loanable funds are identified and described here. Then the sectors that supply loanable funds to the markets are described. Finally, the demand and supply concepts are integrated to explain interest rate movements.

Household Demand for Loanable Funds

Households commonly demand loanable funds to finance housing expenditures. In addition, they finance the consumption of automobiles and

1 An alternative theory for explaining interest rate movements, called *liquidity preference theory,* is described in the appendix. The loanable funds theory receives more attention in this text because of the focus on loanable funds of financial institutions and markets throughout the text.

household items, which results in installment debt. As the aggregate level of household income rises over time, installment debt does as well. The level of installment debt as a percentage of disposable income has been increasing since 1983. It is generally low in recessionary periods (such as 1974–75 and 1982).

If households could be surveyed at any given point in time to indicate the quantity of loanable funds they would demand at various interest rate levels, we would find an inverse relationship between the interest rate and the quantity of loanable funds demanded. This simply implies that at any point in time, households would demand a greater quantity of loanable funds at lower rates of interest. As an example, the quantity of loanable funds demanded increased significantly during recent periods when automobile dealers announced lower "incentive" interest rates.

A hypothetical household demand-for-loanable-funds schedule is shown in Exhibit 2.1. This schedule depicts the amount of funds that would be demanded at various possible interest rates for a given point in time. Various events can cause household borrowing preferences to change and therefore shift the demand schedule. For example, if tax rates on household income are expected to significantly decrease in the future, households might believe that they can more easily afford future loan repayments and thus be willing to borrow more funds. For any interest rate, the quantity of loanable funds demanded by households would be greater as a result of the tax law adjustment. This represents an outward shift in the demand schedule.

Business Demand for Loanable Funds

Businesses demand loanable funds to invest in fixed and short-term assets. The quantity of funds demanded by businesses depends on the number of business projects to be implemented. Businesses evaluate a project by comparing the present value of its cash flows to its initial outlay, as shown here:

$$NPV = -I + \sum_{t=1}^{n} \frac{CF_t}{(1 + i)^t}$$

EXHIBIT 2.1 Relationship between Interest Rates and Household Demand for Loanable Funds at a Given Point in Time

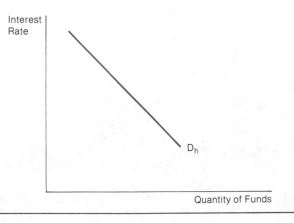

where NPV = net present value of project
I = initial outlay
CF_t = cash flow in period t
i = required rate of return on project

Projects with a positive net present value (NPV) are accepted, because the present value of their benefits outweighs the costs. The required return to implement any given project will be lower if interest rates are lower. Consequently, more projects will have positive NPVs, and a greater amount of financing is required. This implies that businesses will demand a greater quantity of loanable funds when interest rates are lower, as illustrated in Exhibit 2.2.

In addition to projects, businesses also invest in short-term assets (such as accounts receivable and inventory) in order to support ongoing operations. Any demand for funds resulting from this type of investment is positively related to the number of projects implemented and thus inversely related to the interest rate. The opportunity cost of investing in short-term assets is higher when interest rates are higher. Therefore, firms generally attempt to support ongoing operations with less funds during periods of high interest rates. This is another reason why a firm's total demand for loanable funds is inversely related to interest rates at any point in time. While the demand for loanable funds by some businesses may be more sensitive to interest rates than others, all businesses are likely to demand more funds if interest rates are lower at a given point in time.

The business demand-for-loanable-funds schedule can shift in reaction to any events that affect business borrowing preferences. For example, if economic conditions become more favorable, the expected cash flows on various proposed projects will increase. More proposed projects will have expected returns that exceed a particular required rate of return (sometimes called *hurdle rate*). There will be additional acceptable projects as a result of more favorable economic forecasts, causing an increased demand for loanable funds.

EXHIBIT 2.2 Relationship between Interest Rates and Business Demand for Loanable Funds

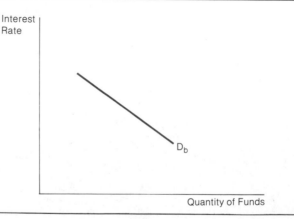

Government Demand for Loanable Funds

Whenever a government's planned expenditures cannot be completely covered by its incoming revenues from taxes and other sources, it demands loanable funds. Municipal (state and local) governments issue municipal bonds to obtain funds, while the federal government and its agencies issue Treasury securities and federal agency securities. These securities represent government debt. The trend in the federal debt level over time shows continual growth (Exhibit 2.3). The debt level as a percentage of annual gross national product (GNP) declined slightly during the late 1970s, but increased from 25 percent in 1980 to 42 percent in 1987.

Federal government expenditure and tax policies are generally thought to be independent of interest rates. Thus, the federal government demand for funds is said to be **interest-inelastic,** or insensitive to interest rates. However, municipal governments sometimes postpone proposed expenditures if the cost of financing is too high, implying that their demand for loanable funds is somewhat sensitive to interest rates.

Like the household and business demand, the government demand for loanable funds can shift in response to various events. For example, assume the federal government demand-for-loanable-funds schedule is D_{g1} in Exhibit 2.4. Assume that new bills were passed that caused a net increase in the deficit of $20 billion. The federal government demand for loanable funds would increase by that amount. The new demand schedule, D_{g2} in the exhibit, would shift inward if the government budget deficit were reduced.

Foreign Demand for Loanable Funds

The demand for loanable funds in a given market also includes foreign demand by foreign governments or corporations. For example, the British

EXHIBIT 2.3 Federal Government Debt Level over Time

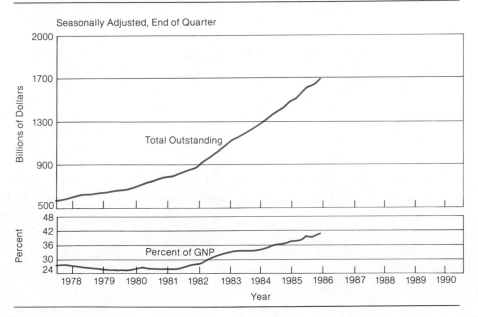

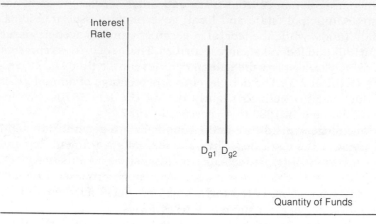

government may obtain financing by issuing British Treasury securities to U.S. investors, representing a British demand for U.S. funds. Because foreign financial transactions are becoming so common, they can have a significant impact on the demand for loanable funds in any given country. A foreign country's demand for U.S. funds is influenced by the differential between its interest rates and U.S. rates (along with other factors). Other things being equal, a larger quantity of U.S. funds would be demanded by foreign governments and corporations if their domestic interest rates were high relative to U.S. rates. Therefore, for a given set of foreign interest rates, the quantity of U.S. loanable funds demanded by foreign governments or firms will be inversely related to U.S. interest rates.

The foreign demand schedule can shift in response to economic conditions. For example, assume the original foreign demand schedule is D_{f1} in Exhibit 2.5. If foreign interest rates rise, foreign firms and governments

EXHIBIT 2.5   Impact of Increased Foreign Interest Rates on the Foreign
Demand for U.S. Loanable Funds

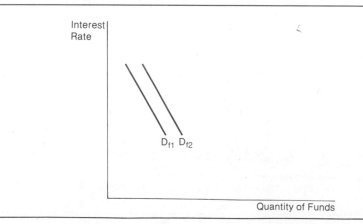

would likely increase their demand for U.S. funds, as represented by a shift from D_{f1} to D_{f2}.

The aggregate demand for loanable funds is the sum of the quantities demanded by the separate sectors at any given interest rate, as shown in Exhibit 2.6. Because most of these sectors are likely to demand a larger quantity of funds at lower interest rates (other things equal), the aggregate demand for loanable funds is inversely related to interest rates at any point in time. If the demand schedule of any sector should change, the aggregate demand schedule will be affected as well.

Supply of Loanable Funds

The "supply of loanable funds" is a commonly used term to represent funds provided to financial markets by savers. The household sector is the largest supplier, but loanable funds are also supplied by some government units that temporarily generate more tax revenues than they spend, or by some businesses whose cash inflows exceed outflows. Households as a group represent a net supplier of loanable funds, however, whereas governments and businesses are net demanders of loanable funds.

Suppliers of loanable funds are willing to supply more funds if the interest rate (reward for supplying funds) is higher, other things being equal (Exhibit 2.7). A supply of loanable funds exists even at a very low interest rate, since some households choose to postpone consumption until later years even when the reward (interest rate) for saving is low.

Foreign households, governments, and corporations commonly supply funds to their domestic markets by purchasing domestic securities. In addition, they have been a major creditor to the U.S. government by purchasing large amounts of Treasury securities. The large foreign supply of

EXHIBIT 2.6 Determination of the Aggregate Demand Schedule for Loanable Funds

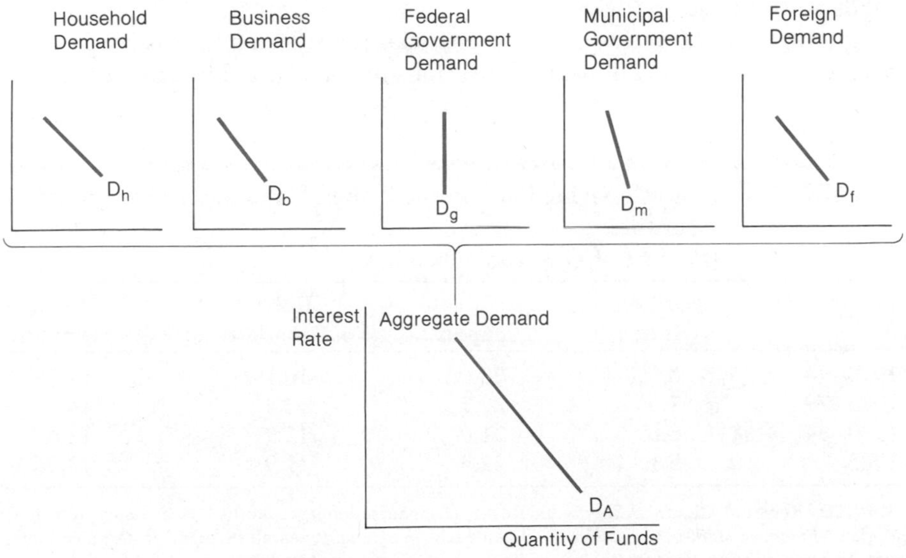

EXHIBIT 2.7 Aggregate-Supply-of-Loanable-Funds Schedule

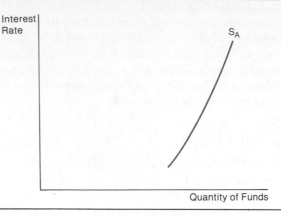

funds to the U.S. market is partially attributed to the high saving rates of foreign households. Exhibit 2.8 compares the personal saving rate of households in the United States to those of three major foreign countries. Percentages for the United Kingdom and West Germany are about twice the U.S. percentage and Japan's about four times.

A second reason for the large foreign supply of loanable funds to the United States is that U.S. interest rates are often relatively high in comparison to many foreign countries. Even if foreign savers do not directly supply loanable funds to the U.S., a portion of the funds they deposit in their local financial institutions will be channeled to the United States.

The supply of loanable funds in the United States is not only influenced by the behavior of savers but also by the monetary policy implemented by the Federal Reserve System. The Fed controls the amount of reserves held by depository institutions and can influence the amount of loanable funds that households, businesses, and governments can supply to the market. The precise manner by which the Fed can influence the supply of loanable funds is discussed in Chapter 12.

Note that the attention given to financial institutions in this section has been minimal. While financial institutions play a critical intermediary role

EXHIBIT 2.8 Personal Saving Rates in the United States and Other Industrial Countries
(Percent of Disposable Income)

	United States	Japan	United Kingdom	West Germany
1970–74	8.5%	20.6%	10.1%	14.9%
1975–79	7.5	22.7	12.4	14.2
1980–84	6.6	21.0	12.9	13.6
1985	5.1	22.5	11.9	13.0

SOURCE: Robert M. Giordano, "Myth and Reality of Japanese Influence on the U.S. Treasury Securities Market," *Financial Market Perspectives*, Goldman Sachs Economic Research (September–October 1986); and *Economic Review*, Federal Reserve of Kansas City, (February 1987): 13.

Part One

Overview of the
Financial Environment

in channeling funds, they do not represent the ultimate suppliers of funds. Any change in the financial institution's supply of funds results only from a change in habits by the ultimate suppliers—the households, businesses, or governments. If we included financial institutions as a supplier of funds, we would be double-counting the funds supplied.

The aggregate supply schedule of loanable funds represents the combination of all sector supply schedules along with the supply of funds provided by the Fed's monetary policy. If any one of these supply schedules is affected, the aggregate supply schedule will be affected as well.

The steep slope of the aggregate supply schedule in Exhibit 2.7 indicates that it is interest inelastic, or somewhat insensitive to interest rates.[2] The quantity of loanable funds demanded is normally expected to be more sensitive to interest rates than the quantity of loanable funds supplied.

Equilibrium Interest Rate

An understanding of equilibrium interest rates is necessary to assess how various events can affect interest rates. Because activities in financial institutions and markets revolve around interest rate projections, the concept of equilibrium interest rates is applicable to all remaining chapters of the text. It is presented first from an algebraic perspective and then from a graphical perspective. Following this presentation, several examples are offered to reinforce the concept.

ALGEBRAIC PRESENTATION OF INTEREST RATE EQUILIBRIUM. The equilibrium interest rate is that which equates the aggregate demand for funds with the aggregate supply of loanable funds. The aggregate demand for funds (D_A) can be written as

$$D_A = D_h + D_b + D_g + D_m + D_f$$

where D_h = gross household demand for loanable funds
D_b = gross business demand for loanable funds
D_g = gross federal government demand for loanable funds
D_m = gross municipal government demand for loanable funds
D_f = gross foreign demand for loanable funds

The aggregate supply of funds (S_A) can be written as

$$S_A = S_h + S_b + S_g + S_m + S_f$$

where S_h = gross household supply of loanable funds
S_b = gross business supply of loanable funds
S_g = gross federal government supply of loanable funds
S_m = gross municipal supply of loanable funds
S_f = gross foreign supply for loanable funds

In equilibrium, $D_A = S_A$. If the aggregate demand for loanable funds increases without a corresponding increase in aggregate supply, there will be a shortage of loanable funds. Interest rates will rise until an additional

2 There is not complete agreement about the interest elasticity of saving. Research by DeFina (listed in the references) summarizes previous studies that attempted to estimate this elasticity measure.

Chapter 2

Determination of
Interest Rates

supply of loanable funds is available to accommodate the excess demand. If the gross supply of loanable funds increases without a corresponding increase in gross demand, there will be a surplus of loanable funds. Interest rates will fall until the quantity of funds supplied no longer exceeds the quantity of funds demanded.

In many cases, both supply and demand for loanable funds are changing. Given an initial equilibrium situation, the equilibrium interest rate should rise when $D_A > S_A$ and fall when $D_A < S_A$.

GRAPHICAL PRESENTATION OF INTEREST RATE EQUILIBRIUM. When combining the aggregate demand and aggregate supply schedules of loanable funds (see Exhibits 2.6 and 2.7), it is possible to compare the total amount of funds that would be demanded to the total amount of funds that would be supplied at any particular interest rate. Exhibit 2.9 illustrates the combined demand and supply schedules. At the equilibrium interest rate of i_e, the supply of loanable funds is equal to the demand for loanable funds.

At any interest rate above i_e, there is a surplus of loanable funds. Some potential suppliers of funds would be unable to successfully supply their funds at the prevailing interest rate. Once the market interest rate is lowered to i_e, the quantity of funds supplied is sufficiently reduced and the quantity of funds demanded is sufficiently increased such that there is no longer a surplus of funds. When a disequilibrium situation exists, market forces should cause an adjustment in interest rates until equilibrium is achieved.

If the prevailing interest rate is below i_e, there will be a shortage of loanable funds. Borrowers will not be able to obtain all the funds that they desire at that rate. Due to the shortage of funds, the interest rate will increase, causing two reactions. First, more savers will enter the market to supply loanable funds, now that the reward (interest rate) is higher. Second, some potential borrowers will decide not to demand loanable funds at the higher interest rate. Once the interest rate rises to i_e, the quantity of loanable funds supplied has increased and quantity of loanable funds demanded has decreased to the extent that a shortage no longer exists. An equilibrium position is achieved once again.

EXHIBIT 2.9   Interest Rate Equilibrium

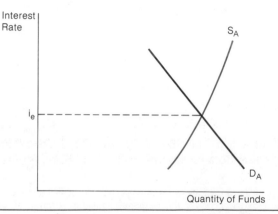

Changes in the Equilibrium Interest Rate

The equilibrium interest rate changes over time due to changes in the demand and supply schedules of loanable funds. Examples illustrating the adjustment in the equilibrium interest rate follow.

Assume that as a result of more optimistic economic projections, most businesses increase their planned expenditures for expansion, which translates into a greater amount of additional borrowing. The aggregate demand schedule would shift outward (to the right). The supply of loanable funds schedule may also shift, but it is more difficult to know how it should shift. It is possible that the increased expansion by businesses could lead to more income for construction crews, and so forth, who service the expansion. Thus, the quantity of savings—and therefore of loanable funds supplied at any possible interest rate—could increase, causing an outward shift in the supply schedule. Yet, there is no assurance that the volume of savings will truly increase. Even if a shift did occur, it would likely be of a smaller magnitude than the shift in the demand schedule.

In summary, the expected impact of the increased expansion by businesses is an outward shift in the demand schedule and no obvious change in the supply schedule (Exhibit 2.10). The shift in the aggregate demand schedule to D_{A2} in the exhibit causes an increase in the equilibrium interest rate to i_{e2}.

In reality, there are no published comprehensive schedules that measure the quantity of funds to be supplied or demanded at every possible interest rate. However, one could still assess the expected impact of a particular event without even knowing the specific numbers that correspond to these schedules. Any event that causes an outward shift in the demand schedule should force interest rates up (as long as the supply schedule is not forced out by an equal or greater degree). Though it is difficult to predict the precise change in the interest rate due to a particular event, an ability to assess the direction of supply or demand schedule shifts can at least help one understand why interest rates changed in a specific direction.

As a second example, consider how a slowdown in the economy would affect the demand and supply schedules of loanable funds and the equilib-

---

EXHIBIT 2.10   Impact of Increased Expansion by Firms

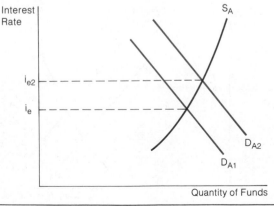

rium interest rate. The demand schedule would shift inward (to the left), reflecting less demand for loanable funds at any possible interest rate. The supply schedule could possibly shift a little, but it is questionable which way it would shift. One could argue that a slowdown should cause increased saving at any possible interest rate as households prepared for the possibility of being laid off. Yet, the gradual reduction in labor income that occurs during an economic slowdown could reduce households' ability to save. Historical data supports this latter expectation. Any shift that did occur would likely be minor relative to the shift in the demand schedule. Therefore, the equilibrium interest rate is expected to decrease, as illustrated in Exhibit 2.11.

Up to this point, the focus has been on shifts in the demand for loanable funds. In some cases, the supply of loanable funds may be significantly affected, which would also cause an adjustment in the equilibrium interest rate. For example, assume that the social security system is deteriorating and that households anticipate that they will not receive any funds from it in the future. This may increase their desire to save. Graphically, such a scenario would represent an outward shift in the supply schedule. It is even possible that the demand schedule could shift inward, since some households may also attempt to borrow less (although we shall assume no change in our demand schedule here). Exhibit 2.12 illustrates the shifts in the supply schedule. As a result of this shift, the equilibrium interest rate would decrease.

THE FISHER EFFECT

More than 50 years ago, Irving Fisher proposed a theory of interest rate determination that is still widely used today. It does not contradict the loanable funds theory, but simply offers an additional explanation for interest rate movements. Fisher proposed that nominal interest payments compensate savers in two ways. First, they compensate for a saver's reduced purchasing power. Second, they provide an additional premium to savers for foregoing present consumption. Savers are willing to forego consump-

EXHIBIT 2.11   Impact of an Economic Slowdown by Firms

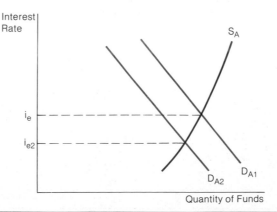

Impact of a Net International Investment Deficit on Interest Rates

The net international investment (NII) measures the difference between a country's accumulated holdings of foreign assets versus its foreign liabilities. Direct foreign investment in real assets and portfolio investment in financial assets are included. The NII changes in response to international capital flows and adjustments in the value of assets owned by foreigners. That value, in turn, is affected by security price and exchange rate movements.

The U.S. NII has historically been positive, due to the large degree of direct foreign investment overseas by U.S.–based corporations in the 1950s and 1960s, and the foreign loans provided by U.S. banks in the 1970s. However, the trend reversed during the 1980s because of a reduced U.S. direct foreign investment relative to that of foreign compa-

nies, a reduced volume of U.S. loans to foreign borrowers, and an increase in foreign purchases of U.S. government assets.

In 1985 the U.S. NII turned negative for the first time since World War I. The implications to the United States of having a negative NII depend on one's perspective. The large capital flows from foreign countries have increased the supply of loanable funds in the United States, keeping interest rates lower than they otherwise would have been. However, this high level of foreign funds can cause future foreign investment decisions to have a greater influence on U.S. interest rates. If for example, most foreign investors that invest in the United States expect a weaker dollar, they may withdraw funds, which could place upward pressure on U.S. interest rates.

tion only if they receive a premium on their savings above the anticipated rate of inflation, as shown in the following equation:

$$i_n = E(I) + i_r$$

EXHIBIT 2.12 Impact of an Increased Desire by Households to Save for Retirement

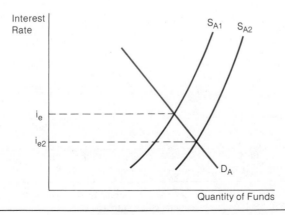

where i_n = nominal or quoted rate of interest

$E(I)$ = expected inflation rate

i_r = premium (often called the real rate of interest)

This relationship between interest rates and expected inflation is often referred to as the **Fisher effect.** The *premium* represents the real return to a saver after adjusting for the reduced purchasing power over the time period of concern. It is referred to as the **real rate of interest,** since, unlike the nominal rate of interest, it adjusts for the expected rate of inflation. The preceding equation can be rearranged to express the real rate of interest as

$$i_r = i_n - E(I)$$

If the normal interest rate was equal to the expected inflation rate, the real interest rate would be zero. Savings would accumulate interest at the same rate that prices are expected to increase, so that the purchasing power of savings would remain stable.

If today's expected inflation can be measured along with today's nominal interest rate, the **ex ante** real interest rate can be estimated. The term *ex ante* means "before the fact." Our discussion focuses on expected inflation rather than actual inflation, since it is expected inflation that influences the habits of savers and borrowers more than actual inflation.

Because the expected inflation rate is difficult to estimate, the ex ante real interest rate is difficult to measure. The actual inflation rate that has occurred can serve as an imperfect substitute for the expected inflation when monitoring the real interest rate over time. If the actual inflation rate is used, the *ex post* ("after the fact") real interest rate is measured.

Exhibit 2.13 illustrates the ex post real interest rate over the 1970–87 period. In some periods it was negative, implying that inflation exceeded the nominal interest rate. This was especially true during the 1973–75 period when oil prices increased substantially, igniting inflation. If investors

EXHIBIT 2.13   Ex Post Real Interest Rates over Time

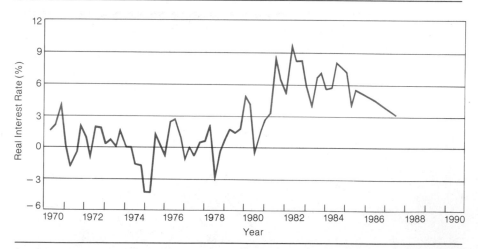

SOURCE: Adapted from Board of Governors; and *Economic Review*, Federal Reserve Bank of Kansas City (November 1985): 35. Data has been updated by author.

had been aware before the fact that inflation was going to be so high, they would have required higher nominal interest rates on their savings. Alternatively, they would have saved less funds, knowing that the purchasing power of their savings was decreasing.

Sometimes the real rate of interest may change in response to changing tax rates. For example, if tax rates increase, savers will need a higher nominal interest rate to maintain their same real return on an after-tax basis. If taxes decrease, a lower nominal interest rate could be sufficient to achieve the after-tax real return desired. During a period of changing tax rates, the before-tax real return might be changing even if savers attempt to simply maintain the same after-tax real return.

KEY ISSUES REGARDING INTEREST RATES

As will be demonstrated throughout the text, interest rate movements are a major concern to all financial institutions and markets. They can affect decision making, performance, and the growth of any particular financial institution. Two of the more common issues regarding interest rates are (1) how a change in expected inflation affects interest rates and (2) how a government budget deficit affects interest rates. A discussion of these issues follows.

Impact of Inflation on Interest Rates

The Fisher effect and loanable funds theory can be used to assess how inflationary expectations could affect nominal interest rates. According to the Fisher effect, expectations of higher inflation cause savers to require a higher nominal interest rate on savings, since this is the only way that they can maintain the existing real rate of interest.

According to loanable funds theory, expectations of higher inflation cause an increase in the demand for loanable funds, as households and businesses are motivated to increase their expenditures before prices increase. For this same reason, households and businesses are less willing to save. The shifts in the supply and demand schedules cause a shortage of funds at the prevailing nominal interest rates—and therefore force an increase in the equilibrium interest rate. While the Fisher effect and loanable funds theory provide different explanations for the same result, they are closely related. The reason for the shift in the demand and supply of loanable funds suggested by loanable funds theory is based on the saver's desire to maintain the existing real rate of interest (as suggested by the Fisher effect).

Notice from Exhibit 2.13 that the ex post real interest rate has been relatively high recently. Thus, the realized rate of inflation may have been lower than anticipated, perhaps because oil prices declined to a greater degree than anticipated.

When the inflation rate is higher than anticipated, the ex post real rate of interest is less than desired for savers. Borrowers benefit, since they were able to borrow at a lower nominal interest rate than would have been offered if inflation had been accurately forecasted. When the inflation rate is lower than anticipated, the ex post real rate of interest is higher than expected for savers, and borrowers are adversely affected.

Throughout the text, the term *interest rate* will be used to represent the nominal, or quoted, rate of interest. Keep in mind, however, that because of inflation, purchasing power is not necessarily increasing during periods of rising interest rates. If one is more concerned with changes in purchasing power, real interest rates should be assessed rather than nominal interest rates.

Impact of a Government Budget Deficit on Interest Rates

Consider how an increase in the federal government deficit would affect interest rates, assuming no other changes in habits by consumers and firms. A higher federal government deficit increases the quantity of loanable funds demanded at any prevailing interest rate, causing an outward shift in the demand schedule. Given no offsetting increase in the supply schedule, interest rates will rise. There is a counter-argument that the supply schedule might shift outward if the government creates more jobs by spending more funds than it collects from the public (this is what causes the deficit in the first place). If this occurred, the deficit might not necessarily place upward pressure on interest rates. Much research has investigated this issue and, in general, has shown that higher deficits place upward pressure on interest rates.[3]

Simultaneous Impact of Several Events on Interest Rates

When assessing the impact of any particular event on interest rates, it is easy to find exceptions to the expected relationship. For example, while the federal government deficit has been consistently increasing in recent years, interest rates have not consistently risen. As a second example, during specific periods when the Federal Reserve System substantially increased money supply (and therefore caused the supply of loanable funds to increase), interest rates were not always decreasing. The reason for these discrepancies is that an assessment of a single event's impact on interest rates assumes that all other factors that could affect the demand and supply of loanable funds are held constant. In reality, all of these factors are changing simultaneously. Some factors place upward pressure on interest rates while other factors place downward pressure. Consequently, the net effect of all factors on interest rates must be assessed. Although financial market participants may not formally list all these factors and weigh their importance, they implicitly run through this exercise when determining why interest rates changed over a particular period of concern.

EVALUATION OF INTEREST RATES OVER TIME

Now that the more important determinants of interest rates have been identified, we can review interest rates over time and explain why they moved as they did. Exhibit 2.14 illustrates nominal interest rates over the last several years. One-year Treasury bill rates were used as a proxy for

3 For example, see Gregory Hoelscher, "New Evidence on Deficits and Interest Rates," Journal of Money, Credit, and Banking (February 1986): 1–17.

Empirical Relationship between the Federal Budget Deficit and Interest Rates

The impact of federal deficits on interest rates has been debated for several years. While it is generally suggested that an increase in the federal government deficit places upward pressure on interest rates, some studies have found little or no relationship between the size of the federal deficit and interest rates.

A recent study by Hoelscher reassessed the relationship between deficits and long-term interest rates over the period from 1953 to 1984.[1] Several regression models were applied to test the relationship, each model specifying a particular measure of the deficit. The analysis found a positive and significant relationship between the size of the deficit and long-term interest rates. For example, one model determined that each $100 billion of the federal deficit is predicted to increase long-term interest rates by 142 basis points (1.42%). While the various models utilized by Hoelscher generated different results, there was a significant positive relationship, regardless of the way in which the federal deficit was defined.

1 Gregory Hoelscher, "New Evidence on Deficits and Interest Rates," *Journal of Money Credit and Banking* (February 1986): 2.

interest rates here. While other securities had different rates, their rate movements were somewhat similar to those of Treasury bills. The rise in interest rates in 1973 was partially due to higher expected inflation (ignited

EXHIBIT 2.14   Nominal Interest Rates over Time (One-year Treasury Bill Rate Used as a Proxy)

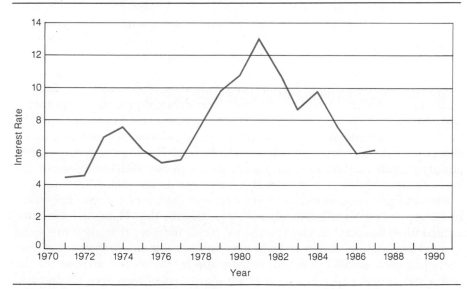

by oil price hikes) which caused a strong demand for loanable funds. In late 1973 and 1974, the economy slowed down and a recession occurred. This led to a reduced demand for loanable funds by firms, since future expansion plans were postponed. In addition, household demand for loanable funds also decreased as spending habits adjusted during the recession. Consequently, interest rates fell. During the 1978–79 period, interest rates increased as a result of high inflation, strong economic growth, and therefore strong demand for loanable funds. In 1980 a mild recession occurred, which reduced the demand for loanable funds and thus reduced interest rates. A quick reversal in interest rates occurred in 1981 as the economy strengthened, only to turn back down in 1982 due to a severe recession. Interest rates remained low during the mid 1980s as oil prices decreased and inflationary expectations subsided.

The supply of loanable funds is also a critical factor that can help explain movements in interest rates. During the mid 1970s, the Federal Reserve System substantially increased money supply, which placed downward pressure on interest rates during that period. However, it is commonly believed that such excessive growth in the money supply could have caused expectations of higher inflation (as will be thoroughly explained in later chapters), which contributed to the strong demand for loanable funds (and rising interest rates) over the late 1970s. This discussion shows how the factors identified in this chapter can be useful for explaining interest rate movements over time.

FORECASTING INTEREST RATES

Exhibit 2.15 summarizes the key factors that are evaluated when forecasting interest rates. With an understanding of how each factor affects interest rates, it is possible to forecast how interest rates may change in the future. When forecasting household demand for loanable funds, it may be necessary to assess consumer credit data to determine the borrowing capacity of households. Seasonal factors (such as Christmas or summer vacations) could also be important, as well as the expected unemployment rate and a host of other factors that affect the earning power of households. The potential supply of loanable funds provided by households may be determined in the same manner.

Business demand for loanable funds can be forecasted by assessing future plans for corporate expansion and the future state of the economy. Federal government demand for loanable funds could be influenced by the future state of the economy, since it affects tax revenues to be received and the amount of unemployment compensation to be paid out, factors that affect the size of the government deficit. The Federal Reserve System's money supply targets may be assessed by reviewing public statements about the Fed's future objectives, although those statements are somewhat vague.

Interest rates are commonly forecasted with the use of *regression analysis*, as illustrated with the following example. Assume that Fighting Irish, Inc., a diversified financial services company, needs to forecast interest rates one quarter ahead. It identifies and compiles historical data on factors that may influence each sector's demand. It then applies regression analysis to the historical data in order to estimate the sensitivity of each sector's demand to each factor. This sensitivity is measured by the estimated regression

EXHIBIT 2.15   Framework for Forecasting Interest Rates

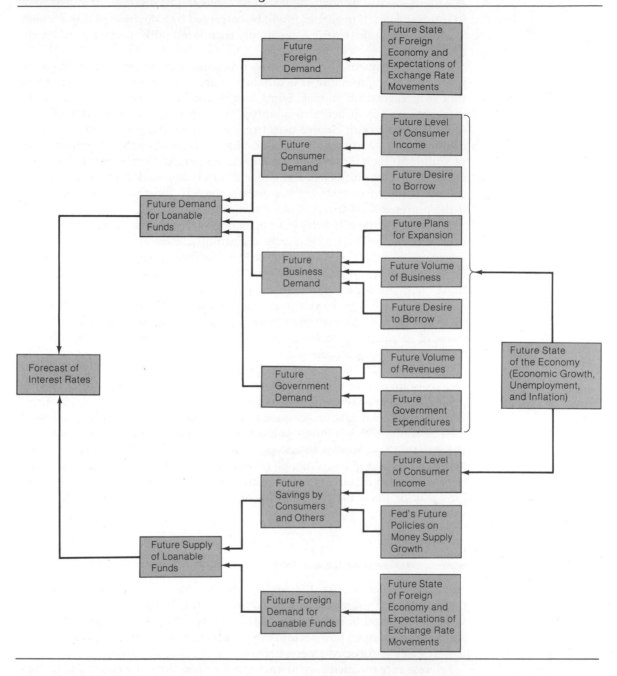

coefficients. Next, the factors are forecasted and used along with the estimated regression coefficients to forecast the sector's future demand for loanable funds. These forecasts can be combined to estimate the aggregate demand for loanable funds simply by replicating the procedure. The resulting projections are then used to forecast net demand:

$$ND_A = D_A - S_A$$
$$= [D_h + D_b + D_g + D_m + D_f] - [S_h + S_b + S_g + S_m + S_f]$$

If the forecasted level of ND_A is positive or negative, a disequilibrium will exist temporarily. If positive, it will be corrected by an upward adjustment in interest rates. If negative, it will be corrected by a downward adjustment. The degree of adjustment is positively correlated with the forecasted magnitude of ND_A.

The limitations of any forecasting procedure can be recognized from the preceding example. First, it is difficult to properly include all relevant factors in a regression model. Some subjective factors such as inflationary expectations are difficult to quantify. In addition, the sensitivity of each sector to factors can change over time. Therefore, the estimated regression coefficients may misspecify the actual sensitivity of each sector's demand or supply to each factor over the forecasted period. Furthermore, forecasts of the factors that influence demand and supply are needed for the forecasted period. If these forecasts are inaccurate, the ND_A forecast will be, too, even if the regression coefficients were accurately estimated.

To illustrate the difficulty in forecasting interest rates, consider how U.S. interest rates will be affected by the simultaneous existence of a higher government deficit, increased growth in the money supply, and increased foreign funds into the United States. There is no clear-cut answer. One can, however, make an educated guess by estimating the individual impact of each event on interest rates and then combining the expected impacts of all these events. Because the impact of some events may be greater than those of others, it is necessary to measure not only the direction but also the magnitude of each impact.

To verify which factors should be considered when forecasting interest rates, obtain a recent business periodical article that provides interest rate projections by various economists and consultants. As an example, a recent article on interest rate projections by 50 top economists cited the following factors contributing to their projections: the Fed's money supply growth, the state of the economy, inflation, the federal budget deficit, the tax reform bill, and oil prices.[4] Even though the economists considered similar factors, they developed different interest rate projections because of their diverse forecasts of these factors and the relative influence the factors have on interest rates.

SUMMARY

As certain events occur, the saving and borrowing habits of households, businesses, and governments (both domestic and foreign) are affected. When the total demand or supply of loanable funds changes, so do interest rates. An understanding of how certain events affect demand and supply schedules is necessary to forecast interest rates.

Interest rate forecasts are always error prone, since the economic factors involved are difficult to forecast. In addition, even if these factors are correctly anticipated, their precise impact on interest rates is difficult to determine, since other events that were not anticipated will simultaneously influence interest rates. Nevertheless, financial institutions and other firms commonly forecast interest rates in an attempt to capitalize on interest rate expectations.

4 See "What's Ahead for Interest Rates?" *Institutional Investor* (September 1986): 321–329.

KEY TERMS

ex ante	loanable funds theory
Fisher effect	real rate of interest
interest-inelastic	

QUESTIONS

2.1. Explain why interest rates changed as they did over the last year.

2.2. Explain what is meant by interest elasticity.

2.3. Would you expect federal government demand for loanable funds to be more or less interest elastic than household demand for loanable funds? Why?

2.4. If the federal government planned to expand the space program, how might this affect interest rates?

2.5. Explain why interest rates tend to decrease during recessionary periods.

2.6. Obtain or develop forecasts of economic growth and inflation. Use this information to forecast interest rates one year from now.

2.7. Jayhawk Forecasting Services analyzed several factors that could affect interest rates in the future. Most factors were expected to place downward pressure on interest rates. Jayhawk also felt that while the annual budget deficit was to be cut by 40 percent from the previous year, it would still be very large. Thus, it believed that the deficit's impact would more than offset the other effects and therefore forecasted interest rates to increase by 2 percent. Comment on Jayhawk's logic.

2.8. Should increasing money supply growth place upward or downward pressure on interest rates? Justify your answer.

2.9. Consider a scenario where inflation is low and is not expected to rise in the future. In addition, assume that the Fed substantially increases the money supply. Explain how this would likely affect interest rates.

2.10. What is the logic behind the Fisher effect's implied positive relationship between expected inflation and nominal interest rates?

2.11. What is the difference between the ex ante and ex post real rate of interest?

2.12. Estimate the ex post real rate of interest over the last year.

2.13. Review historical interest rates to determine how they react to recessionary periods. Explain this reaction.

2.14. Why do forecasts of interest rates differ among experts?

2.15. During the stock market crash in October 1987, interest rates declined. Use the loanable funds framework discussed in this chapter to explain why.

2.16. If foreign investors expected that the U.S. dollar's value would weaken over the next few years, how might this affect (a) the foreign supply of funds to the U.S. markets and (b) U.S. interest rates? Explain.

2.17. A well-known economist recently suggested that lower interest rates will stimulate the economy. Yet, this chapter implied that a strong economy can cause high interest rates. Do these concepts conflict? Explain.

2.18. Assume that if the U.S. dollar strengthens, it can place downward pressure on U.S. inflation. Based on this information, how might expectations of a strong dollar affect the demand for loanable funds in the United

States and U.S. interest rates? Is there any reason to think that expectations of a strong dollar could also affect the supply of loanable funds? Explain.

2.19. If financial market participants overestimate inflation in 1990, will ex post real interest rates be relatively high or low? Explain.

2.20. Why might you expect interest rate movements of various industrialized countries to be more highly correlated in recent years than in earlier years?

PROJECTS

1. FORECASTING INTEREST RATES

Review the "Credit Markets" section of *The Wall Street Journal* (listed in the index of the front page) for the last five days. Use this section to determine the factors likely to have the largest impact on future interest rate movements. Then create your own forecasts as to whether interest rates will increase or decrease from now until the end of this school term, based on your assessment of any factors that affect interest rates. Explain your forecast.

2. ASSESSING THE ACCURACY OF INTEREST RATE FORECASTS

Find a business periodical at least one year old that provided interest rate projections one year ahead.

a. Determine how far off the projected rates were from actual rates.

b. Offer some reasons why the actual rates turned out to be lower or higher than what was projected.

3. MODELING INTEREST RATE MOVEMENTS

Develop a model that measures how nominal interest rates are affected by any economic variables. Indicate whether each variable is expected to have a positive or negative relationship with nominal interest rates when other variables are held constant. Include all relevant variables for which data are available.

REFERENCES

Blinder, Alan. "Distribution Effects and the Aggregate Consumption Function." *Journal of Political Economy* (June 1975): 447–475.

Boskin, Michael. "Taxation, Saving, and the Rate of Interest." *Journal of Political Economy* (April 1978): 3–27.

Ceccheti, Stephen G. "High Real Interest Rates: Can They Be Explained?" *Economic Review* (September–October 1986): 31–41.

DeFina, Robert H. "The Link between Savings and Interest Rates: A Key Element in the Tax Policy Debate." *Business Review*, Federal Reserve Bank of Philadelphia (November–December 1984): 15–21.

DeMagistris, Robin C., and Carl J. Palash. "Impact of IRAs on Saving." FRB of New York: *Quarterly Review* (Winter 1982–83): 24–32.

Hoelscher, Gregory. "New Evidence on Deficits and Interest Rates." *Journal of Money, Credit, and Banking* (February 1986): 1–17.

Holland, Steven A. "Does Higher Inflation Lead To More Uncertain Inflation?" *Review*, Reserve Bank of St. Louis (February 1984): 15–26.

Karp, Richard, and Gregory Miller. "Sadder, but Wiser about Debt." *Institutional Investor* (July 1983): 217–219.

Kopcke, Richard W. "The Determinants of Investment Spending." *New England Economic Review*, Federal Reserve Bank of Boston (July–August 1985): 19–34.

Miller, Preston J. "Budget Deficit Mythology." *Quarterly Review*, Federal Reserve Bank of Minneapolis (Fall 1983): 1–13.

Miller, Preston J. "Higher Deficit Policies Lead to Higher Inflation." *Quarterly Review*, Federal Reserve Bank of Minneapolis (Winter 1983): 8–20.

Mullineaux, Donald J. "Efficient Markets, Interest Rates, and Monetary Policy." *Business Review*, Federal Reserve Bank of Philadelphia (May–June 1981): 3–10.

Tatom, John A. "A Perspective on the Federal Deficit Problem." *Review*, Federal Reserve Bank of St. Louis (June–July 1986): 5–17.

Taylor, Herbert. "Interest Rates: How Much Does Expected Inflation Matter." *Business Review*, Federal Reserve Bank of Philadelphia (July–August 1982): 3–12.

Webster, Charles E., Jr. "The Effects of Deficits On Interest Rates." *Economic Review*, Federal Reserve Bank of Kansas City (May 1983): 19–28.

"What's Ahead for Interest Rates?" *Institutional Investor* (September 1986): 321–329.

Chapter 2

Determination of
Interest Rates

Using the Liquidity Preference Theory to Forecast Interest Rates

The liquidity preference theory, developed by John Maynard Keynes, offers an alternative explanation for interest rate determination. It suggests that the market rate of interest is determined by the demand and supply of money balances. The speculative demand for money balances is thought to be inversely related to interest rates, given any particular level of income. This is shown in Exhibit 2A.1. The higher the market interest rate, the greater is the opportunity cost of holding money. Thus, households and businesses would maintain smaller money (cash and checking account) balances in favor of more interest-bearing securities.

Money demand is also influenced by national income. As national income increases, so does spending, and the transaction and precautionary demand for money increases. This is shown in Exhibit 2A.2. For any particular interest rate, money demand is higher; yet the inverse relationship between money demand and interest rates is sustained.

According to liquidity preference theory, money supply is dictated by monetary policy. The central bank can achieve whatever money supply target it desires, regardless of the prevailing interest rate. A money supply line that is insensitive to interest rates is combined with a money demand line in Exhibit 2A.3. The intersection of the money demand line with the

EXHIBIT 2A.1   **Relationship between the Interest Rate and Money Demand According to Liquidity Preference Theory**

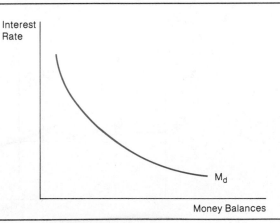

EXHIBIT 2A.2   Effect of an Increase in National Income on the Money Demand Schedule

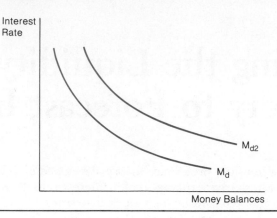

money supply line dictates the equilibrium market interest rate. In Exhibit 2A.3, the equilibrium interest rate is labeled i_e. At lower interest rates, the demand for money would exceed the money supply. Thus, households and businesses would be forced to sell securities in order to attain the money balances they desire. This would reduce the price of securities and increase the market interest rates.

At higher interest rates, the demand for money would be less than the money supply. Households and businesses would convert excess money balances into securities, which would place upward pressure on security prices and downward pressure on interest rates.

The liquidity preference theory can be used to explain how changes in the money supply affect interest rates. See Exhibit 2A.3, where money supply is increased from M_s to M_{s2}. At the higher money supply level, and the initial equilibrium interest rate (i_e), demand for money balances is less than

EXHIBIT 2A.3   Impact of Increased Money Supply on the Interest Rate According to the Liquidity Preference Theory

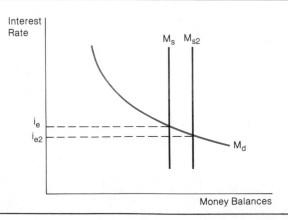

the supply of money balances available. Thus, households and businesses convert excess balances into securities, and interest rates decline. If the money supply is reduced, interest rates will increase.

While the liquidity preference theory is useful for explaining interest rate movements, it is criticized for ignoring possible shifts in the money demand schedule. For example, there is some historical evidence of a positive correlation between money supply growth and inflation. If inflationary expectations are ignited by an increase in money supply, spending may rise, which could cause an outward shift in the money demand line. Therefore, the inverse relationship between money supply and interest rates will not necessarily hold.

Flow of Funds Accounts

The amount of funds channeled to and from various sectors and financial institutions can be monitored by reviewing the *Flow of Funds Accounts*, periodically updated by the Board of Governors of the Federal Reserve System. Flow of funds information is extremely valuable to financial market participants for the following reasons:

1. The information provided on households suggests how their borrowing and saving tendencies are changing over time. This may affect the types of securities issued by a financial institution or the types of services it offers.
2. The flow of funds identifies changes in each type of financial institution's uses or sources of funds over time—useful information to financial institutions monitoring their competitors. It may also indicate whether particular credit instruments are increasing in popularity at various types of financial institutions. The information could affect a particular institution's decision to purchase or sell specific types of securities as well.
3. The historical net increases in U.S. government securities and other fund flow information may be linked with historical interest rate information to specify the relationship between these flows and interest rate movements. This may enhance interest rate forecasting capabilities.

The following discussion briefly introduces some of the information available in *Flow of Funds Accounts*.

Exhibit 2B.1 shows the net flows of households, personal trusts, and nonprofit organizations. Personal income, personal taxes and disposable income consistently increased over time. Annual personal outlays have risen at a similar pace to annual disposable personal income, which is why personal savings has been somewhat stable in recent years.

The forms by which households use their savings are shown from line 19 to line 37 of Exhibit 2B.1. In recent quarters, small deposits and money market shares have increased. Annual investment in corporate bonds and mutual fund shares has generally increased while investment in other corporate equities has decreased.

With regard to liabilities, Exhibit 2B.1 also shows that borrowing in the form of mortgages has substantially increased over time (see lines 40 and 41). Mortgages have consistently represented the largest proportion of net increases in credit market instruments over time.

Exhibit 2B.2 shows a breakdown of net credit market borrowing by various sectors in recent years. The term "net" here reflects the amount of borrowing in excess of savings. The top panel focuses on nonfinancial sectors. The U.S. government was accountable for $141.4 billion of $685.2 billion in total net borrowing by nonfinancial sectors in 1987. The form of

49

EXHIBIT 2B.1 Flow of Funds Accounts for Households, Personal Trusts, and Nonprofit Organizations (billions of dollars)

						1986		1987				Seasonally Adjusted Annual Rates	
	1983	1984	1985	1986	1987	III	IV	I	II	III	IV		
1	2838.6	3108.8	3327.1	3534.3	3746.3	3553.6	3593.6	3662.0	3708.6	3761.0	3853.6	Personal income	1
2	410.5	440.2	485.9	512.3	564.8	515.3	532.0	536.1	577.9	565.7	579.4	– Personal taxes and nontaxes	2
3	2428.1	2668.6	2841.2	3022.1	3181.5	3038.3	3061.6	3125.9	3130.7	3195.3	3274.2	= Disposable personal income	3
4	2297.5	2504.5	2714.1	2891.5	3062.0	2929.4	2952.6	2987.6	3037.5	3106.4	3116.3	– Personal outlays	4
5	130.6	164.1	127.1	130.6	119.6	108.9	109.0	138.3	93.2	88.9	157.9	= Personal saving, NIPA basis	5
6	53.5	63.9	72.3	78.7	80.1	67.6	96.7	85.5	72.2	79.9	82.7	+ Credits from govt. insurance	6
7	4.4	6.0	4.9	17.5	11.1	13.2	38.5	6.1	14.6	13.7	9.9	+ Capital gains dividends	7
8	62.7	98.8	114.1	127.4	114.5	150.3	135.7	105.8	113.1	134.4	104.9	+ Net durables in consumption	8
9	251.2	332.8	318.4	354.1	325.3	340.1	379.8	335.7	293.1	316.9	355.4	= Net saving	9
10	295.3	309.4	332.3	356.2	384.0	358.8	366.6	373.7	380.2	387.7	394.3	+ Capital consumption	10
11	546.5	642.2	650.7	710.3	709.3	698.9	746.4	709.4	673.3	704.6	749.7	= Gross saving	11
12	606.4	729.7	697.5	748.1	727.2	701.4	806.5	760.0	597.8	701.8	846.0	Gross investment	12
13	427.8	505.3	544.1	600.9	636.2	624.9	630.7	615.9	623.3	664.0	641.9	Capital expend. net of sales	13
14	124.9	154.6	159.7	182.0	205.6	180.6	194.2	203.0	197.5	210.3	211.9	Residential construction	14
15	289.1	335.6	368.7	402.4	413.8	427.6	419.8	396.1	409.0	436.8	413.1	Consumer durable goods	15
16	13.9	15.2	15.7	16.5	16.9	16.6	16.7	16.8	16.8	16.9	17.0	Nonprofit plant and equip.	16
17	178.6	224.4	153.4	147.2	91.0	76.5	175.8	144.1	-25.5	37.7	204.0	Net financial investment	17
18	377.5	456.7	465.8	438.1	343.1	434.5	498.8	336.3	271.7	320.7	440.0	Net acq. of financial assets	18
19	291.6	417.4	343.1	263.5	244.6	175.3	411.7	48.1	221.2	245.9	459.9	Dep. & cr. mkt. instr.[1]	19
20	202.5	282.2	181.0	246.5	107.5	278.5	249.7	-76.6	132.1	199.4	171.0	Deposits	20
21	36.8	16.6	39.1	99.8	12.3	86.9	158.2	-61.0	53.7	98.6	-42.2	Checkable dep. & curr.	21
22	210.1	153.3	144.0	120.6	65.0	140.8	113.7	25.5	71.7	68.4	94.5	Small time & svgs. dep.	22
23	-13.3	68.2	-14.2	-16.5	9.1	-12.1	-36.7	-31.8	5.5	10.0	48.6	Large time deposits	23
24	-31.1	44.0	12.1	42.6	21.1	62.8	14.5	-9.3	1.2	22.4	70.2	Money mkt. fund shares	24

	1983	1984	1985	1986	1987	1986 III	1986 IV	1987 I	1987 II	1987 III	1987 IV		
25	89.2	135.3	162.2	17.0	137.1	-103.2	162.0	124.7	89.1	46.5	288.9	Credit mkt. instruments	25
26	59.4	94.8	59.3	-.2	31.5	-111.8	45.8	66.1	47.3	-69.5	83.3	U.S. govt. securities	26
27	39.1	29.5	47.9	-8.2	49.1	36.8	68.5	10.8	25.0	68.5	91.9	Tax-exempt obligations	27
28	-11.6	5.2	11.8	34.7	50.2	-8.6	10.0	40.4	-16.3	72.6	104.1	Corporate & fgn. bonds	28
29	.9	5.8	3.3	1.1	.7	-.1	11.7	2.5	-9.6	10.3	-.4	Mortgages	29
30	1.4	-.1	39.9	-10.4	5.6	-19.5	26.1	4.9	42.7	-35.3	10.0	Open-market paper	30
31	24.0	24.0	69.8	154.1	55.4	144.1	174.8	170.8	91.4	10.0	-50.8	Mutual fund shares	31
32	-19.9	-80.0	-102.7	-132.8	-129.4	-118.3	-170.1	-135.3	-185.8	-118.9	-77.5	Other corporate equities	32
33	8.0	5.2	10.7	17.5	16.0	18.3	19.2	17.9	13.8	19.3	13.1	Life insurance reserves	33
34	145.6	147.2	183.8	184.2	228.5	261.0	160.7	286.7	205.6	238.5	183.3	Pension fund reserves	34
35	-89.5	-72.8	-65.8	-85.2	-97.3	-64.6	-156.1	-68.7	-100.0	-99.9	-120.9	Net inv. in noncorp. bus.	35
36	2.4	-.6	12.5	8.7	.2	-12.7	30.8	-10.1	-2.6	3.0	10.6	Security credit	36
37	15.3	16.3	14.5	28.1	25.0	31.4	27.8	26.9	28.1	22.8	22.3	Miscellaneous assets	37
38	198.9	232.3	312.4	290.9	252.1	358.0	323.0	192.2	297.2	283.0	236.0	Net increase in liabilities	38
39	188.2	234.6	293.4	281.1	245.6	352.6	306.0	199.6	281.2	274.4	227.0	Credit market instruments	39
40	110.8	129.0	151.0	197.4	210.5	241.3	229.6	215.3	233.9	190.8	202.0	Home mortgages	40
41	47.6	73.5	77.7	55.3	35.2	77.5	29.1	5.6	34.3	57.1	43.7	Installment cons. credit	41
42	9.0	16.9	16.8	10.5	-5.1	7.7	6.9	.4	-1.3	-14.9	-4.6	Other consumer credit	42
43	11.4	10.2	30.2	-2.2	-.4	3.6	-2.5	*	-1.3	-.7	.3	Tax-exempt debt	43
44	2.5	2.5	2.4	2.4	2.3	2.3	2.3	2.3	2.3	2.3	2.3	Other mortgages	44
45	3.6	-.4	6.9	11.1	.5	13.9	35.6	-27.1	13.2	37.0	-20.8	Bank loans n.e.c.	45
46	3.3	2.9	8.3	6.6	2.6	6.2	5.0	3.1	.2	2.7	4.2	Other loans	46
47	8.4	-3.1	16.7	8.6	2.7	4.5	15.3	-9.8	12.1	4.7	3.7	Security credit	47
48	1.8	1.8	2.2	2.5	2.9	2.6	2.7	2.8	2.9	3.0	3.0	Trade debt	48
49	.6	-1.0	.1	-1.3	1.0	-1.7	-1.0	-.3	1.0	.9	2.2	Miscellaneous	49
50	-59.9	-87.5	-46.8	-37.8	-17.9	-2.5	-60.0	-50.6	75.5	2.8	-96.2	Discrepancy	50

1 Excludes corporate equities.

SOURCE: Flow of Funds Accounts, Board of Governors; the latest quarter is based on incomplete information.

51

EXHIBIT 2B.2 Flow of Funds Accounts for Sectors That Raised Funds
(billions of dollars)

		Seasonally Adjusted Annual Rates					Net Credit Market Borrowing by Nonfinancial Sectors					Seasonally Adjusted Annual Rates	
							1986		1987				
		1983	1984	1985	1986	1987	III	IV	I	II	III	IV	
1	Total net borrowing by domestic nonfinancial sectors	550.2	753.9	854.8	831.7	685.2	932.5	1036.3	551.4	756.0	633.2	800.4	1
2	U.S. government	186.6	198.8	223.6	215.0	141.4	210.4	235.2	162.3	139.1	68.0	196.1	2
3	Treasury issues	186.7	199.0	223.7	214.7	142.3	208.9	235.0	162.4	141.0	68.5	197.3	3
4	Agency issues & mortgages	-.1	-.2	-.1	.4	-.9	1.5	.2	-.1	-1.9	-.5	-1.2	4
5	Private domestic nonfinancial sectors	363.6	555.1	631.1	616.7	543.9	722.0	801.1	389.1	616.9	565.2	604.2	5
6	Debt capital instruments	253.4	313.6	447.8	452.7	456.5	587.1	492.6	482.6	458.8	458.3	426.2	6
7	Tax-exempt obligations	53.7	50.4	136.4	30.8	31.3	137.1	17.3	46.9	18.6	38.0	21.6	7
8	Corporate bonds	16.0	46.1	73.8	121.5	125.4	113.7	100.8	146.9	108.0	135.3	111.6	8
9	Mortgages	183.6	217.1	237.7	300.6	299.8	336.2	374.5	288.8	332.3	285.0	293.0	9
10	Home mortgages	117.5	129.7	151.9	201.2	212.6	246.4	230.7	217.2	256.6	192.4	204.1	10
11	Multi-family resid.	14.2	25.1	29.2	33.1	23.8	36.8	33.0	28.2	31.5	22.8	12.8	11
12	Commercial	49.3	63.2	62.5	74.6	69.5	59.0	120.2	55.7	70.6	74.0	77.7	12
13	Farm	2.6	-.9	-6.0	-8.4	-6.1	-6.0	-9.4	-12.3	-6.4	-4.1	-1.6	13
14	Other debt instruments	110.2	241.5	183.3	164.0	87.4	135.0	308.5	-93.6	158.1	106.9	178.0	14
15	Consumer credit	56.6	90.4	94.6	65.8	30.1	85.2	36.0	6.0	33.0	42.2	39.1	15
16	Bank loans n.e.c.	23.2	67.1	38.6	66.5	14.2	14.8	226.8	-124.8	75.6	42.0	64.2	16
17	Commercial paper	-.8	21.7	14.6	-9.3	2.3	5.2	-16.3	-1.8	10.8	-12.0	12.2	17
18	Other	31.3	62.2	35.5	41.0	40.8	29.8	61.9	27.1	38.8	34.7	62.5	18
19	By borrowing sector:	363.6	555.1	631.1	616.7	543.9	722.0	801.1	389.1	616.9	565.2	604.2	19
20	State & local governments	34.0	27.4	91.8	44.3	33.3	138.3	30.4	45.7	25.1	39.3	23.1	20
21	Households	188.2	234.6	293.4	281.1	245.6	352.6	306.0	199.6	281.2	274.4	227.0	21
22	Nonfinancial business	141.4	293.0	245.9	291.3	265.0	231.2	464.8	143.8	310.6	251.5	354.2	22
23	Farm	4.1	-.1	-13.9	-15.1	-10.0	-13.4	-13.3	-23.0	-12.7	-8.0	3.5	23
24	Nonfarm noncorporate	77.0	97.0	93.1	116.2	102.5	99.9	171.2	78.9	122.6	99.5	103.9	24
25	Corporate	60.3	196.0	166.7	190.2	172.6	144.6	306.9	87.9	200.7	160.0	241.7	25

	1983	1984	1985	1986	1987	1986		1987				
						III	IV	I	II	III	IV	
26	17.3	8.3	1.2	9.0	3.1	16.5	-23.5	-10.1	-4.6	17.5	9.5	Fgn. net borrowing in U.S.
27	3.1	3.8	3.8	2.6	6.3	2.4	-4.6	2.7	-6.0	4.9	23.5	Bonds
28	3.6	-6.6	-2.8	-1.0	-3.9	-7.7	.6	-2.3	-4.1	-2.9	-6.2	Bank loans n.e.c.
29	6.5	6.2	6.2	11.5	2.1	15.8	-8.1	-4.3	-6.2	21.4	-2.3	Commercial paper
30	4.1	5.0	-6.0	-4.0	-1.5	6.0	-11.4	-6.2	11.7	-5.9	-5.5	U.S. govt. & other loans
31	567.5	762.2	856.0	840.7	688.3	949.0	1012.8	541.3	751.4	650.6	809.9	Total domestic plus foreign

Net Credit Market Borrowing by Financial Sectors

	1983	1984	1985	1986	1987	1986		1987				
						III	IV	I	II	III	IV	
1	99.3	151.9	199.0	295.3	283.4	303.1	393.4	329.8	307.2	264.3	233.3	Total net borrowing by financial sectors
2	67.8	74.9	101.5	178.1	169.3	200.6	239.7	174.8	186.3	153.2	164.0	U.S. government-related
3	1.4	30.4	20.6	15.2	29.9	23.0	20.4	-3.6	19.8	31.4	72.0	Sponsored credit ag. sec.
4	66.4	44.4	79.9	163.3	140.2	179.3	220.7	181.3	166.7	121.8	91.9	Mortgage pool securities
5	—	—	1.2	-.4	-.8	-1.7	-1.3	-2.9	-.1	—	—	Loans from U.S. government
6	31.5	77.0	97.4	117.2	114.1	102.5	153.7	155.0	120.9	111.1	69.4	Private financial sectors
7	17.4	36.2	48.6	69.0	62.0	53.5	78.5	104.1	54.8	70.5	18.7	Corporate bonds
8	*	.4	.1	.1	.3	-.5	-.4	.3	.2	.3	.6	Mortgages
9	-.1	.7	2.6	4.0	-1.1	5.5	2.5	-8.0	-1.5	12.1	-6.9	Bank loans n.e.c.
10	21.3	24.1	32.0	24.2	28.4	34.3	32.5	47.5	51.3	12.8	1.9	Open-market paper
11	-7.0	15.7	14.2	19.8	24.4	9.7	40.7	11.2	16.1	15.3	55.1	Fed. Home Loan Bank loans
12	99.3	151.9	199.0	295.3	283.4	303.1	393.4	329.8	307.2	264.3	233.3	Total, by sector
13	1.4	30.4	21.7	14.9	29.2	21.3	19.0	-6.5	19.6	31.4	72.0	Sponsored credit agencies
14	66.4	44.4	79.9	163.3	140.2	179.3	220.7	181.3	166.7	121.8	91.9	Mortgage pools
15	31.5	77.0	97.4	117.2	114.1	102.5	153.7	155.0	120.9	111.1	69.4	Private financial sectors
16	5.0	7.3	-4.9	-3.6	8.5	1.1	-10.3	6.5	21.7	-19.6	25.4	Commercial banks
17	12.1	15.6	14.5	4.6	4.8	11.8	10.1	26.2	-3.2	13.8	-17.4	Domestic affiliates
18	-2.1	22.7	22.3	29.8	35.2	18.1	49.9	44.5	13.8	28.3	54.2	Savings and loans assns.
19	12.9	18.9	53.9	49.7	26.5	49.0	43.7	12.7	48.9	42.7	1.7	Finance companies
20	-.1	.1	-.7	-.3	.9	-1.3	-1.3	-.4	.3	1.7	2.1	REITs
21	3.7	12.4	12.2	37.1	38.1	23.9	61.7	65.6	39.5	44.2	3.3	CMO Trusts

Total Net Credit Market Borrowing, All Sectors, by Type

	1983	1984	1985	1986	1987	1986		1987				
						III	IV	I	II	III	IV	
1	666.8	914.1	1054.9	1136.0	971.7	1252.1	1406.2	871.1	1058.7	914.9	1043.2	Total net borrowing
2	254.4	273.8	324.2	393.5	311.5	412.8	476.2	340.0	325.5	221.2	360.1	U.S. government securities
3	53.7	50.4	136.4	30.8	31.3	137.1	17.3	46.9	18.6	38.0	21.6	Tax-exempt obligations
4	36.5	86.1	126.1	192.9	193.7	169.6	174.7	253.7	156.8	210.7	153.8	Corporate & foreign bonds
5	183.6	217.4	237.7	300.7	300.1	335.6	374.1	289.1	332.4	285.3	293.6	Mortgages

EXHIBIT 2B.2 Continued

Seasonally Adjusted Annual Rates

						1986		1987						Seasonally Adjusted Annual Rates	
	1983	1984	1985	1986	1987	III	IV	I	II	III	IV				
6	56.6	90.4	94.6	65.8	30.1	85.2	36.0	6.0	33.0	42.2	39.1	Consumer credit	6
7	26.7	61.1	38.3	69.5	9.3	12.6	229.9	−135.1	70.0	51.2	51.2	Bank loans n.e.c.	7
8	26.9	52.0	52.8	26.4	32.8	55.3	8.1	41.3	55.9	22.2	11.8	Open-market paper	8
9	28.4	82.9	44.8	56.5	63.0	43.7	89.9	29.2	66.4	44.2	112.0	Other loans	9
10	−7.1	6.3	14.4	*	3.3	23.7	1.0	−34.3	76.0	−8.0	−20.4	Memo: U.S. govt. cash balance	10
												Totals net of changes in U.S. govt. cash balances:	
11	557.3	747.6	840.4	831.7	681.9	908.8	1035.3	585.6	680.1	641.2	820.7	Net borrowing by dom. nonfin.	11
12	193.7	192.5	209.3	215.0	138.1	186.8	234.1	196.6	63.1	76.0	216.5	By U.S. government	12

External Corporate Equity Funds Raised in U.S. Markets

	1983	1984	1985	1986	1987	III	IV	I	II	III	IV		
1	61.8	−36.4	19.9	91.6	−9.3	82.0	82.7	145.6	23.4	−61.1	−145.3	Total net share issues	1
2	27.2	29.3	85.7	163.3	64.5	156.6	185.6	193.1	101.2	14.9	−51.3	Mutual funds	2
3	34.6	−65.7	−65.8	−71.7	−73.8	−74.6	−102.9	−47.6	−77.7	−75.9	−94.0	All other	3
4	28.3	−74.5	−81.5	−80.8	−76.5	−80.5	−105.0	−57.0	−83.0	−78.0	−88.0	Nonfinancial corporations	5
5	2.6	7.8	12.0	8.3	5.1	10.6	7.7	7.2	3.7	3.6	6.0	Financial corporations	5
6	3.7	.9	3.7	.7	−2.4	−4.7	−5.6	2.2	1.6	−1.6	−12.0	Foreign shares purchased in U.S.	6

SOURCE: *Flow of Funds Accounts*, Board of Governors; the latest quarter is based on incomplete information.

borrowing was predominately Treasury issues. In 1987, state and local governments had a cumulative net borrowing of $33.3 billion, while household net borrowing amounted to $245.6 billion, and nonfinancial business net borrowing amounted to $265.0 billion.

A review of the top panel shows how net borrowing has changed over time. The U.S. government's net borrowing consistently increased each year until 1987. The state and local government's net borrowing increased substantially during 1985 but has declined since then. Household and nonfinancial business net borrowing increased during the mid 1980s but has decreased since then.

The second panel focuses on net borrowing by financial sectors. In 1987, government agencies were accountable for $169.3 billion of the $283.4 billion of net borrowing by financial sectors. The majority of government agency borrowing was used to provide mortgage financing (mortgage pools). Sixty-two billion dollars of the $114.1 billion in private financial net borrowing was achieved by the issuance of corporate bonds.

The third panel displays a breakdown of securities issued by all sectors. The dollar amount of U.S. government securities issued and mortgages make up more than 60 percent of the total net credit market borrowing in 1987. The fourth panel shows the level of equity funds raised in the United States. Mutual funds have consistently received more funding for investment in their portfolios. The increase in 1986 is most pronounced.

Exhibit 2B.3 shows the net flows of the commercial banking sector. Since most commercial banking involves obtaining funds and using them to acquire financial assets, it is not surprising to see the high correlation between annual increases in net acquisition of financial assets and net increase in liabilities. Loans make up a large proportion of the increase in financial assets acquired. Mortgages and consumer credit also represent a significant part of the increase in financial assets.

Exhibit 2B.4 shows the net flows of savings institutions. Their net acquisition of financial assets increased significantly over time. The main use of funds has been for credit market instruments, specifically mortgages, and consumer installment credit.

Exhibit 2B.5 shows the net flows for life insurance companies. Their annual net acquisition of financial assets has generally increased. Credit market instruments such as U.S. government securities, corporate bonds, and mortgages have been the most common uses of funds.

Exhibit 2B.6 shows the net flows of finance companies. Their net acquisition of financial assets more than doubled from 1983 to 1986. Their main uses of funds have been for credit market instruments such as consumer credit and business loans.

Exhibit 2B.7 shows the net flows of mutual funds. Their growth in net acquisition of financial assets increased consistently until 1986 and then declined in 1987 (the year of the stock market crash). The majority of their growth is concentrated in credit market instruments, especially U.S. government securities and tax-exempt obligations. Because mutual funds often specialize in special types of financial assets, their individual composition may differ significantly from the aggregate composition shown here. For example, some mutual funds specialize in corporate equities and do not maintain any credit market instruments.

Exhibit 2B.8 shows the net flows of money market mutual funds. Their annual net acquisition of financial assets increased significantly in 1987,

EXHIBIT 2B.3 Flow of Funds Accounts for Commercial Banking[1]
(billions of dollars)

Seasonally Adjusted Annual Rates

	1983	1984	1985	1986	1987	1986 III	1986 IV	1987 I	1987 II	1987 III	1987 IV		Seasonally Adjusted Annual Rates	
1	7.1	5.8	7.1	9.2	6.9	9.6	9.7	9.2	6.6	6.9	4.7	Current surplus	1
2	8.6	15.7	19.6	22.4	25.1	19.8	24.0	25.3	25.2	25.0	25.0	Fixed nonres. investment	2
3	150.1	199.8	238.8	257.6	123.7	306.8	359.3	-33.9	189.0	225.0	114.7	Net acq. of financial assets	3
4	-.3	-1.1	-.1	.2	.3	.2	.2	.3	.2	.3	.3	Demand deposits and currency	4
5	139.9	170.8	206.9	194.5	113.9	197.2	324.6	-51.3	235.8	170.2	100.7	Total bank credit	5
6	48.6	.6	9.7	43.3	27.5	54.0	70.2	-3.8	33.4	41.3	39.0	U.S. govt. securities	6
7	47.8	1.9	12.1	5.3	8.6	7.8	19.8	-43.2	8.7	28.8	39.9	Treasury issues	7
8	.7	-1.3	-2.4	38.0	18.9	46.1	50.5	39.4	24.7	12.5	-1.0	Agency issues	8
9	4.8	10.8	57.2	-28.5	-22.8	31.2	-104.8	-15.3	3.8	-26.8	-52.8	Tax-exempt obligations	9
10	4.7	4.2	5.8	23.6	18.0	30.6	30.5	31.0	20.2	13.2	7.7	Corporate bonds	10
11	81.9	155.3	134.0	156.1	91.1	81.5	328.6	-63.3	178.5	142.5	106.9	Total loans	11
12	29.2	44.6	49.7	70.1	82.4	64.2	102.9	73.7	98.8	69.3	87.7	Mortgages	12
13	22.7	45.2	37.5	23.3	9.9	25.1	11.4	2.9	5.0	6.9	24.8	Consumer credit	13
14	26.7	61.1	38.3	69.5	9.3	12.6	229.9	-135.1	70.0	51.2	51.2	Bank loans n.e.c.	14
15	.8	-1.4	-2.5	-.9	-1.5	-5.1	2.0	-4.9	2.7	-1.8	-1.8	Open-market paper	15
16	2.4	5.8	11.0	-5.8	-9.0	-15.5	-17.6	.1	1.9	17.0	-55.0	Security credit	16
17	*	-.1	.1	*	*	*	*	*	*	*	*	Corporate equities	17
18	6.9	3.8	-9.5	-5.6	4.6	.1	-10.2	.3	23.4	-9.0	3.7	Cust. liabs. on acceptances	18
19	-3.6	3.6	8.1	19.6	-3.7	21.5	38.1	-32.9	-3.5	14.5	6.9	Vault cash & res. at F.R.	19
20	7.2	22.7	33.4	48.9	8.7	87.9	6.6	49.7	-67.0	49.0	3.1	Miscellaneous assets	20

	1983	1984	1985	1986	1987	1986 III	1986 IV	1987 I	1987 II	1987 III	1987 IV		
21	161.9	206.5	235.7	246.9	121.4	302.9	368.8	-2.7	146.7	284.6	57.2	Net increase in liabilities	21
22	15.9	29.2	53.9	94.1	-19.7	80.8	162.0	-130.5	57.6	94.9	-100.8	Checkable deposits	22
23	-5.3	4.0	10.3	1.7	5.0	19.4	-4.2	-34.7	43.4	21.8	-10.4	U.S. government	23
24	1.6	2.0	1.4	2.9	-.9	3.6	3.1	-1.4	.1	-2.8	.5	Foreign	24
25	19.7	23.2	42.2	89.6	-23.8	57.8	163.0	-94.4	14.2	76.0	-91.0	Private domestic	25
26	130.8	74.6	80.3	71.6	22.1	97.1	51.4	4.8	30.2	38.7	14.8	Small time and savings dep.	26
27	-48.3	38.3	11.8	3.2	42.3	14.3	18.6	34.8	64.3	14.3	55.6	Large time deposits	27
28	14.8	1.6	31.3	19.2	11.8	62.3	-26.9	39.3	11.8	.6	-4.4	Fed. funds and security RPs	28
29	-.1	11.7	21.9	13.8	46.5	-6.9	56.6	58.6	-8.7	111.7	24.2	Net interbank claims	29
30	-1.0	2.0	-.4	-1.2	1.8	-2.7	2.8	23.5	-17.1	-8.1	9.0	To Federal Reserve	30
31	-11.6	7.4	7.7	2.3	-.6	9.8	21.6	-9.6	.8	18.0	-11.7	To domestic banks[2]	31
32	12.5	2.3	14.5	12.7	45.3	-14.0	32.2	44.7	7.6	101.9	27.0	To foreign banks	32
33	.8	1.1	1.4	1.4	1.6	1.4	1.4	1.5	1.6	1.6	1.6	Corporate equity issues	33
34	17.1	22.8	9.6	1.0	13.4	12.8	-.2	32.7	18.5	-5.8	8.1	Credit market debt	34
35	8.4	12.9	16.9	5.6	5.9	12.7	-.4	9.8	-6.6	6.6	13.6	Corporate bonds	35
36	8.7	10.0	-7.3	-4.6	7.5	.1	.2	22.8	25.1	-12.5	-5.5	Open-market paper	36
37	-.1	*	.1	*	.1	*	-.1	.1	*	.1	.1	Profit taxes payable	37
38	31.0	27.2	25.4	42.7	3.5	41.1	106.2	-43.8	-28.6	28.4	58.1	Miscellaneous liabilities	38
39	10.2	-3.1	-15.6	-23.8	-20.5	-14.1	-4.7	15.1	-60.9	41.5	-77.8	Discrepancy	39
40	144.3	168.9	186.3	194.7	127.5	212.7	332.0	-51.1	257.3	144.2	159.5	Memo: Credit mkt. funds adv.	40

1 Consists of U.S.-chartered commercial banks, domestic affiliates (BHC's), Edge Act corporations, agencies and branches of foreign banks, and banks in U.S. possessions. Edge Act corporations and offices of foreign banks appear together in these tables as "foreign banking offices." IBFs are excluded from the banking data.

2 Floats and discrepancies in interbank deposits and loans.

SOURCE: *Flow of Funds Accounts*, Board of Governors; the latest quarter is based on incomplete data.

EXHIBIT 2B.4 Flow of Funds Accounts for Savings Institutions (billions of dollars)

	Seasonally Adjusted Annual Rates					1986		1987				
	1983	1984	1985	1986	1987	III	IV	I	II	III	IV	
1 Current surplus	.5	2.9	5.9	5.1	4.3	4.9	3.7	3.4	4.6	4.1	5.1	1
2 Fixed nonres. investment	1.9	2.0	1.9	2.0	1.5	1.3	3.2	1.4	1.4	1.8	1.4	2
3 Net acq. of financial assets	156.8	184.2	119.5	134.3	135.0	123.7	144.1	113.3	159.9	95.4	171.5	3
4 Demand deposits and currency	3.1	2.3	5.2	4.6	-5.4	.6	16.7	-14.8	-3.3	-3.7	.4	4
5 Time deposits	2.8	-8.1	7.0	11.0	-7.4	15.2	19.0	-25.2	12.4	-7.2	-5.4	5
6 Security RPs	6.4	8.5	4.5	2.3	-6.5	-2.0	-23.1	35.5	-19.9	-35.7	-5.7	6
7 Corporate equities	.3	-.2	-.1	.9	.1	1.5	1.0	2.0	.1	-.6	-1.2	7
8 Credit market instruments	135.6	150.2	83.0	105.5	140.7	121.7	111.5	58.1	150.9	183.7	169.9	8
9 U.S. govt. securities	53.0	21.3	-9.2	52.5	58.0	66.5	67.3	22.9	74.7	59.5	75.0	9
10 Tax-exempt obligations	-.2	-.3	.6	-.3	*	.8	-.7	-.6	-.1	.5	.1	10
11 Corporate bonds	8.3	5.9	.3	.1	13.6	5.1	-4.1	15.0	16.9	15.2	7.5	11
12 Mortgages	53.5	86.6	58.5	24.0	61.7	17.3	29.3	14.3	54.8	81.8	96.0	12
13 Home mortgages	30.0	50.9	33.7	11.4	48.0	11.0	14.6	-10.0	49.4	67.9	84.9	13
14 Multi-family	7.0	14.4	14.5	7.3	8.2	6.3	11.6	8.2	6.4	8.4	9.9	14
15 Commercial	16.6	21.3	10.3	5.3	5.4	.1	3.1	16.1	-1.0	5.5	1.2	15
16 Farm	—	*	.1	*	*	-.1	.1	*	*	—	—	16
17 Consumer install. credit	14.8	23.8	19.0	11.5	13.9	13.7	11.8	7.9	14.2	21.5	11.8	17
18 Consumer noninstall. credit	-.2	.8	2.0	1.9	-.5	-1.7	.6	-.6	2.4	-2.8	-1.1	18
19 Other loans (to business)	2.4	8.7	5.6	6.7	-.2	6.4	9.2	-.5	-.6	4.3	-3.9	19
20 Open-market paper	3.8	3.6	6.1	9.1	-5.8	13.7	-1.7	-.2	-11.2	3.7	-15.4	20
21 Miscellaneous assets	8.5	31.4	19.9	9.9	13.6	-13.3	19.0	57.8	19.7	-41.1	13.5	21
22 Net increase in liabilities	157.7	185.5	116.6	127.2	129.6	115.2	137.8	106.9	153.4	89.0	169.0	22
23 Deposits	132.5	133.1	80.0	74.8	64.0	73.1	66.0	25.5	46.8	61.0	122.9	23
24 Checkable	11.5	7.9	13.0	20.5	7.0	19.4	24.1	12.1	13.3	1.3	1.2	24
25 Small time and savings	85.8	76.3	60.9	52.7	47.6	50.8	63.9	27.2	46.6	30.3	86.4	25
26 Large time	35.3	49.0	6.1	1.6	9.4	2.9	-21.9	-13.8	-13.1	29.4	35.2	26
27 Security RPs	13.9	18.8	-1.9	14.2	25.7	3.6	7.5	16.4	77.0	2.9	6.4	27
28 Cr. mkt. instr. (S&L)	-2.1	22.7	22.3	29.8	35.2	18.1	49.9	44.5	13.8	28.3	54.2	28
29 Profit taxes payable	*	*	.1	*	*	*	-.3	*	-.1	—	*	29
30 Miscellaneous liabilities	13.4	10.9	16.1	8.5	4.7	20.3	14.6	20.5	16.0	-3.2	-14.5	30
31 Discrepancy	-.6	2.2	1.2	-4.0	-2.6	-5.1	-5.8	-4.4	-3.3	-4.1	1.1	31

SOURCE: *Flow of Funds Accounts, Board of Governors; the latest quarter is based on incomplete information.*

SOURCE: *Flow of Funds Accounts*, Board of Governors; the latest quarter is based on incomplete information.

EXHIBIT 2B.5 Flow of Funds Accounts for Life Insurance Companies (billions of dollars)

	Seasonally Adjusted Annual Rates					1986		1987				
	1983	1984	1985	1986	1987	III	IV	I	II	III	IV	
1	4.0	1.9	.9	1.5	1.5	1.4	1.4	1.5	1.5	1.5	1.4	Current surplus
2	2.8	5.0	5.0	5.3	5.1	6.7	4.0	3.5	4.8	5.4	6.5	Fixed nonres. investment
3	59.1	62.5	94.9	104.7	102.8	138.3	99.2	124.2	69.9	121.9	95.1	Net acq. of financial assets
4	-.6	.7	.5	.7	-1.8	.5	1.0	2.3	-4.9	.5	-5.0	Demand deposits and currency
5	-1.9	2.2	.4	1.1	.7	1.2	1.4	1.2	-.1	.6	1.1	Money mkt. fund shares
6	-.4	.5	2.3	2.1	1.5	2.8	2.5	3.7	1.6	.8	-.2	Mutual fund shares
7	3.4	.3	3.7	6.0	3.4	21.3	11.7	16.0	-1.7	-4.9	4.2	Other corporate equities
8	52.5	54.1	76.1	86.8	89.8	104.6	74.2	100.2	63.0	116.7	79.3	Credit market instruments
9	19.3	23.6	23.0	17.9	17.0	19.9	13.8	39.5	-7.0	25.2	10.2	U.S. government securities
10	12.1	12.6	10.5	7.3	9.0	11.8	7.5	27.8	-12.2	10.9	9.4	Treasury issues
11	7.2	11.0	12.5	10.6	8.0	8.0	6.3	11.7	5.2	14.3	.8	Agency issues
12	.9	-1.3	1.0	2.0	.1	3.7	-1.7	-1.0	2.0	-1.3	.8	Tax-exempt obligations
13	16.7	23.7	37.8	40.8	53.6	40.2	39.1	43.9	57.4	57.0	56.0	Corporate & foreign bonds
14	9.0	5.7	15.1	22.0	16.7	26.2	21.4	16.1	16.6	20.2	13.9	Mortgages
15	5.3	1.9	-.6	4.3	2.8	14.7	2.8	3.2	-4.9	15.4	-2.4	Open-market paper
16	1.1	.4	-.1	-.3	-.5	-.1	-1.2	-1.6	-1.1	.2	.7	Policy loans
17	6.1	4.8	12.0	8.0	9.2	8.0	8.4	.8	11.9	8.3	15.7	Miscellaneous assets
18	55.8	66.3	88.3	100.1	102.0	131.0	100.4	119.2	70.3	121.4	96.9	Net increase in liabilities
19	7.8	5.0	10.4	17.2	15.7	18.0	18.9	17.6	13.5	19.0	12.8	Life insurance reserves
20	38.8	46.7	63.4	77.5	82.9	107.2	77.3	93.6	55.6	99.0	83.3	Pension fund reserves
21	-.1	-.2	*	*	.2	-.1	*	.2	.2	.2	.3	Profit taxes payable
22	9.2	14.8	14.4	5.4	3.1	5.9	4.1	7.8	1.0	3.1	.4	Miscellaneous liabilities
23	-2.2	.8	-10.7	-8.4	-4.4	-12.6	-1.5	-6.9	-2.8	-4.5	-3.4	Discrepancy

Seasonally Adjusted Annual Rates

EXHIBIT 2B.6 Flow of Funds Accounts for Finance Companies
(billions of dollars)

Seasonally Adjusted Annual Rates

	1983	1984	1985	1986	1987	1986 III	1986 IV	1987 I	1987 II	1987 III	1987 IV	Seasonally Adjusted Annual Rates	
1	5.0	3.0	3.6	4.6	5.5	4.8	5.0	4.9	5.6	5.5	6.0	Current surplus	1
2	6.1	6.4	9.3	9.3	9.9	10.0	8.2	10.0	10.1	9.7	10.1	Fixed nonres. investment	2
3	26.8	37.8	52.8	58.1	35.7	86.2	34.4	21.7	44.9	38.8	37.5	Net acq. of financial assets	3
4	.1	-.5	.9	1.6	.7	1.4	3.1	-.2	2.1	*	.8	Demand deposits and currency	4
5	26.8	38.3	51.9	56.4	35.0	84.8	31.3	21.8	42.8	38.8	36.7	Credit market instruments	5
6	2.7	5.4	6.8	15.8	-.1	39.5	-5.7	2.5	6.8	-11.5	1.7	Mortgages	6
7	11.0	8.6	24.6	24.2	7.3	43.6	1.9	-2.9	11.0	19.4	1.9	Consumer credit	7
8	13.1	24.4	20.5	16.4	27.8	1.7	35.1	22.2	25.0	31.0	33.1	Other loans (to business)	8
9	19.7	37.6	64.3	79.3	42.4	79.3	55.6	44.7	36.9	55.2	32.9	Net increase in liabilities	9
10	12.9	18.9	53.9	49.7	26.5	49.0	43.7	12.7	48.9	42.7	1.7	Credit market instruments	10
11	5.3	9.6	15.8	22.5	14.5	10.0	18.1	16.1	22.6	16.7	2.6	Corporate bonds	11
12	-5.0	-4.5	-1.0	-1.3	-8.6	5.5	-6.2	-27.2	.1	.7	-8.0	Bank loans n.e.c.	12
13	12.6	13.9	39.1	28.5	20.6	33.6	31.8	23.8	26.2	25.4	7.1	Open-market paper	13
14	*	*	*	*	.1	.1	*	.1	.1	.1	.1	Profit taxes payable	14
15	2.4	12.5	15.0	40.8	.5	28.4	23.8	6.6	-31.3	7.6	18.9	Inv. by parent companies	15
16	4.4	6.2	-4.6	-11.3	15.4	1.9	-11.9	25.3	19.2	4.8	12.1	Other misc. liabilities	16
17	-8.3	-3.5	5.9	16.5	2.2	-12.1	17.9	17.9	-12.5	12.1	-8.7	Discrepancy	17

SOURCE: *Flow of Fixed Accounts*, Board of Governors; the latest quarter is based on incomplete information.

EXHIBIT 2B.7 Flow of Funds Accounts for Mutual Funds
(in billions of dollars)

Seasonally Adjusted Annual Rates

	1983	1984	1985	1986	1987	1986 III	1986 IV	1987 I	1987 II	1987 III	1987 IV		Seasonally Adjusted Annual Rates	
1	−3.2	−5.2	−4.9	−17.3	−10.9	−13.0	−38.2	−5.9	−14.4	−13.6	−9.6	Current surplus	1
2	24.0	24.2	80.8	145.9	53.6	143.6	147.4	187.2	86.8	1.3	−60.9	Net acq. of financial assets	2
3	.6	.4	1.7	2.6	.5	1.6	2.6	5.0	.7	.3	−4.1	Demand deposits and currency	3
4	13.7	5.9	10.3	20.2	26.9	20.1	19.0	40.7	41.9	33.7	−8.6	Corporate equities	4
5	9.8	17.9	68.7	123.1	26.2	121.9	125.8	141.5	44.2	−32.7	−48.3	Credit market instruments	5
6	.6	6.4	52.9	59.3	5.8	57.2	47.9	89.5	−23.3	−34.2	−8.8	U.S. government securities	6
7	.6	5.8	41.4	36.4	5.8	30.8	29.0	71.6	−19.7	−25.9	−2.7	Treasury issues	7
8	—	.5	11.5	22.9	*	26.4	18.9	17.9	−3.6	−8.3	−6.1	Agency issues	8
9	5.5	5.6	14.5	31.8	5.4	32.3	31.6	36.1	−.4	−.1	−13.9	Tax-exempt obligations	9
10	2.7	3.6	3.6	26.8	9.6	30.2	35.6	11.5	64.8	−12.7	−25.2	Corporate & foreign bonds	10
11	1.0	2.4	−2.3	5.3	5.4	2.2	10.8	4.5	3.2	14.4	−.5	Open-market paper	11
12	27.2	29.3	85.7	163.3	64.5	156.6	185.6	193.1	101.2	14.9	−51.3	Net share issues	12

SOURCE: *Flow of Funds Accounts*, Board of Governors; latest quarter based on incomplete information.

EXHIBIT 2B.8 Flow of Funds Accounts for Money Market Mutual Funds
(billions of dollars)

Seasonally Adjusted Annual Rates

	1983	1984	1985	1986	1987	1986 III	1986 IV	1987 I	1987 II	1987 III	1987 IV	Seasonally Adjusted Annual Rates	
1	-40.4	54.2	10.2	48.3	24.0	69.8	21.5	-3.7	.1	24.7	74.7	Net acq. of financial assets	1
2	-.6	-1.0	1.4	-.2	-.3	-4.1	1.3	4.3	-.3	-.9	-4.3	Demand deposits and currency	2
3	-16.8	-.4	-6.8	2.3	14.4	-2.1	6.4	.9	21.6	1.7	33.6	Time deposits	3
4	-3.2	9.7	3.3	6.1	7.1	-9.4	.7	7.0	24.6	6.5	-9.6	Security RPs	4
5	-1.8	-.7	-2.2	3.1	-.6	-.3	1.5	15.2	-8.1	-8.2	-1.2	Foreign deposits	5
6	-17.7	45.0	13.9	34.1	1.8	60.2	-6.2	-18.3	-9.2	3.0	31.8	Credit market instruments	6
7	-18.4	6.2	.3	.5	-1.9	7.9	16.0	-32.1	3.7	9.6	30.6	U.S. government securities	7
8	-19.8	2.6	-.8	3.4	-13.7	6.4	16.3	-38.3	6.9	-19.9	-3.7	Treasury issues	8
9	1.4	3.6	1.1	-3.0	11.9	1.5	-.3	6.2	-3.2	10.3	34.3	Agency issues	9
10	3.6	7.0	12.4	27.5	-2.3	23.2	16.4	9.8	-7.8	-1.1	-10.2	Tax-exempt obligations	10
11	-3.0	31.8	1.2	6.2	6.0	29.1	-38.6	4.0	-5.1	13.8	11.4	Open-market paper	11
12	-.4	1.5	.6	2.9	1.4	25.5	17.8	-12.9	-28.4	22.7	24.4	Miscellaneous	12
13	-40.4	54.2	10.2	48.3	24.0	69.8	21.5	-3.7	.1	24.7	74.7	Net share issues	13

SOURCE: *Flow of Fund Accounts*, Board of Governors; the latest quarter is based on incomplete information.

when investors shifted out of stock mutual funds as a result of the stock market crash. The securities that represent the growth in investment by money market mutual funds are time deposits, security RPs (repurchase agreements), and open-market paper.

The *Flow of Funds Accounts* provide much more data than was presented here. The exhibits shown here simply illustrate the type of information available.

Relationships between Interest Rates and Security Prices

BOND PRICES AND YIELDS IN PERSPECTIVE

After the stock market crash on October 19, 1987, *The Wall Street Journal* reported revised projections of bond prices and yields by economists and analysts. The crash caused a downward revision on economic growth and inflation and also was expected to encourage the Federal Reserve to use a looser monetary policy. These conditions generally caused upward revisions of forecasted bond prices and downward revisions of forecasted bond yields.

On June 16, 1988, the dollar weakened, inflationary expectations increased, and bond prices declined. Some bonds declined as much as $15 per $1,000 par value. Another reason for the decline was the expectation that the Federal Reserve system would tighten credit in the near future.

On June 22, 1988, a government report showed unexpectedly low inflation in the previous month, and the bond markets rallied temporarily.

A review of various issues of *The Wall Street Journal* will demonstrate how quickly bond price projections can change. This should not be surprising since bond prices are closely tied to interest rate movements. As forecasts of the economic factors that influence interest rate movements change, bond price projections are revised in accordance with revised interest rate expectations.

■ How do the factors cited above affect bond prices?

■ How are these factors related to interest rate movements, and how is this relationship relevant to bond market participants?

■ Why are the prices of some types of bonds more sensitive to changing interest rate expectations than others?

■ How does a revised interest rate forecast affect the market value of a bond portfolio?

These and other related questions are addressed in this chapter.

OUTLINE

This chapter explains how security prices are influenced by interest rate movements. The focus here is on securities that reflect a creditor position, such as bonds, rather than an ownership position, such as stocks. The market values of mortgages are also very sensitive to interest rate fluctuations and are closely watched by the financial institutions that originate them (such as mortgage companies or savings and loan associations) and those that purchase them in the secondary market (such as life insurance companies). Since fixed-rate mortgages have cash flow characteristics somewhat similar to those of bonds, the concepts discussed in this chapter could also be applied to them.

BOND VALUATION

Bond valuation is conceptually similar to the valuation of capital budgeting projects, businesses, or even real estate. The appropriate price reflects the present value of cash flows to be received. The discount rate selected to compute present value is critical to accurate valuation. Exhibit 3.1 shows the wide range of present value results yielded by different discount rates—for a $10,000 payment in 10 years. The appropriate discount rate for valuing any asset is the yield that could be earned on alternative investments with similar risk and maturity.

The market price of a bond is determined not only by the size but also the timing of the payments made to bondholders. Funds received sooner can be reinvested to earn additional returns. Thus, a dollar to be received soon has a higher present value than one to be received later. The impact of maturity on the present value of a $10,000 payment is shown in Exhibit 3.2, assuming that a return of 10 percent could be earned on available funds. The $10,000 payment has a present value of $8,264 if it is to be paid in two years. This implies that if $8,264 were invested today and earned 10 percent annually, it would be worth $10,000 in two years. Exhibit 3.2 also shows that a $10,000 payment made 20 years from now has a present value of only $1,486, and a $10,000 payment made 50 years from now has a present value of only $85 (based on the 10 percent discount rate).

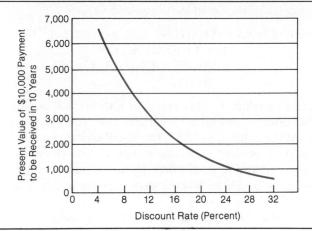

The current price of a bond should be the present value of its remaining
cash flows. The present value (PV) of a bond is

$$PV \text{ of bond} = \frac{C}{(1 + i)^1} + \frac{C}{(1 + i)^2} + \cdots \frac{C + P}{(1 + i)^n}$$

where C = coupon payment provided in each period
P = par value
i = interest rate per period used to discount the bond
n = number of periods to maturity

Consider a bond that has a par value of $1,000, pays $100 at the end of each
year in coupon payments, and has three years remaining until maturity.
Assume that the prevailing annualized yields on other bonds with similar
characteristics is 12 percent. In this case, the appropriate price of the bond

EXHIBIT 3.2   Relationship between Time of Payment and Present Value of
Payment

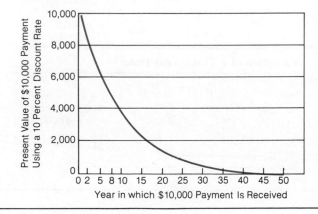

can be determined as follows. The future cash flows to investors who would purchase this bond are $100 in Year 1, $100 in Year 2, and $1,100 (computed as $100 in coupon payments plus $1,000 par value) in Year 3. The appropriate market price of the bond is its present value:

$$PV \text{ of bond} = \$100/(1 + .12)^1 + \$100/(1 + .12)^2$$
$$+ \$1,100/(1 + .12)^3$$
$$= \$89.29 + \$79.72 + \$782.96$$
$$= \$951.97$$

This valuation procedure is illustrated in Exhibit 3.3. Because it was assumed that investors required a 12 percent return, i equals 12 percent for this example. At the price of $951.97, the bondholders purchasing this bond would receive a 12 percent annualized return. The prices of other bonds with three years remaining until maturity and offering a 12 percent return will not necessarily be $951.97, since they may have different coupon payments.

Bond valuation can be simplified with a present-value table, as is shown in Exhibit 3.4. The *present value interest factor (PVIF)* is shown for various interest rates and time periods. Coupon payments and the par value can be multiplied by their respective PVIFs to determine the present value of the bond. For example, the present value of the bond just described is reestimated as follows, using the table in Exhibit 3.4:

$$PV \text{ of bond} = \$100 (PVIF_{i=12\%,n=1}) + \$100 (PVIF_{i=12\%,n=2}) + \$1,100 (PVIF_{i=12\%,n=3})$$
$$= \$100 (.8929) \quad\quad + \$100 (.7972) \quad\quad + \$1,100 (.7118)$$
$$= \$89.29 \quad\quad\quad\quad + \$79.72 \quad\quad\quad\quad + \$782.98$$
$$= \$951.99$$

The slightly different answer is due to rounding.

Valuation of Bonds With Semiannual Payments

In reality, most bonds have semiannual payments. The present value of such bonds can be computed as follows. First, the annualized coupon should be split in half, since two payments are made per year. Second, the annual discount rate should be divided by 2 to reflect two six-month periods per year. Third, the number of periods should be doubled to reflect two times

EXHIBIT 3.3 Valuation of a Three-Year Bond

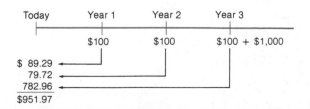

the number of annual periods. Incorporating these adjustments, the present value is determined as follows:

$$\begin{array}{c} PV \text{ of bond} \\ \text{with semiannual} \\ \text{payments} \end{array} = \frac{C/2}{(1 + i/2)^1} + \frac{C/2}{(1 + i/2)^2} + \cdots \frac{C/2 + P}{(1 + i/2)^{2n}}$$

Where $C/2$ is the semiannual coupon payment (one-half of what the annual coupon payment would have been), and $i/2$ is the periodic discount rate used to discount the bond. The last part of the equation shows $2n$ in the denominator exponent to reflect the doubling of periods.

To illustrate the use of bond valuation with semiannual payments, consider the previous example of a bond with $1,000 par value, a 10 percent coupon rate, and three years to maturity. Assuming a 12 percent required return, the present value would be computed as follows:

$$\begin{array}{c} PV \\ \text{of} \\ \text{bond} \end{array} = \frac{\$50}{(1.06)^1} + \frac{\$50}{(1.06)^2} + \frac{\$50}{(1.06)^3} + \frac{\$50}{(1.06)^4} + \frac{\$50}{(1.06)^5} + \frac{\$50 + \$1,000}{(1.06)^6}$$

$$= \$47.17 + \$44.50 + \$41.98 + \$39.60 + \$37.36 + \$740.21$$

$$= \$950.82$$

This example could also have been worked using PVIF tables. The periods in this example are six months in length, and the discount rate is half of the annual 12 percent rate. The present value of the bond with semiannual coupon payments is higher because some of the payments are received by bondholders six months earlier. While the difference in present value is small, it could be significant for bonds with a large par value.

The remaining examples assume annual coupon payments so that we can focus on the concepts presented without concern about adjusting annual payments.

Use of Annuity Tables for Valuation

Any bond can be valued by separating its payments into two components:

$$PV \text{ of bond} = PV \text{ of coupon payments} + PV \text{ of principal payment}$$

A bond's coupon payments represent an **annuity,** or an even stream of payments over a given period of time. The present value of any annuity can be determined by multiplying the annuity amount times the appropriate **present value interest factor of an annuity (PVIFA).** The table in Exhibit 3.5 can be used to identify the appropriate PVIFA. To illustrate, recall the example of the 10 percent coupon bond with annual coupon payments, a $1,000 par value, and three years to maturity. The PVIFA for this example is $PVIFA_{i = 12\%, n = 3} = 2.4018$ as shown in Exhibit 3.5. This is used to determine the present value of the coupon payments:

$$\begin{array}{c} PV \text{ of} \\ \text{coupon} \\ \text{payments} \end{array} = C (PVIFA_{i = 12\%, n = 3})$$

$$= \$100 (2.4018)$$

$$= \$240.18$$

EXHIBIT 3.4 Present Value Interest Factors (PVIF)

Period n	1%	2%	3%	4%	5%	6%	7%	8%	9%	10%	11%	12%
1	.9901	.9804	.9709	.9615	.9524	.9434	.9346	.9259	.9174	.9091	.9009	.8929
2	.9803	.9612	.9426	.9246	.9070	.8900	.8734	.8573	.8417	.8264	.8116	.7972
3	.9706	.9423	.9151	.8890	.8638	.8396	.8163	.7938	.7722	.7513	.7312	.7118
4	.9610	.9238	.8885	.8548	.8227	.7921	.7629	.7350	.7084	.6830	.6587	.6355
5	.9515	.9057	.8626	.8219	.7835	.7473	.7130	.6806	.6499	.6209	.5935	.5674
6	.9420	.8880	.8375	.7903	.7462	.7050	.6663	.6302	.5963	.5645	.5346	.5066
7	.9327	.8706	.8131	.7599	.7107	.6651	.6227	.5835	.5470	.5132	.4817	.4523
8	.9235	.8535	.7894	.7307	.6768	.6274	.5820	.5403	.5019	.4665	.4339	.4039
9	.9143	.8368	.7664	.7026	.6446	.5919	.5439	.5002	.4604	.4241	.3909	.3606
10	.9053	.8203	.7441	.6756	.6139	.5584	.5083	.4632	.4224	.3856	.3522	.3220
11	.8963	.8043	.7224	.6496	.5847	.5268	.4751	.4289	.3875	.3505	.3173	.2875
12	.8874	.7885	.7014	.6246	.5568	.4970	.4440	.3971	.3555	.3186	.2858	.2567
13	.8787	.7730	.6810	.6006	.5303	.4688	.4150	.3677	.3262	.2897	.2575	.2292
14	.8700	.7579	.6611	.5775	.5051	.4423	.3878	.3405	.2992	.2633	.2320	.2046
15	.8613	.7430	.6419	.5553	.4810	.4173	.3624	.3152	.2745	.2394	.2090	.1827
16	.8528	.7284	.6232	.5339	.4581	.3936	.3387	.2919	.2519	.2176	.1883	.1631
17	.8444	.7142	.6050	.5134	.4363	.3714	.3166	.2703	.2311	.1978	.1696	.1456
18	.8360	.7002	.5874	.4936	.4155	.3503	.2959	.2502	.2120	.1799	.1528	.1300
19	.8277	.6864	.5703	.4746	.3957	.3305	.2765	.2317	.1945	.1635	.1377	.1161
20	.8195	.6730	.5537	.4564	.3769	.3118	.2584	.2145	.1784	.1486	.1240	.1037
21	.8114	.6598	.5375	.4388	.3589	.2942	.2415	.1987	.1637	.1351	.1117	.0926
22	.8034	.6468	.5219	.4220	.3418	.2775	.2257	.1839	.1502	.1228	.1007	.0826
23	.7954	.6342	.5067	.4057	.3256	.2618	.2109	.1700	.1378	.1117	.0907	.0738
24	.7876	.6217	.4919	.3901	.3101	.2470	.1971	.1577	.1264	.1015	.0817	.0659
25	.7798	.6095	.4776	.3751	.2953	.2330	.1842	.1460	.1160	.0923	.0736	.0588
26	.7720	.5976	.4637	.3607	.2812	.2198	.1722	.1352	.1064	.0839	.0663	.0525
27	.7644	.5859	.4502	.3468	.2678	.2074	.1609	.1252	.0976	.0763	.0597	.0469
28	.7568	.5744	.4371	.3335	.2551	.1956	.1504	.1159	.0895	.0693	.0538	.0419
29	.7493	.5631	.4243	.3207	.2429	.1846	.1406	.1073	.0822	.0630	.0485	.0374
30	.7419	.5521	.4120	.3083	.2314	.1741	.1314	.0994	.0754	.0573	.0437	.0334
35	.7059	.5000	.3554	.2534	.1813	1301	.0937	.0676	.0490	.0356	.0259	.0189
40	.6717	.4529	.3066	.2083	.1420	.0972	.0668	.0460	.0318	.0221	.0154	.0107
45	.6391	.4102	.2644	.1712	.1113	.0727	.0476	.0313	.0207	.0137	.0091	.0061
50	.6080	.3715	.2281	.1407	.0872	.0543	.0339	.0213	.0134	.0085	.0054	.0035

The present value of the principal must also be determined:

$$PV \text{ of principal} = \frac{\$1{,}000}{(1.12)^3}$$

or $1,000 ($PVIF_{i=12\%, n=3}$)

$$= \$1{,}000 \,(.7118) \text{ [See Exhibit 3.4]}$$
$$= \$711.80$$

When the PV of coupon payments is combined with the principal, the bond's present value is about $951.98 (computed as $240.18 + $711.80).

The use of PVIFA tables is especially efficient for valuing long-term bonds. For example, determine the present value of bonds with an 8 percent coupon

Period	13%	14%	15%	16%	17%	18%	19%	20%	25%	30%	35%	40%	50%
1	.8850	.8772	.8696	.8621	.8547	.8475	.8403	.8333	.8000	.7692	.7407	.7143	.6667
2	.7831	.7695	.7561	.7432	.7305	.7182	.7062	.6944	.6400	.5917	.5487	.5102	.4444
3	.6931	.6750	.6575	.6407	.6244	.6086	.5934	.5787	.5120	.4552	.4064	.3644	.2963
4	.6133	.5921	.5718	.5523	.5337	.5158	.4987	.4823	.4096	.3501	.3011	.2603	.1975
5	.5428	.5194	.4972	.4761	.4561	.4371	.4190	.4019	.3277	.2693	.2230	.1859	.1317
6	.4803	.4556	.4323	.4104	.3898	.3704	.3521	.3349	.2621	.2072	.1652	.1328	.0878
7	.4251	.3996	.3759	.3538	.3332	.3139	.2959	.2791	.2097	.1594	.1224	.0949	.0585
8	.3762	.3506	.3269	.3050	.2848	.2660	.2487	.2326	.1678	.1226	.0906	.0678	.0390
9	.3329	.3075	.2843	.2630	.2434	.2255	.2090	.1938	.1342	.0943	.0671	.0484	.0260
10	.2946	.2697	.2472	.2267	.2080	.1911	.1756	.1615	.1074	.0725	.0497	.0346	.0173
11	.2607	.2366	.2149	.1954	.1778	.1619	.1476	.1346	.0859	.0558	.0368	.0247	.0116
12	.2307	.2076	.1869	.1685	.1520	.1372	.1240	.1122	.0687	.0429	.0273	.0176	.0077
13	.2042	.1821	.1625	.1452	.1299	.1163	.1042	.0935	.0550	.0330	.0202	.0126	.0051
14	.1807	.1597	.1413	.1252	.1110	.0985	.0876	.0779	.0440	.0254	.0150	.0090	.0034
15	.1599	.1401	.1229	.1079	.0949	.0835	.0736	.0649	.0352	.0195	.0111	.0064	.0023
16	.1415	.1229	.1069	.0930	.0811	.0708	.0618	.0541	.0281	.0150	.0082	.0046	.0015
17	.1252	.1078	.0929	.0802	.0693	.0600	.0520	.0451	.0225	.0116	.0061	.0033	.0010
18	.1108	.0946	.0808	.0691	.0592	.0508	.0437	.0376	.0180	.0089	.0045	.0023	.0007
19	.0981	.0829	.0703	.0596	.0506	.0431	.0367	.0313	.0144	.0068	.0033	.0017	.0005
20	.0868	.0728	.0611	.0514	.0443	.0365	.0308	.0261	.0115	.0053	.0025	.0012	.0003
21	.0768	.0638	.0531	.0443	.0370	.0309	.0259	.0217	.0092	.0040	.0018	.0009	.0002
22	.0680	.0560	.0462	.0382	.0316	.0262	.0218	.0181	.0074	.0031	.0014	.0006	.0001
23	.0601	.0491	.0402	.0329	.0270	.0222	.0183	.0151	.0059	.0024	.0010	.0004	.0001
24	.0532	.0431	.0349	.0284	.0231	.0188	.0154	.0126	.0047	.0018	.0007	.0003	.0001
25	.0471	.0378	.0304	.0245	.0197	.0160	.0129	.0105	.0038	.0014	.0006	.0002	.0000
26	.0417	.0331	.0264	.0211	.0169	.0135	.0109	.0087	.0030	.0011	.0004	.0002	.0000
27	.0369	.0291	.0230	.0182	.0144	.0115	.0091	.0073	.0024	.0008	.0003	.0001	.0000
28	.0326	.0255	.0200	.0157	.0123	.0097	.0077	.0061	.0019	.0006	.0002	.0001	.0000
29	.0289	.0224	.0174	.0135	.0105	.0082	.0064	.0051	.0015	.0005	.0002	.0001	.0000
30	.0256	.0196	.0151	.0116	.0090	.0070	.0054	.0042	.0012	.0004	.0001	.0000	.0000
35	.0139	.0102	.0075	.0055	.0041	.0030	.0023	.0017	.0004	.0001	.0000	.0000	.0000
40	.0075	.0053	.0037	.0026	.0019	.0013	.0010	.0007	.0001	.0000	.0000	.0000	.0000
45	.0041	.0027	.0019	.0013	.0009	.0006	.0004	.0003	.0000	.0000	.0000	.0000	.0000
50	.0022	.0014	.0009	.0006	.0004	.0003	.0002	.0001	.0000	.0000	.0000	.0000	.0000

rate, a par value of $100,000, and 20 years to maturity, using a 14 percent required rate of return:

$$PV \text{ of bonds} = PV \text{ of coupon payments} + PV \text{ of principal}$$
$$= \$8,000 \ (PVIFA_{i=14\%, n=20}) + \$100,000 \ (PVIF_{i=14\%, n=20})$$
$$= \$8,000 \ (6.6231) + \$100,000 \ (.0728)$$
$$= \$52,985 + \$7,280$$
$$= \$60,265$$

This implies that investors requiring a 14 percent return would pay no more than $60,265 for these bonds.

Chapter 3

Relationships between
Interest Rates and
Security Prices

EXHIBIT 3.5 Present Value Interest Factors for an Annuity (PVIFA)

Period n	1%	2%	3%	4%	5%	6%	7%	8%	9%	10%	11%	12%
1	0.9901	0.9804	0.9709	0.9615	0.9524	0.9434	0.9346	0.9259	0.9174	0.9091	0.9009	0.8929
2	1.9704	1.9416	1.9135	1.8861	1.8594	1.8334	1.8080	1.7833	1.7591	1.7355	1.7125	1.6901
3	2.9410	2.8839	2.8286	2.7751	2.7232	2.6730	2.6243	2.5771	2.5313	2.4869	2.4437	2.4018
4	3.9020	3.8077	3.7171	3.6299	3.5460	3.4651	3.3872	3.3121	3.2397	3.1899	3.1024	3.0373
5	4.8534	4.7135	4.5797	4.4518	4.3295	4.2124	4.1002	3.9927	3.8897	3.7908	3.6959	3.6048
6	5.7955	5.6014	5.4172	5.2421	5.0757	6.9173	4.7665	4.6229	4.4859	4.3553	4.2305	4.1114
7	6.7282	6.4720	6.2303	6.0021	5.7864	5.5824	5.3893	5.2064	5.0330	4.8684	4.7122	4.5638
8	7.6517	7.3255	7.0197	6.7327	6.4632	6.2098	5.9713	5.7466	5.5348	5.3349	5.1461	4.9676
9	8.5660	8.1622	7.7861	7.4353	7.1078	6.8017	6.5152	6.2469	5.9952	5.7590	5.5370	5.3282
10	9.4713	8.9826	8.5302	8.1109	7.7217	7.3601	7.0236	6.7101	6.4177	6.1446	5.8892	5.6502
11	10.368	9.7868	9.2526	8.7605	8.3064	7.8869	7.4987	7.1390	6.8052	6.4951	6.2065	5.9377
12	11.255	10.575	9.9540	9.3851	8.8633	8.3838	7.9427	7.5361	7.1607	6.8137	6.4924	6.1944
13	12.134	11.348	10.635	9.9856	9.3936	8.8527	8.3577	7.9038	7.4869	7.1034	6.7499	6.4235
14	13.004	12.106	11.296	10.563	9.8986	9.2950	8.7455	8.2442	7.7862	7.3667	6.9819	6.6282
15	13.865	12.849	11.938	11.118	10.380	9.7122	9.1079	8.5595	8.0607	7.6061	7.1909	6.8109
16	14.718	13.578	12.561	11.652	10.838	10.106	9.4466	8.8514	8.3126	7.8237	7.3792	6.9740
17	15.562	14.292	13.166	12.166	11.274	10.477	9.7632	9.1216	8.5436	8.0216	7.5488	7.1196
18	16.398	14.992	13.754	12.659	11.690	10.828	10.059	9.3719	8.7556	8.2014	7.7016	7.2497
19	17.226	15.678	14.324	13.134	12.085	11.158	10.336	9.6036	8.9501	8.3649	7.8393	7.3658
20	18.046	16.351	14.877	13.590	12.462	11.470	10.594	9.8181	9.1285	8.5136	7.9633	7.4694
21	18.857	17.011	15.415	14.029	12.821	11.764	10,836	10.017	9.2922	8.6487	8.0751	7.5620
22	19.660	17.658	15.937	14.451	13.163	12.042	11.061	10.201	9.4424	8.7715	8.1757	7.6446
23	20.456	18.292	16.444	14.857	13.489	12.303	11.272	10.371	9.5802	8.8832	8.2664	7.7184
24	21.243	18.914	16.936	15.247	13.799	12.550	11.469	10.529	9.7066	8.9847	8.3481	7.7843
25	22.023	19.523	17.413	15.622	14.094	12.783	11.654	10.675	9.8226	9.0770	8.4217	7.8431
26	22.795	20.121	17.877	15.983	14.375	13.003	11.826	10.810	9.9290	9.1609	8.4881	7.8957
27	23.560	20.707	18.327	16.330	14.643	13.211	11.987	10.935	10.027	9.2372	8.5478	7.9426
28	24.316	21.281	18.764	16.663	14.898	13.406	12.137	11.051	10.116	9.3066	8.6016	7.9844
29	25.066	21.844	19.188	16.984	15.141	13.591	12.278	11.158	10.198	9.3696	8.6501	8.0218
30	25.808	22.396	19.600	17.292	15.372	13.765	12.408	11.258	10.274	9.4269	8.6938	8.0552
35	29.409	24.999	21.487	18.665	16.374	14.498	12.948	11.655	10.567	9.6442	8.8552	8.1755
40	32.835	27.355	23.115	19.793	17.159	15.046	13.332	11.925	10.757	9.7791	8.9511	8.2438
45	36.095	29.490	24.519	20.720	17.774	15.456	13.606	12.108	10.881	9.8628	9.0079	8.2825
50	39.196	31.424	25.730	21.482	18.256	15.762	13.801	12.233	10.962	9.9148	9.0417	8.3045

IMPACT OF INTEREST RATE MOVEMENTS ON BOND PRICES

Assume that the required rate of return by investors increases from 12 percent to 13 percent, which could occur if interest rates rise, making investors realize that they could earn a return of 13 percent on alternative newly issued securities with similar characteristics. The appropriate price of the bond described earlier can be determined by increasing the discount rate from 12 percent to 13 percent:

$$PV \text{ of bond} = \$100/(1 + .13)^1 + \$100/(1 + .13)^2 + \$1,100/(1 + .13)^3$$
$$= \$88.50 + \$78.31 + \$762.36$$
$$= \$929.17$$

Period n	13%	14%	15%	16%	17%	18%	19%	20%	25%	30%	35%	40%	50%
1	0.8850	0.8772	0.8696	0.8621	0.8547	0.8475	0.8403	0.8333	0.8000	0.7692	0.7407	0.7143	0.6667
2	1.6681	1.6467	1.6257	1.6052	1.5852	1.5656	1.5465	1.5278	1.4400	1.3609	1.2894	1.2245	1.1111
3	2.3612	2.3216	2.2832	2.2459	2.2096	2.1743	2.1399	2.1065	1.9520	1.8161	1.6959	1.5889	1.4074
4	2.9745	2.9137	2.8550	2.7982	2.7432	2.6901	2.6386	2.5887	2.3616	2.1662	1.9969	1.8492	1.6049
5	3.5172	3.4331	3.3522	3.2743	3.1993	3.1272	3.0576	2.9906	2.6893	2.4356	2.2200	2.0352	1.7366
6	3.9975	3.8887	3.7845	3.6847	3.5892	3.4976	3.4098	3.3255	2.9514	2.6427	2.3852	2.1880	1.8244
7	4.4226	4.2883	4.1604	4.0386	3.9224	3.8115	3.7057	3.6046	3.1611	2.8021	2.5075	2.2628	1.8829
8	4.7988	4.6389	4.4873	4.3436	4.2072	4.0776	3.9544	3.8372	3.3289	2.9247	2.5982	2.3306	1.9220
9	5.1317	4.9464	4.7716	4.6065	4.4506	4.3030	4.1633	4.0310	3.4631	3.0190	2.6653	2.3790	1.9480
10	5.4262	5.2161	5.0188	4.8332	4.6585	4.4941	4.3389	4.1925	3.5705	3.0915	2.7150	2.4136	1.9653
11	5.6869	5.4527	5.2337	5.0286	4.8364	4.6560	4.4865	4.3271	3.6564	3.1473	2.7519	2.4383	1.9769
12	5.9176	5.6603	5.4206	5.1971	4.9884	4.7932	4.6105	4.4392	3.7251	3.1903	2.7792	2.4559	1.9846
13	6.1218	5.8424	5.5831	5.3423	5.1183	4.9095	4.7147	4.5327	3.7801	3.2233	2.7994	2.4685	1.9897
14	6.3025	6.0021	5.7245	5.4675	5.2293	5.0081	4.8023	4.6106	3.8241	3.2487	2.8144	2.4775	1.9931
15	6.4624	6.1422	5.8474	5.5755	5.3242	5.0916	4.8759	4.6755	3.8593	3.2682	2.8255	2.4839	1.9954
16	6.6039	6.2651	5.9542	5.6685	5.4053	5.1624	4.9377	4.7296	3.8874	3.2832	2.8337	2.4885	1.9970
17	6.7291	6.3729	6.0472	5.7487	5.4746	5.2223	4.9897	4.7746	3.9099	3.2948	2.8398	2.4918	1.9980
18	6.8399	6.4674	6.1280	5.8178	5.5339	5.2732	5.0333	4.8122	3.9279	3.3037	2.8443	2.4941	1.9986
19	6.9380	6.5504	6.1982	5.8775	5.5845	5.3162	5.0700	4.8435	3.9424	3.3105	2.8476	2.4958	1.9991
20	7.0248	6.6231	6.2593	5.9288	5.6278	5.3527	5.1009	4.8696	3.9539	3.3158	2.8501	2.4970	1.9994
21	7.1016	6.6870	6.3125	5.9731	5.6648	5.3837	5.1268	4.8913	3.9631	3.3198	2.8519	2.4979	1.9996
22	7.1695	6.7429	6.3587	6.0113	5.6964	5.4099	5.1486	4.9094	3.9705	3.3230	2.8533	2.4985	1.9997
23	7.2297	6.7921	6.3988	6.0442	5.7234	5.4321	5.1668	4.9245	3.9764	3.3254	2.8543	2.2989	1.9998
24	7.2829	6.8351	6.4338	6.0726	5.7465	5.4509	5.1822	4.9371	3.9811	3.3272	2.8550	2.4992	1.9999
25	7.3300	6.8729	6.4641	6.0971	5.7662	5.4669	5.1951	4.9476	3.9849	3.3286	2.8556	2.4994	1.9999
26	7.3717	6.9061	6.4906	6.1182	5.7831	5.4804	5.2060	4.9563	3.9879	3.3297	2.8560	2.4996	1.9999
27	7.4086	6.9352	6.5135	6.1364	5.7975	5.4919	5.2151	4.9636	3.9903	3.3305	2.8563	2.4997	2.0000
28	7.4412	6.9607	6.5335	6.1520	5.8099	5.5016	5.2228	4.9697	3.9923	3.3312	2.8565	2.4998	2.0000
29	7.4701	6.9830	6.5509	6.1656	5.8204	5.5098	5.2292	4.9747	3.9938	3.3317	2.8567	2.4999	2.0000
30	7.4957	7.0027	6.5660	6.1772	5.8294	5.5168	5.2347	4.9789	3.9950	3.3321	2.8568	2.4999	2.0000
35	7.5856	7.0700	6.6166	6.2153	5.8582	5.5386	5.2512	4.9915	3.9984	3.3330	2.8571	2.5000	2.0000
40	7.6344	7.1050	6.6418	6.2335	5.8713	5.5482	5.2582	4.9966	3.9995	3.3332	2.8571	2.5000	2.0000
45	7.6609	7.1232	6.6543	6.2421	5.8773	5.5523	5.2611	4.9986	3.9998	3.3333	2.8571	2.5000	2.0000
50	7.6752	7.1327	6.6605	6.2463	5.8801	5.5541	5.2623	4.9995	3.9999	3.3333	2.8571	2.5000	2.0000

If investors required a 13 percent return, they would value the bond at $22.82 less than if they required a 12 percent return.

These examples show that when interest rates rise, the prices of existing bonds decrease. The reason is that higher interest rates cause investors to require higher rates of return, which reduces the present value (and therefore market price) of existing bonds. When interest rates decrease, the required rate of return by investors decreases, and the present values of bonds increase. The inverse relationship between interest rates and prices of existing bonds is a simple but critical concept for all investors. Because interest rates are volatile, so are bond prices. Investors frequently forecast interest rates in order to determine how the required rate of return on bonds will change, and therefore how bond prices will change.

Chapter 3

Relationships between Interest Rates and Security Prices

The relationship between interest rates and bond prices carries important implications for various financial institutions such as commercial banks, savings institutions, and insurance companies that invest in bonds. When interest rates rise, the market value of their bond portfolios decrease, and the converse is true.

The impact of interest rate movements on a financial institution depends on how its asset and liability portfolios are structured, as illustrated in Exhibit 3.6. Financial institutions with interest rate-sensitive liabilities that invest heavily in bonds are exposed to interest rate risk. Many financial institutions attempt to adjust the size of their bond portfolio according to their expectations about future interest rates. The expected return is higher when using unevenly matched rate sensitivities because the mismatch allows an institution to take advantage of the effects of interest rate expectations. When rates are expected to rise, bonds can be sold and the proceeds used to purchase short-term securities, whose market values are less influenced by interest rate movements. When rates are expected to fall, the bond portfolio can be expanded in order to capitalize on the expectations. An aggressive approach offers greater potential for high return but also exposes investors to more risk when their expectations are wrong.

Fixed-rate mortgages generate periodic fixed payments, similar to bonds. Thus, the preceding comments apply to financial institutions such as savings institutions that hold mortgage portfolios. A primary reason for financial problems of savings institutions in the late 1970s was the rise in interest rates, which reduced the market value of their mortgage portfolios. This is a classic example of **interest rate risk,** or the risk that the market value of assets will decline in response to interest rate movements.

Bonds that sell at a price below their par value are called *discount bonds*. In the previous example, the bond price was $929.17, exhibiting a discount of $70.83 (computed as $1,000 minus $929.17). The larger the investor's required rate of return relative to the coupon rate, the larger will be the discount of a bond with a particular par value. As an extreme example, consider a **zero-coupon bond** (which has no coupon payments) with three

---

EXHIBIT 3.6 Potential Returns to Financial Institutions With Different Investment Strategies

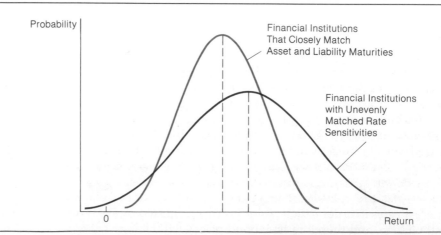

years remaining to maturity and $1,000 par value. Assume the investor's required rate of return on the bond is 13 percent. The appropriate price of this bond can be determined by the present value of its future cash flows:

$$PV \text{ of bond} = \$0/(1 + .13)^1 + \$0/(1 + .13)^2 + \$1,000/(1 + .13)^3$$
$$= \$0 + \$0 + \$693.05$$
$$= \$693.05$$

This very low price of the bond is necessary to generate a 13 percent annualized return to investors. If the bond offered coupon payments, the price would have been higher, since those coupon payments would provide part of the return required by investors. Consider another bond with similar par value and maturity that offers a 13 percent coupon rate. The appropriate price of the bond would now be

$$PV \text{ of bond} = \$130/(1 + .13)^1 + \$130/(1 + .13)^2 + \$1,130/(1 + .13)^3$$
$$= \$115.04 + \$101.81 + \$783.15$$
$$= \$1,000$$

Notice that the price of this bond is exactly equal to its par value. This is because the entire compensation required by investors is provided by the coupon payments.

Finally, consider a bond with a similar par value and term to maturity that offers a coupon rate of 15 percent, which is above the investor's required rate of return. The appropriate price of this bond as determined by its present value is

$$PV \text{ of bond} = \$150/(1 + .13)^1 + \$150/(1 + .13)^2 + \$1,150/(1 + .13)^3$$
$$= \$132.74 + \$117.47 + \$797.01$$
$$= \$1,047.22$$

The price of this bond exceeds its par value because coupon payments are large enough to offset that and still provide a 13 percent annualized return. From the examples provided, the following relationships should now be clear. First, if the coupon rate of a bond is below the investor's required rate of return, the present value of the bond (and therefore the price of the bond) should be below the par value. Second, if the coupon rate equals the investor's required rate of return, the price of the bond should be the same as the par value. Finally, if the coupon rate of a bond is above the investor's required rate of return, the price of the bond should be above the par value. These relationships are shown in Exhibit 3.7 for a bond with a 10 percent coupon and a par value of $1,000. If investors required a return of 5 percent and desired a 10-year maturity, they would be willing to pay $1,390 for this bond. If they required a return of 10 percent on this same bond, they would be willing to pay $1,000. If they required a 15 percent return, they would be willing to pay only $745. The relationships described here hold for any bond, regardless of its maturity.

INFLUENCE OF MATURITY ON BOND PRICE SENSITIVITY

As shown in Exhibit 3.7, as interest rates (and therefore required rates of return) decrease, long-term bond prices increase by a greater degree than

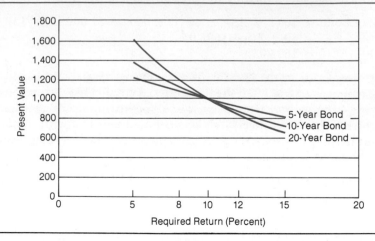

short-term bonds, because the long-term bonds will continue to offer the same coupon rate over a longer period of time than short-term bonds. Of course, if interest rates increase, prices of the long-term bonds would decline by a greater degree.

INFLUENCE OF COUPON PAYMENTS ON BOND PRICE SENSITIVITY

The prices of bonds with relatively low coupon payments are also somewhat more sensitive to interest rate movements than those with higher payments. Exhibit 3.8 compares price sensitivity of ten-year bonds with $1,000 par value and four different coupon rates: 0 percent, 5 percent, 10 percent, and 15 percent. Initially, the required rate of return (i) on the bonds is assumed to be 10 percent. The price of each bond would therefore be the present value of its future cash flows, discounted at 10 percent. The initial price of each bond is shown in Column 2. The top panel shows the effect of a decline in interest rates that reduces the investor's required return to 8 percent. The prices of the bonds based on an 8 percent required return are shown in Column 3. The percentage change in the price of each bond resulting from the interest rate movements is shown in Column 4. Notice that the percentage change is highest for the zero coupon bond and lower for bonds with higher coupon rates.

The sensitivity of bond prices (BP) to changes in the required rate of return (i) is commonly measured by the **bond price elasticity (BP^e),** which is estimated as

$$BP^e = \frac{\text{percent change in } BP}{\text{percent change in } i}$$

If the required rate of return is assumed to change from 10 percent to 8

EXHIBIT 3.8   Sensitivity of Bonds with Different Coupon Rates to Interest Rate Movements

Effects of a Decline in the Required Rate of Return

Bonds with a Coupon Rate of:	Initial Price of Bonds (When i = 10%)	Price of Bonds when i = 8%	Percent Change in Bond Price	Percent Change in i	Bond Price Elasticity (BPᵉ)
0%	$ 386	$ 463	+19.9%	−20.0%	−.997
5	693	799	+15.3	−20.0	−.765
10	1,000	1,134	+13.4	−20.0	−.670
15	1,307	1,470	+12.5	−20.0	−.624

Effects of an Increase in the Required Rate of Return

Bonds with a Coupon Rate of:	Initial Price of Bonds (When i = 10%)	Price of Bonds when i = 12%	Percent Change in Bond Price	Percent Change in i	Bond Price Elasticity (BPᵉ)
0%	$ 386	$ 322	−16.6%	+20.0%	−.830
5	693	605	−12.7	+20.0	−.635
10	1,000	887	−11.3	+20.0	−.565
15	1,307	1,170	−10.5	+20.0	−.525

percent, the bond price of the zero coupon bonds will rise from $386 to $463. Thus, the bond price elasticity (BP^e) is

$$BP^e = \frac{\dfrac{\$463 - \$386}{\$386}}{\dfrac{8\% - 10\%}{10\%}}$$

$$= \frac{+19.9\%}{-20\%}$$

$$= -.997$$

This implies that for each 1 percent change in interest rates, bond prices change by .997 percent in the opposite direction. The price elasticity for each bond is estimated in Exhibit 3.8 according to the assumed change in the required rate of return. The elasticities confirm that prices of bonds with higher coupon rates are less sensitive to interest rate movements.

The estimated bond price elasticity for any particular bond may vary with an adjustment in required rates of return, as illustrated in the lower panel of Exhibit 3.8. Note, however, that the prices of bonds with relatively

Chapter 3

Relationships between
Interest Rates and
Security Prices

low coupon rates are more sensitive regardless of the change in required rates of return.

Also notice from Exhibit 3.8 that the price sensitivity of any particular bond is greater for declining interest rates than rising interest rates. The bond price elasticity is negative in all cases, reflecting the inverse relationship between interest rate movements and bond price movements.

Financial institutions frequently assess the price sensitivity of their existing bond holdings to possible interest rate movements. If their bond portfolio contains a relatively large portion of zero- or low-coupon bonds, they will be more favorably affected by declining interest rates. Of course, they would also be more unfavorably affected by rising rates. Financial institutions can reduce the sensitivity of their bond portfolio to interest rate movements by concentrating on high-coupon bonds.

FORECASTING BOND PRICES

To illustrate how a financial institution can assess the potential impact of interest rate movements on their bond holdings, assume that Longhorn Savings and Loan recently purchased Treasury bonds in the secondary market with a total par value of $40 million. The bonds will mature in five years and have an annual coupon rate of 10 percent. Longhorn is attempting to forecast the market value of these bonds two years from now, since it may sell the bonds at that time. Therefore, it must forecast the investor's required rate of return and use that as the discount rate to determine the present value of the bond's cash flows over the final three years of its life. The computed present value would represent the forecasted price two years from now.

To continue with our example, assume the investor's required rate of return two years from now is expected to be 12 percent. This rate would be used to discount the periodic cash flows over the remaining three years. Given coupon payments of $4 million per year (10% × $40 million) and a par value of $40 million, the predicted present value is determined:

$$
\begin{aligned}
\text{PV of bonds 2 years from now} &= \frac{\$4 \text{ million}}{(1.12)^1} + \frac{\$4 \text{ million}}{(1.12)^2} + \frac{\$44 \text{ million}}{(1.12)^3} \\
&= \$3,571,429 + \$3,188,775 + \$31,318,331 \\
&= \$38,078,535
\end{aligned}
$$

An illustration of this exercise is provided in Exhibit 3.9, using a time line. The market value of the bonds two years ahead is forecasted to be slightly more than $38 million. This is the amount Longhorn expects to receive if it sells the bonds then.

As a second example, assume that Aggie Insurance Company recently purchased corporate bonds in the secondary market with a par value of $20 million, a coupon rate of 14 percent (with annual coupon payments), and three years until maturity. The firm desires to forecast the market value of these bonds in one year, since it may consider selling the bonds at that time. It expects the investor's required rate of return on similar investments to be 11 percent in one year. Using this information, it discounts the bond's cash flows ($2.8 million in annual coupon payments and a par value of $20

EXHIBIT 3.9 Forecasting the Market Value of Bonds

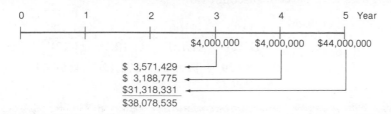

million) over the final two years at 11 percent to determine their present value (and therefore market value) one year from now:

$$\text{PV of bonds 1 year from now} = \frac{\$2.8 \text{ million}}{(1 + 11)^1} + \frac{\$22.8 \text{ million}}{(1.11)^2}$$

$$= \$2,522,522 + \$18,504,991$$

$$= \$21,027,513$$

Thus, the market value of the bonds is expected to be slightly more than $21 million one year from now.

DETERMINATION OF BOND YIELDS

The relationship between bond prices and interest rates can also be useful for determining the yield that a bond with a given price, par value, coupon payments, and maturity is offering. This **yield to maturity** can be determined by solving for the discount rate at which the present value of future payments (coupon payments and par value) to the bondholder would equal the bond's current price. The trial-and-error method can be used by applying a discount rate and computing the present value of the payments stream. If the computed present value is higher than the current bond price, the computation should be repeated using a higher discount rate. Conversely, if the computed present value is lower than the current bond price, try a lower discount rate. Computer programs and bond tables are also available to determine the yield to maturity.

Assume that a bond with $1,000 par value and four years to maturity offers annual coupon payments of $100, and is currently priced at $940. Given that the price (present value), coupon payments, and par value are known, the discount rate can be estimated using trial and error. Since the coupon payments reflect a 10 percent coupon rate (10 percent of the $1,000 par value is $100), and the current price of the bond is less than par value, the yield to bondholders is known to exceed 10 percent. Thus, we will try a discount rate of 11 percent in the present-value formula:

$$\text{PV of bond using an 11\% discount rate} = \frac{\$100}{(1.11)^1} + \frac{\$100}{(1.11)^2} + \frac{\$100}{(1.11)^3} + \frac{\$1,100}{(1.11)^4}$$

$$= \$90.09 + \$81.16 + \$73.11 + \$724.60$$

$$= \$968.96$$

Because the present value of this bond using an 11 percent discount rate exceeds the current price, a higher discount rate should be used. Our second attempt uses a 12 percent discount rate:

$$\begin{aligned} PV \text{ of bond} \\ \text{using a 12\%} \\ \text{discount rate} \end{aligned} = \frac{\$100}{(1.12)^1} + \frac{\$100}{(1.12)^2} + \frac{\$100}{(1.12)^3} + \frac{\$1,100}{(1.12)^4}$$

$$= \$89.29 + \$79.72 + \$71.17 + \$699.07$$

$$= \$939.25$$

Because this present value is approximately equal to the bond's current price, the discount rate of 12 percent is the annualized yield to those who hold the bonds until maturity. The trial-and-error process can be expedited by using the PVIFA table, especially for bonds with several years to maturity.

FORECASTING BOND YIELDS

If bonds are held to maturity, the yield is known. However, if they are sold prior to maturity, the yield is not known until the time of sale. Investors can, however, attempt to forecast the yield with the methods just demonstrated, in which the forecasted required rate of return is used to forecast the market value (and therefore selling price) of the bonds. This selling price can then be incorporated within the cash flow estimates to determine the discount rate at which the present value of cash flows equal the investor's initial purchase price. Suppose that Wildcat Bank purchases bonds with the following characteristics:

- Par value = $30 million
- Coupon rate = 15% (annual payments)
- Remaining time to maturity = 5 years
- Purchase price of bonds = $29 million

The bank plans to sell the bonds in four years. The investor's required rate of return on similar securities is expected to be 13 percent at that time. Given this information, Wildcat forecasts its annualized bond yield over the four-year period in the following stepwise manner.

The first step is to forecast the present value (or market price) of the bonds four years from now. To do this, the remaining cash flows (one final coupon payment of $4.5 million plus the par value of $30 million) over the fifth and final year should be discounted (at the forecasted required rate of return of 13 percent) back to the fourth year when the bonds are to be sold:

$$\begin{aligned} PV \text{ of bonds} \\ 4 \text{ years} \\ \text{from now} \end{aligned} = \frac{\$34.5 \text{ million}}{(1.13)^1}$$

$$= \$30,530,973$$

This predicted present value as of four years from now serves as the predicted selling price in four years.

The next step is to incorporate the forecasted selling price at the end of the bond portfolio's cash flow stream. Then the discount rate that equates the present value of the cash flow stream to the price at which the bonds were purchased will represent the annualized yield. In our example, Wildcat Bank's cash flows are coupon payments of $4.5 million over each of the four years it holds the bonds; the fourth year's cash flows should also include the forecasted selling price of $30,530,973 and therefore sum to $35,030,973. Recall that Wildcat Bank purchased the bonds for $29 million. Given this information, the equation to solve for the discount rate (i) is

$$\$29 \text{ million} = \frac{\$4.5 \text{ million}}{(1 + i)^1} + \frac{\$4.5 \text{ million}}{(1 + i)^2} + \frac{\$4.5 \text{ million}}{(1 + i)^3} + \frac{\$35,030,973}{(1 + i)^4}$$

The trial-and-error method can be used to determine the discount rate if a computer program is not available. The use of PVIF and PVIFA tables can expedite the process. With a discount rate of 17 percent, the present value would be

$$\begin{aligned} \text{\textit{PV} of bonds using a 17\% discount rate} &= \frac{\$4.5 \text{ million}}{(1.17)^1} + \frac{\$4.5 \text{ million}}{(1.17)^2} + \frac{\$4.5 \text{ million}}{(1.17)^3} + \frac{\$35,030,973}{(1.17)^4} \\ &= \$3,846,154 + \$3,287,311 + \$2,809,667 + \$18,694,280 \\ &= \$28,637,412 \end{aligned}$$

This present value is slightly less than the initial purchase price. Thus, the discount rate at which the present value of expected cash flows equals the purchase price is just slightly less than 17 percent. Consequently, Wildcat Bank's expected return on the bonds is just short of 17 percent.

It should be recognized that the process for determining the yield to maturity assumes that any payments received prior to the end of the holding period can be reinvested at the yield to maturity. If, for example, the payments could only be reinvested at a lower rate, the yield to maturity would overstate the actual return to the investor over the entire holding period.

With a computer program, the financial institution could easily create a distribution of forecasted yields based on various forecasts for the required rate of return four years from now. Without a computer, the process illustrated here would need to be completed for each forecast of the required rate of return. The computer actually follows the same steps but can more quickly make the computations.

Financial institutions that forecast bond yields must first forecast interest rates for the point in time at which they plan to sell their bonds. These forecasted rates can be used along with information about the securities to predict the required rate of return that will exist for the securities of concern. The predicted required rate of return is applied to cash flows beyond the time of sale to forecast the present value (or selling price) of the bonds at the time of sale. The forecasted selling price is then incorporated when estimating cash flows over the investment horizon. Finally, the yield to maturity on the bonds is determined by solving for the discount rate that equates these cash flows to the initial purchase price. The accuracy of the forecasted yield depends on the accuracy of the forecasted selling price of the bonds, which in turn depends on the accuracy of the forecasted required rate of return for the time of the sale.

FORECASTING MARKET VALUE OF BOND PORTFOLIOS

Financial institutions can quantitatively measure the impact of possible interest rate movements on the market value of their bond portfolio by separately assessing the impact on each type of bond and then consolidating the individual impacts. Assume that Seminole Financial Inc. has a portfolio of bonds with the required return (*i*) on each type of bond as shown in the upper portion of Exhibit 3.10. Interest rates are expected to increase by one year from today, causing an anticipated increase of 1 percent in the required return of each type of bond. Assuming no adjustment in the portfolio, Seminole's anticipated bond portfolio position is displayed in the lower portion of Exhibit 3.10.

The anticipated market value of each type of bond in the exhibit was determined by discounting the remaining year's cash flows beyond one year by the anticipated required return. The market value of the portfolio is expected to decline by more than $12 million as a result of the anticipated increase in interest rates.

This simplified example assumed a portfolio of only three types of bonds. In reality, a financial institution may have several types of bonds, with several maturities for each type of bond. Computer programs are widely available for assessing the market value of the portfolio. The financial institution gives the computer program input on the cash flow trends of all bond holdings and the anticipated required rates of return for each bond at the future time of concern. The computer uses the anticipated rates to estimate the present value of cash flows at that future time. These present values are then consolidated to determine the forecasted value of the bond portfolio.

The key variable in forecasting the bond portfolio's market value is the anticipated required return for each type of bond. The prevailing interest

---

EXHIBIT 3.10   Measurement and Forecasts of Bond-Portfolio Market Value

Present Bond-Portfolio Position of Seminole Inc.

Type of Bonds	Present *i*	Par Value	Years to Maturity	Present Market Value of Bonds
9%-coupon Treasury bonds	9%	$ 40,000,000	4	$ 40,000,000
14%-coupon corporate bonds	12%	100,000,000	5	107,207,000
10%-coupon gov't agency bonds	10%	150,000,000	8	150,000,000
		290,000,000		297,207,200

Forecasted Bond-Portfolio Position of Seminole Inc.

Type of Bonds	Forecasted *i*	Par Value	Years to Maturity as of One Year from Now	Forecasted Market Value of Bonds in One Year
9%-coupon Treasury bonds	10%	$ 40,000,000	3	$ 39,004,840
14%-coupon corporate bonds	13%	100,000,000	4	102,973,000
10%-coupon gov't agency bonds	11%	150,000,000	7	142,938,000
		290,000,000		284,915,840

rates on short-term securities are commonly more volatile than rates on longer-term securities, so the required returns on bonds with three or four years to maturity may change to a greater degree than the longer-term bonds. In addition, as economic conditions change, the required returns of some risky securities could change even if the general level of interest rates remains stable.

FORECASTING BOND PORTFOLIO RETURNS

Financial institutions measure their overall bond-portfolio returns in various ways. One way is to measure the coupon payments received from the portfolio over the period of concern as a percentage of the market value at the beginning of the period. While this method is simple, it can be misleading. Coupons represent only a portion of the return. As an extreme example, a portfolio of zero-coupon bonds would have a periodic yield of zero when measured by this method. A more appropriate method of measuring returns is to account not only for coupon payments but also for the change in market value over the holding period of concern. The market value at the beginning of the holding period is perceived as the initial investment. The market value at the end of that period is perceived as the price at which the bonds would have been sold. Even if the bonds are retained, the measurement of return requires an estimated market value at the end of the period. Finally, the coupon payments must be accounted for as well. The measurement of a bond portfolio's return is no different than the measurement of an individual bond's return. Mathematically, the bond portfolio return can be determined by solving for i in the following equation:

$$MVP_t = \sum_{t=1}^{n} \frac{C_t}{(1 + i)^t} + \frac{MVP_n}{(1 + i)^n}$$

where MVP_t = today's market value of the bond portfolio
 C_t = coupon payments received at the end of period t
 MVP_n = market value of the bond portfolio at the end
   of the investment period of concern
 i = the discount rate that equates the present value
   of coupon payments and the future portfolio market
   value to today's portfolio market value

To illustrate, recall that Seminole Financial Inc. forecasted its bond portfolio value for one year ahead. Its annual coupon payments (C) sum to $32,600,000 (computed by multiplying the coupon rate of each type of bond by the respective par value). Using this information, along with today's MVP and the forecasted MVP (called MVP^*), its annual return is determined by solving for i as follows:

$$MVP = \frac{C_1 + MVP^*}{(1 + i)^1}$$

$$\$297,207,200 = \frac{\$32,600,000 + \$284,915,840}{(1 + i)^1}$$

$$\$297,207,200 = \frac{\$317,515,840}{(1 + i)^1}$$

The discount rate or i is estimated to be about 7 percent. (Work this yourself for verification.) Therefore, the bond portfolio is expected to generate an annual return of about 7 percent over the one-year investment horizon. The computations to determine the bond portfolio return can be tedious, but financial institutions use computer programs. If this type of program is linked with another program to forecast future bond prices, a financial institution can input forecasted required returns for each type of bond and let the computer determine projections of the bond portfolio's future market value and its return over a specified investment horizon.

BOND PORTFOLIO SENSITIVITY TO INTEREST RATE MOVEMENTS

Some bond portfolio managers choose to **immunize** their portfolio, or insulate it from the effect of interest rate movements. To do this, they must first measure the sensitivity of the bond portfolio. One method of measurement is bond price elasticity, described earlier in the chapter. A second method is **duration,** which has become very popular in recent years. The duration measurement can also be used to compare interest rate sensitivity of various securities, even if they have different coupon rates. As was shown earlier, zero- or low-coupon bonds are more rate-sensitive than high-coupon bonds. The duration measurement represents the term to maturity of a zero-coupon bond with the same sensitivity as the bond being analyzed. The longer a bond's duration, the greater is its rate-sensitivity.

One of the more widely used formulas to measure duration is used here for an individual security:

$$D = \frac{\sum_{t=1}^{n} \dfrac{P_t(t)}{(1 + i)^t}}{\sum_{t=1}^{n} \dfrac{P_t}{(1 + i)^t}}$$

where P_t = the interest or principal payments generated by the bond
t = the time at which the payments are provided
i = the bond's yield to maturity

Once the durations of all securities within the portfolio are determined, the portfolio's duration (D_P) can be estimated as

$$D_P = \sum_{j=1}^{m} w_j D_j$$

where m represents the number of securities in the portfolio, w_j is security j's market value as a percentage of the portfolio market value, and D_j is security j's duration. In other words, the duration of a security portfolio is the weighted average of security durations, weighted according to relative market value. Financial institutions concerned with interest rate risk may compare their asset duration to their liability duration. Assuming that the value of earning assets is approximately equal to liabilities, the difference between their durations can be used to assess the impact of interest rate movements. A positive difference means that the market value of the institution's assets is more rate-sensitive than the market value of its liabilities.

Thus, during a period of rising interest rates, the market value of the assets would be reduced by a greater degree than that of liabilities. The institution's *real net worth* (market value of net worth) would therefore decrease. A detailed discussion of duration is provided in Chapter 18.

SUMMARY

Financial institutions must (1) value individual bonds, (2) forecast bond prices, (3) forecast bond returns, (4) assess the interest rate sensitivity of bonds, (5) value bond portfolios, (6) forecast bond portfolio prices, and (7) forecast bond portfolio returns. These procedures require insight into the following general relationships related to bond prices. An increase in interest rates causes the required rate of return by investors to rise, thereby reducing the present value of bonds and thus their prices. Conversely, a decrease in interest rates reduces investors' required rate of return, increases the present value of bonds, and therefore increases bond prices.

If financial institutions can forecast interest rates accurately, they can also forecast bond prices and adjust their proportion of long-term securities accordingly. While perfect accuracy is impossible, financial institutions can still enhance their performance if their forecasting is fairly accurate a majority of the time. They should reduce their proportion of bonds and/or fixed-rate mortgages if higher interest rates are forecasted and increase it if lower rates are forecasted.

KEY TERMS

bond price elasticity
duration
immunize
interest rate risk

present value interest factor of an
   annuity (PVIFA)
yield to maturity
zero-coupon bond

QUESTIONS

3.1. Based on your forecast of interest rates, would you recommend that investors purchase bonds today? Explain.

3.2. As interest rates decrease, explain the impact on

  a. An investor's required rate of return

  b. The present value of existing bonds

  c. The prices of existing bonds

3.3. Why is the relationship between interest rates and security prices important to financial institutions?

3.4. Determine the direction of bond prices over the last year and explain the reason for it.

3.5. How would a financial institution with a large bond portfolio be affected by falling interest rates? Would it be affected more than a financial institution with a greater concentration of bonds (and less short-term securities)? Explain.

3.6. How is a financial institution with a large portfolio of fixed-rate mortgages affected by rising interest rates? Explain.

3.7. If a bond's coupon rate is above its required rate of return, would its price be above or below its par value? Explain.

3.8. Is the price of a long-term bond more or less sensitive to a change in interest rates than the price of a short-term security? Why?

3.9. Why does the required rate of return for a particular bond change over time?

3.10. Assume that inflation is expected to decline in the near future. How could this affect future bond prices? Would you recommend that financial institutions increase or decrease their concentration in long-term bonds based on this expectation? Explain.

3.11. Explain the concept of bond price elasticity. Would bond price elasticity suggest a higher price sensitivity for zero-coupon bonds or high-coupon bonds that are offering the same yield to maturity? Why? What does this suggest about the market value volatility of mutual funds containing zero-coupon Treasury bonds versus high-coupon Treasury bonds?

3.12. You anticipate that a well-respected analyst will make the following projections: (1) U.S. inflation will decline, and (2) foreign investors expect the dollar to strengthen consistently over the long run. The market has not yet responded to this information, but it will once the news is announced. You plan to purchase either (1) 10-year bonds, (2) 20-year zero-coupon bonds, or (3) one-year securities. Assume you only have funds available for one year. Assume that before the news is announced, each investment had the same expected return for a one-year horizon. If your goal is to maximize return (you don't care about risk), which investment would you choose? Explain.

PROBLEMS

3.1. Assume the following information for an existing bond that provides annual coupon payments:

> Par value = $1,000
> Coupon rate = 11%
> Maturity = 4 years
> Required rate of return by investors = 11%

a. What is the present value of the bond?

b. If the required rate of return by investors were 14 percent instead of 11 percent, what would be the present value of the bond?

c. If the required rate of return by investors were 9 percent, what would be the present value of the bond?

3.2. Assume the following information for existing zero coupon bonds:

> Par value = $100,000
> Maturity = 3 years
> Required rate of return by investors = 12%

$$P = \frac{c}{(1+i)^n} + \frac{Par}{(1+i)^n}$$

$$= \frac{100,000}{(1+.12)^3}$$

$$= 71,178.02$$

How much should investors be willing to pay for these bonds?

3.3. Assume that you require a 14 percent return on a zero-coupon bond with a par value of $1,000 and six years to maturity. What is the price you should be willing to pay for this bond?

3.4. Bulldog Bank has just purchased bonds for $106 million that have a par value of $100 million, three years remaining to maturity, and an annual coupon rate of 14 percent. It expects the required rate of return on these bonds to be 12 percent one year from now.

   a. What could Bulldog Bank sell these bonds for one year from now?

   b. What is the expected annualized yield on the bonds over the next year, assuming they are to be sold in one year?

3.5. Sun Devil Savings has just purchased bonds for $38 million that have a par value of $40 million, five years remaining to maturity, and a coupon rate of 12 percent. It expects the required rate of return on these bonds to be 10 percent two years from now.

   a. What could Sun Devil Savings sell these bonds for two years from now?

   b. What is the expected annualized yield on the bonds over the next two years, assuming they are to be sold in two years?

   c. If the anticipated required rate of return of 10 percent in two years is overestimated, how would the actual selling price differ from the forecasted price? How would the actual annualized yield over the next two years differ from the forecasted yield?

3.6. Spartan Insurance Company plans to purchase bonds today that have four years remaining to maturity, a par value of $60 million, and a coupon rate of 10 percent. Spartan expects that in three years, the required rate of return on these bonds by investors in the market will be 9 percent. It plans to sell the bonds at that time. What is the expected price it will sell these bonds for in 3 years?

3.7. Gator Company plans to purchase either (1) zero-coupon bonds that have ten years to maturity, a par value of $100 million, and a purchase price of $40 million or (2) bonds with similar default risk that have five years to maturity, a 9 percent coupon rate, a par value of $40 million, and purchase price of $40 million.

   Gator can invest $40 million for five years. Assume that the market's required return in five years is forecasted to be 11 percent. Which alternative would offer Gator a higher expected return (or yield) over the five-year investment horizon?

3.8. The portfolio manager of Panther Company has excess cash that is to be invested for four years. He can purchase four-year Treasury notes that offer a 9 percent yield. Alternatively, he can purchase new twenty-year Treasury bonds offering a par value of $3 million and an 11 percent coupon rate with annual payments. The manager expects that the required return on these same twenty-year bonds will be 12 percent four years from now.

   (a) What is the forecasted market value of the twenty-year bonds in four years?

   (b) Which investment is expected to provide a higher yield over the four-year period?

3.9. Doran Investment Company manages a broad portfolio with this composition:

	Par Value	Present Market Value	Years Remaining to Maturity
Zero-coupon bonds	$200,000,000	$ 63,720,000	12
8% Treasury bonds	300,000,000	290,000,000	8
11% corporate bonds	400,000,000	380,000,000	10
		733,720,000	

It expects that in four years, investors in the market will require an 8 percent return on the zero-coupon bonds, a 7 percent return on the Treasury bonds, and a 9 percent return on corporate bonds. Estimate the market value of the bond portfolio four years from now.

PROJECTS

3.1. COMPARING BOND PRICE SENSITIVITY AMONG BONDS WITH DIFFERENT COUPON CHARACTERISTICS

Use a recent business periodical to determine the prices of Treasury bonds with a 10-year maturity and three different coupon rate characteristics: a relatively high coupon rate, a relatively low coupon rate, and a zero-coupon rate. Determine the percentage change in the price that would occur for each bond if interest rates rose by one percentage point? What if interest rates decreased by two percentage points. Based on your results, which type of bond was most sensitive to a change in interest rates? Which type was least sensitive? Explain the results.

3.2. COMPARING BOND PRICE SENSITIVITY AMONG BONDS WITH DIFFERENT MATURITIES

Use a recent business periodical to determine the prices of Treasury bonds with the same coupon rate but three different maturities. Determine the percentage change in the price that would occur for each bond if interest rates rose by one percentage point. What if interest rates decreased by two percentage points? Based on your results, which type of bond was most sensitive to a change in interest rates? Which type was least sensitive? Explain the results.

3.3. EXAMINING RECENT BOND PRICE MOVEMENTS

Review the "Credit Markets" section of *The Wall Street Journal* (listed in the index on the front page) for the last five days. Since bond prices react to expectations of future interest rates, this section attempts to explain why bond prices changed from day to day.

For each day, fill out the following table:

	Did bond prices increase or decrease?	Apparent change in interest rate expectations (higher or lower than previous day?)	Reason for change in interest rate expectations?
One day ago			
2 days ago			
3 days ago			
4 days ago			
5 days ago			

REFERENCES

Bierwag, G. O., George G. Kaufman, Cynthia M. Latta, and Gordon Roberts. "Duration: Response to Critics." *Journal of Portfolio Management* (Winter 1987): 48–52.

Gatti, James F. "Risk and Return on Corporate Bonds: A Synthesis." *Quarterly Review of Economics and Business* 23 (Summer 1983): 53–70.

Lewellen, Wilbur G., and Douglas R. Emery. "On the Matter of Parity Among Financial Obligations." *Journal of Finance* 36 (March 1981): 97–111.

Maloney, Kevin J., and Jess B. Yawitz. "Interest Rate Risk, Immunization, and Duration." *Journal of Portfolio Management* (Spring 1986): 41–48.

McConnell, John J., and Gary G. Schlarbaum. "Returns, Risks, and Pricing of Income Bonds, 1956–76." *Journal of Business* 54 (January 1981): 33–57.

Approximate Annualized Bond Yield

The method to determine a bond's yield to maturity is time-consuming when a computer program is not available, especially when analyzing a bond with semiannual coupon payments and several years until maturity. A more simplified but less accurate method of determining the approximate annualized yield of a bond (Y_B) is based on the coupon payments, the difference between the investor's purchase and selling price, and the number of years the bond was held. It can be computed as

$$Y_B = \frac{\dfrac{S_B - P_B}{n} + C}{\dfrac{P_B + S_B}{2}}$$

where S_B = selling price of bond
$\quad P_B$ = purchase price of bond
$\quad C$ = annual coupon payments received
$\quad n$ = number of years in which the bond was held

Consider a bond with $1,000 par value, current price of $940, with coupon payments of $100 per year and four years to maturity. If the investor holds this bond until maturity, the annualized yield of the bond is

$$Y_B = \frac{\dfrac{\$1,000 - \$940}{4} + \$100}{\dfrac{\$940 + \$1,000}{2}} = \frac{\$115}{\$970} = 11.86\%$$

This estimated annualized yield here is slightly lower than the 12 percent estimate derived from the yield-to-maturity method (as shown in this chapter). A corporation that invests or borrows large sums of money through bonds will normally prefer a more accurate estimate and therefore use the method demonstrated in the chapter.

Structure of Interest Rates

THE STRUCTURE OF INTEREST RATES IN PERSPECTIVE

On June 24, 1988, the following market yields existed:

	Annualized Yield
Ten-year Treasury securities	9.10%
Ten-year government agency securities	9.65%
Ten-year high-quality corporate bonds	10.00%
Ten-year medium-quality corporate bonds	10.31%
Ten-year municipal bonds	7.00%
Thirty-year municipal bonds	7.80%

The yields vary among securities offered. Treasury securities offered a higher yield than municipal bonds. Corporate bonds offered a higher yield than Treasury bonds. Thirty-year municipal bonds offered a higher annualized yield than ten-year municipal bonds. The differences imply that the cost of borrowing funds varies among borrowers at any point in time. In addition, the yields earned by investors vary with the securities purchased.

The differences among yields can change significantly. For example, the difference between government agency securities and Treasury bond yields was much larger during the 1982 recession. In addition, the difference between medium-quality and high-quality corporate bond yields was also larger during the recession.

■ Why can municipal governments issue bonds at a lower cost than the Treasury?
■ Why can the Treasury issue bonds at a lower cost than high-quality corporations or government agencies?
■ Why may thirty-year municipal bonds offer a higher yield than ten-year municipal bonds?
■ What other factors could explain yield differentials among securities?
■ Why do the differences among yields change over time?

This chapter addresses these and other questions related to yields of securities.

OUTLINE

Any security's yield is influenced by prevailing market interest rates and characteristics unique to that security. The factors that affect the general level of market interest rates over time were discussed in Chapter 2. This chapter discusses the characteristics that can cause yields to differ among securities, which are:

- Default risk
- Liquidity
- Tax status
- Maturity
- Special provisions

DEFAULT RISK

Because most securities are subject to the risk of default, investors must consider the creditworthiness of the security issuer. While they always have the option of purchasing risk-free Treasury securities, they may prefer some other securities if the yield compensates them for the risk. Thus, if all other characteristics besides default risk are equal, securities with a higher degree of risk would have to offer higher yields to be chosen. Default risk is especially relevant for longer-term securities that expose creditors to the possibility of default for a longer time.

Default risk premiums of 1 percent, 2 percent, or more may not seem significant. But for corporations borrowing $10 million through the issuance of bonds, an extra percentage point as a premium reflects $100,000 in additional interest expenses per year.

Investors who do not necessarily desire to assess the creditworthiness of corporations that issue bonds can benefit from bond ratings provided by rating agencies. These ratings are based on a financial assessment of the issuing corporation. The higher the rating, the lower is the perceived default risk. As time passes, economic conditions can change, and the perceived default risk of a corporation can change as well. Thus, bonds previously issued by a firm could be rated at one level, while a subsequent issue from

Impact of the Stock Market Crash of October 1987 on Default Risk Premium

During the stock market crash on October 19, 1987, the bond market rallied. Many investors that liquidated their stock holdings purchased bonds, placing upward pressure on the prices of existing bonds. There was also a shift in the *risk perception* of bonds, as shown in the exhibit below. The risk perception can be measured by a bond's *risk premium* (the difference between the bond's yield and a risk-free Treasury bond with the same maturity). Notice from the exhibit how the risk premium on both Baa and AAA bonds increased by almost a full percentage point between October 16 and October 22. The significant jump in the risk premium suggests that investors changed their risk perception of these bonds.

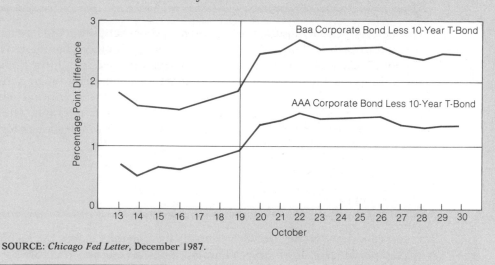

SOURCE: *Chicago Fed Letter*, December 1987.

the same firm could be rated at a different level. The ratings could also differ if the collateral provisions differ among the bonds.

The most popular rating agencies are Moody's Investor Service and Standard and Poor's Corporation. A summary of their rating classification schedules is provided in Exhibit 4.1. Moody's ratings range from Aaa for highest quality to C for lowest quality, while Standard and Poor's range from AAA to D. Since different methods are used by these rating agencies to assess creditworthiness of firms and state governments, a particular bond could be assigned a different rating by each agency; however, differences are usually small.

Some financial institutions such as commercial banks are required by law to invest only in **investment-grade bonds,** which are rated as Baa or better by Moody's and BBB or better by Standard and Poor's. This requirement is intended to limit the portfolio risk of the financial institutions.

Chapter 4

Structure of Interest Rates

EXHIBIT 4.1 Rating Classification by Rating Agencies

	Ratings Assigned by:	
Description of Security	*Moody's*	*Standard and Poor's*
Highest quality	Aaa	AAA
High quality	Aa	AA
High-medium quality	A	A
Medium quality	Baa	BBB
Medium-low quality	Ba	BB
Low quality (speculative)	B	B
Poor quality	Caa	CCC
Very poor quality	Ca	CC
Lowest quality (in default)	C	DDD,D

LIQUIDITY

Investors prefer securities that are **liquid**, meaning that they could be easily converted to cash without a loss in value. Thus, if all other characteristics were equal, securities with lower liquidity would have to offer a higher yield to be preferred. Securities with a short-term maturity or an active secondary market have higher liquidity. For investors who will not need their funds until the securities mature, lower liquidity is tolerable. Other investors, however, are willing to accept a lower return in exchange for a high degree of liquidity.

TAX STATUS

Investors are more concerned with after-tax income than before-tax income earned on securities. If all other characteristics are similar, taxable securities would have to offer a higher before-tax yield to investors than tax-exempt securities to be preferred. The extra compensation required on such taxable securities depends on the tax rates of individual and institutional investors. Investors in high tax brackets benefit most from tax-exempt securities.

When assessing the expected yields of various securities, it is common to convert them into an after-tax form, as shown:

$$Y_{at} = Y_{bt}(1 - t)$$

where Y_{at} = after-tax yield
Y_{bt} = before-tax yield
t = investor's marginal tax rate

Investors retain only a percentage $(1 - t)$ of the before-tax yield once taxes are paid. Consider a taxable security that offers a before-tax yield of 14 percent. When converted into after-tax terms, the yield will be reduced by the tax percentage. The precise after-tax yield is dependent on the tax rate (t). If the tax rate of the investor is 20 percent, the after-tax yield will be

$$Y_{at} = Y_{bt} (1 - t)$$
$$= 14\% (1 - .2)$$
$$= 11.2\%$$

Exhibit 4.2 presents after-tax yields based on a variety of tax rates and before-tax yields. For example, a taxable security with a before-tax yield of 6 percent will generate an after-tax yield of 5.4 percent to an investor in the 10 percent tax bracket, 4.8 percent to an investor in the 20 percent tax bracket, and so on. This exhibit shows why investors in high tax brackets are attracted to tax-exempt securities.

In some cases, investors wish to determine the before-tax yield necessary to match the after-tax yield of a tax exempt security. This can be done by rearranging the terms of the previous equation.

$$Y_{bt} = \frac{Y_{at}}{(1 - t)}$$

Suppose that a firm in the 20 percent tax bracket is aware of a tax-exempt security that is paying a yield of 8 percent. In order to match this after-tax yield, taxable securities must offer a before-tax yield of

$$Y_{bt} = \frac{Y_{at}}{(1 - t)} = \frac{8\%}{(1 - .2)} = 10\%$$

State taxes should be considered along with federal taxes in determining the after-tax yield. Treasury securities are exempt from state income tax, and municipal securities are sometimes exempt as well.[1] Because states impose different income tax rates, a particular security's after-tax yield may vary with the location of the investor.

When comparing different securities, investors should evaluate all expected returns on an after-tax basis. Only after the tax differences are accounted for, should they consider the various other characteristics.

TERM TO MATURITY

Maturity differs among securities and is another reason why security yields differ. The **term structure of interest rates** defines the relationship between maturity and annualized yield, holding other factors such as risk constant.

Any available business periodical can be used to determine the annualized yields of Treasury securities with different terms to maturity. The annualized yields for federal government securities of varied maturities are listed in Exhibit 4.3. A graphic comparison of these maturities and annualized yields is provided in Exhibit 4.4. The connection of points plotted in that exhibit is commonly referred to as a **yield curve.** Because this yield curve is upward sloping, it indiciates that the Treasury securities with longer maturities offered higher annualized yields. A downward sloping curve implies the opposite, and a horizontal yield curve implies that annualized yields are similar for securities with different maturities.

---

[1] The interest income on so-called tax-free municipal bonds is exempt from federal income tax. Yet, the interest on some municipal bonds is subject to federal income tax. Capital gains income is subject to federal income tax. In addition, most states charge income tax on interest from municipal bonds issued in other states.

EXHIBIT 4.2   After-Tax Yields Based on Various Tax Rates and Before-Tax Yields

Tax Rate	Before-Tax Yield:							
	6%	8%	10%	12%	14%	16%	18%	20%
10%	5.40%	7.20%	9.00%	10.80%	12.60%	14.40%	16.20%	18.00%
15	5.10	6.80	8.50	10.20	11.90	13.60	15.30	17.00
20	4.80	6.40	8.00	9.60	11.20	12.80	14.40	16.00
28	4.32	5.76	7.20	8.64	10.08	11.52	12.96	14.40
34	3.96	5.28	6.60	7.92	9.24	10.56	11.88	13.20

Various theories have been used to explain the relationship between maturity and annualized yield of securities, including the pure expectations theory, liquidity premium theory, and segmented markets theory.

Pure Expectations Theory

According to the pure expectations theory, the shape of the yield curve is determined solely by expectations of future interest rates. To understand how interest rate expectations may influence the yield curve, assume that investors who plan to purchase securities must decide between short-term and long-term securities. Assume that the annualized yields of short-term and long-term securities are similar. That is, the yield curve is flat. If investors begin to believe that interest rates will rise, they will invest mostly in short-term securities, so that they can soon reinvest their funds at higher yields after interest rates increase. When investors flood the short-term market and avoid the long-term market, they may cause the yield curve to adjust as shown in Exhibit 4.5. The strong demand for short-term securities will force prices up and annualized yields down. Meanwhile, the lack of demand for long-term securities forces prices down and annualized yields up.

Even though the annualized short-term yields become lower than annualized long-term yields, investors in short-term securities are satisfied since they expect interest rates to rise. They will make up for the lower short-term yield when these securities mature and they reinvest at a higher rate (if interest rates rise) at maturity.

Assuming that the borrowers who plan to issue securities also expect interest rates to increase, they would prefer to lock in the present interest rate over a long period of time. Thus, borrowers would generally prefer to issue long-term securities rather than short-term securities. This places upward pressure on the equilibrium price of short-term securities (due to low supply of short-term securities issued) and downward pressure on the price of long-term securities (due to the large supply of long-term securities issued). The yields of the respective securities would move inversely with the price movements. The pressure on the yield curve from such borrowing activities is similar to that caused by the investing activities. Overall, the expectation of higher interest rates causes the shape of the yield curve to pivot upward (counterclockwise).

Consider how the yield curve would be affected if both investors and borrowers expected interest rates to decrease in the future. Investors would

EXHIBIT 4.3   Comparison of Maturity and Approximate Yield of Government Securities as of May 2, 1988

Maturity	Annualized Yield
1 Month	6.21%
3 Months	6.46
6 Months	6.86
1 Year	7.08
2 Years	7.79
3 Years	7.95
4 Years	8.24
5 Years	8.34
10 Years	8.80
15 Years	9.19
20 Years	9.27

EXHIBIT 4.4   Development of Yield Curve Based on the Data in Exhibit 4.3

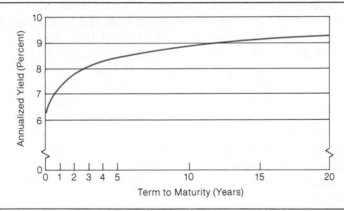

prefer to invest in long-term securities rather than short-term securities, since they could lock in today's interest rate before interest rates fall. Borrowers would prefer to issue short-term securities, so that as these securities mature, new securities could be issued at a lower interest rate.

Based on the expectation of lower interest rates in the future, demand will be low for short-term securities and high for long-term securities. The amount issued by borrowers will be small for long-term securities and large for short-term securities. This would place downward pressure on short-term security prices and upward pressure on short-term yields. The shortage of long-term securities for sale would place upward pressure on their prices and downward pressure on long-term yields. Overall, the expectation of lower interest rates causes the shape of the yield curve to pivot downward (clockwise). Exhibit 4.6 summarizes the impact of interest rate expectations on the slope of the yield curve.

Investors monitor the yield curve to determine the rates that exist for securities with various maturities. They can purchase either a security with a maturity that matches their investment horizon or a security with a shorter

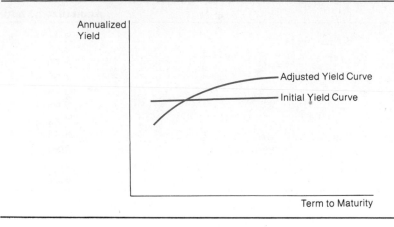

term and reinvest the proceeds at maturity. If a particular investment strategy is expected to generate a higher return over the investment horizon, investors may use that strategy. This could affect the prices and yields of securities with different maturities, realigning the rates so that the expected return over the entire investment horizon would be similar, regardless of the strategy used. If investors were indifferent to security maturities, they would want the return of any security to equal the compounded yield of consecutive investments in shorter-term securities. That is, a two-year security should offer a return that is similar to the anticipated return from investing in two consecutive one-year securities. A four-year security should offer a return that is competitive with the expected return from investing in two consecutive two-year securities, or four consecutive one-year securities, and so on.

EXHIBIT 4.6   Impact of Expected Interest Rate Changes on Slope of the Yield Curve

	Impact of Expected Increase in Interest Rates	Impact of Expected Decrease in Interest Rates
Demand for short-term securities by investors	Upward pressure	Downward pressure
Supply of short-term securities issued by borrowers	Downward pressure	Upward pressure
Price of short-term securities	Upward pressure	Downward pressure
Yield on short-term securities	Downward pressure	Upward pressure
Demand for long-term securities by investors	Downward pressure	Upward pressure
Supply of long-term securities issued by borrowers	Upward pressure	Downward pressure
Price of long-term securities	Downward pressure	Upward pressure
Yield on long-term securities	Upward pressure	Downward pressure
Shape of yield curve	Upward slope	Downward slope

To illustrate these equalities, consider the relationship between interest rates on a two-year security and a one-year security as follows:

$$(1 + {_t}R_2)^2 = (1 + {_t}R_1)(1 + {_{t+1}}r_1)$$

where ${_t}R_2$ = the known annualized interest rate of a two-year security as of time t

${_t}R_1$ = the known annualized interest rate of a one-year security as of time t

${_{t+1}}r_1$ = the one-year interest rate that is anticipated as of time $t + 1$

The term R represents a quoted rate, which is therefore known, whereas r represents a rate to be quoted at some point in the future, which is therefore uncertain. The left side of the equation represents the compounded yield to investors who purchase a two-year security, while the right side of the equation represents the anticipated compounded yield from purchasing a one-year security and reinvesting the proceeds in a new one-year security at the end of one year. If time t is today, ${_{t+1}}r_1$ can be estimated by rearranging terms.

$$1 + {_{t+1}}r_1 = \frac{(1 + {_t}R_2)^2}{(1 + {_t}R_1)}$$

$${_{t+1}}r_1 = \frac{(1 + {_t}R_2)^2}{(1 + {_t}R_1)} - 1$$

The term ${_{t+1}}r_1$, referred to as the **forward rate**, is commonly estimated in order to represent the market's forecast of the future interest rate. As a numerical example, assume that as of today (time t) the annualized two-year interest rate is 10 percent, while the one-year interest is 8 percent. The forward rate is estimated as follows:

$${_{t+1}}r_1 = \frac{(1 + .10)^2}{(1 + .08)} - 1$$
$$= .1203704$$

Conceptually, this rate implies that one year from now, a one-year interest rate must equal about 12.037 percent in order for consecutive investments in two one-year securities to generate a return similar to that of a two-year investment. If the actual one-year rate beginning one year from now (at period $t + 1$) is above (below) 12.037 percent, the return from two consecutive one-year investments will exceed (be less than) the return on a two-year investment.

The forward rate is thought to be a good approximation of the market's consensus interest rate forecast, since if the market had a different perception, demand and supply of today's existing two-year and one-year securities would adjust to capitalize on this information. Of course, there is no guarantee that the forward rate will forecast the future interest rate with perfect accuracy.

The greater the difference between the implied one-year forward rate and today's one-year interest rate, the greater is the expected change in the one-year interest rate. If the term structure of interest rates is solely influenced by expectations of future interest rates, the following relationships hold.

Scenario	Structure of Yield Curve	Expectations About the Future Interest Rate
1. $_{t+1}r_1 > {}_tR_1$	Rising	Higher than today's rate
2. $_{t+1}r_1 = {}_tR_1$	Flat	Same as today's rate
3. $_{t+1}r_1 < {}_tR_1$	Inverted	Lower than today's rate

Forward rates can be determined for various maturities. The relationships described here can be applied when assessing the change in the interest rate of a security with any particular maturity.

The previous example can be expanded to solve for other forward rates. For example, the equality specified by the pure expectations theory for a three-year horizon is

$$(1 + {}_tR_3)^3 = (1 + {}_tR_1)(1 + {}_{t+1}r_1)(1 + {}_{t+2}r_1)$$

where ${}_tR_3$ = the annualized interest rate on a three-year security as of time t,

${}_{t+2}r_1$ = the one-year interest rate that is anticipated as of time $t+2$.

All other terms were already defined. By rearranging terms, we can isolate the forward rate of a one-year security beginning two years from now:

$$1 + {}_{t+2}r_1 = \frac{(1 + {}_tR_3)^3}{(1 + {}_tR_1)(1 + {}_{t+1}r_1)}$$

$$_{t+2}r_1 = \frac{(1 + {}_tR_3)^3}{(1 + {}_tR_1)(1 + {}_{t+1}r_1)} - 1$$

If the one-year forward rate beginning one year from now $({}_{t+1}r_1)$ has already been estimated, this estimate along with actual one-year and three-year interest rates can be used to estimate the one-year forward rate two years from now. Recall that our previous example assumed ${}_tR_1 = 8\%$, and ${}_{t+1}r_1$ was estimated to be about 12.037 percent. Assume that a three-year security has an annualized interest rate of 11 percent $({}_tR_3 = 11\%)$. Given this information, the one-year forward rate two years from now is

$$_{t+2}r_1 = \frac{(1 + {}_tR_3)^3}{(1 + {}_tR_1)(1 + {}_{t+1}r_1)} - 1$$

$$= \frac{(1 + .11)^3}{(1 + .08)(1 + .12037)} - 1$$

$$= \frac{1.367631}{1.21} - 1$$

$$= 13.02736\%$$

Thus the market anticipates a one-year interest rate of 13.02736 percent as of two years from now.

The yield curve can also be used to forecast annualized interest rates for periods other than one year. For example, the information provided in the last example could be used to determine the two-year forward rate beginning one year from now.

According to the pure expectations theory, a one-year investment followed by a two-year investment should offer the same annualized yield over the three-year horizon as a three-year security that could be purchased today. This equality is shown as follows:

$$(1 + {}_tR_3)^3 = (1 + {}_tR_1)(1 + {}_{t+1}r_2)^2$$

where ${}_{t+1}r_2$ = the annual interest rate of a two-year security anticipated as of time $t + 1$

By rearranging terms, ${}_{t+1}r_2$ can be isolated:

$$(1 + {}_{t+1}r_2)^2 = \frac{(1 + {}_tR_3)^3}{(1 + {}_tR_1)}$$

Recall that today's annualized yields for one-year and three-year securities are 8 percent and 11 percent, respectively. With this information, ${}_{t+1}r_2$ is estimated as follows:

$$(1 + {}_{t+1}r_2)^2 = \frac{(1 + {}_tR_3)^3}{(1 + {}_tR_1)}$$

$$= \frac{(1 + .11)^3}{(1 + .08)}$$

$$= 1.266325$$

$$(1 + {}_{t+1}r) = \sqrt{1.266325}$$

$$= 1.1253$$

Thus the market anticipates an annualized interest rate of about 12.53 percent for two-year securities beginning one year from now.

Pure expectations theory is based on the premise that the forward rates are unbiased estimators of future interest rates. If forward rates are biased, investors could attempt to capitalize on the bias. To illustrate, our previous numerical example determined the one-year forward rate beginning one year ahead to be about 12.037 percent. If the forward rate was thought to contain an upward bias, then the expected one-year interest rate beginning one year ahead would be less than 12.037 percent. Therefore, investors with funds available for two years would earn a higher yield by purchasing two-year securities rather than purchasing one-year securities for two consecutive years. Their actions would cause an increase in the price of two-year securities and a decrease in that of one-year securities. The yields of the securities would move inversely with the price movements. The attempt by investors to capitalize on the forward rate bias would essentially eliminate the bias.

If forward rates are unbiased estimators of future interest rates, financial market efficiency is supported, and the information implied by market rates about the forward rate cannot be used to generate abnormal returns. As new information develops, investor preferences would change, yields would adjust, and the implied forward rate would adjust as well.

If a long-term rate is expected to equal a geometric average of consecutive short-term rates covering the same time horizon (as is suggested by pure expectations theory), then long-term rates would likely be more stable than short-term rates. As expectations about consecutive short-term rates change over time, the average of these rates is less volatile than the individual short-term rates—which may explain why long-term rates are in reality much more stable than short-term rates.

Chapter 4

Structure of Interest Rates

Liquidity Premium Theory

Some investors may prefer to own short-term rather than long-term securities, since an earlier maturity represents greater liquidity. In this case, they may be willing to hold long-term securities only if compensated with a premium for the lower degree of liquidity. While long-term securities can be liquidated prior to maturity, their prices are more sensitive to interest rate movements. Short-term securities are normally considered to be more liquid since they are more likely to be converted to cash without a loss in value.

The preference for the more liquid short-term securities places upward pressure on the slope of a yield curve. Liquidity may be a more critical factor to investors at particular points in time, and the liquidity premium will change over time accordingly. As it does, so will the yield curve. This is the **liquidity premium theory.**

Exhibit 4.7 combines the simultaneous existence of expectations theory and a liquidity premium. Each graph shows different interest rate expectations by the market. Regardless of the interest rate forecast, the yield curve is affected in a somewhat similar manner by the liquidity premium.

When expectations theory is combined with the liquidity theory, the yield on a security will not necessarily be equal to the yield from consecutive investments in shorter-term securities over the same investment horizon. For example, the yield on a two-year security can be determined as

$$(1 + {}_tR_2)^2 = (1 + {}_tR_1)(1 + {}_{t+1}r_1) + L_2$$

$$(1 + {}_tR_t)[1 + E({}_{t+1}R_1) + L_2]$$

where L_2 represents the liquidity premium on a two-year security. The yield generated from the two-year security should exceed the yield from consecutive investments in one-year securities by a premium that compensates the investor for less liquidity. The relationship between the liquidity premium and term to maturity can be expressed as follows:

$$0 < L_1 < L_2 < L_3 < \ldots < L_{20}$$

where the subscript represents years to maturity. This implies that the liquidity premium would be more influential on the difference between annualized interest rates on one-year and twenty-year securities than on the difference between one-year and two-year securities.

If liquidity influences the yield curve, the forward rate overestimates the market's expectation of the future interest rate. A more appropriate formula for the forward rate would account for the liquidity premium. Reconsider the example where $R_1 = 8\%$, and $R_2 = 10\%$. Assume that the liquidity premium on a two-year security is .5%. The forward rate is

$$E({}_{t+1}R_1) \qquad {}_{t+1}r_1 = \frac{(1 + {}_tR_2)^2}{(1 + {}_tR_1)} - 1 - L_2$$

$$_{t+1}r_1 = \frac{(1.10)^2}{1.08} - 1 - .005$$

$$= .11537$$

The one-year forward rate as it was estimated earlier (12.037%) should overstate the market's expected interest rate, since a liquidity premium is also included in the longer-term security's interest rate. Forecasts of future interest rates implied by a yield curve are adjusted slightly lower when accounting for the liquidity premium.

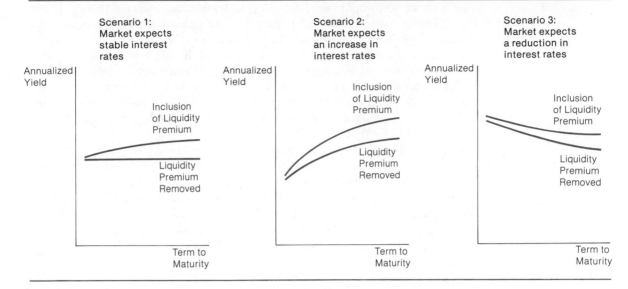

Even with the existence of a liquidity premium, yield curves could still be used to interpret interest rate expectations. A flat yield curve would be interpreted as the market expecting a slight decrease in interest rates (without the effect of the liquidity premium, the yield curve would have had a slight downward slope). A slight upward slope would be interpreted as no expected change in interest rates, since if the liquidity premium were removed, this yield curve would be flat.

Segmented Markets Theory

According to **segmented markets theory,** investors and borrowers choose securities with maturities that satisfy their forecasted cash needs. For example, pension funds and life insurance companies may generally prefer long-term investments that coincide with their long-term liabilities. Commercial banks may prefer more short-term investments to coincide with their short-term liabilities. If investors and borrowers participate only in the maturity market that satisfies their particular needs, markets are segmented. That is, the shifting by investors (or borrowers) from the long-term market to the short-term market or vice versa would only occur if the timing of their cash needs changed. According to segmented markets theory, the choice of long-term versus short-term maturities is predetermined according to *need* rather than expectations of future interest rates.

Assume that most investors have funds available to invest for only a short period of time and therefore desire to invest primarily in short-term securities. Also assume that most borrowers need funds for a long period of time and therefore desire to issue mostly long-term securities. The result would be upward pressure on the price and downward pressure on the yield of short-term securities. In addition, there would be downward pressure on the price and upward pressure on the yield of long-term securities. Overall, the scenario described would create an upward-sloping yield curve.

Chapter 4

Structure of Interest
Rates

105

Now consider the opposite scenario in which most investors wish to invest their funds for a long period of time, while most borrowers need funds for only a short period of time. According to segmented markets theory, there would be downward pressure on the price and upward pressure on the yield of short-term securities. In addition, there would be upward pressure on the price and downward pressure on the yield of long-term securities. Exhibit 4.8 illustrates how the segmented markets theory can explain the shape of the yield curve at any point in time. If there was more balance in the investor's demand and borrower's supply of securities issued between the short-term and long-term markets, the yields of short- and long-term securities would be more similar.

Our example separated the maturity markets into just short-term and long-term. In reality, several maturity markets may exist. Within the short-term market, some investors may prefer maturities of one month or less, while others prefer maturities of one to three months. Regardless of how many maturity markets exist, the yields of securities with various maturities should be somewhat influenced by the desires of investors and borrowers to participate in the maturity market that best satisfies their needs.

The segmented markets theory has support because some participants are likely to choose a maturity based on their needs. A corporation that needs additional funds for 30 days would not consider issuing long-term bonds for such a purpose. Savers with short-term funds are restricted from some long-term investments such as 10-year certificates of deposit or savings bonds that cannot be easily liquidated. Note that this theory of segmented markets conflicts with the general presumption of the pure expectations theory that maturity markets are perfect substitutes for one another.

A limitation of the segmented markets theory is that some borrowers and savers have the flexibility to choose among various maturity markets. For example, corporations that need long-term funds may initially obtain short-term financing if they expect interest rates to decline. Investors with long-term funds may make short-term investments if they expect interest rates

EXHIBIT 4.8   Impact of Different Scenarios on Yield Curve According to Segmented Markets Theory

	Impact of Scenario 1: (Investors have mostly short-term funds available; borrowers want long-term funds)	Impact of Scenario 2: (Investors have mostly long-term funds available; borrowers want short-term funds)
Demand for short-term securities by investors	Upward pressure	Downward pressure
Supply of short-term securities issued by borrowers	Downward pressure	Upward pressure
Price of short-term securities	Upward pressure	Downward pressure
Yield on short-term securities	Downward pressure	Upward pressure
Demand for long-term securities by investors	Downward pressure	Upward pressure
Supply of long-term securities issued by borrowers	Upward pressure	Downward pressure
Price of long-term securities	Downward pressure	Upward pressure
Yield on long-term securities	Upward pressure	Downward pressure
Shape of yield curve	Upward slope	Downward slope

to rise. Some investors with short-term funds available may be willing to purchase long-term securities that have an active secondary market.

Some financial institutions focus on a particular maturity market, while others are more flexible. Commercial banks obtain most of their funds in short-term markets but spread their investments into short-, medium-, and long-term markets. Savings institutions have historically focused on attracting short-term funds and lending funds for long-term periods. Pension funds and insurance companies concentrate on long-term markets for investing.

If maturity markets were completely segmented, an adjustment in the interest rate in one market would have no impact on other markets. Yet, there is clear evidence that interest rates among maturity markets move closely in tandem over time, proving there is some interaction among markets, which implies that funds are being transferred across markets.

While markets are not completely segmented, the preference of particular maturities can affect the prices and yields of securities with different maturities and therefore affect the yield curve's shape. Therefore, the segmented markets theory appears to be a partial explanation for the yield curve's shape, not the sole explanation.

A more flexible perspective of the segmented markets theory, referred to as **preferred habitat theory,** offers a compromising explanation for the term structure of interest rates. This theory suggests that while investors and borrowers may normally concentrate on a particular natural maturity market, certain events may cause them to wander from their natural maturity habitat. For example, commercial banks that obtain mostly short-term funds may select investments with short-term maturities as a natural habitat. However, if they wish to benefit from an anticipated decline in interest rates, they may select medium- and long-term maturities instead. Preferred habitat theory acknowledges that natural maturity markets may influence the yield curve but recognizes that interest rate expectations could entice market participants to stray from preferred maturities.

A Comprehensive Explanation for the Term Structure

To illustrate how all three theories can simultaneously affect the yield curve, assume the following conditions:

1. Investors and borrowers who select security maturities based on anticipated interest rate movements currently expect interest rates to rise.
2. Most borrowers are in need of long-term funds, while most investors have only short-term funds to invest.
3. Investors prefer more liquidity to less.

The first condition, related to expectations theory, suggests the existence of an upward-sloping yield curve, other things being equal. This is shown in Exhibit 4.9 as curve E. The segmented markets information (condition 2), also favors the upward-sloping yield curve. When conditions 1 and 2 are considered simultaneously, the appropriate yield curve may look like curve E + S. The third condition relating to liquidity would then place a higher premium on the longer-term securities due to their lower degree of liquidity. When this condition is included with the first two, the yield curve may look like curve E + S + L.

In our example, all conditions placed upward pressure on long-term yields relative to short-term yields. In reality, there will sometimes be offsetting

EXHIBIT 4.9   Effect of Conditions in Example on Yield Curve

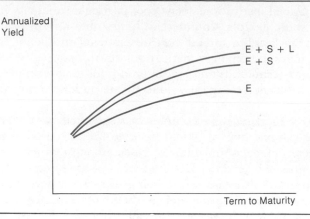

conditions, as one condition places downward pressure on the slope of the yield curve while the others place upward pressure on the slope. For example, if condition 1 were revised to suggest the expectation of lower interest rates in the future, then this condition by itself would result in a downward-sloping yield curve. When combined with the other conditions that favor an upward-sloping curve, it would create a partial offsetting effect. This yield curve would exhibit a downward slope if the effect of the interest rate expectations dominated the combined liquidity premium and segmented markets effects. Conversely, an upward slope would exist if the liquidity premium and segmented markets effects dominated the effects of interest rate expectations.

Use of the Yield Curve

At any point in time, the shape of the yield curve can be used to assess the general expectations of investors and borrowers about future interest rates. Recall from expectations theory that an upward-sloping yield curve generally results from the expectation of higher interest rates, while a downward sloping yield curve generally results from the expectation of lower interest rates. However, the expectations about future interest rates must be interpreted cautiously, since liquidity and specific maturity preferences could influence the yield curve's shape. It is generally believed, though, that interest rate expectations are a major contributing factor to the yield curve's shape, and its shape should provide a reasonable indication (especially if the liquidity premium effect is accounted for) of the market's expectations about future interest rates.

While investors can use the yield curve to interpret the market's consensus expectation of future interest rates, they may have their own interest rate projections. By comparing their projections to those implied by the yield curve, they can attempt to capitalize on the difference. For example, if an upward-sloping yield curve exists, suggesting a market expectation of increasing rates, investors expecting stable interest rates could benefit from investing in long-term securities. From their perspective, long-term securities are undervalued because they reflect the market's expectation of higher

Impact of the Stock Market Crash of October 1987 on Term Structure of Interest Rates

During the stock market crash of October 1987, many investors liquidated their stock holdings and purchased money market securities. The result was an abrupt decline in money market yields. Because securities with longer maturities were not affected as much, the term structure of interest rates was affected. To illustrate the shift in the term structure, the exhibit below shows a trend in the difference between the thirty-year Treasury bond and a three-month Treasury bill over the period of October 13th to 30th. The exhibit suggests that the upward slope of the yield curve must have become steeper over this period. According to expectations theory, such results would imply that investors expected interest rates to rise in the future. The fact that some investors substituted money market securities for capital market securities (stock) during this period suggests that markets are not entirely segmented.

SOURCE: *Chicago Fed Letter*, December 1987

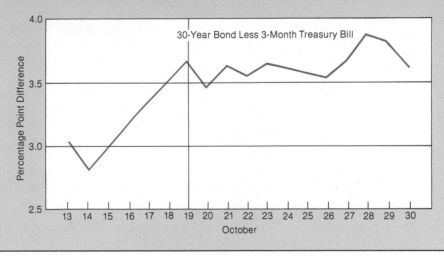

interest rates. Strategies such as this are effective only if the investor can consistently forecast better than the market.

If the yield curve is upward-sloping, some investors may attempt to benefit from the higher yields on longer-term securities, even when they have funds only for a short period of time. The secondary market allows investors the opportunity to do this—it is called **riding the yield curve.** Consider an upward-sloping yield curve such that some one-year securities offer an annualized yield of 7 percent while ten-year bonds can be purchased at par value and offer a coupon rate of 12 percent. An investor with funds available for one year may decide to purchase the bonds and sell them in the secondary market after one year. The investor earns 5 percent more than what was possible on the one-year securities, if the bonds can be sold for what they were purchased for after one year. The risk of this strategy is the uncertainty

Chapter 4

Structure of Interest Rates

of the price at which the security can be sold in the near future. If the upward-sloping yield is interpreted as the market's consensus of higher interest rates in the future, then the price of a security would be expected to decrease in the future. In this case, investors are justified in purchasing a long-term security for a short-term period only if they believe the consensus forecast interpreted from the yield curve is incorrect. While the market's forecast implied by the yield curve often differs from the interest rate that actually occurs, it is difficult to know in advance whether the market will over or underestimate the future interest rate.

The yield curve is commonly monitored by financial institutions whose liability maturities are distinctly different from their asset maturities. Consider a bank that obtains much of its funds through short-term deposits and uses the funds to provide long-term loans or purchase long-term securities. An upward-sloping yield curve is favorable to the bank, since annualized short-term deposit rates are significantly lower than annualized long-term investment rates. The bank's spread is higher than it would be if the yield curve were flat. Some commercial banks may attempt to capitalize on an upward-sloping yield curve by pursuing a greater proportion of short-term deposits and long-term investments. Yet, if the bank believes that the upward slope of the yield curve indicates higher interest rates in the future (as reflected in the expectations theory), then it will expect its cost of liabilities to increase over time as future deposits would be obtained at higher interest rates. Any long-term loans previously provided at a fixed rate would represent a relatively low return in the future if interest rates increase.

The yield curve is also useful for firms that plan to issue bonds. By assessing the prevailing rates on securities for various maturities, they can estimate the rates to be paid on bonds with different maturities. This may enable them to decide the maturity for the bonds they issue.

Historical Review of the Term Structure Relationship

The specific shape of the yield curve changes over time, as illustrated in Exhibit 4.10. Notice that the slope of each yield curve is more pronounced for maturities up to five years and then levels off somewhat for longer maturities. Yield curves are not always upward-sloping. In the late 1970s and early 1980s, securities with shorter maturities commonly offered higher annualized yields, due to the very high interest rates of that period combined with the expectation that they would decrease. While the upward slope has generally persisted since 1982, the degree of slope has changed. In 1985, when nominal interest rates were relatively low, the upward slope became quite pronounced, perhaps because of expectations that interest rates would increase in the future. By 1986 the slope had leveled off.

A **yield surface** can be used to illustrate the yield curves over several points in time on a single graph (see Exhibit 4.11). The foreground of the exhibit shows movements of one-year Treasury securities and the background shows medium- and long-term Treasury securities. The difference in annualized yields among maturities is the vertical gap between the foreground and background. For example, the gap between one-year and longer-term Treasury securities in early 1985 was as much as 3 percent. As interest rates declined over the next two years, the gap narrowed, suggesting that the yield curve not only declined but flattened as well.

Evaluation of the Term Structure Theories

An abundance of research has been conducted on the term structure of interest rates, offering insight into the various theories. Research by Meiselman[1] and others has found that interest rate expectations have a strong influence on the term structure of interest rates. To assess whether other factors are also influential, the forecasting accuracy of the implied forward rates has been evaluated. Accurate forward rates would imply that the market can effectively assess future interest rates and that the expectations theory is, by itself, a proper explanation for the term structure of interest rates. Research has found, however, that forward rates generally are not accurate. To know whether this inaccuracy implies the existence of other factors that affect the term structure of interest rates, the forecasting errors must be more closely evaluated. Presence of a systematic bias is evident which may suggest that other factors are relevant. The liquidity premium, for example, could cause consistent positive forecasting errors, meaning forward rates tend to overestimate future interest rates. Research by Kessel found evidence of this.[2]

Some research has also analyzed liquidity premiums. Van Horne[3] found that the size of liquidity premiums varies inversely with interest rate levels. However, research by Kessel[4] and others found the opposite relationship. The difference in research results can be attributed to different sample periods examined and/or different research methodologies.

While it is difficult to determine whether the term structure of interest rates has been influenced by segmented market forces, some research has been conducted on this topic. A study by Elliot and Echols[5] examined Treasury security data for a variety of maturities and found discontinuities in the yield-maturity relationship. They suggest that the reason could be distinctly different supply and demand conditions for particular maturity segments.

While the results of research differ, there is some evidence that expectations theory, liquidity preference theory, and segmented markets theory all have some validity. Thus, if the term structure is used to assess the market's expectations of future interest rates, investors should first net out the liquidity premium and any unique market conditions for various maturity segments.

1 David Meiselman, *The Term Structure of Interest Rates* (Englewood Cliffs, N.J.: Prentice-Hall, 1962).

2 Reuben A. Kessel, *The Cyclical Behavior of Term Structure of Interest Rates*, Occasional Paper 91 (New York: National Bureau of Economic Research).

3 James C. Van Horne, "Interest Rate Risk and the Term Structure of Interest Rates," *Journal of Political Economy* (August 1965): 344–351.

4 Reuben A. Kessel, *The Cyclical Behavior of Term Structure of Interest Rates*, Occasional Paper 91 (New York: National Bureau of Economic Research).

5 J. W. Elliot and M. E. Echols, "Market Segmentation, Speculative Behavior, and the Term Structure of Interest Rates," *Review of Economics and Statistics*, (February 1976): 40–49.

SPECIAL PROVISIONS

If a security offers any special provision to investors, its yield may be influenced. One type of provision called a **call feature,** allows the issuer of the bonds to buy them back before maturity at a specified price. As an example,

Chapter 4

Structure of Interest Rates

111

EXHIBIT 4.10   Yield Curves at Various Points in Time

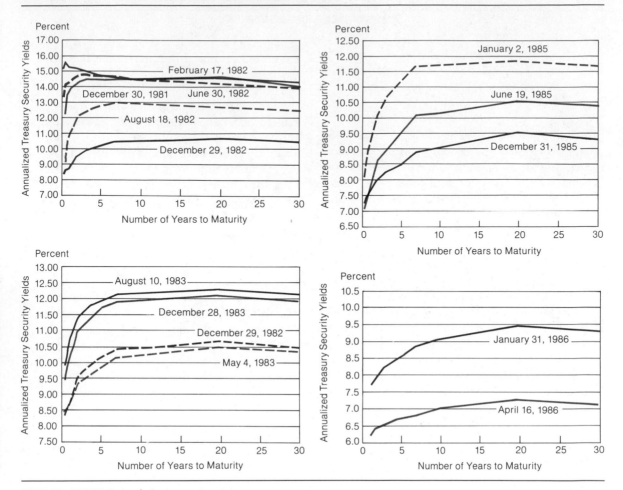

SOURCE: *FRBNY Quarterly Review,* various issues.

Florida Power & Light had issued bonds at close to 16 percent in 1981. By 1986 interest rates had dropped substantially, so the call feature was used to retire its 1981 bonds, and new bonds were issued at a yield of about 9.9 percent. The result was an interest savings of about 6.1 percent, or $61,000 per million dollars borrowed on an annual basis.

Since a call feature could force investors to sell their bonds sooner than they would like, they may require extra compensation in order to purchase them, especially during those periods when interest rates are expected to decrease, making it more likely that the bonds will be called. Thus, the yield on *callable bonds* should be higher than on noncallable bonds, other things being equal.

Another special provision of bonds that can affect the yield is a **convertibility clause,** which allows investors to convert the bond into a specified number of common stock shares. If the market price of the bonds declines, investors who wish to dispose of the bonds have an alternative to selling them in the market. For this reason, investors will accept a lower yield on securities that contain the convertibility feature, other things being equal.

EXHIBIT 4.11 Illustration of a Yield Surface

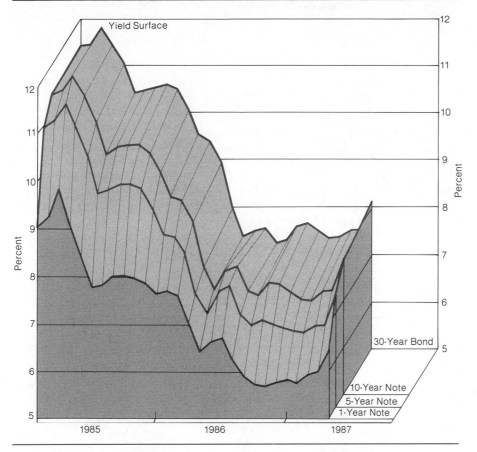

Yield Surface

30-Year Bond
10-Year Note
5-Year Note
1-Year Note

1985   1986   1987

NOTE: A time series representation of the U.S. Treasury's constant-maturity yield curve is presented above. With the horizontal axis representing calendar time and successive maturities lying further away from the viewer, the "nearest" surface shows the history of the bond-equivalent yield to maturity of one-year Treasury securities. At each date, one can compare the yields on 1-, 5-, 10-, and 30-year securities.

SOURCE: *Economic Commentary*, Federal Reserve Bank of Cleveland, (May 1987) P: 19; and Board of Governors.

EXPLANATION OF ACTUAL YIELD DIFFERENTIALS

The differentials in yields among money market securities can be explained by the characteristics just described. Commercial paper and negotiable certificate of deposit (NCD) rates are typically just slightly higher than T-bill (Treasury bill) rates, as investors require a slightly higher return to compensate for default risk and less liquidity. Eurodollar deposit rates are higher than yields on other money market securities with the same maturity because of their lower degree of liquidity and higher degree of default risk.

Exhibit 4.12 illustrates the annualized yields of each money market security (with a three-month maturity). While these yields are quite volatile from year to year, their respective differences do not normally change much

Chapter 4

Structure of Interest Rates

113

EXHIBIT 4.12 Yield Comparison of Securities with Identical (three-month) Maturities Over Time

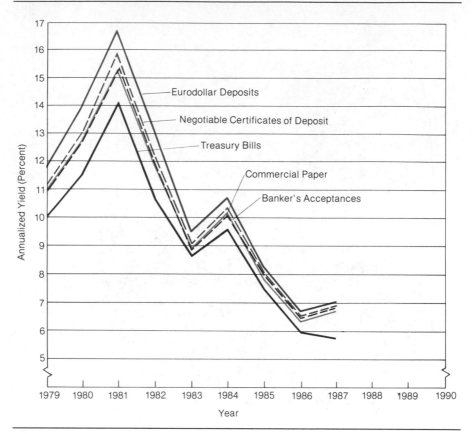

SOURCE: *Federal Reserve Bulletin*, several issues.

over time. The difference between yields on T-bills versus other risky securities was noticeably higher during the recessionary phase in the early 1980s, primarily due to a higher default risk during that period.

Market forces cause the yields of all securities to move in the same direction. To illustrate, assume the Treasury experiences a large increase in the budget deficit and issues a large amount of T-bills to finance the increased deficit. This action creates a large supply of T-bills in the market, placing downward pressure on the price and upward pressure on the T-bill yield. As the yield begins to rise, it approaches the yield of other short-term securities. Businesses and individual investors are now encouraged to purchase T-bills rather than these risky securities, since they can achieve about the same yield while avoiding default risk. The switch to T-bills lowers demand for risky securities, thereby placing downward pressure on their price and upward pressure on their yields. Thus, the risk premium on risky securities would not disappear completely.

With regard to capital market securities, municipal bonds have the lowest before-tax yield. Yet, their after-tax yield is typically above that of Treasury

EXHIBIT 4.13   Yields of Corporate Bonds with Varied Default Risk

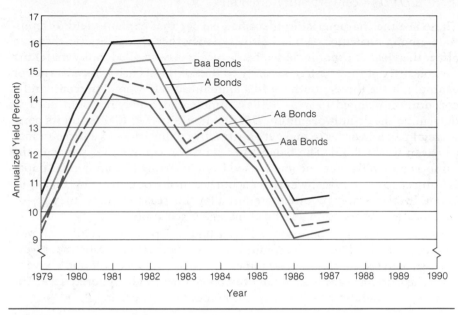

Baa Bonds
A Bonds
Aa Bonds
Aaa Bonds

SOURCE: *Federal Reserve Bulletin*, various issues.

bonds from the perspective of high-tax bracket investors. Treasury bonds are expected to offer the lowest yield because they are free from default risk and can easily be liquidated in the secondary market. Investors prefer municipal or corporate bonds over Treasury bonds only if the after-tax yield is sufficiently higher to compensate for default risk and a lower degree of liquidity.

To further assess how capital market security yields can vary due to default risk, Exhibit 4.13 illustrates yields of corporate bonds in four different risk classes. The yield differentials among capital market securities can change over time as perceptions of risk change. The differential between the highest and lowest risk classes in Exhibit 4.13 is over 2 percent during the 1982 recession but less than 1.5 percent in the mid 1980s.

ESTIMATING THE APPROPRIATE YIELD

When estimating the appropriate yield to be offered on a security, the following formula can be useful:

$$Y_n = RF_n + DP + LP + T + CALLP + COND$$

where Y_n = yield of an n-day security
RF_n = yield of an n-day Treasury (risk-free) security
DP = default premium to compensate for default risk
LP = liquidity premium to compensate for less liquidity
T = adjustment due to the difference in tax status

Chapter 4

Structure of Interest
Rates

115

$CALLP$ = call feature premium to compensate for the possibility that the security will be called

$COND$ = convertibility discount

These are the characteristics identified earlier that explain yield differentials among securities. While maturity is another characteristic that can affect the yield, it is not included here since it is controlled for by matching the maturity of the risk-free security to that of the security of concern. For example, if the three-month T-bill's annualized rate were 8 percent, and a corporation planned to issue 90-day commercial paper, it would need to determine the default premium (DP) and liquidity (LP) to offer on its commercial paper in order to make it as attractive to investors as a three-month (thirteen-week) T-bill. The federal tax status on commercial paper is the same as on T-bills. Yet, income earned from investing in commercial paper is subject to state taxes, whereas income earned from investing in T-bills is not. Investors may require a premium for this reason alone if they reside in a location where state and local income taxes apply.

Assume that the corporation believed that a .7 percent default risk premium, a .2 percent liquidity premium, and a .3 percent tax adjustment were necessary to sell its commercial paper to investors. Since call and convertibility features are applicable only to bonds, they can be ignored here. The appropriate yield to be offered on the commercial paper is

$$Y_n = RF_n + DP + LP + T + CALLP + COND$$
$$= 8\% + .7 + .2\% + .3\% + 0 + 0$$
$$= 9.2\%$$

As time passes, the appropriate commercial paper rate would change, due perhaps to changes in the risk-free rate, default premium, liquidity premium, and tax adjustment.

Some corporations may postpone plans to issue commercial paper until the economy improves, and the required premium for default risk is reduced. Yet, even then, the market rate of commercial paper may increase if interest rates increase. For example, if over time the default risk premium decreases from .7 percent to .5 percent, but RF_n increases from 8 percent to 8.7 percent, the appropriate yield to be offered on commercial paper (assuming no change in the previously assumed liquidity and tax adjustment premiums) would be

$$Y_n = RF_n + DP + LP + T$$
$$= 8.7\% + .5\% + .2\% + .3\%$$
$$= 9.7\%$$

The strategy to postpone issuing commercial paper would backfire in this example. Even though the default premium decreased by .2 percent, the general level of interest rates rose by .7 percent, so the net change in the commercial paper rate is +.5 percent. This example shows that just because a security's yield increases over time, that does not necessarily mean the default premium has increased.

The assessment of yields as described here could also be applied to long-term securities. If for example, a firm desired to issue a 20-year corporate bond, it could identify the yield of a new 20-year Treasury bond and add on the premiums for default risk, liquidity risk, and so on, in order to determine the yield at which it could sell corporate bonds.

SUMMARY

Favorable characteristics of commonly traded securities include a high level of liquidity, a tax-exempt status, a low level of default risk, and a convertibility provision. Buyers of securities make their investment decisions according to these characteristics. Thus, they dictate the premiums that must be offered by various securities. Those with favorable characteristics can offer a lower yield and still appear attractive to investors. The yield of any security fluctuates over time as a result of either a change in market rates, or a change in a premium (or discount) required by investors for the security's particular characteristics.

KEY TERMS

call feature   preferred habitat theory
convertibility clause   riding the yield curve
forward rate   segmented markets theory
investment-grade bonds   term structure of interest rates
liquid   yield curve
liquidity premium theory   yield surface

QUESTIONS

4.1. Identify the relevant characteristics of any security that can affect its yield.

4.2. What effect does a high default risk have on securities?

4.3. Discuss the relationship between the yield and liquidity of securities.

4.4. Do high-tax- or low-tax-bracket investors benefit more from tax-exempt securities? Why?

4.5. Do municipal bonds or corporate bonds offer a higher before-tax yield corp at a given point in time? Why? Which has the higher after-tax yield? depends

4.6. If taxes did not exist, would Treasury bonds offer a higher or lower yield than municipal bonds with the same maturity? Why?

4.7. Explain how a yield curve would shift in response to a sudden expectation of rising interest rates, according to the pure expectations theory.

4.8. What is the meaning of the *forward rate* in the context of the term structure of interest rates?

4.9. Why might forward rates consistently overestimate future interest rates? liq·prem 104 How could such a bias be avoided?

4.10. Assume there is a sudden expectation of lower interest rates in the future. What would be the effect on the shape of the yield curve? Explain.

4.11. Explain the liquidity premium theory.

4.12. If liquidity and interest rate expectations are both important for explaining the shape of a yield curve, what does a flat yield curve indicate about the market's perception of future interest rates?

4.13. If a downward-sloping yield curve is mainly attributed to segmented markets theory, what does that suggest about the demand and supply of funds in the short-term and long-term maturity markets.

4.14. If the segmented markets theory causes an upward-sloping yield curve, what does this imply?

4.15. If markets are not completely segmented, should we dismiss the segmented markets theory as even a partial explanation for the term structure of interest rates? Explain.

4.16. Explain the preferred habitat theory.

4.17. What factors influence the shape of the yield curve?

4.18. Describe how financial market participants use the yield curve.

4.19. Would yields be higher for callable bonds or noncallable bonds that are similar in all other respects? Why?

PROBLEMS

4.1. a. Assume that as of today, the annualized two-year interest rate is 13 percent, while the one-year interest rate is 12 percent. Use only this information to estimate the one-year forward rate.

b. Assume that the liquidity premium on a two-year security is .3 percent. Use this information to reestimate the one-year forward rate.

4.2. Assume that as of today, the annualized interest rate on a three-year security is 10 percent, while the annualized interest rate on a two-year security is 7 percent. Use only this information to estimate the one-year forward rate two years from now.

4.3. If $_tR_1 > _tR_2$, what is the market consensus forecast about the one-year forward rate one year from now? Is this rate above or below today's one-year interest rate? Explain.

PROJECTS

1. EXPLAINING TODAY'S YIELD DIFFERENTIALS

a. Using the most recent issue of *The Wall Street Journal*, review the section called "Money Rates" (listed in the index in the front page). Determine the following interest rates:

Federal funds rate = _____

Commercial paper rate (with shortest maturity) = _____

Certificates of deposit (1-month maturity) = _____

Banker's acceptances (30-day maturity) = _____

London Interbank Offered Rates (LIBOR) (1-month maturity) = _____

Treasury bills (13-week maturity) = _____

b. Rank the securities from highest interest rate to lowest and provide a brief explanation for the differences in yields among these securities.

c. Using the most recent issue of *The Wall Street Journal*, review the "Yield Comparison Table" (sometimes listed in the section entitled "Credit Markets"). Use this table to report the following yields:

Type	Maturity	Yield
Treasury	10-year	_____
Corporate: High Quality	10-year	_____
Corporate: Medium Quality	10-year	_____

If default risk is the only reason for the yield differentials, what is the default risk premium on the corporate high-quality bonds? On the medium-quality bonds?

During the 1982 recession, high-quality corporate bonds offered a yield of .79 percent above Treasury bonds, and medium-quality bonds offered a yield of about 3.11 percent above Treasury bonds. How do these yield differentials compare to the differentials today? Explain the reason for the change in yield differentials.

d. Using the same table from *The Wall Street Journal*, determine the yield on tax-exempt bonds with a 10-year maturity.

Fill out the following table:

Marginal Tax Bracket of Investors	Before-tax yield that would be necessary to achieve existing after-tax yield of tax-exempt bonds.	If the tax-exempt bonds have the same risk and other features as high-quality corporate bonds, which type of bond is preferable for investors in each tax bracket?
10%	_____	_____
15%	_____	_____
20%	_____	_____
28%	_____	_____
34%	_____	_____

2. EXAMINING RECENT ADJUSTMENTS IN DEFAULT RISK

Using the most recent issue of *The Wall Street Journal*, review the section called "Credit Ratings." Report any changes in credit ratings, and for each change explain the following:

a. What was the reason given for the change in credit ratings? How does this reason relate to default risk?

b. How will the change in ratings influence the market price of these securities?

c. How will the change in ratings influence the yield to be earned by investors that previously invested in these securities and are about to sell them?

d. How will the change in ratings influence the expected yield to be earned by investors who now invest in these securities?

3. DETERMINING AND INTERPRETING TODAY'S TERM STRUCTURE

a. Using the most recent issue of *The Wall Street Journal*, review the table called "Treasury Bonds, Notes & Bills (listed in the index in the front page as "Treasury Issues"). Use that table to determine the yields for the various maturities:

Term to Maturity	Annualized Yield
1 year	
2 years	
3 years	

Assuming that the differences in these yields are solely because of interest rate expectations, determine the one-year forward rate as of one year from now and the one-year forward rate as of two years from now.

b. Within the *Wall Street Journal*, a "Treasury Yield Curve" is provided. Use this curve to describe the market's expectations about future interest rates. If a liquidity premium exists, how would this affect your perception of the market's expectations?

REFERENCES

Elliot, J. W. and M. E. Echols. "Market Segmentation, Speculative Behavior, and the Term Structure of Interest Rates." *Review of Economics and Statistics* 58 (February 1976): 40–49.

Ford, Harold D. and Larry D. Wall. "Money Market Account Competition." *Economic Review*, Federal Reserve Bank of Atlanta (December 1984): 4–14.

Garner, C. Alan. "The Yield Curve and Inflation Expectations." *Economic Review*, Federal Reserve Bank of Kansas City (September–October 1987): 3–14.

"How Plummeting Interest Rates are Hoisting the Economy." *Business Week*, March 10, 1986, 28–29.

Keeley, Michael C. and Gary C. Zimmerman. "Interest Sensitivity of MMDAs." Federal Reserve Bank of San Francisco, weekly letter, June 21, 1985.

Kessel, Reuben A. *The Cyclical Behavior of Term Structure of Interest Rates*. Occasional Paper 91. New York: National Bureau of Economic Research.

Meiselman, David. *The Term Structure of Interest Rates*. Englewood Cliffs, N.J.: Prentice-Hall 1962.

Nelson, Charles and Andrew Siegel. "Parsimonious Modeling of Yield Curves." *Journal of Business* (October 1987): 473–489.

Van Horne, James C. *Financial Market Rates and Flows*, 2d ed. Englewood Cliffs, N.J.: Prentice Hall, 1984.

Van Horne, James C. "Interest Rate Risk and the Term Structure of Interest Rates." *Journal of Political Economy* 73 (August 1965): 344–51.

Credit Markets

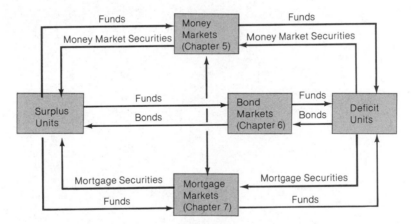

The chapters in Part Two focus on how three types of credit markets facilitate the flow of funds from surplus units to deficit units. Chapter 5 focuses on money markets for investors and borrowers trading short-term securities. Chapters 6 and 7 focus on bond markets and mortgage markets respectively, for investors and borrowers trading long-term securities. Because some financial market participants trade securities in all three markets, there is much interaction between these markets as emphasized throughout these chapters.

Money Markets

MONEY MARKET SECURITIES IN PERSPECTIVE

Most institutional investors not only invest in stocks and bonds but money market securities as well. While money market securities are desirable because of their high degree of liquidity, institutional investors also use money market securities as a temporary investment during periods when stocks and bonds are unattractive.

To illustrate the importance of money market securities for financial institutions that invest in various securities, the following recommendations were made by securities firms as of June 30, 1988:

Recommended Mix of Securities

Securities Firm	Stocks	Bonds	Money Market Securities
Drexel Burnham	58%	25%	17%
A.G. Edwards	25%	50%	25%
Kidder Peabody	40%	10%	50%
Merrill Lynch	40%	45%	15%
Paine Webber	21%	59%	20%
Thomson McKinnan	50%	10%	40%

Thomson McKinnon's large recommended percentage toward money market securities was due to its concern about the potential adverse impact of the Federal Reserve's tightening of credit on bond prices. Kidder Peabody's recommendations for a large investment in money market securities reflected its concerns about the dollar's value, interest rates, and the volatility of other security prices. The large recommended position in money market securities would prevent institutional investors from a major loss if stock and bond prices declined.

■ What types of money market securities are available?
■ How do various money market securities differ regarding degree of liquidity and default risk?
■ Which money market securities offer a higher yield? Why?
These and other related questions are addressed in this chapter.

SOURCE: *The Wall Street Journal*, July 27, 1988, p. 29.

OUTLINE

This chapter first provides a background on the most commonly used money market securities, and then explains their institutional use. Next it describes how money market yields interact and how money markets have become internationalized.

BACKGROUND ON POPULAR MONEY MARKET SECURITIES

Securities are issued by corporations and governments to obtain short-term funds. They are originally issued within the **primary market,** which is a telecommunications network whereby investors can be informed that new securities are for sale. Generally, the issuer has no obligation to repurchase securities until maturity. Yet, investors who purchase them before maturity may be able to sell them through the **secondary market.** Securities that have an active secondary market, and thus can be sold whenever desired, are preferred since they allow investors more flexibility.

Securities with maturities within one year are referred to as **money market instruments.** The more popular ones are

- Treasury bills
- Commercial paper
- Negotiable certificates of deposit
- Repurchase agreements
- Federal funds
- Banker's acceptances

Each of these instruments is described in turn.

Treasury Bills

When the U.S. government needs to borrow funds, the U.S. Treasury frequently issues short-term securities known as Treasury bills (or T-bills).

These are sold weekly through an auction. One-year T-bills are issued on a monthly basis. The par value (amount received by investors at maturity) of T-bills is a minimum of $10,000 in multiples of $5,000 thereafter. T-bills are attractive to investors because they are backed by the federal government and therefore are virtually free of default risk. Another attractive feature of T-bills is their liquidity, due to their short maturity and strong secondary market. Existing Treasury bills can be sold in the secondary market through government securities dealers, who profit by purchasing the bills at a slightly lower price than they sell them for.

TREASURY BILL AUCTION. The primary Treasury bill market is an auction by mail. Investors submit bids on the Treasury bill applications for the maturity of their choice. An example of a 26-week Treasury bill application is shown in Exhibit 5.1. Investors have an option to bid competitively or noncompetitively. Competitive bids must be received by Federal Reserve banks by Monday 1:00 P.M. Eastern time of each week and are then wired to the Treasury. The Treasury has a specified amount of funds that it plans to borrow during the 26-week period, and this dictates the amount of Treasury bill bids it will accept. After accounting for noncompetitive bids, it accepts the highest competitive bids first and works its way down until it has generated the amount of funds from competitive bids that it needs. Any bids that are below that cutoff point are not accepted.

To assure that their bid will be accepted, investors can use a noncompetitive bid. The price they will pay (per $1,000 par value) is the weighted average price paid by all competitive bidders whose bids were accepted. Since noncompetitive bidders do not know this amount in advance, they write a check for the par value of the Treasury bills they have requested. Once the auction results are completed, the Treasury sends a check back to them that represents the difference between par value and the final price.

Noncompetitive bidders are limited to purchasing Treasury bills with a maximum par value of $1 million per auction. Consequently, large corporations typically make competitive bids so they can purchase larger amounts.

Applications to purchase a Treasury bill can be obtained at no charge from a Federal Reserve district or branch bank. Alternatively, investors can ask a broker or a commercial bank to obtain and send in the application for them. The fee charged for this service normally ranges from $25 to $75. This fee can have a significant impact on the yield to an investor that purchases a Treasury bill with a $10,000 par value. For larger denominations, such as $100,000, the yield is less sensitive to a fee.

The results of the weekly auction of 13-week and 26-week Treasury bills are summarized in major daily newspapers each Tuesday. Some of the more commonly reported statistics are the dollar amount of applications and Treasury securities sold, the average price of the accepted competitive bids, and the coupon equivalent (annualized yield) for investors that paid the average price.

The results of a recent Treasury bill auction are shown in Exhibit 5.2. At each auction, the prices paid for six-month T-bills are significantly lower than prices paid for three-month T-bills because the investment term is longer. The lower price results in a higher unannualized yield that compensates investors for their longer-term investment.

EXHIBIT 5.1   Example of a Treasury Bill Application

TREASURY BILL TENDER - 26-WEEK BILLS
FRB CHGO 77-225 (3/14/84)

MAIL TO: FEDERAL RESERVE BANK OF CHICAGO
P.O. BOX 834
CHICAGO IL 60690-0834

P.O. BOX 1059
DETROIT MI 48231-1059

FOR OFFICIAL USE ONLY
FRB Request No. _____
Issue Date _____
Due Date _____
Cusip No. _____

BEFORE COMPLETING THIS FORM READ THE ACCOMPANYING INSTRUCTIONS CAREFULLY

Pursuant to the provisions of Department of the Treasury Circular, Public Debt Series No. 27-76, the public announcement issued by the Department of the Treasury, and the regulations set forth in Department Circular, Public Series No. 26-76, I hereby submit this tender, in accordance with the terms as marked, for currently offered U.S. Treasury bills for my account. (Competitive tenders must be expressed on a yield basis with not more than two decimals. Fractions may not be used.) I understand that noncompetitive tenders will be accepted in full at the average price of accepted competitive bids and that a noncompetitive tender by any one bidder may not exceed $1,000,000.

TYPE OF BID
NONCOMPETITIVE ☐   or   COMPETITIVE ☐   at: Yield _____

AMOUNT OF TENDER $ _____
(Minimum of $10,000. Over $10,000 must be in multiples of $5,000.)

ACCOUNT IDENTIFICATION: (Please type or print clearly using a ball-point pen.)

Depositor(s) _____
_____
_____

Address _____
_____
_____

PRIVACY ACT NOTICE
The individually identifiable information required on this form is necessary to permit the tender to be processed and the bills to be issued, in accordance with the general regulations governing United States book-entry Treasury bills (Department Circular PD Series No. 26-76). The transaction will not be completed unless all required data is furnished.

DEPOSITOR(S) IDENTIFICATION NUMBER

FIRST NAMED   SOCIAL SECURITY NUMBER ☐☐☐ — ☐☐ — ☐☐☐☐   OR   EMPLOYER IDENTIFICATION NO. ☐☐ — ☐☐☐☐☐☐☐

SECOND NAMED   SOCIAL SECURITY NUMBER ☐☐☐ — ☐☐ — ☐☐☐☐

DISPOSITION OF PROCEEDS

The par amount of the account will be paid at maturity unless you elect to have Treasury reinvest (roll-over) the proceeds of the maturing bills. (See below)

☐ I hereby request noncompetitive reinvestment of the proceeds in book-entry Treasury bills.

METHOD OF PAYMENT

TOTAL SUBMITTED	CASH	CHECK	MATURING TREASURY SECURITIES	FOR OFFICIAL USE ONLY	
$	$	$	$	ENTRY DATE	ON

Check the box if you are **NOT** subject to backup withholding under the provisions of section 3406 (a) (i) (c) of the Internal Revenue Code .... ☐

Failure to check the box will result in withholding of 20% of the interest payments.

PREPAYMENT
$

DEPOSITORS AUTHORIZATION

CERTIFICATION - Under the penalties of perjury, I certify that the information provided on this form is true, correct, and complete. Certification must be completed by first named depositor.

Signature ▶ _____

Telephone Number During Business Hours   (____) ____
Area Code

FOR OFFICIAL USE ONLY

Received by _____   Date _____

1-ORIGINAL

126

EXHIBIT 5.2 Example of Treasury Bill Auction Results; Based on the July 11, 1988 Auction

	13-Week Treasury Bill Auction	26-Week Treasury Bill Auction
Applications	$25,244,235,000	$25,025,160,000
Accepted Bids	$ 6,608,185,000	$ 6,607,920,000
Average Price of Accepted Bids (Per $100 Par Value)	$98.301	$96.466
High Price Paid for Accepted Bids (Per $100 Par Value)	$98.309	$96.476
Low Price Paid for Accepted Bids (Per $100 Par Value)	$98.299	$96.461
Coupon Equivalent (Yield)	6.93%	7.35%

SOURCE: *The Wall Street Journal*, July 12, 1988. See *The Wall Street Journal* on any Tuesday for the information above, as well as other information pertaining to Monday's Treasury Bill auction. The results are usually reported in the section called "Credit Markets."

ESTIMATING THE YIELD. T-bills do not offer coupon payments but are sold at a discount from par value. Their yield is influenced by the difference between the selling price and purchase price. If an investor purchases a newly issued T-bill and holds it until maturity, the return is based on the difference between the par value and the purchase price. If the T-bill is sold prior to maturity, the return is based on the difference between the price for which the bill was sold in the secondary market and the purchase price.

The annualized yield from investing in a T-bill (Y_T) can be determined as

$$Y_t = \frac{S - P}{P} \times \frac{365}{n}$$

where S = selling price
P = purchase price
n = number of days of the investment (holding period)

Assume that an investor purchases a T-bill with a six-month (182-day) maturity and $10,000 par value for $9,600. If this T-bill is held to maturity, its yield is

$$Y_T = \frac{\$10,000 - \$9,600}{\$9,600} \times \frac{365}{182} = 8.36\%$$

If the T-bill is sold prior to maturity, the selling price and therefore the yield are dependent on market conditions at the time of the sale. Suppose the investor plans to sell the T-bill after 120 days and forecasts a selling price of $9,820 at that time. The expected annualized yield based on this forecast is

$$Y_T = \frac{\$9,820 - \$9,600}{\$9,600} \times \frac{365}{120} = 6.97\%$$

The higher the forecasted selling price, the higher will be the expected annualized yield.

Business periodicals frequently quote the T-bill discount (or T-bill rate) along with the T-bill yield. The T-bill discount (D_T) represents the percent discount of the purchase price from par value *(par)* for newly issued T-bills and is computed as

$$D_T = \frac{par - P}{par} \times \frac{360}{n}$$

A 360-day year is used to compute the T-bill discount. Using the information from the previous example, the T-bill discount is

$$D_T = \frac{\$10,000 - \$9,600}{\$10,000} \times \frac{360}{182} = 7.91\%$$

For a newly issued T-bill that is held to maturity, the T-bill yield will always be higher than the discount. The difference occurs because the purchase price is the denominator of the yield equation, while the par value is the denominator of the T-bill discount equation, and the par value will always exceed the purchase price of a newly issued T-bill. In addition, the yield formula uses a 365-day year versus a 360-day year for the discount computation.

Commercial Paper

Commercial paper is issued only by well-known creditworthy firms and is typically unsecured. It is normally issued to provide liquidity or finance a firm's investment in inventory and accounts receivable. In recent years, some firms have been backing commercial paper with assets. This so-called *collateralized commercial paper* reduces the risk to investors and thus is easier to sell. Some commercial paper is backed by standby *letters of credit* (L/C) from banks.

The minimum denomination of commercial paper is $25,000, although denominations of $100,000 or more are common. Maturities are normally between 20 and 45 days but can be as short as 1 day or as long as 270 days. The 270-day maximum is due to a Securities and Exchange Commission (SEC) ruling that paper with a maturity exceeding 270 days must be registered.

An active secondary market for commercial paper does not exist. However, it is sometimes possible to sell the paper back to the dealer who initially helped to place it. In most cases, commercial paper is held until maturity by investors. Financial institutions such as finance companies and bank holding companies are major issuers of commercial paper. Exhibit 5.3 shows the dominance of financial commercial paper issues over time. In recent years, nonfinancial corporations have relied more heavily on commercial paper as a source of short-term funds.

RATINGS. In 1970 Penn Central Transportation Company defaulted on $82 million of commercial paper. Since that time, corporations have found that it is easier to place commercial paper if they have it rated. Companies such as Moody's Investors Service, Standard & Poor's Corporation, and Fitch Investor Service perform this service. Some potential investors use the rat-

EXHIBIT 5.3   Comparison of U.S. Commercial Paper Outstanding by Issuer

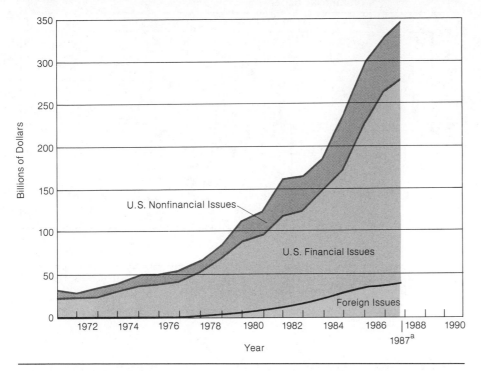

a 1987 data is as of October 1.

SOURCE: Board of Governors of the Federal Reserve System, *Flow of Funds*, and *FRBNY Quarterly Review* (Autumn 1987): 25.

ings as a measure of default risk, while others prefer to assess the risk themselves.

A higher risk classification can increase a corporation's commercial paper rate by as much as 150 basis points. Exhibit 5.4 illustrates the difference between high-grade and medium-grade commercial paper. The difference reached 150 basis points during the 1974 and 1982 recessions but has been less than 50 basis points over recent years. Fees charged by rating services typically range between $5,000 and $25,000 per year, depending on how often the firm issues paper.

PLACEMENT. Some firms place commercial paper directly with investors. Others use commercial paper dealers, at a cost of usually one-eighth of 1 percent of the face value. This transaction cost is generally less than it would cost to create a department within the firm to place commercial paper directly. Of course, those companies that frequently issue commercial paper may reduce expenses by creating such a department. Most nonfinancial companies prefer to use commercial paper dealers rather than in-house resources to place their commercial paper. Their liquidity needs, and therefore their commercial paper issues, are cyclical, so an in-house direct-placement department would not be efficiently used throughout the year.

Chapter 5

Money Markets

EXHIBIT 5.4 Difference between High-Grade and Medium Grade Commercial Paper

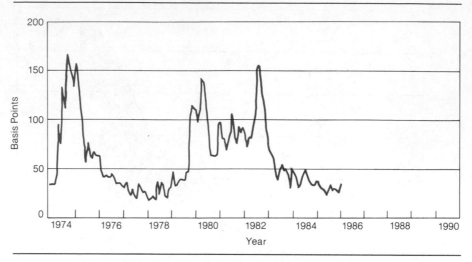

SOURCE: *Money Market Instruments*, Federal Reserve bank of Richmond, Sixth Edition, 115 and the Board of Governors of the Federal Reserve System.

Finance companies typically maintain an in-house department, since they frequently borrow in this manner regardless of the business cycle.

A comparison of the directly issued and dealer-placed commercial paper outstanding, in Exhibit 5.5, shows that the amounts of both types have consistently increased since 1970, with the exception of the recessionary period in 1982. The proportion of directly issued paper to dealer-placed paper has been fairly even over the last several years.

BACKING COMMERCIAL PAPER. Issuers of commercial paper typically maintain backup lines of credit in case they for some reason cannot roll over (reissue) commercial paper at a reasonable rate. Such an event could occur if their assigned rating was lowered. A backup line of credit provided by a commercial bank allows the company the right (but not the obligation) to borrow a specified maximum amount of funds over a specified period of time. The fee for the line can either be a direct percentage of the total accessible credit (such as .5 percent), or it can be in the form of required compensating balances (such as 10 percent of the line).

ESTIMATING THE YIELD. At a given point in time, the yield on commercial paper is slightly higher than the yield on a T-bill with the same maturity, since commercial paper carries some default risk and is less liquid. Like T-bills, commercial paper is sold at a discount from par value. The nominal return to investors who retain the paper until maturity is the difference between the price paid for the paper and the par value. Thus, the yield received by a commercial paper investor can be determined in a manner similar to the T-bill yield, although a 360-day year is usually used. For

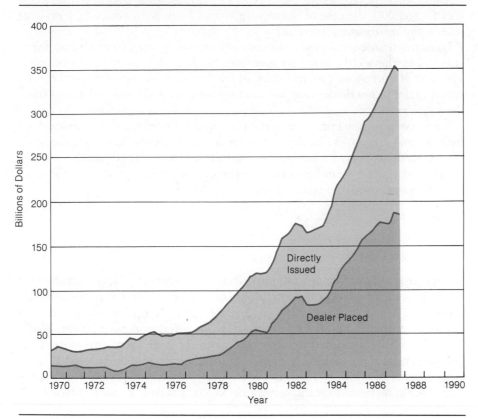

SOURCE: Federal Reserve Bank of New York; and *FRBNY Quarterly Review* (Autumn 1987).

example, if an investor purchases 30-day commercial paper with a par value
of $1,000,000 for a price of $990,000, the yield is

$$Y_{cp} = \frac{\$1,000,000 - \$990,000}{\$990,000} \times \frac{360}{30}$$
$$= 12.12\%$$

When a firm plans to issue commercial paper, the price (and therefore
yield) to investors is uncertain. Thus, the cost of borrowing funds is uncertain until the paper is issued. Consider the case of a firm that plans to issue
90-day commercial paper with a par value of $5,000,000. It expects to sell
the commercial paper for $4,850,000. The yield it expects to pay investors
(its cost of borrowing) is estimated to be

$$Y_{cp} = \frac{par - P}{P} \times \frac{360}{n}$$
$$= \frac{\$5,000,000 - \$4,850,000}{\$4,850,000} \times \frac{360}{90}$$
$$= 12.37\%$$

Chapter 5

Money Markets

When firms sell their commercial paper at a lower (higher) price than projected, their cost of raising funds will be higher (lower) than what they initially anticipated. Using the previous example, if the actual selling price was $4,865,000, the cost of borrowing would have been about 11.1 percent (check the math as an exercise).

Ignoring transaction costs, the cost of borrowing with commercial paper is equal to the yield earned by investors holding the paper until maturity. The cost of borrowing can be adjusted for transaction costs (charged by the commercial paper dealers) by subtracting the nominal transaction fees from the price received.

Some corporations prefer to issue commercial paper rather than borrow from a bank since it is usually a cheaper source of funds. Yet, even the large creditworthy corporations that are able to issue commercial paper normally obtain some short-term loans from commercial banks in order to maintain a business relationship with banks.

Negotiable Certificates of Deposit (NCDs)

The **negotiable certificate of deposit (NCD)** is issued by large commercial banks and other depository institutions as a short-term source of funds. Its minimum denomination is $100,000, although a $1 million denomination is more common. Nonfinancial corporations often purchase NCDs. While NCD denominations are typically too large for individual investors, they are sometimes purchased by money market funds that have pooled individual investors' funds. Thus, the existence of money market funds allows individuals to be indirect investors in NCDs, making a more active NCD market.

Maturities on NCDs normally range from two weeks to one year. A secondary market for NCDs exists, providing investors with some liquidity. However, institutions prefer not to have their newly issued NCDs compete with their previously issued NCDs that are being resold in the secondary market. The oversupply of NCDs for sale can force them to sell their newly issued NCDs at a lower price.

PLACEMENT. Some issuers place their NCDs directly; others use a correspondent institution that specializes in placing NCDs. Another alternative is to sell NCDs to securities dealers, who in turn resell them. A portion of unusually large issues is commonly sold to NCD dealers. However, NCDs can normally be sold to investors directly at a higher price.

MEASUREMENT OF THE PREMIUM. NCDs must offer a premium above the Treasury bill yield to compensate for less liquidity and safety. Exhibit 5.6 shows the premiums paid on three-month NCDs versus Treasury bills. The premiums were generally higher during recessionary periods. The premiums also reflect the market's perception about the safety of the financial system. The higher premiums in 1984 relative to other recent nonrecessionary years were likely due to the rescue of Continental Illinois Bank.

Repurchase Agreements

A **repurchase agreement** (or *repo*) represents the sale of securities by one party to another with an agreement to repurchase the securities at a specified date and price. In essence, the repo transaction represents a loan backed by the securities. If the borrower defaults on the loan, the lender has claim to the securities. Most repo transactions use government securities, although some involve other securities such as commercial paper or NCDs. A *reverse repo* refers to the purchase of securities by one party from another with an agreement to sell them. Thus, a repo and reverse repo can represent the same transaction but from different perspectives. These two terms are sometimes used interchangeably, so a description of a repo transaction may actually reflect a reverse repo, and vice versa.

Repo transactions are negotiated through a telecommunications network. Dealers and repo brokers act as financial intermediaries to create repos for firms with deficient and excess funds, receiving a commission for their services.

When the borrowing firm can find a counterparty to the repo transaction, it avoids the transaction fee involved in having a government securities dealer find the counterparty. Some companies that commonly engage in repo transactions have an in-house department for finding counterparties and executing the transactions. These same companies that borrow through repos may, from time to time, serve as the lender. That is, they purchase the government securities and agree to sell them back in the near future. Because the cash flow of any large company changes on a daily basis, it is not unusual for a firm to act as an investor one day (when it has excess funds) and a borrower the next (when it has a cash shortage).

EXHIBIT 5.6 Premium Offered on NCD Rates (Relative to Treasury Bill Rates) Over Time

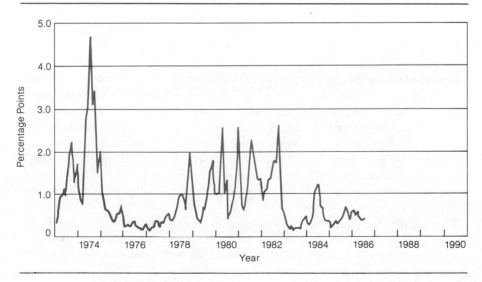

The repo rate is determined by the difference between the initial selling price of the securities and the agreed-upon repurchase price, annualized with a 360-day year. For example, securities initially purchased by an investor at a price *(P)* of $9,852,217 with an agreement to sell them back at a price *(S)* of $10,000,000 at the end of a 60-day period, offers a yield (or repo rate) of

$$\text{repo rate} = \frac{S - P}{P} \times \frac{360}{n}$$

$$= \frac{\$10,000,000 - \$9,852,217}{\$9,852,217} \times \frac{360}{60}$$

$$= 9\%$$

Financial institutions such as banks, savings and loan associations, and money market funds often participate in repurchase agreements. Many non-financial institutions are active participants as well. The dollar volume of repos has almost tripled in the last five years, even surpassing the volume of commercial paper in 1985. Transaction amounts are usually, though not always, for $10 million or more. The most common maturities are from one day to fifteen days and for one, three, and six months. Because of the short maturities, a secondary market for repos does not exist. Some firms in need of funds will set the maturity on a repo to be the minimum time period for which they need temporary financing. If they still need funds when the repo is about to mature, they will borrow additional funds through new repos and use these funds to fulfill their obligation on maturing repos.

Federal Funds

The federal funds market allows depository institutions to effectively lend or borrow short-term funds from each other at the so-called **federal funds rate.** The negotiations between two depository institutions may take place directly over the telephone or may occur through a federal funds broker. Once a loan transaction is agreed upon, the lending institution can instruct its district Federal Reserve bank to debit its reserve account and to credit the borrowing institution's reserve account by the amount of the loan. If the loan is for just one day, it will likely be based on an oral agreement between the parties, especially if the institutions commonly do business with each other.

Commercial banks are the most active participant in the federal funds market. Federal funds brokers serve as financial intermediaries in the market, matching up institutions that wish to sell (lend) funds with those that wish to purchase (borrow) them. The brokers receive a commission for their service. The transactions are negotiated through a telecommunications network that links federal funds brokers with the participating institutions. Most loan transactions are for $5 million or more and usually have a one- to seven-day maturity (although the loans may often be extended by the lender if the borrower desires).

The importance of lending between depository institutions can be realized by measuring the volume of interbank loans on commercial bank balance sheets over time. The interbank loan volume has been reported in the *Federal Reserve Bulletin* since 1984 and is disclosed here:

End of Year	Interbank Loans Outstanding
1984	$126.9 billion
1985	149.6 billion
1986	168.9 billion
1987	175.8 billion

The level of interbank loan lending continues to increase over time. Some commercial banks make loan transactions with other depository institutions on a daily basis.

Banker's Acceptances

A **banker's acceptance** represents a bank accepting responsibility for a future payment. It is commonly used for international trade transactions. Exporters often prefer that banks act as guarantor before sending goods to importers whose credit rating is not known. The bank therefore facilitates international trade by stamping ACCEPTED on a draft, which obligates payment at a specified point in time. In turn, the importer will pay the bank what is owed to the exporter along with a fee to the bank for guaranteeing the payment.

Exporters can hold the banker's acceptance until the date at which payment is to be made. Yet, they frequently sell the acceptance before then at a discount, in order to obtain cash immediately. The investor who purchases the acceptance then receives the payment guaranteed by the bank in the future. The investor's return on a banker's acceptance, like that of commercial paper, is derived from the difference between the discounted price paid for the acceptance versus the amount to be received in the future. Maturities on banker's acceptances often range from 30 to 270 days. Since there is a possibility of banks defaulting on payment, investors are exposed to a slight degree of default risk. Thus, they deserve a return above the T-bill yield as compensation.

Because acceptances are often discounted and sold by the exporting firm prior to maturity, an active secondary market exists. Dealers match up companies that wish to sell acceptances with other companies that wish to purchase them. The bid price of dealers is less than their ask price, which creates their *spread*, or their reward for doing business. The spread is normally between one-eighth and seven-eighths of 1 percent.

The sequence of steps involved in a banker's acceptance is illustrated in Exhibit 5.7. To understand the sequence of steps, consider the example of a U.S. importer of Japanese goods. First, the importer places a purchase order for the goods (Step 1). If the Japanese exporter is unfamiliar with the U.S. importer, it may demand payment before delivery of goods, which the U.S. importer may be unwilling to make. A compromise may be reached through the creation of a banker's acceptance. The importer requests that a *letter of credit (L/C)* be issued on its behalf in favor of the exporter (Step 2). The L/C represents a commitment by a bank to back the payment owed to the Japanese exporter. Then the L/C is presented to the exporter's bank (Step 3), which informs the exporter that the L/C has been received (Step 4). The exporter then sends the goods to the importer (Step 5) and sends the shipping documents to its bank (Step 6), which passes them along to the

EXHIBIT 5.7 Sequence of Steps in the Creation of a Banker's Acceptance

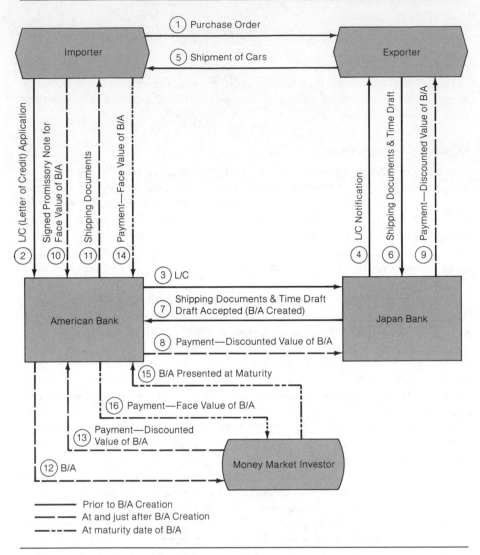

SOURCE: Adapted from *Instruments of the Money Market*, Federal Reserve Bank of Richmond, Sixth Edition, 127.

importer's bank (Step 7). At this point, the banker's acceptance is created. This importer's bank sends payment to the exporter's bank (Step 8). The payment is discounted because it is earlier than the date for which payment was promised on the L/C. The exporter's bank passes payment along to the exporter (Step 9). The importer's bank passes the shipping documents on to the importer in exchange for a note to pay the amount specified in the L/C (Steps 10 and 11) to the bank at maturity.

The importer's bank can hold the acceptance until maturity, or it can sell it to the money market investor at a discount (Steps 12 and 13). Potential purchasers of acceptances are short-term investors. When the acceptance matures, the importer pays its bank (Step 14), which in turn pays the money market investor who presents the acceptance (Steps 15 and 16).

There are several variations of this sequence. For example, the exporter may be willing to hold the acceptance and therefore await payment until the acceptance matures. Or the importer's bank may hold the acceptance until maturity. In either of these cases, the importer's bank does not make payment until the acceptance matures.

Regardless of the specifics, the creation of a banker's acceptance allows the importer to receive goods from an exporter without sending immediate payment. The selling of the acceptance creates financing for the exporter. Even though banker's acceptances are often created to facilitate international transactions, they are not limited to money market investors with international experience. Investors that purchase acceptances are more concerned with the credit of the bank that guarantees payment than with the credit of the exporter or importer. For this reason, the default risk on a banker's acceptance is somewhat similar to that of NCDs issued by commercial banks. Yet, because acceptances have the backing of the bank as well as the importing firm, they may be perceived as having slightly less default risk than NCDs. Also, there may be a difference in the risk of the banks involved.

While acceptances are initially created by banks, they are perceived by some other firms as a potential source of funds. Firms that receive the acceptance as a result of exporting goods or that purchase the acceptance in the market shortly after it has been created can sell the acceptance in the market whenever they need funds.

Exhibit 5.8 shows the trend in banker's acceptances outstanding. The dollar volume is considerably less than that of commercial paper or repurchase agreements. However, banker's acceptances have become quite common, averaging more than $70 billion outstanding since 1981. As long as the commercial banks that create acceptances are favorably perceived by

EXHIBIT 5.8   Volume of Banker's Acceptances Outstanding Over Time

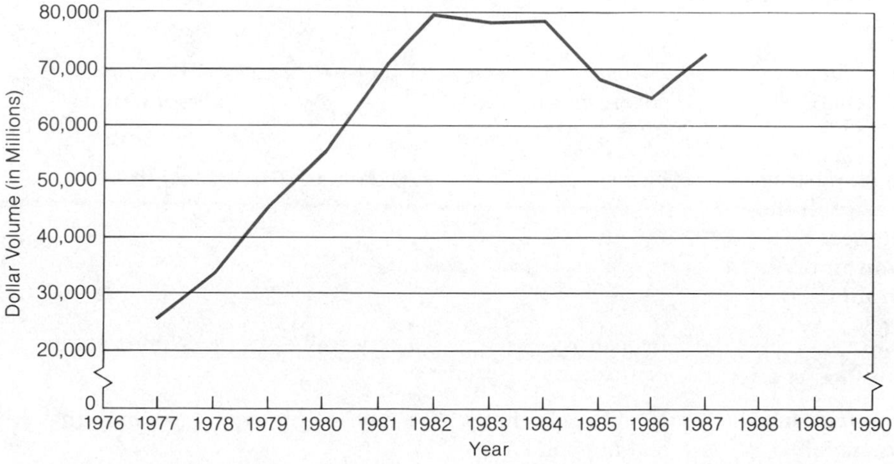

investors, the secondary market for acceptances should continue to be active.

Comparison of Money Market Securities

The key characteristics of money market securities are summarized in Exhibit 5.9. The differences in these characteristics cause the risk-return attributes to vary among money market securities. The default risk of money market securities varies with the type of issuer. In addition, even though all money market securities have short-term maturities, their degrees of liquidity vary with the maturity and secondary market activity.

For investors who wish to compare yields among money market securities, money market rates are commonly quoted in business periodicals. An example is shown in Exhibit 5.10. Investors consider the default risk, liquidity, and the quoted yields of money market securities when making their investment decisions.

INSTITUTIONAL USE OF MONEY MARKET SECURITIES

The institutional use of money market securities is summarized in Exhibit 5.11. Financial institutions purchase money market securities in order to simultaneously earn a return and maintain adequate liquidity. They issue

EXHIBIT 5.9   Characteristics of Money Market Securities

Money Market Securities	Issued by	Common Investors	Common Maturities	Secondary Market Activity
Treasury bills	Federal government	Consumers and firms	13 weeks, 26 weeks, 1 year	High
NCDs	Large banks and savings institutions	Firms	2 weeks to 1 year	Low
Commercial paper	Bank holding companies, finance companies, and other companies	Firms	1 day to 270 days	Low
Eurodollar deposits	Banks located outside the U.S.	Firms, governments, and some banks	1 day to 1 year	Low or sometimes nonexistent
Banker's acceptances	Banks (exporting firms can sell the acceptances at a discount in order to obtain funds)	Firms	30 days to 270 days	High
Federal funds	Depository institutions	Depository institutions	1 day to 7 days	Nonexistent
Repurchase agreements	Nonfinancial firms and financial institutions	Nonfinancial firms and financial institutions	1 day to 15 days	Nonexistent

EXHIBIT 5.10   Sample of Money Market Rates (August 8, 1988)

	Maturity	Annualized Yield
Banker's acceptances	30-day	7.85%
	60-day	7.92%
	180-day	8.19%
Certificates of deposit	30-day	7.84%
	90-day	7.91%
	180-day	8.12%
Commercial paper	30-day	7.85%
	90-day	7.89%
	180-day	8.21%
Discount rate		6.00%
Federal funds rate		7.65%
Prime rate		9.52%
Treasury bills	91-day	7.36%
	182-day	7.55%

money market securities when experiencing a temporary shortage of cash. Because money markets serve businesses, the average transaction size is very large and is typically executed through a telecommunications network.

Money market securities can be used to enhance liquidity in two ways. First, newly issued securities generate cash. The institutions that issue new securities have created a short-term liability in order to boost their cash balance. Second, institutions that previously purchased money market securities will generate cash upon liquidation of the securities. In this case, one type of asset (the security) is replaced by another (cash).

Most financial institutions maintain sufficient liquidity by either holding some securities that have very active secondary markets and/or securities with short-term maturities. Treasury bills are the most popular money market instrument because of their marketability, safety, and short-term maturity. While Treasury bills are purchased through an auction, other money market instruments are commonly purchased through dealers or specialized brokers. For example, commercial paper is purchased through commercial paper dealers or directly from the issuer, NCDs are usually purchased through brokers specializing in NCDs, federal funds are purchased (borrowed) through federal funds brokers, and repurchase agreements are purchased through repo dealers.

Financial institutions whose future cash inflows and outflows are more uncertain will generally maintain additional money market instruments for liquidity. For this reason, depository institutions such as commercial banks allocate a greater portion of their asset portfolio to money market instruments than pension funds.

Financial institutions are acting as a creditor to the initial issuer of the securities. For example, when they hold Treasury bills, they are creditors to the Treasury. Yet, the Treasury bill transactions in the secondary market commonly reflect a flow of funds between two non-government institutions. Treasury bills represent a source of funds for those financial institutions

EXHIBIT 5.11 Institutional Use of Money Markets

Type of Financial Institution	Participation in the Money Markets
Commercial banks and savings institutions	▪ Bank holding companies issue commercial paper. ▪ Some banks and savings institutions issue NCDs, borrow or lend funds in the federal funds market, engage in repurchase agreements, and purchase Treasury bills. ▪ Commercial banks create banker's acceptances. ▪ Commercial banks provide backup lines of credit to corporations that issue commercial paper.
Finance companies	▪ Issue large amounts of commercial paper
Money market mutual funds	▪ Use proceeds from shares sold to invest in Treasury bills, commercial paper, NCDs, repurchase agreements, and banker's acceptances
Insurance companies	▪ May maintain a portion of its investment portfolio as money market securities for liquidity
Pension funds	▪ May maintain a portion of its investment portfolio as money market securities that may be liquidated when portfolio managers desire to increase their investment in bonds or stocks

that liquidate some of their Treasury bill holdings. In fact, this is the main reason why Treasury bills are held by financial institutions. Other money market instruments are also purchased by financial institutions in order to provide liquidity, including federal funds (purchased by depository institutions), repurchase agreements (purchased by depository institutions and money market funds), bankers acceptances, and CDs (purchased by money market funds).

Some financial institutions issue their own money market instruments in order to obtain cash. For example, depository institutions issue CDs, while bank holding companies and finance companies issue commercial paper. Depository institutions also obtain funds through the use of repurchase agreements, or in the federal funds market.

Many money market transactions involve two financial institutions. For example, a federal funds transaction involves two depository institutions. Money market funds commonly purchase CDs from banks and savings institutions. Repurchase agreements are frequently negotiated between two commercial banks.

The issuer of a money market security should first consider whether direct placement is possible, so that additional transaction costs can be avoided.

Direct placement requires knowledge of institutions that commonly purchase the security of concern and a department that can properly execute the sale. If direct placement is not possible, a dealer specializing in trading this type of security must be informed about the maturity, par value, and so forth, of the securities to be sold. For each type of money market security, a group of specialized dealers exists. Their primary function is to receive sell requests and accommodate those requests by locating a buyer.

Institutions with excess temporary funds represent the potential buyers of money market securities. They anticipate having a specific amount of funds available for a specific period of time. They also know the degree of default risk and interest rate risk they are willing to accept. Using this information, they can call institutions or dealers that often sell the securities they are interested in, inquire about the yields presently being offered, and make their investment decisions.

INTERACTION AMONG MONEY MARKET YIELDS

Companies investing in money markets closely monitor the yields on the various instruments. Because the instruments serve as reasonable substitutes for each other, the investing companies may exchange instruments in order to achieve a more attractive yield. This causes yields among these instruments to be somewhat similar. If a disparity in yields arises, companies will avoid the low-yield instruments in favor of the high-yield instruments. This places upward pressure on the low-yield security and downward pressure on the high-yield securities, causing realignment.

In some cases, money market yields are affected by events in the capital markets. For example, during the stock market crash in October 1987, many investors liquidated their stock holdings and purchased money market securities, placing upward pressure on money market prices and downward pressure on money market yields.

Exhibit 5.12 shows the yields of money market securities over time. The high degree of correlation among security yields is obvious. T-bill yields consistently offer lower yields than the other securities because they are very liquid and free from default risk.

INTERNATIONALIZATION OF MONEY MARKETS

Market interest rates vary among countries, as shown in Exhibit 5.13. The interest rate differentials occur because geographic markets are somewhat segmented. However, since many markets are accessible to foreign investors and borrowers, interest rate differentials have encouraged international money market transactions. The growth in such transactions is also attributed to tax differences among countries, speculation on exchange rate movements, and a reduction in government barriers that were previously imposed on foreign investment in securities. U.S. Treasury bills and commercial paper are very accessible to foreign investors. In addition, securities such as Eurodollar deposits, Euronotes, and Euro-commercial paper are widely traded throughout the international money markets, as will be discussed.

INTERNATIONAL

ASPECTS

Chapter 5

Money Markets

141

EXHIBIT 5.12   Money Market Yields (Averages, Annualized)

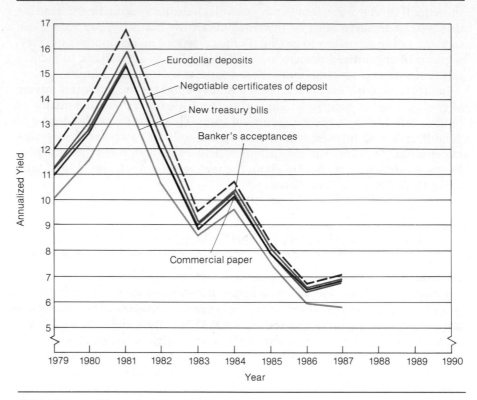

SOURCE: *Federal Reserve Bulletin*, various issues.

EXHIBIT 5.13   Comparison of International Interest Rates

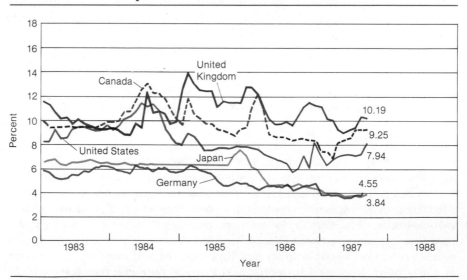

SOURCE: Morgan Guaranty Trust Company; and *International Economic Conditions* (January 1988): 60.

Interest Rate Linkage between the United States and Pacific Basin Countries

Countries in the Pacific Basin, such as Hong Kong, Singapore, Japan, and Taiwan, have loosened their restrictions on international financial transactions. Consequently, financial markets have become more globally integrated. A recent study by Glick evaluated the linkage between Pacific Basin real rates of interest and U.S. real rates of interest. He found that the linkage between the Pacific Basin and the United States is somewhat similar to the linkage between European countries and the United States. This suggests that not only can financial market conditions in the United States affect real interest rates in Pacific Basin countries, but that conditions in Pacific Basin countries can affect real interest rates in the United States.

The relationship between the U.S. and Pacific Basin real interest rates was not perfect, since remaining restrictions and transactions costs discourage some financial flows between these countries. Nevertheless, the results of this study suggest that in forecasting U.S. real interest rates, analysts must monitor conditions in other countries that may affect fund flows to the United States.

SOURCE: Reuven Glick, "Interest Rate Linkages in the Pacific Basin," *Economic Review*, Federal Reserve Bank of San Francisco (Summer 1987): 31–42.

Eurodollar Deposits

As corporations outside the United States (especially in Europe) increased international trade transactions in U.S. dollars, the U.S. dollar deposits in non–U.S. banks (called **Eurodollar certificates of deposit** or Eurodollar CDs) grew. Furthermore, because interest rate ceilings were historically imposed on dollar deposits in U.S. banks, corporations with large dollar balances often deposited their funds overseas to receive a higher yield.

Eurodollar CD volume has grown substantially over time, as a significant portion of international trade and investment transactions involve the U.S. dollar as a medium of exchange. Some firms overseas receive the U.S. dollars as payment for exports and invest in Eurodollar CDs. Because these firms may expect to need dollars to pay for future imports, they retain dollar-denominated deposits rather than converting dollars to their home currency.

In the so-called **Eurodollar market,** banks channel the deposited funds to other firms that need to borrow them in the form of Eurodollar loans. The deposit and loan transactions in Eurodollars are typically $1 million or more per transaction so only governments and large corporations participate in this market. Since transactions amounts are large, investors in the market avoid some costs associated with the continuous small transactions that occur in retail-oriented markets. In addition, Eurodollar CDs are not subject to reserve requirements, which means that banks can lend out 100 percent of the deposits that arrive. For these reasons, the spread between the rate banks pay on large Eurodollar deposits and what they charge on Eurodollar loans is relatively small. This allows attractive interest rates for

Chapter 5

Money Markets

143

Impact of the Stock Market Crash on the Difference in U.S. and Foreign Interest Rates

During the stock market crash in October 1987, some investors liquidated their stock holdings and used the proceeds to purchase money market securities. This caused higher prices and lower yields on money market securities. Consequently, the spread between some foreign money market rates and U.S. money market rates shifted, as shown in the exhibit below. The British money market rate was already higher than the U.S. rate, and the gap grew during the crash. The French rate was lower than the U.S. rate but surpassed it during the crash. The money market rates of West Germany, Switzerland, and Japan were below the U.S. rate, but the gap narrowed during the crash. Shifts in money market spreads are significant because they help determine the choices of money market investors and thus influence exchange rate movements.

SOURCE: *Chicago Fed Letter* (December 1987).

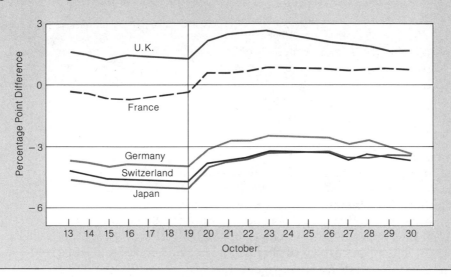

both depositors and borrowers in the Eurodollar market. The rates offered on Eurodollar deposits are slightly higher than rates offered on negotiable certificates of deposit.

Unlike other CDs, Eurodollar transactions represent a loan from one commercial bank to another. While this seems to overlap the function of the federal funds market, Eurodollar CDs provide funding for longer maturities.

A secondary market for Eurodollar CDs exists, allowing the initial investors to liquidate their investment if necessary. The growth in Eurodollar volume has made the secondary market more active.

Over the last 15 years, interest rates have fluctuated to a great degree. Consequently, investors in fixed-rate Eurodollar CDs were adversely affected by rising market interest rates, while issuers of these CDs were adversely affected by decreasing rates. To deal with this interest rate risk,

Part Two

Credit Markets

Eurodollar floating-rate CDs (called FRCDs) have been used in recent years. The rate adjusts periodically to the London Interbank Offer Rate (LIBOR), which is the interest rate charged on interbank dollar loans. As with other floating-rate instruments, the rate on FRCDs assures that the borrower's cost and investor's return reflect prevailing market interest rates.

Over time, the volume of deposits and loans denominated in other foreign currencies has also grown due to an increased international trade, increased flows of funds among subsidiaries of multinational corporations, and existing differences among country regulations on bank deposit rates. Consequently, the so-called **Eurocurrency market** was developed, made up of several banks (called **Eurobanks**) that accept large deposits and provide large loans in foreign currencies. These same banks also make up the **Eurocredit market,** which is mainly distinguished from the Eurocurrency market by the longer maturities on loans.

The Eurobanks participating in the Eurocurrency market are located not only in Europe, but also in the Bahamas, Canada, Japan, Hong Kong, and some other countries. Exhibit 5.14 provides the estimated dollar value of commercial bank liabilities in the Eurocurrency market. This exhibit shows that since 1978 liabilities have about quadrupled. Over this time period, the value of dollar liabilities has represented between 70 percent and 80 percent of the market value of all Eurocurrency liabilities. In recent years, the percentage has declined slightly, due to the growth in non-dollar Eurocurrency deposits.

Short-term Euronotes are issued in bearer form, with common maturities of one, three, and six months. The typical investors in Euronotes often include the Eurobanks that are hired to place the paper. These Euronotes are sometimes underwritten, thereby guaranteeing the issuer a specific price. In addition, the underwriters may even guarantee a price at which the notes can be rolled over (reissued at maturity). The Euronotes described here differ from the traditional meaning of medium-term loans provided by Eurobanks.

EXHIBIT 5.14   Estimated Dollar Value of Commercial Bank Liabilities in the Eurocurrency Market

Year	Dollar Value of Liabilities (in Billions of Dollars)
1978	$ 673
1979	904
1980	1,172
1981	1,470
1982	1,645
1983	1,711
1984	1,793
1985	2,112
1986	2,786
1987	2,986

NOTE: 1987 figures are as of March 1987.

SOURCE: *International Economic Conditions*, Federal Reserve Bank of St. Louis, various issues.

Euro-Commercial Paper

Euro-commercial paper (CP) is issued without the backing of a banking syndicate. Maturities can be tailored to satisfy investors. Dealers that place commercial paper have created a secondary market by being willing to purchase existing Euro-CP before maturity. The Euro-CP market is used by large corporations that wish to hedge future cash inflows in a particular foreign currency. For example, if a U.S. corporation expects to receive 3 million marks as payment for goods in three months, it may borrow marks today and convert them to dollars to support U.S. operations. Then the marks to be received in three months can be used to repay the loan. If the German interest rates are lower than the U.S. interest rates, this strategy allows the U.S. corporation to reduce its financing cost without being exposed to exchange rate risk. Even if corporations do not have future cash inflows in a foreign currency, they may still consider borrowing from a foreign market if they expect that foreign currency to decline.

The Euro-CP rate is typically between 50 and 100 basis points above LIBOR. Euro-CP is sold by dealers, at a transaction cost ranging between 5 and 10 basis points of the face value. This market is tiny compared to the U.S. commercial paper market. Yet, some non–U.S. companies can more easily place their paper here, where they have a household name.

The amount of short-term Euronotes and the Euro-CP outstanding has grown dramatically in just the last few years, reaching about $30 billion in mid-1986. It has been estimated that U.S. businesses account for as much as $6 billion of these securities.

Regulatory Issues

While a lack of regulation led to the initial growth of the Eurocurrency market, it also poses a concern. If some of the large Eurobanks were to experience financial problems, this could have a devastating impact on the Eurocurrency market, and therefore on all who participate in it. A greater degree of regulation might enhance the safety of Eurobanks and thus the confidence of corporations and governments that use it. Of course, country governments would have to agree on any regulations imposed. Also, any government that desired more Eurobanking business for its country could neglect to enforce the regulations, thereby offering comparative advantages.

SUMMARY

Money markets serve the liquidity needs of financial and nonfinancial corporations. There are various markets for money market instruments since each instrument is issued by a particular type of institution. Their diverse characteristics benefit investors, whose preferences for marketability and default risk differ—they can choose the type that fits their needs.

Financial institutions such as commercial banks, finance companies, and savings institutions are common issuers of some money market instruments. In addition, all financial institutions maintain some money market instruments for liquidity purposes.

Because money market instruments often serve as substitutes for each other, some investors will switch their money market portfolio if the yields of certain instruments become more attractive than those of others (unless the higher yield reflects higher risk or some other unfavorable characteristic). Such a substitution process stabilizes yield differentials among money market instruments.

KEY TERMS

banker's acceptance
commercial paper
Eurobanks
Eurocredit market
Eurocurrency market
Eurodollar certificates of deposits
Eurodollar floating-rate CDs

Eurodollar market
federal funds rate
money market instruments
negotiable certificate of deposit
primary market
repurchase agreement
secondary market

QUESTIONS

5.1. Explain how the Treasury uses the primary market to obtain adequate funding.

5.2. How can investors using the primary Treasury bill market be assured that their bid will be accepted?

5.3. Why do large corporations typically make competitive bids for Treasury bills rather than noncompetitive bids?

5.4. Describe the activity in the secondary Treasury bill market. How can this degree of activity benefit investors in Treasury bills?

5.5. Who issues commercial paper?

5.6. Why do some firms create a department that can directly place commercial paper? What criteria affect the decision to create such a department?

5.7. Why are ratings assigned by rating agencies on commercial paper?

5.8. What types of financial institutions issue commercial paper?

5.9. Explain how investors' preferences for commercial paper will change during a recession. How should this reaction affect the difference between commercial paper rates and Treasury bill rates during recessionary periods?

5.10. How can small investors participate in the investment of negotiable certificates of deposits (NCDs)?

5.11. Based on what you know about repurchase agreements, would you expect them to have a lower or higher annualized yield than commercial paper? Why?

5.12. What is the use of a banker's acceptance to (a) exporting firms, (b) importing firms, (c) commercial banks, and (d) investors?

5.13. Explain how money markets can accommodate the desired cash positions of institutions.

5.14. Why might Treasury bills sometimes be considered as a "potential source of funds" to a financial institution when they can be issued only by the Treasury?

PROBLEMS

5.1. Assume an investor purchased a six-month T-Bill with $10,000 par for $9,000 and sold it ninety days later for $9,100. What is the yield?

5.2. Newly issued three-month T-bills with a par value of $10,000 sold for $9,700. Compute the T-bill discount.

5.3. Assume an investor purchased six-month commercial paper with a face value of $1,000,000 for $895,000. What is the yield?

5.4. Stanford Corporation arranged a repurchase agreement in which it purchased securities for $4,900,000 and will sell the securities back for $5,000,000 in 40 days? What is the yield (or repo rate) to Stanford Corporation?

1) $Y = \dfrac{9100 - 9000}{9000} \cdot \dfrac{365}{90}$

    4.5%

2) $D = \dfrac{10{,}000 - 9700}{10{,}000} \cdot \dfrac{360}{90}$

    12%

3) $\dfrac{1000K - 895K}{895K} \cdot \dfrac{360}{182}$

    23.21%

4) $\dfrac{5000 - 4900}{4900} \cdot \dfrac{360}{40}$

    18.37%

PROJECT

1. COMPARING MONEY MARKET YIELDS

Review the "Money Rates" section of *The Wall Street Journal* for the last five days. For each day, fill out the following table:

	90-day commercial paper	Three-month CDs	90-day banker's acceptances	13-week Treasury bills
1 day ago				
2 days ago				
3 days ago				
4 days ago				
5 days ago				

Did the money market rates change in the same direction over time? Which of the money market securities had the highest rate? Why? Which of the money market securities had the lowest rate? Why?

Taking Positions in the Repo Market

The dealers that serve as financial intermediaries in the repo (repurchase agreement) market sometimes take a "long" or "short" position in securities, rather than simply matching up two parties. For example, assume that as of March 1, BOR institution desires to borrow through a repo for three months, while LEN institution desires to lend that same amount for two months. Since their wishes do not perfectly correspond, the only way in which the dealer can match them up is to take a position as well. On March 1, the dealer creates two repos, one with BOR for three months and a second with LEN for two months. Because the dealer has taken a long position (with BOR) for three months, and a short position (with LEN) for two months, it has created an offset over the first two months but has a net long position over the third month. To continue with the example, assume the following:

1. On March 1, BOR agrees to sell the dealer Treasury securities for $25 million and repurchase them three months later (June 1) for $25,625,000. This represents a repo rate of

$$\text{repo rate} = \frac{\$25,625,000 - \$25,000,000}{\$25,000,000} \times \frac{360 \text{ days}}{90 \text{ days}}$$
$$= 10\%$$

2. On March 1, LEN agrees to purchase Treasury securities from the dealer for $25 million, and resell them two months later (May 1) for $25,417,000. This represents a repo rate of

$$\text{repo rate} = \frac{\$25,417,000 - \$25,000,000}{\$25,000,000} \times \frac{360 \text{ days}}{60 \text{ days}}$$
$$= \text{about } 10\%$$

To simplify this example, transaction fees charged by the dealer are not included here. As of May 1, the dealer must purchase the Treasury securities from LEN, but it cannot sell Treasury securities back to BOR for another month. To finance its position over the month of May, the dealer creates a repo with ZEN financial institution as of May 1. Assume the repo calls for an initial purchase price of $25,417,000 and a repurchase price one month later of $25,586,950, representing a repo rate of

$$\text{repo rate} = \frac{\$25,586,950 - \$25,417,000}{\$25,417,000} \times \frac{360 \text{ days}}{30 \text{ days}}$$
$$= 8\%$$

Notice that the proceeds received by the dealer from this repo can be used to repurchase the securities from LEN. This way the dealer does not tie up any of its own funds. On June 1, the dealer will receive $25,625,000 from BOR (as BOR repurchases the securities it sold earlier) and will pay $25,586,950 to ZEN. The difference between these payments ($38,050) represents the dealer's nominal return. This difference was generated from the dealer's position; additional earnings would have occurred if the transaction fees charged by the dealer for these transactions had been included.

The dealer's transactions in this example are summarized in Exhibit 5A.1. The gain on the dealer's position resulted from a decrease in interest rates. The dealer's initial repos as of March 1 were based on a 10 percent repo rate. Yet, by May 1, interest rates had declined, allowing the dealer to obtain funds during May at 8 percent. If interest rates had increased by May 1, the dealer would have been borrowing funds during May at a higher rate than what was being earned during May on the repo with BOR.

The situation for the dealer is similar to that of other financial institutions whose cost of funds is more interest rate–sensitive than income received

EXHIBIT 5A.1 Summary of Repo Transactions in the Example

1. March 1: A three-month repo is initiated between the dealer and BOR, and a simultaneous two-month repo is initiated between the dealer and LEN.

2. May 1: The two-month repo between the dealer and LEN is completed, and a new one-month repo is initiated between the dealer and ZEN.

3. June 1: The three-month repo between the dealer and BOR is completed, and the one-month repo between the dealer and ZEN is completed.

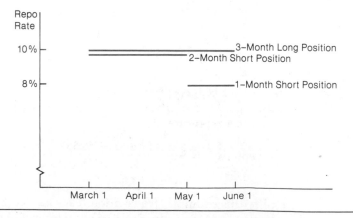

on funds used. The dealer benefits if interest rates decrease over the time period of concern but is adversely affected if interest rates rise. To illustrate the risk involved, assume that as of May 1, interest rates increased to 12 percent. In this case, ZEN would be willing to purchase the securities only if it would receive $25,671,170. Thus, the dealer would lose $46,170 (computed as $25,625,000 − $26,671,170).

The previous example assumed initial repo rates of 10 percent for both the two-month and three-month repos, as if the yield curve were flat over this short-term horizon. If the yield curve were upward-sloping, the two-month repo would have had a lower annualized rate than the three-month repo. This would be an advantage to the dealer. However, recall that an upward-sloping yield curve may be interpreted as the market's expectation of rising interest rates. If the one-month repo rate as of May 1 is high, the dealer's gain over the first two months could be offset.

If a dealer anticipates interest rates to rise substantially, it may consider a position opposite to the previous example. That is, it may simultaneously create a two-month repo in which it represents the lender and a three-month repo in which it represents the borrower. In two months, its lending position will terminate, and it will create a new one-month repo to match the remaining month on the other existing repo. If rates have risen by the time the new repo is created, it will benefit.

Dealers can decide whether to take such positions by using information on existing market rates for repos of various maturities and the forecasted rates on repos to be executed in the future. Assume again the information from our previous numerical example. On March 1, the dealer knows the prevailing repo rates on two-month and three-month repos that begin on that day. The only uncertain variable of concern is the one-month repo rate as of May 1. Assume that on March 1, the dealer's best guess is that the interest rates will decrease, and that the one-month repo rate as of May 1 will be 8 percent. Yet, because of the uncertainty involved, the dealer develops a probability distribution for the repo rate. This information is then used to determine the funds to be generated from that one-month repo and the gain (or loss) from taking a position as shown in Exhibit 5A.2. For each possible repo rate outcome, the repurchase price and earnings have been estimated. The expected value of the earnings is $17,372 (shown in Column 5). There is an 80 percent chance that positive earnings will result from the position contemplated by the dealer. The generally favorable outlook on the proposed strategy is based on the relatively low interest rate possibilities. The outlook would not be as favorable if interest rates were more likely to be around the 12 percent range.

EXHIBIT 5A.2 Estimating the Probability Distribution of Earnings on a Repo Position

(1) Possible one-month repo rate as of May 1	(2) Probability of that repo rate occurring	(3) Repurchase price if that repo rate occurs	(4) Earnings if that repo rate occurs	(5) Estimated expected value of earnings = (2) × (4)
7%	10%	$ 25,565,266	$25,625,000 − $25,565,266 = $59,734	$59,734 × 10% = $ 5,973
8	40	$ 25,586,447	$25,625,000 − $25,586,447 = $38,553	$38,553 × 40% = $15,421
9	30	$ 25,607,628	$25,625,000 − $25,607,628 = $17,372	$17,372 × 30% = $ 5,212
12	20	$425,671,170	$25,625,000 − $25,671,170 = −$46,170	−$46,170 × 20% = −$ 9,234
			Expected Value =	$17,372

Bond Markets

BOND MARKETS IN PERSPECTIVE

To illustrate the typical bond market activity on a given day, the activity on June 21, 1988 (which was reported in *The Wall Street Journal* on the following day) is summarized below:

■ A government report disclosed lower inflation than what was expected. Bond prices rose in response to this report but declined later in the day.

■ The Treasury was only about $1.5 billion short of the maximum amount of bonds it had the authority to issue.

■ There was speculation that Congress would not act quickly to allow the Treasury to issue more long-term bonds. If the Treasury substitutes medium-term or short-term securities for long-term bonds, it could influence the term structure of interest rates.

■ In the corporate market, corporations issued almost $1 billion of new debt. Continental Corporation had a $300 million issue which was priced to yield .74% above Treasury securities with a similar maturity. Salomon Brothers played a major role in placing the debt in financial markets.

Other corporations that issued debt on this day included Quantum Chemical Corporation and Morgan Stanley Group Inc.

■ A New Jersey Turnpike issue was priced to yield 7.20 percent in the municipal bond market. The City of New York issued $455 million of debt. Merrill Lynch facilitated the placement of this debt.

■ In the foreign markets, West German and Japanese government bond prices increased. West German government bonds were priced to yield 6.59 percent, while Japanese government bonds were priced to yield 4.73 percent.

■ What provisions differentiate the bonds that were issued?
■ What factors affect bond prices?
■ How do financial institutions participate in bond markets?
■ How have bond markets become internationalized over time?

These and other related questions are addressed in this chapter.

OUTLINE

Bonds are debt obligations issued by governments or corporations with long-term maturities. Bond markets are needed to facilitate the flow of long-term funds from surplus units to deficit units. This chapter describes the different types of bonds and explains the risks for each. It also discusses bond portfolio management and the participation of financial institutions in bond markets. Finally, it discusses the internationalization of bond markets, addressing the key aspects involved in trading foreign bonds.

Bonds are often classified according to the type of issuer:

- Treasury bonds issued by the Treasury
- Municipal bonds issued by state and local governments
- Corporate bonds issued by corporations

A discussion of each type of bond follows.

TREASURY BONDS

The U.S. Treasury commonly issues Treasury notes or Treasury bonds to finance federal government expenditures. The key difference between a note and bond is that note maturities are usually less than 10 years, while bond maturities are 10 years or more. An active secondary market allows investors to sell Treasury notes or bonds prior to maturity.

The yield from holding a Treasury bond, as with other bonds, depends on the coupon rate and on the difference between the purchase price and selling price. (Examples of bond yield calculations were provided in Chapter 3.) Investors in Treasury notes and bonds receive semiannual interest payments from the Treasury. Although the interest is taxed by the federal

Impact of Issuer Sophistication on the Net Interest Cost of Bonds

A study by Roden and Bland assessed whether a municipality's net interest cost incurred when issuing bonds is affected by its previous experience in issuing bonds (referred to as *issuer sophistication*). Some analysts suggest that as an issuer becomes more sophisticated in the placement of bonds, it will negotiate for a higher price with investment bankers. The authors of the study applied regression analysis to determine how a variety of variables, including issuer sophistication, affected net interest cost of municipal bonds. For each previous bond issue negotiated (measured up to 10 years), the net interest cost decreased by 7.27 basis points (up to three issues). Therefore, there was an inverse relationship between issuer sophistication and net interest cost, but the incremental benefits from increasing sophistication became negligible after three issues.

SOURCE: Peyton Foster Roden and Robert L. Bland, "Issuer Sophistication and Underpricing in the Negotiated Municipal Bond Market," *Journal of Financial Research* (Summer 1986): 163–169.

government as ordinary income, it is exempt from state and local taxes, if any exist. Domestic and foreign firms and individuals are common investors in Treasury notes and bonds.

MUNICIPAL BONDS

Like the federal government, state and local governments frequently spend more than the revenues they receive. To finance the difference, they issue **municipal bonds,** most of which can be classified as either **general obligation bonds** or **revenue bonds.** Payments on general obligation bonds are supported by the municipal government's ability to tax, whereas payments on revenue bonds must be generated by revenues of the project (tollway, tollbridge, state college dormitory, etc.) for which the bonds were issued. If insufficient revenues are generated, revenue bonds could default, as happened in the summer of 1983 with bonds issued by the Washington Public Power Supply System (called "WHOOPS") to finance the construction of two nuclear power plants. Because the project's costs became higher than expected, the plants were never completed and the Washington Public Power Supply System defaulted on the bonds.

Revenue bonds and general obligation bonds typically promise interest payments on a semiannual basis. Common purchasers of these bonds include financial and nonfinancial institutions, as well as individuals. The minimum denomination of municipal bonds is typically $5,000. A secondary market exists for them, although it is less active than the one for Treasury bonds. One of the most attractive features of municipal bonds is that the interest income they provide is normally exempt from federal taxes and in some cases is exempt from state and local taxes.

Chapter 6

Bond Markets

The volume of state and local government bonds issued is displayed in Exhibit 6.1. Revenue bonds have consistently dominated since 1975. The total amount of bond financing by state and local governments has generally increased over the 1980s and peaked in 1985 because of concern by state and local governments that tax reform would repeal the tax-exempt status of newly issued bonds, requiring them to offer a higher before-tax yield. In anticipation, they issued a particularly large volume of bonds.

The Tax Reform Act of 1986 did limit the use of tax-exempt bonds. Consequently, state and local governments desiring to finance projects (such as housing and airports) that were not purely for government purposes were sometimes forced to sell taxable bonds (called *taxable munis*). These bonds had a before-tax yield of about 2 percent above the tax-exempt yields in 1987.

CORPORATE BONDS

When corporations need to borrow for long-term periods, they issue **corporate bonds,** which usually promise the owner interest on a semiannual basis. The minimum denomination is $1,000. The degree of secondary market activity varies; some large corporations have a much larger amount of

EXHIBIT 6.1   Dollar Volume of State and Local Government Securities Issued

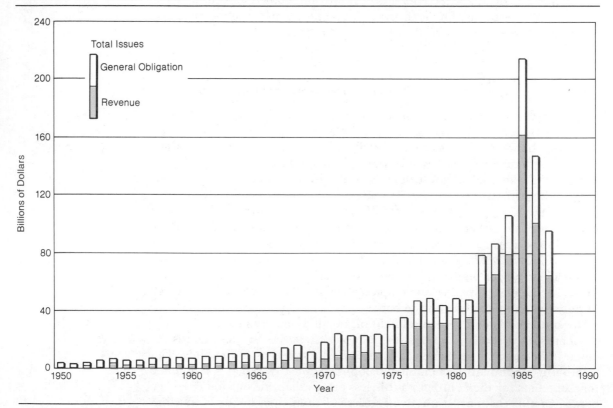

SOURCE: *1987 Federal Reserve Chart Book* updated by author.

bonds outstanding in the market, which increases secondary market activity and the bond's liquidity. Common purchasers of corporate bonds include many financial and some nonfinancial institutions, as well as individuals.

Characteristics of Corporate Bonds

Corporate bonds can be described according to a variety of characteristics. The bond *indenture* is a legal document specifying the rights and obligations of both the issuing firm and the bondholders. It is very comprehensive (normally several hundred pages) and is designed to address all matters related to the bond issue (collateral, payment dates, default provisions, call provisions, etc.).

Federal law requires that for each bond issue of significant size a *trustee* be appointed to represent the bondholders in all matters concerning the bond issue. This includes monitoring the issuing firm's activities to ensure compliance with the terms of the indenture. If the terms of the indenture are violated, the trustee initiates legal action against the issuing firm and represents the bondholders in that action. Bank trust departments are frequently hired to perform the duties of trustee.

Bond indentures frequently include a *sinking-fund provision*, or a requirement that the firm retire a certain amount of the bond issue each year. This provision is considered to be an advantage to the remaining bondholders since it reduces the payments necessary at maturity.

Specific sinking-fund provisions can vary significantly among bond issues. For example, a bond with 20 years until maturity could have a provision to retire 5 percent of the bond issue each year. Or, it could have a requirement to retire 5 percent each year beginning in the fifth year, with the remaining 20 percent to be retired at maturity. The actual mechanics of bond retirement are carried out by the trustee.

Bond indentures normally place restrictions on the issuing firm that are designed to protect the bondholders from being exposed to increasing risk during the investment period. These so-called **protective covenants** frequently limit the amount of dividends and corporate officer's salaries the firm can pay and also restrict the amount of additional debt the firm can issue. Other financial policies may be restricted as well.

Most bonds include an indenture provision allowing the firm to **call** the bonds (force bondholders to sell their bonds back to the firm). A **call provision** normally requires the firm to pay a price above par value when it calls its bonds. The difference between the bond's par value and call price is the **call premium**—typically one year's interest, although the premium may decline as the bond approaches maturity. There are two principal uses of a call provision. First, if market interest rates decline after a bond issue has been sold, the firm might end up paying a higher rate of interest than the prevailing rate for a long period of time. Under these circumstances, the firm may consider selling a new issue of bonds with a lower interest rate and using the proceeds to retire the issue by calling the old bonds.

The second principal use of the call provision is to retire bonds as required by a sinking-fund provision. Many bonds have two different call prices: a lower price for calling the bonds to meet sinking-fund requirements and a higher price if the firm calls the bond for any other reason.

A call provision is normally viewed as a disadvantage to bondholders since it can disrupt their investment plans and reduce their investment returns. As a result, firms must pay slightly higher rates of interest on bonds that are callable, other things being equal.

Bond Collateral

Bonds can be classified according to whether they are secured by collateral and by the nature of that collateral. Usually it is a mortgage on real property (land and buildings). A **first mortgage bond** has first claim on the specified assets. If the bond issue is an **open-end mortgage bond,** the firm can issue additional bonds in the future using the same assets as collateral, and giving the same priority of claim against those assets. A **closed-end mortgage bond** prohibits the firm from issuing additional bonds with the same priority of claim against those assets. However, the assets can be used as collateral to secure additional bonds if a lower priority of claim is given against those assets. Between these two extremes is the **limited open-ended mortgage** bond whereby the firm is permitted to issue an additional specified amount of new debt with the same priority of claim against the assets. In some cases, specific property is not designated as collateral against a bond issue. Instead, a **blanket mortgage** is used, in which the bond issue is backed by all of the firm's real property.

Bonds can also be secured with a **chattel mortgage,** which is a mortgage secured by personal property. For example, **collateral trust bonds** are a special type of chattel mortgage bonds that are normally secured by common stock and/or bonds issued by subsidiaries of the issuing firm. These securities are held as collateral by a trustee and are to be liquidated if the issuing firm defaults.

Debentures

Bonds unsecured by specific property are called **debentures** (backed only by the general credit of the issuing firm). These bonds are normally issued by large, financially sound firms whose ability to service the debt is not in question. Debentures that have claims against the firm's assets that are junior to the claims of both mortgage bonds and regular debentures are called **subordinated debentures.** Owners of these debentures receive nothing until the claims of mortgage bondholders, regular debenture owners, and secured short-term creditors have been satisfied.

Junk Bonds

In recent years, the volume of low-grade bonds, or **junk bonds,** being issued has increased substantially. Financial institutions such as life insurance companies, savings institutions, and pension funds purchase junk bonds. In addition, some mutual funds maintain portfolios concentrated in junk bonds.

One apparent reason for the surge in junk bond issues is related to mergers and acquisitions. Some companies have issued junk bonds to obtain necessary funds for pursuing acquisition targets. Other companies have issued junk bonds to restructure their capital in a manner that would discourage

Low-Grade Bonds and Takeovers

Low-grade bonds became the center of public attention because of their association with corporate takeover attempts. In a takeover, one firm or a set of investors acquires the stock (and thus ownership) of another firm. When the stock purchase is not financed with cash or newly issued stock of the acquiring firm, the acquisition is financed by borrowing funds. As a result, equity in the combined firm is replaced with debt and its debt-equity ratio rises. Many of these cases involve so-called "leveraged buyouts" (LBOs), in which a group of investors, usually including the management of the firm being acquired, buy out stockholders in order to take the firm private.[a]

In the past, there was little LBO borrowing and what there was took the form of bank loans. However, because an increased debt-equity ratio raises the default risk of a firm's debt, bank loans usually come with a lot of restrictions and collateral requirements. In response to an increased demand for LBO financing, Drexel Burnham Lambert, in late 1983, started using its extensive network of private and institutional buyers of low-grade debt to float LBO bonds. These bonds are frequently rated below investment grade, especially when they are junior to already existing debt, and when cash flow projections barely exceed the higher required interest payments. The flexibility of this new source of LBO financing allows some investors to attempt acquisitions of firms several times their own size.[b]

In contrast to the amount of public discussion about this topic, low-grade bond issues actually involved in takeovers make up only a small part of the market. During 1984, LBOs amounted to only $10.8 billion, compared with $122.2 billion in total merger and acquisition activity.[c] Drexel estimates that of about $14 billion in publicly issued low-grade bonds in 1984, only "approximately 12% was issued in acquisition or leveraged buyout transactions, of which a de minimis amount was connected with the financing of unsolicited acquisitions."[d] By 1985, however, other analysts had estimated that the proportion of new low-grade issues used to finance acquisitions and LBO transactions had risen to 38 percent.[e]

a For details, see Carolyn K. Brancato and Kevin F. Winch, "Merger Activity and Leveraged Buyouts: Sound Corporate Restructuring or Wall Street Alchemy?" U.S. Congress, House, Committee on Energy and Commerce, Subcommittee on Telecommunications, Consumer Protection, and Finance, 98th Congress, 2nd Session (November 1984).

b Early in 1986, the Board of Governors of the Federal Reserve System ruled that bonds that are issued by a corporation with no business operations and no assets other than the stock of the target company, are functionally equivalent to borrowing to buy stock (that is, buying stock on margin). Therefore, these bonds are subject to a 50 percent margin as required by Regulation G. That is, only 50 percent of the stock purchase can be financed with borrowed funds. However, the Board specifically excluded bonds that are issued simultaneously with the consummation of the merger or LBO—a standard practice in LBOs—because the assets of the firm, and not its stock, would be the source of repayment of the bond issue. For details, see Federal Reserve System 12 C.F.R Part 207 (Regulation G; Docket No. R-0562).

c W. T. Grimm & Co. "1984 Merger/Acquisitions Set Ten-Year Record: Total Dollar Value Rose to 67% to a Record-Breaking $122.2 Billion," (Chicago: W. T. Grimm & Co., 1985). Press release, undated, duplicated.

d Drexel Burnham Lambert, Inc., "Acquisitions and High Yield Bond Financing," submitted to the Subcommittee on Telecommunications, Consumer Protection, and Finance (March 20, 1985) p. 14.

e Martin Fridson and Fritz Wahl, "Plain Talk About Takeovers," *High Performance* (February 1986) p. 2. Fridson and Wahl use a more restrictive definition of the size of the low-grade market than Drexel does.

SOURCE: *Economic Review*, Federal Reserve Bank of Philadelphia (November–December 1986): 9. Jan Loeys, "Low-Grade Bonds: A Growing Source of Corporate Funding."

Chapter 6

Bond Markets

takeover attempts. Many firms issued junk bonds simply to benefit from the relatively low interest rates in the mid 1980s, commonly using the proceeds to retire some outstanding stock.

Junk bonds are generally perceived to offer high returns with high risk. During the mid 1980s, junk bond defaults were relatively infrequent, which may have renewed public interest in them and encouraged corporations to issue more. As their popularity grew, various innovative features were implemented. Some junk bonds were convertible into the corporation's stock. Others were offered at yields that adjusted to market interest rates or even to commodity price indices over time.

A study by Christopher Ma and Garry Weed provides evidence that junk bonds have outperformed high-grade bonds on a risk-adjusted basis. In addition, a recent study by Altman and Nammacher found that even after adjusting for risk, junk bonds generated a return of 5 percentage points more than government securities. While the abnormal performance of junk bonds might be interpreted as a sign of market inefficiency, it might also suggest that the default rate on such bonds turned out to be less than expected. There is no guarantee, however, that such results will occur in the future.

After the stock market crash of October 1987, the market became more concerned about the risk of junk bonds, so issuers had to lower the price (allowing a higher yield) to compensate for the higher perceived risk.

Exhibit 6.2 illustrates the breakdown of bonds issued by rating. Note the substantial increase in low-rated bonds during the five-year period. Government regulators of the financial markets have become concerned that investors do not fully recognize the degree of default risk exhibited by junk bonds. During an economic downturn, the market's risk perception increases, which could adversely affect those investors (including financial institutions) that maintain large holdings of junk bonds.

Low- and Zero-Coupon Bonds

In the early 1980s, firms began issuing bonds with coupons roughly half the size of the prevailing rate and later with zero coupons. These **low-coupon** or **zero-coupon bonds** are therefore issued at a deep discount from par value. Investors are taxed annually on the amount of interest earned, even though much or all of it will not be received until maturity. The amount of interest taxed is the amortized discount (the gain at maturity is prorated over the life of the bond). Low- and zero-coupon corporate bonds are purchased mainly for tax-exempt investment accounts (pension funds, individual retirement accounts etc.).

To the issuing firm, these bonds have the advantage of requiring low or no cash outflow during their life. Additionally, the firm is permitted to deduct the amortized discount as interest expense for federal income tax purposes, even though it does not pay interest. This adds to the firm's cash flow. Finally, the demand for low- and zero-coupon bonds has been great enough that firms can, in most cases, issue them at a lower cost than regular bonds. The major disadvantage to the firm is that at maturity of the bond it must pay an amount equal to both principal and interest (the discount), which can be substantial.

EXHIBIT 6.2   Volume of Bonds Classified by Risk Rating

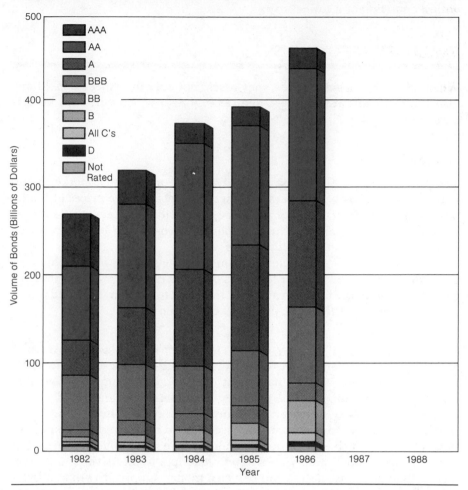

SOURCE: Economic Trends Federal Reserve Bank of Cleveland (July 1987): 16, and *Standard and Poor's Bond Guide*, various issues.

Variable-Rate Bonds

The highly volatile interest rates experienced during the 1970s inspired the development of **variable-rate bonds,** which affect the investor and borrower as follows: (1) they allow investors to benefit from rising market interest rates over time, and (2) they allow issuers of bonds to benefit from declining rates over time.

Convertible Bonds

Another type of bond, known as the **convertible bond,** allows investors to exchange a bond for a stated number of shares of the firm's common stock. This conversion feature offers investors the potential for high returns if the price of the firm's common stock rises. Investors are therefore willing to accept a lower rate of interest on these bonds, which allows the firm to obtain financing at a lower cost.

EVALUATING BOND RISK

When investors consider bonds, they assess not only the expected yield but also the risk—interest rate risk and default risk, which will both be discussed in detail.

Interest Rate Risk

The precise impact of interest rate movements on a bond's market value depends on the cash flow characteristics of the bond. The prices of bonds with longer terms to maturity are more susceptible to interest rate movements. In addition, prices of low-coupon or zero-coupon bonds are more susceptible to interest rate movements.

Bond-portfolio managers closely monitor interest rate movements and make decisions based on their forecasts of future rates. Any factors that are expected to influence interest rates are often used to explain why bond prices rise or fall. Some of the more critical factors follow.

IMPACT OF MONEY SUPPLY GROWTH. When money supply growth is increased by the Federal Reserve System, three reactions are possible. First, the increased money supply may result in an increased supply of loanable funds. If demand for loanable funds is not affected, the increased money supply should place downward pressure on interest rates, causing bond-portfolio managers to expect an increase in bond prices and thus purchase bonds based on such expectations. An alternative reaction is to expect that the increased money supply growth will lead to a higher level of inflation. A historical positive relationship between money supply growth and inflation substantiates this expectation. On this basis, bond-portfolio managers may expect a large increase in the demand for loanable funds (as a result of inflationary expectations), causing an increase in interest rates and lower bond prices. Such forecasts would encourage immediate sale of long-term bonds.

IMPACT OF OIL PRICES. Oil prices have a major impact on a variety of wholesale and consumer prices. Bond-portfolio managers therefore forecast oil prices and their potential impact on inflation in order to forecast interest rates. A forecast of high oil prices results in expectations of higher interest rates, causing bond-portfolio managers to sell some of their bond holdings. A forecast of lower oil prices results in expectations of lower interest rates, causing bond-portfolio managers to purchase more bonds.

IMPACT OF THE DOLLAR. To the extent that fluctuations in the dollar affect interest rates, they affect U.S. bond prices. Holding other things equal, expectations of a weaker dollar are likely to increase inflationary expectations, because they increase the prices of imported supplies. Such expectations also price foreign competitors out of the market, allowing U.S. firms to increase their prices with more abandon. Thus, U.S. interest rates are expected to rise and bond prices are expected to decrease when the dollar is expected to weaken. Foreign investors expecting dollar depreciation are less willing to hold U.S. bonds, because the coupon payments will convert to less of their home currency in that event, and this could cause an immediate net sale of bonds, placing further downward pressure on bond prices.

Expectations of a strong dollar should have the opposite results. A stronger dollar reduces the prices paid for foreign supplies, thus lowering retail prices. In addition, because a stronger dollar makes the prices of foreign products more attractive, domestic firms must maintain low prices in order to compete. Consequently, low inflation, and therefore low interest rates, are expected, and bond portfolio managers are likely to purchase more bonds.

SIMULTANEOUS IMPACT OF ALL FACTORS. If investors could correctly predict the interest rate for a certain point in time, they could predict how bond prices would be affected at that time with a high degree of accuracy. However, they are limited in their ability to forecast interest rates by two main factors. First, it is impossible to accurately predict all changes in all factors (such as money supply, oil prices, and the dollar value) that influence inflation and therefore interest rates. Second, even if these factors could be predicted with perfect accuracy, their impact on interest rates cannot. To deal with the uncertainty, bond portfolio managers often develop a variety of possible interest rate scenarios for a future point in time and estimate bond prices for each scenario. In this way, they can create a probability distribution of forecasted bond prices that can be used to help them decide whether to buy or sell bonds.

Default Risk

Bond portfolio managers also monitor factors that reduce the bond issuer's ability to meet its payment obligations. At one extreme, Treasury bonds are normally perceived to have zero default risk, because they are backed by the federal government. However, the default risk of municipal and corporate bonds must be measured by investors. Small investors frequently rely on bond ratings provided by rating agencies such as Moody's or Standard & Poor's. Exhibit 6.3 shows the number of changes in Moody's bond ratings over time. Since 1976 the number of downgrades has exceeded the number of upgrades. The difference was most pronounced during the 1982 recession and in 1986 when several corporations were perceived to have an excessive amount of debt.

Bond portfolio managers who trade millions of dollars of bonds on a daily basis may both monitor bond ratings and also conduct their own evaluation of the bonds. Their own evaluation would include an assessment of the bond issuer's financial ratios over time. Ratios that compare cash flow to interest owed would be most useful. Historical financial ratios are not necessarily proper indicators of the future, so bond portfolio managers may attempt to forecast the bond issuer's future earnings and cash flow and determine from that whether the debt payments can be covered.

Perceived Reliability of Bond Ratings

A recent study by Ederington, Yawitz, and Roberts examines the informational content of bond ratings. Some of the more relevant results of their study are summarized below:

1. When market participants evaluate a bond issue's creditworthiness, they consider recent financial information about the company of concern above and beyond the information embedded within the ratings by Moody's or Standard & Poor's.

2. When compared for reliability, neither Moody's nor Standard & Poor's ratings were found to be clearly superior to the other.

3. When existing bonds have not been rated for a long period of time, market participants tend to place more emphasis on publicly available financial information and less on the ratings assigned by ratings agencies. This suggests that a rating is perceived to be more reliable for assessing the short-term creditworthiness of the bond issue than the long-term creditworthiness. Perhaps ratings would be consistently emphasized by market participants if they were updated more frequently by the rating agencies.

SOURCE: Louis H. Ederington, Jess B. Yawitz, and Brian E. Roberts, "The Informational Content of Bond Ratings," *Journal of Financial Research* (Fall 1987): 211–226.

INTERACTION AMONG BOND MARKET YIELDS

Yields among bonds can vary according to default risk, marketability, tax status, and other factors. Yet, the differential remains somewhat stable over time, because investors will switch to bonds that are perceived as more favorable. For example, if the Treasury issues an unusually large number of Treasury bonds in the primary market, such a large supply places downward pressure on the market price and upward pressure on the market yield of these bonds. Consequently, holders of corporate bonds with default risk may then switch to Treasury bonds, since they can achieve almost the same yield without being exposed to default risk. This tendency places downward pressure on the Treasury bond yields and upward pressure on corporate bonds, restoring the yield differential between the two. Thus, because some investors perceive various bonds as substitutes, their buy and sell decisions will stabilize yield differentials among the bonds.

Exhibit 6.4 compares yields on various types of bonds over time. The high correlation among yields is noticeably broken in specific periods, namely, during the poor economic periods of 1930, 1973–1974, and 1982, when investors required a higher default risk premium.

Yield differentials among bonds can change when investors perceive a characteristic of a particular type of bond to be more or less favorable than before. For example, if interest rates suddenly rise, those existing bonds that have a call feature are more likely to be called. Thus, the call feature characteristic is perceived as more unfavorable, and bonds with this char-

EXHIBIT 6.3   Changes in Moody's Corporate Bond Ratings

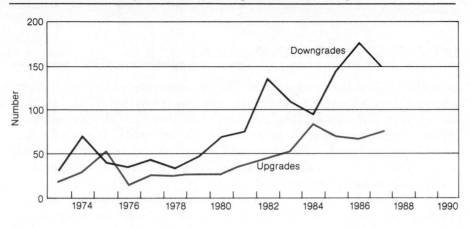

SOURCE: *Federal Reserve Bulletin* (January 1988): 4; and *Moody's Investor Service*. Data for 1987 is through the second quarter.

EXHIBIT 6.4   Long-term Bond Yields

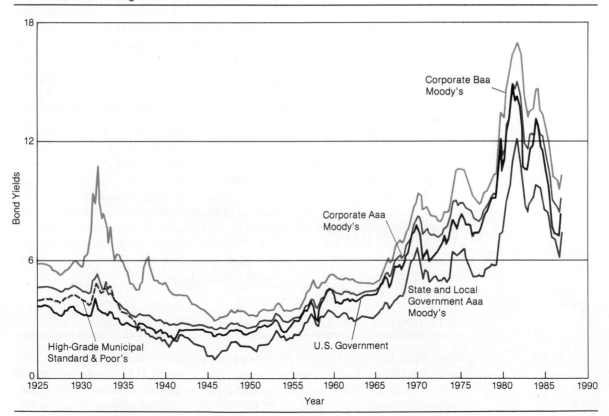

SOURCE: *1987 Federal Reserve Chart Book,* 97.

acteristic will sell only if the price is lowered. This implies that the yield differential reacts to the changing perception of the factor that caused the differential.

BOND PORTFOLIO MANAGEMENT

Some bond-portfolio managers will actively restructure their portfolio in anticipation of economic conditions. If they expect favorable economic conditions, they will increase their holdings of bonds with higher default risk. When the economic outlook is more pessimistic, they will shift toward bonds with low or no default risk. Others take a more passive approach in which their mix of bonds with different degrees of risk remains somewhat constant (except in unusual circumstances).

If bond portfolio managers anticipate lower interest rates, they may attempt to benefit from that by replacing short-maturity bonds with long-maturity bonds, or high-coupon bonds with low- or zero-coupon bonds. If they anticipate higher interest rates, they may concentrate on short-maturity and/or high-coupon bonds. In addition, they may temporarily liquidate part of their bond portfolio and use the proceeds to invest in money market securities. When their expectations of future interest rates change, they can liquidate the money market securities and invest in more bonds.

A more passive strategy would be to diversify among bonds that exhibit varied degrees of sensitivity to interest rate movements. Such a mix might even be permanently maintained. Although this strategy would have a lower potential return than an actively managed bond portfolio, it would not be as adversely affected if interest rates moved in the opposite direction of what was expected. Furthermore, transaction costs would be much lower.

PARTICIPATION OF FINANCIAL INSTITUTIONS IN BOND MARKETS

All financial institutions participate in the bond markets, as summarized in Exhibit 6.5. Commercial banks, bond mutual funds, insurance companies, and pension funds are dominant participants in the bond market activity on any given day. A financial institution's investment decisions will often affect bond market and other financial market activity simultaneously. For example, an institution's anticipation of higher interest rates may cause a sale of its bond holdings and a purchase of either money market securities or stocks. Conversely, expectations of lower interest rates may encourage financial institutions to shift investment from their money market security and/or stock portfolios to their bond portfolio.

INTERNATIONALIZATION OF BOND MARKETS

Bond markets have become increasingly integrated among countries. Exhibit 6.6 shows that foreign purchases and sales of U.S. bonds increased substantially in recent years. The value of foreign transactions during the 1985–1987 period was more than double the value of transactions during the 1982–1984 period.

INTERNATIONAL

ASPECTS

Part Two

Credit Markets

Benefits from Diversifying among Bonds

Because the market values of bonds are inversely related to interest rate movements, it may seem that diversification among bonds would not reduce risk. However, a study by McEnally and Boardman found that a bond portfolio's risk (as measured by variance of returns) can be substantially reduced by diversifying. This study estimated the mean variance of a set of one-bond, two-bond, three-bond, . . . forty-bond portfolios. The general relationship between the mean variance and number of bonds in the portfolio is shown in the exhibit below. As the number of bonds in the portfolio was increased, the mean variance of the bond portfolio declined. The degree of risk-reduction became smaller as the number increased.

SOURCE: Richard W. McEnally and Calvin M. Boardman, "Aspects of Corporate Bond Portfolio Diversification," *Journal of Financial Research* (Spring 1979): 27–36.

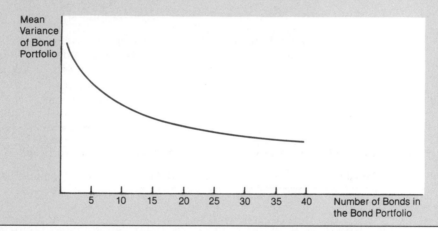

The increased volume in the foreign trading of U.S. securities is partially because U.S. corporations are issuing more securities in foreign markets. In addition, mutual funds containing U.S. securities are accessible to foreign investors. Furthermore, primary dealers of U.S. Treasury notes and bonds have opened offices in London, Tokyo, and other foreign cities to accommodate the foreign demand for these securities.

In 1963 U.S.–based corporations were limited to the amount of funds they could borrow in the United States for overseas operations. Consequently, these corporations began to issue bonds in the so-called **Eurobond market.** Various currencies are commonly used to denominate Eurobonds. The U.S. dollar is used the most, denominating 70 to 75 percent of the Eurobonds.[1] Non-dollar currencies have become more popular during the mid 1980s, when the dollar began to weaken.

---

1 See Frederick H. Jensen, "Recent Developments in Corporate Finance," *Federal Reserve Bulletin* (November 1986): 745–756.

EXHIBIT 6.5   Participation of Financial Institutions in Bond Markets

Financial Institution	Participation in Bond Markets
Commercial banks and savings and loan associations (S&Ls)	■ Purchase bonds for their asset portfolio ■ Sometimes place municipal bonds for municipalities ■ Sometimes issue bonds as a source of secondary capital
Finance companies	■ Commonly issue bonds as a source of long-term funds
Mutual funds	■ Use funds received from the sale of shares to purchase bonds; some bond mutual funds specialize in particular types of bonds while others invest in all types
Brokerage firms	■ Facilitate bond trading by matching up buyers and sellers of bonds in the secondary market
Investment banking firms	■ Place newly issued bonds for governments and corporations; they may underwrite the bonds and therefore assume the risk of market price uncertainty or place the bonds on a best-efforts basis in which they do not guarantee a price for the issuer
Insurance companies	■ Purchase bonds for their asset portfolio
Pension funds	■ Purchase bonds for their asset portfolio

Non–U.S. investors who desire dollar-denominated bonds may use the Eurobond market if they prefer the bearer form to the registered form of corporate bonds issued in the United States. Alternatively, they may use the Eurobond market because they are more familiar with bond placements within their own country.

Before 1984, foreign investors that directly purchased U.S.–placed bonds were subject to a 30 percent withholding tax; that is, the issuers retained 30 percent of the interest payments. A variety of tax treaties between the United States and other countries caused this withholding tax to affect investors in some countries more than others. Because of the withholding tax, many U.S. bonds were issued in the Eurobond market through financing subsidiaries in the Netherlands Antilles. A tax treaty allowed interest payments from Antilles subsidiaries of U.S.–based corporations to non–U.S. investors to be exempt from the withholding tax, and U.S. firms that used this method of financing were able to sell their bonds at a higher price. Thus, they obtained funds at a relatively low cost. Some U.S. firms did not use this financing method, since there was a cost of establishing a financing subsidiary in the Netherlands Antilles, and because they knew that this method of circumventing the withholding tax might be prohibited by the U.S. government at some point in the future.

EXHIBIT 6.6   Foreign Trading of U.S. Bonds (in Billions of Dollars)

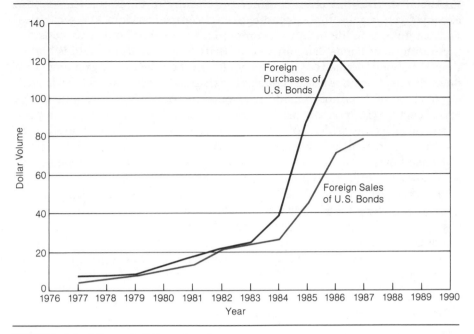

SOURCE: *Federal Reserve Bulletin*, various issues.

In July 1984 the U.S. government abolished the withholding tax and allowed U.S. corporations to issue bearer bonds directly to non–U.S. investors. This caused a large increase in the volume of bonds sold to non–U.S. investors. In addition, the general worldwide decline in interest rates during the 1980s prompted a large increase in bond issuance by corporations, compounding the impact of the removal of the withholding tax on the volume of bonds issued in the Eurobond market.

An underwriting syndicate of investment banks participates in the Eurobond market by placing the bonds issued. They normally underwrite the bonds, guaranteeing a particular value to be received by the issuer. Thus, they are exposed to *underwriting risk*, or the risk that they will be unable to sell the bonds above the price that they guaranteed the issuer.

The issuer of Eurobonds can choose the currency in which the bonds should be denominated. The issuer's periodic coupon payments and repayment of principal will normally be in this currency. Moreover, the financing cost from issuing bonds depends on the currency chosen. In some cases, a firm may denominate the bonds in a currency with low interest rate and use earnings generated by one of its subsidiaries to cover the payments. For example, the coupon rate on a Eurobond denominated in Swiss francs may be 5 percentage points lower than a dollar-denominated bond. A U.S. firm may consider issuing Swiss franc–denominated bonds and converting the francs to dollars for use in the United States. Then it could instruct a subsidiary in Switzerland to cover the periodic coupon payments with earnings that the subsidiary generates. In this way, a lower financing rate would be achieved without exposure to exchange rate risk.

Impact of Exchange Rates on Returns of Foreign Bonds

Financial institutions often consider purchasing foreign securities whose expected returns are higher than expected returns on domestic securities. For example, U.S. life insurance companies or pension funds may consider the purchase of bonds denominated in British pounds if the yield is higher than U.S. bond yields. However, the yield will be affected by exchange rate fluctuations. Consider a U.S. financial institution's purchase of bonds with a par value of 2 million pounds, a 10 percent coupon rate (payable at the end of each year), presently priced at par value, and with six years remaining until maturity. Consider how the dollar cash flows to be generated from the investment will differ under the three scenarios shown in Exhibit 6.7. The cash flows in the last year also account for the principal payment. The sensitivity of dollar cash flows to the pound's value is obvious.

From the perspective of the investing institution, the most attractive foreign bonds offer a high coupon rate and are denominated in a currency that strengthens over the investment horizon. While the coupon rates of some bonds are fixed, the future value of any foreign currency is uncertain. Thus, there is a risk that the currency will depreciate and more than offset any coupon rate advantage.

Diversifying Bonds Internationally

Financial institutions may attempt to reduce their exchange rate risk by diversifying among foreign securities denominated in various foreign currencies. In this way, a smaller proportion of their foreign security holdings

EXHIBIT 6.7   Dollar Cash Flows Generated from a Foreign Bond under Three Scenarios

Scenario I (stable pound)	Year					
	1	2	3	4	5	6
Forecasted value of pound	$1.50	$1.50	$1.50	$1.50	$1.50	$1.50
Forecasted dollar cash flows	300,000	300,000	300,000	300,000	300,000	3,300,000
Scenario II (weak pound)						
Forecasted value of pound	$1.48	$1.46	$1.44	$1.40	$1.36	$1.30
Forecasted dollar cash flows	296,000	292,000	288,000	280,000	272,000	2,860,000
Scenario III (strong pound)						
Forecasted value of pound	$1.53	$1.56	$1.60	$1.63	$1.66	$1.70
Forecasted dollar cash flows	306,000	312,000	320,000	326,000	332,000	3,740,000

will be exposed to the depreciation of any particular foreign currency. Because the movements of many foreign currency values are highly correlated, U.S. investors may reduce exchange rate risk only slightly when diversifying among European securities. For this reason, U.S. financial institutions commonly attempt to purchase securities across continents rather than within a single continent, as a review of the foreign securities purchased by pension funds, life insurance companies, or most international mutual funds would show.

Institutional investors also diversify their bond-portfolio internationally in order to reduce exposure to interest rate risk. If all bonds were from a single country, the values of all bonds in the portfolio would be systematically affected by interest rate movements in that country. International diversification of bonds reduces the sensitivity of the overall bond portfolio to any single country's interest rate movements.

Use of Interest Rate Swaps in International Bond Markets

An **interest rate swap** enables firms to exchange fixed interest rate payments for variable-rate payments. These swaps are used by bond issuers because they may reconfigure the future bond payments to a more preferable structure. As an example, consider two firms that desire to issue bonds:

- Quality Company is a highly rated firm that prefers to borrow at a variable rate.
- Risky Company is a low-rated firm that prefers to borrow at a fixed rate.

Assume the rates these companies would pay for issuing either variable-rate or fixed-rate Eurobonds are as follows:

	Fixed-Rate Bond	Variable-Rate Bond
Quality Company	9%	LIBOR + ½%
Risky Company	10½%	LIBOR + 1%

LIBOR is the interbank offer rate, which changes over time. Based on the information given, Quality Company has a comparative advantage when issuing either fixed-rate or variable-rate bonds, but its advantage is greater when issuing fixed-rate bonds. Quality Company could issue fixed-rate bonds while Risky Company issues variable-rate bonds. Quality could provide variable-rate payments to Risky in exchange for fixed-rate payments.

Assume that Quality negotiated with Risky to provide variable-rate payments at LIBOR plus ½ percent in exchange for fixed-rate payments of 9½ percent. This interest rate swap is shown in Exhibit 6.8. Quality Company benefits, since its fixed-rate payments received on the swap exceed the payments owed to bondholders by ½ percent. Its variable-rate payments to Risky Company are the same as what it would have paid if it had issued variable-rate bonds. Risky is receiving LIBOR plus ½ percent on the swap, which is ½ percent less than what it must pay on its variable-rate bonds. Yet, it is making fixed payments of 9½ percent, which is 1 percent less than it would have paid if it had issued fixed-rate bonds. Overall, it saves ½ percent per year on financing costs.

EXHIBIT 6.8   Illustration of Interest Rate Swap

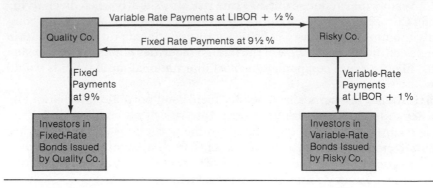

Two limitations of the swap just described are worth mentioning. First, there is a cost of time and resources associated with searching for a suitable swap candidate and negotiating the swap terms. Second, there is a risk to each swap participant that the counter-participant could default on payments. For this reason, financial intermediaries are usually involved in swap agreements. They match up participants (for a fee) and sometimes assume the default risk involved.

Use of Currency Swaps in International Bond Markets

Another swap used to complement bond issues, the **currency swap,** enables firms to exchange currencies at periodic intervals. To illustrate why currency swaps occur, consider a U.S. firm called Philly Company that desires to issue a German mark–denominated bond (since it could make payments with mark inflows to be generated from ongoing operations). However, assume that this firm is not well-known to investors that would consider purchasing mark-denominated bonds. Also, consider a firm called Windy Company that desires to issue dollar-denominated bonds because its inflow payments are mostly in dollars. However, it is not well-known to the investors that would purchase these bonds. If Philly is known within the dollar-denominated market while Windy is known within the mark-denominated market, the following transactions would be appropriate. Philly could issue dollar-denominated bonds while Windy issues mark-denominated bonds. Philly could exchange marks for dollars to make its bond payments. Windy would receive marks in exchange for dollars to make its bond payments. This type of currency swap is illustrated in Exhibit 6.9.

The Federal Reserve has reported that swaps may correspond with 50 to 75 percent of new Eurobond issues in recent years. The Fed also reported that the amount of principal representing swap transactions has increased from $3 billion in early 1982 to $200 billion by 1986. The large commercial banks that serve as financial intermediaries sometimes take positions. That is, they may agree to swap fixed payments for variable payments or swap currencies with a firm rather than simply search for a suitable swap candidate.

EXHIBIT 6.9 Illustration of a Currency Swap

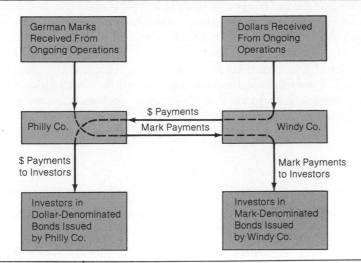

Deregulation of International Bond Markets

Monetary and regulatory authorities of most major countries have moved toward internationalizing their securities markets in recent years. Consequently, investors have more flexibility to invest in foreign countries, and borrowers have more flexibility to borrow in foreign countries. Some examples of financial deregulation within the international markets follow.

Bundesbank, the West German central bank, has approved the use of floating-rate notes and zero-coupon bonds. It also allows foreign-owned underwriters based in West Germany to be the lead manager of security issues. A Frankfurt interbank offer rate (FIFOR) is continually updated to price floating-rate notes.

Authorities in the Netherlands recently approved floating-rate securities. Foreign-owned investment banks based in the Netherlands can now act as lead-manager on security underwritings. The Amsterdam interbank offer rate (AIBOR) is updated to price floating-rate securities.

The Japanese government is planning to lift a ban on the Japanese trading of U.S. financial futures. Because Japanese investors hold such a large amount in U.S. bonds, they may sometimes desire to take futures positions in order to reduce interest rate risk. These developments will likely result in continued growth in the volume of international financial transactions.

SUMMARY

This chapter described the main types of bonds and the characteristics that differentiate them. Because bond characteristics can vary significantly, so can their yields. A main reason for differences in yield is default risk. Treasury bonds have no default risk, while junk bonds have a high degree, with other types of bonds falling in between these two extremes.

While bond yields differ, they generally move in the same direction in response to interest rate movements. The prices of bonds with long maturities and/or low (or no) coupon payments are most sensitive to interest rate risk. Because interest rate risk is so influential, bond portfolio managers closely monitor all factors that affect interest rates, including money supply, the value of the dollar, and oil prices.

International bond markets have become internationally integrated in recent years. Financial institutions such as commercial banks, insurance companies, and pension funds that maintain a bond portfolio are increasing their investment in foreign bonds.

KEY TERMS

blanket mortgage
call
call premium
call provision
chattel mortgage
closed-end mortgage bond
collateral trust bonds
convertible bond
corporate bonds
currency swap
debentures
Eurobond market
first mortgage bond

general obligation bonds
interest rate swap
junk bonds
limited open-ended mortgage
low-coupon bonds
municipal bonds
open-end mortgage bond
protective covenants
revenue bonds
subordinated debentures
variable-rate bonds
zero-coupon bonds

QUESTIONS

6.1. What is a bond indenture?

6.2. What is the function of a trustee, as related to bond issues?

6.3. Explain the use of a sinking-fund provision. How can it reduce the risk of investors?

6.4. What are protective covenants?

6.5. Explain the call feature of bonds. How can it affect the price of a bond?

6.6. Explain the common types of collateral for bonds.

6.7. What are debentures? How do they differ from subordinated debentures?

6.8. What are the advantages and disadvantages to a firm that issues low- or zero-coupon bonds.

6.9. Are variable-rate bonds attractive to investors who expect interest rates to decrease? Explain.

6.10. Why can convertible bonds be issued by firms at a higher price than other bonds?

6.11. Explain how bond prices may be affected by money supply growth, oil prices, and the expected value of the dollar.

6.12. Explain why a passive strategy in bond-portfolio management would result in lower transaction costs than a more aggressive strategy.

6.13. Explain why some companies that issue bonds engage in interest rate swaps in financial markets. Why do they not simply issue bonds that require the type of payments (fixed or variable) that they prefer to make?

6.14. Explain why some companies that issue bonds engage in currency swaps. Why do they not simply issue bonds in the currency that they would prefer to use for making payments?

6.15. Assume that oil-producing countries have agreed to reduce their oil production by 30 percent. How would bond prices be affected by this announcement? Explain.

6.16. Assume that the bond market participants suddenly expect the Fed to substantially increase money supply.

a. Assuming no threat of inflation, how would bond prices be affected by this expectation?

b. Assuming that inflation may result, how would bond prices be affected?

6.17. During 1987 and 1988, the trade deficit figures were closely watched by bond portfolio managers.

a. When the trade deficit figure was higher than anticipated, bond prices typically declined. Explain why this reaction may have occurred.

b. In some cases, the trade deficit figure was very large, but the bond markets did not respond to the announcement of it. Assuming that no other information offset its impact, explain why the bond markets may not have responded to the announcement.

6.18. Assume that the bond yields in Japan rise. How might U.S. bond yields be affected? Why?

6.19. Assume that the Japanese government announces plans to impose a special high tax on income earned by Japanese investors who have purchased non-Japanese bonds. How might this announcement affect U.S. bond prices immediately, even before the plan is finalized?

6.20. Assume that news is announced that causes bond portfolio managers to suddenly expect much higher economic growth. How might bond prices be affected by this expectation? Explain.

6.21. Assume that news is announced that causes bond portfolio managers to suddenly anticipate a recession. How might bond prices be affected? Explain.

6.22. A U.S. insurance company chose to purchase British 20-year Treasury bonds instead of U.S. 20-year Treasury bonds because the coupon rate was 2 percent higher on the British bonds. Assume that the insurance company sold the bonds after five years. Its yield over the five-year period was substantially less than the yield it would have received on the U.S. bonds over the same five-year period. Assume that the U.S. insurance company had hedged its exchange rate exposure. Given that the lower yield was not because of default risk or exchange rate risk, explain how the British bonds could possibly generate a lower yield than the U.S. bonds. (Assume that either type of bond could have been purchased at the par value.)

PROBLEMS

6.1. Cardinal Company, a U.S.–based insurance company, considers purchasing bonds denominated in Canadian dollars, with a maturity of six years, a par value of C$50 million, and a coupon rate of 12 percent. The bonds can be purchased at par by Cardinal and would be sold four years from now. The current exchange rate of the Canadian dollar is $.80. Cardinal expects that the required return by Canadian investors on these bonds four years from now will be 9 percent. If Cardinal purchases the bonds, it will sell them in the Canadian secondary market four years from now. The following exchange rates are forecast as follows:

Year	Exchange Rate of C$
1	$.80
2	.77
3	.74
4	.72
5	.68
6	.66

a. Determine the expected U.S. dollar cash flows to Cardinal over the next four years. Refer to Chapter 3 to determine the present value of a bond as of a particular time in the future.

b. Does Cardinal expect to be favorably or adversely affected by the interest rate risk? Explain.

c. Does Cardinal expect to be favorably or adversely affected by exchange rate risk? Explain.

PROJECT

1. EXAMINING RECENT BOND PRICE MOVEMENTS.

Review the "Credit Markets" section of *The Wall Street Journal* (listed in the index on the front page) for the last five days. This section describes how bond prices changed on the previous day. Since bond prices react to expectations of future interest rates, it also attempts to explain why bond prices changed on the previous day.

For each day, fill out the following table:

	Did bond prices increase or decrease?	Apparent change in interest rate expectations (higher or lower than previous day?)	Reason for change in interest rate expectations?
1 day ago			
2 days ago			
3 days ago			
4 days ago			
5 days ago			

REFERENCES

Altman, Edward I. and Scott A. Nammacher. "The Default Rate Experience on High-Yield Corporate Debt." *Financial Analysts Journal* (July–August 1985): 25–42.

Andrews, Suzanna. "The Creative Surge in Tax-Exempt Finance." *Institutional Investor* (December 1984): 211–222.

Bierwag, G., George Kaufman and Cynthia Latta. "Bond Portfolio Immunization: Tests of Maturity, One- and Two-Factor Duration Matching Strategies." *Financial Review* (May 1987): 203–219.

Dyl, Edward A. and Michael D. Joehnk. "Refunding Tax Exempt Bonds." *Financial Management* (Summer 1976): 59–66.

Ederington, Louis. "Negotiated versus Competitive Underwritings of Corporate Bonds." *Journal of Finance* (March 1976): 17–26.

Ederington, Louis, Jess Yawitz and Brian Roberts. "The Informational Content of Bond Ratings." *Journal of Financial Research* (Fall 1987): 191–209.

Fabozzi, F. J. and R. R. West. "Negotiated vs. Competitive Underwriting of Public Utility Bonds: Just One More Time." *Journal of Financial and Quantitative Analysis* (September 1981): 323–339.

Fons, Jerome. "The Default Premium and Corporate Bond Experience." *Journal of Finance* (March 1987): 81–98.

Hawthorne, Fran. "The Battle of the Bond Indexes." *Institutional Investor* (April 1986): 117–118, 122.

Hess, Alan C. and Peter A. Frost. "Tests of Price Effects of New Issues of Seasoned Securities." *Journal of Finance* 37 (March 1982): 11–26.

Hoffmeister, J. Ronald, Patrick Hays and Gary Kelley. "Conditions Affecting the Timing of Convertible Bond Sales." *Journal of Business Research* (February 1987): 101–106.

Jensen, Frederick H. "Recent Developments in Corporate Finance." *Federal Reserve Bulletin* (November 1986): 745–756.

Karp, Richard and Gregory Miller. "Sadder But Wiser About Debt." *Institutional Investor* (July 1983): 217–219.

Kidwell, David, Eric Sorensen and John Wachowicz. "Estimating the Signaling Benefits of Debt Insurance: The Case of Municipal Bonds." *Journal of Finance and Quantitative Analysis* (September 1987): 299–314.

Levy, Yvonne. "Default for Washington Power?" *Weekly Letter*, Federal Reserve Bulletin of San Francisco (April 22, 1983).

Liu, Pu and William Moore. "The Impact of Split Bond Ratings on Risk Premia." *Financial Review* (February 1987): 71–85.

Logue, Dennis E. and Robert A. Jarrow. "Negotiation vs. Competitive Bidding in the Sale of Securities by Public Utilities." *Financial Management* (Fall 1978): 31–39.

Ma, Christopher K. and Garry M. Weed. "Fact and Fancy of Takeover Junk Bonds." *Journal of Portfolio Management* (Fall 1986): 34–37.

Milligan, John W. "A One-Man Assault on the Muni Guarantee Business." *Institutional Investor* (June 1986): 251–243.

Ogden, Joseph. "Determinants of the Ratings and Yields on Corporate Bonds: Tests of the Contingent Claims Model." *Journal of Financial Research* (Winter 1987): 329–339.

Pieptea, Dan. "Leveraged Bond Portfolio Optimization Under Uncertainty." *Financial Review* (February 1987): 87–109.

Pozdena, Randall J. "Municipal Bond Behavior." *Weekly Letter*, Federal Reserve Bank of San Francisco (February 22, 1985).

Proctor, Allen J. and Julie N. Rappaport. "Public and Private Debt Accumulation: A Perspective," *Quarterly Review*, Federal Reserve Bank of New York (Autumn 1985): 1–15.

Ronn, Ehud. "A New Linear Programming Approach to Bond Portfolio Management." *Journal of Financial and Quantitative Analysis* (December 1987): 439–466.

Schaefer, Stephen and Eduardo Schwartz. "Time-Dependent Variance and the Pricing of Bond Options." *Journal of Finance* (December 1987): 1113–1128.

Shapiro, Harvey D. "The Financial Fallout From Whoops." *Institutional Investor* (December 1983): 213–218.

Stover, Roger D. "The Interaction between Pricing and Underwriting Spread in the New Issue Convertible Debt Market." *Journal of Financial Research* (Winter 1983): 323–332.

Wilcox, James A. "Inflation Proof Long-Term Bonds." *Weekly Letter*, Federal Reserve Bank of San Francisco (November 30, 1984).

Zwick, Burton. "Yields on Privately Placed Corporate Bonds." *Journal of Finance* 35 (March 1980): 23–29.

Part Two

Credit Markets

Mortgage Markets

MORTGAGE MARKETS IN PERSPECTIVE

On June 9, 1988, prices of mortgage-backed securities (securities issued by financial institutions which are backed by mortgages as collateral) declined, mainly because of concern about higher inflation. On June 15, their prices again declined, as the reported increase in commodity prices heightened inflationary concerns. High-coupon securities were less affected by the pessimistic outlook. On the morning of June 23, inflationary concerns were reduced by expectations of a stronger dollar, causing a price increase in mortgage-backed securities. However, the prices declined later in the day as the dollar's value declined. On June 27, prices of mortgage-backed securities decreased, but by a smaller degree than the decline in Treasury bonds.

On July 11, mortgage-backed security prices increased in response to lower prices of oil and other commodities, which reduced inflationary expectations. At this time, these securities were offering a yield of about one percentage point above Treasury bonds.

On July 28, the yields offered on newly-issued mortgage-backed securities declined in response to rumors that the Fed was concerned with inflationary pressure and had planned to tighten credit. The market reaction was also attributed to a report that gross national product was rising at a higher pace than expected, which could further ignite inflationary fears.

■ What other factors not cited above affect the prices and therefore yields of mortgage-backed securities?
■ What are some key financial instruments, other than mortgage-backed securities, used in mortgage markets?
■ What financial institutions participate in the mortgage markets?

These and other related questions are addressed in this chapter.

OUTLINE

Mortgages are securities used to finance housing purchases, originated by various financial institutions, such as savings institutions and mortgage companies. A secondary mortgage market accommodates originators of mortgages that desire to sell their mortgages prior to maturity. Both the origination process and the secondary market activities for mortgages have become much more complex in recent years.

This chapter provides an overview of the mortgages offered and describes the activities in the secondary mortgage market. First, a brief background is provided and the various types of mortgages are discussed. Second, the key characteristics of residential mortgages are summarized. Third, the secondary mortgage market is described, and its main participants are identified. Finally, a breakdown of mortgage holdings by financial institution is provided.

BACKGROUND ON MORTGAGES

Exhibit 7.1 discloses the mortgage debt outstanding over time by type of property. The majority of mortgage debt outstanding is on one- to four-family properties, while commercial properties are a distant second. The level of mortgage debt has generally risen over time, although not at a constant rate. The effects of the mild recession in 1980 and severe recession in 1982 on mortgage debt are obvious. Families tend to avoid housing purchases that would increase their debt during recessionary periods. Because *residential mortgages* (one- to four-family and multifamily) dominate the mortgage market, they receive the most attention in this chapter.

CHARACTERISTICS OF RESIDENTIAL MORTGAGES

When financial institutions originate residential mortgages, the mortgage contract created should specify whether the mortgage is federally insured, the amount of the loan, whether the interest rate is fixed or adjustable, the interest rate to be charged, the maturity, and other special provisions that may vary among contracts. Over time, financial institutions have become more aware of the specific borrowing preferences of those who purchase residential housing. Yet, each family requesting a mortgage may have a different preference for the loan structure.

Insured versus Conventional Mortgages

Mortgages are often classified as federally insured or conventional. *Federally insured mortgages* guarantee loan repayment to the lending financial institution, thereby covering it against the possibility of default by the borrower. An insurance fee of .5 percent of the loan amount is applied to cover the cost of insuring the mortgage. The guarantor can be either the Federal Housing Administration (FHA) or the Veterans Administration (VA). Borrowers applying for FHA and VA mortgage loans from a financial institution must meet various requirements specified by those government agencies in order to qualify. In addition, the maximum mortgage amount is limited by

EXHIBIT 7.1 Volume of Mortgage Debt by Type of Property (in Billions of Dollars)

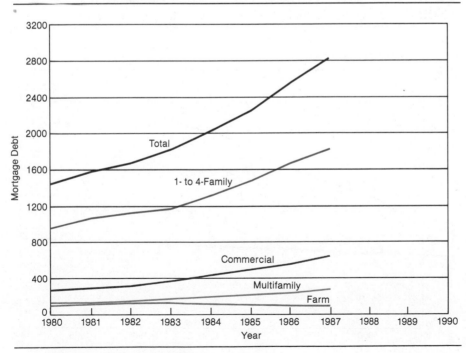

a October estimates were used for 1987.

SOURCE: *Federal Reserve Bulletin.*

law (although the limit varies among states to account for cost of housing differences). The dollar volume of FHA and VA mortgage loans is displayed in Exhibit 7.2. The volume of FHA loans has consistently exceeded that of VA loans since 1960. Both types of mortgages have become increasingly popular over the last 30 years.

Conventional mortgages are also provided by financial institutions. Although they are not federally insured, they can be privately insured so that the lending financial institutions can still avoid exposure to default risk. The insurance premium paid for such private insurance would likely be passed on to the borrowers. They can choose to incur the default risk themselves, and avoid the insurance fee. Yet, most participants in the secondary mortgage market will purchase only those conventional mortgages that are privately insured (unless the mortgage's loan-to-value ratio is less than 80 percent).

Fixed versus Adjustable-Rate Mortgages

One of the most important provisions in the mortgage contract is the interest rate. It can be specified as a fixed rate or can allow for periodic rate adjustments over time. The **fixed-rate mortgage** locks in the borrower's interest rate over the life of the mortgage. Thus, the periodic interest payment received by the lending financial institution is constant, regardless of how market interest rates change over time. Financial institutions that hold fixed-rate mortgages in their asset portfolio are exposed to interest rate risk,

EXHIBIT 7.2   Dollar Volume of FHA and VA Mortgages Over Time

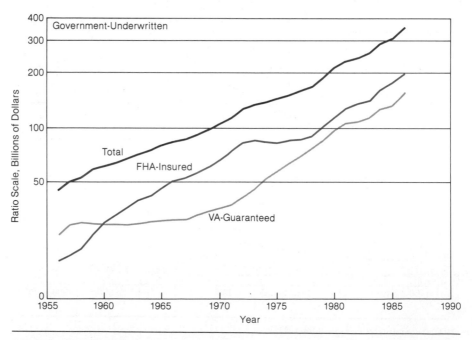

SOURCE: *1987 Federal Reserve Chart Book.*

since they commonly use funds obtained from short-term customer deposits to make long-term mortgage loans. If interest rates increase over time, the financial institution's cost of obtaining funds (from deposits) will increase. Yet, the return on its fixed-rate mortgage loans will be unaffected, causing its profit margin to decrease.

Borrowers with fixed-rate mortgages do not suffer from the effects of rising interest rates, but they also fail to benefit from declining rates. While they could attempt to refinance (obtain a new mortgage to replace the existing mortgage) at the lower prevailing market interest rate, transaction costs (such as closing costs and an origination fee) would be incurred.

In contrast to the fixed-rate mortgage, the **adjustable-rate mortgage (ARM)** allows the mortgage interest rate to adjust to market conditions. Its contract will specify a precise formula for this adjustment. The formula and the frequency of adjustment can vary among mortgage contracts. A common ARM uses a one-year adjustment, with the interest rate tied to the average Treasury bill rate over the previous year (for example, the average T-bill rate plus 2 percent may be specified).

Because the interest rate of the ARM moves with prevailing interest rates, financial institutions can stabilize their profit margin. If their cost of funds rises, so does their return on mortgage loans. For this reason, ARMs have become very popular over time, making up more than 60 percent of all new conventional single-family mortgages during 1984. However, during 1985 and 1986, the percentage declined as borrowers wanted to lock in the low market rates that existed at that time. The use of ARMs increased in 1987 once mortgage rates had risen.

Most ARMs specify a maximum allowable fluctuation in the mortgage rate per year and over the mortgage life, regardless of what happens to market interest rates. These so-called *caps* are commonly 2 percent per year and 5 percent for the mortgage lifetime. To the extent that market interest rates move outside these boundaries, the financial institution's profit margin on ARMs could be affected by interest rate fluctuations. Yet, this interest rate risk is significantly less than that of fixed-rate mortgages.

While the ARM reduces the uncertainty about the financial institution's profit margin, it creates uncertainty for the borrower, whose future mortgage payments will depend on future interest rates. Because some home purchasers prefer fixed-rate mortgages, lending institutions continue to offer them.

Some ARMs now contain an option clause that allows mortgage holders to switch to a fixed-rate within a specified period, such as one to five years after the mortgage is originated (the specific provisions vary).

Determination of Mortgage Rates

The mortgage rate quoted by a financial institution depends primarily on the prevailing market interest rates for similar mortgages, which in turn is influenced by the market cost of funds. Thus, the average market rate for a particular type of mortgage is used as a base and then is adjusted according to various factors. For example, if local competitors are offering lower rates than the national market, the rate may have to be adjusted downward. (Indeed, some institutions use just the local area as a more appropriate market rate than the national average.)

In addition to considering a market rate, the lending institution should also evaluate its flow of funds. If it has excess funds available to finance mortgages, it may reduce its mortgage rate slightly in order to attract more mortgage applications. The risk of the mortgage applicant does not have much impact on the mortgage rate, although it is evaluated to determine whether the mortgage application should be approved.

Exhibit 7.3 illustrates how mortgage rates have changed over time, following the pattern of long-term government security rates. They typically have a premium of from 1.3 to 3 percent, which compensates the mortgage holder for the additional credit risk and lower degree of marketability.

Another factor that affects the mortgage rate is whether the mortgage specifies a fixed or adjustable interest rate. Mortgage lenders normally charge a higher initial interest rate on the fixed-rate mortgage to compensate for incurring more interest rate risk. Exhibit 7.4 compares the interest rates of fixed versus adjustable-rate mortgages. The difference has generally been 1.5 to 3 percent.

Mortgage Maturities

During the 1970s, mortgages typically were originated with a 30-year maturity. However, the 15-year mortgage has recently become very popular due to the potential savings in total interest expenses. Exhibit 7.5 compares the payments necessary for 15- and 30-year mortgages based on various mortgage loan amounts and an 11 percent rate. For example, a $100,000

EXHIBIT 7.3   Comparison of Mortgage Rates to Other Rates Over Time

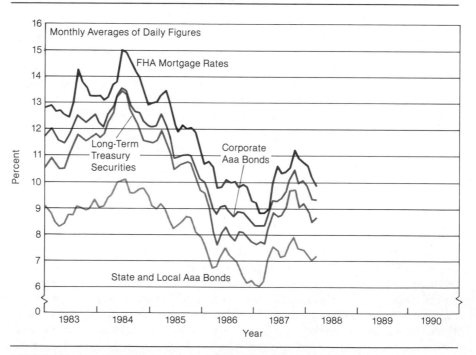

SOURCE: *Monetary Trends*, Federal Reserve Bank of St. Louis (April 1988): 12.

EXHIBIT 7.4   Mortgage Rates on New Fixed-Rate Mortgages versus New ARMs Over Time

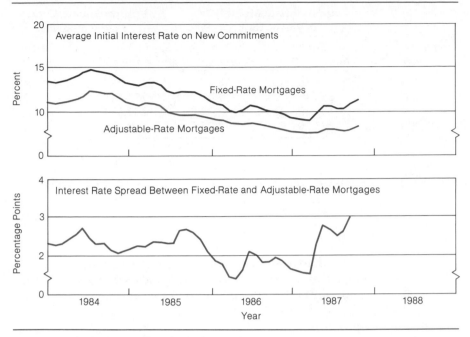

SOURCE: *Federal Reserve Bulletin* (December 1987): 899.

mortgage at 11 percent requires monthly payments (excluding taxes and insurance) of $952.32 over 30 years. The same mortgage would require monthly payments of $1,136.60 over 15 years, totaling $204,588 versus $342,835. The reduction in total payments on mortgages with shorter lives is due to the more rapid amortization and consequent lower cumulative interest. While mortgages with shorter lives can reduce total payments, their higher monthly payments represent an opportunity cost, as the additional funds could have been put to some other use. Yet, many borrowers believe that this disadvantage is outweighed by favorable features.

From the perspective of the lending financial institution, there is a lower degree of interest rate risk on a 15-year fixed-rate mortgage than on a 30-year fixed-rate mortgage, since the former exists for only half the period of the latter. Accordingly, financial institutions generally charge a lower interest rate on a 15-year loans than on 30-year loans, other provisions being equal.

An alternative to mortgages with 15- and 30-year maturities is the **balloon-payment mortgage,** which requires interest payments for a three- to five-year period. At the end of this period, full payment of the principal (the "balloon payment") is required. Because principal payments are not made until maturity, the monthly payments are lower. Realistically, most borrowers have not saved enough funds to pay off the mortgage in three to five years, so the balloon payment in effect forces them to request new mortgages and therefore subjects them to refinancing risk. In essence, the financial institution is providing a long-term loan, but it can periodically revise the

EXHIBIT 7.5 Comparison of Payments Necessary for 15- and 30-Year Mortgages (Based on an Interest Rate of 11 Percent)

Amount of Mortgage	Approximate Monthly Payment for a:		Approximate Total Payments for a:	
	15-Year Mortgage	30-Year Mortgage	15-Year Mortgage	30-Year Mortgage
$ 50,000	$ 568.30	$ 476.17	$102,294	$171,421
75,000	852.45	717.48	153,441	258,293
100,000	1,136.60	952.32	204,588	342,835
200,000	2,273.20	1,913.26	409,176	688,774

mortgage provisions (including the interest rate) at the time of each balloon payment.

Amortizing Mortgages

Given the maturity and interest rate on a mortgage, the **amortization schedule** can be developed to determine monthly payments broken down into principal and interest. During the early years of a mortgage, most of the payment reflects interest. Over time, as some of the principal has been paid off, the interest proportion decreases.

The lending institution that holds a fixed-rate mortgage will receive a fixed amount of equal periodic payments over a specified period of time. The amount depends on the principal amount of the mortgage, the interest rate, and the maturity. If insurance and taxes are to be included in the mortgage payment, then they, too, influence the amount. As an example, consider a 30-year (360 months) $100,000 mortgage that specifies an annual interest rate of 11 percent. In order to focus on the mortgage principal and interest payments, insurance and taxes are not included in this example. A breakdown of monthly principal versus monthly interest paid is shown in Exhibit 7.6. Note the larger proportion of interest paid in the earlier years and of principal paid in the later years. Computer programs are widely available to determine the amortization schedule for any type of mortgage.

CREATIVE MORTGAGE FINANCING

Exhibit 7.7 shows that the average purchase price of new homes has increased over time. The increase results from either (1) a trend toward building higher-quality homes or (2) increased land, labor, and material costs, or both. As the average purchase price increases, so does the average loan amount on new homes, as verified by the exhibit. Various methods of creative financing have been developed to make housing more affordable, including

- Graduated-payment mortgage
- Growing-equity mortgage
- Second mortgage
- Shared-appreciation mortgage

EXHIBIT 7.6 Example of Amortization Schedule for Selected Years
(Based on a 30-Year $100,000 Mortgage at 11 Percent)

Payment Number	Payment of Interest	Payment of Principal	Total Payment	Remaining Loan Balance
1	$916.67	$ 35.65	$952.32	$99,964.35
2	916.34	35.98	952.32	99,928.37
.	.	.	.	.
.	.	.	.	.
.	.	.	.	.
100	864.34	87.98	952.32	94,202.62
101	863.53	88.80	952.32	94,113.82
.	.	.	.	.
.	.	.	.	.
.	.	.	.	.
200	733.18	219.14	952.32	79,764.19
201	731.17	221.16	952.32	79,543.03
.	.	.	.	.
.	.	.	.	.
.	.	.	.	.
300	406.55	545.77	952.32	43,804.89
301	401.54	550.78	952.32	43,254.12
.	.	.	.	.
.	.	.	.	.
.	.	.	.	.
359	17.30	935.02	952.32	951.73
360	8.72	943.60	952.32	–0–

While these methods are the most common, several other innovative techniques exist. Moreover, as the needs and preferences of borrowers change over time, additional methods of creative financing are likely to emerge.

Graduated-Payment Mortgage (GPM)

The **graduated-payment mortgage (GPM)** allows borrowers to repay their loan on a graduated basis over the first 5 to 10 years; payments then level off from there on. GPMs are tailored for families who anticipate higher income and thus the ability to make larger monthly mortgage payments as time passes. In a sense, they are delaying part of their mortgage payment.

Growing-Equity Mortgage

A **growing-equity mortgage** is similar to the GPM in that the initial monthly payments are low and increase over time. Yet, unlike the GPM, the payments

EXHIBIT 7.7   Average Price and Loan Amounts on New Homes (in Thousands of Dollars)

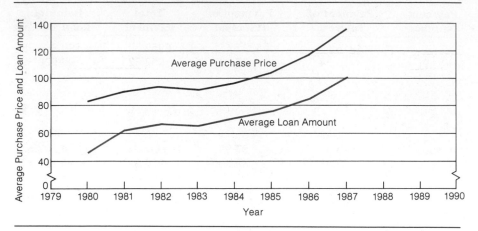

SOURCE: Federal Reserve Bulletin, various issues.

never level off but continue to increase (typically by about 4 percent per year) throughout the life of the loan. With such an accelerated payment schedule, the entire mortgage may be paid off in 15 years or less.

Second Mortgage

A second mortgage can be used in conjunction with the primary or first mortgage. Financial institutions may place a limit on the first mortgage amount based on the borrower's income. Yet, other financial institutions may consider offering a second mortgage, with a maturity shorter than on the first mortgage. In addition, the interest rate on the second mortgage is higher, because the second mortgage is behind the existing first mortgage in priority claim against the property in the event of default. The higher interest rate reflects greater compensation as a result of higher risk to providers of second mortgages.

Sellers of a home sometimes offer the buyers a second mortgage. This is especially common if the old mortgage is assumable, and if the selling price of the home is much higher than the remaining balance on the first mortgage. Through offering a second mortgage, the seller can make the house more affordable and therefore more marketable. The specific interest rate and maturity terms are negotiated between the seller and buyer.

Shared-Appreciation Mortgage

A **shared-appreciation mortgage** allows a home purchaser to obtain a mortgage at a below-market interest rate. In return, the lender providing the attractive loan rate will share in the price appreciation of the home. The precise percentage of appreciation allocated to the lender is negotiated at the origination of the mortgage.

RISK FROM HOLDING MORTGAGES

Financial institutions that hold mortgages in their asset portfolio are exposed to two types of risk. First, they incur interest rate risk, or the sensitivity of earnings (and net worth) to interest rate fluctuations. Because mortgages are long-term in nature, and deposits are commonly short-term, this interest rate risk is a primary concern. Of course, institutions with this type of balance sheet structure are not just adversely affected by rising interest rates; they also benefit from declining rates. Yet, the favorable impact is somewhat dampened, as a large proportion of mortgages are refinanced when interest rates decrease.

The second risk of mortgages is possible late payments or even default, referred to as credit or default risk. Exhibit 7.8 illustrates the delinquency rate of all mortgages over time. Note the somewhat consistent increase over the last 25 years. The most pronounced increases occur in recessionary periods such as 1974 and 1982. There is some concern that while ARMs reduce interest rate risk, they may increase credit risk, as borrowers may be unable to make mortgage payments during periods of increasing interest rates. Yet, lending financial institutions can obtain insurance to cover against default risk, if they are willing to pay the insurance premiums.

SECONDARY MORTGAGE MARKET ACTIVITIES

Financial institutions that originate mortgages sometimes sell them if they are short of cash. In addition, they may prefer to reduce their holdings of fixed-rate mortgages if interest rates are expected to increase. Some financial institutions such as mortgage companies may simply desire to service

short on cash
int rates ↑
service only,
no finance

EXHIBIT 7.8   Delinquency Rate of Mortgages Over Time

SOURCE: Adapted from *Economic Review*, Federal Reserve Bank of Kansas City (July–August 1985): 16.

mortgages (originate them, process payments, etc.), but not finance them. They periodically pool their recently originated mortgages together and sell them, but commonly continue to service them. For all these reasons, a secondary market for mortgages is desirable. It is not, however, as active as the secondary markets for other capital market instruments (such as stocks and bonds), because differing mortgage characteristics cannot be standardized as easily. In addition, the amount of each mortgage is small. Compare this to a financial institution's holdings of a corporation's bonds, which may represent an amount of $20 million or more. If it were to sell these bonds, a potential purchaser would need only one credit evaluation before making its decision. While a potential purchaser could buy a group of mortgages, it would need to evaluate the credit on each mortgage involved. If the mortgages were insured against default risk, then this credit check would not be necessary. Yet, the selling of a group of mortgages in the secondary market is still difficult, since the mortgages may have different interest rates, maturities, and so forth, complicating the evaluation process. However, mortgages with similar characteristics can be pooled to offer a more standardized product.

The financial institutions that ultimately finance mortgages may differ from the institutions that service them. Suppose USA Savings and Loan originates and services mortgages for a few years, then sells the mortgages to Safety Insurance Company but continues to service them. The borrowers continue to send their monthly mortgage payments to USA Savings Association, even though it is no longer holding claim to the mortgages. It processes the payments and charges the new holder of the mortgages (Safety Insurance Company) a fee for the processing. It deducts this fee from the mortgage payments received and sends the remainder to Safety Insurance Company.

Use of Mortgage-Backed Securities

As an alternative to selling their mortgages outright in the secondary market, financial institutions can issue *mortgage-backed securities*. While these securities come in various forms, the more common are **mortgage pass-through securities.** A group of mortgages held by a trustee of the issuing institution serves as collateral for these securities. The interest and principal payments on the mortgages are sent to the financial institution, which then transfers (passes through) the payments to the owners of the mortgage-backed securities, after deducting fees for servicing and for guaranteeing payments to the owners.

The issuance of pass-through securities can reduce interest rate risk, since it ties the payments received from mortgages to the payments sent to security owners. To the extent that the financial institutions use pass-through securities to finance mortgages holdings, they can insulate their profit margin from interest rate fluctuations. The interest and principal payments to owners of pass-through securities can vary over time. For example, if a higher-than-normal proportion of the mortgages backing the securities are prepaid in a specific period, these payments received by the financial institution will be passed through (after deducting a servicing fee) to the security owners.

Five of the more common types of pass-through securities are

- Ginnie Mae
- Fannie Mae
- Publicly issued
- Participation certificates
- Collateralized mortgage obligations (CMOs)

Each type is described in turn.

GINNIE MAE MORTGAGE-BACKED SECURITIES. Financial institutions issue securities that are backed by FHA and VA mortgages. The Government National Mortgage Association (GNMA), frequently referred to as Ginnie Mae, guarantees timely payment of principal and interest to investors that purchase these securities. The funds received from their sale are used to finance the mortgages. All mortgages pooled together to back Ginnie Mae pass-throughs must have the same interest rate. Then the interest rate received by purchasers of the pass-throughs is slightly less (typically 50 basis points) than that rate. This difference reflects a fee to the financial institution servicing the loan and to GNMA for guaranteeing full payment of interest and principal to the security purchasers.

FANNIE MAE MORTGAGE-BACKED SECURITIES. The Federal National Mortgage Association (FNMA), commonly referred to as Fannie Mae, issues mortgage-backed securities and uses the funds to purchase mortgages. In essence, Fannie Mae channels funds from investors to financial institutions that desire to sell their mortgages. These financial institutions may continue to service the mortgages and would earn a fee for this service, while Fannie Mae receives a fee for guaranteeing timely payment of principal and interest to the holders of the mortgage-backed securities. The mortgage payments on mortgages backing these securities are sent to the financial institutions that service the mortgages. The payments are channeled through to the purchasers of mortgage-backed securities, which may be collateralized by conventional or federally insured mortgages. Exhibit 7.9 illustrates Fannie Mae's increasing use of mortgage-backed securities. By 1988 there were more than $140 billion outstanding in them.

PUBLICLY ISSUED PASS-THROUGH SECURITIES (PIPs). Another type of pass-through security, called PIPs are similar to GNMA mortgage-backed securities, except that they are backed by conventional rather than FHA or VA mortgages. The mortgages backing the securities are insured through private insurance companies.

PARTICIPATION CERTIFICATES (PCs). The Federal Home Loan Mortgage Association, called **Freddie Mac,** sells **participation certificates (PCs)** and uses the proceeds to finance the origination of conventional mortgages from financial institutions. This provides another outlet (in addition to Fannie Mae) for savings associations and savings banks that desire to sell their conventional mortgages in the secondary market.

EXHIBIT 7.9 Fannie Mae's Use of Mortgage-backed Securities (Outstanding at End of Quarter)

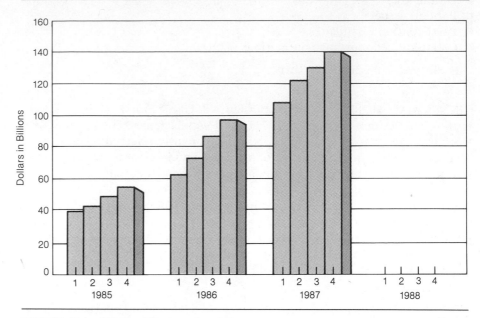

SOURCE: Federal National Mortgage Association

COLLATERALIZED MORTGAGE OBLIGATIONS (CMOs). In 1983 **collateralized mortgage obligations (CMOs)** were developed. They have semiannual interest payments, unlike other mortgage-backed securities that have monthly payments. The CMOs that represent a particular mortgage pool are segmented into classes (or *tranches*). The first class has the quickest payback. Any repaid principal is initially sent to owners of the first-class CMOs, until the total principal amount representing that class is fully repaid. Then any further principal payments are sent to owners of the second-class CMOs, until the total principal amount representing that class is fully repaid. This process continues until principal payments are made to owners of the last-class CMOs. CMO issues commonly have between 3 and 10 classes.

The attractive feature of CMOs is that investors can choose a class that will fit their maturity desires. Even though investors are still uncertain as to when the securities will mature, they have a better feel for the maturity structure than with other pass-through securities. Investors who purchase third-class CMOs know that they will not receive any principal payments until the first- and second-class CMO owners are completely paid off. CMOs have become quite popular in the short period in which they have been in existence and are likely to be used even more frequently in the future.

Tailoring Mortgage-Backed Securities for the Small Investor

Pass-through securities have been historically restricted to large investors. Ginnie Mae pass-throughs, for example, come in minimum denominations

Fannie Mae's Battle against Interest Rate Risk

Fannie Mae has historically made a secondary market for mortgages. It was created in 1938 with the intent of purchasing government-guaranteed mortgages from financial institutions that desired to sell them. Since it reorganized into a privately owned corporation in 1968, it also has purchased conventional mortgage loans. To finance its purchases, Fannie Mae issues short-term notes as well as intermediate and long-term securities to investors. It pays slightly lower interest rates on the securities it issues than the rates received on the mortgages it buys. Its asset-portfolio profits are generated from this interest rate spread. Fannie Mae's actions result in a transfer of funds from investors to those financial institutions that are selling mortgages. Fannie Mae holds the mortgages, and the investors hold the debt securities it issues.

In 1981 and 1982 Fannie Mae experienced losses of more than $100 million, primarily because the average lifetime of mortgages purchased exceeded that of the securities it issued. Consequently, its cost of funds was more sensitive to interest rate movements than its return on mortgages. When interest rates increased, the cost of funds increased, but its return on mortgages remained somewhat stable, and its interest margin became negative.

To reduce its exposure to interest rate risk, Fannie Mae now commonly buys adjustable-rate mortgages. The return generated by these mortgages moves in tandem with interest rate fluctuations. In addition, Fannie Mae now buys 15-year mortgages, and second mortgages, which have shorter maturities than the traditional 30-year mortgages. The market values of these mortgages are less sensitive than 30-year mortgages to interest rate movements. Fannie Mae also increased the maturities on the securities it issues to make them more similar to the maturities of its mortgage holdings. Now that its return on mortgages and its cost of funds are similarly sensitive to interest rate changes, its interest rate spread has been somewhat stable in recent years. Fannie Mae is now more capable of insulating itself against interest rate fluctuations.

of $25,000, with $5,000 increments above. In recent years, however, unit trusts have been created that allow small investors to participate. For example, a portfolio of Ginnie Mae pass-through securities is sold in $1,000 pieces. Each piece represents a tiny fraction of the overall portfolio of securities. These unit trusts have become very popular in recent years. The composition of the portfolio is not adjusted over time.

Some mutual funds offer Ginnie Mae funds, which like the unit trusts, represent a portfolio of GNMA pass-through securities. Yet, unlike the unit trust, the composition of the mutual fund's portfolio can be actively managed (adjusted) by the securities firm over time. As would be expected, the market values of Ginnie Mae unit trusts and mutual funds are inversely related to interest rate movements. The Ginnie Mae unit trust is more sensitive to increasing interest rates since its composition cannot be adjusted. A mutual fund can modify the Ginnie Mae portfolio composition (shift to shorter-term maturities) if it anticipates increasing interest rates.

Chapter 7

Mortgage Markets

Some mutual funds also invest in Fannie Mae mortgage-backed securities and PCs (participation certificates), allowing the small investor access to them.

Pass-through securities are attractive because they can be purchased in the secondary market without purchasing the servicing of the mortgages that back them. In addition, the holders of pass-throughs are insured in the event of default. Furthermore, they are very liquid and can be used as collateral for repurchase agreements. Yet, the performance of pass-throughs is susceptible to the borrower's prepayment habits. Prepayments increase when market interest rates fall below the mortgage rates, because of the high frequency of refinancing, and decrease when market interest rates exceed mortgage rates. Thus, the maturities of pass-throughs will be shorter during the former periods and longer during the latter. Investors in pass-through securities would prefer just the opposite situation. They benefit most when market interest rates fall below mortgage rates, since their return remains fixed.

BREAKDOWN OF MORTGAGE HOLDINGS AMONG INSTITUTIONS

Financial institutions such as savings institutions and commercial banks originate and service mortgages. Yet, other financial institutions also participate by investing in mortgages. Exhibit 7.10 provides a breakdown of financial institutions that purchase and hold mortgages. Note that savings institutions dominate. The financial institutions identified here hold in aggregate about 62 percent of the entire dollar amount of all mortgages.

Exhibit 7.11 classifies the mortgages of the financial institutions into four types of borrower categories. The savings institutions dominate the one- to four-family and multifamily markets. They also participate in commercial mortgages, but to a lesser degree. They have continually increased their participation in commercial mortgages in recent years, however. Commercial banks dominate the commercial mortgage market, with life insurance companies behind them. Commercial banks also heavily participate in residential mortgages but are far behind savings institutions in that market.

Another type of financial institution that participates in the mortgage business is the mortgage company. Because it quickly sells the mortgages it originates, it does not maintain a large mortgage portfolio. The majority of its earnings are generated from origination and servicing fees. Because

EXHIBIT 7.10   Breakdown of Mortgages by Holder (in Millions of Dollars)

Holder	Dollar Amount of Mortgages Held	Percent of Total Mortgages Held
Savings institutions	$ 840,251	51.0%
Commercial banks	563,553	34.2
Life insurance companies	204,632	12.5
Finance companies	38,328	2.3
Total financial institutional holdings	$1,646,764	100.0%

SOURCE: *Federal Reserve Bulletin* (March 1988): A39.

EXHIBIT 7.11 Breakdown of Mortgage Holdings among Financial Institutions (in Millions of Dollars)

	Mortgages Allocated to:				
	1- to 4-Family	Multifamily	Commercial	Farm	Total
Savings institutions	$580,605	$107,629	$151,213	$ 804	$840,251
Commercial banks	264,983	30,995	253,261	14,314	563,553
Life insurance companies	12,745	21,863	159,811	10,213	204,632
Finance companies	38,328	0	0	0	38,328

SOURCE: *Federal Reserve Bulletin* (March 1988): A39.

mortgage companies do not typically finance mortgages themselves, they are not as exposed to interest rate risk as other financial institutions. Yet, risk is still a major concern.

As mortgage companies originate mortgages, they pool them together and then sell the entire pool at once. When a mortgage is originated, it has market value similar to the face value. As market interest rates change, though, the market value of the mortgage changes. Investors are willing to pay more for a given fixed-rate mortgage if market interest rates are lower, since that mortgage offers locked-in payments. Conversely, investors would pay less for such mortgages if market interest rates are higher at the time. The mortgage company's concern is that market interest rates might increase from the time the mortgage is originated until it is sold. Even though mortgage companies tend to sell the mortgages they originate within a short period of time, just a small change in interest rates over this period can significantly affect the value of the mortgages.

Exhibit 7.12 discloses the federal and related agency holdings of mortgages. Fannie Mae dominates these holdings. Yet, its mortgage holdings are lower than those of three types of financial institutions shown in Exhibit 7.10. In addition to financial institutions and federal-related agencies, mortgages are also held by individuals and other investors. Investor interest in mortgages has increased since the creation of Ginnie Mae unit trusts and mutual funds.

INSTITUTIONAL USE OF MORTGAGE MARKETS

The discussion up to this point has implied how some types of financial institutions participate in the mortgage markets. A summary of the institutional use of mortgage markets is provided in Exhibit 7.13. Most institutional participation could be broadly classified as either (1) originating and servicing or (2) financing. Commercial banks and savings institutions are the primary originators of mortgages. These institutions along with credit unions, finance companies, mutual funds, and insurance companies help finance mortgages by maintaining them in their investment portfolios.

Some institutional participation in mortgage markets represents neither origination nor financing of mortgages. Brokerage firms participate by matching up sellers and buyers of mortgages in the secondary market. Investment banking firms participate by helping institutional investors hedge their mortgage holdings against interest rate risk. They offer interest rate

EXHIBIT 7.12 Breakdown of Federal and Related Agency Holdings of Mortgages (in Millions of Dollars)

Federal and Related Agencies	Dollar Amount	Percent of Federal and Agency Related Holdings
Federal National Mortgage Association (FNMA)	$ 94,884	49.5%
Government National Mortgage Association (GNMA)	654	.4
Federal land banks	34,930	18.2
Other	61,093	31.9
Total federal and related agency holdings	191,561	100.0

NOTE: These figures do not include mortgage-backed securities outstanding, of which Ginnie Mae has over $229 billion, Fannie Mae has $81 billion, and Freddie Mac has $100 billion.

SOURCE: *Federal Reserve Bulletin* (March 1988): A39.

EXHIBIT 7.13 Institutional Use of Mortgage Markets

Type of Financial Institution	Participation in Mortgage Markets
Commercial banks and savings institutions	■ Originate commercial and residential mortgages, service mortgages, and maintain mortgages within their investment portfolios ■ Issue mortgage-backed securities to finance some of their mortgage holdings
Credit unions and finance companies	■ Originate mortgages and maintain mortgages within their investment portfolios
Mutual funds	■ Have sold shares and used the proceeds to construct portfolios of pass-through securities
Brokerage firms	■ Serve as financial intermediaries between sellers and buyers of mortgages in the secondary market
Investment banking firms	■ Offer techniques to help institutional investors in mortgages hedge against interest rate risk
Insurance companies	■ Commonly purchase mortgages in the secondary market

swaps to these institutions, which provide a stream of variable-rate payments in exchange for fixed-rate payments. Savings institutions are the most common users of interest rate swaps. The manner by which savings institutions use swaps to hedge interest rate risk is discussed in Chapter 21.

INTERNATIONALIZATION OF MORTGAGE MARKETS

Mortgage market activity is not confined within a single country. For example, non–U.S. financial institutions hold mortgages on U.S. property, and vice versa. Large U.S. banks often maintain mortgage-banking subsidiaries in foreign countries. In addition, the use of interest rate swaps to hedge mortgages in the U.S. often involves a non–U.S. counterpart. While investment banking firms may serve as the financial intermediary, they commonly search for a non–U.S. financial institution that desires to swap variable-rate payments in exchange for fixed-rate payments.

Participants in mortgage markets closely follow international economic conditions because of the potential impact on interest rates. Bond- and mortgage-portfolio decisions are highly influenced by announcements related to the value of the dollar. In general, any announcements that imply a potentially weaker dollar tend to cause expectations of higher U.S. inflation and therefore higher U.S. interest rates. The demand for fixed-rate mortgages would likely decline in response to such announcements. Announcements that imply a potentially stronger dollar tend to cause the opposite expectations and effects. However, it is difficult to show evidence of these relationships, because expectations do not always occur and often change from one day to the next.

SUMMARY

Sweeping changes have occurred in the mortgage markets in recent years. New types of mortgages have been created to better accommodate the borrowers as well as the financial institutions that offer mortgages. In addition, recent innovative strategies have allowed financial institutions to sell their mortgages more easily in the secondary market. The changing structure of mortgage markets enables financial institutions to adjust the balance of their mortgage lending and servicing functions to whatever degree they desire.

KEY TERMS

adjustable-rate mortgage (ARM)
amortization schedule
balloon-payment mortgage
collateralized mortgage
    obligations (CMOs)
fixed-rate mortgage
Freddie Mac

graduated-payment mortgage
    (GPM)
growing-equity mortgage
mortgage pass-through securities
participation certificates (PCs)
shared-appreciation mortgage

QUESTIONS

7.1. Distinguish between FHA and conventional mortgages.

7.2. Explain how mortgage lenders can be affected by interest rate movements. Also explain how they can insulate against interest rate movements.

Chapter 7

Mortgage Markets

7.3. Explain how "caps" on adjustable-rate mortgages can affect a financial institution's exposure to interest rate risk.

7.4. What is the general relationship between mortgage rates and long-term government security rates.

7.5. How does the initial rate on adjustable rate mortgages differ from the rate on fixed-rate mortgages? Why?

7.6. Why is the 15-year mortgage attractive to homeowners?

7.7. Is the interest rate risk to the financial institution higher for a 15-year or 30-year mortgage? Why?

7.8. Explain the use of a balloon-payment mortgage. Why might a financial institution prefer to offer this type of mortgage?

7.9. Describe the graduated-payment mortgage. What type of homeowners would prefer this type of mortgage?

7.10. Describe the growing-equity mortgage. How does it differ from a graduated-payment mortgage?

7.11. Why are second mortgages offered by some home sellers?

7.12. Describe the shared-appreciation mortgage.

7.13. Mortgage lenders with fixed-rate mortgages should benefit when interest rates decline. Yet, research has shown that such a favorable impact is dampened. By what?

7.14. Describe the trend in mortgage delinquencies over the last several years.

7.15. Explain why some financial institutions prefer to sell the mortgages they originate.

7.16. Compare the secondary market activity for mortgages to the other capital market instruments (such as stocks and bonds). Provide a general explanation for the difference in the activity level.

7.17. Describe how mortgage pass-through securities are used. How can the use of pass-through securities reduce a financial institution's interest rate risk?

7.18. Describe how collateralized mortgage obligations (CMOs) are used and why they have been popular.

7.19. Explain how the maturity on pass-through securities can be affected by interest rate movements.

7.20. What type of financial institution finances the majority of one- to four-family mortgages? What type of financial institution finances the majority of commercial mortgages?

7.21. Explain how the mortgage company's degree of exposure to interest rate risk differs from other financial institutions.

7.22. Explain Fannie Mae's participation in the mortgage market. Explain why Fannie Mae experienced losses in 1981 and 1982. How has Fannie Mae reduced its exposure to interest rate risk in recent years?

PROJECT

1. ASSESSING MORTGAGE RATES.

In the "Money Rates" section of *The Wall Street Journal* (WSJ), rates on conventional fixed-rate mortgages are quoted (see "Federal Home Loan Mortgage Corporation). Obtain data on this rate and the 30-year Treasury bond rate (quoted in the section of the WSJ called "Yield Comparisons") for the beginning of each of the last six months. Describe any movements in the mortgage rates over this six-month period. Have mortgage rates changed because of a general change in market interest rates, a change in the risk perception of mortgages, or both? Explain.

REFERENCES

"ARMs: Their Financing Rate and Impact on Housing." *FRBNY Quarterly Review* (Autumn 1985): 39–49.

Bennett, Barbara. "Fannie Mae's New Standards." *FRBSF Weekly Letter*, November 19, 1985.

Brick, John R. "A Primer on Mortgage-Backed Securities." *The Bankers Magazine* (January–February 1984): 44–52.

Buynak, Thomas M. *Economic Commentary*, Federal Reserve Bank of Cleveland, January 15, 1985.

"Call to ARMs." *FRBSF Weekly Letter*, October 5, 1984.

Cassidy, Henry J., "Monte Carlo Simulation Estimates of the Expected Value of the Due-on-Sale Clause in Home Mortgages." *Housing Finance Review* (January 1983): 33–52.

Dietrich, J. Kimball, Terrence C. Langetieg, David Dale-Johnson, and Tim S. Campbell. "The Economic Effects of Due-on-Sale Clause Invalidation." *Housing Finance Review* (January 1983): 19–32.

"Fannie Mae's New Standards." *FRBSF Weekly Letter*, November 29, 1985.

Furlong, Frederick T. "Savings and Loan Asset Composition and the Mortgage Market." *Economic Review*, Federal Reserve Bank of San Francisco (Summer 1985): 14–24.

Green, Jerry and John B. Shoven. "The Effects of Interest Rates on Mortgage Prepayments." *Journal of Money, Credit, and Banking* (February 1986): 41–59.

Hendershott, Patrick H. and Sheng Hu. "Accelerating Inflation and Nonassumable Fixed-Rate Mortgages: Effects on Consumer Choice and Welfare." *Public Finance Quarterly* (April 1982): 158–184.

Hendershott, Patrick H., Sheng Hu, and Kevin E. Villani. "The Economics of Mortgage Terminations: Implications for Mortgage Lenders and Mortgage Terms." *Housing Finance Review* (April 1983): 127–142.

Loud, James F. "Automating the Mortgage Origination Process." *The Bankers Magazine* (May–June 1984): 34–37.

Kau, James, Donald Keenan, Walter Muller III, and James Epperson. "The Valuation and Securitization of Commercial and Multifamily Mortgages." *Journal of Banking and Finance* (September 1987): 525–546.

Manchester, Joyce. "Mortgage Finance: Why Not PLAMs" *Economic Review*, Federal Reserve Bank of Kansas City (September–October 1984): 31–44.

Palash, Carl J. and Robert B. Stoddard. "ARMs: Their Financing Rate and Impact on Housing." *FRBNY Quarterly Review* (Autumn 1984): 39–49.

Pozdena, Randall J. "Call to ARMs." *FRBSF Weekly Letter*, October 5, 1984.

Roberts, William and Michael J. Stutzer. "Adjustable Rate Mortgages." *Quarterly Review*, Federal Reserve Bank of Minneapolis (Summer 1985): 10–20.

Stutzer, Michael J. and William Roberds. "Adjustable Rate Mortgages: Increasing Efficiency More Than Housing Activity." *Quarterly Review*, Federal Reserve Bank of Minneapolis (Summer 1985): 10–20.

"The New Appeal of Mortgage Securities." *Business Week*, March 12, 1984, 136–138.

"The Rise of Quick Pay Mortgages." *Newsweek*, December 10, 1984: 72.

"Why Fannie Mae No Longer Wears Red." *Business Week*, January 30, 1984, 65–68.

APPENDIX 7

Mortgage Securitization & REMICs

Increasingly, the assets of traditional lenders such as banks and thrifts are being used to back traded securities—a process known as securitization. (See the *Weekly Letter* dated July 4, 1986.) Nowhere is this trend more evident than in the mortgage arena. Up until a decade ago, it was common practice for mortgage lenders to keep the mortgages they originated in their own portfolios. Increasingly, however, *mortgages are being "securitized"—a process that involves creation of a security backed by mortgage loans.* Holders of these securities receive interest and principal payments that are supported by the underlying mortgages and the securities often can be traded freely in the marketplace. Individual savers, pension funds, and other financial institutions invest in mortgage-backed securities.

With the passage of the 1986 Tax Act, the pace of mortgage securitization is likely to quicken still further. The new tax law permits creation of Real Estate Mortgage Investment Conduits (REMICs), legal devices that allow mortgage-backed securities to be better tailored to the needs of investors and issuers. This *Weekly Letter* discusses the major forms of mortgage securitization, and role of REMICs in this process.

BACKGROUND: MORTGAGE-BACKED SECURITIES

Securitization of mortgages is motivated by two forces. First, the banks and thrifts that originate mortgages can employ securitization to achieve desired changes in their balance sheet. For example, if mortgage assets can be "sold out of portfolio", compliance with regulators' capital/risk-asset ratio regulation can be facilitated. The simplest securitization process that achieves this goal involves creation of a Mortgage Pass-through Security (MPS). This process involves selling the mortgages into a trust (called a "grantor" trust) that then issues securities backed by the underlying mortgages. The payments made on the underlying mortgage are "passed through" unaltered to the security holder.

Second, mortgage securitization potentially permits transformation of mortgage debt into securities that satisfy the diverse tastes of investors for different patterns of cash-flow, risk and other investment features. A simple MPS can do little to transform the underlying mortgage into more attractive instruments. (Indeed, by its very nature it takes on precisely the features of the underlying mortgages, including an uncertain effective maturity because of the possibility of prepayment of the mortgages.) Two other devices, the Mortgage-Backed Bond and the Collateralized Mortgage Obligation, however, offer the means of transforming mortgage assets in a more radical way.

THE MORTGAGE-BACKED BOND

The Mortgage-Backed Bond (MBB) does not pass the payments through untransformed; rather, the issuer of an MBB creates a fixed-term ("call protected") instrument with fixed coupon payments. Unlike the case of the MPS, therefore, the payment flows generated by the underlying mortgages will not match precisely the timing of the coupon and principal payment obligations of the MBB. Thus the market requires that issuers of the MBBs (the holders of the underlying mortgages) overcollateralize MBB issues so that a "buffer" of extra mortgage payments and principal is available to meet unanticipated deviations between the two payment streams. The difference between the value of the collateral and the value of the MBB liabilities issued represents, in effect, an equity investment on the part of the issuer.

Thus, although the mortgage-backed bond provides investors with a more-nearly "bond like" instrument than the MPS, it does not relieve the issuer of mortgage assets on his books; they remain there as collateral for the MBB liabilities sold by the issuer. In addition, some argue that the degree of overcollateralization required by security-rating agencies for the MBBs to achieve investment-grade ratings is more than the market itself would require. This limits the extent to which a given dollar value of mortgage assets can be securitized. These considerations likely are responsible for the trivial size of the MBB market in comparison to other mortgage-backed securities.

MULTI-CLASS PASSTHROUGHS: THE CMO

To ideally serve both the portfolio-management goals of the originator of the mortgage and the needs of investors, mortgage securitization would both create an asset "sale" out of portfolio (as the MPS does) and permit transformation of the mortgage payment stream (as the MBB does). An obvious way to achieve both results would be to use mortgages to back *multiclass* passthrough securities; the mortgages would be "sold" into a trust which then would issue security classes with different priorities to the mortgage payment flows or different seniority of claims on the collateral of the mortgages. The transaction would generate the desired asset sale from the viewpoint of the issuer, while creating instruments with an attractive range of maturity and default characteristics.

In an important Internal Revenue Service ruling in the early 1980's, however, several impediments against the issuance of such multiclass pass-throughs were posed. The IRS ruled that trusts set up to hold mortgages and issue such securities would not be given the favorable tax treatment afforded grantor trusts, namely, insulation from corporate income tax liability. Accordingly, the only way that a pool of mortgages could be securitized effectively into multiple class securities was by issuing a variety of debt obligations collateralized by mortgages although this, of course, did not achieve the goal of effecting "sale" of the mortgage assets out of portfolio.

Such multiclass debt obligations are referred to as Collateralized Mortgage Obligations (CMOs). The CMO works by using the interest and principal payments flowing from the mortgage loans to service several classes or "tranches" of debt securities. Specifically, interest and principal payments are used first to service and retire the first CMO security class (typically, Class A). No retirement of the next class (Class B) occurs until all Class A securities are retired and so on through the various classes of CMOs, implicitly endowing each successive class with increasing call protection. The last CMO security class (sometimes called a "Z-bond") is an instrument that receives no interest coupons and is only retired ("reaches maturity") after all other classes have been retired.

LIMITATIONS ON CMOS

CMOs have been attractive alternatives to MPs and MBBs for both issuers and investors. Like the MBB, the multi-class nature of the CMO permits those buyers of CMOs who wish it to obtain some call protection. The CMO has an advantage over the MBB, however, in that its coupon and principal payments are linked to the underlying mortgage payments. This permits the issuer to hold relatively little equity in the CMO, so that funds more nearly equal to the full amount of the underlying mortgage collateral can be raised by selling the CMOs.

The main disadvantage of CMOs is that, as debt obligations, they remain on the balance sheet of the issuer as liabilities (and the mortgages remain as assets). This makes it harder for the issuer to achieve standards of capital adequacy employed by regulators or rating agencies. In addition, in order not to violate the IRS definition of collateralized debt (and thus be classified as a taxable multiclass trust), other criteria had to be met by CMOs that had the effect of limiting their application. Specifically, issuers could not issue tranches with high default risk potential (that is, with a junior claim on the underlying mortgages in the event of default). Also, in order to qualify as true "debt", the mortgage-backed instruments had to use a semi-annual payment convention. These and other restrictions limited the usefulness and flexibility of CMOs.

ENTER REMICS

Subtitle H of the Tax Reform Act of 1986 dramatically alters these circumstances by creating a new legal device called a Real Estate Mortgage Conduit (REMIC). The REMIC is a separate legal entity for tax purposes into which issuers can "sell" mortgage assets and which can issue mortgage-backed securities. It is not a taxable entity if it is used as a conduit for passing mortgage payments to holders of mortgage-backed securities even if those securities are multi-class securities. Indeed, the securities can be very complex, with diverse claims on the interest, principal and real estate collateral of the underlying mortgages. The REMIC thus offers all of the opportunity to effect a "sale" of mortgage assets out of the issuer's portfolio as well as the ability to issue multi-class securities in whatever form is attractive to the marketplace—all without the previous constraints imposed by tax law.

REMICs will facilitate the securitization of the traditional mortgage into instruments with various degrees of call protection and cash flow characteristics. They obviously will facilitate the issuance of the traditional CMO-like securities backed by conventional mortgages, since they remove the previous impediments to multiclass passthroughs. By removing the restrictions on the nature of the securities that can be issued without adverse tax consequences, however, a wider variety of mortgages should be able to be securitized. Adjustable rate mortgages, for example, have been difficult to securitize as single-class passthroughs because of the uncertainty in payment flows created by the interest rate caps, payment caps and negative amoritization features associated with these mortgages. Although there currently is legal debate over the applicability of the new law in this area, with REMICs, adjustable rate mortgages potentially could be "unbundled" into component securities attractive to the investor marketplace.

REMICS AND GOVERNMENT MORTGAGE POLICY

REMICs also may present an opportunity to reduce the level of government involvement in the secondary mortgage markets. At the present time, various Federal credit agencies and government-sponsored intermediaries are involved in the business of guaranteeing mortgages or securities backed by qualifying mortgages. One rationale for this involvement is that, without such guarantees, the default risk potential of certain types of mortgages would deter the average investor for investing in mortgage-backed securities. This, in turn, would restrain development of a liquid secondary market for mortgage assets and, indirectly, the mortgage market generally.

Securitization offers an alternative means of dealing with the risk in the mortgage market. A pool of mortgages could be transformed into a family of securities which differ in the seniority of their claim to the underlying mortgages and, hence, their default potential. This would effectively "unbundle" the mortgage debt into low- and high-risk securities better tailored to the diversity of risk/return preferences that exist among investors. Under previous tax law, the issuance of "junior" claims exposed issuers to adverse tax treatment (although a limited number of uninsured mortgage pools were securitized in this way nonetheless). With REMICs, these barriers can be removed, facilitating this type of securitization. In such an environment, the role of government as guarantor may not be as necessary to stimulate liquid markets for mortgage assets.

SOURCE: This appendix is a reprint of the *FRBSF Weekly Letter*, May 8, 1987. The author of the article is Randall Pozdena.

Other Financial Markets

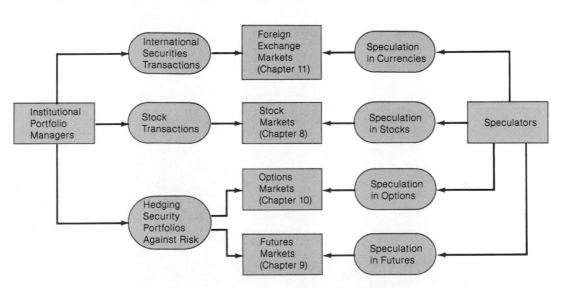

The chapters in Part Three focus on financial markets other than credit markets. Each of these chapters explains how institutional portfolio managers and speculators use particular markets. Many financial market participants simultaneously use all four types of markets, as is emphasized throughout these chapters.

Stock Markets

STOCK MARKETS IN PERSPECTIVE

Stock markets around the world generally rallied for several months after the October 19, 1987, crash. Several explanations were offered for the rally in U.S. stock prices. The explanations often changed from one day to the next. *The Wall Street Journal* offered the following reasons for the rally on June 23, 1988:

■ Foreign investors expected that the dollar's value had little potential to decline and much potential to rise. Thus, they became more willing to invest in dollar-denominated assets such as U.S. stocks.
■ Some foreign investors expected that Japanese stock prices had peaked out, and the investors switched to U.S. stocks.

On this same day, stock prices of major companies changed in different directions and to different degrees. *The Wall Street Journal's* explanation of these price movements identifies some of the key factors that affect individual stock prices.

■ Large banks such as Citicorp and Chase Manhattan experienced gains because of anticipated increases in 1988 earnings.
■ GAF's stock price fell in response to concern about a possible securities law violation that was being investigated.
■ UAL stock increased by $3.50 per share as Merrill Lynch increased its estimate of UAL's 1988 earnings.
■ Rorer Group stock increased by over 5 percent on this single day as a result of takeover rumors.
■ Birmingham Steel stock decreased by about $1.60 per share, possibly in response to its plans to issue more stock in the market.

■ What factors affect the general stock market trends?
■ What caused the stock market crash on October 19, 1987?
■ What other factors, in addition to those cited above, affect stock prices of individual companies?
■ What financial institutions participate in the stock markets?
■ How have stock markets become internationalized over time?

These and other related questions are addressed in this chapter.

OUTLINE

This chapter first provides a background on common stock and preferred stock, then describes how stocks are publicly placed in the market. Next, it describes the secondary market trading of stocks at security exchanges and explains how financial institutions participate in stock markets. Finally, it explains how stock markets have become internationalized.

BACKGROUND ON COMMON STOCK

Like other securities, common stock is a medium by which funds can be obtained. However, the purchaser of stock becomes part owner, rather than just a creditor. While the issuing corporation is not obligated to repurchase this stock at any time in the future, stockholders can sell it to other investors within the secondary market.

The ownership of common stock entitles stockholders to a number of rights not available to other individuals. Normally, only the owners of common stock are permitted to vote on certain key matters concerning the firm. Among those key matters are the election of the board of directors, authorization to issue new shares of common stock, approval of amendments to the corporate charter, and adoption of by-laws and merger proposals. While the exercise of control is important to the stockholders of smaller firms, it is frequently unimportant to the stockholders of large firms. The reason is that management of large firms normally request that stockholders

How Changes in Risk Ratings Affect Stock Returns

Bond ratings serve as a measurement of a firm's risk. If they contain useful information not known by the market, then they should influence the perceived risk of the stock. Thus, the stock price should change also. If they do not provide new information, they should not influence stock prices.

A recent study by Holthausen and Leftwich used *cumulative average residual (CAR)* analysis to determine whether stock returns were influenced by downgrades in ratings by Moody's and Standard and Poor's. (See the appendix of Chapter 18 for more information on CAR analysis.) The analysis detected negative abnormal stock returns for two days, beginning with the day that a downgrade in bond ratings was announced. An upgrade announcement, however, produced little evidence of abnormal performance. The results suggest that the downgrade announcements signal more valuable information than upgrade announcements.

SOURCE: Robert W. Holthausen and Richard W. Leftwich, "The Effect of Bond Rating Changes on Common Stock Prices," *Journal of Financial Economics* (September 1986): 57–89.

transfer their right to vote to management. Many investors comply by assigning their vote to management through the use of a *proxy*. Many other stockholders simply fail to vote at all. As a result, management normally receives the majority of the votes and can elect its own candidates as directors. If investors become dissatisfied with the firm's performance, they can compete with management in the solicitation of proxy votes in what is known as a *proxy fight*. If the dissident stockholders can gain enough votes, they can elect one or more directors who share their views. In this case, stockholders are truly exercising their control.

Investors can purchase stock *on margin*, or with borrowed funds, by signing up for a margin account with their broker. The margin limit is 50 percent, meaning they can use as much as 50 percent borrowed funds (from the brokerage firm) to purchase stocks. Over a short-term period, the return on stocks purchased on margin *(R)* can be estimated as follows:

$$R = \frac{SP - I - LP + D}{I}$$

where SP = selling price

I = initial investment by investor, not including borrowed funds

LP = loan payments paid on borrowed funds, including both principal and interest

D = dividend payments

Consider a stock priced at $40 that pays an annual dividend of $1 per share. Investors purchase the stock on margin, paying $20 per share and borrowing the remainder from the brokerage firm at 10 percent annualized.

Chapter 8

Stock Markets

If after one year, the stock is sold at a price of $60 per share, the return on the stock would be

$$R = \frac{\$60 - \$20 - \$22 + 1}{\$20}$$
$$= \frac{\$19}{\$20}$$
$$= 95\%$$

The brokerage firm has the right to demand more collateral (more cash or stocks) or to sell the stock if the stock price declines by a specified amount. Investors must respond to this so-called **margin call** if the market is crashing. During the stock market crash in October 1987, those who did not have cash available to respond to the margin call sold their stock, causing additional downward pressure on stock prices.

BACKGROUND ON PREFERRED STOCK

Since all creditors and preferred stockholders must be compensated before common stockholders, owners of common stock have a *residual claim* on firm income. All or part of the earnings available to common stockholders is paid out in the form of cash dividends. The remaining portion is reinvested in the firm and appears on the balance sheet as an increase in retained earnings. The expectation of higher future dividends as a result of reinvested earnings can cause a more rapid increase in the market price of the firm's common stock. Therefore, stockholders should benefit from both the payment of dividends and the retention of earnings.

When a firm is liquidated as a result of bankruptcy (or for any other reason), all creditors are paid the principal and interest owed to them, then preferred stockholders are repaid for their initial investment before common stockholders receive anything. The amount of payment to preferred stockholders is based on either the *par value* or the *liquidation value* of the preferred stock, depending on which is specified at the time of issue.

Unlike creditors, who can force the liquidation of the firm in order to satisfy their claims, preferred stockholders technically share the ownership of the firm with common stockholders and are therefore compensated only when earnings have been generated. Therefore, if the firm does not have sufficient earnings from which to pay the preferred stock dividends, it may omit the dividend without fear of being forced into bankruptcy. A **cumulative provision** on most preferred stock prevents dividends from being paid on common stock until all preferred stock dividends (both current and those previously omitted) have been paid.

Since the payment of dividends on preferred stock can be omitted, firms assume less risk when they issue it than when they issue bonds. Moreover, preferred stock acts as a cushion for creditors in that money raised through its sale can be used by the firm to purchase assets that will generate income for paying the creditors first.

Counterbalancing the advantages of preferred stock is the fact that if a firm omits the payment of preferred stock dividends, it may be unable to raise new capital until the omitted dividends have been paid, since investors will be reluctant to make new investments in a firm unable to compensate

Investment in Initial Public Offerings

A recent study by Chalk and Pearry assessed returns on stocks just after initial public offerings. On the first day, returns averaged over 20 percent, which was clearly abnormal. The second day the mean return was much lower but still about 1 percent above the overall stock market return. On subsequent days the returns were lower. Thus it appeared that abnormally high returns occurred only during the first two days.

The authors also compared stocks in different price groups to determine whether the market reaction to initial public offerings depended on price level. The return on the first day was abnormally high regardless of the price group, but especially for stocks priced at $1 per share or less. The returns on low-priced stocks averaged over 55 percent on the first day of the initial public offering. Because transactions costs are higher for low-priced stocks, the high returns of newly issued low-priced stocks is overstated. Yet, even when accounting for these transaction costs, the authors found that the low-priced stocks generated abnormally high returns on the first day.

SOURCE: Andrew J. Chalk and John W. Pearry III, "Initial Public Offerings: Daily Returns, Offering Types and the Price Effect," *Financial Analysts Journal* (September–October 1987): 65–69.

its existing sources of capital. Also, from a cost perspective, preferred stock is a less desirable source of capital than bonds. Since there is no legal requirement for the firm to pay preferred stock dividends, investors must be enticed to assume the risk involved by receiving higher dividends. In addition, preferred stock dividends are technically compensation to owners of the firm. Therefore, payment of dividends is not a tax-deductible expense to the firm, whereas interest on bonds is tax-deductible.

Preferred Stock Compared with Common Stock and Bonds

In a sense, preferred stock is a cross between common stock and bonds. One similarity between common and preferred stock is that the holders of both cannot force the firm into bankruptcy for failure to pay dividends, since they are "owners" of the firm. Another similarity is that both types of stock provide dividends (as opposed to the interest paid to creditors). A final similarity is that both are permanent sources of financing. That is, neither has a maturity date (there are some rare exceptions to this for preferred stock).

Preferred stock also shares two characteristics with bonds. First, the owners of preferred stock typically do not have voting rights and therefore lack control of the firm. Second, the owners of preferred stock do not normally participate in the profits of the firm beyond the stated fixed annual dividend. All profits above those needed to pay dividends on preferred stock belong to the owners of common stock.

Chapter 8

Stock Markets

211

PUBLIC PLACEMENT OF STOCK IN THE MARKET

When a corporation obtains funds through issuing stocks, it normally uses the services of investment banking firms (IBFs) and possibly brokerage firms in placing the securities with purchasers. Exhibit 8.1 shows the dollar value of publicly placed common and preferred stock over time. In general, the volume of stock issued has increased. However, in some periods, such as 1984 when interest rates were low, some corporations issued bonds instead of stocks as a form of long-term financing.

Corporations sometimes focus their sales of stock toward a particular group of people, such as their existing shareholders, giving them **preemptive rights** (first priority) to purchase the new stock. By placing newly issued stock with existing shareholders, the firm avoids diluting ownership. Preemptive rights are exercised by purchasing new shares during the subscription period (which normally lasts a month or less) at the price specified by the rights. Alternatively, the rights can be sold to someone else.

Shelf-Registration

Due to a 1982 Securities and Exchange Commission (SEC) rule, corporations can publicly place securities without the time lag often caused by registering with the SEC. This so-called **shelf-registration** fulfills SEC requirements up to two years before issuing new securities. The registration statement contains financing plans over the upcoming two years. The securities are in a sense, "shelved," until the firm needs to issue them. Shelf-registrations allow firms quick access to funds without repeatedly being slowed by the registration, enabling those corporations anticipating higher market interest rates to quickly lock in their financing costs. While this is beneficial to issuing corporations, potential purchasers must realize that the information disclosed in the registration may not accurately reflect the firm's financial status over the two-year shelf period, since it is not continually updated.

TRADING AT SECURITY EXCHANGES

In addition to the primary markets where stocks are initially placed, secondary markets exist to facilitate the trading of existing stocks. Organized security exchanges are used to execute secondary market transactions.

The more popular organized exchanges are the New York Stock Exchange, the American Stock Exchange, the Midwest Stock Exchange, and the Pacific Stock Exchange. The New York Stock Exchange is by far the largest, controlling 80 percent of the volume of all organized exchange transactions in the United States. Over 2,300 different stocks are traded on this exchange. Each of the exchanges has a trading floor, where the buying and selling of securities takes place.

Exhibit 8.2 shows the daily trading volume on the New York Stock Exchange over a sixty-seven year period since 1920. The trading has consistently increased over time, implying that stock markets are becoming more active. A primary reason for the active trading in the mid 1980s was the

EXHIBIT 8.1   Value of Publicly Placed Stock

	Value of Stock Placed (Millions of Dollars)	
Year	Preferred Stock	Common Stock
1979	$ 3,574	$ 7,751
1980	3,631	16,858
1981	1,796	22,846
1982	5,113	25,449
1983	7,213	44,366
1984	4,118	18,510
1985	6,505	29,010
1986	11,514	50,316
1987	10,123	43,228

EXHIBIT 8.2   Stock Market Trading Volume

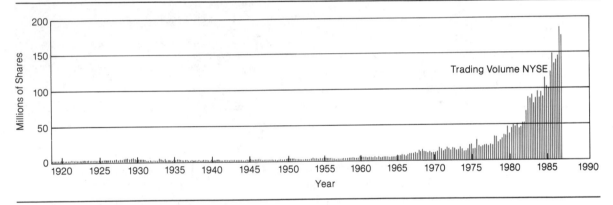

SOURCE: *1987 Federal Reserve Chart Book.*

bullish market that existed at that time. Trading in the secondary markets tends to increase when stock prices are generally rising.

Individuals or firms that purchase a *seat* on the stock exchange are provided the right to trade securities there. (The term *seat* is somewhat misleading since all trading is carried out by individuals standing in groups.) Each brokerage firm must own a seat on the exchange so that it can purchase or sell the securities requested by its clients.

The trading that takes place on the floor of an organized exchange resembles an auction. Those members of the exchange attempting to sell a client's stock strive to obtain the highest price possible, while members purchasing stock for their clients aim for the lowest possible price. When members of the floor of the exchange announce the sale of a certain number of shares of a certain stock, they receive bids for that stock by other members. They either accept the highest bid or hold the stock until an acceptable bid is offered. Any member of the organized exchange can act both as a seller and buyer.

Chapter 8

Stock Markets

Market Reaction to Companies Listing on the New York Exchange

A recent study by Grammatikos and Papaioannou assessed the market price reaction to companies listing on the New York Stock Exchange. When a company applies for approval to be listed, this may signal to the market that the company has confidence in its future performance. In addition, the company may appear more prestigious. However, there are also costs associated with being listed.

Cumulative abnormal residual (CAR) analysis was performed on newly listed companies. If there is favorable market reaction to such an event, the company's stock returns should be abnormally high. The authors found the following results:

■ Stock returns of high-performing companies were not abnormally high just before or after these companies were approved to be listed on the New York Stock Exchange.
■ Stock returns of low-performing companies were abnormally high during the period between application and approval of the New York Stock Exchange listing. These companies also experienced some abnormally low returns after approval.

In general, there is no clear evidence that companies can increase their value by listing on the New York Stock Exchange.

SOURCE: Theoharry Grammatikos and George J. Papaioannou, "The Informational Value of Listing on the New York Stock Exchange," *Financial Review* (November 1986) 485–499.

To have their stock traded on an organized exchange, firms must have it **listed.** Each organized exchange has its own listing requirements, related to a specified minimum number and minimum market value of outstanding shares. In addition to satisfying security exchange requirements, the firm must satisfy SEC requirements as well. The advantages and disadvantages of exchange listing are indicated as follows:

Advantages of Exchange Listing

■ Some institutional investors are permitted to purchase only shares of listed securities. Therefore, listing could increase the demand for a firm's stock, resulting in a higher stock price and a lower cost of capital for the firm. However, the evidence is not clear on whether this actually happens.
■ Securities listed on a securities exchange can be sold in these markets, which could make them more marketable.

Disadvantages of Exchange Listing

■ Stock exchanges require the payment of fees and the filing of additional reports, adding to the firm's expenses.
■ Exchanges can require the publication of more information about the firm than the firm might otherwise desire to expose to the public (and its competitors).

Tracking Insider Trading

The New York Stock Exchange has the ability to monitor, record, and analyze automatically every trade that takes place every day, both on an intramarket and intermarket basis.

This surveillance capability begins in the Stock-Watch area. Using computers, Stock-Watch monitors every trade on the New York Stock Exchange's trading floor as it happens. Historical trading patterns for each stock are established. Trades that fall outside those patterns are flagged by the computer for examination.

Sometimes it is just an error—such as a clerk on the trading floor pushing the wrong button as he records the trade. Or it could be the result of a news story or corporate announcement. Other times there is no explanation for the stock's unusual movement. But that is when an initial analysis begins.

First, the market trading analysts will contact the company whose stock is exhibiting unusual behavior to see if there are any announcements pending. At the same time, analysts also have the Intermarket Surveillance Information System (ISIS), which is a consolidated automated database to house the market data of all the cooperating exchanges and the NASD.

ISIS was developed in 1981 as a result of the securities industry's expanding customer base, increased sophistication, and growing interdependency of the various markets. Overseeing trading was growing to mean looking at the marketplace. With that in mind, the NYSE played a major role in establishing a cooperative relationship with seven other national securities exchanges and the NASD to coordinate sharing of market data and enhance intermarket surveillance. The focus was to assure the integrity of trading in options and equities and to improve public protection in the marketplace. Thus, ISIS was born.

Using sophisticated programs to access the vast array of data it contains, ISIS has become a key source of industrywide information for the purpose of reviewing and analyzing overall market activity.

Included in ISIS is an electronic audit trail component that captures and records the details of every NYSE trade—from execution through comparison. From ISIS, one can determine the trade or quote in the stock, where it occurred, which brokerage firms participated, and whether the NYSE trade was for the account of the member firm or for one of its customers. ISIS can even identify the broker on the exchange floor who executed the trade.

Using ISIS and its audit trail capability, analysts are able to determine which transactions from the entire spectrum of trades in a particular stock are suspect. When necessary, NYSE analysts coordinate their activities with their opposite numbers at the options exchanges, as well. Once a suspicious transaction is detected and the customer is identified by the member firm, Automated Search and Match (ASAM) can be put into play.

ASAM contains easily retrievable public data on about 75,000 companies and subsidiaries and roughly 500,000 business executives. It is designed to cross-check electronically customers against the public information in its database to reveal connections that might indicate insider trading, including corporate links, civic and social affiliations, and even school ties.

Last year, 6,000 instances of trading flagged by the Stock-Watch unit were reviewed. About 10 percent of them actually became the subjects of inquiries. And about 10 percent of those—or sixty-five—cases were eventually referred to the SEC for consideration.

SOURCE: Reprinted with permission from *Bankers Magazine*, Nov/Dec 1986, Copyright © 1986, Warren, Gorham, & Lamont, Inc., 210 South Street, Boston MA, 02111. All Rights Reserved.

In addition to the organized exchanges, the over-the-counter (OTC) market also facilitates secondary market transactions, and securities not listed on organized exchanges are traded here. Unlike the organized exchanges, the OTC market does not have a trading floor. Instead, the buy and sell orders are completed through a telecommunications network. Since there is no trading floor, it is not necessary to buy a "seat" to trade within this exchange. However, it is necessary to register with the SEC.

Regulation of Trading at Security Exchanges

The Securities Exchange Acts of 1933 and 1934 were created to prevent unfair or unethical trading practices on the security exchanges. These acts gave the SEC authority to monitor the exchanges and required listed companies to file a registration statement and financial reports with the SEC and the exchanges. In addition, directors and major stockholders of firms were required to file monthly reports on any changes in stock holdings.

INSTITUTIONAL USE OF STOCK MARKETS

Exhibit 8.3 summarizes the participation of various types of financial institutions in the stock market. Some of these finance their growth by issuing stock. Insurance companies, pension funds, and stock mutual funds are common purchasers of newly issued stock in the secondary markets on a daily basis. Their performance is highly dependent on the returns generated by their stock portfolios.

Many stock market transactions involve two financial institutions. For example, an insurance company may purchase the newly issued stocks of a commercial bank. If the insurance company someday sells this stock in the secondary market, a mutual fund or pension fund may possibly act as the purchaser. Because some financial institutions hold large amounts of stock, their collective sales or purchases of stocks can significantly affect stock market prices.

The high volume of trading of secondary stock market activity is attributed to institutional buying and selling. Thus, financial institutions increase the marketability of stocks by creating such an active secondary market.

The use of stock index futures by financial institutions is one form of so-called **portfolio insurance.** Just before the stock market crash in October 1987, it was estimated that portfolio insurance was protecting $60 to $90 billion in assets. Two months later, it was protecting only half that amount. Portfolio managers became skeptical because portfolio insurance was not as effective as anticipated. More information about portfolio insurance and the stock market crash is provided in the appendix.

EVALUATION OF STOCK PERFORMANCE

In many cases, stocks are evaluated by comparing their *risk-adjusted returns*. For this reason, a stock's risk must be measured. One common proxy for risk is the beta, which measures sensitivity of the stock's returns to market

EXHIBIT 8.3   Institutional Use of Stock Markets

Type of Financial Institution	Participation in Stock Markets
Commercial banks	■ Issue stock to boost their capital base ■ Manage trust funds that usually contain stocks
Stock-owned savings institutions	■ Issue stock to boost their capital base
Savings banks	■ Invest in stocks for their investment portfolios
Finance companies	■ Issue stock to boost their capital base
Stock mutual funds	■ Use the proceeds from selling shares to invest in stocks
Investment banking firms (IBFs) and brokerage firms	■ Issue stock to boost their capital base ■ IBFs place new issues of stock ■ IBFs offer advice to corporations that consider purchasing large blocks of stock from other companies (takeover attempts) ■ Brokerage firms execute buy and sell orders of investors.
Insurance companies	■ Issue stock to boost their capital base. ■ Invest a large proportion of their premiums in the stock market.
Pension funds	■ Invest a large proportion of pension fund contributions in the stock market.

returns. This can be computed from historical data using the following regression model:

$$R_j = b_o + B R_m + e$$

where R_j = return of stock j

   R_m = market return

   b_o = intercept

   B = regression coefficient that serves as an estimate of beta

   e = error term

An alternative risk measure of a stock is the standard deviation of its historical returns. Both forms of risk measure the variability of stocks. The beta accounts only for the variability that is systematically related to market returns, often referred to as **systematic risk.** This measure of risk would be most appropriate if any unsystematic variability were diversified away. The standard deviation measures total variability of a stock's returns.

Once a stock's risk is measured, its risk-adjusted returns can be determined by consolidating the return and the risk measurement. There are two commonly used techniques to measure risk-adjusted returns:

■ Sharpe Index (reward-to-variability ratio)
■ Treynor Index (reward-to-systematic risk ratio)

Impact of the October 1987 Stock Market Crash on Financial Markets

On October 19, 1987, the Dow Jones Industrial Average declined to 1738.42 from 2246.74 on the previous trading day. This represents a 22.6 percent decline, significantly exceeding the 12.8 percent one-day decline on October 28, 1929. Various financial markets and institutions were affected by the stock market crash:

■ Most foreign stocks markets experienced a somewhat similar downturn as the U.S. market.

■ Many investors that sold stocks placed their funds in short-term money market securities; consequently, yields on newly issued commercial paper Treasury bills and bank CDs declined.

■ Other investors that sold stocks placed their funds in other capital market securities, such as bonds and mortgages; consequently, prices of existing bonds increased.

■ The market value of assets in insurance companies and pension funds was substantially reduced, because of their large holdings of stocks. Investment companies that held stock in their own accounts were also adversely affected. Investment companies that manage stock mutual funds were forced to sell stocks in the funds in order to cover redemptions by fund shareholders. Yet, investors that sold stock mutual fund shares often placed their money in other mutual funds managed by the same investment company (such as bond funds and money market funds).

■ The underwriting activity of investment banking firms declined as corporations postponed new issues of stock (since the market price per share of stock was so low).

■ Interest in acquisitions increased as many companies were perceived as bargains, with their stock prices so low.

■ Interest in leveraged buyouts increased as managers and other investors were more able to retire a company's stock and convert it into a privately held company. However, leveraged buyouts often necessitate a large amount of financing. Creditors were more skeptical after the crash and less willing to provide funds needed for leveraged buyouts.

Some critics have suggested that the decline in stock prices on October 19, 1987, was more pronounced because of portfolio insurance strategies, which attempt to limit potential losses on a portfolio. Positions in stock index futures are commonly taken as a form of portfolio insurance. As the stock prices began to decline on October 19th, the stock markets could not handle the volume of trades required to implement the insurance. Portfolio insurance was not as effective as anticipated, and portfolio managers reacted by selling stocks, creating more downward

Sharpe Index

If total variability is thought to be the appropriate measure of risk, a stock's risk-adjusted returns can be determined by the so-called reward-to-variability ratio (also called the **Sharpe Index**), computed as

$$\text{Sharpe Index} = \frac{\bar{R} - \bar{R}_f}{SD}$$

pressure on stock prices. Portfolio insurance accounted for an estimated 12 percent to 24 percent of activity on October 19, 1987.

Brokerage firms sustained huge losses on their own security holdings. However, these losses were at least partially offset by fees earned from a high volume of securities transactions and from advisory fees on mergers and acquisitions during the fourth quarter of 1987.

Shortly after the crash, corporations such as Genetech, Birmingham Steel, Symbol Tech, and BusinessLand shifted from the over-the-counter (OTC) market to the New York Stock Exchange (NYSE). Approximately 4,800 corporations have their stocks listed on the OTC, versus about 1,660 on the NYSE. The recent shift of corporations from the OTC to the NYSE was partially because OTC traders reportedly failed to answer their phones during the stock market crash. Consequently, some investors were temporarily prevented from selling their stock holdings, and by the time their requests were accommodated, stock values declined further.

The National Association of Securities Dealers (NASD), which oversees the OTC market, has responded to the criticism by improving its computer capabilities. By February 1988, when stock prices began to rise, OTC stocks generally performed well, sug-gesting investors' renewed confidence in the OTC market.

One of the key differences between the stock market crash of October 1987 and the crash in 1929 was the effect on bank deposits. In 1929 the reduced public confidence caused not only a liquidation of stocks but massive deposit withdrawals as well. This did not occur in 1987, due to the deposit insurance of up to $100,000 per bank account. In addition, borrowing margins on stocks were limited to 50 percent in 1987, versus 78 percent in 1929. Furthermore, a much larger percentage of investors represents margin buyers in 1929 as compared to 1987.

Share volume on the New York Stock Exchange exceeded 600 million shares on the day of the crash, which was almost twice the previous record of trading volume on a given day. Share volume for this week was 2.3 billion shares. Because of the huge increase in trading volume, brokerage firms were unable to keep up with the processing of orders. The New York and American stock exchanges closed early so that the processing of orders could catch up. The trading of some stocks stopped because of the imbalances of orders. While the markets calmed shortly after, the crash has created some concern about the capabilities, risk, and regulations of the securities industry.

where $\bar{R}$ = average return on the stock
$\bar{R}_f$ = average risk-free rate
SD = standard deviation of the stock's returns

The higher the stock's mean return is relative to the mean risk-free rate, and the lower the standard deviation, the higher the Sharpe Index. This index measures the excess return above the risk-free rate per unit of risk.

Assume the following information for two mutual funds over holding periods:

- Average return for Sooner mutual fund   =   16%
- Average return for Longhorn mutual fund   =   14%
- Average risk-free rate   =   10%
- Standard deviation of Sooner stock returns   =   15%
- Standard deviation of Longhorn stock returns   =   8%

$$\text{Sharpe Index for Sooner mutual fund} = \frac{16\% - 10\%}{15\%}$$
$$= .40$$

$$\text{Sharpe Index for Longhorn mutual fund} = \frac{14\% - 10\%}{8\%}$$
$$= .50$$

Even though Sooner stock had a higher average percentage return, Longhorn stock had a higher performance because of its lower risk. If a stock had an average return that was less than the average risk-free rate, the Sharpe index for that stock would be negative.

Treynor Index

If beta is thought to be the most appropriate type of risk, a stock's risk-adjusted returns can be determined by the **Treynor Index** computed as

$$\text{Treynor Index} = \frac{\bar{R} - \bar{R}_f}{B}$$

where B = the stock's beta

The Treynor Index is similar to the Sharpe Index, except that it uses beta rather than standard deviation to measure the stock's risk. The higher the Treynor Index is, the higher the return relative to the risk-free rate, per unit of risk.

Reconsider the information provided earlier on Sooner stock and Longhorn stock. Using this information, and assuming that Sooner's stock beta = 1.2 while Longhorn's beta = 1.0, the Treynor index is computed for each stock as follows:

$$\text{Treynor Index for Sooner stock} = \frac{16\% - 10\%}{1.2}$$
$$= .05$$

$$\text{Treynor Index for Longhorn stock} = \frac{14\% - 10\%}{1.0}$$
$$= .04$$

Based on the Treynor Index, Sooner stock had higher performance. The choice of the fund with higher performance depends on the preferred measure of risk, and therefore on the preferred index. In some cases, the indexes will lead to the same results. As with the Sharpe Index, the Treynor Index is negative for a stock whose average return is less than the average risk-free rate.

STOCK MARKET EFFICIENCY

If stock markets are efficient, the prices of stocks at any point in time should fully reflect all available information. As investors must attempt to capitalize on new information that is not already accounted for, stock prices should adjust immediately. Investors commonly over- or under-react to information. This does not mean markets are inefficient unless the reaction is biased (consistently over- or under-reacting). In this case, investors that recognized the bias would be able to earn abnormally high risk-adjusted returns.

Efficient markets can be classified into three forms: weak, semistrong, and strong. The *weak-form* efficient-market hypothesis states that security prices reflect all market-related data, such as historical security price movements, and volume of securities trades. If it holds, investors will not be able to earn abnormal returns on a trading strategy that is solely based on past price movements.

The semistrong efficient market hypothesis states that security prices fully reflect all public information. The difference between public information and market-related information is that public information also includes announcements by firms, economic news or events, and political news or events. Market-related information is a subset of public information. Thus, if semistrong efficiency holds, weak-form efficiency must hold as well. Yet, weak-form efficiency could possibly hold while semistrong form efficiency does not. In this case, investors could earn abnormal returns by using the relevant information that was not immediately accounted for by the market.

The strong-form efficient market hypothesis states that security prices fully reflect all information, including private or insider information. If strong-form efficiency holds, then semistrong efficiency must hold as well. However, semistrong efficiency could hold while strong-form efficiency does not, if insider information leads to abnormal returns. Such a finding would suggest that markets are not perfect, since some relevant information is not disseminated to all investors simultaneously.

Tests of the Efficient Market Hypothesis

Weak-form efficiency has been tested by searching for a nonrandom pattern in security prices. If the future change in price is related to recent changes, then historical price movements could be used to earn abnormal returns. In general, studies have found that historical price changes are independent over time. Therefore, historical information is already reflected by today's price and cannot be used to earn abnormal profits. Even for those cases where some dependence was detected, the transaction costs were expected to offset any excess return earned.

Semistrong form efficiency has been tested by assessing how security returns adjust to particular announcements. One type of announcement is related specifically to the firm, such as an announced dividend increase, acquisition, or stock split. Another type of announcement is economy-related, such as an announced decline in the Fed's discount rate. In general, security prices immediately reflected the information from the announcements. That is, the securities were not consistently over- or under-valued. Consequently, abnormal returns could not consistently be achieved. This is especially true when considering transaction costs.

Methodology for Testing Market Efficiency

To determine whether a trading strategy (one based on either historical stock price movements or specific announcements) earns abnormal returns, we must first determine normal returns. This can be accomplished by using a pricing model. The **capital asset pricing model** (CAPM) is commonly used to estimate what a stock's return should have been, as shown here:

$$\hat{r}_j = R_f + B(r_m - R_f)$$

where $\hat{r}_j$ = estimated return on asset j
R_f = the risk-free rate
r_m = the market return
B = beta

The beta represents the sensitivity of the individual asset's return to the market return. It reflects the relevant risk of a stock for any investor holding a diversified portfolio of investments. Once the asset's estimated return is derived from the CAPM, it can be compared to the return that actually occurred (called r_j):

$$e = r_j - \hat{r}_j$$

where e = the residual, representing an excess above the expected return after accounting for the stock's risk

Suppose that a particular trading strategy was tested in which a particular stock was purchased after a particular announcement. The stock's beta was estimated to be 1.2, based on historical data, and during the period after the announcement the risk-free rate was 6 percent and the market return (as measured here by the Dow Jones Industrial Average) was 8 percent. The expected return of asset j based on the CAPM is

$$\begin{aligned}
\hat{r}_j &= R_f + B(r_m - R_f) \\
&= 6\% + 1.2\,(8\% - 6\%) \\
&= 8.4\%
\end{aligned}$$

If the actual return of asset j over this period was 10 percent, then there was an excess return of

$$\begin{aligned}
e &= r_j - \hat{r}_j \\
&= 10\% - 8.4\% \\
&= 1.6\%
\end{aligned}$$

Based on this single period, it appears that the strategy can generate an abnormally high risk-adjusted return. However, a single period does not provide sufficient evidence. The strategy should be tested in several periods to determine whether abnormal returns can be achieved on average, over time. This requires estimating the expected return for each period, based on the security's estimated beta, along with the risk-free rate and market return over the period of concern. For each period, the excess return is

What Caused the Stock Market Crash in October 1987?

Institutional Investor magazine conducted phone interviews of chief investment officers and other senior officials at over 100 large financial institutions regarding the crash in October 1987. Some of the major results of the survey are summarized below:

■ Sixty-five percent of the respondents thought that an extremely overpriced stock market was a very important factor causing the stock market crash, and another 28 percent thought it was a somewhat important factor.

■ The second most influential factor was the growing trade deficit; 40 percent thought that this was a very important factor, while another 41 percent thought it was a somewhat important factor.

■ Most respondents also believed that the lack of action on the federal budget deficit and the growing lack of confidence in the Reagan administration were important factors.

■ Some other factors thought to be important by some respondents included portfolio insurance, rising interest rates, and a restrictive monetary policy

In addition to the causes of the crash, respondents were also asked if and how the proportion of their securities portfolio changed. Those respondents that indicated a shift in securities generally reduced their stock holdings and increased their holdings of bonds and cash.

SOURCE: *Institutional Investor* (January 1988): 36.

estimated, and tested to see if it differs significantly from zero (using the t-test for statistical significance). If excess returns are positive and significant, this would imply that purchasing the asset just after particular public announcements can yield abnormally high profits. Under these circumstances, the hypothesis that the market is efficient must be rejected.

A few limitations of this testing procedure deserve to be mentioned. First, the estimation of the excess return depends on the estimation of the expected return. If the pricing model does not appropriately measure the normal risk-adjusted return, the estimated excess return will be inaccurate as well.

If the pricing model is appropriate, and excess returns are not detected, this does not prove that markets are efficient. The analysis suggests only that the trading rule examined does not lead to excess profits. It says nothing about an infinite number of other possible trading strategies that could be attempted. If an analysis detects no significant excess returns, this supports but does not prove the efficient market hypothesis.

Evaluation of Stock Prices during Bull Market Periods

A comparison of the 1924–1929 to the 1982–1987 bull market periods is shown in Exhibit 8.4. Both bull markets lasted for 21 quarters and peaked in the third quarter, with the subsequent crash in the fourth quarter. Some

Chapter 8

Stock Markets

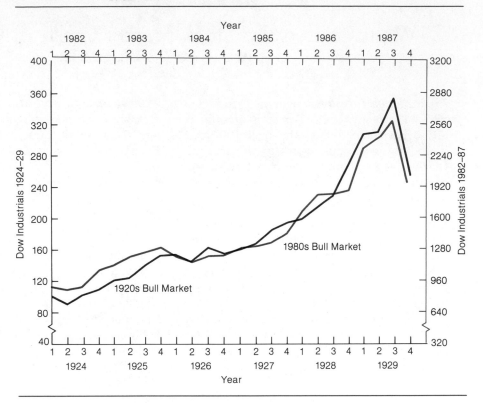

SOURCE: *Review*, Federal Reserve Bank of St. Louis, November 1987, p. 18.

critics suggest that the bull markets represented speculative bubbles, where market prices rose in response to trading fads rather than fundamental reasons. The concern with speculative bubbles is that they will inevitably burst once market prices become sufficiently above their fundamental values. A recent study by Santoni[1], however, addressed this issue and found no evidence of speculative bubbles.

The Stock Market as an Economic Indicator

While expectations of economic conditions can affect stock prices, stock market movements can also affect economic activity. For example, the stock market crash in October 1987 significantly reduced the net worth of many individual investors, forcing them to revise their spending behavior. Consequently, economic growth slowed.

There is some question as to whether stock market movements can be used to forecast economic activity. Exhibit 8.5 compares stock market movements to recessionary periods (shaded areas), and Exhibit 8.6 describes the

1 See G. J. Santoni, "The Great Bull Markets 1924–29 and 1982–87: Speculative Bubbles or Economic Fundamentals?" *Review*, Federal Reserve Bank of St. Louis (November 1987): 16–30.

EXHIBIT 8.5 Relationship between Stock Market Movements and Recessions

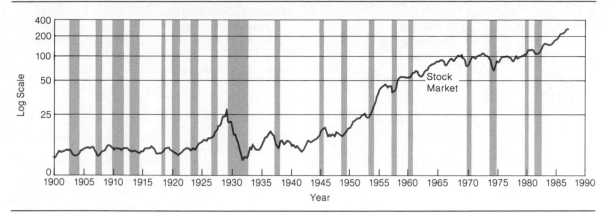

NOTE: Shaded areas represent recessions

SOURCE: *Economic Review*, Federal Reserve Bank of Kansas City (January 1988): 12–13.

stock market activity preceding each recession. Some recessions were preceded by declining stock market prices, suggesting that the stock market might serve as a useful economic indicator. However, other recessions were not preceded by a stock market decline, and some stock market declines occurred without a subsequent recession.

IMPACT OF THE DOLLAR'S VALUE ON STOCK PRICES

INTERNATIONAL
ASPECTS

The dollar's value can affect U.S. stock prices for a variety of reasons. First, foreign investors tend to purchase U.S. stocks when the dollar is weak and sell them when it is near its peak. Thus, the foreign demand for any given U.S. stock may be higher when the dollar is expected to strengthen, other things being equal. Also, stock prices are affected by the impact of the dollar's changing value on cash flows. Stock prices of U.S. firms primarily involved in exporting could be favorably affected by a weak dollar and adversely affected by a strong dollar. U.S. importing firms could be affected in the opposite manner.

Stock prices of U.S. companies may also be affected by exchange rates if stock market participants measure performance by reported earnings. A multinational corporation's consolidated reported earnings would be affected by exchange rate fluctuations even if its cash flows were not affected. A weaker dollar tends to inflate the reported earnings of a U.S.–based company's foreign subsidiaries. Some analysts would argue that any effect of exchange rate movements on financial statements is irrelevant unless cash flows were also affected.

The changing value of the dollar can also affect stock prices by affecting expectations of economic factors that influence the firm's performance. For example, if a weak dollar stimulates the U.S. economy, it may enhance the value of a U.S. firm whose sales are dependent on the U.S. economy. A strong dollar could adversely affect such a firm if it dampens U.S. economic growth.

Chapter 8

Stock Markets

EXHIBIT 8.6 Statistics on Stock Market Declines and Recessions

Periods of Declining Stock Prices[a]	Recessions	Decline in Stock Prices (Percent Change, S&P 500)		Association of Stock Price Decline and Recessions
		Total	Before Recession	
1902:3-03:4	1902:4-04:3	27	0	No lead
1906:4-07:4	1907:2-08:2	35	11	Successful prediction
1909:4-10:3	1910:1-12:1	14	3	Successful prediction
1912:3-15:1	1913:1-14:4	23	7	Successful prediction
1916:4-17:4	—	28	—	False signal
—	1918:3-19:1	—	—	No decline
1919:4-21:3	1920:1-21:3	29	7	Successful prediction
1923:1-23:3	1923:2-24:3	12	5	Successful prediction
—	1926:4-27:4	—	—	No decline
1929:3-32:2	1929:3-33:1	82	0	No lead
1934:1-35:1	—	13	—	False signal
1937:1-38:2	1937:2-38:2	42	9	Successful prediction
1938:4-39:2	—	11	—	False signal
1939:4-42:2	—	34	—	False signal
—	1945:1-45:4	—	—	No decline
1946:2-48:1	—	23	—	False signal
1948:2-49:2	1948:4-49:4	10	3	Successful prediction
—	1953:3-54:2	—	—	No decline
1956:3-57:4	1957:3-58:2	15	4	Successful prediction
—	1960:2-61:1	—	—	No decline
1961:4-62:3	—	18	—	False signal
1966:1-66:4	—	13	—	False signal
1968:4-70:3	1970:1-70:4	25	16	Successful prediction
1973:1-74:4	1973:4-75:1	40	11	Successful prediction
1976:3-78:1	—	14	—	False signal
—	1980:1-80:3	—	—	No decline
1980:4-82:3	1981:3-82:4	14	6	Successful prediction
1987:3-87:4	—	—	20	—

a Periods were selected by the following criteria:
   —Peaks must be 10 percent higher than the preceding and following troughs.
   —Troughs must be 10 percent lower than the preceding and following peaks.

SOURCE: *Economic Review*, Federal Reserve Bank of Kansas City (January 1988): 15.

Since inflation affects some firms, a weak dollar value could indirectly affect a firm's stock by placing upward pressure on inflation. A strong dollar would have the opposite indirect impact.

Expectations about the dollar could also affect stock prices by their influence on interest rates. Holding other things equal, expectations of a weak dollar may cause a decrease in capital flows to the U.S., and therefore place upward pressure on interest rates. It may also ignite inflationary fears, which have a similar effect on nominal interest rates. Expectations of a strong dollar may cause a net increase in capital flows to the United States and therefore place downward pressure on interest rates (other things being equal). The expected impact of a given interest rate forecast on U.S. firms will vary because of their different financial characteristics.

In summary, the effect of expectations about the dollar's value on a company's stock value depends on

- Degree of exporting or importing conducted
- Composition of export and import markets
- Availability of export or import substitutes
- Degree to which the company hedges its anticipated cash flows against exchange rate movements
- Relative amount of sales and earnings generated by subsidiaries in foreign countries
- Locational composition of subsidiaries
- Company's exposure to economic factors, such as inflation or interest rates

Some companies attempt to insulate the exposure of their stock price to the changing value of the dollar, while other companies purposely remain exposed with the intent to benefit from it.

INTERNATIONALIZATION OF STOCK MARKETS

U.S. corporations have increasingly tapped foreign markets for funds by issuing stock overseas. Non–U.S. corporations are also following the same strategy, using the U.S. market as a source of funds. The placement of stocks across markets allows a new issue to be more easily absorbed by investors. It also allows investors access to foreign securities.

The secondary market for stocks has become internationalized as well, primarily due to the growth in international mutual funds (IMFs). These IMFs allow investors to invest in foreign stocks without incurring excessive transaction and information costs. Furthermore, the foreign securities are selected by the fund's managers, so individual investors may invest internationally without having to assess foreign companies themselves. Due to the increased availability of foreign securities, the flow of funds between countries should increase.

The international stock market has grown dramatically in recent years. Investment banks underwrite stocks through one or more syndicates across countries. Because the global distribution of stock can reach a much larger market, greater quantities of stock can be issued at a given price. In addition, some foreign markets perceive a company's characteristics differently. Even when U.S. investors are not interested in a particular type of stock, investors in other countries may still have an interest, possibly because of differences among country tax laws, which affect the desirability of stocks.

Some companies may consider issuing stock in foreign countries to avoid flooding the local market. In addition, international distribution can spread a company's name across the world, which is especially important for firms that concentrate in international trade or direct foreign investment. One concern of international stock distribution is that much of the stock intended for foreign markets can eventually flow back to the local market, causing downward pressure on its price.

The degree to which stock trading is becoming internationalized is illustrated in Exhibit 8.7, which shows the increase in U.S. stocks purchased and sold by foreign investors. The volume of trading has more than tripled in the last three years.

Around-the-Clock Global Security Trading

In October 1986, a major deregulatory event affected London's stock market. This event was known as the "Big Bang." A computerized network (similar to the NASDAQ over-the-counter system in the United States) was established. The system is called **SEAQ** (pronounced see-yak), where international traders are hooked up by telephones and computers to conduct trading. In addition to the establishment of a computerized network, the London exchange now allows investment firms that trade in the United States and

EXHIBIT 8.7   Foreign Trading of U.S. Stocks (in Billions of Dollars)

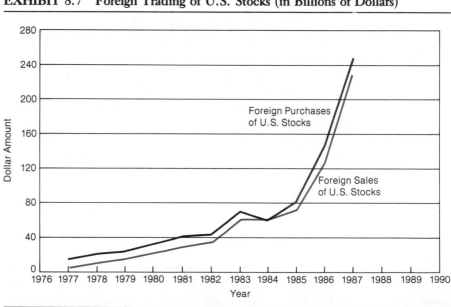

a Not available

SOURCE: *Federal Reserve Bulletin*, various issues.

Japan to trade in London (formerly forbidden). This deregulatory step was very significant to large investment firms that trade on the New York and Tokyo exchanges, because it allowed them to create a nearly 24-hour market. They can use the New York Stock Exchange 9:30 A.M. to 4 P.M. Eastern time, the Tokyo Stock Exchange from 7 P.M. to 1 A.M. Eastern time, and the London Stock Exchange from 4 A.M. to 10:30 A.M. Eastern time. Those shares traded on all exchanges could be bought or sold almost any time of the day. As of 1987, about 50 non-Japanese companies were listed on the Tokyo Stock Exchange. In the future, it is likely that shares of most major companies will be available on these three major exchanges.

The "Big Bang" also eliminated the fixed commission structure. That is, the commissions paid on stock transactions in London were deregulated (similar to the deregulated commissions in the United States in 1975). The expected result of this move is more intense competition and lower profit margins. Over time, the reduced profit margins may eliminate some of the competitors.

A market for **American depository receipts** (ADRs) has been established in the United States, which also facilitates U.S. investment in foreign companies. An ADR is a certificate that represents ownership of a foreign stock. ADRs for more than 500 different foreign stocks are now traded on U.S. stock exchanges.

ADRs are sometimes a preferable method for U.S. investors to invest in foreign companies, for the following reasons. First, they are closely followed by U.S. investment analysts. Second, companies represented by ADRs are required by the Securities and Exchange Commission (SEC) to file financial statements consistent with the generally accepted accounting principles in the United States. These statements may not be available for other non–U.S. companies. Third, reliable quotes on ADR prices are consistently available, with existing currency values factored in to translate the price into dollars. While ADRs have advantages, there is only a limited amount to select from. Also, the ADR market is less active than other stock markets. Consequently, ADRs are less liquid than most listed U.S. stocks.

Integration of Country Stock Markets During the 1987 Crash

Exhibit 8.8 compares the U.S. stock market movements to three foreign stock markets during October 1987. While the U.S. market suffered the biggest decline, the other three markets were severely affected as well. The high correlation among country stock markets is partially due to the integration among the markets. Many institutional investors buy and sell stocks on numerous stock exchanges. If they anticipate a general decline in stocks, they may liquidate some stocks from all markets, rather than just the U.S. market.

Even if stock markets were not integrated, country economies are. If U.S. investors are concerned about the U.S. economy, there should also be concern about the foreign economies that are influenced by the U.S. economy. Therefore, investors in various countries may react to news or expectations about the U.S. economy.

EXHIBIT 8.8 Impact of the Crash on Four Stock Markets

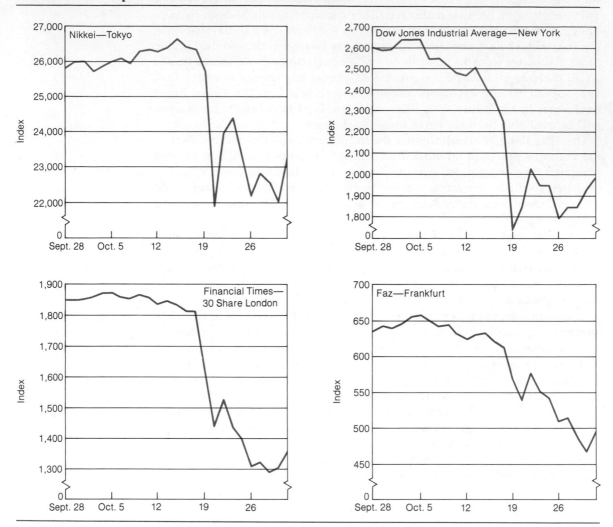

SOURCE: *Economic Trends*, Federal Reserve Bank of Cleveland, (November 1987): 17.

SUMMARY

Stock is issued in the primary capital markets to provide long-term sources of funds for corporations. It is commonly sold in the secondary markets by investors that either are substituting investments or need to obtain funds. The active secondary market increases the liquidity of stocks, which in turn creates a greater willingness of investors to purchase these securities in the primary market. Investment banking firms (IBFs) play a crucial role in placing newly issued stock. Many other financial institutions use a substantial portion of their funds to invest in stock. Institutional trading of securities represents a large proportion of the total trading volume.

KEY TERMS

American depository receipts (ADRs)	**portfolio insurance**
	preemptive rights
capital asset pricing model (CAPM)	**SEAQ**
	Sharpe Index
cumulative provision	**shelf-registration**
listed	**systematic risk**
margin call	**Treynor Index**

QUESTIONS

8.1. Explain the rights of common stockholders that are not available to other individuals.

8.2. What is the danger of issuing too much stock?

8.3. How is preferred stock similar to common stock?

8.4. How is preferred stock similar to bonds?

8.5. Explain the "distribution" role of investment banking firms during a public placement of stock.

8.6. What are some advantages and disadvantages of being listed on the New York Stock Exchange?

8.7. Are organized stock exchanges used to place newly issued stock? Explain.

8.8. Explain the difference between weak-form, semistrong form, and strong-form efficient market hypotheses. Which hypothesis is most difficult to test? Which is most likely to be rejected?

8.9. Explain how to test weak-form efficiency in the stock market.

8.10. It has been suggested that stock returns are abnormally high shortly after an announced increase in dividends. If so, there is evidence to reject the semistrong form of efficiency. Explain the strategy that can be used to attempt to benefit from this suggestion. How can we test whether the strategy generated abnormal returns? (Explain in your answer how normal returns can be estimated.)

8.11. A consulting firm was hired to determine whether a particular trading strategy could generate abnormal returns. The strategy involved taking positions based on recent historical movements in stock prices. The strategy did not achieve abnormal returns. Consequently, the consulting firm concluded that the stock market is weak-form efficient. Do you agree? Explain?

8.12. How do you think the U.S. stock prices would react to expectations of a weak dollar, assuming that inflation was not a major concern? What if inflation was a major concern?

8.13. If you expected the dollar to strengthen, would you expect stock returns of U.S. exporting companies or importing companies to be higher? Why?

8.14. Would foreign investors find U.S. stocks more attractive if they expected the dollar to strengthen or weaken? Explain.

8.15. How have international mutual funds (IMFs) increased the degree of international integration of capital markets among countries?

8.16. Describe the pattern in the volume of foreign investment in U.S. stocks.

8.17. Explain the significance of the "Big Bang" with regard to deregulation in financial markets.

8.18. Explain ADRs.

8.19. During 1987 and 1988, many stock portfolio managers closely monitored the U.S. trade deficit figures. When the trade deficit was announced to be higher than expected, the stock market often declined significantly.

a. Why might the market react in such a manner even when the trade figures announced have already occurred?

b. In some periods, the announced trade deficit was large, but the market did not respond. Offer a possible explanation for this lack of response.

8.20. Stock prices seem to be more volatile since the crash than they were before the crash. Why? Do you think it is because economic conditions are more volatile, or because investors now react more than before to financial news?

PROBLEMS

8.1. Assume that Vogl stock is priced at $50 per share and pays a dividend of $1 per share. Investors purchased the stock on margin, paying $30 per share and borrowing the remainder from the brokerage firm at 10 percent annualized. If after one year, the stock is sold at a price of $60 per share, what is the return to the investors?

8.2. Assume that Duever stock is priced at $80 per share and pays a dividend of $2 per share. Investors purchased the stock on margin, paying $50 per share and borrowing the remainder from the brokerage firm at 12 percent annualized. If after one year, the stock is sold at a price of $90 per share, what is the return to the investors?

8.3. Assume the following information over a five-year period.

- Average risk-free rate = 6 %
- Average return for Crane stock = 11%
- Average return for Load stock = 14%
- Standard deviation of Crane stock returns = 2%
- Standard deviation of Load stock returns = 4%
- Beta of Crane stock = .8
- Beta of Load stock = 1.1

Which stock has higher risk-adjusted returns when using the Sharpe Index? Which stock has higher risk-adjusted returns when using the Treynor Index? Show your work.

8.4. Assume Mess stock has a beta of 1.2. If the risk-free rate is presently 7 percent, and the market return is 10 percent, what is the expected return on Mess stock?

PROJECT

1. ASSESSING STOCK MARKET MOVEMENTS

Review the section "Abreast of the Market" in *The Wall Street Journal* (listed in the index on the first page) as of the last five trading days. For each day, explain whether the market went up or down, and identify the factors contributing to the change.

	Did the stock market rise or fall? By how much?	Reasons given for the rise or fall in the stock market.
1 day ago		
2 days ago		
3 days ago		
4 days ago		
5 days ago		

REFERENCES

Akgiray, Vedat and Geoffrey Booth. "Compound Distribution Models of Stock Returns: An Empirical Comparison." *Journal of Financial Research* (Fall 1987): 269–280.

Amihud, Yakov and Haim Mendelson. "Trading Mechanisms and Stock Returns: An Empirical Investigation." *Journal of Finance* (July 1987): 533–553.

Baron, David P. "A Model of the Demand for Investment Banking and Advising, and Distribution Services for New Issues." *Journal of Finance* 37 (September 1982): 955–976.

Barrett, W. Brian, Andrea Heuson, Robert Kolb, and Gabriele Schropp. "The Adjustment of Stock Prices to Completely Unanticipated Events." *Financial Review* (November 1987): 345–354.

Bhagat, Sanjai. "The Effect of Pre-emptive Right Amendments on Shareholder Wealth." *Journal of Financial Economics* 12 (November 1983): 289–310.

Benesh, Gary and Robert Pari, "Performance of Stocks Recommended on the Basis of Insider Trading Activity." *Financial Review* (February 1987): 145–158.

Cho, D. Chinhyung and William Taylor. "The Seasonal Stability of the Factor Structure of Stock Returns." *Journal of Finance* (December 1987): 1195–1212.

Davidson, Lawrence S. and Richard T. Froyen. "Monetary Policy and Stock Returns: Are Stock Markets Efficient?" *Review*, Federal Reserve Bank of St. Louis (March 1982): 3–12.

DeBondt, Werner F. M. and Richard Thaler. "Further Evidence on Investor Overreaction and Stock Market Seasonability." *Journal of Finance* (July 1987): 557–581.

Etebari, Ahmad, James Horigan and Jan Landwehr. "To Be or Not to Be—Reaction of Stock Returns to Sudden Deaths of Corporate Chief Executive Officers." *Journal of Business Finance & Accounting* (Summer 1987): 255–278.

French, Kenneth, G. William Schwert and Robert Stambauh. "Expected Stock Returns and Volatility." *Journal of Financial Economics* (September 1987): 3–30.

Gordon, Laurence A., David F. Larcker, and George E. Pinches. "Testing for Market Efficiency." *Journal of Financial and Quantitative Analysis* (June 1980): 262–287.

Grinblatt, Mark and Sheridan Titman. "The Relation Between Mean-Variance Efficiency and Arbitrage Pricing." *Journal of Business* (January 1987): 97–112.

Grube, R. Corwin, O. Maurice Joy and John Howe. "Some Empirical Evidence on Stock Returns and Security Credit Regulation in the OTC Equity Market." *Journal of Banking and Finance* (March 1987): 17–32.

Gultekin, Mustafa and Bulent Gultekin. "Stock Return Anomalies and the Tests of the APT." *Journal of Finance* (December 1987): 1213–1224.

Hamilton, James. "Off-Board Trading of NYSE-Listed Stocks: The Effects of Deregulation

233

and the National Market System." *Journal of Finance* (December 1987): 1331–1346.

Hansen, Robert S. and John M. Pinkerton. "Direct Equity Financing: A Resolution of a Paradox." *Journal of Finance* 37 (June 1982): 651–665.

Heath, Robert S. and Robert Jarrow. "Ex-Dividend Stock Price Behavior and Arbitrage Opportunities." *Journal of Business* (January 1988): 95–108.

Kawaller, Ira, Paul Koch and Timothy Koch. "The Temporal Price Relationship Between S&P 500 Futures and S&P 500 Index." *Journal of Finance* (December 1987): 1309–1330.

Kim, Moon. "Macro-Economic Factors and Stock Returns." *Journal of Financial Research* (Summer 1987): 87–98.

Kim, Wi Saeng, Jae Won Lee and Jack Clark Francis. "Investment Performance of Common Stocks in Relation to Insider Ownership." *Financial Review* (February 1988): 53–64.

Laderman, Jeffrey. "Protecting Stock Profits if the Bear Attacks." *Businessweek* (March 31, 1986): 62.

Lamoureux, Christopher and James Wansley. "Market Effects of Changes in the Standard & Poor's 500 Index." *Financial Review* (February 1987): 53–69.

MacMinn, Richard. "Forward Markets, Stock Markets, and the Theory of the Firm." *Journal of Finance* (December 1987): 1167–1186.

Marsh, Terry and Robert Merton. "Dividend Behavior for the Aggregate Stock Dividend Market." *Journal of Business* (January 1987): 1–40.

McConnell, John and Gary Sanger. "The Puzzle in Post-Listing Common Stock Returns." *Journal of Finance* (March 1987): 119–140.

McDaniel, William R. "Sinking Fund Preferred Stock." *Financial Management* 13 (Spring 1984): 45–52.

Mulhern, John J. "The National Stock Market: Taking Shape." *Business Review*, Federal Reserve Bank of Philadelphia (September–October 1980): 3–11.

Pearce, Douglas. "Challenges to the Concept of Stock Market Efficiency." *Economic Review*, Federal Reserve Bank of Kansas City (September–October 1987): 16–30.

Pearce, Douglas K. "Stock Prices and the Economy." *Economic Review*, Federal Reserve Bank of Kansas City (November 1983): 7–22.

Pearce, Douglas K. "The Impact of Inflation on Stock Prices." *Economic Review*, Federal Reserve Bulletin of Kansas City (March 1982): 3–18.

Peterson, David. "Security Price Reactions to Initial Reviews of Common Stock by the Value Line Investment Survey." *Journal of Financial & Quantitative Analysis* (December 1987): 483–494.

Rappaport, Alfred. "Stock Market Signals to Managers." *Harvard Business Review* (November–December 1987): 57–62.

Rogers, Ronald. "The Relationship Between Earnings Yield and Market Value: Evidence from the American Stock Exchange." *Financial Review* (February 1988): 65–80.

Rozeff, Michael and Mir A. Zaman. "Market Efficiency and Insider Trading: New Evidence." *Journal of Business* (January 1988): 25–44.

Santoni, G. J. "The Great Bull Markets 1924–1929 and 1982–1987: Speculative Bubbles or Economic Fundamentals?" *Review*, Federal Reserve Bank of St. Louis (November 1987): 16–30.

Seyhun, H. Nejat. "The Information Content of Aggregate Insider Trading." *Journal of Business* (January 1988): 1–24.

Smith, Clifford W., Jr. "Alternative Methods for Raising Capital: Rights versus Underwritten Offerings." *Journal of Financial Economics* (December 1977): 273–307.

Wilson, Jack and Charles Jones. "A Comparison of Annual Common Stock Returns: 1871–1925 with 1926–1985." *Journal of Business* (April 1987): 239–258.

Zivney, Terry and Donald Thompson II. "Relative Stock Prices and the Firm Size Effect." *Journal of Financial Research* (Summer 1987): 99–110.

Part Three

Other Financial Markets

A Simple Guide to Understanding Portfolio Insurance

In the aftermath of the events surrounding October 19, portfolio insurance, or dynamic hedging, has received a close examination by the equity investment community. The reassessment of this strategy by some groups has shifted portfolio insurance from being one of the hottest investment strategies in 1986–87 to the possible villain of the October crash. Additionally, critics of portfolio insurance have stated that it was ineffective in protecting its users, who were sold a "false bill of goods." These extreme views concerning this strategy and its impact on the marketplace have neither been fully substantiated nor adequately assessed.

This guide will not attempt to answer the question of whether portfolio insurance was a cause of the downturn, other than to say that the evidence does not support this contention. For a discussion of these issues, the reader is referred to the Chicago Mercantile Exchange (CME) blue ribbon panel paper which concludes that there is no support for the beliefs that portfolio insurance and/or futures caused the crash. This conclusion also was reached by the Commodity Futures Trading Commission (CFTC), which found "no evidence to support the frequently cited argument that the combined trading strategies of index arbitrage and portfolio insurance selling caused the market break on October 19 or that these strategies combined to cause a downturn spiral or cascade in stock prices."[1]

With a twofold purpose, this guide focuses on micro-level costs associated with portfolio insurance. First, the risk-return tradeoff inherent in dynamic hedging strategies is explained. Second, how costs associated with portfolio insurance change with the market environment is addressed.

1 "Preliminary Report of the Committee on Inquiry Appointed to the Chicago Mercantile Exchange to Examine the Events Surrounding October 19, 1987"; Merton H. Miller, University of Chicago; John D. Hawke, Jr., Arnold & Porter; Burton Malkiel, Yale University; Myron Scholes, Stanford University; December 22, 1987. If you are interested in an excerpt from this report, please refer to the article, "October 19, 1987; The Facts," which appeared in the December/January 1988 issue of *Market Perspectives*.

DEFINING PORTFOLIO INSURANCE

Portfolio insurance is best defined as any of a group of strategies that attempts to adjust the payoff structure of a portfolio in a manner that will reduce or eliminate downside returns while still allowing for the capture of upside returns. The effectiveness of portfolio insurance as a hedging strategy can best be assessed through discussion of the tradeoffs between its costs and associated benefits.

Portfolio insurance programs are designed to reduce the chance of returns falling below a minimum or floor level over some specified time horizon. Inherently, this alteration is a "safety-first" strategy; it lowers the probability of returns falling below a specified level. This safety-first technique has been used effectively by hedgers in all commodity and financial futures markets and has been extensively used by investment managers.

Portfolio insurances' novel twist is its dynamic nature, which allows its return payoff to mimic that of an option. The portfolio insurance strategy replicates the payoff from holding stocks and buying puts. Certainly, while this strategy strives to provide protection like an "insurance policy," the dynamic nature of portfolio insurance distinguishes it from the static act of buying an insurance policy. Dynamic hedging is a form of self-insurance. It is a hedging strategy that gives the desired payoff only when properly executed. Dynamic hedging is a more descriptive name for this strategy of continuous adjustment. In exchange for this protection of providing a floor level for returns, the cost of the insurance program to the user is the underperformance of the portfolio returns in up markets.

EXHIBIT 8A.1   Tradeoff Between Portfolio and Market Returns

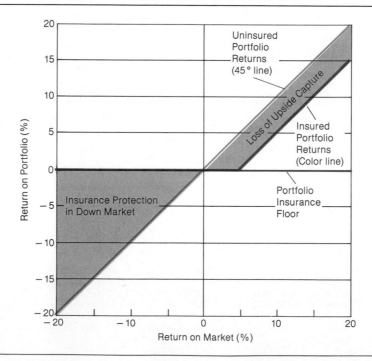

A dynamic hedging program attempts to alter the payoff structure by adding an insurance floor. (See Exhibit 8A.1.) If the pension manager hedges all of the time and holds the market portfolio, the resulting portfolio returns will be unaffected by changes in equity values. A selective hedge program may attempt to pick broad market moves in order to protect the portfolio in down markets and allow for gains in up markets. Nevertheless, it is unclear whether managers have the ability to pick market swings. Portfolio insurance does not attempt to have the investment manager market time. Rather, the objective of the portfolio insurance program is to limit the downside risk to some prespecified level. The strategy is a purer form of hedging. It allows managers to meet their fiduciary responsibility of protecting their portfolios without having to forecast or speculate on market moves. Pension funds and trusts are provided with the advantages of having clear objectives and decision rules for use in the implementation of the strategy. Of course, the cost of this technique is that managers cannot get this protection without giving up some return.

Exhibit 8A.1 shows the benefit and cost of the portfolio insurance program. The program provides a return tradeoff that is similar to a call option, (i.e., a combination of holding stock and buying put options). The protection provided is illustrated by the shaded area below the floor level. The insurance cost in an up market is the shaded area below the linear return line and above the floor. This is the "loss of upside capture."

COSTS OF PORTFOLIO INSURANCE

Unlike a static options program based on buying puts, where the cost of insurance is the price of the put, the portfolio insurance strategy cost is not known in advance, with certainty. However, even a dynamic option strategy will have variable costs based on the premiums that have to be paid for the options.

Any portfolio insurance program will affect the risk-return structure of the portfolio. Exhibit 8A.2 displays the effect of a portfolio insurance strategy on the probability distribution of returns. The two-tailed log-normal distribution shows the possible returns from holding an uninsured portfolio. The second distribution shows the impact of setting a floor on portfolio returns. The program affects the return distribution by reducing the probability of receiving returns lower than the floor. For perfect protection, there is no probability of returns going below the floor return. The portfolio-insurance tradeoff is that managers will have returns that will not go below the floor, but there also will be lower probabilities associated with higher returns. The distribution of returns will not be symmetric.

The cost of a portfolio insurance program can be divided into two major areas. First, there are variables that can be controlled by the manager, such as the protection horizon and floor level. Second, there are variables like market conditions which are outside the managers' control.

VARIABLES CONTROLLED BY MANAGERS

The simplest way to alter the effect of the insurance program is to change the target floor returns. By lowering the floor, the program costs will de-

EXHIBIT 8A.2   Return for Insured and Uninsured Portfolios

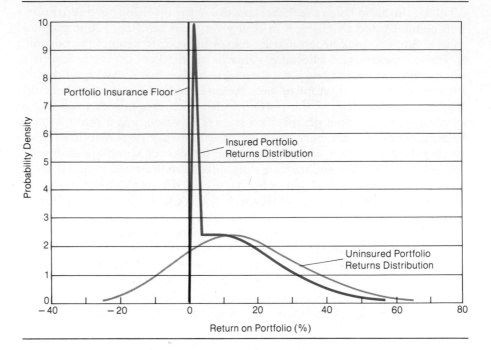

crease. This is similar to changing the deductible in an insurance policy. Protecting against catastrophe is cheaper than protecting against lower returns.

Another way to reduce the cost of a program is to assume partial insurance or "coinsurance." With this implementation strategy, portfolio insurance is only applied to a portion of the portfolio. Of course, the returns distribution will be affected so that there is the possibility that the floor level will be violated.

The cost for a given level of protection can change with the protection horizon. If the same level of protection is extended over a longer time period, the chances of hitting the floor for the total portfolio returns over the program's time horizon is lower; hence, there is a reduction in the cost of the program. When a floor return is based on a one-year horizon, only a small market downturn will force the portfolio to hit the floor causing an increase in trading costs. The manager has to make decisions based on the tradeoff between short-run protection and costs when he is holding the portfolio for longer-term goals.

COSTS OUTSIDE MANAGERS' CONTROL

Changing market conditions will greatly affect the cost of insurance; however, these costs are out of the control of the manager. Thus these costs have to be closely examined. Clearly, these costs most dramatically affected the ability of managers to meet their targets during the October crash.

As a practical matter, implementation of portfolio insurance requires selling (stocks or futures) following a market decline and repurchasing with rebounds. Thus volatility is the most important variable that cannot be controlled in an insurance program. An increase in volatility will increase the probability of hitting the program floor. Hence the manager will have to enter the market more often, thereby increasing transaction costs and the possibility of being "whipsawed."

Short-term interest rates also will affect the portfolio returns level. An increase in a money market interest rate, which is the return that the hedger trades into when hedging the market portfolio, will reduce the probability of falling below the floor return. Higher interest rates effectively reduce the floor level for the insurance program.

Transactions costs play an important role in affecting the overall returns of the hedged portfolio. If the actual cost of transacting is higher, the cost of the insurance program will be higher. In fact, the rationale for using futures for portfolio insurance is based on the lower cost of transacting. Costs for portfolio insurance also will be affected by mispricing between cash and futures markets (i.e., where prices deviate from fair value). The costs of a hedging program will increase significantly if when trying to sell futures the futures price is selling at a discount to cash, and conversely, when trying to buy futures the futures price is trading at an excessive premium. Another hidden cost is the price pressure effect of the market transaction. If there is a lack of liquidity in a market, then attempts to hedge a large portfolio will have a market impact. Finally, jumps or discontinuities in price will affect the ability of managers to place a hedge at the desired price.

CONCLUSIONS

Portfolio insurance as a dynamic hedging strategy can provide good protection for pensions and trusts in a manner that is independent of future market expectations. However, this insurance is not free. It is not designed as a strategy to enhance total returns but to protect existing returns. Managers have to pay for eliminating risk through reduced returns. The costs of these programs can be controlled through setting a proper mix between floor levels and program time horizons. Nevertheless, users have to be aware of costs that are outside their control and are market determined. Portfolio insurance is not like "buying" traditional insurance, but it does serve as a useful tool for managers who desire protection from market changes and want to mold the payoff characteristics of their portfolios to meet specific objectives.

SOURCE: Reprinted from "A Simple Guide To Understanding Portfolio Insurance," *Market Perspectives*, March 1988, Chicago Mercantile Exchange, by Mark Rzepczynski.

Financial Futures Markets

FINANCIAL FUTURES IN PERSPECTIVE

The following list contains just some of the types of financial futures contracts available to investors:

- Treasury Bond Futures
- Treasury Note Futures
- Treasury Bill Futures
- Muni Bond Index Futures
- S&P 500 Index Futures
- NYSE Composite Index Futures
- KC Value Line Index Futures
- Major Market Index Futures

While these futures contracts can be traded for speculative purposes, they are commonly traded by financial institutions to reduce portfolio risk. For example, in 1987 San Diego Gas & Electric Company took positions in financial futures contracts to hedge its pension fund portfolio against a potential decline in stock prices. Yet when stock prices declined, the pension portfolio value was adversely affected. Stock portfolios of other companies such as Manville and Honeywell also were adversely affected by the crash, even though they were hedged by futures positions.

While the effectiveness of financial futures during the crash has been questioned, many portfolio managers still use futures as a hedging device.

- How can financial futures be used to hedge against a stock market downturn?
- How can financial futures be used to hedge bond portfolios?
- How do speculators use financial futures?

These and other related questions on the use of financial futures are addressed in this chapter.

OUTLINE

In recent years, financial futures markets have received much attention because of their potential to generate large returns to speculators and their high degree of risk. However, these markets can also be used to reduce the risk of financial institutions and other corporations, and this chapter describes how. The participation of financial institutions in the financial futures markets is emphasized.

BACKGROUND ON FINANCIAL FUTURES CONTRACTS

A **financial futures contract** (or *interest rate futures*) is a standardized agreement to deliver or receive a specified amount of a specified financial instrument at a specified price and date. Financial futures contracts are traded on organized exchanges, which establish and enforce rules for such trading.

The Chicago Board of Trade (CBT) introduced financial futures in 1975 with the Government National Mortgage Association—Collateralized Depository Receipt (GNMA-CDR) futures contract, which allowed for the future purchase of GNMA bonds at a fixed price. Other financial futures contracts were created over time. All CBT financial futures contracts specify delivery (or settlement) dates of the underlying securities in either March, June, September, or December, up to at least two years in the future. Contract prices are quoted as a percentage of par, with minimum increments of one thirty-second of 1 percent. The Treasury bond futures contract represents Treasury bonds that have an 8 percent coupon rate, and mature or are noncallable for at least 15 years from the futures delivery date. The GNMA futures contract also uses an 8 percent coupon rate.

The more popular futures contracts are available for the Treasury bills, Treasury notes, Treasury bonds, and Eurodollar CDs. The appropriate type of contract depends on the participant's objective.

Part Three

Other Financial Markets

242

For financial futures contracts representing a $100,000 face value, a one percent change reflects a $1,000 change in value. A single day's price movement is generally limited to 3 percentage points or $3,000 per contract on these contracts.

Various futures contracts are purchased and sold through an open outcry auction. Each contract price is measured as 100 minus the interest rate represented by that instrument. For example, a futures rate of 7.5 percent would reflect a futures price of 92.50 for contracts representing short-term securities.

For every buyer of a futures contract, there is a corresponding seller. Brokers act as intermediaries. They receive requests to purchase or sell futures and communicate this information to the futures trading locations (exchanges) where trades are negotiated. A clearinghouse facilitates the trading process by recording all transactions and guaranteeing timely payments on futures contracts. This precludes the need for a purchaser of a futures contract to check the creditworthiness of the contract seller. In fact, purchasers of contracts do not even know who the sellers are, and vice versa. The clearinghouse also supervises the delivery of contracts as of settlement date.

Only the members of a futures exchange can engage in futures transactions on the exchange floor, unless such privileges have been leased to someone else. The purchase of a seat on the exchange entitles membership. In January 1988 the price of a seat on the CBT was $382,500; on the Chicago Mercantile Exchange, $380,000. The price of a seat on any exchange fluctuates over time. Prices declined dramatically for exchanges that trade instruments related to stock after the stock market crash of October 1987.

Members of a futures exchange can be classified as either **commission brokers** (also called *floor brokers*) or **floor traders.** Commission brokers execute orders for their customers. Many of them are employees of brokerage firms, while others work independently. Floor traders (also called *locals*) trade futures contracts for their own account.

As the market price of the financial asset represented by the financial futures contract changes, so will the value of the contract. For example, if the prices of Treasury bonds rise, the value of an existing Treasury bond futures contract should rise, since the contract has locked in the price at which Treasury bonds can be purchased.

Customers who request financial futures transactions are required by the exchanges to establish a margin deposit with their respective brokers before the transaction can be executed. The initial margin is typically between 3 and 10 percent of a futures contract's full value. Brokers commonly require margin requirements above those established by the exchanges. As the futures contract price changes on a daily basis, its value is "marked to market." When the contract's value moves in an unfavorable direction, participants in futures contracts receive a **margin call** from the broker, requiring additional margin money in order to satisfy the so-called **maintenance margin.** These margin requirements reduce the risk that participants will later default on their obligations.

Financial futures activity has grown so much that it now dominates futures contract trading. Exhibit 9.1 shows the volume of financial futures contracts and nonfinancial futures contracts at the CBT in three different periods. In 1976 less than 1 percent of the futures contracts were financial, by 1981 one-third were, and by 1986 more than three-fourths were.

EXHIBIT 9.1 Volume of Futures Contracts Outstanding at the Chicago Board of Trade (CBT)

Type of Futures Contracts	1976		1981		1986	
	Volume	*Percentage*	*Volume*	*Percentage*	*Volume*	*Percentage*
Financial instruments	128,568	.68%	16,362,735	33.30%	78,057,678	77.40%
Agricultural, metals, and other nonfinancial instruments	18,766,588	99.32	32,723,028	66.70	22,756,155	22.60
Total volume at CBT	18,895,156	100.00	49,085,763	100.00	100,813,833	100.00

Participants in financial futures markets can normally· be classified as *hedgers* or *speculators*. Hedgers take positions to reduce their exposure to movements in interest rates or stock prices. Speculators take positions to profit from expected changes in the contract price over time.

INTERPRETING FINANCIAL FUTURES TABLES

Prices of interest rate futures contracts vary from day to day, and are reported in the financial pages of newspapers. *The Wall Street Journal* provides a comprehensive summary of trading activity on various financial futures contracts. Assume the information in Exhibit 9.2 is disclosed on a particular day in May 1989, which refers to the previous trading day. From this exhibit, the futures contract specifying delivery of the Treasury bills for June opened at 94.00 (per $100 par value). The highest trading price for the day was 94.26, while the low was 94.00, with a closing price ("settle" price in Column 5) of 94.20 at the end of the day. The change in Column 6 reflects the difference between settle price and the quoted settle price on the previous trading day. The reported discount in Column 7 is based on the settle price, and represents the percentage difference between the purchase price and par value. The change in the discount in Column 8 represents the difference between quoted discount and the discount on the previous day. The "open interest" in Column 9 represents the number of outstanding futures contracts for the settlement date of concern.

Exhibit 9.2 provides information for T-bill futures contracts with four different settlement months. Once the June settlement date passes, the other months would be moved up one row in the table, and information on T-bill futures with a settlement date for the following June would be shown in the fourth row.

Futures on Treasury bonds and notes are also available and can be used for hedging portfolio positions or for speculation. Specific characteristics of these contracts are disclosed in Exhibit 9.3. Both Treasury bond and note futures traded on the CBT represent a face value of $100,000, which is substantially less than the $1 million face value of securities underlying the T-bill futures contracts.

EXHIBIT 9.2 Example of Treasury Bill Futures Quotations

Treasury Bill Futures

(1)	(2)	(3)	(4)	(5)	(6)	(7)	(8)	(9)
						Discount		Open
	Open	High	Low	Settle	Change	Settle	Change	Interest
June 1989	94.00	94.26	94.00	94.20	+.30	5.80	−.30	16,000
Sept 1989	93.80	94.05	93.80	94.05	+.28	5.95	−.28	2,519
Dec 1989	93.62	93.79	93.62	93.75	+.24	6.25	−.24	287
March 1990	93.45	93.60	93.45	93.60	+.23	6.40	−.23	206

EXHIBIT 9.3 Characteristics of Treasury Bond and Note Futures Traded on the Chicago Board of Trade (CBT)

Characteristic of Futures Contract	U.S. Treasury Bond Futures	U.S. Treasury Note Futures
Size	$100,000 face value	$100,000 face value
Deliverable grade	U.S. Treasury bonds maturing at least 15 years from date of delivery if not callable; coupon rate is 8%	U.S. Treasury notes maturing at least 6½ years but not more than 10 years from the first day of the delivery month; coupon rate is 8%
Price quotation	In points ($1,000) and thirty-seconds of a point	In points ($1,000) and thirty-seconds of a point
Minimum price fluctuation	One-thirty-second (¹⁄₃₂) of a point, or $31.25 per contract	One-thirty-second (¹⁄₃₂) of a point, or $31.25 per contract
Daily trading limits	Three points ($3,000) per contract above or below the previous day's settlement price	Three points ($3,000) per contract above or below the previous day's settlement price
Settlement months	March, June, September, December	March, June, September, December

SPECULATING WITH FINANCIAL FUTURES

The use of financial futures for speculating can be explained with the following example. In February, Jim Sanders forecasts that interest rates will decrease over the next month. If his expectation is correct, the market value of Treasury bills should increase. Jim calls a broker and requests the purchase of a Treasury bill futures contract. Assume that the price of the T-bill futures contract purchased was 94.00 (a 6 percent discount), and the price of T-bills as of the March settlement date is 94.90 (a 5.1 percent discount). Jim could accept delivery of the T-bills and sell them for 90 basis points (.9 percent) more than he purchased them for. Since T-bill futures represent $1 million of par value, the nominal dollar difference between

Chapter 9

Financial Futures Markets

the selling and purchase price of T-bills is $9,000 (computed as $949,000 − $940,000).

In this example, Jim benefited from his speculative strategy because interest rates declined from the time the futures position was taken until the settlement date. If interest rates had risen over this period, the price of T-bills as of settlement date would have been below $94.00 (reflecting a discount above 6 percent), and Jim would have incurred a loss. For example, if the price of T-bills as of the March settlement date was 92.50 (representing a discount of 7.5 percent), the nominal dollar difference between the selling price and purchase price of T-bills would have been − $15,000 (computed as $925,000 − $940,000).

If Jim had, as of February, anticipated that interest rates would rise by March, he would have sold a Treasury bill futures contract with a March settlement date, obligating him to provide Treasury bills to the purchaser as of the delivery date. If Treasury bill prices had actually declined by March, Jim would have been able to obtain Treasury bills at a lower market price in March than what he was obligated to sell those bills for. Again, there is always the risk that interest rates (and therefore Treasury bill prices) will move contrary to expectations. In that event, Jim would have paid a higher market price for the Treasury bills than what he could sell them for.

The potential payoffs from purchasing futures contracts are illustrated in Exhibit 9.4. The term "S" represents the initial price at which a futures position is created. The points along the horizontal axis represent the market value of the securities represented by futures contract as of the delivery date. The maximum possible loss when purchasing futures is the amount to be paid for the securities. Yet, this loss would occur only if the market value of the securities became zero. The amount of gain (or loss) to a speculator that initially purchased futures would equal the loss (or gain) to a speculator that initially sold futures on the same date (assuming zero transaction costs).

CLOSING OUT A FINANCIAL FUTURES CONTRACT

Most buyers and sellers of financial futures contracts do not actually make or accept delivery of the financial instrument, but rather offset their positions by the settlement date. For example, purchasers of Treasury bond futures contracts could sell Treasury bond futures contracts by settlement date. Because they now own a contract to receive and a contract to deliver, the obligations net out. The gain or loss from involvement in the futures positions depends on the futures price at the time of the purchase versus the futures price at the time of the sale. If the price of the securities represented by the futures contract has risen over time, speculators would likely have paid a lower futures price than what they can sell the futures contract for. Thus, a positive gain would have resulted, and the size of the gain would depend on the degree of movement in prices of the securities underlying the contract.

Consider an opposite situation (referred to as a *short* position) where the sale of financial futures was followed by a purchase of futures a few months later in order to offset the initial short position. If security prices rose over this period, the earlier contract to sell futures would be priced lower than the later contract to purchase futures. Thus, a loss would have been incurred.

EXHIBIT 9.4   Potential Payoffs from Speculating in Financial Futures

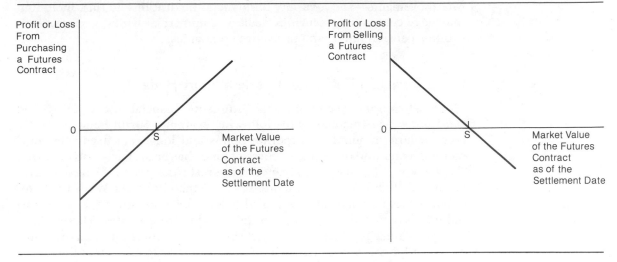

It has been estimated that only 2 percent of all futures contracts actually involve delivery. Yet, this does not reduce the effectiveness of futures contracts for speculation or hedging. Because the contract prices move with the financial instrument representing the contract, an offsetting position at settlement date generates the same gain or loss as if the instrument were delivered.

As an example of taking an offsetting position, assume the futures contract on Treasury bonds was purchased, specifying 90–00, or 90 percent of the $100,000 par value as the price to be paid. This reflects a nominal purchase price of $90,000. One month later, the same futures contract is sold in order to close out the position. At this time, the futures contract specifies 92–10, or 92 and 10/32nds percent of the par value as the price. This reflects a nominal selling price of $92,312.50 and a gain of $2,312.50, ignoring transaction costs.

If the initial position was a sale of the futures contract, then a purchase of that same type of contract would close out the position. Using the numbers in the previous example, a loss of $2,312.50 (ignoring transaction costs) would result from closing out the position. A position is closed out at a loss by participants who expect that a larger loss will occur if the position is not closed out. If the short position is not closed out before settlement date, the investor assuming that position is obligated to deliver the securities underlying the futures contract at that time.

HEDGING WITH FINANCIAL FUTURES

Financial institutions can classify their assets and liabilities by the sensitivity of their market value to interest rate movements. The difference between their volume of rate-sensitive assets and rate-sensitive liabilities represents their exposure to interest rate risk. Over the long run, they may attempt to restructure their assets or liabilities to balance the degree of rate sensitivity. Yet, restructuring the balance sheet takes time. In the short run, they may consider using financial futures to hedge their exposure to interest rate movements—and a variety of financial institutions do this, including mortgage companies, securities dealers, commercial banks, savings institutions, pension funds, and insurance companies.

Using Financial Futures to Create a Short Hedge

The most common use of financial futures by financial institutions is the *short hedge*, as explained by the following example. Austin Bank currently holds a large amount of corporate bonds and long-term fixed-rate commercial loans, and its primary source of funds has been short-term deposits. The bank will be adversely affected if interest rates rise in the near future, because its liabilities are more rate-sensitive than its assets. While the bank believes that its bonds are a reasonable long-term investment, it prefers to reduce its sensitivity to the potential rise in interest rates. Therefore, it hedges against the interest rate risk by selling futures on securities that have similar characteristics to the securities it is hedging, so that the future prices will change in tandem with these securities. One possible strategy is to sell Treasury bond futures, since the price movements of Treasury bonds are highly correlated with movements in corporate bond prices.

If interest rates rise as expected, the market value of existing corporate bonds held by the bank will decline. Yet, this could be offset by the favorable impact of the futures position. The bank locked in the price at which it could sell Treasury bonds. It can purchase Treasury bonds at a lower price just prior to termination of the futures contract period (since the value of bonds has decreased) and profit from fulfilling its futures contract obligation. Alternatively, it could offset its short position by purchasing futures contracts similar to the type that it sold earlier.

If interest rates decrease over this period, the market value of Treasury bonds will increase and Austin bank will be forced to purchase them at a higher price than it could sell them for. Yet, its corporate bonds will increase in value, thereby offsetting the loss incurred on the futures position.

As another example, Charlotte Insurance Company plans to satisfy cash needs in six months by selling its U.S. Treasury bond holdings for $5 million at that time. It is concerned that interest rates might increase over the next three months, which would reduce the market value of bonds by the time they are sold. To hedge against this possibility, Charlotte plans to sell U.S. Treasury bond futures. It sells 50 Treasury bond futures contracts with a face value of $5 million ($100,000 per contract) for 98–16, or $98,500 per contract. This represents a total of $4,925,000 ($98,500 × 50 contracts) to be received.

Suppose that the actual price of the futures contract declined to 94–16 because of an increase in interest rates. Charlotte can close out its short futures position by purchasing contracts identical to those that it has sold. If it purchases 50 Treasury bond futures contracts at the prevailing price of 94–16, it pays $94,500 per contract, or $4,725,000 ($94,500 × 50 contracts). Comparing the price of the futures contracts at the time they were sold versus when they were purchased, Charlotte has earned $200,000 ($4,925,000 − $4,725,000). This gain on the futures contract position offsets the reduced market value of Charlotte's bond holdings.

If interest rates rise by a greater degree over the six-month period, the market value of Treasury bond holdings will decrease further. However, the price of Treasury bond futures contracts will also decrease by a greater degree, creating a larger gain from the futures position. If interest rates increase, the futures prices will rise, causing a loss on the futures position. But this will be offset by a gain in market value of Treasury bond holdings.

This example presumes that the *basis*, or differences between the price of a security and the price of a futures contract, remains the same. In reality, the price of the security may fluctuate more or less than the futures contract used to hedge it. If so, a perfect offset will not result when hedging a given face value amount of securities with the same face value amount of futures contracts.

When one considers both the rising and declining interest rate scenarios, the advantages and disadvantages of financial futures are obvious. Financial futures can hedge against adverse events but also hedge against favorable events. Exhibit 9.5 compares two probability distributions of returns generated by a financial institution whose liabilities are more rate-sensitive than its assets. If the institution hedges its exposure to interest rate risk, its probability distribution of returns is narrower than if it does not hedge. The return from hedging would have been higher than without hedging if interest rates increased (see left portion of graph) but lower if interest rates decreased (see right portion of graph).

A financial institution that hedges with financial futures is less sensitive to economic events. Thus, financial institutions that frequently use financial futures may be able to reduce the variability of their earnings over time, which reflects a lower degree of risk. Yet, it should be recognized that hedging will not likely reduce all uncertainty, since it is virtually impossible to perfectly hedge the sensitivity of all cash flows to interest rate movements.

EXHIBIT 9.5 Comparison of Probability Distributions of Returns: Hedged versus Unhedged Positions

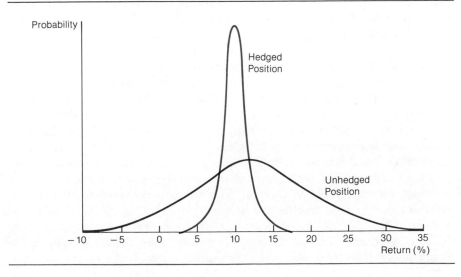

Using Financial Futures to Create a Long Hedge

Some financial institutions use a *long hedge* to reduce exposure to the possibility of declining interest rates. Consider government securities dealers that plan to purchase long-term bonds in a few months. If the dealers are concerned that prices of these securities will rise, they may purchase Treasury bond futures contracts. These contracts lock in the price at which Treasury bonds can be purchased, regardless of what happens to market rates prior to the actual purchase of the bonds.

As another example, consider a bank that has obtained a large amount of its funds from large CDs with a maturity of one year. Also assume that most of its assets represent loans with rates that adjust every six months. This bank would be adversely affected by a decline in interest rates, since interest earned on assets would be more sensitive than interest paid on liabilities. To hedge against the possibility of lower interest rates, the bank could purchase Treasury bill futures to lock in the price on Treasury bills at a specified future date. If interest rates decline, the gain on the futures position could partially offset any reduction in the bank's earnings due to the reduction in interest rates.

Hedging Net Exposure

Because financial futures contracts result in transaction costs, they should be used only to hedge *net exposure*, which reflects the difference between asset and liability positions. Consider a bank that has $300 million in long-term assets and $220 million worth of long-term fixed-rate liabilities. If interest rates rise, the market value of long-term assets will decline, while the bank benefits from the fixed rate on the $220 million in long-term liabilities. Thus, the net exposure is only $80 million (assuming that the long-term assets and liabilities are similarly affected by rising interest rates). The financial institution should therefore focus on hedging its net exposure of $80 million by creating a short hedge.

Complications of Hedging with Financial Futures

While the concept of using financial futures is logical, the actual implementation is difficult. In many situations, the characteristics of the assets being hedged differ from the assets represented by the financial futures contract. Because the impact of changing interest rates on the prices of the two types of assets may differ, a perfect offsetting effect is unlikely. To deal with this problem, financial institutions attempt to identify an asset represented by futures contracts whose market value moves closely in tandem with that of the assets they want to hedge. Their use of a futures contract on one financial instrument to hedge their position in a different financial instrument is known as **cross-hedging.** The effectiveness of a cross-hedge depends on the degree of correlation between the market values of the two financial instruments. If the price of the underlying security of the futures contract moves closely in tandem with the security hedged, the futures contract can provide an effective hedge.

Even when the futures contract is highly correlated with the portfolio being hedged, the value of the futures contract may change by a higher or lower percentage than the portfolio's market value. If the futures contract value is less volatile than the portfolio value, hedging will require a greater amount of principal represented by the futures contracts. For example, assume that for every percentage movement in the portfolio, the price of the futures contract changes by .8 percent. In this case the value of futures contracts to fully hedge the portfolio would be 1.25 times the principal of the portfolio (computed as 1 divided by .8). Over time, this so-called **hedge ratio** will change, forcing the portfolio manager to adjust by liquidating some of the futures contracts.

Another problem arises when the assets to be hedged may be prepaid earlier than their designated maturity. Suppose a commercial bank sells Treasury bond futures in order to hedge its holdings of corporate bonds, and just after the futures position is created, the bonds are called by the corporation that initially issued them. If interest rates subsequently decline, the bank would incur a loss from its futures position without a corresponding gain from its bonds position (since the bonds were called earlier).

As a second example, consider a savings and loan association with large holdings of long-term fixed-rate mortgages that are mostly financed by short-term funds. It sells Treasury bond futures to hedge against the possibility of rising interest rates; then, after the futures position is established, interest rates decline, and many of the existing mortgages are prepaid by homeowners. The savings and loan association would incur a loss from its futures position without a corresponding gain from its fixed-rate mortgage position (since the mortgages were prepaid).

There are strategies to deal with the complications identified here. An explanation of these strategies would require an entire textbook itself. This chapter is simply intended to suggest some advantages and complications that financial institutions must recognize when hedging with financial futures.

HEDGING WITH INDEX FUTURES

Index futures allow one to purchase or sell an index for a specified price at a specified date. The index is defined according to prices of a specified security portfolio. Futures contracts are available for both stock indexes and bond indexes, and they are commonly used by some financial institutions to hedge their positions, as explained next.

Stock Index Futures

The **Major Market Index (MMI)** represents 20 stocks, and its movements are very similar to that of the Dow Jones Industrial Average. Like other futures contracts, the MMI futures contract is standardized. It represents an index reflecting prices of 20 stocks, not the stocks themselves. An MMI futures position can be closed by taking an offsetting position at any point until the settlement date. If the position is not closed out prior to settlement date, it will automatically be settled in cash on the settlement date. The initial margin for stock index futures has typically ranged from 3 to 10 percent.

For institutions that concentrate on stocks other than those making up the Dow Jones Industrial Index, MMI futures may not be appropriate be-

Portfolio Insurance and the Crash of October 1987

The stock market crash on Monday, October 19, 1987, has raised questions both about how effectively portfolio insurance limited downside risk and about its possible systemic repercussions to the underlying stock market. On October 19, "Black Monday," the Dow Jones Industrial Average plunged a record 508 points (22 percent) and the S&P 500 Index dropped 57.6 points (20.5 percent), proportionately almost as much. In the following weeks, both stock-index arbitrage and portfolio insurance were widely blamed for exacerbating the market's turmoil.

Some critics have raised a well-founded concern that the *interaction* of portfolio insurance and stock-index arbitrage may be destabilizing. Stock-index arbitrage should be thought of as a trading link between the futures and stock markets that aligns index futures and stock index prices. Stock-index arbitrage is a straightforward form of arbitrage: buying a good or asset in a market where it is cheap and selling it in a market where it is dear. If the futures price is sufficiently below (above) the index price, arbitrageurs buy (sell) the futures and sell (buy) the index. In theory, ensuring that the "law of one price" holds cannot be destabilizing; in practice, however, the volume and timing

of stock-index arbitrage could conceivably contribute to intraday volatility. Coupling index arbitrage with portfolio insurance may create destabilizing price movements. The critics' argument goes as follows: A large market decline triggers futures selling by portfolio insurers, which drives the futures price down relative to the index price. This in turn sets off arbitrage trading because the futures become underpriced relative to the index. Stock-index arbitrageurs buy the futures and sell short a basket of stocks that replicates the current composition of the index. Stock sales by arbitrageurs drive the index price down. Thus, stock-index arbitrage transmits the selling pressure from futures to the stock market. Arbitrage-induced price declines in the stock market then induce further portfolio-insurance futures selling, setting off a downward price spiral between the stock and futures markets.

What actually happened on October 19 is more complicated than the above scenario. Right at the opening of trade on "Black Monday," the S&P 500 futures market was exposed to great selling pressure. After the previous Friday's 106 point decline on the Dow, portfolio managers and others may have anticipated further futures selling by insurers

cause the MMI may not closely track the market values of their stocks. An alternative stock futures index, known as NASDAQ-100 futures, may be more suitable. This index is composed of the 100 largest and most actively traded nonfinancial stocks exchanged in the over-the-counter (OTC) market. In addition, another index, known as the SPOC, is designed to track the activity of the overall OTC market. This index is determined by the prices of 250 stocks that are sold on the OTC. The S&P 500 futures index is still another alternative, representing the weighted average of the 500 stocks comprising the Standard and Poor's listing. Because of the variety of stock index futures, institutional investors can use an index that provides the best

Part Three

Other Financial Markets

and tried to get their own futures and stock sales in ahead of them.

The chaotic market conditions on Black Monday led to a breakdown of stock-index arbitrage because it became very risky. The volatility in both the futures and stock markets made it difficult to know what the current futures and index prices were. Trades based on incorrect prices could translate into large losses on what theoretically are riskless transactions. The record trading volume of 605 million shares on the New York Stock Exchange (NYSE) also compounded the risk, as orders could not be executed immediately and simultaneously in the two markets. The NYSE "uptick" rule restricted opportunities to sell stock short during the huge market decline on October 19. Arbitrageurs who executed their stock market trades by short selling had to wait for component stock prices to rise before having their sell orders executed. Severe order backlogs developed on the NYSE.

Preliminary survey data collected by the regulatory agency that oversees stock-index futures trading, the Commodity Futures Trading Commission (CFTC), indicate that index arbitrage constituted only 9 percent of total NYSE volume on that day. On the following day, after the Chicago Mercantile Exchange temporarily suspended trading in stock-index futures, the NYSE effectively banned arbitrage by prohibiting brokerage houses from executing orders through direct computer links to the exchange floor; arbitrage trading dropped to 2 percent of volume.[1]

According to preliminary CFTC trader position data, futures selling by institutional investors accounted for a greater volume of trades in the S&P 500 futures than stock-index arbitrage: their futures sales on October 19 represented between 12 and 24 percent of that day's total volume in the S&P 500 contract and between 19 and 26 percent on October 20.[2] Portfolio insurance-related futures sales were a portion of that hedging-related activity. Only careful study of market events surrounding the crash may uncover what role portfolio insurance played in the market turmoil.

1 U.S. Commodity Futures Trading Commission, *Interim Report on Stock Index Futures and Cash Market Activity During October 1987*, November 9, 1987, p. 74.
2 Ibid.

SOURCE: *Economic Review*, Federal Reserve Bank of Atlanta (November–December 1987): 19.

hedge. The index that most closely tracks the stocks they are holding or planning to purchase would be most appropriate.

Stock index futures contracts have four expiration dates in a given year—the third Friday in March, June, September, and December. The securities underlying the stock index futures contracts are not deliverable; settlement occurs through a cash payment. On the settlement date, the futures contract is valued according to the quoted stock index. The net gain or loss on the stock index futures contract is the difference between the futures price when the initial position was created and the value of the contract as of the settlement date. If a position is closed out prior to the settlement date, the

Chapter 9

Financial Futures Markets

Do Stock Index Futures Increase Stock Market Volatility?

A recent study by Edwards attempted to determine whether the trading stock index futures increases stock market volatility. For much of the period in which stock index futures have existed (since 1982), stock market volatility was found to be relatively low. Edwards concludes that the stock index futures trading is not likely to be the primary cause of the recent increase in stock market volatility. While he acknowledges that there is no clear explanation for the higher degree of stock market volatility, he suggests that it may be because of the large U.S. balance of trade deficit, the substantial decline in the value of the dollar, and the large federal budget deficit. These are the same factors that contributed to the stock market crash in October 1987. The volatility in the stock market was even higher for several months after the crash than during the months before the crash. Perhaps this increase in volatility is the result of the crash itself and simply reflects more frequent transactions into and out of the stock markets.

SOURCE: Franklin R. Edwards. "Does Futures Trading Increase Stock Market Volatility?" *Financial Analysts Journal* (January–February 1988): 63–69.

net gain or loss on the stock index futures contract is the difference between the futures price when the position was created and the futures price when the position was closed out.

Some speculators prefer to trade stock index futures rather than actual stocks because of substantially smaller transaction costs. The commission cost of a purchase and subsequent sale of 100 S&P 500 futures contracts is about $2,500, compared to $45,100 for equivalent stocks contained in the S&P 500.

Assume Boulder Insurance Company plans to purchase a variety of stocks in December, once cash inflows are generated. While it does not have cash to purchase the stocks immediately, it is anticipating a large jump in stock market prices before December. Given this situation, it decides to purchase S&P 500 index futures. The futures price on the S&P 500 index with a December settlement date is presently 305. The value of an S&P contract is $500 times the index, or $152,500 ($500 × 305). Because the S&P 500 futures prices should move with the stock market, it will rise over time if the company's expectations are correct. Assume that the S&P 500 index rose to 340 on the settlement date. The futures contract is therefore valued at $170,000 ($500 × 340), resulting in a gain of $17,500 ($170,000 − $152,500). This gain can be used to offset the higher prices that will be paid for stocks in December.

If the stock prices had decreased over the period of concern, the S&P 500 futures index would have decreased, and Boulder Insurance Co. would have incurred a loss on its futures position. However, it would have been able to purchase stocks at relatively low prices because of the market's decline.

Part Three

Other Financial Markets

Bond Index Futures

For financial institutions that trade in municipal bonds, the Chicago Board of Trade offers **Municipal Bond Index (MBI)** futures. The index is based on the **Bond Buyer Index** of 40 actively traded general obligation and revenue bonds. The specific characteristics of MBI futures are disclosed in Exhibit 9.6. Because MBI futures are based on an index rather than the bonds themselves, there is no physical exchange of bonds. Instead, these futures contracts are settled in cash.

Consider an insurance company that will be receiving large cash flows in the near future. While it plans to use some of the incoming funds to purchase municipal bonds, it is concerned that because of the likely downward trend in interest rates, municipal bond prices may increase before it can purchase them. Thus, it purchases MBI futures. If the company's expectation is correct, the futures position will generate a gain, which can be used to pay for the higher-priced bonds once it has sufficient funds. Conversely, if bond prices fall, the company will incur a loss from its futures position. Yet, this loss is somewhat offset since the company can purchase bonds at low market prices.

As a second example, consider an investment banking firm that has agreed to underwrite bonds for various municipalities. Assume that it expects the market prices of bonds to decline in the near future. Such an event could reduce underwriting profits if the market price falls before these bonds are sold. To hedge this risk, it could sell MBI futures. The futures position would generate a gain and offset the reduced underwriting profits if its expectations are correct.

EXHIBIT 9.6   Characteristics of Municipal Bond Index Futures

Characteristic of Futures Contract	Municipal Bond Index Futures
Trading unit	1,000 times the Bond Buyer Municipal Bond Index. A price of 90-00 represents a contract size of $90,000.
Price quotation	In points and thirty-seconds of a point.
Minimum price fluctuation	One thirty-second ($\frac{1}{32}$) of a point, or $31.25 per contract.
Daily trading limits	Three points ($3,000) per contract above or below the previous day's settlement price
Settlement months	March, June, September, and December.
Settlement procedure	Municipal Bond Index futures settle in cash on the last day of trading. The settlement price is based on the Bond Buyer Municipal Bond Index value of that day.

INSTITUTIONAL USE OF FUTURES MARKETS

Exhibit 9.7 summarizes the manner by which various types of financial institutions participate in futures markets. Financial institutions generally use futures contracts to reduce risk, as has already been illustrated by several examples. Some commercial banks and savings institutions use a short hedge to protect against a possible increase in interest rates. Some bond mutual funds, pension funds, and life insurance companies take futures positions to insulate their bond portfolios from a possible increase in interest rates. Stock mutual funds, pension funds, and insurance companies take positions in stock index futures to partially insulate their respective stock portfolios from adverse stock market movements.

INTERNATIONALIZATION OF FUTURES MARKETS

INTERNATIONAL

ASPECTS

The trading of financial futures involves the assessment of international financial market conditions. The foreign flow of funds into and out of the United States can affect interest rates and therefore the market value of Treasury bonds, corporate bonds, mortgages, and other long-term debt securities. Portfolio managers assess international flows of funds to forecast changes in interest rate movements, which in turn affect the value of their respective portfolios. Even speculators assess the international flows of funds

EXHIBIT 9.7 Institutional Use of Futures Markets

Type of Financial Institution	Participation in Futures Markets
Commercial banks	■ Take positions in futures contracts to hedge against interest rate risk
Savings institutions	■ Take positions in futures contracts to hedge against interest rate risk
Securities firms	■ Execute futures transactions for individuals and firms ■ Take positions in futures to hedge their own portfolios against stock market or interest rate movements
Mutual funds	■ Take positions in futures contracts to speculate on future stock market or interest rate movements ■ Take positions in futures contracts to hedge their portfolios against stock market or interest rate movements
Pension funds	■ Take positions in futures contracts to hedge their portfolios against stock market or interest rate movements
Insurance companies	■ Take positions in futures contracts to hedge their portfolios against stock market or interest rate movements

to forecast interest rates so that they can determine whether to take short or long futures positions.

The trading of stock index futures can also be influenced by the dollar's value, since it affects the strength of the U.S. economy, and therefore the anticipated stock prices of U.S. companies. In addition, the international business performance of U.S.–based multinational corporations is affected by the dollar's value.

Foreign Stock Index Futures

Foreign stock index futures have been created to either speculate on or hedge against potential movements in foreign stock markets. Expectations of a strong foreign stock market would encourage purchasing futures contracts on the representative index. Conversely, if firms expected a decline in the foreign market, they would consider selling futures on the representative index. In addition, financial institutions with substantial investment in a particular foreign stock market could hedge against a temporary decline in that market by selling foreign stock index futures.

Some of the more popular foreign stock index futures contracts are identified in Exhibit 9.8. Numerous other foreign stock index futures contracts will likely be created over time.

Currency Futures Contracts

A futures contract on a foreign currency is a standardized agreement to deliver or receive a specified amount of a specified foreign currency at a specified price (exchange rate) and date. The settlement months, as noted earlier, are March, June, September, and December. Some companies act as hedgers in the currency futures market by purchasing futures on currencies that they will need in the future to cover payables or by selling futures on currencies that they will receive in the future. Speculators in the currency futures market may purchase futures on a foreign currency that they expect to strengthen against the U.S. dollar or sell futures on currencies that they expect to weaken against the U.S. dollar.

EXHIBIT 9.8   Popular Foreign Stock Index Futures Contracts

Name of Stock Futures Index	Description
Nikkei 225	225 Japanese stocks
Toronto 35	35 stocks on Toronto stock exchange
Financial Times-Stock Exchange 100	100 stocks on London stock exchange
Barclays share price	40 stocks on New Zealand stock exchange
Hang Seng	33 stocks on Hong Kong stock exchange
Osaka	50 Japanese stocks
All ordinaries share price	307 Australian stocks

SOURCE: *The Wall Street Journal*, September 18, 1987, 42d

Resolving the Uncertainty Associated with Program Trading

Program trading discouraged some investors from participating in the stock market after the crash. On July 7, 1988, the boards of directors at the New York Stock Exchange (NYSE) and Chicago Mercantile Exchange (CME) announced plans that would boost the confidence of individual investors in financial markets. Some of the key components for the plan are:

■ Giving priority to individual investor orders when the Dow Jones Industrial Average moves 25 points
■ Provision of program trading statistics

■ The NYSE and CME will attempt to control the link between stock prices and stock futures prices. Price limits on S&P 500 futures contracts were established to reduce the swings in prices of these contracts

While the joint agreement by the NYSE and CME was experimental, it was a first step toward encouraging individual investors to re-enter the stock market. In addition, it showed that the two exchanges could work together to resolve the market uncertainty that persisted since the crash.

Purchasers of **currency futures contracts** can hold the contract until settlement date and accept delivery of the foreign currency at that time, or can close out their long position prior to the settlement date by selling the identical type and number of contracts before then. If they close out their long position, their gain or loss is determined by the futures price when they created a long position versus the price at the time the position was closed out. Sellers of currency futures contracts either decide to deliver the foreign currency at the settlement date or close out their position by purchasing the identical type and number of contracts prior to the settlement date. Currency futures contracts are discussed in more detail in Chapter 11.

SUMMARY

Futures contracts are not only used by speculators but also by financial institutions that desire to hedge against risk. Portfolio managers of various financial institutions are concerned with the impact of general stock market or interest rate movements on the value of their respective portfolios. Futures on various types of securities or on indexes are used to hedge against adverse stock market or interest rate movements. The most appropriate type of futures contract for hedging a given portfolio depends on the characteristics of that portfolio.

Futures contracts are not normally able to provide a perfect portfolio hedge, but they can substantially reduce the uncertainty of a portfolio's future performance. However, along with preventing very poor portfolio performance, they also prevent very high performance. Therefore, financial

Part Three

Other Financial Markets

institutions that use futures contracts must be willing to forego higher potential return in exchange for less risk.

KEY TERMS

Bond Buyer Index	hedge ratio
commission brokers	index futures
cross-hedging	maintenance margin
currency futures contracts	Major Market Index (MMI)
financial futures contract	margin call
floor traders	Municipal Bond Index (MBI)

QUESTIONS

9.1. Describe the general characteristics of a futures contract.

9.2. How does a clearinghouse facilitate the trading of financial futures contracts?

9.3. How does the price of a financial futures contract change as the market price of the security it represents changes? Why?

9.4. Explain why some futures contracts may be more suitable than others for hedging exposure to interest rate risk.

9.5. Would speculators buy or sell Treasury bond futures contracts if they expected interest rates to increase? Explain.

9.6. What is the maximum loss to a purchaser of a futures contract?

9.7. Explain how purchasers of financial futures contracts can offset their position. How is their gain or loss determined?

9.8. Explain how sellers of financial futures contracts can offset their position. How is their gain or loss determined?

9.9. Assume a financial institution had a larger amount of rate-sensitive assets than rate-sensitive liabilities. Would it likely be more adversely affected by an increase or decrease in interest rates? Should it purchase or sell financial futures contracts in order to hedge its exposure?

9.10. Assume a financial institution had a larger amount of rate-sensitive liabilities than assets. Would it likely be more adversely affected by an increase or decrease in interest rates? Should it purchase or sell financial futures contracts in order to hedge its exposure?

9.11. Why do some financial institutions remain exposed to interest rate risk, even when they believe that the use of financial futures could reduce their exposure?

9.12. Explain the difference between a long hedge and a short hedge used by financial institutions. When is a long hedge more appropriate than a short hedge.

9.13. Explain how the probability distribution of a financial institution's returns is affected when it uses financial futures to hedge. What does this imply about its risk?

9.14. Describe the act of cross-hedging. What determines the effectiveness of a cross-hedge?

9.15. How might a savings association use Treasury bond futures to hedge its fixed-rate mortgage portfolio (assuming that its main source of funds is short-term deposits)? Explain how prepayments on mortgages can limit the effectiveness of the hedge.

9.16. Describe stock index futures. How could they be used by a financial institution that is anticipating a jump in stock prices but does not yet have sufficient funds to purchase large amounts of stock?

9.17. Why would a pension fund or insurance company even consider selling stock index futures?

9.18. Blue Devil Savings & Loan Association has a large portion of 10-year fixed-rate mortgages and obtains most of its funds from short-term deposits. It uses the yield curve to assess the market's anticipation of future interest rates. It believes that expectations of future interest rates are the major force in affecting the yield curve. Assume that an upward-sloping yield curve exists with a steep slope. Based on this information, should Blue Devil consider using financial futures as a hedging technique? Explain.

PROBLEMS

9.1. Spratt Company purchased Treasury bill futures contracts when the quoted price was $93.50. When this position was closed out, the quoted price was $94.75. Determine the profit or loss per contract, ignoring transaction costs.

9.2. Suerth Investments Inc. purchased Treasury bill futures contracts when the quoted price was $95.00. When this position was closed out, the quoted price was $93.60. Determine the profit or loss per contract, ignoring transaction costs.

9.3. Toland Company sold Treasury bill futures contracts when the quoted price was $94.00. When this position was closed out, the quoted price was $93.20. Determine the profit or loss per contract, ignoring transaction costs.

9.4. Rude Dynamics Inc. sold Treasury bill futures contracts when the quoted price was $93.26. When this position was closed out, the quoted price was $93.90. Determine the profit or loss per contract, ignoring transaction costs.

9.5. Egan Company purchased a futures contract on Treasury bonds that specified a price of 91–00. When the position was closed out, the price of the Treasury bond futures contract was 90–10. Determine the profit or loss, ignoring transaction costs.

9.6. R. C. Clark sold a futures contract on Treasury bonds that specified a price of 92–10. When the position was closed out, the price of the Treasury bond futures contract was 93–00. Determine the profit or loss, ignoring transaction costs.

9.7. Marks Insurance Company sold S&P 500 stock index futures that specified an index of 290. When the position was closed out, the index specified by the futures contract was 320. Determine the profit or loss, ignoring transaction costs.

PROJECT

1. ASSESSING CHANGES IN FUTURES PRICES

Use *The Wall Street Journal* to determine the recent future prices on Treasury bonds and on the S&P 500 index. Also obtain the futures prices that existed six weeks ago. Then fill out the following table.

	Recent Futures Price	Futures Price 6 weeks ago	Profit or Loss on a Long Position Over this Six-Week Period	Reason for Change in the Futures Price
Treasury Bonds				
S&P 500 Index				

REFERENCES

Andrews, Suzanna. "Can Banks Succeed in Futures?" *Institutional Investor* (February 1984): 173–186.

Andrews, Suzanna. "Were Muni Index Futures Worth the Wait?" *Institutional Investor* (June 1985): 261–262.

Barnhul, Theodore, James Jordan and William Seale. "Maturity and Refunding Effects on Treasury-Bond Futures Price Variance." *Journal of Financial Research* (Summer 1987): 121–132.

Belongia, Michael J. and G. J. Santoni. "Hedging Interest Rate Risk with Financial Futures: Some Basic Principles." *Review*, Federal Reserve Bank of St. Louis (October 1984): 15–25.

Belongia, Michael J. and G. J. Santoni. "Cash Flow or Present Value: What's Lurking Behind that Hedge?" *Review*, Federal Reserve Bank of St. Louis (January 1985): 5–13.

Block, Stanley B. and Timothy J. Gallagher. "The Use of Interest Rate Futures and Options by Corporate Financial Managers." *Financial Management* (Autumn 1986): 73–78.

Bollenbacher, George M. "Using Stock Index Products in Trust Banking." *Banker's Magazine* (July–August 1984): 57–61.

Booth, James R., Richard L. Smith, and Richard W. Stolz. "Use of Interest Rate Futures by Financial Institutions." *Journal of Bank Research* (Spring 1984): 15–20.

Ferris, Stephen and Don Chance. "Trading Time Effects in Financial and Commodity Futures Markets." *Financial Review* (May 1987): 281–294.

Franckle, Charles T. and George M. McCabe. "The Effectiveness of Rolling the Hedge Forward in the Treasury Bill Futures Market." *Financial Management* (Summer 1983): 21–29.

Goodman, Laurie S. "New Options Markets." *Quarterly Review*, Federal Reserve Bank of New York (Autumn 1983): 35–43.

Hartzmark, Michael. "Returns to Individual Traders of Futures: Aggregate Results." *Journal of Political Economy* (December 1987): 1292–1306.

Hedge, Shantaram. "The Forecast Performance of Treasury Bond Futures Contracts." *Journal of Business Finance and Accounting* (Summer 1987): 291–304.

Kamara, Abraham. "Optimal Hedging in Futures Markets with Multiple Delivery Specifications." *Journal of Finance* (September 1987): 1007–1021.

Kawaller, Ira G. "The Futures Contract Alternative." *Banker's Magazine* (March–April): 67–71.

Koppenhaver, G. D. "Futures Market Regulation." *Economic Perspectives*, Federal Reserve Bank of Chicago (January–February 1987): 3–16.

Laderman, Jeffrey. "Protecting Stock Profits If the Bear Attacks." *Businessweek*, March 31, 1986, 62.

Marton, Andrew. "Cashing in on Futures Fever." *Institutional Investor* (July 1983): 155–160.

Marton, Andrew. "Making It in Financial Futures." *Institutional Investor* (August 1983): 191–199.

Morris, Bailey. "Getting Tough with the Futures Exchanges." *Institutional Investor* (February 1985): 145–148.

Pearlman, Ellen. "Getting Acquainted with

Stock-Index Futures." *Institutional Investors* (August 1983): 202–208.

Petero, Ed. "The Growing Efficiency of Index Futures Markets." *Journal of Portfolio Management* (Summer 1985): 52–56.

"Recent and Prospective Growth of Money Market Mutual Funds." *Financial Letter*, Federal Reserve Bank of Kansas City, June 16, 1981.

Reich, Cary. "Futures." *Institutional Investor* (March 1983): 51–66.

"The Dawning of the Stock-Index Era." *Institutional Investor* (July 1982): 166–171.

Walmsley, Julian. "The New Options Markets." *Bankers Monthly* (November 1986): 12–13.

Williams, Jeffrey. "Futures Markets: A Consequence of Risk Aversion or Transactions Costs?" *Journal of Political Economy* (October 1987): 1000–1023.

Worthy, Ford S. "Big New Players in Financial Futures." *Fortune* September 17, 1984, 109–110, 118.

October 19, 1987: The Facts

STATEMENT OF THE CHICAGO MERCANTILE EXCHANGE

On Monday, October 19, specialists at New York exchanges were faced with an overwhelming influx of sell orders at the opening bell. These opening imbalances lasted for the better part of two hours and paralyzed trading in many important stocks.

For example, over 30% of the stocks in the Dow Jones Industrial Average were still closed an hour after the opening of the market. During that day and those that followed, similar imbalances occurred for extended periods of time. As a result, investors experienced great difficulty in selling or buying stocks.

In contrast, our market opened promptly at 8:30 AM (CST) on Monday, the 19th. We, also, experienced unusual conditions with large opening sell orders. Still, the S&P futures contract was able to maintain an orderly market with a bid/ask spread that, while unusually large, compared favorably with other markets.

Although our prices were substantially below the previous day's settlement, our market immediately provided a necessary refuge for investment hedging. And, of equal importance, our market offered an opportunity to those investors who wanted to buy at a time when other markets were not yet fully open for business. Thus, pension fund and other portfolio managers, as well as individual investors turned to our market to adjust their investment exposure.

The CME's S&P 500 futures and options contracts served as a pressure valve on Monday, October 19, the day the stock market declined over 500 Dow points, as well as during the days that followed. Our risk transfer mechanism was tested during one of the most turbulent periods in economic history. It worked. Our index markets provided institutions and individual investors a way to hedge their risk. Those funds that used futures to hedge their positions protected their customers from the full impact of the market decline.

Program Trading

There are some who believe program trading was a major factor in the stock market decline. Program trading is little understood, has many faces, and is often used in conjunction with stock market applications that have nothing to do with futures and options. Program trading has become a buzzword of vague and variable definition. In fact, its only relation to futures is in a strategy called index arbitrage.

Our preliminary estimates from October 19 show that index arbitrage involving CME futures probably resulted in the sale of about 50 million out of 600 million shares of stock on the New York Stock Exchange (NYSE). Thus, program trading represented less than 10% of total stock sales on the NYSE on Monday. A full 90% of the total share traded on the NYSE had nothing to do with futures activity at the CME.

In addition, index arbitrage transferred to New York only a fraction of the total selling pressure experienced in Chicago. Institutional and retail investors at the CME absorbed the equivalent of at least another 75 million shares on October 19 that were not arbitraged to New York. Without the stock index futures market, selling pressure on the NYSE could only have increased and resulted in further imbalances.

Moreover, on Monday, October 26, one week after the initial shock, the U.S. stock market suffered its second worst decline in history. This time, however, futures cannot be blamed since there was a very low level of futures-related trading. On this day, the S&P 500 futures contract traded less than half its normal volume, and NYSE rules virtually precluded index arbitrage. These facts thus contradict the charge that program trading plays a contributing role in abrupt market declines.

Finally, the experience of foreign stock markets also demonstrates that stock index futures did not cause the current market turmoil. During the week ending October 23, most major foreign stock markets suffered declines and volatility comparable to that in the U.S. Between October 16 and October 23, the U.K. market declined by 22%, the German market by 12%, the Japanese market by 12%, the French market by 10%, and the U.S. market by 13%. Furthermore, all of these markets suffered abrupt one day drops. Yet, aside from the U.S., none of these countries has a well-developed stock index futures market. In Hong Kong, another market without program trading, the decline was even more severe—but one can ascribe its cause to the fact that this market closed for four consecutive days.

This is the third time in recent memory that program trading has been invoked as the cause of a market decline. Program trading was supposed to have been the villain in the September 11 and 12, 1986 declines as well as the January 23, 1987 price move. These events were subjected to extensive scrutiny to determine the role of program trading. The SEC firmly concluded:

the magnitude of the September decline was a result of changes in investors' perceptions of fundamental economic conditions, rather than artificial forces arising from index-related trading strategies.[1]

1 The Role of Index-Related Trading in the Market Decline on September 11 and 12, 1986. *SEC Div. of Market Regulation, March 1987.*

The CFTC study of the January 23 market move was equally clear in vindicating program trading:

The staff found that index-related trading was not very significant during the narrow time period in which the stock and futures markets peaked and began to fall rapidly. Furthermore, for the entire day, such trading was smaller in magnitude and relative to total volume than what was found on either September 11 or 12.

Additionally, the CFTC's more recent "Interim Report on Stock Index Futures and Cash Market Activity During October 1987," which was published on November 9, 1987 states (pages 5–6):

This interim report focuses on one aspect of the recent events—futures market activity during the historic decline in the stock market—and has found that futures-related trading apparently was not a major part of NYSE volume on October 19 and following days during the week ending October 23, 1987. Moreover, many institutional investors have maintained that; absent the hedging facility provided by the futures market, the stock market decline of October 19 might have been greater.

Despite all this, index arbitrage continues to serve as a convenient explanation for the panic. Negative assertions about program trading are simple and convenient, but dangerous and wrong. The vocal critics of program trading: (1) divert attention from fundamental underlying economic factors that have burdened our economy; (2) obscure the important role futures and options markets played in acting as a first line of defense for the investment community; and (3) threaten the viability of an industry whose success has already drawn a host of foreign imitators and competitors eager for the thousands of jobs and billions of deposits created by our energies.

Margin Policy

Margin levels at futures exchanges are variously blamed for increasing prices, falling prices, and/or higher volatility levels.

It is true that the purchaser of a futures index contract must in the initial instance *deposit* between 10% and 20% of the underlying value of the contract while a stock buyer may only *borrow* 50% of the value of his stock. But, that difference neither explains recent market gyrations nor adequately describes the differences between the concepts.

Critics suggest that over-extended investors were forced out of the futures market by margin calls and that a downward spiral followed. This, however, is contrary to fact. Speculators bought, not sold, futures; our total open interest (or amount of contracts outstanding) increased.

Critics have also alleged that low futures margins encouraged speculative demand for stock index products, which in turn led to an overpricing of U.S. equities. The charge that speculation is linked to market instability has been studied at length by our nation's finest economists.[2] Direct tests

2 *See*, A Review and Evaluation of Federal Margin Regulations, *A Study by the staff of the Board of Governors of the Federal Reserve Bank, December, 1984, or for a comprehensive bibliography see S. Figlewski*, Margins and Market Integrity: Margin Setting for Stock Index Futures and Options, *Columbia University's Center for the Study of Futures Working Paper Series #csfm-83, 1984.*

of the effect of margin requirements on price volatility in the stock market have found little apparent relationship.

Moreover, in this instance, the behavior of prices on foreign stock exchanges contradict this simplistic claim. Generally, foreign markets experienced greater appreciation than the U.S. market both in price levels and price/earnings ratios during the 1980s. Those foreign markets were not fueled by stock index products. The presence of an efficiently margined, strong stock index futures market in the U.S. did nothing to push U.S. stock values out of line with the rest of the world.

More fundamentally, "margin" in stock and "margin" in futures are two substantially different things—only the word is the same. Stock margins limit the extension of credit to purchase an asset. A futures contract is not an asset—it has no value when purchased. It is therefore not logically possible to discuss futures margin in the context of credit extension. Instead, futures margins are good faith deposits for contract performance. Yet, even in this capacity, futures margins play a substantially different role than securities margins. In contrast to securities markets, futures markets maintain a virtual "no debt" financial system. All futures market positions are marked-to-market at least on a daily basis, i.e., any price changes in futures positions representing losses must be paid for in cash at least on a daily basis.

For example, pursuant to normal procedures in volatile market periods, during recent weeks, our exchange has called for margin payments two and sometimes three times during a single trading session. This financial system, substantially safer than other systems that allow losses to accumulate for many days, avoids the need for high initial margins to maintain financial integrity.

Thus, the differences between the role, function and level of futures and stock margins exist as a natural and necessary result of the very different functions these two markets perform. They are not the result of a regulatory gap or loophole. Perhaps the clearest evidence of this comes from securities options markets whose purpose and function is, in many respects, similar to that of futures markets and whose margins are regulated by the Federal Reserve Board and the Securities and Exchange Commission. Securities options margins are, if anything, lower than comparable futures market margins.

SEC/CFTC Merger

There has been a call from some quarters to eliminate the CFTC as the regulator of futures market equity-based indices or as regulator for other financial futures such as U.S. Treasury bond futures. Two reasons have been advanced to support this demand.

First it is claimed that the recent market actions would not have occurred, or would have been less extreme, if there had been a single regulator. The claim that a single regulator would have mitigated the market's movement is not supported by the facts. The record is absolutely clear that the SEC, the CFTC, the NYSE and the CME were in constant and complete communication during the relevant period. The markets and the agencies worked together without friction and for a single purpose. The greater understanding of market subtlety and workings that existed by reason of the specialized knowledge of the separate agencies was a plus in managing the situation rather than a detriment that needs to be cured. No one regulator suggested an action which was rejected by another regulator or by any of the exchanges.

A second ground for the elimination of the CFTC as a regulator of futures contracts based on securities-type products is the assertion that these futures contracts are functionally equivalent to the securities that underlay them. This argument is groundless. It is exactly like arguing that ocean shipping insurance ought to be regulated by the Maritime Commission because both relate to boats. The fact is that futures trading is a species of insurance. The method by which the product is traded, marketed and regulated is completely different than comparable securities transactions.

Futures markets are composed of an array of different underlying instruments. There are agricultural products, currency products, interest rate products, metal products, energy products, as well as the equity index products. It is not rational to argue that each of these product lines should be governed by a different regulator—one whose primary responsibility is to regulate the underlying product. The result of such disjointed jurisdiction must lead to confusion, inefficiency, and duplicative regulations—all to the complete disservice of the marketplace.

The only sensible allocation of regulatory responsibility is the one presently adopted by Congress. Since all futures markets have a common denominator—all are traded in the same fashion under the same set of rules and apply a similar system of financial safeguards—they should all be regulated by a single regulator with the same common denominator who will govern with a unified set of regulations.

Finally, the CME has spoken at length with legislators who are firmly convinced that the CFTC is not as experienced, or as firm, or as knowledgeable—you can substitute your own adjective—as the SEC. These legislators are simply reluctant to trust the CFTC with the sensitive job of regulating financial futures contracts. We have the same response to all who have criticized the CFTC. Stop talking generalities, step back from rumors, ignore unsupported editorials and look at the facts. The facts and the record are clear. In every identifiable area of regulation, the CFTC compares favorably with the SEC.

Accelerations, Strategies and Systems

Finally, some critics point to "portfolio insurance" as the culprit. They argue that such market strategies (usually associated with large pension and mutual fund managers), accelerated the decline. There are at least four very good reasons why such assertions are either false or specious.

First, the facts, as previously noted, do not bear out the charge. Futures market selling did not translate into significant additional stock market selling. The futures market absorbed those sales. We stopped rather than accelerated the decline.

Second, the argument is intellectually incorrect. The exclusive focus on the implementation of selling strategies that are employed after price decreases is a grossly inadequate model of the actual market. Falling prices invoke as many buying strategies as selling strategies. Corporations bought back undervalued stocks. Investors sought bargains. Traders found opportunities.

Third, eliminating or impeding the use of portfolio insurance as a market strategy would serve to increase market volatility rather than reduce it. Without portfolio insurance, institutional managers would be forced to actually liquidate portions of their underlying portfolio whenever they fear, or are faced, with a market decline. Such additional selling pressure would clearly increase market volatility and add stress to the already burdened specialist system.

Finally, so-called "portfolio insurance" is nothing more than a stop-loss strategy. Stop-loss strategies take many forms. They represent market applications that are as old as the marketplace itself. Without question such strategies have an impact on the market as does every other strategy that is carried out by market participants. But to suggest that this indicates a fault in the system is nonsense. If such an assertion is carried to its logical conclusion, it would mean that all strategies should be banned from the marketplace since they all have an impact on the market, or in the alternative, no market should exist that permits strategies to be carried out.

We suggest a different form of analysis should be undertaken. Rather than blaming the strategy employed, our resources should be turned to an examination of the ability of our futures market system as compared to that of any other system to meet investor demands during the adverse and panic conditions existing on October 19. If such an objective comparison is made, we have little doubt that the system under which our futures market functioned will come out on top.

Conclusion

Those who ignore economic conditions and world tensions and blame traders and trading techniques for the market decline are at best naive and at worst irresponsible.

Our nation is burdened with some basic fundamental economic problems, including the largest budget deficit in our history, a massive trade deficit, a weakened U.S. dollar, rising interest rates, inflationary expectations, and a large dependence on foreign capital. Clearly, these problems could not have continued indefinitely without major market consequences.

Moreover, these serious problems were recently exacerbated by a trend toward trade protectionism, hostilities in the Persian Gulf, and finally by falling foreign stock markets and a disagreement between the U.S. and Germany about interest rates and dollar values. The cumulative effect of the foregoing set the stage for the volatile markets which ensued.

To suggest that stock index futures and options, program trading, portfolio insurance, computers, etc. caused the stock market decline is incorrect. Certainly computers were a factor in last week's market decline, but only in the same sense as telephones, facsimiles, quote machines and other modern-day technological tools. Stock index futures and options markets responded to investor demands and facilitated the continued functioning of U.S. capital markets. Human decisions still determined the direction of stock prices.

We are confident that, as in previous analyses, program trading and our stock index futures and options markets will not only be exonerated, but be proved to have been an essential factor in providing investor protection.

SOURCE: Reprinted from the Chicago Mercantile Exchange's publication, *Market Perspectives* (December–January 1988).

Options Markets

OPTIONS MARKETS IN PERSPECTIVE

As a result of increasing price volatility of bonds, mortgages, and stocks, the options market has become very popular. Stock options are widely used, not only by speculators, but also by financial institutions that desire to reduce the risk of their stock portfolios.

In recent years, several new types of options on futures contracts have been created. Some of the more popular types used by financial institutions include:

- Options on Treasury bill futures
- Options on Treasury note futures
- Options on Treasury bond futures
- Options on municipal "index" futures
- Options on the NYSE composite "index" futures
- Options on the S&P 500 stock "index" futures.

These contracts are commonly used by financial institutions to reduce the risk of their mortgage and bond portfolios. Because options on futures contracts are relatively new, their hedging capabilities and limitations are still not completely clear.

It is likely that additional types of options contracts will become available over time, in order to further accommodate the desire of financial institutions to reduce the risk of their security portfolios.

- How can options be used to reduce risk?
- How effective are they?
- How do options on futures differ from financial futures in reducing the risk of a financial institution's security portfolio?

These and other related questions are addressed in this chapter.

OUTLINE

This chapter first provides a background on stock options, then explains how they can be used to speculate on expected stock price movements. The factors that affect the price (or *premium*) of stock options are identified, then the way financial institutions utilize the stock options markets is described. Finally, options on futures contracts are explained, followed by a discussion of the international aspects of options markets.

BACKGROUND ON STOCK OPTIONS

Options are classified as *calls* or *puts*. A **call option** grants the owner the right to purchase a specified financial instrument for a specified price (called the **exercise price** or **strike price**) within a specified period of time. There are two major differences between purchasing an option and a futures contract. First, the option requires that a premium be paid in addition to the price of the financial instrument. Second, owners can choose to let the option expire without using it. That is, call options grant a right, but not an obligation, to purchase a specified financial instrument. The seller (sometimes called the *writer*) of a call option is obligated to provide the specified financial instrument at the price specified by the option contract if the owner exercises the option. Sellers of the call options receive an upfront fee (the premium) from the purchaser as compensation.

A call option is often referred to as "in the money" when the market price of the underlying security exceeds the exercise price, as "at the money" when it is equal to the exercise price, and "out of the money" when it is below the exercise price.

The second type of option is known as a **"put" option.** It grants the owner the right to sell a specified financial instrument for a specified price within a specified period of time. As with call options, owners pay a premium to obtain put options. They can exercise the options at any time up to the expiration date, but are not obligated to exercise the contract.

A put option is often referred to as "in the money" when the market price of the underlying security is below the exercise price, "at the money" when it is equal, and "out of the money" when it exceeds the exercise price.

Call and put options specify 100 shares for the stocks to which they are assigned. Premiums paid for call and put options are determined on the trading floor of exchanges through competitive open outcry between exchange members. The premium for a particular option changes over time as it becomes more or less desirable to traders.

Option contracts are guaranteed by a clearinghouse to assure that option writers fulfill their obligations. Participants can close out their option positions by making an offsetting transaction. For example, purchasers of an option can offset their positions at any point in time by selling an identical option. The gain or loss is determined by the premium paid when purchasing the option versus the premium received when selling an identical option.

Sellers of options can offset their positions at any point in time by purchasing an identical option. In addition to the "American-style" stock options just described, "European-style" stock options are also available that can be exercised only on the expiration date.

SPECULATING WITH STOCK OPTIONS

To illustrate how options can be used to speculate, consider Pat Jackson, who expects IBM stock to increase from its present price of $113 per share but does not want to tie up her available funds by investing in stocks. She purchases a call option on IBM with an exercise price of $115 for a premium of $4 per share. Before the option's expiration date, IBM's price rises to $121. At that time, Pat exercises her option, purchasing shares at $115 per share. She then immediately sells those shares at the market price of $121 per share. Her gain on this transaction is $6 per share. Yet, considering that she paid $4 per share to obtain the call option, her net gain is only $2 per share, or $200 for one call option contract.

If the price of IBM stock had not risen above $115 before the option's expiration data, Pat would have let the option expire. Her net loss would have been the $4 per share she initially paid for the option, or $400 for one option contract.

The potential gains or losses from this call option are shown in the top portion of Exhibit 10.1, based on the assumptions that (1) the call option is exercised on the expiration date, if at all, and (2) if the call option is exercised, the shares received are immediately sold. Exhibit 10.1 shows that the maximum loss when purchasing this option is the premium of $4 per share. For stock prices between $115 and $119, the option is exercised, and the purchaser of a call option incurs a net loss of less than $4 per share. The stock price of $119 is a break-even point, since the gain from exercising the option exactly offsets the premium paid for it. At stock prices above $119, a net gain would be realized.

The lower portion of Exhibit 10.1 shows the net gain or loss to a writer of the same call option, assuming that the writer obtains the stock only when the option is exercised. Under this condition, the call option writer's net gain (loss) is the call option purchaser's net loss (gain), assuming zero transaction costs. The maximum gain to the writer of a call option is the premium received.

Several call options are available for a given stock, and the risk-return potential will vary among them. Assume that three types of call options were available on IBM stock with a similar expiration date, as described in Exhibit 10.2. The potential gains or losses per unit for each option are

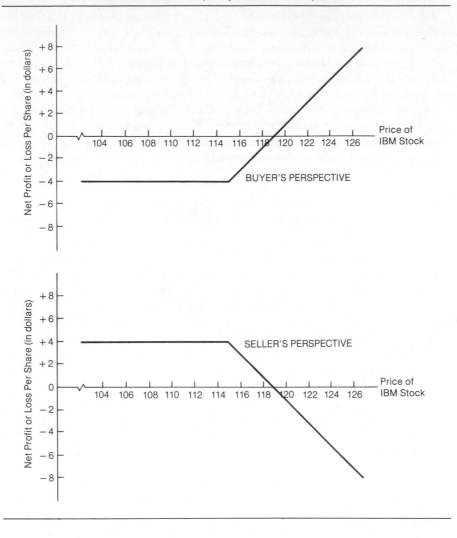

also shown in Exhibit 10.2, assuming that the option is exercised on the expiration date, if at all. It is also assumed that if the speculators exercise the call option, they immediately sell the stock. Exhibit 10.2 shows that Call Option 3 has the smallest possible loss to the speculator but also the least potential for return. In addition, the break-even stock price at which a zero profit per share is achieved is higher than that of the other two options. Option 1 has the lowest break-even stock price, and also offers the highest potential profit per share. However, the potential loss is much greater than the maximum possible loss of Option 3. Option 2 has a higher potential return than Option 3 but less than Option 1. Its maximum loss is less than that of Option 1, but more than that of Option 3. The comparison of various options for a given stock illustrate the various risk-return trade-offs that speculators can choose from.

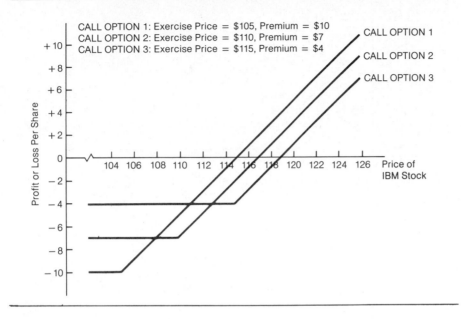

CALL OPTION 1: Exercise Price = $105, Premium = $10
CALL OPTION 2: Exercise Price = $110, Premium = $7
CALL OPTION 3: Exercise Price = $115, Premium = $4

If speculators had expected the price of IBM stock to decrease, they might have considered purchasing a put option. For example, assume that a put option on IBM was available with an exercise price of $110 and with a premium of $2. If the price of IBM stock falls below $110, speculators could purchase the stock and then exercise their put options to benefit from the transaction. However, they would need to make at least $2 per share on this transaction in order to fully recover the premium paid for the option. For example, if they exercised the option when the market price was $109, they would earn $1 per share on the transaction but lose $1 per share on a net basis (when accounting for the premium paid for the put option). If the market price declined to $106 before the option's expiration date, they could earn $4 per share when exercising their option, and $2 per share on a net basis.

The potential gains or losses from the put option described here are shown in the top portion of Exhibit 10.3, based on the assumptions that (1) the put option is exercised on the expiration date, if at all, and (2) the shares would be purchased just before the put option is exercised. Exhibit 10.3 shows that the maximum loss when purchasing this option is $2 per share. For stock prices between $108 and $110, the purchaser of a put option incurs a net loss of less than $2 per share. The stock price of $108 is a break-even point, since the gain from exercising the put option would exactly offset the $2 per share premium. At stock prices below $108, a net gain would be realized.

The lower portion of Exhibit 10.3 shows the net gain or loss to a writer of the same put option, assuming that the writer sells the stock received as the put option is exercised. Under this condition, the put option writer's

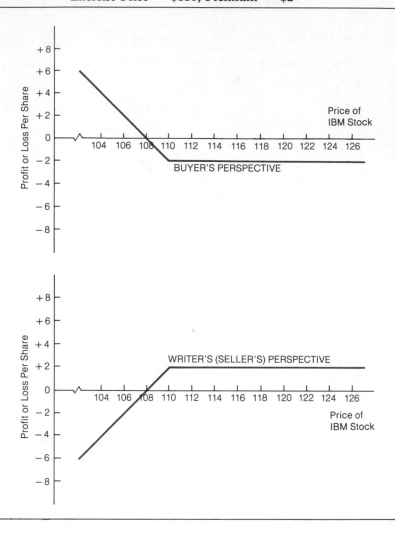

net gain (loss) is the put option purchaser's net loss (gain), assuming zero transaction costs. The maximum gain to the writer of a put option is the premium received.

As with call options, there are normally several put options available for a given stock, and the risk-return potential will vary among them. Suppose that three types of put options were available on IBM stock with a similar expiration date, as described in Exhibit 10.4. The potential gains or losses per unit for each option are also shown in Exhibit 10.4, assuming that the option is exercised on the expiration date, if at all. It is also assumed that the speculators would purchase the stock just before they exercise the put option. Exhibit 10.4 shows that Put Option 1 has the smallest possible loss to the speculator but also the least potential for return. Option 3 has the largest possible loss but also the highest potential return. The potential loss

EXHIBIT 10.4   Risk-Return Trade-Off for Three Put Options

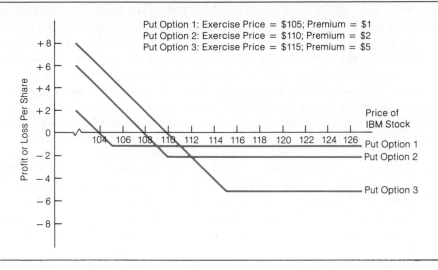

Put Option 1: Exercise Price = $105; Premium = $1
Put Option 2: Exercise Price = $110; Premium = $2
Put Option 3: Exercise Price = $115; Premium = $5

and return for Option 2 is more than those of Option 1 but less than those of Option 3.

When comparing Exhibit 10.4 with Exhibit 10.2, the call options appear to be more expensive. This is because the existing price of IBM stock at the time the option data were obtained was about $113. Two of the three call options described in Exhibit 10.2 were "in the money," while only one of the put options described in Exhibit 10.4 was.

DETERMINANTS OF OPTION PREMIUMS

Any characteristics that increase the probability of the call option owner exercising the option will result in a higher premium. The following factors influence the premium:

1. The greater the existing price of the financial instrument of concern relative to the exercise price, the higher will be the call option premium, other things being equal.
2. The greater the variability of the instrument's market value, the higher will be the call option premium, other things being equal.
3. The longer the maturity is of the option, the higher will be the call option premium, other things being equal.
4. The higher the prevailing interest rate, the higher will be the call option, other things being equal.

A financial instrument's value has a higher probability of increasing above the exercise price by a large degree if (1) it is already close to or above the exercise price, (2) it is volatile, and (3) a long time period is allowed by the option. Under these circumstances, the sellers of a call option require a higher premium.

To illustrate the influence of the stock price on the call option premium, a call option on IBM stock with an exercise price of $140 and January

Chapter 10

Options Markets

expiration is shown for two different dates in Exhibit 10.5. The first date is shortly before the stock market crash, and the second date is one day after the crash. When the stock price was $134.50 per share, the call option premium was $7.75. On the next trading day, the price declined to $103.24 per share, and the option premium declined to $5.25, or by about 32 percent.

The relationship between the exercise price and the call option premium is shown in Exhibit 10.6 for IBM call options quoted on May 5, 1988, with a similar expiration date. The premium for the call option with the $105 exercise price was more than $8 higher than the premium for the option with the $120 exercise price. The difference reflects the more favorable price at which the option with the $105 exercise price can be purchased.

The relationship between the time to maturity and the call option premium is shown in Exhibit 10.7 for IBM call options quoted on May 5, 1988, with a similar exercise price. The premium was $6.87 per share for the call option with a July expiration month versus $3.87 per share for the call option with a May expiration month. The difference of $3.00 per share reflects the additional two months time in which the call option can be exercised.

The premium paid on a put option is dependent on the same factors that affect call option premiums, with a slight adjustment. The lower the existing price is of the financial instrument relative to the exercise price, the higher will be the put option premium, other things being equal. This influence on the put option differs from the influence on the call option, since a lower market price is preferable from the perspective of a put option purchaser. The remaining three determinants of call option premiums have a similar influence on put option premiums.

The relationship between the stock price and a put option on IBM with an exercise price of $140 and January expiration date is shown for two

---

EXHIBIT 10.5   Comparison of Stock Prices and Call Option Prices of IBM Just Before and After the Stock Market Crash

Date	Price Per Share of IBM Stock	Premium Per Share of IBM Call Options With a $140 Exercise Price and a January Expiration Date
October 16, 1987	$134.50	$7.75
October 19, 1987 (Crash)	103.25	5.25

EXHIBIT 10.6   Relationship between Exercise Price and Call Option Premium on IBM Stock

Exercise Price	Premium for June Expiration Date
$105	9⅜
110	5⅜
115	2⅞
120	1³⁄₁₆

SOURCE: *The Wall Street Journal*, May 5, 1988.

different dates in Exhibit 10.8. When the stock price declined on the day of the stock market crash, the put option premium increased from $10.75 per share to $27.50 per share.

The relationship between the exercise price and the put option premium is shown in Exhibit 10.9 for IBM put options on a given day with a similar expiration date. The premium for the call option with the $120 exercise price was $6.75 per share higher than the premium for the option with the $105 exercise price. The difference reflects the more favorable price at which the option with the $120 exercise price can be sold.

The relationship between the time to maturity and the put option premium is shown in Exhibit 10.10 for IBM put options quoted on a given day with a similar exercise price. The premium was $3.00 per share for the put option with a July expiration month versus $1.12 per share for the put option with a May expiration month. The difference of $1.88 per share reflects the additional two months time in which the put option can be exercised.

EXHIBIT 10.7 Relationship between Time To Maturity and Call Option Premium on IBM Stock

	Premium for:		
Exercise Price	May Expiration Date	June Expiration Date	July Expiration Date
$110	3⅞	5⅜	6⅞

SOURCE: *The Wall Street Journal*, May 5, 1988.

EXHIBIT 10.8 Comparison of Stock Prices and Put Option Prices of IBM Just Before and After the Stock Market Crash

Date	Price Per Share of IBM Stock	Premium Per Share of IBM Put Options With a $140 Exercise Price and a January Expiration Date
October 16, 1987	$134.50	$10.75
October 19, 1987 (Crash)	103.25	27.50

EXHIBIT 10.9 Relationship between Exercise Price and Put Option Premium on IBM Stock

Exercise Price	Premium for June Expiration Date
$105	1
110	2¼
115	4⅝
120	7¾

SOURCE: *The Wall Street Journal*, May 5, 1988.

EXHIBIT 10.10 Relationship between Time to Maturity and Put Option Premium on IBM Stock

	Premium for:		
	---	---	---
Exercise Price	May Expiration Date	June Expiration Date	July Expiration Date
$110	1⅛	2¼	3

SOURCE: *The Wall Street Journal*, May 5, 1988.

HEDGING WITH STOCK OPTIONS

Call and put options on selected stocks and stock indexes are commonly used for hedging. Consider an example in which Tallahassee Pension Fund expects to receive funds from its participants in the near future. It plans to purchase a large amount of IBM stock but cannot make the purchase until more funds arrive. It is also concerned that the stock price may rise before its future time of purchase. For this reason, it would like to lock in the maximum price that it would have to pay on this stock, which it could accomplish by purchasing enough options on this stock to cover its future planned stock purchases.

The creation of a call option contract requires participation by not only interested purchasers of such a contract, but interested sellers as well. A likely seller of a call option on IBM stock may be another financial institution that already owns that stock and is concerned about a potential decline in its price over the next few months. The sale of a call option can hedge against such a potential loss. This is known as a *covered call*, since the option is "covered," or backed, by stocks already owned. If the market price of IBM stock rises, the call option will likely be exercised, and the institution that sold the call option will fulfill its obligation by selling its IBM stock to the purchaser of the call option at the exercise price. Conversely, if the market price of the stock declines, the option will not be exercised. Consequently, the institution would not have to sell its IBM stock, and the premium received from selling the call option would represent a gain that could partially offset the decline in the price of the stock. In this case, although the market value of the institution's stock portfolio is adversely affected, it is at least partially offset by the premium received from selling the call option.

To illustrate the use of covered call writing, assume that Portland Pension Fund has purchased shares of IBM stock at market price of $112 per share, and that call options with an exercise price of $110 presently have a premium of $5 per share. The net profit or loss per share without covered call writing is shown in Exhibit 10.11 as the solid diagonal line, assuming that the stock is to be sold on the option's expiration date. The dotted line represents the profit from covered call writing, assuming that the purchaser of the call option would exercise the option on the expiration date, if at all.

The table below the graph in Exhibit 10.11 explains the profit or loss per share from covered call writing. At any price above $110 per share as of

EXHIBIT 10.11 **Risk-Return Trade-off from Holding IBM Stock: With Covered Call Writing versus Without It**

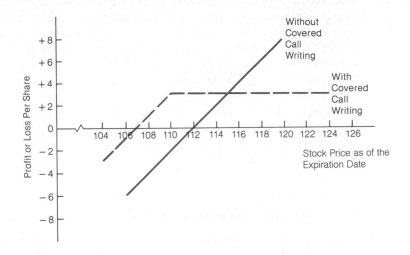

Explanation of Profit Per Share from Covered Call Writing:

Market Price of IBM as of the Expiration Date	Price at Which Portland Pension Fund Sells IBM Stock		Premium Received from Writing the Call Option		Price Paid for IBM Stock		Profit or Loss Per Share
$104	$104	+	$5	−	$112	=	− $3
105	105	+	5	−	112	=	− 2
106	106	+	5	−	112	=	− 1
107	107	+	5	−	112	=	0
108	108	+	5	−	112	=	1
109	109	+	5	−	112	=	2
110	110	+	5	−	112	=	3
111	110	+	5	−	112	=	3
112	110	+	5	−	112	=	3
113	110	+	5	−	112	=	3
114	110	+	5	−	112	=	3
115	110	+	5	−	112	=	3
116	110	+	5	−	112	=	3
117	110	+	5	−	112	=	3
118	110	+	5	−	112	=	3
119	110	+	5	−	112	=	3
120	110	+	5	−	112	=	3

the expiration date, the call option would be exercised, and Portland would have to sell its holdings of IBM stock at the exercise price of $110 per share to the purchaser of the call option. The net gain to Portland would be $3 per share, determined as the premium of $5 per share, received when writing the option, minus the $2 per share difference between the price paid for IBM stock versus the price at which it is sold. Exhibit 10.11 demonstrated how covered call writing limits the upside potential return on stocks but also reduces the risk.

Chapter 10

Options Markets

Put options on stock are also used to hedge stock positions. For example, consider a life insurance company that has large holdings of a particular stock. While the stock is likely to perform well over the long run, it may possibly experience a decline in the next few months. To hedge against a potential decline in the price of the stock, the institution could purchase a put option on the stock, thereby locking in the price at which it could sell the stock. If the price falls significantly, the company would likely exercise the option. If the price remains high, the option would expire without being exercised.

Some speculators who expect the stock's price to rise sell put options, which obligates them to purchase the stock at the specified exercise price if the options are exercised. If the market price remains above the exercise price, the put option expires, and their gain is the option premium received.

OPTIONS ON FUTURES CONTRACTS

A **call option on financial futures** grants the right to purchase a futures contract at a specified price within a specified period of time. This "option on futures" differs from a "futures" contract that it offers a right rather than an obligation. The institution can choose to let the contract expire. A **put option on financial futures** grants the right (again, not an obligation) to sell a particular financial futures contract at a specified price within a specified period of time. Because many futures contracts can hedge interest rate risk, options on futures might be considered by any financial institution that is exposed to this risk, including savings institutions, commercial banks, life insurance companies, and pension funds.

Options on Treasury bill, note, and bond futures are available. These contracts have become popular because the maximum loss to a purchaser of options on Treasury bond futures is the premium paid. In addition, purchasers of options are not subject to margin calls. Options on Treasury bonds are especially desirable because the market for these options is liquid. The average daily trading volume in Chicago Board of Trade options on Treasury bond futures exceeds 80,000 contracts. Because of the high level of activity, the premium paid on these options should not be substantially affected by a single firm's transactions.

Assume that Emory Savings and Loan Association has a large number of long-term fixed-rate mortgages that are mainly supported by short-term funds and would therefore be adversely affected by rising interest rates. It was shown in the previous chapter that the sales of Treasury bond futures could partially offset the adverse effect of rising interest rates in this situation. However, if interest rates declined, the potential increase in Emory's interest rate spread (difference between interest revenues and expenses) would be partially offset by the loss on the futures contract.

The put option on futures is attractive because it can hedge in the event that interest rates rise, yet go unexercised if interest rates fall. Of course, a premium must be paid up front to obtain the option. Financial institutions must determine whether the benefits are worth the premium charged.

The option on futures premium is quoted as a percentage of the $100,000 par value of the securities represented by the futures contract, in increments of one sixty-fourth. For example, a premium of $1\frac{32}{64}$ equals $1,500. Like other option premiums, the premium of an option on futures is determined by the market. The more desirable a long position in futures is, the higher the premium charged for a call option on futures. The more desirable a short position on futures, the greater would be the premium charged for a put option on futures. Options on futures specify expiration dates for the same months as futures contracts, although their actual settlement date is earlier in the month.

Some speculators may be willing to sell a put option on futures if they expect interest rates to remain stable or decline. If their expectations are correct, the price of a futures contract will likely remain stable or rise, and the put option will not be exercised. Therefore, sellers of the put option would earn the premium charged.

The risk to sellers of a put option is that interest rates might rise, which would likely cause a decline in financial futures prices and encourage buyers of put options on futures to exercise them. Sellers of put options would then be forced to purchase the futures contract at the exercise price. Their gain or loss is determined by comparing the premium received from selling the put option to the difference between the purchase price of the futures contract (the exercise price) and the selling price.

As a numerical example of using options on futures, assume that a speculator purchases a put option on Treasury bond futures with a December delivery date and a strike price of 89–16 ($89,500). Assume the put option has a premium of 1–48 (1 and $48/64$ percent of $100,000), or $1,750. Assume that the price of the Treasury bond futures contract decreases to 85–00 ($85,000). The speculator could purchase Treasury bond futures at this time for $85,000 and simultaneously exercise the put option, enabling him or her to sell that futures contract for $89,500. The difference is a gain of $4,500. However, when accounting for the option premium of $1,750, the net gain is $2,750 ($4,500 − $1,750). If interest rates decrease, the futures price would likely increase above 89–16. In this case, the speculator would let the option contract expire, incurring a loss of $1,750 (the premium paid for the put option).

If speculators anticipated a decrease in interest rates but were unwilling to purchase Treasury bond futures because of the risk of being wrong, they could purchase call options on Treasury bond futures. For example, assume a call option on the Treasury bond futures contract described in the previous example has a premium of 1–56 (1 and $56/64$ percent of $100,000), or $1,875. Assume that interest rates decrease as expected and the price of the Treasury bond futures contract rises to 93–00 ($93,000). Speculators could exercise their option to purchase futures at the exercise price of $89,500 and simultaneously sell the contract for $93,000. The net gain after considering the call option premium is $1,625 ($93,000 − $89,500 − $1,875). If the futures price reached only 91–00 ($91,000) the option would still be exercised, but the gain of $1,500 ($91,000 − $89,500) would not fully offset the option premium. If the futures price did not exceed the exercise price over the period of concern, the call option would not be exercised, and a loss of $1,875 (the option premium) would be incurred.

Options are also available on index futures. They have become very popular over the short period of time they have been in existence. As an example, assume that Gainesville Insurance Co. considered the purchase of S&P (Standard and Poor's) 500 Index futures, because of anticipated optimism about the stock market. Yet, because it was somewhat concerned about the potential market downturn, it was unwilling to take this position. Instead, it purchased an option on this futures contract. Assume the option premium is quoted as 7.40. The dollar value of the premium is $500 times this quote, or $3,700 ($500 × 7.40). Assume the exercise price is 310. Since the value of the futures contract is $500 times the index, the dollar value of the exercise price is $155,000. If the index on the futures contract increased to 335, the futures contract could be sold for $167,500 (500 × 335), resulting in a gain of $12,500. When accounting for the $3,700 premium paid, the net gain is $8,800 (12,500 − $3,700).

The net gain would be higher if Gainesville had initially purchased the futures contract rather than an option on the futures contract. However, the option offers Gainesville the flexibility to avoid the futures position in the event of a market downturn and lower prices on the index futures contract.

INSTITUTIONAL USE OF OPTIONS MARKETS

Exhibit 10.12 summarizes the uses of options by various types of financial institutions, some of which the previous examples have illustrated. While options positions are sometimes taken by financial institutions for speculative purposes, they are more commonly intended for hedging. Savings institutions and bond mutual funds use options on futures in order to hedge interest rate risk. Stock mutual funds, insurance companies, and pension funds use stock options and options on stock index futures in order to hedge their stock portfolios.

TRIPLE WITCHING HOUR

On the third Fridays of March, June, September, and December, options and futures on stock indexes expire, igniting heavy trading. Known as **triple witching hour,** this time is of great significance to investors and regulators. As an example, on the third Friday in March 1986, between 3:30 P.M. to 4:30 P.M., a record of 57 million shares were traded, and the Dow Jones Industrial average fell by 36 points.

OPTIONS FROM AN INTERNATIONAL PERSPECTIVE

INTERNATIONAL

ASPECTS

Part Three

Other Financial Markets

The trading of stock options involves the assessment of international financial market conditions. The foreign flow of funds into and out of the United States can affect economic conditions and therefore the market value of corporate stocks. Portfolio managers assess the potential impact of international factors on U.S. economic conditions to forecast the value of their respective portfolios. Speculators also assess the international flows of funds to forecast stock prices so that they can determine whether to take a position in call options or put options.

Options on futures contracts are also affected by international conditions. Because the value of securities underlying futures contracts are sensitive to interest rate movements, participants who trade options on futures con-

EXHIBIT 10.12   Institutional Use of Options Markets

Type of Financial Institution	Participation in Options Markets
Commercial banks	■ sometimes offer currency options to businesses.
Savings institutions	■ sometimes take positions in options on futures contracts in order to hedge interest rate risk.
Mutual funds	■ stock mutual funds take positions in stock options to hedge against a possible decline in prices of stocks within their portfolios. ■ stock mutual funds sometimes take speculative positions in stock options in an attempt to increase their returns. ■ bond mutual funds sometimes take positions in options on futures to hedge interest rate risk.
Brokerage firms	■ execute stock option transactions for individuals and businesses.
Pension funds	■ take positions in stock options to hedge against a possible decline in prices of stocks within their portfolio. ■ take positions in options on futures contracts in order to hedge their bond portfolios against interest rate movements.
Insurance companies	■ take positions in stock options to hedge against a possible decline in prices of stocks within their portfolio. ■ take positions in options on futures contracts in order to hedge their bond portfolios against interest rate movements.

tracts closely monitor the international flow of funds when forecasting interest rate movements. The decisions to buy or sell options on futures and the performance of options on futures both depend on the international flow of funds.

Currency Options Contracts

A **currency call option** provides the right to purchase a specified currency for a specified price within a specified period of time. Corporations involved in international business transactions use currency call options to hedge future payables. If the exchange rate at the time payables are due exceeds the exercise price, corporations can exercise their options by purchasing the currency at the exercise price. Conversely, if the prevailing exchange rate is lower than the exercise price, they can purchase the currency at the prevailing exchange rate and let the options expire.

Use of Options by Pension Funds

A recent survey of pension funds found that about 64 percent of the respondents using options purchased them on individual stocks, 42 percent on stock indexes, and 39 percent on stock index futures. About 78 percent of pension funds using options cited hedging as a major reason. They used covered call writing (selling call options) more than purchasing puts, by about a 3 to 1 margin, for hedging against downward stock price movements. Some of the respondents also trade options on bond futures, primarily to hedge their bond positions. More than 65 percent of the respondents using options hired an independent investment counselor to manage their options program.

SOURCE: "Slow Gains for Options," *Institutional Investor* (September 1986): 151–154.

Speculators purchase call options on currencies that they expect to strengthen against the dollar. If the foreign currency strengthens as expected, they can exercise their call options to purchase the currency at the exercise price and then sell the currency at the prevailing exchange rate.

A **currency put option** provides the right to sell a specified currency for a specified price within a specified period of time. Corporations involved in international business transactions may purchase put options to hedge future receivables. If the exchange rate at the time they receive payment in a foreign currency is less than the exercise price, they can exercise their option by selling the currency at the exercise price. Conversely, if the prevailing exchange rate is higher than the exercise price, they can sell the currency at the prevailing exchange rate and let the options expire.

Speculators purchase put options on currencies they expect to weaken against the dollar. If the foreign currency weakens as expected, the speculators can purchase the currency at the prevailing spot rate and exercise their put options to sell the currency at the exercise price.

For every buyer of a currency call or put option, there must be a seller (or *writer*). A writer of a call option is obligated to sell the specified currency at the specified strike price if the option is exercised. A writer of a put option is obligated to purchase the specified currency at the specified strike price if the option is exercised. Speculators may be willing to write call options on foreign currencies that they expect to weaken against the dollar or put options on those they expect to strengthen against the dollar. If a currency option expires without being exercised, the writer keeps the up-front premium received. Currency options are discussed in more detail in the following chapter.

SUMMARY

Options markets are widely used by both speculators and hedgers. Speculators purchase call options on stocks whose prices are expected to rise and put options on those expected to decrease. They purchase options on financial futures contracts when they expect interest rates to decrease. They buy currency call options when they expect foreign currencies to strengthen and currency put options when they expect foreign currencies to weaken.

Options markets are also widely used by financial institutions to hedge positions. If the institutions desire to hedge against rising interest rates, they may purchase put options on financial futures. Financial institutions such as pension funds and insurance companies can use stock options to hedge their stock portfolios. To hedge against a potential short-term decline in stock prices, they may purchase put options or sell call options. To hedge against a potential rise in the stocks they plan to purchase, they may purchase call options. By accommodating the hedging needs of financial institutions, options markets can reduce the risk of these institutions and enhance the public's confidence in the financial system.

KEY TERMS

call option
call option on financial futures
currency call option
currency put option
exercise price

put option
put option on financial futures
triple witching hour

QUESTIONS

10.1. Describe the general differences between a call option and a futures contract. *280*

10.2. How are call options used by speculators? Describe the conditions in which their strategy would backfire. *284*

10.3. How are put options used by speculators? Describe the conditions in which their strategy would backfire. *284*

10.4. Describe the maximum loss that could occur for a purchaser of a call option.

10.5. Under what conditions would speculators sell a call option?

10.6. What is the risk to speculators who sell put options?

10.7. Identify the factors affecting the premium paid on a call option. Describe how each factor affects the size of the premium. *275*

10.8. Identify the factors affecting the premium paid on a put option. Describe how each factor affects the size of the premium.

10.9. How can financial institutions with stock portfolios use stock options when they expect stock prices to rise substantially but do not yet have sufficient funds to purchase more stock?

10.10. Why would a financial institution holding ABC stock consider buying a put option on this stock rather than simply selling the stock?

10.11. Describe a call option on financial futures. How does it differ from purchasing a futures contract? *280*

10.12. Describe a put option on financial futures. How does it differ from selling a futures contract?

10.13. Assume a savings institution had a large amount of fixed-rate mortgages and obtained most of its funds from short-term deposits. How could it use options on financial futures to hedge its exposure to interest rate movements? Would futures or options on futures be more appropriate if the institution was concerned that interest rates would decrease, causing a large number of mortgage prepayments?

PROBLEMS

10.1. A call option on Illinois stock specifies an exercise price of $38. Today's price of the stock is $40. The premium on the call option is $5. Assume the option will not be exercised until maturity, if at all. Fill out the table below:

Assumed stock price at the time the call option is about to expire	Net profit or loss per share to be earned by the writer (seller) of the call option
$37	
39	
41	
43	
45	
48	

10.2 A call option on Michigan stock specifies an exercise price of $55. Today's price of the stock is $54 per share. The premium on the call option is $3. Assume the option will not be exercised until maturity, if at all. Fill out the table below for a speculator that purchases the call option:

Assumed stock price at the time the call option is about to expire	Net profit or loss per share to be earned by the speculator
$50	−3
52	−3
54	−3
56	−2
58	0
60	2
62	4

10.3. A put option on Iowa stock specifies an exercise price of $71. Today's price of the stock is $68. The premium on the put option is $8. Assume the option will not be exercised until maturity, if at all. Fill out the table below for a speculator who purchases the put option (and presently does not own the stock):

Assumed stock price at the time the put option is about to expire	Net profit or loss per share to be earned by the speculator
$60	
64	
68	
70	
72	
74	
76	

10.4. A put option on Indiana stock specifies an exercise price of $23. Today's price of the stock is $24. The premium on the put option is $3. Assume the option will not be exercised until maturity, if at all. Fill out the table below:

Assumed stock price at the time the put option is about to expire	Net profit or loss per share to be earned by the writer (or seller) of the put option
$20	
21	
22	
23	
24	
25	
26	

10.5a. Assume that Evanston Insurance Inc. has purchased shares of Stock E at $50 per share. It will sell the stock in six months. It considers using a strategy of covered call writing to partially hedge its position in this stock. The exercise price is $53, the expiration date is six months, and the premium on the call option is $2. Fill out the table below:

279

Possible price of Stock E in six months	Profit or loss per share if a covered call strategy is used	Profit or loss per share if a covered call strategy is not used
$47	2 -3= -1	-3
50	2 = 2	0
52	2+2= 4	2
55	2 +3 =5	5
57	2 +3 =5	7
60	2 +3 =5	10

10.5b. Assume that each of the six stock prices in the first column in the table have an equal probability of occurring. Compare the probability distribution of the profits (or losses) per share when using covered call writing versus not using it. Would you recommend covered call writing in this example? Explain.   yes

3.33

10.6. Purdue Savings and Loan Association purchases a put option on Treasury bond futures with a September delivery date and an exercise price of 91–16. Assume the put option has a premium of 1–32. Assume that the price of the Treasury bond futures decreases to 88–16. Should Purdue exercise the option or let the option expire? What is Purdue's net gain or loss after accounting for the premium paid on the option?

prem = 2000
EP = 92,125
P = 93,125

10.7. Wisconsin Inc. purchased a call option on Treasury bond futures at a premium of 2–00. The exercise price is 92–08. If the price of the Treasury bond futures becomes 93–08, should Wisconsin Inc. exercise the call option or let it expire? What is Wisconsin's net gain or loss after accounting for the premium paid on the option?   exercise

281

net loss = (1000)

10.8. DePaul Insurance Company purchased a call option on an S&P 500 futures contract. The option premium is quoted as $6. The exercise price is $330. Assume the index on the futures contract becomes $340. Should DePaul exercise the call option or let it expire? What is the net gain or loss to DePaul after accounting for the premium paid for the option?

PROJECTS

1a. Obtain the stock options data just before and after the stock market crash of October 19, 1987, for a particular stock you are interested in (or assigned by your professor). Fill in the table below:

Name of company _____

Exercise Price of Call Option _____

Call Option Premium as of October 16, 1987 (Use the October 19, 1987 issue of *The Wall Street Journal*.) _____

Put Option Premium as of October 16, 1987 (Use the October 19, 1987 issue of *The Wall Street Journal*.) _____

Call Option Premium as of October 19, 1987 (Use the October 20, 1987 issue of *The Wall Street Journal*.) _____

Put Option Premium as of October 19, 1987 (Use the October 20, 1987 issue of *The Wall Street Journal*.) _____

1b. What was the percentage change in the call option premium? What was the percentage change in the put option premium?

2a. Obtain recent stock options data for a particular stock you are interested in. Use a recent issue of *The Wall Street Journal* to fill in the table below (use the same expiration month for all quoted premiums):

Name of Stock	Exercise Price	Premium on Call Option	Premium on Put Option

2b. Explain the relationship between the options exercise price and (a) the call option premium and (b) the put option premium.

3a. Obtain recent stock options data for a particular stock you are interested in. Use a recent issue of *The Wall Street Journal* to fill in the table below (use the same exercise price for all quoted premiums):

Name of Stock _____

Expiration Month	Premium on Call Option	Premium on Put Option

3b. Explain the relationship between the option's time to maturity and (1) the call option premium and (2) the put option premium.

4a. Obtain recent stock options data for a particular stock you are interested in. Using the *The Wall Street Journal*, fill in the table below.

Name of Stock _____

	Recently quoted premium for a particular exercise price and expiration month	Quoted premium for that same exercise price and expiration month as of one month ago
Call option		
Put option		

4b. Explain why the call option premium increased or decreased. Determine the percentage change in the premium. Do the same for the put option premium.

REFERENCES

Black, Fisher. "Fact and Fantasy in the Use of Options." *Financial Analysts Journal* (July–August 1975): 36–41.

Black, Fisher and Myron Scholes. "The Valuation of Option Contracts and a Test of Market Efficiency." *Journal of Finance* (May 1972): 399–417.

———. "The Pricing of Options and Corporate Liabilities." *Journal of Political Economy* (May–June 1973): 637–654.

Dawson, Frederic S. "Risk and Returns in Continuous Option Writing." *Journal of Portfolio Management* (Winter 1979): 58–63.

Finnerty, Joseph E. "The Chicago Board Options Exchange and Market Efficiency." *Journal of Financial and Quantitative Analysis* (March 1978): 29–38.

French, Dan W. and Glenn V. Henderson. "Substitute Hedged Option Portfolios: Theory and Evidence." *Journal of Financial Research* (Spring 1981): 21–31.

Galai, Dan. "Tests of Market Efficiency of the Chicago Board Options Exchange." *Journal of Business* (April 1977): 167–197.

Gastineau, Gary L. "An Index of Listed Option Premiums." *Financial Analysts Journal* (May–June 1977): 70–75.

Gambola, Michael J., Rodney L. Roenfeldt, and Philip L. Cooley. "Spreading Strategies in CBOE Options: Evidence on Market Performance." *Journal of Financial Research* (Winter 1978): 35–44.

Hettenhouse, George W. and Donald J. Puglisi. "Investor Experience with Put and Call Options." *Financial Analysts Journal* (July–August 1975): 53–58.

Johnson, Herb and David Shanno. "Option Pricing When the Variance is Changing." *Journal of Finance and Quantitative Analysis* (June 1987): 143–152.

Johnson, Herb and Rene Stulz. "The Pricing of Options with Default Risk." *Journal of Finance* (June 1987): 281–300.

Lo, Andrew. "Semi-Parametric Upper Bounds for Option Prices and Expected Payoffs." *Journal of Financial Economics* (December 1987): 373–387.

Ma, Christopher and Ramesh Rao. "Information Asymmetry and Options Trading." *Financial Review* (February 1988): 39–51.

Merton, Robert. "The Theory of Rational Option Pricing," *The Bell Journal of Economics and Management Science* (Spring 1973a): 141–183.

———. "Option Pricing When Underlying Stock Returns are Discontinuous," *Journal of Financial Economics* (January–March 1976): 125–144.

Rao, Ramesh and Christopher Ma. "The Effect of Call-Option-Listing Announcement on Shareholder Wealth." *Journal of Business Research* (October 1987): 449–461.

Reback, Robert. "Risk and Return in Option Trading." *Financial Analysts Journal*, (July–August 1975): 42–52.

Rendleman, Richard J., Jr. "Optimal Long-Run Option Investment Strategies." *Financial Management* (Spring 1981): 61–76.

Scholes, Myron. "Taxes and the Pricing of Options." *Journal of Finance* (May 1976): 319–332.

Scott, Louis. "Option Pricing When the Variance Changes Randomly: Theory, Estimation and an Application." *Journal of Financial and Quantitative Analysis* (December 1987): 419–438.

Smith, Clifford W., Jr. "Option Pricing: A Review." *Journal of Financial Economics*, (January–March 1976): 3–51.

Strong, Robert and William P. Andrew. "Further Evidence of the Influence of Option Expiration on the Underlying Common Stock." *Journal of Business Research* (August 1987): 291–302.

Wiggins, James. "Option Values Under Stochastic Volatility: Theory and Empirical Estimates." *Journal of Financial Economics* (December 1987): 351–372.

Wolf, Avner. "Optimal Hedging with Futures Options." *Journal of Economics and Business* (May 1987): 141–158.

APPENDIX 10

Option Valuation

In 1973 Black and Scholes devised an option-pricing model that motivated further research on option valuation pricing that continues to this day. Their formula for the value of an American call option *(C)* is

$$C = SN(d_1) - Xe^{-rT}N(d_2)$$

where S = stock price
$N(d_1)$ and $N(d_2)$ = probabilities from the cumulative normal distribution evaluated at d_1 and d_2
X = exercise price of the call option
e = base e antilog or 2.7183
r = risk-free rate of return for one year
T = time to maturity of the call option expressed as a fraction of a year

The terms $N(d_1)$ and $N(d_2)$ deserve further elaboration. N represents a cumulative probability for a unit normal variable, where

$$d_1 = \frac{\ln(S/X) + rT}{\sigma\sqrt{T}} + \frac{1}{2}\sigma\sqrt{T}$$

where $\ln(S/X)$ represents the natural logarithm and σ represents the standard deviation of the continuously compounded rate of return on the underlying stock; and

$$d_2 = d_1 - \sigma\sqrt{T}$$

Some of the key assumptions underlying the Black-Scholes option-pricing model are

- The risk-free rate is known and constant over the life of the option.
- The probability distribution of stock prices is log normal.
- The variability of a stock's return is constant.
- The option is to be exercised at maturity, if at all.

- There are no transaction costs involved in trading options.
- Tax rates are similar for all participants who trade options.
- The stock of concern does not pay cash dividends.

Several variants of the Black-Scholes model have been developed to account for alternative assumptions, such as that stocks do pay dividends. The references at the end of Chapter 10 identify several articles that offer more specific details about option-pricing models.

To illustrate the application of the Black-Scholes option-pricing model, assume the following information:

- Current stock price is $72.
- Exercise price of the American call option is $70.
- Annual risk-free rate of interest is 7 percent.
- Time to maturity of the call option is one-half of the year.
- Standard deviation of the continuously compounded rate of return on stock is .10.

First, d_1 must be determined, as follows:

$$d_1 = \frac{\ln\left(\frac{S}{X}\right) + rT}{\sigma\sqrt{T}} + \frac{1}{2}\sigma\sqrt{T}$$

$$= \frac{\ln(72/70) + .07(.50)}{.10\sqrt{.50}} + \frac{1}{2}(.10)(\sqrt{.50})$$

$$= .8934 + .0353$$

$$= .9287$$

$$d_2 = d_1 - \sigma\sqrt{T}$$
$$= .9287 - .10\sqrt{.50}$$
$$= .8580$$

Using a table that identifies the area under the standard normal distribution function (see Exhibit 10A.1), the cumulative probability can be determined. Since $d_1 = .9287$, the cumulative probability from zero to .9287 is about .3231 (from Exhibit 10A.1, using interpolation). Since the cumulative probability for a unit normal variable from minus infinity to zero is .50, the cumulative probability from minus infinity to .9287 is .50 + .3231 = .8231.

For d_2, the cumulative probability from zero to .8580 is .3042. Therefore, the cumulative probability from minus infinity to .8580 is .50 + .3042 = .8042.

Now that $N(d_1)$ and $N(d_2)$ have been estimated, the call option value can be estimated:

$$C = S\,N(d_1) - Xe^{-rT}\,N(d_2)$$
$$= \$72\,(.8231) - \$70\,(2.7183)^{-.07(.50)}\,(.8042)$$
$$= \$59.26 - \$54.36$$
$$= \$4.90$$

Various computer programs are available to expedite the estimation of option values. As the characteristics represented by the pricing formula

EXHIBIT 10A.1 Cumulative Probabilities of the Standard Normal Distribution Function

d	0.00	0.01	0.02	0.03	0.04	0.05	0.06	0.07	0.08	0.09
0.0	0.0000	0.0040	0.0080	0.0120	0.0160	0.0199	0.0239	0.0279	0.0319	0.0359
0.1	0.0398	0.0438	0.0478	0.0517	0.0557	0.0596	0.0636	0.0675	0.0714	0.0753
0.2	0.0793	0.0832	0.0871	0.0910	0.0948	0.0987	0.1026	0.1064	0.1103	0.1141
0.3	0.1179	0.1217	0.1255	0.1293	0.1331	0.1368	0.1406	0.1443	0.1480	0.1517
0.4	0.1554	0.1591	0.1628	0.1664	0.1700	0.1736	0.1772	0.1808	0.1844	0.1879
0.5	0.1915	0.1950	0.1985	0.2019	0.2054	0.2088	0.2123	0.2157	0.2190	0.2224
0.6	0.2257	0.2291	0.2324	0.2357	0.2389	0.2422	0.2454	0.2486	0.2517	0.2549
0.7	0.2580	0.2611	0.2642	0.2673	0.2704	0.2734	0.2764	0.2794	0.2823	0.2852
0.8	0.2881	0.2910	0.2939	0.2967	0.2995	0.3023	0.3051	0.3078	0.3106	0.3133
0.9	0.3159	0.3186	0.3212	0.3238	0.3264	0.3289	0.3315	0.3340	0.3365	0.3389
1.0	0.3413	0.3438	0.3461	0.3485	0.3508	0.3531	0.3554	0.3577	0.3599	0.3621
1.1	0.3643	0.3665	0.3686	0.3708	0.3729	0.3749	0.3770	0.3790	0.3810	0.3830
1.2	0.3849	0.3869	0.3888	0.3907	0.3925	0.3944	0.3962	0.3980	0.3997	0.4015
1.3	0.4032	0.4049	0.4066	0.4082	0.4099	0.4115	0.4131	0.4147	0.4162	0.4177
1.4	0.4192	0.4207	0.4222	0.4236	0.4251	0.4265	0.4279	0.4292	0.4306	0.4319
1.5	0.4332	0.4345	0.4357	0.4370	0.4382	0.4394	0.4406	0.4418	0.4429	0.4441
1.6	0.4452	0.4463	0.4474	0.4484	0.4495	0.4505	0.4515	0.4525	0.4535	0.4545
1.7	0.4554	0.4564	0.4573	0.4582	0.4591	0.4599	0.4608	0.4616	0.4625	0.4633
1.8	0.4641	0.4649	0.4656	0.4664	0.4671	0.4678	0 4686	0.4693	0.4699	0.4706
1.9	0.4713	0.4719	0.4726	0.4732	0.4738	0.4744	0.4750	0.4756	0.4761	0.4767
2.0	0.4773	0.4778	0.4783	0.4788	0.4793	0.4798	0.4803	0.4808	0.4812	0.4817
2.1	0.4821	0.4826	0.4830	0.4834	0.4838	0.4842	0.4846	0.4850	0.4854	0.4857
2.2	0.4861	0.4866	0.4830	0.4871	0.4875	0.4878	0.4881	0.4884	0.4887	0.4890
2.3	0.4893	0.4896	0.4898	0.4901	0.4904	0.4906	0.4909	0.4911	0.4913	0.4916
2.4	0.4918	0.4920	0.4922	0.4925	0.4927	0.4929	0.4931	0.4932	0.4934	0.4936
2.5	0.4938	0.4940	0.4941	0.4943	0.4945	0.4946	0.4948	0.4949	0.4951	0.4952
2.6	0.4953	0.4955	0.4956	0.4957	0.4959	0.4960	0.4961	0.4962	0.4963	0.4964
2.7	0.4965	0.4966	0.4967	0.4968	0.4969	0.4970	0.4971	0.4972	0.4973	0.4974
2.8	0.4974	0.4975	0.4976	0.4977	0.4977	0.4978	0.4979	0.4979	0.4980	0.4981
2.9	0.4981	0.4982	0.4982	0.4982	0.4984	0.4984	0.4985	0.4985	0.4986	0.4986
3.0	0.4987	0.4987	0.4987	0.4988	0.4988	0.4989	0.4989	0.4989	0.4990	0.4990

change, the option value would change as well. The following relationships hold when all other factors are constant:

- The higher the stock price (S), the higher is the call option value.
- The higher the exercise price, the lower is the call option value.
- The higher the standard deviation of the return on the stock, the higher is the call option value.
- The greater the time to maturity, the higher is the call option value.
- The higher the risk-free rate, the higher is the call option value.

These relationships can be verified by reviewing the call option pricing formula. The value of any particular call option can change as a result of (1) a change in the underlying stock's price, (2) a change in the perceived volatility of the stock by investors, (3) decline in the remaining time to maturity on the option, and (4) a change in the prevailing risk-free rate.

Research by Rubinstein and others has detected that the Black-Scholes model undervalues some options and overvalues others. While a variety of alternative option-pricing models have been developed, none has been found to properly value all options. Nevertheless, their accuracy rate is high enough to make them useful; and, in addition to valuing options, they can be used for assessing the market's perception of a particular stock's risk. By using today's option price, exercise price, the underlying stock's price, the risk-free rate, and the remaining time to maturity, the so-called *implied standard deviation* can be determined to assess the market's perception of the stock's volatility. For example, the implied standard deviations just after the stock market crash of 1987 were much higher than those a year or so before the crash, indicating an increase in investors' risk perception of stocks.

Foreign Exchange Markets

FOREIGN EXCHANGE MARKETS IN PERSPECTIVE

On April 15, 1988, the announcement of a larger than expected U.S. merchandise trade deficit caused the dollar to decline by 2.3 percent against the Japanese yen and 2 percent against the German mark. The reaction to the announcement reflected expectations of continued weakness in the dollar, which in turn caused strong reactions in the stock and bond markets. Stock prices declined sharply, and long-term Treasury bond prices declined by 1.5 percent over the course of this day.

On June 10, 1988, the value of the dollar declined against foreign currencies. Some market participants believed that central bank intervention in the foreign exchange markets was a reason for the decline.

On June 15, 1988, the value of the dollar surged against major foreign currencies. One of the key reasons for the stronger dollar was an announcement that the U.S. trade deficit in March 1988 was $11.7 billion (seasonally adjusted), which was the smallest monthly deficit since December 1984. High interest rates in the U.S. relative to some other countries was another reason for the surge.

On July 27, 1988, the dollar declined on reports that central banks were intervening to weaken the dollar. The reports apparently encouraged multinational corporations and speculators to liquidate dollar positions and take positions in foreign currencies.

■ How do the factors cited above affect the dollar's value?
■ How can central banks intervene in the foreign exchange markets?
■ Can central banks control the dollar's value?
■ Why do participants in the stock markets, bond markets, mortgage markets and money markets closely monitor movements in the dollar's value?

These and other related questions are addressed in this chapter.

OUTLINE

This chapter explains how foreign exchange markets facilitate foreign currency transactions among institutions and individuals. In addition, it identifies factors that affect exchange rates and describes the foreign exchange instruments available. Finally, it discusses the use and effects of arbitrage in the foreign exchange markets, and explains how financial institutions participate in these markets.

BACKGROUND ON FOREIGN EXCHANGE MARKETS

As international trade and investing has increased over time, so has the need to exchange currencies. Foreign exchange markets represent a global telecommunications network among the large commercial banks that serve as financial intermediaries for such exchange. These banks are located in New York, Tokyo, Hong Kong, Singapore, Frankfurt, Zurich, and London. Foreign exchange transactions at these banks have been increasing, as shown by Exhibit 11.1.

At any point in time, the price at which banks will buy a currency (bid price) is slightly lower than the price at which they will sell it (ask price). As with markets for other commodities and securities, the market for foreign currencies is more efficient because of financial intermediaries (commercial banks). Otherwise, individual buyers and sellers of currency would be unable to identify counterparties to accommodate their needs.

Exchange Rate Quotations

Exhibit 11.2 shows the approximate foreign exchange rates of the major currencies that existed as of May 5, 1988. These exchange rates are listed in any major newspaper on a daily basis. Directly across from the currency name (in the second column) is the **spot exchange rate,** for immediate de-

EXHIBIT 11.1 Foreign Exchange Turnover in the New York Foreign Exchange Market

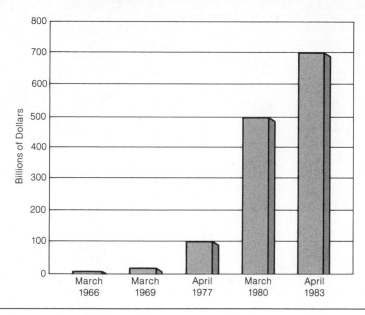

SOURCE: Federal Reserve Bank of New York, Annual Report, 1985.

livery. The exchange rates in this column define the value of a foreign currency in terms of U.S. dollars. The exchange rates in the third column are expressed as the number of units per dollar. According to the foreign exchange table, the British pound's value is $1.8632, which implies that .5367 pounds equal $1. The West German mark is worth $.5941, which implies that 1.6833 marks equal $1. Each exchange rate in the third column is simply the reciprocal of what is shown in the second column.

For widely used currencies such as the British pound and West German mark, **forward rates** are available and are listed just below the respective spot rates. The use of forward exchange rates is described later in this chapter.

Types of Exchange Rate Systems

From 1944 to 1971, the exchange rate at which one currency could be exchanged for another was maintained by governments within 1 percent of a specified rate. This period was known as the *Bretton Woods era*, since the agreement among country representatives occurred at the Bretton Woods Conference. The manner by which governments were able to control exchange rates is discussed later in this chapter.

By 1971 the U.S. dollar was clearly overvalued. That is, its value was maintained only by central bank intervention. In 1971 an agreement among all major countries (known as the *Smithsonian Agreement*) allowed for devaluation of the dollar. In addition, the Smithsonian Agreement called for a widening of the boundaries from 1 percent to 2¼ percent around each currency's set value.

EXHIBIT 11.2   Foreign Exchange Rate Quotations, May 5, 1988

Country (currency)	U.S. $ Equiv.	Currency per U.S. $
Argentina (Austral)	.1639	6.10
Australia (Dollar)	.7670	1.3038
Austria (Schilling)	.08482	11.79
Bahrain (Dinar)	2.6525	.377
Belgium (Franc)		
Commercial rate	.02849	35.09
Financial rate	.02832	35.31
Brazil (Cruzado)	.007030	142.24
Britain (Pound)	1.8632	.5367
30-Day Forward	1.8621	.5370
90-Day Forward	1.8586	.5380
180-Day Forward	1.8526	.5398
Canada (Dollar)	.8106	1.2337
30-Day Forward	.8095	1.2354
90-Day Forward	.8072	1.2389
180-Day Forward	.8041	1.2436
Colombia (Peso)	.003518	284.22
Denmark (Krone)	.1547	6.4640
Finland (Markka)	.2499	4.0010
France (Franc)	.1746	5.7275
30-Day Forward	.1745	5.7310
90-Day Forward	.1742	5.7405
180-Day Forward	.1739	5.7500
Greece (Drachma)	.007446	134.30
Hong Kong (Dollar)	.1281	7.8085
India (Rupee)	.07523	13.29
Ireland (Punt)	1.5905	.6287
Israel (Shekel)	.6394	1.5640
Italy (Lira)	.0007955	1257.00
Japan (Yen)	.008013	124.80
30-Day Forward	.008037	124.42
90-Day Forward	.008083	123.72
180-Day Forward	.008155	122.63
Kuwait (Dinar)	3.6643	.2729
Malta (Lira)	3.0994	.3226
Mexico (Peso)	.0004405	2270.00
Netherlands (Guilder)	.5295	1.8885
New Zealand (Dollar)	.6865	1.4567
Norway (Krone)	.1625	6.1525
Pakistan (Rupee)	.05682	17.60
Peru (Inti)	.0303	33.00
Philippines (Peso)	.04756	21.025
Portugal (Escudo)	.007273	137.50
Saudi Arabia (Riyal)	.2666	3.7505
Singapore (Dollar)	.4993	2.0030
South Africa (Rand)		
Commercial rate	.4521	2.2120
Financial rate	.3436	2.9100
South Korea (Won)	.001352	739.90
Spain (Peseta)	.009009	111.00
Sweden (Krona)	.1702	5.8760

EXHIBIT 11.2   Continued

Country (currency)	U.S. $ Equiv.	Currency per U.S. $
Switzerland (Franc)	.7124	1.4038
30-Day Forward	.7155	1.3977
90-Day Forward	.7214	1.3861
180-Day Forward	.7308	1.3684
Taiwan (Dollar)	.03498	28.59
Thailand (Baht)	.03981	25.12
Turkey (Lira)	.0007888	1267.80
Venezuela (Bolivar)		
Official rate	.1333	7.50
Floating rate	.03384	29.55
W. Germany (Mark)	.5941	1.6833
30-Day Forward	.5960	1.6778
90-Day Forward	.5998	1.6671
180-Day Forward	.6058	1.6507
	– – –	
SDR	1.37988	0.724703
ECU	1.23693	. . . .

At one time, governments intervened in the foreign exchange market whenever exchange rates threaten to wander outside the boundaries. However, in 1973 the boundaries were eliminated. Since then, the exchange rates of major currencies have been floating without any government-imposed boundaries. Yet, governments may still intervene in the foreign exchange market in order to influence the market value of their currency. A system whereby exchange rates are market-determined without boundaries but subject to government intervention is called a **dirty float.** This can be distinguished from a **freely floating** system, in which the foreign exchange market is totally free from government intervention. Governments continue to intervene in the foreign exchange market from time to time.

Some currencies are still pegged to another currency or a unit of account and maintained within specified boundaries. For example, many European currencies are pegged to a multi-currency unit of account known as the **European Currency Unit (ECU)** Because these currencies are pegged to the same unit of account, they are essentially pegged to each other. Governments intervene to assure that exchange rates between these currencies are maintained within the established boundaries.

FACTORS AFFECTING EXCHANGE RATE MOVEMENTS

The value of a currency adjusts to changes in demand and supply conditions, moving toward equilibrium. In equilibrium, there is no excess or deficiency of that currency. For example, a large increase in the U.S. demand for German goods and German securities would result in an increased demand for German marks. Because the demand for marks would then exceed the supply of marks for sale, the market makers (commercial banks) would experience a shortage of marks and would respond by increasing their price. Therefore, the mark would **appreciate,** or increase in value.

As a second example, assume that German corporations begin to purchase more U.S. goods, and that German investors purchase more U.S. securities. These actions reflect an increased sale of marks in exchange for dollars, causing a surplus of marks in the market. The value of the mark would therefore **depreciate,** or decline in order to once again achieve equilibrium. In reality, both the demand for marks and the supply of marks for sale can change simultaneously. The adjustment in the exchange rate will depend on the direction and magnitude of these changes.

Supply and demand for a currency are influenced by a variety of factors, including (1) differential inflation rates, (2) differential interest rates, (3) differential income levels, and (4) government intervention. Each of these factors is discussed in turn.

Differential Inflation Rates

Begin with an equilibrium situation, and consider what would happen to the U.S. demand for marks and the supply of German marks for sale if U.S. inflation suddenly became much higher than German inflation. The U.S. demand for German goods would increase, reflecting an increased U.S. demand for German marks. In addition, the supply of marks to be sold for dollars would decline, as the German desire for U.S. goods decreased. Both forces would place upward pressure on the value of the mark.

Under the reverse situation, where German inflation suddenly becomes much higher than U.S. inflation, the U.S. demand for marks would decrease, while the supply of marks for sale would increase, placing downward pressure of the value of the mark.

A well-known theory regarding the relationship between inflation and exchange rates, **purchasing power parity (PPP),** suggests that the exchange rate will, on average, change by a percentage that reflects the inflation differential between the two countries of concern. For example, assume an initial equilibrium situation where the British pound's spot rate is $1.60, U.S. inflation is 3 percent, and British inflation is also 3 percent. If U.S. inflation suddenly increased to 5 percent, the British pound would appreciate against the dollar by approximately 2 percent according to PPP. The rationale is that the U.S. would increase its demand for British goods as a result of the higher U.S. prices, placing upward pressure on the pound's value. Once the pound appreciated by 2 percent, the purchasing power of U.S. consumers would be the same whether they purchased U.S. goods or British goods. While the U.S. goods would have risen in price by a higher percentage, the British goods would then be just as expensive to U.S. consumers because of the pound's appreciation. Thus, a new equilibrium exchange rate results from the change in U.S. inflation.

In reality, exchange rates do not always change as suggested by the PPP theory. The other factors that influence exchange rates (discussed next) can distort the PPP relationship. Thus, all these factors must be considered when assessing why an exchange rate changed. Furthermore, forecasts of future exchange rates must account for the potential direction and magnitude of changes in all factors that affect exchange rates.

Differential Interest Rates

Consider what would happen to the U.S. demand for marks and the supply of marks for sale if U.S. interest rates suddenly become much higher than German interest rates. The demand by U.S. investors for German interest-bearing securities would decrease as these securities would become less attractive. In addition, the supply of marks to be sold in exchange for dollars would increase as German investors increased their purchases of U.S. interest-bearing securities. Both forces would place downward pressure on the mark's value. Under the reverse situation, opposite forces would occur, resulting in upward pressure on the mark's value. In general, the currency of the country with a higher increase (or smaller decrease) in interest rates is expected to appreciate, other factors held constant.

Differential Income Levels

Consider how the U.S. demand for marks and the supply of marks for sale would be affected if the U.S. income level suddenly increased by a much larger amount than the German income level. The U.S. demand for German goods would increase by a greater degree than the German demand for U.S. goods, due to the higher increase in income in the U.S. Consequently, the increase in U.S. demand for marks would likely exceed any increase in the supply of marks for sale, thereby placing upward pressure on the mark's value. Under a reverse scenario, where the German increase in income exceeded the U.S. increase in income, the increase in the supply of marks for sale would likely exceed the increase in the U.S. demand for marks, thereby placing downward pressure on the mark value. In general, the currency of the country with the higher increase in income will depreciate, other factors held constant.

Government Intervention

A country's government can intervene to affect a currency's value. Direct intervention occurs when a country's central bank (such as the Federal Reserve Bank for the United States or the Bank of England for Great Britain) sells some of its currency reserves for a different currency. For example, if the Federal Reserve Bank desired to weaken the dollar, it could sell some of its dollar reserves in exchange for foreign currencies. In essence, it would thereby increase the U.S. demand for foreign currencies, which could cause those currencies to appreciate against the dollar. To strengthen the dollar, it could sell some of its foreign currency reserves in exchange for dollars.

As an indirect method of intervention, the government could influence those factors (such as inflation, interest rates, or income) that affect a currency's value. Alternatively, it could place restrictions on international trade or on international investments. For example, if the U.S. government imposed trade restrictions on U.S. imports, this would limit the U.S. demand for foreign currencies and would place downward pressure on those currencies' values.

Central bank intervention can be overwhelmed by market forces, however, and therefore may not always succeed in reversing exchange rate movements. Yet, it may significantly affect the foreign exchange markets in two ways. First, it may slow the momentum of exchange rate movements. Second, it may cause commercial banks and other corporations to reassess their foreign exchange strategies if they believe the central banks will continue intervention.

In September 1985 central banks of the five major industrial powers (the *Group of Five*) developed an intervention strategy to weaken the U.S. dollar value. Within two weeks, the dollar depreciated by 13 percent against the Japanese yen and 9 percent against the German mark. Each country's central bank sold $1 billion or more during this intervention period. This amount seems insignificant in light of the estimated equivalent of $150 billion per day traded in foreign exchange markets. Yet, foreign exchange traders suggest that skill and timing are more important than the amount spent during the intervention process. If central banks work together and use proper timing, they can have a more lasting impact on currency values then if they do not. Many intervention efforts prior to September 1985 just temporarily jolted the markets, only to have exchange rates continue their pattern the following day. Yet, the intervention in September 1985 was the beginning of the dollar's reversal. While the transactions were not sufficient for a long-term reversal, they may have affected the strategies of the market participants, leading to a sustained weakening of the dollar.

Central banks often combine an adjustment of interest rates with intervention in the foreign exchange markets. To understand why this makes their intervention more effective, consider how commercial banks speculate with foreign exchange. If a commercial bank expects the mark to depreciate against the dollar, it may take a *short* position in marks and a *long* position in dollars. That is, it will first borrow marks from another bank, then exchange the marks for dollars to provide a short-term dollar loan to a bank that needs dollars. When the loan period is over, it receives dollars back with interest, converts them back to marks, and pays off its debt in marks with interest. If the dollar strengthens over this period, the bank receives more marks per dollar than the number of marks needed to purchase each dollar in the first place. As a numerical example, assume the following information:

- Interest rate on borrowed marks is 6 percent annualized.
- Interest rate on dollars loaned out is 7 percent annualized.
- Spot rate is 2 marks per dollar.
- Expected spot rate in six days is 2.05 marks per dollar.
- Bank can borrow 20 million marks.

The following steps can be taken to determine the profit from "shorting" marks and "going long" on dollars;

STEP 1. Borrow 20 million marks, and convert to $10 million (at $.50 per mark).

STEP 2. Invest the $10 million for one week at 7 percent annualized or (.11667 percent over six days), which will generate $10,011,667.

STEP 3. After six days, convert the $10,011,667 into marks at the spot rate that exists at that time. Based on the expected rate of 2.05 marks per dollar, the dollars would convert to 20,523,917 marks.

STEP 4. Pay back the loan of 2 million marks plus interest of 6 percent annualized (.1 percent over six days), which equals 20,020,000 marks.

Impact of the Stock Market Crash on Central Bank Intervention

During the stock market crash in October 1987, central banks were attempting to boost the value of the dollar. While such attempts frequently occurred during the 1985–1988 period, there was even greater concern just after the crash. The coordinated intervention effort was apparently aimed at boosting the confidence of non–U.S. investors that were holding U.S. securities, so that they would not sell them and cause greater turmoil in the markets. The effort to strengthen the dollar may also have been designed to reduce inflationary expectations in the U.S.

Shortly after the crash, both the stock markets and foreign exchange markets stabilized to a degree. Yet, they were still noticeably more volatile on a day-to-day basis after the crash than before the crash. The higher degree of volatility continued for several months after the crash.

The result is that the bank earned 503,917 marks profit over a six-day period. While potential profits are attractive, the speculative performance will depend on the uncertain future spot rate at the time the short and long positions are closed out.

If central banks wish to strengthen a currency, they may increase the cost of overnight financing so that commercial banks and other corporations do not "short" the currency. The idea of borrowing a potentially weak currency becomes less attractive when financing rates are high. As an extreme example, in 1981 there was downward pressure on the French franc as Francois Mitterrand became president. The French central bank (Banque de France) raised overnight borrowing rates to 3,000 percent annualized to discourage speculators from shorting the franc.

MOVEMENTS IN EXCHANGE RATES

The foreign exchange market has received much attention in recent years because of the degree to which currency movements can affect a firm's performance or a country's economic conditions. Exhibit 11.3 shows the trend in various foreign currency values over time. Most foreign (non–U.S.) currencies strengthened against the dollar in the late 1970s, weakened during the early 1980s, and began to strengthen again in 1985. Periods of increased foreign currency values reflect a weak dollar, while periods of decreased foreign currency values reflect a strong dollar.

Movements in the Dollar Index

In order to generalize the dollar's movement against foreign currencies, it can be compared to a composite of foreign currencies. The most common

Chapter 11

Foreign Exchange Markets

EXHIBIT 11.3 Exchange Rate Movements of Various Currencies

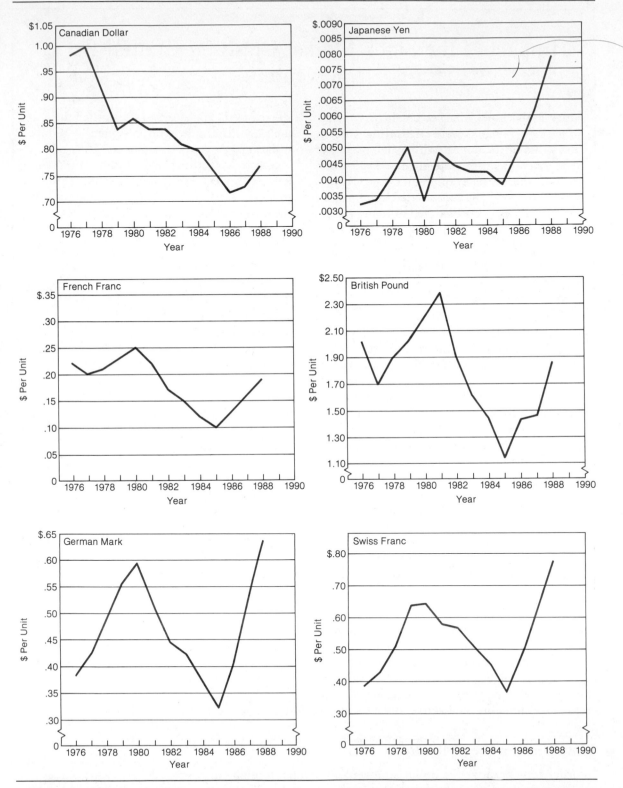

SOURCE: *Federal Reserve Chart Book.*

type of composite assigns weights to each currency that reflect their relative importance in trade. This is the approach used to measure the Federal Reserve Board (FRB) index. Exhibit 11.4 shows the relative importance in trade between the United States and other major countries. The FRB index weights also account for the volume of trade between these countries and non–U.S. countries. For this reason, the Canadian dollar is assigned a lower weight than what is reflected by its trade with the United States, while the German mark is assigned a higher weight (as it has a relatively high volume of trade with non–U.S. countries).

An index measurement of the dollar is commonly used to monitor the dollar's general movement against major currencies. To assess the dollar's movement against any particular foreign currency, the exchange rate movements of that currency should be monitored.

IMPACT OF EXCHANGE RATES ON INTERNATIONAL TRADE

A weak home currency is favorable for exporters because it can increase the foreign demand for their products. For example, consider U.S–produced calculators that are selling wholesale in the U.S. for $20 and also sold to firms in West Germany for the same price. Given a German mark value of

EXHIBIT 11.4 Composition of Trade-Weighted Index to Measure Value of Dollar

Country	Percentage of U.S. World Trade[a]		FRB Index Weight
	1974	1984	
Japan	13.7	17.2	13.6
Canada	15.8	14.9	9.2
Germany	7.0	5.6	20.8
United Kingdom	5.3	4.7	11.9
Mexico	5.1	4.6	
Taiwan	2.2	4.2	
Republic of Korea	1.9	3.3	
France	3.2	3.0	13.1
Hong Kong	1.6	2.4	
Italy	2.9	2.4	9.0
Netherlands	3.1	2.2	8.3
Brazil	3.0	2.2	
Belgium/Luxembourg	2.4	1.7	6.4
Singapore	0.9	1.6	
Australia	2.0	1.5	
Saudi Arabia	0.5	1.2	
Switzerland	1.2	1.2	3.6
China, People's Republic	0.6	1.1	
Sweden	1.1	1.0	4.2
	73.5	76.0	100.0

a Exports plus imports, minus oil trade, minus auto trade with Canada.

SOURCE: U.S. Department of Commerce, Bureau of the Census; and the Federal Reserve Bank of Cleveland.

Use of ECUs and SDRs in Foreign Exchange Markets

Some products, services, and financial instruments are denominated in several currencies rather than a single currency. There are several so-called *multi-currency units of account* used for this purpose, the most popular of which are the European Currency Unit (ECU) and the **SDR (Special Drawing Rights).**

The European Currency Unit (ECU) is commonly used to denominate products and financial instruments. Its value at any point in time is the weighted average of ten European currencies. The weight assigned to each currency depends on its country's relative gross national product and intra-European trade. For example, from 1985 to 1988, European currencies generally appreciated against the dollar. Since the ECU is valued as a portfolio of European currencies, its value increased against the dollar over this period.

The exchange rate between the ECU and any particular European currency also changes. However, since the exchange rates between European currencies are somewhat stable, so is the rate between any single European currency and the ECU. Central banks of some European currencies attempt to maintain the value of their home currency within 2.25 percent of its initially established value relative to the ECU. This implies that the central bank is attempting to stabilize its home currency relative to other European currencies. Consequently, intra-

European trade patterns are not likely to be highly influenced by exchange rate movements.

The ECU may serve as an appropriate unit for denominating products exported by one European country to another. To illustrate its use, suppose a British firm purchases products from a German firm. If the products are invoiced in marks, the British firm may be concerned about the potential strengthening of the mark against the pound by the time payment is required. The German firm could reduce this concern by invoicing the product in ECUs. The potential movement of the pound against the ECU is less than against the mark, since the ECU's value is based on a portfolio.

The special drawing right (SDR) is an international reserve asset created by the International Monetary Fund (IMF) and allocated to countries to supplement currency reserves. The SDR is now used as a unit of account to denominate some bonds, deposit accounts, international airline fares, and other products and services. In 1981 its valuation was simplified from a 16-currency formula to a 5-currency formula. Now its value at any point in time is based on the values of the U.S. dollar, German mark, French franc, Japanese yen, and British pound. The weights assigned to each currency represent their relative degree of importance in international trade and finance.

$.40, the calculator could be purchased by exchanging 50 marks to obtain $20 (2½ marks per dollar times $20). If the German mark appreciates to $.50 (which reflects a weaker dollar), the $20 calculators could be purchased for 40 marks. This should increase the foreign demand for calculators without reducing the profit margin to the exporter.

If exporting is a major business in the country of concern, a weak home currency value can have a very favorable impact on the country's economy

and also benefit corporations facing competition from foreign exporters. For example, if the dollar weakens, U.S. customers would find goods exported to their country more expensive (since they would need more dollars to match the amount of foreign currency required). Consequently, they are more likely to purchase goods from U.S. producers. To the degree that domestic producers export to other countries, or face foreign competition in their home country, the home country's economy can be stimulated by a weaker home currency. Some economists have even attempted to quantify the number of jobs created by each 1 percent decrease in the home currency's value. Yet, the impact is not always immediate or even guaranteed. A weak currency can also cause higher inflation in the home country. As it reduces foreign competition (by making foreign products more expensive), it allows local producers more flexibility to raise their prices.

A strengthening home currency is expected to have the opposite impact on the economy. Foreign customers have to pay more to purchase goods produced by the home country. In addition, domestic customers can purchase foreign goods at a lower price. Both forces reduce the demand for U.S. goods in favor of foreign goods, hurting local production and employment levels (and helping foreign production and employment).

The preceding discussion implies that a strong dollar can dampen economic growth. However, it can also dampen U.S. inflation, for two reasons. First, foreign materials can be obtained at a lower price, which may allow corporations to reduce the price of a finished product. Second, U.S. producers are forced to maintain low prices since they are aware of how attractive their foreign competitor's prices are to U.S. consumers when the dollar is strong.

Fluctuating exchange rates are sometimes thought to serve as a self-correcting mechanism on a country's balance of trade. A balance-of-trade deficit should place downward pressure on the value of a country's currency. A weakening home currency should then make the foreign-produced goods less attractive to home consumers. Consequently, the balance of trade could adjust in response to the changing currency value.

The relationship between the balance of trade and the exchange rate is not as precise as this, however. Factors in addition to international trade affect the value of a currency. For example, the home currency of a country with a balance-of-trade deficit and attractive interest rates could appreciate if the increase in net financial inflows exceeds the increase in net trade outflows.

Even if a country's currency does weaken in response to its balance-of-trade deficit, the deficit may still continue. Some foreign trade transactions are ordered six months ahead of time or longer, so the volume of these transactions will not be affected by exchange rate fluctuations until some point in the future. This suggests that there may be a lagged impact of a weak home currency on the economy.

When foreign goods become more expensive due to a weaker dollar, there may not be adequate substitutes for them. Even when substitutes are available at home, foreign competitors may compensate for the exchange rate fluctuations by reducing their profit margin. As an example, when the U.S. dollar weakened during 1986, U.S. importers of Japanese goods needed more dollars to obtain the yen to pay for their periodic imports. Some Japanese producers responded by reducing the prices of these goods in order to offset the weakened value of the dollar. This way, some Japanese products remained attractive to U.S. customers—another example of how a balance-of-trade position will not necessarily improve in response to a weaker home currency.

FOREIGN EXCHANGE INSTRUMENTS

To accommodate the various international transactions by individuals, firms, and other institutions, various foreign exchange instruments have been created, the most popular being

- Forward contracts
- Currency futures contracts
- Currency options contracts

Each of these instruments is described in turn.

Forward Contracts

The forward market allows participants to buy or sell a specified currency for a specified price on a specified date. Large commercial banks that offer foreign exchange on a spot basis also offer forward transactions for the widely traded currencies. By enabling a corporation to lock in the price to be paid for a foreign currency, forward purchases can hedge the corporation's risk that the currency's spot rate may appreciate over time. In addition, a corporation receiving a particular foreign currency in the future could lock in the price at which the currency could be sold by selling that currency forward. Again, large banks will accommodate such a request. They are buying forward from some firms and selling forward to others for a given date. They profit from the difference between the bid price at which they buy a currency forward and the slightly higher ask price at which they sell that currency forward.

The forward rate of a currency will sometimes exceed the existing spot rate, thereby exhibiting a *premium*. At other times, it will be below the spot rate, exhibiting a *discount*. Forward contracts are sometimes referred to in terms of their percentage premium or discount rather than their actual rate. For example, assume that the spot rate *(SR)* of the German mark is \$.50 while the 180-day $(n=180)$ forward rate *(FR)* is \$.51. The forward rate premium would be

$$\text{Forward rate premium} = \frac{FR - SR}{SR} \times \frac{360}{n}$$
$$= \frac{\$.51 - \$.50}{\$.50} \times \frac{360}{180}$$
$$= 4\%$$

This premium simply reflects the percentage by which the forward rate exceeds the spot rate on an annualized basis.

Using the forward rate and spot rate information for the British pound and German mark as disclosed in Exhibit 11.2, forward rate premiums and discounts are computed in Exhibit 11.5. This exhibit shows that the pound's forward rates had discounts while the mark's forward rates had premiums.

EXHIBIT 11.5   Estimation of Forward Rate Premiums and Discounts (May 5, 1988)

Currency	Maturity	Forward Rate (FR)	Estimated Forward Premium or Discount
British pound	30-day	$1.8621	−.71%
	90-day	1.8586	−.99
	180-day	1.8526	−1.14
German mark	30-day	.5960	3.84
	90-day	.5998	3.84
	180-day	.6058	3.94

The size of a forward rate's premium or discount is influenced by interest rate differentials, as explained later in this chapter. The computation is annualized so that forward rates with various maturities can more easily be compared.

If a bank's forward purchase and sale contracts do not even out for a given date, it is exposed to exchange rate risk. Consider a U.S. bank which has contracts committed to selling 100 million German marks and purchasing 150 million marks 90 days from now. It will receive 50 million marks more than it sells. An increase in the mark value 90 days from now would be advantageous, but if the mark depreciated instead, the bank would be adversely affected by its exposure to the *exchange rate risk*.

Currency Futures Contracts

An alternative to the forward contract is a currency futures contract, which requires an amount of a currency to be delivered on a specified date and at a specified exchange rate. A firm can purchase a futures contract to hedge payables by locking in the price at which it could purchase a specific currency at a particular point in time. To hedge receivables, it could sell futures, thereby locking in the price at which it could sell a foreign currency. A futures contract represents a standard number of units, as shown in Exhibit 11.6. Currency futures contracts also have specific maturity dates from which the firm must choose.

Futures contracts differ from forward contracts in that they are standardized, whereas forward contracts can specify whatever amount and maturity date the firm desires. Forward contracts have this flexibility because they are negotiated with commercial banks, rather than on a trading floor.

Currency Options Contracts

Another instrument used for hedging is the currency option. Its primary advantage over forward and futures contracts is that it provides a *right* rather than an *obligation* to purchase or sell a particular currency at a specified price within a given period.

To hedge payables, a *call option* could be used. It provides the right to purchase a currency at a specified price (called the *exercise price*) within a specified period. If the spot rate remains below the exercise price, the option would not be exercised, since the firm could purchase the foreign currency

EXHIBIT 11.6 **Foreign Currencies for Which Futures Contracts Are Available (on the International Monetary Market)**

Currency	Number of Foreign Currency Units Per Contract
British pound	25,000
Canadian dollar	100,000
Japanese yen	12,500,000
Swiss franc	125,000
West German mark	125,000

at a lower cost in the spot market. Flexibility is thus provided by a currency option contract. However, options can be obtained only for a fee (or *premium*), so there is a cost to a firm hedging with options, even if the options are not exercised. To hedge receivables, a *put option* could be purchased, since it functions like a call option except that it provides the right to sell rather than purchase. If the spot rate remains above the exercise price, the option would not be exercised since the firm could sell the foreign currency at a higher price in the spot market. Conversely, if the spot rate is below the exercise price at the time the foreign currency is received, the firm could exercise its put option.

When deciding whether to use the forward, futures, or options contracts for hedging, the following characteristics of each contract should be considered. First, if the firm requires a tailor-made hedge that cannot be matched by existing futures contracts, a forward contract may be preferred. Otherwise, forward and futures contracts should generate somewhat similar results.

The choice of either an obligation-type contract (forward or futures) or options contract depends on the expected trend of the spot rate. If the currency denominating payables appreciates, the firm will benefit more from a futures or forward contract than from a call option contract. The call option contract requires an up-front fee, but it is a wiser choice when the firm is less certain of the future direction of a currency. The call option can hedge the firm against possible appreciation but still allow it to ignore the contract and use the spot market if the currency depreciates. Put options may be preferred over futures or forward contracts for hedging receivables when future currency movements are very uncertain.

Use of Foreign Exchange Instruments for Speculating

The forward, currency futures, and currency options markets may be used for not only hedging but speculating as well. For example, a speculator who expects the German mark to appreciate could consider any of these strategies:

1. Purchase marks forward and, when received, sell them in the spot market.
2. Purchase futures contracts on marks; when the marks are received, sell them in the spot market.
3. Purchase call options on marks; at some point before the expiration date, when the spot rate exceeds the exercise price, exercise the call option and then sell the marks received in the spot market.

Conversely, a speculator who expects the mark to depreciate could consider any of these strategies:

1. Sell marks forward and then purchase them in the spot market just before fulfilling the forward obligation.
2. Sell futures contracts on marks; purchase marks in the spot market just before fulfilling the futures obligation.
3. Purchase put options on marks; at some point before the expiration date, when the spot rate is less than the exercise price, purchase marks in the spot market and then exercise the put option.

SPECULATING WITH CURRENCY FUTURES. As an example of speculating with currency futures, consider the following information:

- Spot rate of British pound is $1.56 per pound.
- Price of futures contract is $1.57 per pound.
- Expectation of pound's spot rate as of maturity date of the futures contract is $1.63 per pound.

Given that the future spot rate is expected to be higher than the futures price, you could buy currency futures. You would receive pounds on the maturity date for $1.57. If your expectations are correct, you would then sell the pounds for $.06 more per unit than you paid for them (assuming that you sold the pounds at that time). Your gain would be $1,500 per contract ($.06 × 25,000 units).

The risk of your speculative strategy is that the pound may decline rather than increase in value. If it declines to $1.55 by the maturity date, you would have sold the pounds for $.02 less per unit than what you paid, causing a loss of $500 per contract.

To account for uncertainty, speculators may develop a probability distribution for the future spot rate:

Future Spot Rate of British Pound	Probability
$1.50	10%
1.59	20
1.63	50
1.66	20

This probability distribution suggests that four outcomes are possible. For each possible outcome, the anticipated gain or loss can be determined:

Possible Outcome for Future Spot Rate	Probability	Gain or Loss per Unit
$1.50	10%	− $.07
1.59	20	.02
1.63	50	.06
1.66	20	.09

Efficiency of Currency Options, Forwards, and Futures

Due to the popularity of currency options as a speculative tool, much research has been devoted to assessing whether the currency options market is efficient. If currency options are not priced efficiently, excess risk-adjusted returns may be achievable. Recent research by Bodurtha and Courtadon and by Tucker found that when accounting for transaction costs, the currency options market is efficient. This does not prevent speculators from achieving gains, but only suggests that option prices generally reflect all available information.

The forward market, however, was not found to be efficient by research. A study by Kaen, Simos, and Hackey found that the forward rate is a poor forecaster of the future spot rate. A study by Chiang on the forward rates of the British pound, Canadian dollar, French franc, and German mark determined that these rates do not incorporate all relevant information. Bear in mind, though, that the results of such a study tend to vary with the time period and currencies analyzed.

To assess the efficiency of the currency futures market, Thomas developed a trading strategy based on interest rate differentials. This strategy generated a return of about 10.3 percent above the three-month Treasury bill rate on average, suggesting that currency futures are not priced efficiently (if the excess return is assumed to more than compensate for the risk involved).

See the following references for more details on this subject:

Bodurtha, James N. Jr., and George R. Courtadon. "Efficiency Tests of the Foreign Currency Options Market." *Journal of Finance* (March 1986): 151–161.

Tucker, Alan L. "Empirical Tests of the Efficiency of the Currency Option Market." *Journal of Financial Research* (Winter 1985): 275–285.

Kaen, Fred R., Erangelos O. Simos, and George A. Hackey. "The Response of Forward Exchange Rates to Interest Rate Forecasting Errors." *Journal of Financial Research* (Winter 1984): 281–290.

Chiang, Thomas. "On the Predictions of the Future Spot Rates." *The Financial Review* (February 1986): 69–83.

Thomas, Lee R. "A Winning Strategy for Currency Futures Speculation." *Journal of Portfolio Management* (Fall 1985): 65–69.

This analysis measures the probability and potential magnitude of a loss from the speculative strategy.

SPECULATING WITH CURRENCY OPTIONS. Consider the information from the previous example, and also assume that a British call option is available with an exercise price of $1.57 and a premium of $.03 per unit. Recall that your best guess of the future spot rate was $1.63. If your guess is correct, you will earn $.06 per unit on the difference between what you paid (the exercise price of $1.55) and what you could sell a pound for ($1.63). After the premium paid for the option ($.03 per unit) is deducted, the net gain is $.03 per unit.

The risk of purchasing this option is that the pound's value might decline over time. If so, you will be unable to exercise the option, and your loss will be the premium paid for it. To assess the risk involved, a probability distribution could be developed. In Exhibit 11.7 the probability distribution from the previous example is applied here. The distribution of net gains from the strategy is shown in the sixth column.

Part Three

Other Financial Markets

Speculators should always compare the potential gains from currency options and currency futures contracts to determine which type of contract (if any) to trade. It is possible for two speculators to have similar expectations about potential gains from both types of contracts, yet because they have different degrees of risk aversion, prefer different types of contracts.

ARBITRAGE IN THE FOREIGN EXCHANGE MARKETS

Exchange rates in the foreign exchange market are market-determined. If they become misaligned, market forces will cause realignment. Some examples follow.

Suppose the exchange rates of the mark quoted by two banks differ, as shown in Exhibit 11.8. The ask quote is higher than the bid quote to reflect transactions cost charged by each bank. Because Baltimore Bank is asking $.499 for marks, and Sacramento Bank is willing to pay (bid) $.500 for marks, an institution could execute **locational arbitrage.** That is, it could achieve a risk-free return without tying funds up for any length of time by buying marks at one location (Baltimore Bank) and simultaneously selling them to the other location (Sacramento Bank).

As location arbitrage is executed, Baltimore Bank will begin to raise its ask price on marks in response to the strong demand. In addition, Sacramento Bank will begin to lower its bid price in response to its excess supply of marks recently received. Once the ask price of Baltimore Bank is at least as high as the bid price by Sacramento Bank, locational arbitrage will no longer be possible. Because some financial institutions (particularly the foreign exchange departments of commercial banks) watch for locational arbitrage opportunities, any discrepency in exchange rates among locations should quickly be alleviated.

EXHIBIT 11.7   Estimating Speculative Gains from Options Using a Probability Distribution

(1)	(2)	(3)	(4)	(5)	(6)
Possible Outcome for Future Spot Rate	Probability	Will the Option be Exercised Based on This Outcome?	Gain per Unit from Exercising Option	Premium Paid per Unit for the Option	Net Gain or Loss per Unit
$1.50	10%	No	—	$.03	− $.03
1.59	20	Yes	$.02	.03	− .01
1.63	50	Yes	.06	.03	.03
1.66	30	Yes	.09	.03	.06

EXHIBIT 11.8   Bank Quotes Used for Locational Arbitrage Example

	Bid Rate on Marks	Ask Rate on Marks
Sacramento Bank	$.500	$.507
Baltimore Bank	$.491	$.499

The coexistence of international money markets and forward markets force a special relationship between a forward rate premium and the interest rate differential of two countries, known as **interest rate parity.** The equation for interest rate parity can be written as

$$p = \frac{(1 + i_h)}{(1 + i_f)} - 1$$

where p = forward premium of foreign currency
i_h = home country interest rate
i_f = foreign interest rate

For example, assume that the spot rate of the German mark is $.50, the one-year U.S. interest rate is 9 percent, and the one-year German interest rate is 6 percent. Under conditions of interest rate parity, the forward premium of the mark would be

$$p = \frac{(1 + 9\%)}{(1 + 6\%)} - 1$$
$$= \text{approx. } 2.8\%$$

This means that the forward rate of the mark would be about $.514 to reflect a 2.8 percent premium above the spot rate. When one reviews the equation for interest rate parity, the following relationship is obvious. If the interest rate is lower in the foreign country than in the home country, the forward rate of the foreign currency will have a premium. In the opposite situation, it will have a discount.

Interest rate parity suggests that the forward rate premium (or discount) should be about equal to the differential in interest rates between the countries of concern. To illustrate this relationship, assume that both the spot rate and one-year forward rate of the Canadian dollar was $.80. Also assume that the Canadian interest rate was 10 percent while the U.S. interest rate was 8 percent. U.S. investors could take advantage of the higher Canadian interest rate without being exposed to exchange rate risk by executing **covered interest arbitrage.** Specifically, they would exchange U.S. dollars for Canadian dollars and invest at the rate of 10 percent. They would simultaneously sell Canadian dollars one year forward. Because they are able to purchase and sell Canadian dollars for the same price, their return is the 10 percent interest earned on their investment.

As the U.S. investors demand Canadian dollars in the spot market, while selling Canadian dollars forward, they place upward pressure on the spot rate and downward pressure on the one-year forward rate of the Canadian dollar. Thus, the Canadian dollar's forward rate will exhibit a discount. Once the discount becomes large enough, the interest rate advantage in Canada will be offset. What U.S. investors gain on the higher Canadian interest rate is offset by having to buy Canadian dollars at a higher (spot) rate than the selling (forward) rate. Consequently, covered interest arbitrage will no longer generate a return that is any higher for U.S. investors than an alternative investment within the U.S. Once the forward discount (or premium) offsets the interest rate differential in this manner, interest rate parity exists.

We can use the interest rate parity equation to determine the forward discount that the Canadian dollar must exhibit in order to offset the interest rate differential:

$$p = \frac{(i + i_h)}{(1 + i_f)} - 1$$

$$= \frac{(1 + 8\%)}{(1 + 10\%)} - 1$$

$$= \text{approx.} - 1.82\%$$

If the forward rate is lower than the spot rate by 1.82 percent, the interest rate is offset, and covered interest arbitrage would yield a return to U.S. investors similar to the U.S. interest rate.

The existence of interest rate parity prevents investors from earning higher returns from covered interest arbitrage than can be earned in the United States. Yet, international investing may still be feasible if the investing firm does not simultaneously cover in the forward market. Of course, failure to do so usually exposes the firm to exchange rate risk; if the currency denominating the investment depreciates over the investment horizon, the return on the investment is reduced.

INSTITUTIONAL USE OF FOREIGN EXCHANGE MARKETS

The manner by which financial institutions utilize the foreign exchange market is summarized in Exhibit 11.9. The degree of international investment by financial institutions is influenced by potential return, risk, and government regulations. Commercial banks use international lending as their primary form of international investing. Mutual funds, pension funds, and insurance companies purchase foreign securities. In recent years, technology has reduced information costs and other transaction costs associated with purchasing foreign securities, prompting an increase in institutional purchases of foreign securities.

The degree of regulation imposed on investment in foreign securities varies with the institutional investor and its home country government. For example, pension funds are typically subject to constraints as to how and where they invest their funds. Regulations on pension funds are liberal in some countries, such as the United Kingdom and the Netherlands, and are more restrictive in others, such as Canada and Japan.

SUMMARY

International trade and capital flows require the exchange of foreign currencies. A foreign exchange market serves this purpose. Commercial banks make a market for foreign exchange by purchasing and selling a variety of currencies. The rate at which they will exchange one currency for another is determined by supply and demand and therefore changes over time. If a particular exchange rate differs distinctly among banks, locational arbitrage will cause the rates to become realigned.

In recent years, foreign exchange instruments have been commonly used for hedging or speculating. Forward contracts are available to corporations that desire to hedge future inflows or outflows in a foreign currency. Futures contracts are available for the same purpose and are also traded to speculate

EXHIBIT 11.9   Institutional Use of Foreign Exchange Markets

Type of Financial Institution	Uses of Foreign Exchange Markets
Commercial banks	■ Serve as financial intermediaries in the foreign exchange market by buying or selling currencies to accommodate customers ■ Speculate on foreign currency movements by taking long positions in some currencies and short positions in others ■ Provide forward contracts to customers ■ Some commercial banks offer currency options to customers; these options can be tailored to a customer's specific needs, unlike the standardized currency options traded on an exchange
Mutual funds	■ International mutual funds commonly need to exchange currencies when reconstructing their portfolios ■ Some international mutual funds use foreign currency futures and/or options to hedge a portion of their exposure
Brokerage firms and Investment banking firms	■ Some brokerage firms and investment banking firms engage in foreign security transactions for their customers or for their own accounts
Insurance companies	■ Require an exchange of currencies for their international operations ■ Require foreign exchange when investing in foreign securities for their investment portfolio or when selling foreign securities
Pension funds	■ Require foreign exchange of currencies when investing in foreign securities for their stock or bond portfolios

on forecasted movements in exchange rates. Options contracts can also lock in the future rate at which currencies can be exchanged, but they offer more flexibility in that there is a right but no obligation to the option holder. For this advantage, options require an up-front premium.

KEY TERMS

appreciate	freely floating
covered interest arbitrage	interest rate parity
depreciate	locational arbitrage
dirty float	purchasing power parity (PPP)
European Currency Unit (ECU)	SDR (Special Drawing Rights)
forward rates	spot exchange rate

QUESTIONS

11.1. Explain the exchange rate system that existed during the 1950s and 1960s. How did the Smithsonian Agreement in 1971 revise it? How does today's exchange rate system differ?

11.2. Explain the difference between a freely floating system and dirty float. Which type is more representative of the United States?

11.3. Assume that France places a quota on goods imported from the United States, and the United States does not plan to retaliate. How could this affect the value of the French franc? Explain.

11.4. Assume that stocks in Great Britain become very attractive to U.S. investors. How could this affect the value of the British pound? Explain.

11.5. Assume that West Germany suddenly experiences high and unexpected inflation. How would this affect the value of the German mark according to purchasing power parity (PPP) theory?

11.6. Assume that Switzerland has a very strong economy (with a large increase in national income), placing upward pressure on both inflation and interest rates. Explain how each of these factors could place pressure on the value of the Swiss franc, and determine whether the franc's value will rise or fall.

11.7. The Bank of Japan desires to decrease the value of the Japanese yen against the dollar. How could it use direct intervention to do this?

11.8. When would a commercial bank take a short position in a foreign currency? A long position?

11.9. Seattle Bank was long in German marks and short in Canadian dollars. Explain a possible future scenario that could adversely affect the bank's performance.

11.10. How does a weak dollar affect U.S. inflation? Explain.

11.11. Explain why a system of floating exchange rates is sometimes thought to serve as a self-correcting mechanism on the balance of trade. Why does the exchange rate system not necessarily correct a balance-of-trade deficit over time?

11.12. Assume a horizontal yield curve exists. How do you think the yield curve would be affected if foreign investors of short-term securities and long-term securities suddenly anticipate that the value of the dollar will strengthen? (Refer back to a discussion of the yield curve in Chapter 4 if it would help develop your opinion).

PROBLEMS

11.1. Assume the following information:

	Interbank Interest Rate	Spot Rate	Expected Spot Rate in 5 days
Canadian dollars	6%	$ .80	$ .79
British pounds	7%	$1.50	$1.52

Explain how Minnesota Bank could speculate, based on this information, by taking a short position in one currency and a long position in the other. What would be the gain if expectations come true, assuming that the bank could borrow 1 million units of either currency?

11.2. Assume that a U.S. firm issues three-year notes in West Germany with a par value of 60 million marks and a 6 percent annual coupon rate, priced at par. The forecasted exchange rate of the mark is $.50 at the end of Year 1, $.53 at the end of Year 2, and $.57 at the end of Year 3. Estimate the dollar cash flows needed to cover these payments.

11.3. Using the following information, determine the probability distribution of per unit gains from selling in French franc (FF) futures.

- Spot rate of FF is $.10
- Price of FF futures per unit is $.102.
- Your expectation of FF spot rate at maturity of futures contract is

Possible Outcome for Future Spot Rate	Probability
$.09	10%
.095	70%
.11	20%

11.4. Using the following information, determine the probability distribution of net gains per unit from purchasing a call option on British pounds

- spot rate of British pound = $1.45
- premium on British pound option = $.04 per unit
- exercise price of a British pound option = $1.46
- your expectation of British pound spot rate prior to the expiration of option is:

Possible outcome for future spot rate	Probability
$1.48	30%
1.49	40%
1.52	30%

11.5. Assume the following exchange rate quotes on British pounds:

	Bid	Ask
Orleans Bank	$1.46	$1.47
Kansas Bank	1.48	1.49

Explain how locational arbitrage would occur. Also explain why this arbitrage will realign the exchange rates.

11.6. Assume the following information:

British pound spot rate = $1.58
British pound one-year forward rate = $1.58

British one-year interest rate = 11%
U.S. one year interest rate = 9%

Explain how covered interest arbitrage could be used by U.S. investors to lock in a higher yield than 9%. What would be their yield? As covered interest arbitrage occurs, explain how the spot and forward rates of the pound would change.

11.7. Assume the following information:

French one-year interest rate = 15%
U.S. one-year interest rate = 11%

If interest rate parity exists, what would be the forward premium or discount on the French franc's forward rate? Would covered interest arbitrage be more profitable to U.S. investors than investing at home? Explain.

PROJECTS

11.1. Review the section called "Foreign Exchange" in *The Wall Street Journal* (listed in the index on the first page) over the last five trading days. Fill in the following table.

	General movement in value of major foreign currencies	Explanation for the movement
1 day ago		
2 days ago		
3 days ago		
4 days ago		
5 days ago		

11.2 Choose a major foreign currency of your choice (or assigned by your professor) and determine how that currency's value has changed against the dollar over the last six months. Offer an explanation for the general trend in this currency over the last six months.

REFERENCES

Adler, Michael and Bruce Lehmann. "Deviations from Purchasing Power Parity in the Long Run." *Journal of Finance* (December 1983): 1471–1487.

Bodurtha, James N., Jr. and George R. Courtadon. "Efficiency Tests of the Foreign Currency Options Market." *Journal of Finance* (March 1986): 151–161.

Chiang, Thomas. "On the Predictions of the Future Spot Rates." *The Financial Review* (February 1986): 69–83.

Dornbusch, Rudiger. "Expectations and Exchange Rate Dynamics." *Journal of Political Economy* (December 1976): 1161–1174.

Ehrlich, Edna E. "Foreign Pension Fund Investment in the United States." *Quarterly*

Review, Federal Reserve Bank of New York (Spring 1983): 1–12.

Evans, Paul. "Is the Dollar High Because of Large Budget Deficits?" *Journal of Monetary Economics* 18 (November 1986): 227–250.

Fama, Eugene. "Forward and Spot Exchange Rates." *Journal of Monetary Economics* (November 1984): 319–383.

Hakkio, Craig. "Does the Exchange Rate Follow a Random Walk? A Monte Carlo Study of Four Tests for a Random Walk." *Journal of International Economics* (June 1986): 221–230.

Helpman, Elhanan. "An Exploration in the Theory of Exchange Rate Regimes." *Journal of Political Economy* (October 1981): 865–890.

Kaen, Fred R., Erangelos O. Simos, and George A. Hackey. "The Response of Forward Exchange Rates to Interest Rate Forecasting Errors." *Journal of Financial Research* (Winter 1984): 281–290.

Morris, Frank E. "The Changing World of Central Banking." *New England Economic Review*, Federal Reserve Bank of Boston (March–April 1986): 3–6.

Sender, Henry. "Games Central Banks Play with Currencies." *Institutional Investor* (November 1985): 100–110.

Stockman, Alan. "A Theory of Exchange Rate Determination." *Journal of Political Economy* (August 1980): 673–698.

Stockman, Alan. "Recent Issues in the Theory of Flexible Exchange Rates: A Review Article." *Journal of Money, Credit, and Banking* (August 1985): 401–410.

Stockman, Alan and Lars Svensson. "Capital Flows, Investment, and Exchange Rates." *Journal of Monetary Economics* 19 (March 1987): 171–202.

Thomas, Lee R. "A Winning Strategy for Currency Futures Speculation." *Journal of Portfolio Management* (Fall 1985): 65–69.

Tucker, Alan L. "Empirical Tests of the Efficiency of the Currency Option Market." *Journal of Financial Research* (Winter 1985): 275–285.

Government Influence on Financial Markets

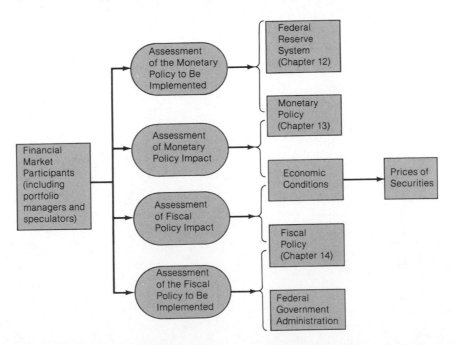

The chapters in Part Four explain how the two key components of the U.S. federal government, the Federal Reserve System and the Administration, affect economic conditions. Because the policies implemented by the federal government can influence security prices, they are closely monitored by financial market participants. The expected government policies to be implemented and their expected impact on security prices are used by participants to value securities and make investment decisions.

The Fed and Monetary Policy

THE FED IN PERSPECTIVE

The high level of economic growth during the first nine months of 1987 caused the Federal Reserve System ("the Fed") to utilize a moderately tight monetary policy. Because the Fed's main concern was potential inflation, it was unwilling to use a loose money policy that could ignite inflation.

In October 1987, the stock market crash caused concern about a possible recession. Consequently, the Fed was more willing to increase the money supply if the economy deteriorated, or if the financial system lacked sufficient liquidity.

In early 1988, the Fed tightened its credit policy, somewhat reversing the policy implemented in response to the stock market crash. Throughout the various changes in policy, there was some dissension among Fed members. One member, Vice Chairman Johnson, implied that the Fed concentrates on three financial indicators. Another member, Mr. Angell, focuses on commodity prices as an economic indicator. Some other members prefer not to focus on one or a few variables.

During the summer of 1988, a drought throughout the Midwest affected the prices of farm products, and the Fed was again concerned about inflation. In July 1988, Chairman of the Fed Alan Greenspan suggested that if the Fed errs in its decisions to control money supply, it should err on the tighter side in order to assure that inflationary momentum is prevented. Some other Fed members would have preferred a somewhat looser monetary policy to prevent a possible recession.

■ How does the Fed tighten or loosen credit?
■ What part of the Fed determines whether credit should be loosened or tightened?
■ Why do Fed members sometimes disagree on the appropriate policy to be implemented?
■ Why is the Fed's policy sometimes criticized by the Administration?

These and other related questions are addressed in this chapter.

OUTLINE

The Federal Reserve System (or *Fed*), as the central bank of the United States, has the responsibility of conducting national monetary policy. Such policy influences interest rates and other economic variables that determine the prices of securities. Participants in the financial markets therefore monitor the Fed's monetary policy closely. This chapter provides a background on the Fed and explains how it controls the money supply. Financial market participants must understand how the Fed operates in order to predict its impact on the market and implement the proper policies.

ORGANIZATION OF THE FED

In 1791 the First Bank of the United States was created to oversee the commercial banking system and attempt to maintain a stable economy. Because its 20-year charter was not renewed by Congress, First Bank was terminated in 1811. A major criticism of this central bank was that it interfered with the development of the banking system and economic growth. Its termination, however, reduced public confidence in the banking system. In 1816 the Second Bank of the United States was established, and since its 20-year charter also was not renewed by Congress, it was terminated in 1836.

During the late 1800s and early 1900s, several banking panics occurred, culminating with a major crisis in 1907. This motivated another attempt to establish a central bank. Accordingly, in 1913 the Federal Reserve Act was passed, establishing reserve requirements for those commercial banks that desired to become members. It also specified 12 districts across the United States, as well as a city in each district where a Federal Reserve district bank was to be established. Each district bank had the ability to buy and sell government securities, which could affect the money supply (as will be explained later in this chapter). Each district bank focused on its particular district, without much concern for other districts. Over time,

Part Four

Government Influence
on Financial Markets

324

a more centralized system was organized, where money supply decisions were assigned to a particular group of individuals rather than across 12 district banks. The Fed as it exists today has five major components:

- Federal Reserve district banks
- Member banks
- Board of Governors
- Federal Open Market Committee (FOMC)
- Advisory committees

Each component is discussed in turn.

Federal Reserve District Banks

The 12 Federal Reserve districts are identified in Exhibit 12.1, along with the city where each district bank is located and the district branches. The New York district bank is considered the most important because many large banks are located in this district. Commercial banks that become members of the Fed are required to purchase stock in their **Federal Reserve district bank.** This stock, which is not traded in a secondary market, pays a maximum dividend of 6 percent annually.

Each Fed district bank has nine directors. Six of them are elected by member banks in that district. Of these six directors, three are professional bankers and the other three are businesspeople. Besides these six directors, three other directors are appointed by the Board of Governors (to be discussed shortly). The nine directors appoint the president of their Fed district bank.

Fed district banks facilitate operations within the banking system by clearing checks, replacing old currency, and providing loans (through the *discount window*) to depository institutions in need of funds. They also collect economic data and conduct research projects on commercial banking and economic trends.

Member Banks

Commercial banks can elect to become member banks if they meet specific requirements of the Board of Governors. All national banks (chartered by the Comptroller of the Currency) are required to be members of the Fed, while other banks (chartered by their respective states) are not. Member banks currently represent about 35 percent of all banks, and about 70 percent of all bank deposits are in these member banks.

Board of Governors

The **Board of Governors** (sometimes called the Federal Reserve Board) is made up of seven individual members with offices in Washington D.C. Each member is appointed by the president of the United States (and confirmed by the Senate) and serves a nonrenewable 14-year term. Such a long term is thought to reduce political pressure on these members and thus encourage the development of policies that will benefit the U.S. economy over the long run. Each member's starting terms have been staggered so that one term expires in every even-numbered year.

EXHIBIT 12.1 Locations of Federal Reserve District Banks and Branches

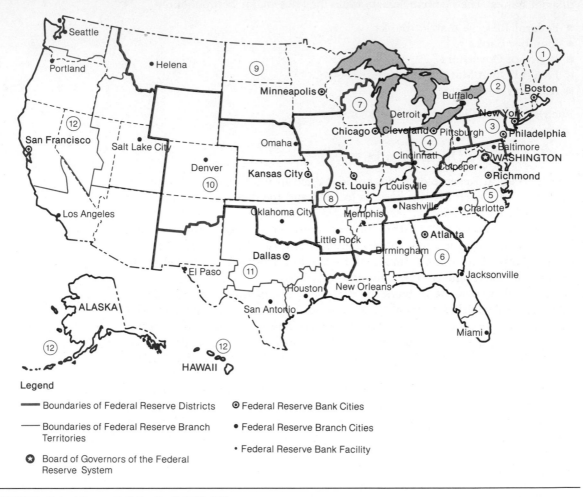

Legend

— Boundaries of Federal Reserve Districts
⊚ Federal Reserve Bank Cities

— Boundaries of Federal Reserve Branch Territories
• Federal Reserve Branch Cities

✪ Board of Governors of the Federal Reserve System
· Federal Reserve Bank Facility

SOURCE: *Federal Reserve Bulletin*, (April 1988): 85A.

One of the seven board members is selected by the president to be Federal Reserve chairman for a four-year term, which may be renewed. While the chairman has no more voting power than any other member, he may have more influence. As an example, Paul Volcker, who served as chairman from 1979 to 1987, was very persuasive.

The board has two main roles: (1) regulating commercial banks and (2) controlling monetary policy. It supervises and regulates commercial banks that are members of the Fed and bank holding companies. It oversees the operation of the 12 Federal Reserve districts banks in their provision of services to depository institutions and their supervision of specific commercial banks. It also establishes regulations in consumer finance. It was previously responsible for determining ceiling interest rates on bank deposits; those ceilings were completely phased out by 1986 as a result of the Depository Institutions Deregulation and Monetary Control Act of 1980. The

Board continues to participate in the supervision of member banks and in setting credit controls such as margin requirements (percentage of a purchase of securities that must be paid with nonborrowed funds).

With regard to monetary policy, the Board has direct control in two monetary policy tools and participates in the control of a third tool. First, it has the power to revise reserve requirements imposed on depository institutions. Second, it authorizes changes in the **discount rate,** or the interest rate charged on Fed district bank loans to depository institutions. Any changes in the discount rate or reserve requirements can affect the money supply level, as explained later in this chapter. The Board can also control money supply by participating in the decisions of the Federal Open Market Committee, discussed next.

Federal Open Market Committee (FOMC)

The **Federal Open Market Committee (FOMC)** is made up of the seven members in the Board of Governors, plus presidents of five Fed district banks (the New York district bank plus four of the other eleven Fed district banks as determined on a rotating basis). Presidents of the seven remaining Fed district banks typically participate in the FOMC meetings but are not allowed to vote on policy decisions. The chairman of the Board of Governors serves as chairman of the FOMC.

The main goals of the FOMC are to promote high employment, economic growth, and price stability. Achievement of these goals would stabilize financial markets, interest rates, foreign exchange values, and so on. Because the FOMC may not be able to achieve all of its main goals simultaneously, it may concentrate on resolving a particular economic problem.

The FOMC attempts to achieve its goals through control of the money supply. It meets about every six weeks to review economic conditions and determine appropriate monetary policy to improve economic conditions and/or prevent potential adverse conditions from erupting. Its decision will be forwarded to what is called the *Trading Desk* (or the *Open Market Desk*) at the New York Fed district bank. It is here that "open market operations," or the Fed's trading of government securities, is carried out. The specific manner by which this trading affects money supply is discussed later in this chapter.

Advisory Committees

The Federal Advisory Council consists of one member from each Federal Reserve district. Each district's member is elected each year by the board of directors of the respective district bank. The council meets in Washington, D.C., at least four times a year and makes recommendations to the Fed about economic and banking-related issues.

The Consumer Advisory Council is made up of 30 members, representing the financial institutions industry and its consumers. This committee normally meets with the board four times a year to discuss consumer-related issues.

The Thrift Institutions Advisory Council is made up of representatives of savings banks, savings and loan associations, and credit unions. Its purpose is to offer views on issues specifically related to these types of institutions.

Summary of Recent FOMC Meetings

The short-run money growth rates specified by the FOMC are shown in the exhibit below for various periods. For each FOMC meeting, any dissension by the FOMC members regarding the specified growth ranges is summarized in the footnotes.

The exhibit illustrates how (1) target ranges are sometimes adjusted at FOMC meetings and (2) FOMC members often disagree about the appropriate degree of money supply growth.

EXHIBIT   FOMC Short-Run Operating Specifications

Meeting Date	Target Period	Expected Growth Rates			Intermeeting Federal Funds Range	Degree of Reserve Pressure
		M1	M2	M3		
December 16–17, 1985[1]	November 1985— March 1986	7–9%	about 6–8%	about 6–8%	6–10%	decrease somewhat
February 11–12, 1986[2]	November 1985— March 1986	about 7	about 6	about 7	6–10	unchanged
April 1, 1986	March 1986— June 1986	about 7–8	about 7	about 7	6–10	unchanged
May 20, 1986[3]	March 1986— June 1986	about 12–14	about 8–10	about 8–10	5–9	unchanged
July 8–9, 1986[4]	June 1986— September 1986	not specified[5]	about 7–9	about 7–9	4–8	decrease somewhat

1 Mr. Black dissented because he felt that a decrease in the degree of reserve pressure was undesirable, given the rapid growth of M1.

2 Mr. Martin and Ms. Seger dissented because they believed that the risks to the economic expansion would be lessened by reductions in short-term interest rates, including an eventual reduction in the discount rate. They favored some easing of reserve conditions in order to facilitate these reductions.

3 Mr. Wallich dissented because he was concerned about the inflationary implications of rapid monetary expansion and felt that open-market operations should be directed toward somewhat greater restraint.

4 Mr. Melzer dissented because he felt that easing under current circumstances could have an adverse impact on inflationary expectations and lead to an undesirably sharp depreciation in the value of the dollar on foreign exchange markets. He also

Integration of Federal Reserve Components

Exhibit 12.2 shows the relationships between the various components of the Federal Reserve System. The advisory committee advises the board, while the board oversees operations of the district banks. The board and representatives of the district banks make up the FOMC.

EXHIBIT Continued

Meeting Date	Target Period	Expected Growth Rates			Intermeeting Federal Funds Range	Degree of Reserve Pressure
		M1	M2	M3		
August 19, 1986[6]	June 1986— September 1986	not specified	about 7–9	about 7–9	4–8	decrease slightly
September 23, 1986[7]	August 1986— December 1986	not specified	7–9	7–9	4–8	unchanged
November 5, 1986	September 1986— December 1986	not specified	7–9	7–9	4–8	unchanged
December 15–16, 1986	November 1986— March 1987	not specified	about 7	about 7	4–8	unchanged

noted that the outlook for the quarters ahead appeared to be consistent with the economy's long-run growth potential, and that further ease, in his view, would generate inflationary pressures without encouraging much faster growth in real output. He therefore favored maintaining the existing degree of reserve pressure.

5 The directive stated that "While growth in M1 is expected to moderate . . . that growth will continue to be judged in the light of the behavior of M2 and M3 and other factors." See Record (October 1986), p. 711, and subsequent Records referenced in the footnotes to the text.

6 Mr. Melzer dissented because he was concerned that further ease might heighten inflationary expectations and put excessive downward pressure on the foreign exchange value of the dollar. He also felt that the prospects for economic growth had improved during the intermeeting period. Mr. Wallich dissented because he felt that policy should be directed toward slowing the growth of the monetary aggregates and reducing the potential for inflation. Mr. Wallich and Mr. Melzer preferred to maintain the existing degree of pressure on reserve positions.

7 Mr. Wallich dissented because he believed that a slight tightening of reserve conditions was desirable in light of the persistence of rapid monetary growth and the threat that it presented to continued price stability.

SOURCE: *Review*, Federal Reserve Bank of St. Louis (February 1987): 23.

MONETARY POLICY TOOLS

The Fed can use three monetary policy tools to either increase or decrease the money supply:

- Open market operations
- Adjusting the discount rate
- Adjusting the reserve requirement ratio

Each of these tools is described in turn.

EXHIBIT 12.2   Integration of Federal Reserve Components

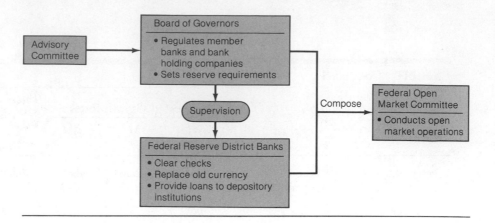

Open Market Operations

The FOMC's target money supply level is forwarded to the trading desk through a statement called the *policy directive*. The FOMC objectives are specified in the form of a target range—such as an annualized growth rate of 3 to 5 percent in the money supply over the next few months—rather than one specific money supply level. The FOMC may also specify a desired target range for the federal funds rate, even though this rate is not set by the Fed. The manager of the Trading Desk uses the policy directive as a guideline to instruct traders on the amount of government securities to buy or sell. These open market operations are the Fed's usual way of controlling the money supply.

FED PURCHASE OF SECURITIES. When traders at the Trading Desk are instructed to purchase a specified amount of securities, they call government securities dealers. The dealers provide a list of securities for sale that gives the denomination and maturity of each, as well as the *ask price* quoted by the dealer (the price at which the dealer is willing to sell the security). From this list, the traders attempt to purchase those that are most attractive (lowest prices for whatever maturities are desired) until they have purchased the amount requested by the manager of the Trading Desk. The accounting department of the New York district bank then notifies the government bond department to receive and pay for those securities.

When the Fed purchases securities through the government securities dealers, the commercial banks that handle securities transactions for the dealers will be credited this amount on their reserve accounts maintained at the Fed. Consequently, total reserves of commercial banks will increase by the dollar amount of security purchases by the Fed. Exhibit 12.3 shows this adjustment for a deal in which the Trading Desk paid $1 billion on securities. The increase of $1 billion in reserves represents demand deposits of $1 billion for government securities dealers.

The Fed's purchase of government securities has a different impact than another institution's purchase, since it results in additional bank reserves,

EXHIBIT 12.3   Impact of a Fed Purchase of Government Securities

Federal Reserve Bank of New York

Assets	Liabilities
+ $1 billion in Treasury securities	+ $1 billion in reserve accounts of the security dealers' clearing bank

The Dealers' Clearing Banks

Assets	Liabilities
+ $1 billion in reserve accounts at the Fed	+ $1 billion in demand deposits of dealers

and increases the ability of banks to make loans and create new deposits. An increase in reserves can allow for a net increase in deposit balances and therefore an increase in money supply. Conversely, the purchase of government securities by someone other than the Fed results in offsetting reserve positions at commercial banks.

FED SALE OF SECURITIES.   If the Trading Desk is instructed to decrease the money supply, its traders can sell government securities (obtained from previous purchases) to government securities dealers. The securities would be sold to the dealers that submitted the highest bids. As the dealers pay for the securities, the reserve balances that their clearing banks maintain at the Fed would be reduced.

The balance sheet effects of this event are shown in Exhibit 12.4, assuming that the total sale amounted to $1 billion. As the clearing banks of the dealers pay for the government securities, their level of reserves is reduced. In addition, the demand deposit accounts of government securities dealers are reduced.

FED USE OF REPURCHASE AGREEMENTS.   If the Fed desires to just temporarily increase the aggregate level of bank reserves, the Trading Desk may use *repurchase agreements*. It would purchase Treasury securities from government securities dealers with an agreement to sell back the securities at a specified date in the near future. Initially, the reserve level would rise as

EXHIBIT 12.4   Impact of a Fed Sale of Government Securities

Federal Reserve Bank of New York

Assets	Liabilities
− $1 billion in Treasury securities	− $1 billion in reserve accounts of the security dealers' clearing bank

The Dealers' Clearing Banks

Assets	Liabilities
− $1 billion in reserve accounts at the Fed	− $1 billion in demand deposits of dealers

Chapter 12

The Fed and Monetary Policy

Excerpts of FOMC Policy Directives

Excerpts of recent policy directives (shown below) reveal a general vagueness. This vagueness allows the manager of the Trading Desk flexibility in adjusting the money supply in accordance with economic business cycles. While target levels of money supply were reported, the notes for each meeting (see last column) suggest that the Fed may revise its tentative targets if economic conditions differ from what is anticipated.

Every six weeks or so, the manager at the Trading Desk may receive a new policy directive from the FOMC. If the money supply targets in new policy directive differ from those in the previous directive, the manager will need to adjust instructions to the traders. New targets may be necessary if the FOMC foresees a significant change in economic conditions.

Date of Meeting	Period for Which Money Growth is Specified	Annualized Money Growth Specifications for M_2	Notes
8/18/87	June to September	5%	The Committee sought to maintain the existing degree of pressure on reserve positions. Somewhat greater reserve restraint would, or slightly lesser reserve restraint might, be acceptable depending on indications of inflationary pressures, the strength of the business expansion, developments in foreign exchange markets, as well as the behavior of the aggregates.
9/22/87	August to December	4%	The Committee sought to maintain the slightly firmer degree of pressure on reserve positions that had been sought in recent weeks. Somewhat greater/lesser reserve restraint would be acceptable depending on the indications of inflationary pressures, the strength of the business expansion, developments in foreign exchange markets, as well as the behavior of the aggregates.
11/3/87	September to December	6% to 7%	The Committee sought to maintain the degree of pressure on reserve positions that had been sought in recent days. The Committee recognized that the volatile conditions in

the securities were sold; then it would be reduced when the dealers repurchased the securities. Repurchase agreements are used by the Trading Desk during holidays and other such periods to correct temporary imbalances in

Date of Meeting	Period for Which Money Growth is Specified	Annualized Money Growth Specifications for M₂	Notes
			financial markets and uncertainties in the economic outlook might continue to call for a special degree of flexibility in open market operations, depending, in particular, on demands for liquidity growing out of recent or prospective developments in financial markets. Apart from such considerations, somewhat lesser reserve restraint would, or slightly greater reserve restraint might, be acceptable depending on the strength of business expansion, indications of inflationary pressures, developments in foreign exchange markets, as well as the behavior of the monetary aggregates.
12/15/87	November to March	5%	The Committee sought to maintain the existing degree of pressure on reserve positions and to phase open market operations into a more normal approach to policy implementation keyed increasingly to a desired degree of reserve pressure while giving less emphasis than recently to money market conditions. The Committee recognized that still sensitive conditions in financial markets and uncertainties in the economic outlook may continue to call for a special degree of flexibility in open market operations. Taking account of conditions in financial markets, somewhat lesser or somewhat greater reserve restraint would be acceptable depending on the strength of the business expansion, indications of inflationary pressures, developments in foreign exchange markets, as well as the behavior of the monetary aggregates.

SOURCE: The exhibit above was adapted from *FRBNY Quarterly Review*, Spring 1988, p. 52.

the level of bank reserves. To correct a temporary excess of reserves, it sells some of its Treasury security holdings to securities dealers and agrees to repurchase them at a specified future date.

DYNAMIC VERSUS DEFENSIVE OPEN MARKET OPERATIONS. The intent of open market operations can be classified as either *dynamic* or *defensive*. Dynamic operations are implemented to increase or decrease the level of reserves; defensive operations offset the impact of other conditions that affect the level of reserves. For example, if the Fed expects a large inflow of cash into commercial banks, it could offset this inflow by selling some of its Treasury security holdings.

Adjusting the Discount Rate

The **discount window** of the Fed offers depository institutions three types of credit. *Adjustment credit* is offered for short-term liquidity problems, *seasonal credit* for a seasonal liquidity squeeze, and *extended credit* for severe liquidity problems that will not be resolved in the near future. Any type of credit extended by the Fed represents an increase in reserves at depository institutions, as shown in Exhibit 12.5. If, on the other hand, depository institutions borrow from each other, there is simply a transfer of funds among institutions, and the total level of reserves is not increased.

To increase money supply, the Fed (specifically the Board of Governors) could authorize a reduction in the discount rate. This would encourage depository institutions that are short on funds to borrow from the Fed rather than from other sources such as the federal funds market. To decrease money supply, it could attempt to discourage use of the discount window by increasing the discount rate. Depository institutions in need of short-term funds would likely obtain funding from alternative sources. As existing discount window loans were repaid to the Fed while new loans were obtained from sources other than the discount window, there would be a decrease in the level of reserves.

Adjusting the Reserve Requirement Ratio

A third method of controlling the money supply is for the Board of Governors to adjust the *reserve requirement ratio*. Depository institutions are then able to lend out a greater percentage of their deposits. As the funds loaned out are spent, a portion of them will return to the depository institutions in the form of deposits. The lower the reserve requirement ratio, the greater is the lending capacity of depository institutions, so any initial increase in money

---

EXHIBIT 12.5 Effect of Increased Use of Discount Window

Federal Reserve Bank

Assets	Liabilities
Increase in loans provided	Increase in the reserve accounts at depository institutions

Depository Institutions

Assets	Liabilities
Increase in reserves maintained at the Fed	Increase in loan payables due

Reaction of the Fed to the Stock Market Crash in 1987

On October 19, 1987, the Dow Jones Industrial Index declined by more than 500 points, the largest decline in history. The Federal Reserve System took action to prevent further adverse effects. On the morning after the crash, the Fed issued a statement that it was prepared to provide liquidity to the financial markets. It became actively involved in open market operations to assure adequate liquidity. Because it was concerned that economic growth would be adversely affected by the crash, the Fed loosened money supply.

The Fed also monitored bank deposit balances to assure that the crash did not cause runs on bank deposits. It monitored credit relationships between commercial banks and securities firms, since such relationships can change abruptly during a financial crisis. In general, the financial fears that caused the crash did not escalate, and financial markets stabilized shortly after the crash. The calming of the markets may have been partially because of the Fed's efforts to assure adequate liquidity and restore confidence in the financial system.

supply can multiply by a greater degree. An example is provided in the appendix.

Comparison of Monetary Policy Tools

Exhibit 12.6 compares the ways that monetary policy tools increase or decrease money supply growth. The Fed does not need to simultaneously use all three tools. In fact, it typically chooses to use open market operations, although it does have the option of using the other tools if necessary.

The frequent use of open market operations as a monetary policy tool is due mainly to its convenience and the disadvantages of using the alternative tools. An adjustment in the discount rate will only affect the money supply if depository institutions respond (borrow more or less from the Fed than normal) due to the adjustment. In addition, borrowings through the discount window are for a very short term, so that any adjustment in reserves resulting from an increase or decrease in loans from the Fed is only temporary. An adjustment in the reserve requirement ratio can cause erratic shifts in money supply. Thus, there is a higher probability of missing the target money supply level when using the reserve requirement ratio.

Open market operations do not suffer from these limitations. In addition, open market operations can be used without signaling the Fed's intentions and can easily be reversed without the public knowing. A reverse adjustment in the reserve requirement ratio or the discount rate, however, could cause more concern by the public and reduce the Fed's credibility.

Because the rate by which injected funds will multiply is uncertain (even when leaving the reserve requirement ratio unchanged), open market operations are not guaranteed to accomplish the money growth target. Even so, they can be continuously used over time to manipulate the money supply toward the desired money supply target.

Chapter 12

The Fed and Monetary Policy

335

EXHIBIT 12.6   Comparison of Monetary Policy Tools

Monetary Policy Tool	To Increase Money Supply Growth	To Decrease Money Supply Growth
Open market operations	Fed should (through the Trading Desk) purchase government securities in the secondary market.	Fed should (through the Trading Desk) sell government securities in the secondary market.
Adjusting the discount rate	Fed should lower the discount rate to encourage borrowing through the discount window.	Fed should raise the discount rate to discourage borrowing through the discount window.
Adjusting reserve requirements	Fed should lower the reserve requirement ratio to cause money to multiply at a higher rate.	Fed should raise the reserve requirement ratio to cause money to multiply at a lower rate.

IMPACT OF TECHNICAL FACTORS ON RESERVES

Even if the Fed did not intervene, the volume of reserves can change as a result of so-called *technical factors*, such as currency in circulation and Federal Reserve float. When the amount of *currency in circulation* increases (such as during the holiday season), the corresponding increase in net deposit withdrawals reduces reserves. When it decreases, the net addition to deposits increases reserves. *Federal Reserve float* is the amount of checks credited to banks' reserves that have not yet been collected. A rise in float causes an increase in bank reserves, and a decrease in float causes a reduction in bank reserves.

A staff at the Federal Reserve Bank of New York along with a staff at the Board of Governors in Washington, D.C., provide daily forecasts of how technical factors such as these will affect the level of reserves. Because these factors affect the reserve level, the Fed must account for such influences when implementing monetary policy. The manager of the Trading Desk incorporates the expected impact of technical factors on reserves into the instructions to traders. If the policy directive calls for growth in reserves, but technical factors are expected to increase reserves, the instructions would reflect a smaller injection of reserves than if the technical factors were ignored. Conversely, if technical factors are expected to reduce reserves, the instructions would reflect a larger injection of reserves to offset the impact of technical factors.

FED CONTROL OF MONEY SUPPLY

When the Fed manipulates money supply to influence economic variables, it must decide what form of money to manipulate. The optimal form of money should (1) be controllable by the Fed, and (2) have a predictable impact on economic variables when adjusted by the Fed. The most narrow form of money, known as **M₁**, includes currency held by the public and checkable deposits (such as demand deposits, NOW accounts, and automatic transfer balances) at depository institutions. While M_1 has received the most attention in recent years, it does not include all funds that can be used for transactions purposes. For example, checks can be written against a **money market deposit account (MMDA)** offered by depository institutions or against a money market mutual fund. In addition, funds can easily be withdrawn from savings accounts to make transactions. For this reason, a broader measure of money, called **M₂**, also deserves consideration. It includes everything in M_1, as well as savings accounts and small time deposits, MMDAs, money market funds, and some other items. While there are even a few other broader measures of money (such as M_3), M_1 and M_2 receive the most attention. A comparison of M_1, M_2, and M_3 is provided in Exhibit 12.7.

During the deregulation phase (early 1980s) in the depository institutions industry, various new deposit accounts were created, and consumers were switching among accounts. The transfer of funds from *demand deposit accounts* to MMDAs caused a reduction in M_1, even without the Fed taking any action to reduce it. A transfer of funds from savings into NOW accounts, for example, would cause an increase in M_1 due simply to a change in consumer habits rather than monetary policy actions. The M_1 measure became quite volatile over this period and was difficult for the Fed to control. The broader M_2 measure was not as sensitive to the consumer's change of habits, since most deposit accounts are included under M_2. Even though individual components of M_2 (such as MMDAs, NOW accounts, etc.) were affected by deregulation, the overall level of M_2 was not.

Fed Emphasis on Money Supply Rather Than Interest Rates

In the 1970s the Fed attempted to simultaneously control the money supply and interest rates within specified target ranges. It used the **federal funds rate** as its representative interest rate to control, which in turn can influence other interest rates. Simultaneous control of the money supply and federal

---

EXHIBIT 12.7   Comparison of Money Supply Measures

Money Supply Measure		Dollar Level (in billions) as of March 1988
M₁		$ 763.1
	+ savings deposits, MMDAs, overnight repurchase agreements, Eurodollars, noninstitutional money market mutual funds, and small time deposits	$2204.5
	= M₂	2967.6
M₂		
	+ institutional money market mutual funds, large time deposits, and repurchase agreements and Eurodollars lasting more than one day	773.7
	= M₃	3741.3

funds rate is not always possible. Consider Exhibit 12.8, which shows hypothetical target ranges for the money supply growth and federal funds rate. Notice that both variables are near the upper boundary of their respective ranges. If the Fed desires to maintain the federal funds rate within its range, it would likely inject more funds into the economy (increase money supply growth). Yet, this will force the money supply growth above its upper boundary. If it instead maintains money supply growth within its range, it may be unable to prevent the federal funds rate from rising above its upper boundary.

The Fed recognized that it could not simultaneously control both variables and as of October 1979 chose to focus primarily on money supply. Though it continued to monitor the federal funds rate, it did not feel compelled to maintain it within a narrow range. Exhibit 12.9 shows how the federal funds rate range was widened as of October 1979. The increased emphasis on the money supply was intended to achieve a more stable economy over the long run.

MONEY SUPPLY TARGET SHOOTING

To illustrate the Fed's ability to control the money supply, Exhibit 12.10 shows target growth boundaries for M_1. While the Fed did not always maintain M_1 within the boundaries, this does not necessarily mean that the money supply was uncontrollable. Rather, the Fed may have been willing to let the money supply wander outside the previously established target range, since any adjustment might have had an adverse impact on economic variables.

Because M_2 is also considered by the Fed to have an important impact on the economy, it is assigned target ranges as well, as shown in Exhibit

EXHIBIT 12.8 Dilemma of Controlling Money Supply and Interest Rates Simultaneously

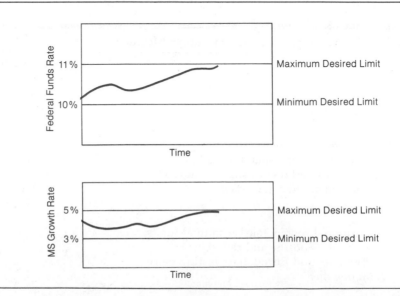

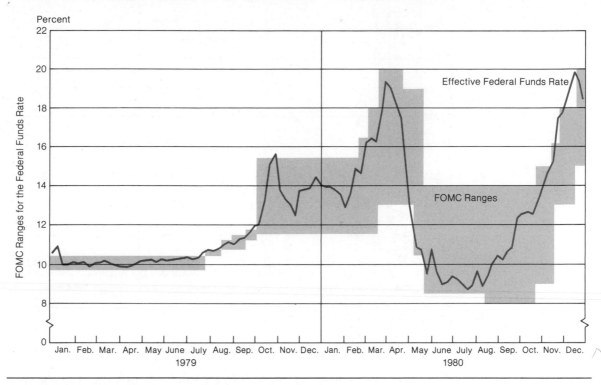

SOURCE: *Review*, Federal Reserve Bank of St. Louis (August–September 1981): 9.

12.11. Note that the Fed maintained M_2 within its bands to a greater degree than M_1. The Fed has both short-term and long-term target ranges for money supply. Even though it may overshoot or undershoot its short-term targets, its long-term targets have been hit with some success. Of course, this does not guarantee that the monetary growth will influence the economy as expected. Yet, it at least suggests that the Fed is capable of controlling long-term growth of money supply within ranges.

MONETARY CONTROL ACT OF 1980

In 1980 the Depository Institutions Deregulation and Monetary Control Act (DIDMCA) was passed. Commonly referred to as the *Monetary Control Act*, it had two key objectives. First, it was intended to deregulate some aspects of the depository institutions industry (discussed in the chapters on depository institutions). Second, it was intended to enhance the Fed's ability to control the money supply.

Before DIDMCA, member banks of the Federal Reserve were subject to its reserve requirements, while nonmember banks were subject to the reserve requirements of their respective states. Nonmember banks were often

Chapter 12

The Fed and Monetary Policy

EXHIBIT 12.10   Comparison of Recent M₁ Levels to Target Range

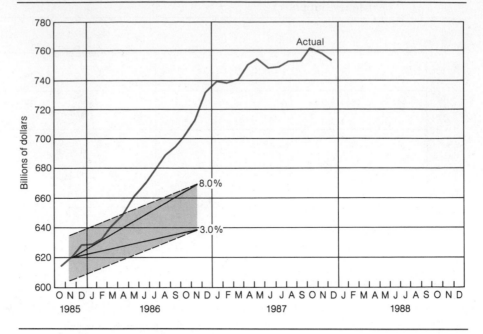

SOURCE: FRBNY Quarterly Review, Spring 1988, p. 43.

at an advantage in that they could typically maintain their required reserves in some interest-bearing form (such as in the form of Treasury securities). A member bank's required reserves could only be held as balances at the Fed or vault cash and therefore could not earn interest. This disadvantage to member banks became more pronounced in the 1970s, when interest rates were generally higher than in previous years. The opportunity cost of tying up funds in a noninterest-bearing form increased. As a result, some member banks dropped their membership.

As Fed memberships decreased, so did the Fed's ability to control the money supply through reserve requirement adjustments, since it could adjust reserve requirements only of *member* banks to manipulate money supply. The Monetary Control Act mandates that all depository institutions be subject to the same reserve requirements imposed by the Fed. The reserve requirements were reduced relative to what the Fed previously required; yet, all required reserves were still to be held in a noninterest-bearing form. The revised reserve requirements were phased in over an eight-year period. Because the Fed normally controls money supply growth using open market operations rather than reserve requirement adjustments, there is some question as to whether this revision will actually improve the Fed's control of the money supply.

A related provision of the Monetary Control Act is that all depository institutions must report their deposit levels promptly to the Fed. This improves the Fed's knowledge of the current level of deposits in the banking system at any point in time. In the past, the Fed may have underestimated the prevailing money supply at times and thus increased the money supply

EXHIBIT 12.11   Comparison of M₂ Levels to Target Range

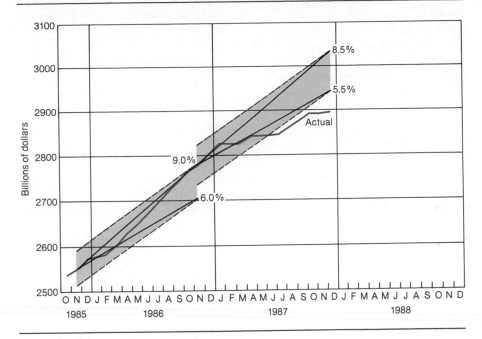

SOURCE: FRBNY Quarterly Review, Spring 1988, p. 43.

above the level desired. With the improved reporting system, it should have a better feel for the prevailing money supply level and therefore make better adjustments.

In addition to reserve requirement and reporting laws, the Monetary Control Act allows all depository institutions that offer transaction accounts (such as demand deposits or NOW accounts) access to the discount window. Previously, only member banks were allowed access. This provision might give the Fed additional control over the money supply, since more institutions will have access to the discount window. However, the Fed does not frequently use the discount-window technique to control money supply.

SUMMARY

The key components of the Federal Reserve are district banks, member banks, the Board of Governors, and the FOMC. While the Fed participates in the regulation and supervision of commercial banks, it is also responsible for controlling the money supply. The Fed can adjust money supply growth by using open market operations, adjusting the discount rate, or adjusting the reserve requirement ratio. Since it can manipulate the money supply, and money supply adjustments can significantly affect the economy, the Fed has substantial influence over the economy. The manner by which money supply adjustments affect the economy is discussed in the following chapter.

Chapter 12

The Fed and Monetary Policy

KEY TERMS

Board of Governors
discount rate
discount window
federal funds rate
Federal Open Market Committee
(FOMC)

Federal Reserve district banks
M₁
M₂
money market deposit account

QUESTIONS

12.1. Briefly describe the origination of the Federal Reserve System.

12.2. Describe the functions of the Fed district banks.

12.3. What are the main goals of the Federal Open Market Committee? How does it attempt to achieve these goals?

12.4. Explain how the Fed increases the money supply through open market operations.

12.5. What is the policy directive, and who carries it out?

12.6. How is the money supply adjusted through the discount window?

12.7. How is money supply growth affected by an increase in the reserve requirement ratio?

12.8. What are the disadvantages of using the discount window or reserve requirement ratio to adjust the money supply?

12.9. Describe the characteristics that would be desirable for a measure of money to be manipulated by the Fed.

12.10. Explain the dilemma of attempting to simultaneously control money supply and the federal funds rate.

12.11. What are the two key objectives of the Monetary Control Act?

12.12. Have the reserve requirement revisions of the Monetary Control Act improved the Fed's ability to manipulate the money supply? Explain.

12.13. How does the Monetary Control Act help the Fed avoid improper adjustments of the money supply?

PROJECT

1. ASSESSING REVISIONS IN FOMC MONEY SUPPLY TARGETS

Review recent articles in the *Federal Reserve Bulletin* or the *FRBNY Quarterly Review* to determine whether money supply targets have been recently revised by the FOMC. What explanation is given for revisions?

REFERENCES

Batten, Dallas S., and Daniel L. Thornton. "M₁ and M₂: Which Is the Better Monetary Target?" *Review*, Federal Reserve Bank of St. Louis (June–July 1983): 36–42.

Keeley, Michael C., and Gary Zimmerman. "Deposit Rate Deregulation and the Demand for Transactions Media." *Economic Review* (Summer 1986): 47–62.

McNees, Stephen K. "Modeling the Fed: A Forward-Looking Monetary Policy Reaction Function." *New England Economic Review*, Federal Reserve Bank of Boston (November–December 1986): 3–8.

Miller, Richard B. "Henry Reuss Talks about the Fed and Other Problems." *The Bankers Magazine* (May–June 1983): 43–47.

Roth, Howard L. "Federal Reserve Open Market Techniques." *Economic Review*, Federal Reserve Bank of Kansas City (March 1986): 3–15.

Sellon, Gordon H. "The Instruments of Monetary Policy." *Economic Review*, Federal Reserve Bank of Kansas City (May 1984): 3–20.

Taylor, Herb. "The Discount Window and Money Control." *Business Review*, Federal Reserve Bank of Philadelphia (May–June 1983): 3–12.

Thornton, Daniel L. "The Discount Rate and Market Interest Rates: What's the Connection?" *Review*, Federal Reserve Bank of St. Louis (June–July 1982): 3–14.

Thornton, Daniel L. "The Discount Rate and Market Interest Rates: Theory and Evidence." Federal Reserve Bank of St. Louis (August–September 1986): 5–21.

Wallich, Henry C. "Recent Techniques of Monetary Policy." *Economic Review*, Federal Reserve Bank of Kansas City (May 1984): 21–30.

Use of the Reserve Requirement Ratio for Monetary Policy

EXAMPLE OF ADJUSTING THE RESERVE REQUIREMENT RATIO

To explain how adjustments in the reserve requirement ratio can affect money supply growth, a simplified example follows. Assume the following information:

Assumption 1. Banks obtain all their funds from demand deposits and use all funds except required reserves to make loans.

Assumption 2. The public does not store any cash; any funds withdrawn from banks are spent, and any funds received are deposited in banks.

Assumption 3. The reserve requirement ratio on demand deposits is 10 percent.

Based on these assumptions, 10 percent of all bank deposits are maintained as required reserves, and the other 90 percent are loaned out (zero excess reserves). Now assume that the Fed initially uses open market operations by purchasing $100 million worth of government securities.

As the government securities dealers sell securities to the Fed, their deposit balances at commercial banks increase by $100 million. Banks maintain 10 percent of the $100 million, or $10 million, as required reserves, and lend out the rest. As the $90 million lent out is spent, it returns to banks as new demand deposit accounts (by whoever receives the funds that were spent). Banks maintain 10 percent, or $9 million, of these new deposits as required reserves and lend out the remainder ($81 million). Because of this cycle, the initial increase in demand deposits (money) multiplies into a much larger amount. Exhibit 12A.1 summarizes this cycle. This cycle will not continue forever. Every time the funds lent out return to a bank, a portion (10 percent) is retained as required reserves. Thus, the amount of new deposits created is less for each round. Under the previous assumptions, the initial money supply injection of $100 million would multiply by 1/

EXHIBIT 12A.1   Illustration of Multiplier Effect

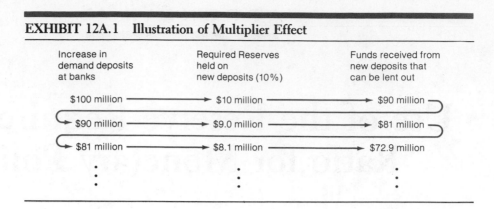

Increase in demand deposits at banks	Required Reserves held on new deposits (10%)	Funds received from new deposits that can be lent out
$100 million	$10 million	$90 million
$90 million	$9.0 million	$81 million
$81 million	$8.1 million	$72.9 million

reserve requirement ratio, or 1/.10, to equal 10, so that the total change in money supply once the cycle is complete is $100 million × 10 = $1 billion.

The simplified example demonstrates that an initial injection of funds will multiply into a larger amount. The reserve requirement controls the amount of loanable funds that can be created from new deposits. If the reserve requirement was 20 percent instead of 10 percent, new deposits created for each round would be less than in the original example. So a higher reserve requirement ratio causes an initial injection of funds to multiply by a smaller amount. Conversely, a lower reserve requirement ratio causes it to multiply by a greater amount. In this way, the Fed adjusts money supply growth by adjusting the reserve requirement ratio.

Our example exaggerates the amount by which money multiplies. Consumers sometimes hold cash, and banks sometimes hold excess reserves, contradicting the assumptions of banks holding only demand deposits and zero excess reserves. Consequently, leakages occur, and money does not multiply to the extent shown in the example. Exhibit 12A.2 displays the trend of the money multiplier over a recent period. The money multiplier can change over time because of changes in the excess reserve level and in consumer preferences of demand deposits versus time deposits (which are not included in the M_1 definition of money). This complicates the task of forecasting how an initial adjustment in bank reserves will ultimately affect the money supply level.

CONTEMPORANEOUS RESERVE REQUIREMENTS

In February 1984 *contemporaneous reserve requirements (CRR)* replaced *lagged reserve requirements (LRR)* in order to strengthen the relationship between reserves of depository institutions and the money supply. Under the CRR system, reserve requirements are determined according to the deposits held over 14-day periods (called the *computation period*) that end every other Monday. Depository institutions must maintain a daily average of required reserves (based on this 14-day period) over a 14-day maintenance period that ends every other Wednesday. The reserve requirements on transaction deposits are based on the 14-day period ending two days prior to the end of that maintenance period. Reserve requirements on specified time deposits

EXHIBIT 12A.2   Measurement of the Actual Money Multiplier Over Time

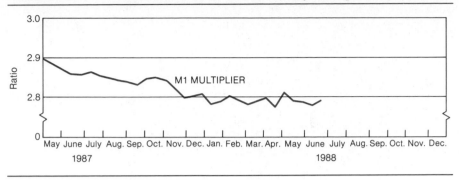

SOURCE: *U.S. Data*, Federal Reserve Bank of St. Louis, July 14, 1988, p. 4.

and Eurocurrency deposits are based on average deposits for the 14-day period ending 17 days before the beginning of its maintenance period. Vault cash is counted as reserves over this same 14-day period, ending 17 days before the beginning of its maintenance period.

The difference between the CRR and LRR is illustrated in Exhibit 12A.3. The maintenance period of the LRR began 8 days after the computation period. Conversely, the computation and maintenance periods of the CRR overlap to a great degree. If the Fed adjusts the reserve requirements ratio under the LRR system, the impact on reserves will not occur immediately, because the maintenance period lags the computation period. Under the CRR system, the reserves would be affected instantaneously by an adjustment in the reserve requirement ratio.

EXHIBIT 12A.3   Comparison of Lagged and Contemporaneous Reserve
                Requirement Systems

The Timing of Lagged and Contemporaneous Reserve Accounting

Lagged Reserve Requirements, 1968–1984

Contemporaneous Reserve Requirements since February 1984

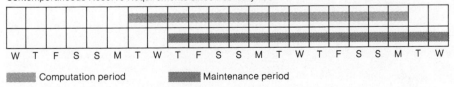

▨ Computation period   ▨ Maintenance period

SOURCE: *Economic Commentary*, Federal Reserve Bank of Cleveland, May 15, 1985.

Financial Market Reaction to Monetary Policy

MONETARY POLICY EFFECTS IN PERSPECTIVE

Some critics blamed the stock market crash of October 1987 on the uncertainty about the Fed's future policy by financial market participants. This is a dramatic example of how important the Fed's policy can be to financial market participants.

Subsequent to the crash, the Administration was increasingly concerned about a possible recession. The Administration reacted by attempting to influence the Federal Reserve. In February 1988, Assistant Treasury Secretary Michael Darby sent a letter to members of the Fed, prior to the Fed's February meeting to determine monetary policy. Mr. Darby's letter criticized the Fed for using too tight a monetary policy which would dampen economic growth. Alan Greenspan, chairman of the Fed, responded by suggesting that the Fed would resist pressure by the Administration and would make its own policy decisions. He also mentioned his concern about how financial markets would react to continued confrontations between the Fed and the Administration.

On July 20, 1988, Alan Greenspan suggested that the economic statistics in re-

cent weeks have not revised the plans of the Fed. This was favorable news to financial market participants who previously thought the Fed would decide to tighten credit. Stock prices rose in response to Greenspan's statements. The Dow Jones Industrial Average increased by 28.63 points, the largest daily increase in the last month. Such an abrupt market reaction to statements by Federal Reserve officials is quite common.

■ Does the Fed use a monetary policy that is typically too tight?
■ What are the potential dangers of a looser monetary policy?
■ How do financial markets react to monetary policies perceived as too tight or too loose?
■ What types of financial institutions closely monitor the Fed's policies?
■ What financial markets appear to be most sensitive to the Fed's policies?

These and other related questions on effects and reaction to monetary policy are addressed.

OUTLINE

The previous chapter discussed the Fed and how it controls money supply, information essential to financial market participants. It is just as important for them to know how changes in money supply affect the economy, which is the subject of this chapter. First, the economic impact of monetary policy is discussed, with a focus on a trade-off frequently faced by the Fed when implementing monetary policy. Then, financial market assessment and reaction to monetary policy are discussed.

RELATIONSHIPS BETWEEN MONEY SUPPLY AND THE ECONOMY

Exhibit 13.1 shows the lagged positive relationship between money supply growth (using M_1 as a proxy) and real (inflation-adjusted) GNP. Exhibit 13.2 shows the level of relative money growth prior to recessions (the shaded areas) over time. The top graph in Exhibit 13.2 uses M_1 as a measure of money while the lower graph uses M_2. Notice that each recession is preceded by a relatively low level of growth in M_1 and M_2.

Exhibits 13.1 and 13.2 give the impression that a *loose-money* (high-growth) policy is appropriate to strengthen an economy and reduce the possibility of a recession. However, as illustrated in Exhibit 13.3, high money supply growth usually precedes high inflation. During the oil crisis of 1973–1974, inflation responded more to high money growth than in other years. Some level of inflation would have existed even without the high money growth.

In the early 1980s, a high money growth policy was implemented without any inflationary consequences, perhaps because of the reduction in oil prices. Also, the U.S. dollar was highly valued during this period, so foreign goods could be purchased cheaply. This allowed U.S. producers that purchase foreign supplies to keep their cost (and therefore prices) low. It also forced U.S. firms that compete with foreign firms to maintain low prices.

Any factor that affects inflation can affect the relationship between money supply and inflation. Even though this relationship is not as strong as it

EXHIBIT 13.1 Historical Relationship between Money Supply Growth and GNP.

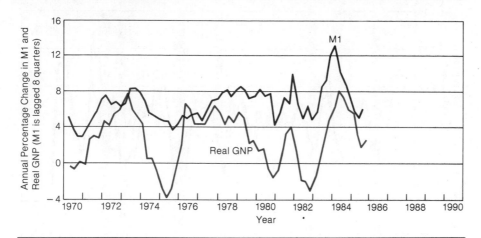

SOURCE: *Economic Review*, Federal Reserve Bank of Kansas City (December 1985): 20.

used to be , there is still concern that consistently excessive money supply growth will lead to higher inflation.

TRADE-OFF FACED BY THE FED

The Fed monitors over time, such as inflation, unemployment, and gross national product (GNP). While it does not have direct control over these variables, it can attempt to influence them by manipulating the money supply.

Ideally, the Fed would like to maintain low inflation, steady GNP growth, and low unemployment. Because GNP growth can lead to low unemployment, these two goals may be achieved simultaneously. Yet, it has often been suggested that low inflation and low unemployment cannot be consistently maintained. For over 200 years, economists have recognized a possible trade-off between the two. In 1958, in an article that became famous, Professor A. W. Phillips compared the annual percentage change in average unemployment rate and wages in the United Kingdom from 1861 to 1913. His research confirmed a negative relationship between the two variables. This relationship suggested that government policies designed to cure unemployment appear to place upward pressure on wages. In addition, government policies designed to cure inflation can cause more unemployment. This negative relationship came to be known as the **Phillips curve.** The concept provided a new framework for the central bank and the Administration to determine government policies.

Research on the U.S. inflation and unemployment data revealed that the relationship was frequently changing. Shifts in the Phillips curve were attributed to unionization, changing productivity, and, more recently, changing expectations about inflation.

EXHIBIT 13.2 Level of Real Money Supply Growth Prior to Recessions

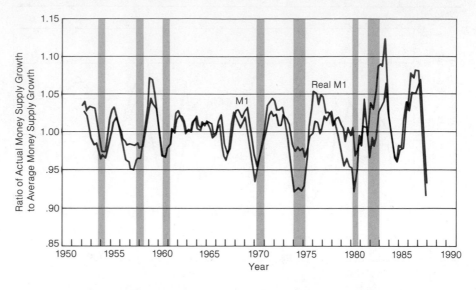

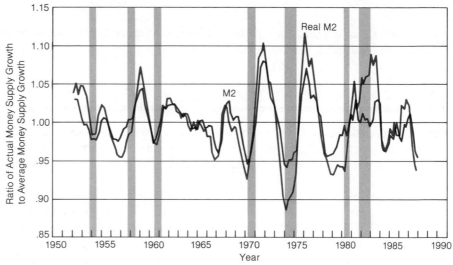

SOURCE: *Economic Review*, Federal Reserve Bank of Kansas City (January 1988): 7.

When inflation is higher than the Fed deems acceptable, it may consider implementing a *tight-money* policy in order to reduce economic growth. As economic growth slows, producers cannot as easily raise their prices and still maintain sales volume. Similarly, workers are not in demand and do not have much bargaining power on wages. Thus, the use of tight money to slow economic growth can reduce the inflation rate. A possible cost of the lower inflation rate is higher unemployment. If the economy becomes stagnant due to the tight-money policy, sales decrease, inventories accumulate, and firms may reduce their workforce to reduce production.

EXHIBIT 13.3 Relationship between Money Supply Growth and Inflation

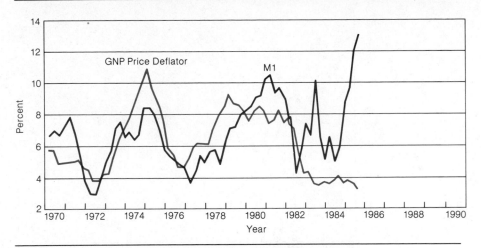

SOURCE: *Economic Review,* Federal Reserve Bank of Kansas City (December 1985): 19.
NOTE: The GNP price deflator was used as a measure of inflation. M_1 is lagged eight quarters.

Given that a loose-money policy can reduce unemployment, while a tight-money policy can reduce inflation, the Fed must determine whether unemployment or inflation is a more serious problem. It may not be able to cure both problems simultaneously. In fact, it may not be able to fully eliminate either problem. While a loose-money policy can stimulate the economy, it does not guarantee that unskilled workers will be hired. While a tight-money policy can reduce inflation caused by excessive spending, it cannot reduce inflation caused by factors such as an agreement among the oil cartel to keep oil prices high.

The Fed has sometimes been criticized for using "quick fix" policies that cause more volatile business cycles. In other words, it may remedy one problem but cause a new one. The 1982 recession was a case where it tried to avoid that mistake. Afraid that inflation would result from stimulating the economy with a loose-money policy, it was initially unwilling to allow excessive growth in the money supply.

To illustrate the trade-off involved, consider a situation where because of specific cost factors (higher energy and insurance costs, etc.) inflation will be at least 3 percent. This amount of inflation will exist no matter what type of monetary policy the Fed implements. Also assume that due to the number of unskilled workers and people between jobs, the unemployment rate will be at least 4 percent. A loose-money policy sufficiently stimulates the economy to maintain unemployment at that minimum level of 4 percent. However, such a stimulative policy may also cause additional inflation beyond the 3 percent level. Or a tight-money policy could maintain inflation at the 3 percent minimum, but unemployment would likely rise above the 4 percent minimum.

This trade-off is illustrated in Exhibit 13.4. Here the Fed can use a very stimulative (loose-money) policy that is expected to result in point A (9 percent inflation and 4 percent unemployment). Alternatively, it can use a very restrictive (tight-money) policy that is expected to result in point B (3

Chapter 13

Financial Market Reaction to Monetary Policy

EXHIBIT 13.4 Trade-off between Reducing Inflation versus Unemployment

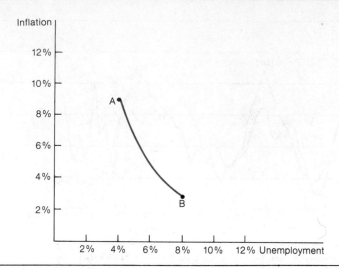

percent inflation and 8 percent unemployment). Or it can enact a more compromising policy that would result in some point along the curve extending from point A to point B.

Historical inflation and unemployment rates on a yearly basis show that when one of these problems worsens, the other does not automatically improve. Both variables can rise or fall over time. Yet, this does not refute the trade-off faced by the Fed. It simply means that some outside factors have affected inflation and/or unemployment. To illustrate, recall that the Fed could have achieved point A, point B, or somewhere along the curve connecting these points during a particular time period. Now assume that oil prices have substantially increased and several product-liability lawsuits have occurred. These events will affect consumer prices such that the minimum inflation rate would be, say, 6 percent. In addition, assume that various training centers for unskilled workers have been closed down, leaving a higher number of unskilled workers. This forces the minimum unemployment rate to 6 percent. Now the Fed's trade-off position has changed. Its new set of possibilities is shown as curve CD in Exhibit 13.5. Notice that the points reflected on curve CD are not as desirable as the points along curve AB that were previously attainable. No matter what type of monetary policy the Fed uses, both the inflation and unemployment rates will be higher than in the previous time period. Yet, this is not the fault of the Fed. In fact, the Fed 'is still faced with a trade-off among point C (11 percent inflation, 6 percent unemployment), point D (6 percent inflation, 10 percent unemployment), and somewhere within those points along curve CD.

To appreciate the complexity involved in determining the appropriate monetary policy, review Exhibit 13.6, which focuses on real GNP (inflation-adjusted GNP) as the ultimate measure of economic conditions. This variable implicitly incorporates inflation, unemployment, and economic growth. It is shown to be dependent on the factors (across the top of Exhibit 13.6)

EXHIBIT 13.5 Adjustment in the Trade-off between Unemployment and Inflation Over Time

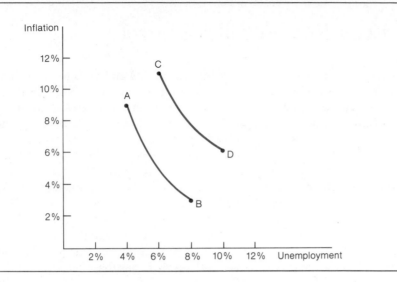

EXHIBIT 13.6 Economic Relationships to Consider When Determining Monetary Policy

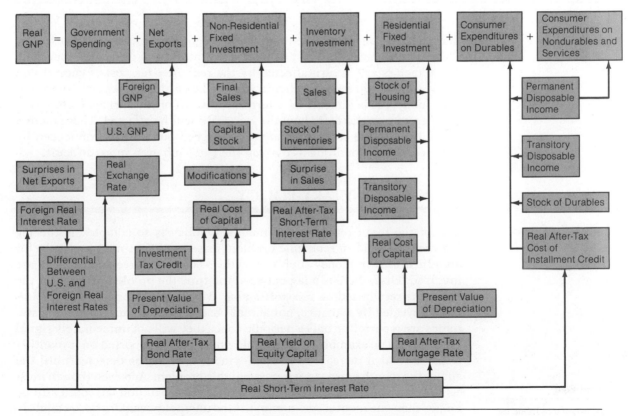

SOURCE: *Economic Review,* Federal Reserve Bank of San Francisco (Winter 1985): 29.

Fed's Role to Calm Markets

During the stock market crash in October 1987, the Fed injected funds into the banking system in order to provide more liquidity. The Fed was somewhat limited in its ability to use public announcements to calm the markets, because market participants had conflicting fears about the crash. Some feared potentially high inflation, while others feared potentially high unemployment. If the Fed had announced monetary policy adjustments, it might have reduced some participants' fears but ignited others.

On October 20, 1987, Alan Greenspan, chairman of the Fed, stated that the Fed was ready to provide liquidity to support the financial system. This statement appeared to temporarily calm the market.

While providing immediate liquidity, the Fed was confronted with a policy dilemma. Should it raise interest rates in an attempt to boost the value of the U.S. dollar, or should it reduce interest rates in order to stimulate the economy? Before the crash, the dollar was a higher priority. However, the crash raised concerns of a recession and forced the Fed to rethink its strategy. It decided to use a somewhat stimulative monetary policy and closely monitored economic conditions after the crash. Because economic growth continued for several months after the crash, the Fed did not need to drastically revise its monetary policy.

that influence aggregate demand, such as government spending, exports, business investment in machinery and inventory, and consumer spending. These factors are in turn affected by the real after-tax cost of capital and installment credit (among other factors). When proposing a particular monetary policy, it is difficult to determine how all of the various factors will be affected and therefore how the real GNP will be affected. These factors are not under the complete control of the Fed but are also influenced by other economic conditions—making the Fed's job even more difficult.

LAGS IN MONETARY POLICY

One of the main reasons why monetary policy is so complex is the lag between the time an economic problem arises and the time it will take for an adjustment in money supply growth to solve it. Three specific lags are involved. First, there is a lag between the time the problem arises and the time it is recognized—a **recognition lag.** Most economic problems are initially revealed by statistics, not actual observation. Because economic statistics are reported on only a periodic basis, they will not immediately signal a problem. For example, the unemployment rate is reported on a monthly basis. A sudden increase in unemployment may not be detected until the end of the month when statistics reveal this problem. And even though most economic variables are updated monthly, the recognition lag could still be longer than one month. For example, if the unemployment increases slightly each month for two straight months, the Fed may not necessarily act on this information, since it may not appear to be significant. Only after a few more months of steadily increasing unemployment might the Fed recognize that a serious problem exists. In this case, the recognition lag may be four months or longer.

The time from which a serious problem is recognized until the time the Fed implements a policy to resolve it is known as the **implementation lag.** Then, even after the Fed implements a policy, there will be an **impact lag** until it has its full impact on the economy. For example, an adjustment in money supply growth may have an immediate impact of some degree on the economy, but its full impact may not be manifested until a year or so after the adjustment.

These lags hinder the Fed's control of the economy. Suppose the Fed uses a loose-money policy to stimulate the economy and reduce unemployment. By the time the implemented monetary policy begins to take effect, the unemployment rate may have already reversed itself as a result of some other outside factor (such as a weakened dollar that increased foreign demand for U.S. goods and created U.S. jobs). Thus, a problem of more concern may now be inflation (since the economy is heating up again). And the loose-money policy implemented by the Fed may further ignite inflation. If not for monetary policy lags, implemented policies would have a higher rate of success.

ASSESSING THE IMPACT OF MONETARY POLICY

Financial market participants will not all necessarily react to monetary policy in the same manner because they trade different securities. The expected or actual impact of monetary policy on long-term mortgage rates may differ from corporate and municipal bond rates, money market rates, and stock prices. Exhibit 13.7 shows the various components of the financial environment that are affected by monetary policy. This exhibit implies that the most influential economic variable on the performance for many financial markets is interest rates, although other variables such as economic growth and inflation are also important.

Even financial market participants that trade the same securities may react differently to the monetary policy, since they may have different expectations about the impact of monetary policy on economic variables. They have only limited success in forecasting economic variables due to the difficulty in forecasting (1) money supply movements and (2) how future money supply movements will affect economic variables. Each of these forecasting aspects is discussed in turn.

Forecasting Money Supply Movements

Business periodicals will from time to time specify the weekly ranges of M_1 and M_2 based on the Fed's most recent disclosure of its target range. The Fed is less concerned about meeting its targets on a weekly basis than about meeting its long-term targets. Yet, some financial participants compare the actual money supply levels with weekly ranges that can be estimated from the Fed's longer-term target ranges. Weekly ranges represent the path that the Fed would follow over time if it moves toward its targets at a constant

EXHIBIT 13.7 Impact of Monetary Policy and Other Variables on Financial Markets and the Economy

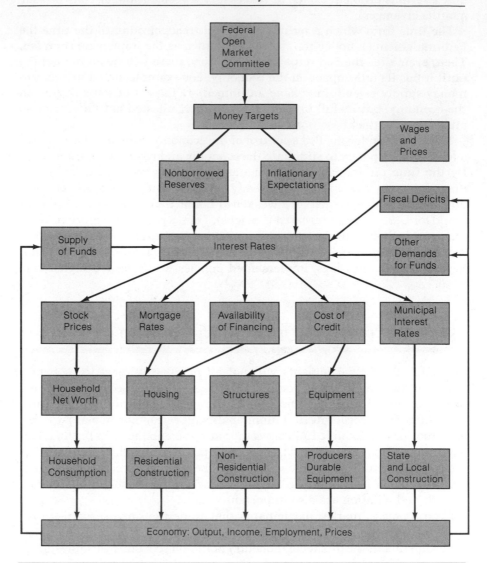

SOURCE: Paul Meek, *Open Market Operations*, Federal Reserve Bank of New York (August 1985): 24.

rate. For example, if the target growth range is specified as 4 percent to 6 percent annually, the money supply should grow at a weekly rate of between 4%/52 and 6%/52 (given 52 weeks per year). If the Fed consistently over-or undershoots these weekly ranges, it may desire to offset that at some point in the future.

When the actual money supply is not within the target range, it could be due to a change in the Fed's range that has not yet been publicly announced. The Fed may be meeting its new targets, while financial market participants believe it plans to adjust money to meet its previously announced range.

Normally, the Fed attempts to avoid revising target ranges, since if it changes them too often it may lose some credibility. Persistent changes might suggest that it is unsure of how money supply fluctuations affect the economy.

In some periods, the Fed is more willing than usual to let the money supply wander outside its target range. For example, during the initial stage of deregulated deposit accounts in 1982–1984, the Fed was less concerned than usual when the reported money supply was above its target range. It felt that the reported money supply level may have been distorted, and focused its policy actions on whatever would improve the economy rather than on meeting its money supply targets.

Any changes in the Fed's monetary policy plans are publicized about 45 days later in the *Federal Reserve Bulletin*. In addition, statistical measures of the money supply are not completely up to date. Thus, financial market participants cannot confirm from any changes in these money supply statistics whether the Fed has recently adjusted its money supply targets. Given the lack of information, financial market participants sometimes guess at the Fed's monetary policy plans and make their decisions according to this guess. Some participants may take a passive approach and presume that the most recently publicized money supply targets set by the Fed are still intact. Other participants may have reason to suspect that the Fed recently revised its money supply targets.

MARKET REACTION TO REPORTED MONEY SUPPLY LEVELS. On every Thursday afternoon, the most up-to-date money supply figures are released. Financial market participants will often use these newly released figures to predict how the Fed will adjust money supply in the future, and therefore how interest rates and security prices may be influenced. Consider the role of bond portfolio managers who work for financial institutions. When they expect interest rates to rise, they should also expect that the values of their current holdings of bonds will decrease and may therefore reduce their bond holdings in favor of short-term securities. They could replenish their bond portfolio once interest rates increase and prices of existing bonds decline.

As an example, Exhibit 13.8 shows movements in the money supply over time. The dotted lines form the Fed's most recently disclosed money supply target range. This range was disclosed in Week 1. The range specifies money supply growth of between 3 percent and 6 percent on an annualized basis. In Weeks 1 through 5, the Fed managed to control money supply within its target. In Week 6, bond portfolio managers are awaiting the release of the money supply figures. If the reported money supply is near point A, this suggests that the Fed overshot its target range, and may tighten money supply in the near future to push it back within the target range. Given the expectation of the Fed pursuing a tight-money policy, bond portfolio managers may expect higher interest rates in the near future and thus sell some of their bonds before prices decline.

As a second possibility, the reported money supply level may be near point B, which would suggest that the Fed undershot its target range. If so, the Fed may loosen money supply in the near future to push it back within the target range. Given the expectation of a future loose-money policy, bond portfolio managers may expect lower interest rates in the near future (assuming that the loose money does not ignite inflationary expectations) and thus purchase more bonds now. Some portfolio managers may wait until

EXHIBIT 13.8   Possible Money Supply Movements Over Time

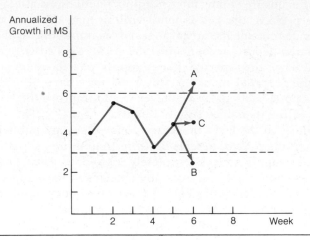

the Fed is consistently above or below its range before they anticipate a concerted Fed effort to move back within the range.

As a third possibility, the reported money supply level may be near point C, which would suggest that the Fed has remained within its target range. This does not offer much of a hint as to whether the Fed will tighten or loosen money supply in the future. Thus, bond portfolio managers may react less to this scenario than the previous two.

Because all bond portfolio managers receive the report on money supply at the same time, they may not be able to capitalize as easily on the information. For example, if the reported money supply leads all of them to expect higher interest rates, they will all try to simultaneously sell some of their bonds. Consequently, there could be a large amount of bonds for sale but very little demand for the bonds, which would force the price of these bonds down immediately. When the reported money supply leads bond portfolio managers to expect lower interest rates, they will all try to purchase more bonds, which could force the market price of bonds up immediately.

ANTICIPATING REPORTED MONEY SUPPLY LEVELS. Bond portfolio managers recognize that it is difficult to capitalize on a money supply report unless they react before other bond portfolio managers. The only way this could be done is to forecast what the money supply announcements will be on each Thursday afternoon. As an example, reconsider Exhibit 13.8, and assume that you are a bond portfolio manager, assessing the situation during Week 6. On Wednesday, the day before the money supply figures are released, you have completed your assessment. You believe that the Fed has overshot its money supply targets and will therefore tighten money supply in the near future in order to get back within its range. This would lead to higher interest rates and lower bond prices in the future. Based on your expectations, you sell your bonds on Wednesday. If your expectation is correct, you will be able to sell some of your bonds at a higher price on Wednesday than if you had waited until after the money supply was reported

Market Reaction to Money Supply Announcements

Recent research by Loeys examined how financial markets react to money supply announcements. When the announced M_1 measure was above what was anticipated, interest rates usually increased. When it was lower, interest rates usually declined. Financial market participants were apparently using money supply announcements to forecast future money supply movements.

Loeys also mentions that financial market participants, recognizing the potential adverse consequences of volatile money supply movements, monitor the volatility to anticipate and protect themselves from such adverse conditions. Signs of greater volatility may also signal an adjustment in the Fed's policy.

Before October 1979 the Fed often allowed M_1 to stray outside its range in order to maintain the federal funds rate within its range. Therefore, financial market participants did not react as much to money supply announcements, since the announcements did not necessarily signal future money supply movements.

After October 1979 the Fed emphasized control of M_1 more than the federal funds rate, and the markets reacted more to money supply announcements because more useful information was contained therein. In January 1982 the market response to money supply announcements declined. A recession had just begun and could have led the markets to believe that the Fed would concentrate on resolving the recession rather than adhering to monetary targets. Thus, a money supply announcement would not indicate new information about the future course of money movements.

In December 1982 short-term securities markets became less responsive to money supply announcements, possibly due to the technical problems of controlling M_1, since the introduction of new depository accounts caused a substantial public shift of funds in and out of M_1. Therefore, the Fed had less control over M_1, or was not as concerned with achieving its M_1 targets.

The long-term market participants became more responsive to M_1 announcements during this period. Loeys mentions that there was much uncertainty about the future course of monetary policy at this time and concern that the Fed would allow money supply growth to accelerate. Perhaps the long-term market participants were reacting to M_1 because of this concern, even if there was some distortion in the measurement of M_1.

SOURCE: Jan G. Loeys, "Market Views of Monetary Policy and Reactions to M_1 Announcements", *Business Review*, Federal Reserve Bank of Philadelphia (March–April 1984): 9–17.

on Thursday. Assume that you sold $1 million worth of bonds on Wednesday, and on Thursday, after the money supply was reported, bond prices fell by 2 percent. In this case you would receive $20,000 more than if you had waited until after the money supply was reported to sell your bonds. This is an example of the potential benefits of correctly forecasting the money supply figure before it is released.

Various consulting firms forecast the money supply level based on information from a sample of banks and then sell their forecasts to bond portfolio managers. Some bond portfolio managers purchase these forecasts, since

Chapter 13

Financial Market
Reaction to Monetary
Policy

POINT OF INTEREST

Should the Fed Announce Its Monetary Policy Immediately?

Financial market participants would prefer that any revision in the Fed's money supply target range be announced immediately. They would also prefer that all matters regarding monetary policy be disclosed immediately, since then they could make decisions based on more accurate information. There would be less guessing, and movements in security prices might be less volatile. Guessing often causes overreaction in the financial markets and thus more volatile security price movements.

The Fed might reply that if it immediately disclosed its monetary policy plans, security prices would be more volatile. Under the current situation, where there is less information disclosed and financial market participants are more uncertain of the future, there are usually some buyers and some sellers of

all securities, since there is disagreement about which way interest rates and security prices will move. If everyone had accurate information about the Fed's plans, there would be a more pronounced movement into or out of certain securities, and the prices would be very sensitive to such volatile movements. If prices of securities were more volatile, their perceived risk would be greater, and the public would have less confidence in holding securities. The Fed might further argue that much of whatever impact it does have on interest rates is completed by the time the financial markets are aware of the Fed's intentions. At this time, it is difficult to conclude which argument has more support. This issue will surely continue to be debated in the future.

the fee is small relative to the potential return that can be generated if the right strategy (buy versus sell) is implemented. Others are more doubtful of the accuracy of these forecasts, so they either develop their own or simply wait until the money supply figure is reported.

Even if forecasts of the reported money supply could be perfected, bond portfolio managers might incorrectly guess the Fed's future monetary policy plans. For example, if the most recently reported money supply showed that the Fed had overshot its money supply target range, it would be rational for financial market participants to expect the Fed to push the money supply back within its initially established range. However, the money supply might be within a newly established but not yet publicized target range.

MARKET REACTION TO DISCOUNT RATE ADJUSTMENTS. Besides the comparison of the most recently reported (or anticipated) money figures to the money supply growth targets, financial market participants have other methods of forecasting future money supply movements. One of the more common methods is to monitor actual or potential changes in the discount rate by the Fed. A change in the discount rate is often thought to signal a change in money supply targets. A decrease in the discount rate may signal a stimulative monetary policy designed to reduce interest rates. An increase in the discount rate may signal a tight-money policy designed to increase interest rates. It is not the revision in the discount rate, but the potentially revised money supply targets accompanying this revision that are so important.

Some discount rate adjustments are policy-related while others are *technical* (intended to bring the discount rate in line with other market rates). Exhibit 13.9 classifies recent discount rate adjustments as policy-related or technical. Six of the nine adjustments were policy-related. Since the Fed normally does not announce whether the adjustment is policy-related or technical, financial market participants must interpret each adjustment themselves.

Because a change in the discount rate is often thought to signal the Fed's future monetary policy, financial market participants attempt to predict when the Fed will change the discount rate and by how much. If they can accurately forecast a future adjustment, they can take advantageous positions in securities prior to the actual adjustment.

Some critics contend that the financial markets often overreact to discount rate revisions, since the revision may indicate nothing about the future course of monetary policy and economic conditions. This is because the Fed commonly revises the discount rate to move it back in line with other interest rates. In these situations, there may be no adjustment in money supply targets; and a change in the discount rate without any other adjustments is not likely to significantly affect the economy.

Recent research by Roley and Troll has found that since 1980 discount rate changes often precede market interest rate movements in the same direction. Thus, market participants are often justified in interpreting discount rate adjustments as a signal about future interest rate movements, regardless of whether the Fed planned such movements.

Does a Reported Money Supply Level Mean Anything?

While there is a definite link between money supply and a variety of economic variables, some critics contend that financial market participants take the money supply data too seriously. They suggest that while money supply trends over time are important, the money supply figure for any given week is not significant. Others rationalize the significance in a single money supply announcement as follows. Even if that single money supply level will not have much of an impact on the future economy, many participants in the financial markets think it does. Because they will make buy or sell decisions based on that figure, prices of existing securities will be affected.

Forecasting the Impact of Monetary Policy on the Economy

Even if financial market participants could correctly anticipate changes in money supply movements, they might not be able to predict future economic conditions. The historical relationship between money supply and economic variables has not remained perfectly stable over time. Thus, there is no guarantee as to how money supply fluctuations will affect the economy or how long the impact will lag.

Consider the anticipated impact of an increase in money supply on interest rates. If the Fed increases the supply of loanable funds without af-

EXHIBIT 13.9 Classification of Recent Discount Rate Changes

Date Effective	Change	Classification	Reason
October 12, 1982	10% to 9.5%	Technical related	Action taken to bring the discount rate into closer alignment with short-term market interest rates
November 22, 1982	9.5% to 9%	Policy related	Action taken against the background of continued progress toward greater price stability and indications of continued sluggishness in business activity and relatively strong demand for liquidity
December 14, 1982	9% to 8.5%	Policy related	Action taken in light of current business conditions, strong competitive pressures on prices and further moderation of cost increases, a showing of private credit demands and present indications of some tapering off in growth of the broader monetary aggregates
April 9, 1984	8.5% to 9%	Technical related	Action taken to bring discount rate into closer alignment with short-term interest rates
November 21, 1984	9% to 8.5%	Policy related	Action taken in view of slow growth of M1 and M2 and the moderate pace of business expansion, relatively stable prices and a continued strong dollar internationally
December 24, 1984	8.5% to 8%	Policy related	Essentially the same as before plus to bring the discount rate into more appropriate alignment with short-term market interest rates
May 20, 1985	8% to 7.5%	Policy related	Action taken in the light of relatively unchanged output in the industry sector stemming from rising imports and a strong dollar. Rate reduction is consistent with declining trend in market interest rates
March 7, 1986	7.5% to 7%	Policy related	Action taken in context of similar action by other important industrial countries and for closer alignment with market interest rates. A further consideration was a sharp decline in oil prices
April 21, 1986	7% to 6.5%	Technical related	Action taken to bring discount rate into closer alignment with prevailing levels of market rates

SOURCE: *Review*, Federal Reserve Bank of St. Louis (August–September 1986): 14; and *Federal Reserve Bulletin*, paraphrased from statements in various issues, and *The Wall Street Journal*.

fecting the demand schedule for loanable funds, interest rates should decrease. However, it is possible that the increase in money supply might also affect the demand for loanable funds. The higher money supply can cause consumers and firms to expect future inflation (because of the historical relationship that has existed between these variables) and therefore modify their borrowing habits today. Expectations of future inflation can cause a higher demand for loanable funds. When combining this shift with the previously mentioned shift in the supply schedule, the net impact of the Fed's increase in money supply is uncertain.

From this discussion, it appears that if participants in financial markets could correctly predict whether the Fed's increase in money supply will cause inflationary expectations, they could determine how the Fed's actions will affect interest rates. There are also some other economic conditions that may determine whether an increase in money supply will ignite inflationary expectations. It might not if the conditions currently show no potential for higher inflation—for example, decreasing oil prices, very little potential for huge wage increases to labor unions, low prices paid for imported goods, etc.

Participants in the financial markets commonly disagree on whether an increase in money supply growth will affect inflationary expectations and therefore how interest rates will react. Well-known economists even tend to disagree.

Up to this point, our discussion has focused on increased money supply. The Fed may also reduce the money supply, which reduces the supply of loanable funds and places upward pressure on interest rates. However, it can also lower the demand for loanable funds if it reduces inflationary expectations, and it therefore could offset any decrease in the supply of loanable funds.

Combining Forecasts of Monetary Policy with Forecasts of its Impact

Exhibit 13.10 can be used to summarize why financial market participants are often unable to determine future interest rate movements. To forecast future interest rate movements one must forecast the future money supply

---

EXHIBIT 13.10   Forecasts Required to Assess Future Interest Rate Movements

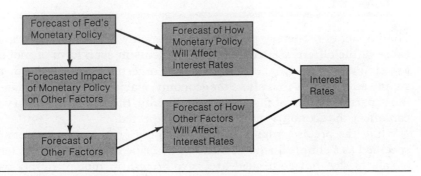

amount, as well as other factors (such as the size of the federal deficit, the strength of the economy, etc) that affect interest rates. Then it is necessary to determine how these variables will affect interest rates. If the forecasts of the variables are correct, but the assessment of how they will affect interest rates is incorrect, the forecast of interest rates will be inaccurate.

It is virtually impossible to forecast accurately not only the values of all future relevant variables, but also how they will affect interest rates. However, being able to at least determine the general direction of future interest rates greatly improves investment and financing decisions.

INTERNATIONAL CONSIDERATIONS IN U.S. MONETARY POLICY

INTERNATIONAL ASPECTS

The type of monetary policy to be implemented by the Fed is somewhat dependent on various international factors. For example, a weak dollar can stimulate U.S. exports, discourage U.S. imports, and therefore stimulate the U.S. economy. In addition, it tends to exert inflationary pressure in the United States. Thus, the Fed would be less likely to use a stimulative monetary policy when the dollar is weak. A strong dollar tends to reduce inflationary pressure but also dampen the U.S. economy. Therefore, the Fed is more likely to use a stimulative policy during a strong-dollar period.

The Fed's policies may also depend partly on foreign economies. For example, in 1987 and 1988, U.S. government officials requested that governments of other industrialized countries stimulate their respective economies. If, over time, these foreign governments comply, there will be an indirect stimulus to the United States through a greater demand for U.S. exports. Consequently, the Fed may not need to use a stimulative monetary policy. Of course, foreign governments may not comply with U.S. requests, just as the U.S. government policies do not necessarily comply with foreign government requests. But the point of this discussion is that because economies are integrated, one country's monetary policy may depend partly on government policies in other countries.

International flows of funds can also affect the Fed's monetary policy. If there is upward pressure on U.S. interest rates that can be offset by foreign inflows of funds, the Fed may not feel compelled to use a loose-money policy. However, if foreign investors reduce their investment in U.S. securities, the Fed may be forced to intervene in order to prevent interest rates from rising.

SUMMARY

The impact of monetary policy on the economy is extremely complex because of the different effects that adjustments in each form of money (M_1, M_2, etc.) can have. In addition, there are other factors along with money supply adjustments that affect the economy, making it difficult to determine the separate impact of money supply. Finally, the lags in monetary policy can affect the economy differently than expected.

While the precise impact of money supply on the economy cannot be specified as a simple formula, it can be described in more general terms. It is safe to say that continued excessive growth in money supply can put upward pressure on inflation, while an extremely tight money policy can force an economic slowdown. Any attempt to be more precise leads to controversy. Suffice it to say, the Fed faces an economic trade-off in attempting to simultaneously maintain low unemployment and inflation. If financial market participants can pinpoint the Fed's main concern, they may be able to predict the monetary policy and thus improve their forecast of future economic conditions. In this way, they could improve lending, borrowing, and investing decisions.

Many explanations of recent movements, and forecasts of future movements in interest rates or other economic variables are based on the Fed's monetary policy. It can affect a variety of economic variables, which in turn affect the values of securities traded in financial markets. In reality, no one knows the Fed's future monetary policy with certainty or precisely how it will affect interest rate movements. However, those financial market participants who best predict the Fed's policies and their effects will benefit the most.

KEY TERMS

impact lag
implementation lag
Phillips curve
recognition lag

QUESTIONS

13.1. How does the Fed's monetary policy affect economic conditions?

13.2. Describe the economic trade-off faced by the Fed in achieving its economic goals.

13.3. What is a criticism of using "quick fix" policies?

13.4. When does the Fed use a loose-money policy and a tight-money policy?

13.5. Briefly summarize the pure Keynesian philosophy and identify the key variable considered. (See the appendix.)

13.6. Briefly summarize the Monetarist approach. (See the appendix.)

13.7. Why may the Fed have difficulty in controlling the economy in the manner desired? Be specific.

13.8. What is the recognition lag? Explain why it occurs.

13.9. When does the implementation lag occur?

13.10. Assume that the Fed's primary goal is to cure inflation. How can it use open market operations to achieve its goal? What is a possible adverse effect of this action by the Fed (even if it achieves its goal)?

13.11. When it was announced on June 2, 1987, that Paul Volcker would resign as chairman of the Federal Reserve, the dollar weakened substantially. Why do you think this may have occurred?

13.12. Why do financial market participants closely monitor money supply movements?

13.13. Why do financial market participants that monitor monetary policy have only limited success in forecasting economic variables?

13.14. Why might the Fed allow the money supply to continue outside the target range?

13.15. Why would the Fed try to avoid frequent changes in the money supply?

13.16. Explain why an increase in money supply can affect interest rates in different ways. Incorporate the potential impact of money supply on the supply of loanable funds and demand for loanable funds when answering this question.

13.17. What other factors may be considered by financial market participants that are assessing whether an increase in money supply growth will affect inflation?

13.18. How do financial market participants use the up-to-date money supply figures released every Thursday afternoon?

13.19. Describe how portfolio managers in the bond market scenario may react if the Fed overshoots its target range.

13.20. Research discussed in this chapter found less market reaction to money supply announcements before 1979. Explain why this would occur.

13.21. Why would financial markets react less to money supply announcements during a recessionary period?

13.22. Why did financial markets react less to money supply announcements during the period of deregulation when new types of deposits were introduced by depository institutions?

13.23. Explain how some bond portfolio managers attempt to capitalize on their projections of money supply announcements.

13.24. If you were a bond portfolio manager, would you allocate any of your time for monitoring weekly money supply announcements or forecasting weekly money supply announcements? Defend your answer.

13.25. If a change in the discount rate is not likely to directly affect market interest rates, why do financial markets sometimes react to such a change?

PROJECT

1. MARKET ASSESSMENT OF FED POLICY

Review the "Credit Markets" section of *The Wall Street Journal* (listed in the index on the first page) over the last five days. Summarize the market assessments of the Fed on each day. Also summarize the market's expectations about future interest rates. Are these expectations primarily because of the Fed's monetary policy or because of other factors? The following table can be used for your analysis:

	Market assessment of the Fed	Market expectations of future interest rates	Are the market's interest rate expectations due to Fed policy?
1 day ago			
2 days ago			
3 days ago			
4 days ago			
5 days ago			

REFERENCES

Batten, Dallas S. and Daniel L. Thornton. "M$_1$ or M$_2$: Which Is the Better Monetary Target?" *Review*, Federal Reserve Bank of St. Louis (June–July 1983): 36–42.

Brown, W. W. and G. J. Santoni. "Monetary Growth and the Timing of Interest Rate Movements," *Review*, Federal Reserve Bank of St. Louis (August–September 1983): 16–25.

———. "Money Supply Announcements and Interest Rates: Another View," *Journal of Business* (January 1983): 1–23.

Cacy, J. A. "Recent M$_1$ Growth and Its Implications," *Economic Review*, Federal Reserve Bank of Kansas City (December 1985): 18–24.

Davidson, Lawrence S. and Richard T. Froyen. "Monetary Policy and Stock Returns: Are Stock Markets Efficient?," *Review*, Federal Reserve Bank of St. Louis (March 1982): 3–12.

Engel, Charles and Jeffrey Frankel. "Why Interest Rates React to Money Announcements: An Explanation from the Foreign Exchange Market," *Journal of Monetary Economics* (January 1984): 31–39.

Gilbert, Alton R. "Access to the Discount Window for All Commercial Banks: Is It Important for Monetary Policy?" *Review*, Federal Reserve Bank of St. Louis (February 1980): 15–24.

Grossman, Jacob. "The Rationality of Money Supply Expectations and the Short-Run Response of Interest Rates to Monetary Surprises." *Journal of Money, Credit, and Banking* (November 1981): 409–424.

Higgins, Bryon. "Should the Federal Reserve Fine-Tune Monetary Growth?" *Economic Review*, Federal Reserve Bank of Kansas City (January 1982): 3–16.

Horrigan, Brian and Aris Protopapadakis. "Federal Deficits: A Faulty Gauge of Government's Impact on Financial Markets," *Business Review*, Federal Reserve Bank of Philadelphia (March–April 1982): 3–16.

Hein, Scott E. "The Response of Short-term Interest Rates to Weekly Money Announcements: A comment." *Journal of Money, Credit, and Banking* (May 1985): 264–271.

Judd, John P. "Money Supply Announcements, Forward Interest Rates and Budget Deficits," *Economic Review*, Federal Reserve Bank of San Francisco (Fall 1984): 36–46.

Kahn, George A. "Investment in Recession and Recovery," *Economic Review*, Federal Reserve Bank of Kansas City (November 1985): 25–38.

Kopcke, Richard W. "Inflation and the Choice of 'Monetary' Guidelines," *New England Economic Review*, Federal Reserve Bank of Boston (January–February): 5–14.

Lane, Timothy D. "Instrument Instability and Short-term Monetary Control." *Journal of Monetary Economics* 14, no. 2 (1984): 209–224.

Litterman, Robert B. "How Monetary Policy in 1985 Affects the Outlook." *Quarterly Review* (Fall 1985): 2–13.

Loeys, Jan G. "Market Views of Monetary Policy and Reactions to M$_1$ Announcements," *Business Review*, Federal Reserve Bank of Philadelphia (March–April 1984): 9–17.

McNees, Stephen K. "Modeling the Fed: A Forward-Looking Monetary Policy Reaction Function." *New England Economic Review*, Federal Reserve Bank of Boston (November–December 1986): 3–8.

McNees, Stephen K. "The Current Expansion in Historical Perspective," *New England Economic Review*, Federal Reserve Bank of Boston (November–December 1984): 5–8.

Miller, Richard B. "Henry Reuss Talks about the Fed and Other Problems." *The Bankers Magazine* (May–June 1983): 43–47.

Mullineaux, Donald J. "Efficient Markets, Interest Rates, and Monetary Policy." *Business Review*, Federal Reserve Bank of Philadelphia (May–June 1981): 3–10.

Peterson, Susan B. "Long-Run Targets and FOMC Policy Decisions," *Akron Business and Economic Review* (Winter): 20–26.

Puckett, Richard H. "Federal Open Market Committee Structure and Decisions." *Journal of Monetary Economics* 14, no. 1 (1984): 97–104.

Roley, V. Vance. "The Response of Short-Term Interest Rates to Weekly Money Announcements: A Note." *Journal of Money, Credit, and Banking* (August 1983): 344–354.

Roley, V. Vance and Rick Troll. "The Impact of Discount Rate Changes on Market Interest Rates." *Economic Review*, Federal Reserve Bank of Kansas City (January 1984): 27–39.

Roley, V. Vance and Carl E. Walsh. "Unanticipated Money and Interest Rates." *American Economic Review* (May 1984): 49–54.

Roth, Howard. "Effects of Financial Deregulation on Monetary Policy," *Economic Review*, Federal Reserve Bank of Kansas City (March 1988): 17–29.

Roth, Howard L. "Federal Reserve Open Market Techniques." *Economic Review*, Federal Reserve Bank of Kansas City (March 1986): 3–15.

Roth, Howard L. "Recent Experience with M_1 as a Policy Guide." *Economic Review*, Federal Reserve Bank of Kansas City (March 1984): 17–29.

Sellon, Gordon H. and Ronald L. Teigen. "The Choice of Short-Run Targets for Monetary Policy." *Economic Review*, Federal Reserve Bank of Kansas City (May 1981): 3–12.

Sheehan, Richard G. "Weekly Money Announcements: New Information and Its Effects." *Review*, Federal Reserve Bank of St. Louis, (August–September: 1985).

Taylor, Herb. "The Discount Window and Money Control." *Business Review*, Federal Reserve Bank of Philadelphia (May–June 1983): 3–12.

Thornton, Daniel L. "The Discount Rate and Market Interest Rates: What's the Connection?" *Review*, Federal Reserve Bank of St. Louis (June–July 1982): 3–14.

Thornton, Daniel L. "The Discount Rate and Market Interest Rates: Theory and Evidence." *Review*, Federal Reserve Bank of St. Louis (August–September 1986): 5–21.

Urich, Thomas J. and Paul Wachtel. "Market Response to the Weekly Money Supply Announcements in the 1970s." *Journal of Finance* (December 1981): 1063–1072.

Urich, Thomas J. "The Information Content of Weekly Money Supply Announcements." *Journal of Monetary Economics* (July 1982): 73–88.

Wallich, Henry C. "Recent Techniques of Monetary Policy," *Economic Review*, Federal Reserve Bank of Kansas City (May 1984): 21–30.

Weiner, Stuart E. "The Natural Rate of Unemployment: Concepts and Issues." *Economic Review*, Federal Reserve Bank of Kansas City (January 1986): 11–24.

Monetary Policy Theories

The type of monetary policy implemented by the Fed depends on the economic philosophies of the FOMC members. Some of the more popular theories that can influence the Fed's policies are described in this appendix.

PURE KEYNESIAN APPROACH

At one extreme is the *Keynesian theory*, developed by John Maynard Keynes, a British economist. To do justice to explaining this theory would require an entire text. Briefly, though, the Keynesian theory suggests how the demand for money interacts with the supply of money to affect the economy. The demand for money for speculative purposes is thought to be inversely related to interest rates. When interest rates are low, there is a greater chance that they will increase in the future. Households and corporations therefore prefer to hold money rather than bonds, since bond prices will decrease if interest rates rise. When interest rates are high, households and corporations are more willing to hold bonds, because they expect interest rates to decrease (and bond prices to increase). This inverse relationship is represented by the money demand curve (M_d) in the left graph of Exhibit 13A.1.

   Money supply is highly influenced by the actions of the Federal Reserve System. An increase in the supply of money as shown in the left graph of Exhibit 13A.1 should place downward pressure on the equilibrium interest rate (assuming that the money demand line remains unchanged). Conversely, a reduction should cause a shortage of funds at the prevailing interest rate, and therefore force the equilibrium interest rate to rise.

   The level of capital investment rises when a corporation's required rate of return is low; and this, in turn, is strongly influenced by the prevailing interest rate, which reflects the cost of financing the projects. If a change in money supply can affect interest rates, it can affect the level of capital investment (on equipment, buildings, machinery, etc.), as illustrated in Exhibit 13A.1. If money supply is increased, corporate required rates for return will decrease, and the level of capital investment will increase.

Aggregate demand includes corporate consumption and capital investment and government expenditures. Since the Fed is able to influence capital investment by adjusting the money supply, it can use monetary policy to affect aggregate demand. The Keynesian philosophy advocates an active role of the federal government in doing just that in order to correct economic problems. It conflicts with the *classical theory* that production (supply) creates its own demand, and gained support during the Great Depression when the existing level of production had clearly exceeded demand, causing massive layoffs. Under such conditions, the Keynesian theory would have prescribed stimulative federal government policies, such as high monetary growth.

If excessive inflation is the main concern, the pure Keynesian philosophy would still focus on aggregate demand as the variable that must be adjusted. A portion of the high inflation is possibly due to excessive aggregate demand that is pulling up prices, commonly referred to as **demand-pull inflation.** The Keynesian approach would prescribe a federal government policy to reduce aggregate demand (such as relatively low money supply growth) and therefore reduce inflation. Critics charge, however, that if the Fed follows a pure Keynesian approach, money supply movements over time may be quite volatile, as the money supply target range would be frequently revised in reaction to existing problems. This contention is supported by recent research by Roley and Troll.

QUANTITY THEORY OF MONEY AND THE MONETARIST APPROACH

The quantity theory is applicable to monetary policy because it suggests a particular relationship between money supply and the degree of economic activity. It is based on the so-called **equation of exchange** specified below:

$$MV = PQ$$
where M = amount of money in the economy
  V = velocity of money
  P = weighted average price of goods and services in the economy
  Q = quantity of goods and services sold

Velocity represents the average number of times each dollar changes hands per year. The right side of the equation of exchange represents the total value of goods and services produced. If velocity is constant, a given *adjustment* in money supply will produce a predictable change in the total value of goods and services. Thus, a direct relationship between money supply and gross national product is evident.

An early form of the theory assumed Q constant in the short run, which implied a direct relationship between money supply and prices. If the money supply is increased, the average price level will increase. However, the assumption of a stable quantity is not realistic today. The original quantity theory has been revised by so-called *Monetarists* into what is referred to as the *modern quantity theory of money.* Milton Friedman and others relaxed

EXHIBIT 13A.1   Impact of Increased Money Supply on Business Investment According to Keynesian Approach

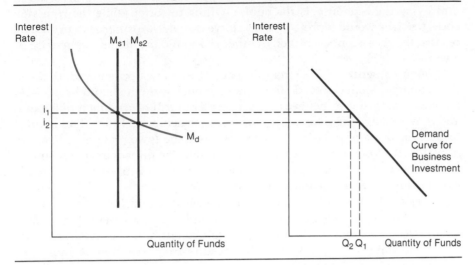

the stable-quantity assumption to suggest that a given increase in money supply leads to a predictable increase in the value of goods and services produced.

Because velocity represents the ratio of money stock to nominal output, it is affected by any factor that influences this ratio. Income patterns can affect velocity because they influence the amount of money held by households. Factors that increase the ratio of money holdings to income of households reduce velocity, while factors that reduce this ratio increase velocity. Households maintain more money if their income is received less frequently. Credit cards can reduce the need to hold money balances. Expectations of high inflation encourage households to hold less money balances, thereby increasing velocity. Yet, Friedman has found that velocity changes in a predictable manner and is not related to fluctuations in money supply. Therefore, the equation of exchange can be applied to assess how money can affect aggregate spending.

The Monetarist approach advocates a stable, low growth in the money supply. It may be criticized for being too passive, but its supporters contend that it allows economic problems to resolve themselves without causing additional problems. Suppose the United States experiences a recession. While the typical Keynesian monetary policy prescription would be high money growth, Monetarists would avoid a loose money policy on the grounds that it tends to ignite inflationary expectations, which can increase the demand for money and place upward pressure on interest rates. The Monetarist cure for the recession would not call for any revision in the existing monetary policy. Instead, Monetarists would expect the stagnant economy to reduce corporate and household borrowing and thus result in lower interest rates. Once interest rates are reduced to a low enough level, they will encourage borrowing and therefore stimulate economic growth. Since the Monetarist approach to achieve lower interest rates does not require an increase in money supply growth, inflationary expectations should not be ignited as they might be under the Keynesian approach.

A major limitation of the Monetarist approach is the timing involved in improving the economy. Is the public willing to suffer while the recession cures itself, or would it prefer a more active (Keynesian) approach to quickly resolve the recession, even though other economic problems might arise as a result?

Though recognizing the strong impact of money supply fluctuations on the economy, Monetarists do not believe money growth should be actively adjusted. Instead they believe in accepting a natural rate of unemployment, and they criticize the government for trying to achieve a lower than natural rate at the price of inflation—especially since the lower rate is unlikely to prevail in the long run. Friedman has found that the impact of money supply growth on economic growth has a long lag time and is uncertain, which is why he advocates a constant rate of monetary growth.

A major difference in the beliefs of Keynesians and Monetarists is the perceived relative importance of inflation and unemployment. Keynesians tend to focus on maintaining low unemployment and are therefore more willing to tolerate any inflation that results from stimulative monetary policies. Monetarists are more concerned about maintaining low inflation and are therefore more willing to tolerate what they refer to as a natural rate of unemployment.

MONETARIST PROPOSAL TO STABILIZE MONEY SUPPLY GROWTH

A strong form of monetarism would be to set the money supply growth level at a particular rate and permanently maintain it at that rate. This is often referred to as the **fixed money supply rule.** If implemented, this would have significant implications for financial markets. There would no longer be a need for financial market participants to monitor the Fed, since the Fed's importance would be greatly reduced. Instead, the focus could shift to all the other factors that affect economic conditions. Because the Fed would not be able to revise monetary policy, it could not be blamed for a poor economy. The fiscal policymaking group would be solely responsible for the state of the economy.

There are some concerns about a fixed money supply rule. First, what form of money supply should be controlled at a fixed-growth rate. Second, what is the appropriate rate? The decision must be an arbitrary one, which if proved wrong over the years could be harmful. In addition, a severe problem could arise in the future that would require a change in monetary policy, yet, change would be prohibited by a fixed money supply rule. Finally, a fixed money supply rule would increase the power of the fiscal policy side, which is more politically motivated. The existing power of the Fed allows more of a long-run concern about economic conditions than what would be the case if all power were held by the fiscal side.

A compromise may be to employ a fixed money supply rule that is subject to adjustment if it is not working well. However, this dampens the advantages of a fixed rule. The financial markets would again have to follow the Fed and forecast when the rule might be revised, since any revision would have an impact on the economy. This compromise essentially represents the system as it is today, where a money supply target is set, but changed periodically at the discretion of the Fed.

RATIONAL EXPECTATIONS

The *theory of rational expectations* implies that the public accounts for all existing information when forming its expectations. As applied to a monetary policy, this theory suggests that households and business, having witnessed historical effects of monetary policy actions, will use this information to forecast the impact of an existing policy and act accordingly. For example, if the Fed uses a loose monetary policy to stimulate the economy, households will respond by increasing their spending, as they anticipate that higher inflation will result from the policy. In addition, businesses will increase their investment in machinery and equipment in an attempt to beat impending higher costs of borrowing. Further, participants in the labor market will negotiate for higher wages to compensate for higher anticipated inflation, and the level of savings will be reduced while the level of borrowing will increase. These forces will offset the impact of an increase in money supply. Therefore, the policy will not affect interest rates or economic growth. In general, rational expectations supports the contention by Friedman and some other monetarists that changes in monetary policy are unlikely to have any sustained positive impact on the economy.

In reality, all households and businesses may not anticipate the effects of a particular monetary policy. Many do, however—a fact ignored by monetary theory in the past. Today's monetary theories account for decisions that are based on expectations.

A MORE BALANCED APPROACH

The FOMC as a whole is not thought to be pure Keynesian or pure Monetarist. FOMC members adjust monetary growth targets when they see fit (in line with the Keynesian philosophy) but are quite aware of the potential adverse consequence of excessive money supply growth (as suggested by Monetarists). If a stimulative boost is needed, and if severe inflation does not appear to be a potential consequence, a loose money policy may be implemented. However, if inflation is a major concern, the Fed must weigh the costs and benefits of a stimulative monetary policy.

The decisions by the FOMC members may also be influenced by the political party that appointed them. Recent research by Puckett found that dissenting votes by FOMC members appointed by Democratic U.S. presidents were in favor of looser monetary policy while those members appointed by Republican U.S. presidents were in favor of tighter monetary policy. The dissenting votes by presidents of the Federal Reserve district banks were similar to those of members appointed by Republican presidents.

It is important for financial market participants to keep track of the FOMC member personalities over time. As members of the FOMC are replaced, there can be a shift in the overall philosophy of the FOMC, which can result in a different monetary policy.

Financial Market Reaction to Fiscal Policy

FISCAL POLICY EFFECTS IN PERSPECTIVE

Many analysts who evaluated the stock market crash of October 1987 suggest that the federal government's budget deficit was a primary reason for the crash. Financial market participants became increasingly worried about the potential impact of the budget deficit on interest rates, inflation, and economic growth, and therefore on stock prices. This example illustrates the potential influence of fiscal policy on financial markets.

As a less dramatic example, consider the Treasury's announced plans in May 1988 to issue new debt amounting to $26 billion. Prices on all types of bonds declined in reaction to this announcement, as bond traders became concerned about the potential impact that the Treasury's additional borrowing would have on interest rates and other economic variables.

On August 1, 1988, the *Wall Street Journal* reported a forecast circulating on Wall Street that the economy will continue to grow steadily through 1993, U.S. budget deficits will nearly disappear, and social security surpluses will mount as a result of strong economic growth. This report was provided in the "Credit Markets" section, since bond and stock market participants react to such information related to U.S. fiscal policy.

■ How does the federal budget deficit affect economic conditions?
■ How can the Federal Reserve attempt to offset the potential adverse economic impact of a larger budget deficit?
■ How might such a policy by the Fed backfire?

These and other related questions are addressed in this chapter.

OUTLINE

Financial market participants are well aware that fiscal policy actions can have a significant influence on interest rates and other economic variables. Therefore, their economic forecasts must incorporate forecasts of those fiscal policies and their impact.

This chapter first introduces the decision makers behind fiscal policy. Then, it describes the trade-off involved in implementing fiscal policy. Finally, it discusses how financial markets assess fiscal policy, and how fiscal and monetary policies are integrated.

DECISION MAKERS OF FISCAL POLICY

Fiscal policy is primarily dictated by the president of the United States, the Senate, and the House of Representatives. At the beginning of each calendar year the president sends Congress his budget proposal for the upcoming fiscal year (starting October 1). This budget represents a financial plan of the size and allocation of government spending. Over the nine-month period preceding the new fiscal year, Congress evaluates the budget.

The budget is prepared during the nine-month period prior to the calendar year. The director of the Office of Management and Budget (OMB) meets with the president and administrators of government agencies to discuss existing and proposed programs.

The agencies provide appropriation requests to the OMB, which in turn presents them to the president. Approximately two months before the new calendar year, the administration provides Congress with a current-services budget, which estimates government spending over the following five years. Projections of government receipts are also determined, based on assumptions of economic growth, tax rates, and interest rates. Congress considers the government spending plans on a case-by-case basis.

Congress authorizes legislation to establish or continue a federal program and authorize appropriation. The appropriations requests are evaluated by the House of Representatives Appropriations Committee, while proposed sources of revenues are examined by the Ways and Means Committee. The approved appropriations and revenue bills are then assessed by the Senate. Any differences between the House and Senate are resolved by a committee of members from both sides. This committee provides a proposal for approval by the House and Senate, which is then presented to the president for approval or veto.

Just as monetary policy uses the control of money supply to influence the economy, fiscal policy uses taxes and government expenditures. In general terms, a stimulative fiscal policy involves reducing tax rates and/or increasing government expenditures. Conversely, a fiscal policy designed to slow economic growth would likely increase tax rates and reduce government expenditures. These solutions to economic problems do not always work, as will be illustrated later.

Fiscal policy, like monetary policy, faces a trade-off in attempting to cure unemployment and inflation simultaneously. A policy of low tax rates and high government expenditures may stimulate the economy and reduce unemployment, but it can also ignite inflation. A policy of higher tax rates and low government expenditures may slow an economy and reduce any inflation attributable to economic growth, but it can cause higher unemployment.

FINANCIAL MARKET ASSESSMENT OF FISCAL POLICY

Because any significant changes in tax rates or government expenditures are well publicized, financial markets do not need to guess at the existing fiscal policy. Monetary policy, on the other hand, is not publicized until a month and a half after it is decided.

Even if fiscal policy occurs as planned, there is still uncertainty as to how it will affect economic growth, interest rates, and other economic variables. Thus, financial market participants may react differently from one another to any significant news about future fiscal policy.

Suppose a large income tax cut is likely. Some analysts may expect that this would stimulate the economy, as consumers would now have more funds to spend (their disposable, or after-tax, income would rise). Yet, a cut in taxes could reduce tax revenues, which could force a reduction in government expenditures and offset the stimulative impact of increased consumer spending.

If tax revenues are reduced and the government does not reduce expenditures, the federal budget deficit will increase, placing upward pressure on interest rates, since the government is forced to borrow more funds. Given a certain amount of loanable funds supplied to the market (through savings), excessive government demand for these funds tends to "crowd out" the private demand (by consumers and corporations) for funds. The federal government may be willing to pay whatever is necessary to borrow these funds, while the private sector may not. This impact is known as the **crowding-out effect.** Exhibit 14.1 illustrates the flow of funds between the federal government and the private sector.

While lower tax rates should increase disposable income and spending, the higher budget deficit (due to a reduction in tax revenues) could increase interest rates, discourage private-sector borrowing, and reduce spending. Thus, the overall impact of a tax cut is uncertain. The purpose of this discussion is not to resolve this issue of how a tax cut affects the economy, but to illustrate why financial market participants will not necessarily agree on the economic impact of a particular fiscal policy.

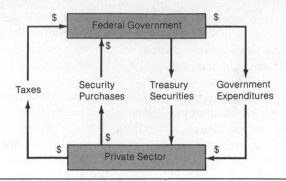

A key issue of our discussion is whether a tax cut will lead to a lower level of tax revenues. Some argue that a tax cut may instead increase tax revenues. Consider a situation where corporate taxes are reduced, so that for each dollar of earnings, the federal government receives a few cents less. This lower corporate tax rate may encourage corporations to expand, as some proposed projects that were previously thought to be unfeasible may now be feasible (since expected *after-tax* earnings may now be sufficiently large). As a result of greater corporate expansion, corporate earnings could rise, and the corporate tax revenues could increase, even though the tax rate applied to these earnings is now lower.

Financial market participants who understand the complex set of economic relationships will do a better job of assessing the economic impact of fiscal policy. Even the components of fiscal policy (tax policy and government expenditure policy) are interrelated. A higher level of proposed government expenditures will affect economic growth and overall earnings, and therefore influence tax revenues. Economic growth, interest rates, and any other economic variables are influenced not only by the level of tax receipts and government expenditures resulting from fiscal policy, but also by outside factors such as oil prices, strikes, the value of the U.S. dollar, and so on. The tax decision affects unemployment and economic growth, which in turn have feedback effects on tax receipts, since they affect the volume of earnings to which tax rates are applied.

Some built-in fiscal stabilizers can stabilize economic conditions without any explicit adjustments in fiscal policy. For example, a U.S. recession reduces income and therefore the amount of taxes paid to the federal government. In addition, government spending on unemployment benefits and welfare increases. Thus, the impact of the recession is less severe.

FINANCIAL MARKET ASSESSMENT OF THE BUDGET DEFICIT

The size of the federal budget deficit is largely determined by fiscal policy. It will continue to receive much attention by financial market participants, since it is thought to have an impact on interest rates. Exhibit 14.2 illustrates

EXHIBIT 14.2 Federal Budget Deficit Levels Over Time

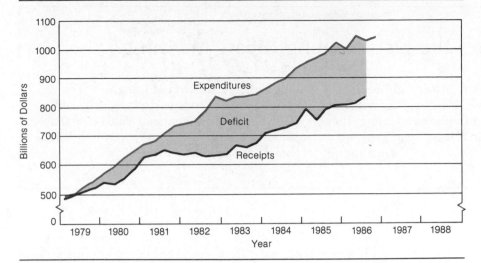

SOURCE: *Federal Reserve Chart Book* (1987).

the abrupt increase in the annual federal budget deficit in the early 1980s. Until then, an annual deficit of $40 billion would have seemed high. By the mid 1980s an annual deficit of $200 billion no longer seemed unnatural, although there was concern for the long-run economic impact it might have.

It has sometimes been suggested that the growth in the annual federal deficit is an illusion. Exhibit 14.3 shows the annual expenditures, tax receipts, and the deficit as a percent of GNP. The deficit does not seem as large from this perspective. However, the increase during the 1980s is still noticeable. The shaded areas in Exhibit 14.3 represent recessionary periods. Note that the deficit as a percent of GNP is relatively high in those periods.

The trend in the deficit over time can be more thoroughly assessed by examining the trends of components that make it up. Exhibit 14.4 shows the main components of federal government receipts. Personal and business taxes have typically been the primary source of revenues.

Exhibit 14.5 shows the main components of federal government expenditures. Transfer payments (such as social security payments, Medicare, and interest on the national debt) have become a more important use of federal government funds, while grants-in-aid have become less important.

While a precise relationship between the federal budget deficit and economic variables (such as interest rates) does not exist, financial market participants would likely make more accurate economic assessments if they could properly forecast the federal budget deficit. In this endeavor, they could choose to develop an individual forecast for the main components of federal government receipts and expenditures (shown in Exhibits 14.4 and 14.5) and then derive the overall deficit forecast from that. Or they could obtain a deficit forecast constructed by a consulting firm or a government agency. Although deficit forecasts are widely available, a *consistently accurate* one is unavailable. To illustrate the potential margin of error, the federal deficit in 1982 was forecasted by the government to be in the range of $40 billion, but it exceeded $100 billion.

Does the Debt Ceiling Mean Anything?

The federal debt has historically been subject to a debt ceiling. If this ceiling were permanent, it would provide useful information as to the maximum allowable federal deficit in the future. (A revision of the ceiling requires the permission of Congress.) For this reason, some critics ask why a debt ceiling even exists, and financial market participants tend to ignore it in forecasting future federal debt levels.

Exhibit 14.6 illustrates potential differences in opinion regarding budget deficit projections. One set of forecasts is provided by the Congressional Budget Office (CBO) while the other set is provided by the Office of Management and Budget (OMB). The difference in projections occurs because of different assumptions about the underlying variables (such as gross national product and unemployment) that affect government expenditures

EXHIBIT 14.3   Annual Federal Government Revenues and Expenditures as a Percent of GNP

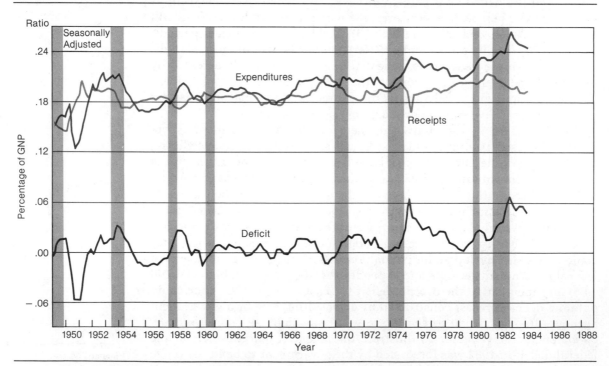

SOURCE: *Review,* Federal Reserve Bank of St. Louis (June–July 1984): 7.

EXHIBIT 14.4   Breakdown of Federal Government Receipts

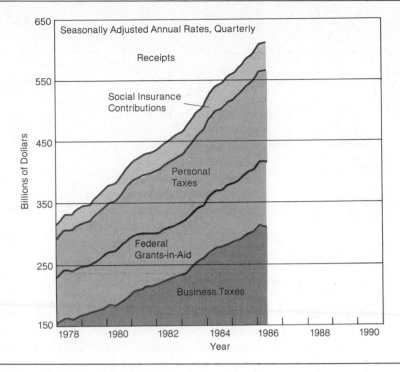

SOURCE: *Federal Reserve Chart Book* (1986).

EXHIBIT 14.5   Breakdown of Federal Government Expenditures

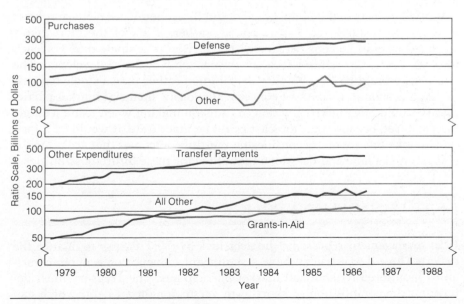

SOURCE: *Federal Reserve Chart Book* (1987).

EXHIBIT 14.6   Comparison of Federal Deficit Projections

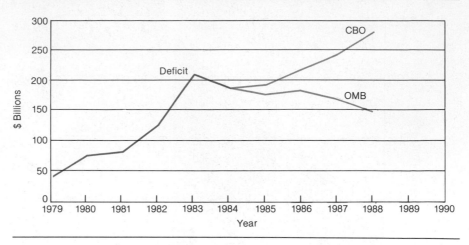

SOURCE: *FRBSF Weekly Letter*, November 23, 1984.

and receipts. Federal budget deficit projections by a given group may change over time, as the assumptions about economic variables are revised. As an example, Exhibit 14.7 shows the deficit forecasts by the CBO at three different points in time. The downward adjustment in their forecasts was because of (1) downward adjustment in projected inflation (mainly due to lower oil prices), which reduced the forecasted national defense expenditures, and (2) a downward adjustment in interest rates, which reduced the forecasted level of federal borrowing necessary to cover future interest payments. As projections of the deficit are changed, projections of interest rates and other economic variables by financial market participants will change as well.

While forecasts of the budget deficit and its economic impact are subject to error, they should not be neglected; rather, a few of the more likely scenarios should be considered together instead of a single one. For each forecast, a set of possible effects on the economy could be developed. The end result would be a probability distribution rather than a single forecast for each economic variable of concern. Obviously, financial market participants would have more direction in decision making when using a single forecast. Yet, because that forecast could be inaccurate, it would be a mistake to take this route. By considering multiple outcomes that are possible, one can make financial decisions that allow for these future possibilities.

DEBT MANAGEMENT POLICY

Debt management represents the decisions by the Treasury to finance the deficit. These decisions can have a significant influence on economic variables monitored by financial market participants. The Treasury must determine the composition of short-term versus long-term debt, which can affect the term structure of interest rates, and therefore the relative desir-

Empirical Evidence on Budget Deficits

Research by Miller has led to the following major conclusions about federal budget deficits:

■ Higher deficits tend to cause higher inflation.

■ Deficits result from policy actions (such as defense expenditures or tax law adjustments), rather than from changing economic conditions.

■ The adverse effects of deficits cannot be cured by monetary policy.

Research by Thornton found that debt monetization occurred only when the Fed used interest rate targeting (before 1980) as higher deficits placed upward pressure on interest rates. Since the Fed began to target money supply rather than interest rates, there is no evidence of debt monetization.

Webster, in assessing recent research on the relationship between budget deficits and interest rates, suggests that results are mixed.

In addition, studies generally found that budget deficits did not have much effect on debt monetization even during the interest rate targeting period. Research by Hein found that deficits cause inflation only when they are monetized.

Research by Carlson found that

■ Nominal interest rates are affected by monetary policies but not significantly by fiscal policies.

■ Output is affected by monetary policies in the short run but not significantly by either monetary or fiscal policies in the long run.

■ The level of investment is affected only temporarily by monetary policy but permanently by fiscal policy.

SOURCE: Keith M. Carlson, "The Mix of Monetary and Fiscal Policies: Conventional Wisdom vs. Empirical Reality," *Review*, Federal Reserve Bank of St. Louis (October 1982): 7–20; Scott Hein, "Deficits and Inflations," *Review*, Federal Reserve Bank of St. Louis (March 1981): 19–24; Preston J. Miller, "Higher Deficit Policies Lead to Higher Inflation", *Quarterly Review*, Federal Reserve Bank of Minneapolis (Winter 1983): 8–20; Daniel L. Thornton, "Monetizing the Debt," *Review*, Federal Reserve Bank of St. Louis (December 1984): 30–43; and Charles E. Webster, Jr. "The Effects of Deficits on Interest Rates," *Economic Review*, Federal Reserve Bank of Kansas City (May 1983): 19–28.

ability of various securities. The composition can also affect the level of investment and therefore aggregate demand. For example, if the Treasury uses a relatively large proportion of long-term debt, this would place upward pressure on long-term yields. Because long-term investment is sensitive to long-term financing rates, corporations may reduce their investment in fixed assets. Conversely, if the Treasury uses mostly short-term securities to finance its deficit, long-term interest rates may be relatively low, thereby stimulating corporate investment in fixed assets.

The degree to which the Treasury's debt management policy will affect the term structure of interest rates depends on the degree of segmentation between markets. If investors and borrowers are willing to switch to different maturities, the impact will be reduced. To illustrate, assume that the current term structure of interest rates can be characterized by an upward-sloping yield curve. Also assume that the Treasury restructures its debt by using the proceeds of newly issued short-term securities to retire long-term securities. There is initial upward pressure on short-term yields and down-

Chapter 14

Financial Market
Reaction to Fiscal Policy

EXHIBIT 14.7   Deficit Forecasts by the CBO at Three Points in Time

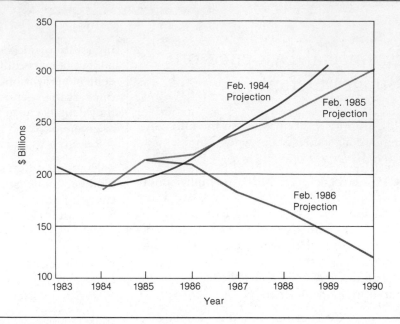

SOURCE: *FRBSF Weekly Letter*, August 1, 1986.

ward pressure on long-term yields. However, some investors may switch from long-term securities to short-term securities in response to the changing yield curve. In addition, some borrowers may switch from short-term debt to long-term debt to capitalize on the changing yield curve. These reactions partially offset the initial pressure caused by the Treasury's debt management strategy.

INTEGRATION OF FISCAL AND MONETARY POLICIES

The presidential administration has historically been most concerned with the objective of maintaining strong economic growth and low unemployment. The Fed generally shared the same concern in the early 1970s. A year before President Nixon's reelection in 1972, the economy was somewhat stagnant, and inflation was higher than in previous years. Nixon's Administration and the Fed combined their power to resolve their problems. The administration enforced wage-price controls (although many exceptions were allowed) in order to limit inflation, while the Fed used a stimulative monetary policy to reduce unemployment. While such a stimulative policy can normally lead to higher inflation, the wage-price controls temporarily prevented inflationary consequences. By the time of reelection, economic conditions had improved, which was a primary reason for Nixon's victory. Yet, when wage-price controls were lifted in 1973, inflation increased.

By 1980 and 1981, inflation was close to 10 percent annually, and unemployment was also high. At this time, the present administration attempted to stimulate the economy by reducing tax rates. Yet, the Fed used a relatively tight monetary policy in order to reduce inflation. As expected, the tight money policy slowed economic growth and effectively reduced inflation. While the Fed was given partial credit for lowering inflation, it was also criticized for causing the 1982 recession, and for not resolving the 1982 recession as quickly as it could have. However, if the Fed had used a stimulative policy to eliminate the recession, inflation could have reignited.

The Fed's increased concern for inflation during the early 1980s relative to the 1970s was partially attributed to the appointment of Paul Volcker as chairman in 1979. He was a strong believer in reducing the inflationary spiral that continued throughout the 1970s. Financial market participants who understood his beliefs may have been able to forecast the Fed's anti-inflationary monetary policy during the early 1980s.

The Fed and the administration sometimes differ in whether economic growth (and unemployment) or inflation deserve the most attention. Some of their most intense arguments occurred during the 1982–1983 recession, and the 1984 election period. The frequent arguments during this period are briefly summarized below with the following hypothetical conversation:

Administration:	We are receiving all the criticism from the farmers, auto workers, etc. who are out of work. If you would loosen money supply, interest rates would decline, spending would increase, and jobs would be created.
Fed:	First of all, we are receiving as much criticism from the unemployed as you are. Second, if you didn't create such a large federal deficit, interest rates would already be lower, and you wouldn't have to rely on a loose monetary policy to stimulate the economy.
Administration:	We are currently trying to reduce our budget deficit. In the meantime, your sole concern to reduce inflation is causing millions of people to be unemployed and is therefore reducing our tax revenues and increasing our deficit.
Fed:	If we don't attempt to reduce inflation, who will? You are more interested in the next election, and you believe that higher unemployment causes more lost votes than higher inflation would cause. If we allow excessive growth in the money supply now, the long-term consequences of higher inflation could be devastating. We have witnessed how sustained inflation can force interest rates up, possibly leading to a stagnant economy over time. Thus, the ultimate result could be both high unemployment and inflation if we don't reduce inflation now.
Administration:	We agree that excessive growth in the money supply can lead to continued inflation. But you have been too tight with money lately. Do you think the public is satisfied with your tight money policy?
Fed:	The public may not understand that while our policy is painful now, it will benefit them over the long run.
Administration:	Do you think that unemployed people are going to believe that?
Fed:	Probably not. And you certainly don't make it any easier by claiming that it is our fault that they are unemployed.
Administration:	So when are you going to loosen up in order to end this severe recession?
Fed:	When it appears that loosening up will not reignite inflation.
Administration:	How long are you willing to wait for such conditions, while millions of people are without jobs?
Fed:	As long as necessary!

To conclude this argument, the Fed did loosen money supply in 1983, causing a significant decline in interest rates. The economy subsequently improved, and inflation remained low. Looking back at the results, some critics use these results as evidence to claim that the Fed could have loosened money supply earlier to more quickly eliminate the recession, without reigniting inflation. Others suggest that the Fed's policy worked only because it was implemented after inflation had fully subsided. Finally, others claim that the Fed purposely maintained a relatively tight monetary policy to demonstrate that it makes its own decisions and will not surrender to pressure by any presidential administration.

Up to this point, it has been suggested that the Fed is independent of the administration. With regard to decision making, the Fed makes its own decisions; however, its decisions may be influenced by actions of the administration. Assume that the Fed has set monetary growth targets which under existing conditions are expected to achieve their long-term goals. Then the administration decides to implement a new fiscal policy that will result in more government expenditures, without increasing tax revenues. Consequently, the federal deficit will now become larger than what was originally expected. The Fed must first assess the potential impact that this new fiscal policy will have on the economy. One possible effect is that the increased government spending could stimulate the economy. If this is the most likely impact, the Fed's only concern may be that the policy could lead to higher inflation, in which case it may adjust its monetary policy to counter the stimulative impact of the new fiscal policy and thus avoid inflationary consequences. That is, it would consider tightening money more than originally planned.

A second and more likely concern of the Fed is that the new fiscal policy would increase the budget deficit and therefore increase interest rates. In this case, it could counter by loosening money supply, which might offset the increased demand for loanable funds by the federal government. This action is known as **monetizing the debt,** as the Fed is partially financing the federal deficit. Exhibit 14.8 illustrates how this works. As the Treasury issues new Treasury securities in the primary market in order to finance the deficit, there may be upward pressure on interest rates. The Fed could offset this pressure by using open market operations to purchase Treasury securities (from government securities dealers) in the secondary market. Before the Fed monetizes the debt, it may first monitor how the additional borrowing by the Treasury is affecting interest rates. If there is no significant change in interest rates, the Fed may decide not to intervene.

When the Fed purchases Treasury securities, the Treasury must repurchase the securities at maturity just as if an individual or a firm owned them. Thus, Treasury securities held by the Fed still reflect debt from the Treasury's perspective. However, the Treasury may sometimes prefer for the Fed to monetize the debt, since if it does not, interest rates could rise and reduce economic growth.

Market Reaction to Integrated Policies

Financial market participants must consider the potential policies of both the administration (fiscal) and the Fed (monetary) when assessing future economic conditions. Exhibit 14.9 provides a broad overview of how the

Does Debt Monetization Depend on the Debt Level?

When government budget deficits grow, central banks may desire to monetize the debt. Such action could relieve the upward pressure on interest rates caused by the budget deficit. However, it can also ignite inflationary fears. A recent study by Protopapadakis and Siegel examined the historical relationship between the budget deficit and the money supply growth. A positive correlation between the budget deficit and excess money supply growth would suggest that central banks are more likely to monetize the debt during periods of excessive government borrowing.

The authors defined average excess debt growth as the average debt growth minus average real output. They defined average excess money growth as average monetary base (currency plus reserves) growth minus average real output. A rank correlation test was conducted to determine if there was any positive association between the two variables for ten different countries. The test found no significant association. Therefore, the degree of excess money supply growth does not appear to be related to the level of excess debt growth, suggesting that central banks can implement monetary policies that are not directly in response to fiscal policies.

SOURCE: Aris Protopapadakis and Jeremy J. Siegel, "Are Government Deficits Monetized?" *Business Review*, Federal Reserve Bank of Philadelphia (November–December 1986): 13–22.

EXHIBIT 14.8   Monetization of Debt by the Fed

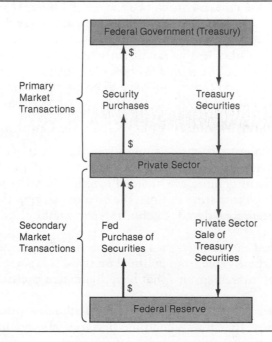

EXHIBIT 14.9   Simultaneous Assessment of Fiscal and Monetary Policies

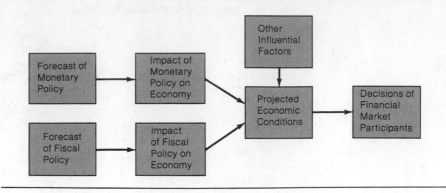

participants monitor monetary and fiscal policy actions. They forecast the type of monetary and fiscal policies that will be implemented and then determine how these anticipated policies will affect future economic conditions. For example, they must forecast shifts in the supply and demand for loanable funds, and this requires a forecast of the factors that affect them. The supply of loanable funds can be affected by the Fed's adjustment of the money supply or any changes in tax policies by the administration. The demand for loanable funds is affected by any change in inflationary expectations, which can be influenced by fluctuations in money supply or aggregate demand. In addition, the demand for loanable funds is affected by government expenditures. Tax revisions could also affect the demand for loanable funds if they affect the incentive for firms or individuals to borrow.

Once forecasts of the supply and demand for loanable funds are completed, interest rate movements can be forecasted. Interest rate projections are necessary to forecast the aggregate demand for goods and services, which will influence the level of economic growth, the unemployment rate, and inflation rate. Other factors not directly related to government policies also have an impact on the economic variables, such as oil prices and labor contract situations, and these, too, have to be considered.

Should Fiscal and Monetary Policy Goals Be Combined?

The U.S. government structure is unique in that its monetary and fiscal policymaking agencies are independent of each other. In other countries, monetary and fiscal policies are blended together in order to achieve congruent objectives. From time to time, the idea of merging the Fed with the Treasury has been considered. Such a merger would eliminate the Fed's independence.

Because the Fed can make its own decisions, it can implement a monetary policy that is virtually free from political motives. It is somewhat insulated from the special interest groups that have significant political influence on fiscal policy.

However, since the Fed and the presidential administration are independent of each other, they may sometimes disagree on economic remedies to the extent that the monetary policy implemented will offset the fiscal policy, or vice versa. The power of each agency can reduce the ability of the other to control the economy in the manner desired. The ultimate result of their combined policy actions may therefore fail to achieve what either side desired.

There is no consensus as to whether the Fed should remain independent. If it merged with the Treasury, perhaps the two sides could work together toward a common goal. Yet, because of the differences between them, their goals might never be completely compatible.

SUMMARY

Since fiscal policy can have a significant impact on economic conditions, financial market participants attempt to forecast both the future policy and its impact and both are very difficult to forecast with precision. Yet, even imperfect forecasts can provide valuable input for borrowing and investing decisions.

KEY TERMS

crowding-out effect
debt management
monetizing the debt

QUESTIONS

14.1. What is a primary role of the Office of Management and Budget (OMB)?

14.2. How can fiscal policy be used to influence economic growth?

14.3. Discuss the economic trade-off involved in fiscal policy actions taken to reduce inflation and unemployment.

14.4. Explain how an increase in government expenditures can affect tax revenues.

14.5. Compare the approximate average annual deficit in the late 1970s to the average annual deficit in the mid 1980s. Explain in general terms why it has grown.

14.6. Why does the deficit as a percent of GNP increase during recessionary periods?

14.7. Should the debt ceiling influence market projections of the future level of federal debt? Explain.

14.8. At times, the monetary and fiscal policies can complement each other. Describe how this happened in 1972.

14.9. Do you think the Fed used a monetary policy in the early 1980s that was too tight? Explain.

14.10. Is the Fed independent of the presidential administration? Explain.

14.11. Explain the meaning of monetizing the debt. How can this action improve economic conditions? What is the risk involved?

14.12. Describe the crowding-out effect. What causes it, and what are its implications?

14.13. Explain why a cut in the corporate tax rate might increase corporate tax revenues. (See the appendix.)

14.14. Compare the time frames of each lag between fiscal policy and monetary policy. (See the appendix.)

14.15. How could the Treasury's decision to finance its deficit with mostly long-term funds affect the term structure of interest rates? If short-term and long-term markets are segmented, would the Treasury's decision have a more or less pronounced impact on the term structure? Explain.

14.16. Assess the economic situation today. Is the administration more concerned with reducing unemployment or inflation? Does the Fed have a similar opinion? If not, is the administration publicly criticizing the Fed? Is the Fed publicly criticizing the administration? Explain.

PROJECT

1. The Treasury will periodically issue new bonds to finance its deficit. Review recent issues of *The Wall Street Journal* or check its index in your library to find a recent article on such financing. Does the article suggest that financial markets are expecting upward pressure on interest rates as a result of the Treasury financing? Is the Fed expected to intervene in order to reduce the potential impact on interest rates (according to the article)? What happened to prices of existing bonds when the Treasury announced its intentions to issue new bonds?

REFERENCES

Carlson, John B. and E. J. Stevens. "The National Debt: A Secular Perspective." *Economic Review*, Federal Reserve Bank of Cleveland (3rd Quarter 1985): 11–24.

Carlson, Keith M. "The Mix of Monetary and Fiscal Policies: Conventional Wisdom vs. Empirical Reality." *Review*, Federal Reserve Bank of St. Louis (October 1982): 7–20.

Cunningham, Thomas J. and Rosemary Thomas Cunningham. "Projecting Federal Deficits and the Impact of The Gramm-Rudman-Hollins Budget Cuts." *Economic Review*, Federal Reserve Bank of Atlanta (May 1986): 19–24.

Hein, Scott. "Deficits and Inflation." *Review*, Federal Reserve Bank of St. Louis (March 1981): 3–10.

Horrigan, Brian R. "The Tax Reform Controversy: A Guide for the Perplexed." *Business Review*, Federal Reserve Bank of Philadelphia (May–June 1985): 3–15.

Horrigan, Brian and Aris Protopapadakis. "Federal Deficits: A Faulty Gauge of Government's Impact on Financial Markets." *Business Review*, Federal Reserve Bank of Philadelphia (March–April 1982): 3–16.

Huang, Roger D. "Does Monetization of Federal Debt Matter?" *Journal of Money, Credit, and Banking* (August 1986): 275–289.

Kahn, George A. "Investment in Recession and Recovery." *Economic Review*, Federal Reserve Bank of Kansas City (November 1985): 25–38.

McHugh, Richard. "Productivity and the Prospects for Outgrowing the Budget Deficit." *Business Review*, Federal Reserve Bank of Philadelphia (January–February 1986): 15–23.

McNees, Stephen K. "The Current Expansion in Historical Perspective." *New England Economic Review*, Federal Reserve Bank of Boston (November–December 1984): 5–8.

Miller, Glenn H., Jr. "The Value-Added Tax: Cash Cow or Pig in a Poke." *Economic Review*, Federal Reserve Bank of Kansas City (September–October 1986): 3–15.

Miller, Preston J. "Budget Deficit Mythology." *Quarterly Review*, Federal Reserve Bank of Minneapolis (Fall 1983): 1–13.

Miller, Preston J. "Higher Deficit Policies Lead to Higher Inflation." *Quarterly Review*, Federal Reserve Bank of Minneapolis (Winter 1983): 8–20.

Miller, Richard B. "Henry Reuss Talks About the Fed and Other Problems." *The Bankers Magazine* (May–June 1983): 43–47.

Munnell, Alicia H. "The Economics of Tax Simplification: An Overview." *New England Economic Review*, Federal Reserve Bank of Boston (January–February): 12–27.

Protopapadakis, Aris. "Supply–Side Economics: What Chance for Success?" *Business Review*, Federal Reserve Bank of Philadelphia (May–June 1981): 11–23.

Protopapadakis, Aris and Jeremy J. Siegel. "Are Government Deficits Monetized?" *Business Review*, Federal Reserve Bank of Philadelphia (November–December 1986): 13–22.

Roley, Vance V. "The Financing of Federal Deficits: An Analysis of Crowding Out." *Economic Review*, Federal Reserve Bank of Kansas City (July–August 1981): 16–30.

Siegel, Jeremy J. and Aris Protopapadakis. "Are Government Deficits Monetized? Some International Evidence." *Business Review*, Federal Reserve Bank of Philadelphia (November–December 1986): 13–22.

Tatom, John A. "A Perspective on the Federal Deficit Problem." *Review*, Federal Reserve Bank of St. Louis (June–July 1984): 5–17.

Thornton, Daniel L. "Monetizing the Debt." *Review*, Federal Reserve Bank of St. Louis (December 1984): 30–43.

Tobin, James. "The Monetary and Fiscal Policy Mix." *Economic Review*, Federal Reserve Bank of Atlanta (August–September 1986): 4–16.

Webster, Charles E., Jr. "The Effects of Deficits on Interest Rates." *Economic Review*, Federal Reserve Bank of Kansas City (May 1983): 19–28.

Weiner, Stuart E. "The Natural Rate of Unemployment: Concepts and Issues." *Economic Review*, Federal Reserve Bank of Kansas City (January 1986): 11–24.

APPENDIX 14

Special Topics on Fiscal Policy

THEORIES ABOUT FISCAL POLICY

Recall that aggregate demand is composed of consumption, capital investment (by corporations) and government expenditures. If a government policy can increase any one of these components without offsetting the others, aggregate demand can be increased. Fiscal policy can affect aggregate demand in various ways. First, a reduction in taxes could increase household consumption. Second, a reduction in business taxes could increase business investment. Third, an increase in government expenditures represents an increase in aggregate demand. While any components of aggregate demand can be influenced, the net impact of fiscal policy actions is debatable. A reduction in tax rates may result in a reduction in tax revenues, which may result in a reduction in government expenditures.

An increase in government expenditures requires either more tax revenues or borrowing from the public. Monetarists suggest that while a fiscal policy that increases government expenditures would increase aggregate demand, the government spending causes a crowding-out effect that decreases consumption and capital investment. The additional borrowing by the government to support increased expenditures places upward pressure on interest rates. Spending by consumers and businesses is reduced as a result of the higher cost of borrowing. Monetarists claim that the reduction in these components of aggregate demand will completely offset the increase in government expenditures. This is described as a *complete crowding-out effect*. Keynesians agree that interest rates would increase as a result of the additional government spending but do not believe that a complete offset takes place.

Because monetarists believe additional government spending is completely offset, they do not recommend government intervention. They suggest that the economy can correct itself. Conversely, Keynesians see a potential net benefit from adjusting government expenditures and therefore recommend government intervention to resolve economic problems. Moreover, because they have a shorter-run view than Monetarists, they are less willing to wait for self-correcting mechanisms to take effect. For obvious reasons, Keynesians are sometimes called activists and Monetarists non-activists. While both strive for similar economic objectives, their methods differ completely; and it is difficult to determine from historical data which approach has had better results, since the two cannot be implemented simultaneously (and no two historical situations are identical). In addition, there are different opinions within the Keynesian and Monetarist groups as to the precise solution to an economic problem.

DEMAND VERSUS SUPPLY-SIDE FISCAL POLICIES

Demand-management policies that affect that level of aggregate spending have historically been used often. However, supply-side policies, which are designed to affect the total supply of goods and services offered, did not become popular until the early 1980s. Supply-siders believe that, for example, a reduction in business taxes should encourage businesses to offer a greater supply of goods and services at any given price level, because more projects appear feasible when the tax rates are lower. A special tax deduction (such as the investment tax credit) reduces the after-tax purchase price of a project. In either case, the incentive for additional production exists.

Arthur Laffer, a well-known economist and proponent of supply-side economics, advised President Reagan to reduce corporate tax rates in the early 1980s. The precise corporate tax rate that would maximize corporate tax revenues is difficult to determine. As it is increased to 5 percent, 10 percent, etc., corporate tax revenues are expected to increase. At some point, the corporate tax revenues will be maximized. Any average tax rate beyond that point would result in lower tax revenues, as corporations would have less incentive to increase their earnings (since much of it would be taxed away). At extremely high average tax rates, corporate tax revenues would be very low, since there would be very little incentive to do business.

Tax revenues do not automatically increase because of higher corporate tax rates or decrease because of lower corporate tax rates. Therefore, the impact of a tax change on the federal budget deficit and on interest rates is unclear. This discussion is intended to illustrate further the complexity involved in assessing how fiscal policy actions affect the economy.

LAGS IN FISCAL POLICY

As with monetary policy, fiscal policy is subject to lags. The *recognition lag*, which lasts from the time an economic problem occurs until it is recognized, should be somewhat similar for both fiscal and monetary policy, since the administration and the Fed monitor the same measures of GNP growth, unemployment, inflation, etc. The *implementation lag*, which is the period from when an economic problem is recognized until policy action is implemented, is typically longer for fiscal policy than for monetary policy, since fiscal policy actions (such as a tax cut or changes in government spending plans) must work their way through Congress before they can be implemented. Finally, the *impact lag*, which is the time from when action is taken until it has an impact, is typically shorter for fiscal policy than monetary policy. Financial market participants must account for lags in fiscal policy so that they can anticipate the timing of fiscal policy's impact on economic variables.

Commercial Banking

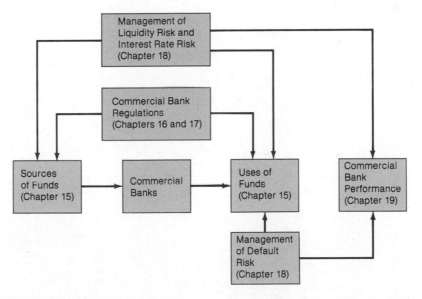

The chapters in Part Five focus on commercial banking. Chapter 15 identifies the common sources and uses of funds for commercial banks while Chapters 16 and 17 describe the regulations imposed on sources and uses of funds and other banking operations. Chapter 18 explains how sources and uses of funds are managed by banks to deal with risk. Chapter 19 explains how commercial bank performance can be measured and monitored to assess previous managerial policies. Chapter 20 describes commercial bank regulation, management, and performance from an international perspective.

Commercial Bank Financial Structure

BANK FINANCIAL STRUCTURE IN PERSPECTIVE

The key to any commercial bank's success is the selection of its sources and uses of funds. First Union Bank's 1987 annual report substantiates the importance of sources and uses of funds. This annual report suggests the following:

■ One of First Union's greatest strengths is its level of customer deposits. Its emphasis on customer deposits rather than alternative sources of funds enabled it to achieve a lower cost of funds.

■ Deposits are the key to First Union's growth potential. Total deposits have increased substantially over time, amounting to $17.4 billion at the beginning of 1988. First Union also had $9 billion in other funds at that time.

■ First Union typically reinvests 70 to 76 percent of its earnings back into the corporation, distributing the remainder to shareholders in the form of dividends. This policy has enabled First Union to build its capital base and exceed the minimum capital guidelines imposed by regulators.

■ First Union prefers to use equity (such as retained earnings) rather than long-term debt as a source of capital. It monitors its long-term debt to equity ratio, attempting to maintain the ratio at less than 50 percent.

■ In addition to the traditional lending operations, First Union has diversified into trusts, discount brokerage, and the origination of mortgages.

■ What other sources of funds does First Union or any other commercial bank have access to?

■ How does the selection of fund sources affect the cost of funds?

■ How do sources and uses of funds affect the risk of First Union or any other bank?

■ How do large banks differ from small banks with respect to sources of funds?

■ How do large banks differ from small banks with respect to uses of funds?

These and other related questions concerning commercial bank operations are addressed in this chapter.

OUTLINE

Commercial banks represent the most important financial intermediary when measured by total assets. Like other financial intermediaries, they perform a critical function of facilitating the flow of funds from surplus units to deficit units. This chapter describes the financial structure of commercial banks, first addressing the common sources of funds and then the common uses of funds. This information offers a foundation for understanding bank regulations (Chapters 16 and 17), management (Chapter 18), and performance (Chapter 19).

BANK SOURCES OF FUNDS

The major sources of commercial bank funds are

Deposit accounts

1. Transaction deposits
2. Savings deposits
3. Time deposits
4. Money market deposit accounts

Borrowed funds

1. Federal funds purchased (borrowed)
2. Borrowing from the Federal Reserve banks
3. Repurchase agreements
4. Eurodollar borrowings

Long-term sources of funds

1. Bonds issued by the bank
2. Bank capital

Each source of funds is briefly described in turn.

Transaction Deposits

The *demand deposit account* or "checking account" is offered to customers who desire to write checks against their account. The conventional type of demand deposit account requires a small minimum balance and pays no interest. In addition, service fees are usually charged. From the bank's perspective, demand deposit accounts are classified as *transaction accounts* that provide a source of funds that can be used until withdrawn by customers (as checks are written).

In the early 1970s, some financial institutions in the New England area were allowed by their respective state regulatory agencies to offer **negotiable order of withdrawal (NOW) accounts,** which provided checking services as well as interest. These accounts proved popular, and as of 1981, commercial banks (and other depository institutions) throughout the entire country were given the authority to offer them. Because NOW accounts at most financial institutions require a minimum balance beyond what some consumers are willing to maintain in a transaction account, the traditional demand deposit account is still popular. Until 1986 an interest rate ceiling of 5.25 percent was imposed on NOW accounts by regulators, but in January 1986 the ceiling was eliminated. Businesses are not allowed to set up NOW accounts, although regulatory proposals to remove this prohibition are presently being developed.

In January 1983 commercial banks were allowed to offer *SUPER NOW accounts*, which offered an interest rate close to the prevailing market rates but required a minimum balance of $2,500. In 1986 the minimum balance was eliminated, which along with the deregulated rate ceiling on NOW accounts, removed any distinct difference between NOWs and SUPER NOWs. Consequently, banks began to offer just one type of NOW account.

Exhibit 15.1 shows the rapid growth of NOW accounts (including SUPER NOWs) since their inception. Measured here as a percentage of total personal checking balances, NOWs make up almost 70 percent of the total balances, versus less than 5 percent in 1978.

Savings Deposits

The traditional type of savings account is the passbook savings account, which does not permit check-writing. Until 1986 Regulation Q restricted the interest rate banks could offer on passbook savings with the intent of preventing excessive competition that could cause bank failures. Actually, the ceilings hurt commercial banks, because it prevented them from competing for funds during periods of higher interest rates. In 1986 Regulation Q was eliminated. The passbook savings account continues to attract savers with a small amount of funds, as it often has no required minimum balance. While it legally requires a 30-day written notice by

EXHIBIT 15.1 Comparison of Transaction Account Balances Over Time

Deposits Shift into NOWs and Super NOWs

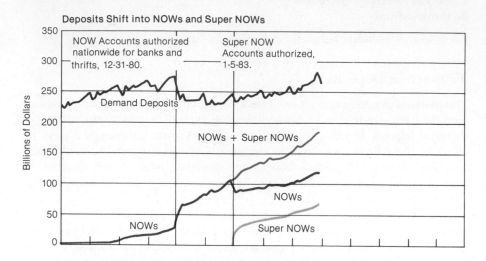

The Changing Composition of Personal Checking Account Balances

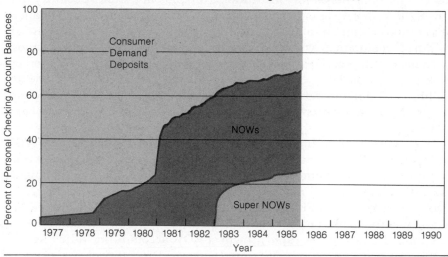

SOURCE: *FRBSF Weekly Letter*, November 14, 1986.

customers to withdraw funds, most banks will allow withdrawals from these accounts on a moment's notice.

Another type of savings account is the *automatic transfer service (ATS) account*, created in November 1978. It allows customers the ability to maintain an interest-bearing savings account that automatically transfers funds to their checking account when checks are written. Only the amount of funds needed is transferred to the checking account. Thus, the ATS provides interest and check-writing ability to customers. Some ATS accounts were eliminated when the NOW accounts were established.

Time Deposits

A common type of time deposit, known as a **retail certificate of deposit** (or *retail CD*), requires a specified minimum amount of funds to be deposited for a specified period of time. When the first short-term retail CDs were created in 1978, their minimum balances were enforced by industry regulators. In addition, their interest rates were tied to the T-bill rate, and only three- and six-month maturities were available. Throughout the early 1980s, the interest rate, maturity, and minimum balance regulations on retail CDs began to loosen, and they no longer exist today. Banks are now able to offer a CD that better meets an individual's needs. Most offer a wide variety, with maturities as short as 7 days and annualized interest rates that vary among banks, and even among maturity types within a single bank. An organized secondary market for retail CDs does not exist. Depositors must leave their funds in the bank until the specified maturity, or they will normally forego a portion of their interest as a penalty.

The interest rates on retail CDs have historically been fixed. However, in 1987, a CD was offered with a rate that would vary each year in accordance with market rates. Other CDs offered savers a minimum guaranteed return and an option to earn a higher rate at a particular point in time if market rates had risen by then. Some CD rates are tied to the performance of a stock market index but guarantee a minimum rate (such as 4 percent or so) regardless of the stock market's performance. There are *bull-market CDs* that reward depositors if the market performs well and *bear-market CDs* that reward depositors if the market performs poorly. These new types of retail CDs typically have a minimum deposit of $1,000 to $5,000. Like the more conventional CDs, they qualify for deposit insurance (assuming that the depository institution of concern is insured). Only time will tell whether these innovative CDs become popular.

Another type of time deposit is the **negotiable CD (NCD),** offered by some large banks to corporations. NCDs are similar to retail CDs in that they require a specified maturity date and a minimum deposit. Their maturities are typically short-term, and their minimum deposit requirement is $100,000 or more. A secondary market for NCDs does exist.

Exhibit 15.2 illustrates recent trends in small and large time deposits. The level of large time deposits is much more volatile, since investors with large sums of money frequently shift their funds to wherever they can receive higher rates. Small investors do not have as many options as large investors and are less likely to shift in and out of small time deposits.

A comparison of time and savings deposit volume as a percentage of total sources of funds is displayed in Exhibit 15.3. Demand deposits now make up about 20 percent of funds, versus 70 percent in 1950. Time and savings deposits now account for over 50 percent of funds, versus about 23 percent in 1950.

Money Market Deposit Accounts

The *money market deposit account (MMDA)* was created by a provision of the Garn–St Germain Act of December, 1982. It differs from conventional time deposits in that it does not specify a maturity. MMDAs are available to individuals and businesses. They are more liquid than retail CDs from

EXHIBIT 15.2   Level of Small and Large Time Deposits Over Time

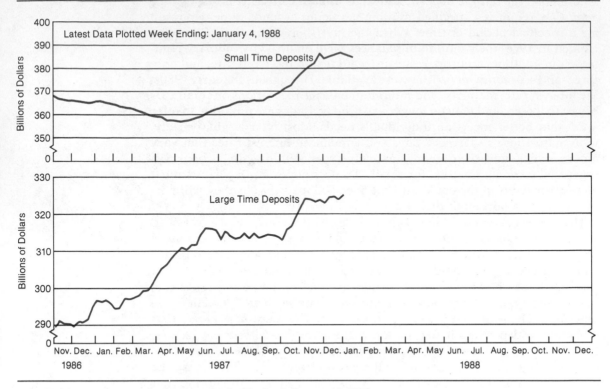

SOURCE: *Financial Data*, Federal Reserve Bank of St. Louis (January 14, 1988).

the depositor's point of view. Because banks would prefer to know how long they will have use of a depositor's funds, they normally pay a higher interest rate on CDs. MMDAs differ from NOW accounts in that they have limited check-writing ability (they only allow a limited number of transactions per month), require a larger minimum balance, and offer a higher yield. The bank's cost of funds obtained through MMDAs is volatile, since its MMDA rate quickly adjusts to market conditions.

The remaining sources of funds to be described are of a nondepository nature. Such sources are necessary when a bank temporarily needs more funds than are being deposited. It should be mentioned that some banks use nondepository funds as a permanent source of funds.

Federal Funds Purchased

The federal funds market allows depository institutions to accommodate the short-term liquidity needs of other financial institutions. Federal funds "purchased" (or borrowed) represent a liability to the borrowing bank and an asset to the lending bank that "sells" them. Loans in the federal funds market are often for one to seven days. Such loans can be rolled over, so that a series of one-day loans could take place. Yet, the intent of federal funds transactions is to correct short-term fund imbalances experienced by banks. A bank may act as a lender of federal funds on one day and as a borrower shortly thereafter, as its fund balance changes on a daily basis.

EXHIBIT 15.3 **Comparison of Demand Deposits and Time and Savings Deposits as a Percentage of Total Fund Sources at Commercial Banks**

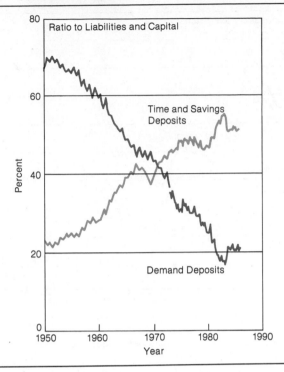

SOURCE: Federal Reserve Chart Book (1987): 83.

The interest rate charged in the federal funds market is called the **federal funds rate.** Like other market interest rates, it moves in reaction to changes in the demand and/or supply. If many banks have excess funds and few banks are short of funds, the federal funds rate will be low. Conversely, a high demand by many banks to borrow federal funds relative to a small supply of excess funds available at other banks will result in a higher federal funds rate. Whatever rate exists will typically be the same for all banks borrowing in the federal funds market, although a financially troubled bank may have to pay a higher rate in order to obtain federal funds (to compensate for its higher risk). The federal funds rate is quoted in multiples of one-sixteenth, on an annualized basis (using a 360-day year). Exhibit 15.4 shows that the federal funds rate is generally between .25 percent and 1.00 percent above the Treasury bill rate. The difference normally increases when the perceived risk of banks increases.

The federal funds market is typically most active on Wednesday, since it is the final day of each particular settlement period for which each bank must maintain a specified volume of reserves required by the Fed. Those banks that were short of required reserves on average over the period must compensate with additional required reserves before the settlement period ends. Large banks frequently need temporary funds and therefore are common borrowers in the federal funds market.

Chapter 15

Commercial Bank
Financial Structure

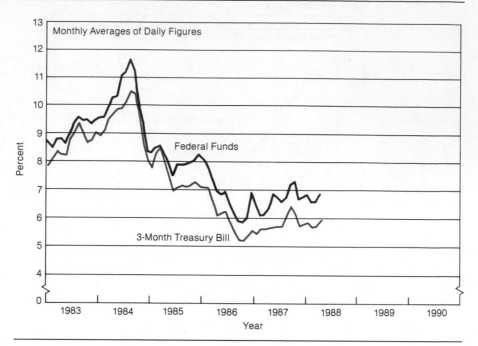

SOURCE: *Monetary Trends*, Federal Reserve Bank of St. Louis (May 1988).

Borrowing from the Federal Reserve Banks

Another temporary source of funds for banks is the Federal Reserve System, which serves as the U.S. central bank. Along with other bank regulators, the Federal Reserve district banks regulate certain activities of banks. Yet, they will also provide short-term loans to banks (as well as to some other depository institutions). This form of borrowing by banks is often referred to as "borrowing at the discount window." The interest rate charged on these loans is known as the **discount rate.**

Loans from the discount window are short-term, commonly from one day to a few weeks. Banks that wish to borrow at the discount window must first be approved by the Fed before a loan is granted. This is intended to make sure that the bank's need for funds is justified. Like the federal funds market, the discount window is mainly used to resolve a temporary shortage of funds. If a bank needed more permanent sources of funds, it would develop a strategy to increase its level of deposits.

When a bank needs temporary funds, it must decide whether borrowing through the discount window is more feasible than alternative nondepository sources of funds, such as the federal funds market. Exhibit 15.5 shows that the federal funds rate is more volatile than the discount rate. This is because it is market-determined, as it adjusts to demand and supply conditions on a daily basis. Conversely, the discount rate is set by the Federal Reserve and adjusted only periodically to keep it in line with other market rates (such as the federal funds rate).

Part Five

Commercial Banking

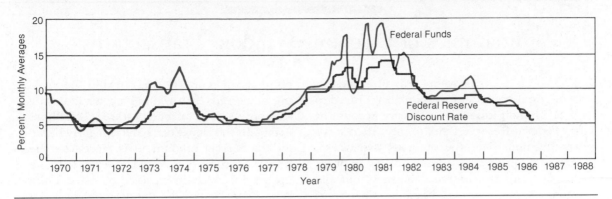

EXHIBIT 15.5   Movements in the Federal Funds Rate and Discount Rate Over Time

SOURCE: *Economic Trends*, Federal Reserve Bank of Cleveland (1987).

Banks commonly borrow in the federal funds market rather than through the discount window even though the federal funds rate typically exceeds the discount rate. This is because the Fed offers the discount window as a source of funds for banks that experience *unanticipated* shortages of reserves. If a bank frequently borrows to offset reserve shortages, these shortages should have been anticipated. Such frequent borrowing implies that the commercial bank has a permanent rather than temporary need for funds and should therefore satisfy this need with a more permanent source of funds. The Fed may disapprove of continuous borrowing by a bank unless there were extenuating circumstances, such as if the bank was experiencing financial problems and could not obtain temporary financing from other financial institutions.

Repurchase Agreements

A repurchase agreement *(repo)* represents the sale of securities by one party to another with an agreement to repurchase the securities at a specified date and price. Banks often use a repo as a source of funds, when they expect to need funds for just a few days. They would simply sell some of their government securities (such as their Treasury bills) to a corporation with a temporary excess of funds, and buy those securities back shortly thereafter. The government securities involved in the repo transaction serve as collateral for the corporation providing funds to the bank.

Repurchase agreement transactions occur through a telecommunications network connecting large banks, other corporations, government securities dealers, and federal funds brokers.The federal funds brokers match up those firms or dealers who need funds (wish to sell and later repurchase their securities) with those who have excess funds (are willing to purchase securities now and sell them back on a specified date). Transactions are typically in blocks of $1 million. Like the federal funds rate, the yield on repurchase agreements is quoted in multiples of one-sixteenth on an annualized basis (using a 360-day year). The yield on repurchase agreements is slightly less than the federal funds rate at any given point in time, since the funds loaned out are backed by collateral and are therefore less risky.

Examples of Discount Window Transactions

EXAMPLE 1. It is Wednesday afternoon at a regional bank, and the bank is required to have enough funds in its reserve account at its Federal Reserve Bank to meet its reserve requirement over the previous two weeks. The bank finds that it must borrow in order to make up its reserve deficiency, but the money center (that is, the major New York, Chicago, and California) banks have apparently been borrowing heavily in the federal funds market. As a result, the rate on fed funds on this particular Wednesday afternoon has soared far above its level earlier that day. As far as the funding officer of the regional bank is concerned, the market for funds at a price she considers acceptable has "dried up." She calls the Federal Reserve Bank for a discount window loan.

EXAMPLE 2. A West Coast regional bank, which generally avoids borrowing at the discount window, expects to receive a wire transfer of $300 million from a New York bank, but by late afternoon the money has

not yet shown up. It turns out that the sending bank had, due to an error, accidentally sent only $3,000 instead of the $300 million. Although the New York bank is legally liable for the correct amount, it is closed by the time the error is discovered. In order to make up the deficiency in its reserve position, the West Coast bank calls the discount window for a loan.

EXAMPLE 3. It is Wednesday reserve account settlement at another bank, and the funding officer notes that the spread between the discount rate and fed funds rate has widened slightly. Since his bank is buying fed funds to make up a reserve deficiency, he decides to borrow part of the reserve deficiency from the discount window in order to take advantage of the spread. Over the next few months, this repeats itself until the bank receives an "informational" call from the discount officer at the Federal Reserve Bank, inquiring as to the reason for the apparent pattern in discount window borrowing. Tak-

Eurodollar Borrowings

If a U.S. bank is in need of short-term funds, it may borrow from those banks outside the United States that accept dollar-denominated deposits, or **Eurodollars.** Some of these so-called **Eurobanks** are foreign banks or foreign branches of U.S. banks that participate in the Eurodollar market by accepting large short-term deposits and making short-term loans in dollars. Because U.S. dollars are widely used as an international medium of exchange, the Eurodollar market is very active. Some U.S. banks commonly obtain short-term funds from Eurobanks.

Bonds Issued by the Bank

Like other corporations, banks own some fixed assets such as land, buildings, equipment, etc. These assets often have an expected life of 20 years or

ing the hint, the bank refrains from continuing the practice on subsequent Wednesday settlements.

EXAMPLE 4. A money center bank acts as a clearing agent for the government securities market. This means that the bank maintains book-entry securities accounts for market participants, and that it also maintains a reserve account and a book-entry securities account at its Federal Reserve Bank, so that securities transactions can be cleared through this system. One day, an internal computer problem arises that allows the bank to accept securities but not to process them for delivery to dealers, brokers, and other market participants. The bank's reserve account is debited for the amount of these securities, but it is unable to pass them on and collect payment for them, resulting in a growing overdraft in the reserve account. As close of business approaches, it becomes increasingly clear that the problem will not be fixed in time to collect the required payments from the securities buyers. In order to avoid a negative reserve balance at the end of the day, the bank estimates its anticipated reserve account deficiency and goes to the Federal Reserve Bank discount window for a loan for that amount. The computer problem is fixed and the loan is repaid the following day.

EXAMPLE 5. Due to mismanagement, a privately insured savings and loan association fails. Out of concern about the condition of other privately insured thrift institutions in the state, depositors begin to withdraw their deposits, leading to a run. Because they are not federally insured, some otherwise sound thrifts are not able to borrow from the Federal Home Loan Bank Board in order to meet the demands of the depositors. As a result, the regional Federal Reserve Bank is called upon to lend to these thrifts. After an extensive examination of the collateral the thrifts could offer, the Reserve Bank makes loans to them until they are able to get federal insurance and attract back enough deposits to pay back the discount window loans.

SOURCE: *Economic Review*, Federal Reserve Bank of Richmond (May–June 1986): 3.

more and are usually financed with long-term sources of funds, such as through the issuance of bonds. Common purchasers of such bonds are consumers and various financial institutions, including life insurance companies and pension funds. Banks do not finance with bonds as much as most other corporations, since their fixed assets are less than those of corporations that use industrial equipment and machinery for production. Therefore, they have less of a need for long-term funds.

Bank Capital

Bank capital generally represents funds attained through the issuance of stock or through retaining earnings. Either form has no obligation to pay out funds in the future. This distinguishes bank capital from all the other bank sources of funds that represent a future obligation by the bank to pay out funds. Bank capital as defined here represents the equity or net worth of the bank. Capital can be classified into primary or secondary types. Primary capital results from issuing common or preferred stock or retaining earnings, while secondary capital results from issuing subordinated notes and debentures.

A bank's capital must be sufficient to absorb operating losses in the event that expenses and/or losses have exceeded revenues, regardless of the reason for the losses. While long-term bonds are sometimes considered as secondary capital, they are a liability to the bank and therefore do not appropriately cushion against operating losses.

When banks issue new stock, they dilute the ownership of the bank, since the proportion of the bank owned by existing shareholders decreases. In addition, the bank's reported earnings per share is reduced when additional shares of stock are issued, unless earnings increase by a greater proportion than the increase in outstanding shares. For these reasons, banks generally attempt to avoid issuing new stock unless it is absolutely necessary.

Bank regulators are concerned that banks may maintain a lower level of capital than they should and have therefore imposed capital requirements on them. Because capital can absorb losses, a higher level of capital is thought to enhance the bank's safety and may increase the public's confidence in the banking system. In 1981 regulators imposed a minimum primary capital requirement of 5.5 percent of total assets and a minimum total capital requirement of 6 percent of total assets. Due to regulatory pressure, banks have increased their capital ratios in recent years. Exhibit 15.6 shows that the average capital ratio of the 25 largest bank holding companies increased from less than 4.5 percent in 1980 to about 6.5 percent five years later.

Regulatory pressure may sometimes create a dilemma for banks, since they must manage their capital level to satisfy their corporate objectives, but also abide by any capital requirements imposed. Regulators have historically allowed bonds to qualify as capital when determining whether banks have at least maintained the minimum acceptable level.

Summary of Bank Sources of Funds

Because banks cannot completely dictate the amount of deposits to be received, they may experience a shortage of funds. For this reason, the nondepository sources of funds are useful. To support the acquisition of fixed assets, long-term funds are obtained by either issuing long-term bonds, issuing stock, or retaining a sufficient amount of earnings.

COMPARISON OF FUND SOURCES AMONG BANKS

Exhibit 15.7 shows the percentage distribution of fund sources for three different bank size samples, as well as for all banks in the samples examined. Smaller banks rely more heavily on deposits than larger banks. In particular, time and savings deposits make up 66 percent of small bank funds but only about 35 percent of funds for the largest class of banks. This results from small bank concentration on household savings and therefore on small deposits. Much of this differential is made up in foreign deposits, which comprise 19.4 percent of funds for very large banks but zero percent for

EXHIBIT 15.6 Average Capital Ratio of Large Banks Over Time

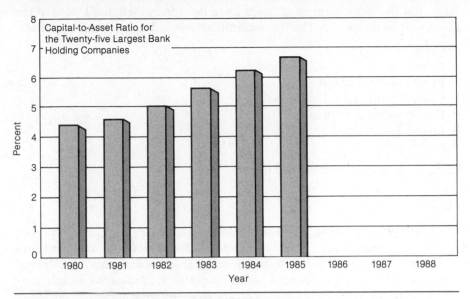

SOURCE: Federal Reserve Bank of New York, Annual Report, 1985, 23.

*Nine months of 1985, annualized.
†September 30, 1985.

EXHIBIT 15.7 Distribution of Bank Fund Sources (by Percentage) among Size Categories

| | Asset Size of Bank | | | |
Source of Funds	$100 Million to $1 Billion	$1 Billion to $5 Billion	$5 Billion or More	All Banks in Sample
Demand deposits	17.7%	20.7%	14.8%	15.8%
Time deposits (greater than $100,000)	12.4	12.1	10.6	11.0
Other time deposits	26.6	21.4	10.4	12.7
Savings deposits	27.0	22.9	13.9	15.8
Foreign deposits	.0	1.7	19.4	16.0
Total deposits	83.7	78.8	69.1	71.3
Short-term borrowings	6.4	11.4	15.1	14.2
Long-term borrowings	1.8	1.3	4.0	3.5
Other liabilities	1.6	2.3	6.5	5.6
Stockholders' equity	6.4	6.2	5.1	5.3
Total liabilities and stockholders' equity	100.0%	100.0%	100.0%	100.0%

SOURCE: *Federal Reserve Bulletin (December 1985).*

small banks. In addition, the larger banks rely more on short-term borrowings (15.1 percent) than small banks (6.4 percent). The impact of the differences in composition of fund sources on bank performance is discussed in Chapter 18.

Chapter 15

Commercial Bank
Financial Structure

USES OF FUNDS BY BANKS

Now that the main sources of funds have been identified, bank uses of the funds will be described. The more common uses of funds by banks include:

- Cash
- Loans
- Investment securities
- Federal funds sold (loaned out)
- Repurchase agreements
- Eurodollar loans
- Fixed assets

Each of these uses is discussed in turn.

Cash

Banks are required to hold some cash as reserves, since they must abide by reserve requirements enforced by the Federal Reserve. Banks also hold cash in order to maintain some liquidity and accommodate any withdrawal requests by depositors. Because banks do not earn income from cash, they will hold only as much cash as necessary to maintain a sufficient degree of liquidity. They can tap various sources for temporary funds and therefore are not overly concerned with maintaining excess reserves.

Banks hold cash in their vaults and at their Federal Reserve district bank. Vault cash is useful for accommodating withdrawal requests by customers or for qualifying as required reserves, while cash placed at the Federal Reserve district banks represents the major portion of required reserves. The required reserves are mandated by the Fed, since they provide a medium by which it can control the money supply. Exhibit 15.8 displays the present reserve requirement percentage applied to each type of deposit. The required reserves of each bank are dependent on the bank's composition of deposits.

Bank Loans

The main use of bank funds is for loans. The loan amount and maturity can be tailored to the borrower's needs.

TYPES OF BUSINESS LOANS. A common type of business loan is the **working capital loan** (sometimes called a "self-liquidating" loan), which is designed to support ongoing business operations. There is a lag between the point at which a firm needs cash to purchase raw materials used in production and receives cash inflows from the sales of finished products. A working capital loan can support the business until sufficient cash inflows are generated. These loans are typically short-term. Yet, they may be needed by businesses on a frequent basis.

Banks also offer **term loans,** primarily to finance the purchase of fixed assets such as machinery. A term loan involves a specified amount of funds to be loaned out, for a specified period of time, and for a specified purpose. The assets purchased with the borrowed funds may serve as partial or full collateral on the loan. Maturities on term loans commonly range from two to five years, and are sometimes as long as ten years.

EXHIBIT 15.8   Reserve Requirements[1]

Type of Deposit, and Deposit Interval[2]	Depository Institution Requirements after Implementation of the Monetary Control Act	
	Percent of Deposits	*Effective Date*
Net transaction accounts[3,4]		
$0 million–$36.7 million	3	12/30/86
More than $36.7 million	12	12/30/86
Nonpersonal time deposits[5]		
By original maturity		
Less than 1½ years	3	10/6/83
1½ years or more	0	10/6/83
Eurocurrency liabilities		
All types	3	11/13/80

1 Reserve requirements in effect on Dec. 31, 1986. Required reserves must be held in the form of deposits with Federal Reserve Banks or vault cash. Nonmembers may maintain reserve balances with a Federal Reserve Bank indirectly on a pass-through basis with certain approved institutions. For previous reserve requirements, see earlier editions of the *Annual Report* and of the FEDERAL RESERVE BULLETIN. Under provisions of the Monetary Control Act, depository institutions include commercial banks, mutual savings banks, savings and loan associations, credit unions, agencies and branches of foreign banks, and Edge corporations.

2 The Garn-St Germain Depository Institutions Act of 1982 (Public Law 97-320) requires that $2 million of reservable liabilities (transaction accounts, nonpersonal time deposits, and Eurocurrency liabilities) of each depository institution be subject to a zero percent reserve requirement. The Board is to adjust the amount of reservable liabilities subject to this zero percent reserve requirement each year for the succeeding calendar year by 80 percent of the percentage increase in the total reservable liabilities of all depository institutions, measured on an annual basis as of June 30. No corresponding adjustment is to be made in the event of a decrease. On Dec. 30, 1986, the exemption was raised from $2.6 million to 2.9 million. In determining the reserve requirements of depository institutions, the exemption shall apply in the following order: (1) net NOW accounts (NOW accounts less allowable deductions); (2) net other transaction accounts; and (3) nonpersonal time deposits or Eurocurrency liabilities starting with those with the highest reserve ratio. With respect to NOW accounts and other transaction accounts, the exemption applies only to such accounts that would be subject to a 3 percent reserve requirement.

3 Transaction accounts include all deposits on which the account holder is permitted to make withdrawals by negotiable or transferable instruments, payment orders of withdrawal, and telephone and preauthorized transfers in excess of three per month for the purpose of making payments to third persons or others. However, MMDAs and similar accounts subject to the rules that permit no more than six preauthorized, automatic, or other transfers per month, of which no more than three can be checks, are not transaction accounts (such accounts are savings deposits subject to time deposit reserve requirements).

4 The Monetary Control Act of 1980 requires that the amount of transaction accounts against which the 3 percent reserve requirement applies be modified annually by 80 percent of the percentage increase in transaction accounts held by all depository institutions, determined as of June 30 each year. Effective Dec. 30, 1986, the amount was increased from $31.7 million to $36.7 million.

5 In general, nonpersonal time deposits are time deposits, including savings deposits, that are not transaction accounts and in which a beneficial interest if held by a depositor that is not a natural person. Also included are certain transferable time deposits held by natural persons and certain obligations issued to depository institution offices located outside the United States. For details, see section 204.2 of Regulation D.

SOURCE: *Federal Reserve Bulletin* (July 1987): A8.

Because of the long-term nature of a term loan, sufficient documentation is needed to specify any conditions that the borrower must abide by. These conditions, often referred to as **protective covenants,** may specify a maximum level of dividends that borrower can pay to shareholders per year, require bank approval on some of the borrowing firm's major decisions (such as mergers), and limit the additional debt that the firm can accumulate. Term loans can be amortized so that fixed periodic payments are made by the borrower over the life of the loan. Alternatively, the bank can request interest payments periodically with the loan principal to be paid off in one lump sum (called a **balloon payment**) at a specified date in the future. This is known as a **bullet loan.** There are also several combinations of these payment methods possible. For example, a portion of the loan may be amortized over the life of the loan, while the remaining portion could be covered with a balloon payment.

As an alternative to providing a term loan, the bank may consider purchasing the assets and leasing them to the firm in need. This method, known as a **direct lease loan,** may be especially appropriate when the firm wishes to avoid further additions of debt on its balance sheet. Because the bank would serve as owner of the assets, it could depreciate the assets over time for tax purposes.

A flexible financing arrangement between banks and businesses, the **informal line of credit,** allows the business to borrow up to a specified amount within a specified period of time. This is useful for firms that may experience a sudden need for funds but do not know precisely when. The interest rate charged on any borrowed funds is typically adjustable in accordance with prevailing market rates. Banks are not legally obligated to provide funds to the business. Yet, They usually honor the arrangement to avoid harming their reputation.

An alternative financing arrangement to the informal line of credit is the **revolving credit loan,** which obligates the bank to offer up to some specified maximum amount of funds over a specified period of time (typically less than five years). Because the bank is committed to provide funds when requested, it normally charges businesses a commitment fee (of about ½ percent) on any unused funds.

CHANGING COLLATERAL REQUIREMENTS ON BUSINESS LOANS. Commercial banks are increasingly accepting intangible assets—such as patents, brand names, and licenses to franchise and distributorships—as collateral for commercial loans. This change is especially important to service-oriented companies that do not have the tangible assets.

LENDER LIABILITY ON BUSINESS LOANS. In recent years, businesses that previously obtained loans from banks are filing lawsuits, claiming that the banks terminated further financing without sufficient notice. These so-called *lender liability* suits have been prevalent in the farming industry. Some farmers claimed that they were encouraged by banks to borrow, yet were cut off from additional financing necessary to make their projects successful and thus lost the land and equipment representing collateral. Lender liability lawsuits have also been filed by companies in other industries, including grocery, clothing, and oil.

TYPES OF CONSUMER LOANS. Commercial banks provide **installment loans** to individuals to finance purchases of cars and household products. These loans require the borrowers to make periodic payments over time.

Banks also provide credit cards to consumers who qualify, enabling purchases of various goods without the customer reapplying for credit on each purchase. A maximum limit is assigned to credit card holders depending on their income and employment record, and a fixed annual fee is usually charged. This service often involves an agreement with VISA or MasterCard. If they pay off the balance each month, they are not normally charged interest. State regulators can impose **usury laws** that restrict the maximum rate of interest charged by banks, and these usury laws may be applied to credit card loans as well. A federal law requires that banks abide by the usury laws of the state where they are located rather than the state of the consumers. Many states have recently lifted their ceilings on credit card loans.

The process of credit assessment on consumer loan applicants is much easier than on corporate loan applicants. An individual's cash flow situation is typically simpler and more predictable than corporate cash flow. In addition, the average loan amount to individuals is relatively small, warranting a less detailed credit analysis.

REAL ESTATE LOANS. Another type of loan provided by banks is the *real estate loan*. For residential real estate loans, the maturity on a mortgage is typically 15 to 30 years, although shorter-term mortgages with a balloon payment are also common. The loan is backed by the residence purchased. Banks also provide some commercial real estate loans to finance commercial development.

TRENDS IN LOANS PROVIDED BY BANKS. Exhibit 15.9 shows the trends of commercial, individual (consumer), and real estate loan volume over time. The volume of commercial loans has consistently dominated. The proportion of funds allocated to commercial, consumer, and real estate loans has been somewhat stable since 1983.

Exhibit 15.10 provides a breakdown of loans for banks in three different size categories, as well as for the entire sample in aggregate. The small banks are more localized and therefore concentrate on individual and real estate loans to a much greater degree than large banks. Conversely, the large banks concentrate more heavily on foreign loans.

Investment Securities

Banks purchase Treasury securities as well as securities issued by the agencies of federal government. Government agency securities can be sold in the secondary market, but the market is not as active as it is for Treasury securities. Furthermore, government agency securities are not a direct obligation of the federal government. Therefore, default risk exists, although it is normally thought to be very low. Banks that are willing to accept the slight possibility of default risk and less liquidity from investing in government agency securities can earn a higher return than on Treasury securities with a similar maturity.

Federal agency securities are commonly issued by federal agencies, such as the Federal Home Loan Mortgage Association, (called *Freddie Mac*) and the Federal National Mortgage Association (called *Fannie Mae*). Funds received by the agencies issuing these securities are used to purchase mortgages from various financial institutions. Such securities can range from one month to 25 years. Unlike interest income of Treasury securities, interest income of federal agency securities is subject to state and local income taxes.

Along with Treasury and federal government agency securities, banks also purchase corporate and municipal securities. While corporate bonds are subject to default risk, they offer a higher return than Treasury or govern-

---

EXHIBIT 15.9   Breakdown of Loans by Banks Over Time

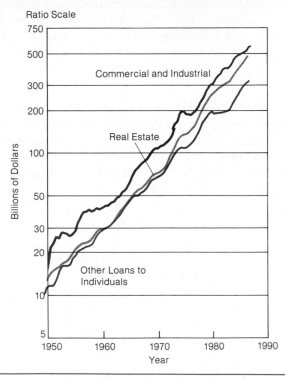

SOURCE: *Federal Reserve Chart Book* (1987).

EXHIBIT 15.10   Distribution of Loans among Bank Size Categories

| Type of Loan | Bank Asset Size | | | |
	$100 Million to $1 Billion	$1 Billion to $5 Billion	$5 Billion or More	All Banks in Sample
Commercial and industrial loans	34.3%	33.4%	30.0%	30.6%
Loans to individuals	22.5	23.1	14.6	16.0
Real estate loans	34.6	30.2	19.8	21.7
All other domestic loans	8.4	11.9	10.0	10.2
Foreign loans	.0	1.4	25.7	21.5
Total	99.8%	100.0%	100.1%	100.0%

SOURCE: *Federal Reserve Bulletin* (December 1985): 227. Totals may not always sum to 100 percent due to rounding.

ment agency securities. Municipal bonds exhibit some degree of risk, but can also provide an attractive return to banks, especially when considering their after-tax return. The interest income earned from municipal securities is exempt from federal taxation. While these types of securities could default, the overall risk to banks is limited in that they only purchase *investment-grade* securities (as determined by bond rating agencies), which have a low degree of default risk.

Exhibit 15.11 compares the volume of loans and cash and securities (as a percentage of total assets) for all banks. Cash and securities made up approximately 70 percent of bank assets in 1950, but less than 30 percent in 1986. These figures suggest a general tendency toward higher potential return and higher risk, although such performance characteristics can be properly evaluated only by assessing the entire balance sheet.

Federal Funds Sold

Banks often lend funds in the federal funds market. The funds "sold," or lent out, will be returned at the time specified in the loan agreement, with interest. Small banks are common providers of funds in the federal funds market. If the transaction was executed by a broker, the borrower's cost on a federal funds loan is slightly higher than the lender's return, since the federal funds broker matching up the two parties would charge a transaction fee.

EXHIBIT 15.11   Bank Concentration in Loans and Securities Over Time

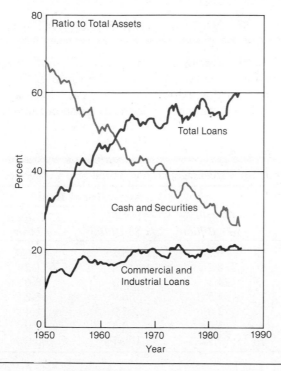

SOURCE: *Federal Reserve Chart Book* (1987): 83.

Repurchase Agreements

Recall that from the borrower's perspective, the repurchase agreement (repo) transaction involves repurchasing the securities it had previously sold. From a lender's perspective, the repo represents a sale of securities that it had previously purchased. Banks can act as the lender (on a repo) by purchasing a corporation's holdings of Treasury securities and selling them back at a later date. This provides short-term funds to the corporation, and the bank's loan is backed by these securities.

Eurodollar Loans

Branches of U.S. banks located outside the United States and some foreign-owned banks provide dollar-denominated loans to corporations and governments. These so-called *Eurodollar loans* are common since the dollar is frequently used for international transactions. Eurodollar loans are of a short-term nature and denominated in large amounts, such as $1 million or more. Some U.S. banks may even establish Eurodollar deposits at a foreign bank as a temporary use of funds.

Fixed Assets

Banks must maintain some amount of fixed assets, such as office buildings and land, so that they can conduct their business operations. However, this is not a concern to those bank managers who decide how day-to-day incoming funds shall be used. They will direct these funds into the other types of assets already identified.

COMPARISON OF USES OF FUNDS AMONG BANKS

Exhibit 15.12 shows the average allocation of bank funds among three size classes, as well as for all banks included in the sample. The term "money market investments" in this exhibit includes repurchase agreements and federal funds sold. The dominance of loans as a use of funds is obvious for

---

EXHIBIT 15.12 Allocation of Bank Funds (by Percentage) among Three Size Categories

Use of Funds	Asset Size of Bank			
	$100 Million to $1 Billion	*$1 Billion to $5 Billion*	*$5 Billion or More*	*All Banks in Sample*
Cash	6.7%	8.2%	6.6%	6.9%
Money market investments	8.2	10.9	11.2	11.0
Investment securities	24.5	19.6	8.6	10.9
Loans	55.5	56.0	65.2	63.4
Premises and equipment	2.0	1.9	1.4	1.5
Other assets	3.0	3.5	7.0	6.3
Total assets	99.9%	100.1%	100.0%	100.0%

The loan account also includes leases.
Totals may not always sum to 100 percent due to rounding.

SOURCE: *Federal Reserve Bulletin* (1985): 928.

all size classes, especially large banks, since they have potential corporate customers across the nation (or world). Small and moderate-sized banks do not concentrate as heavily on loans, as they maintain a significantly higher percentage of investment securities.

SUMMARY

Banks offer a variety of accounts, so that consumers can select the one that best fits their needs. Banks then allocate the funds they receive from these accounts to consumers, corporations, and governments in the form of loans or purchases of securities.

Banks survive by earning a higher return on their uses of funds than what they pay for their sources of funds. While this sounds like a simple operation, managing the risk involved is not. While maintaining risk at a tolerable level, the bank must manage fund sources and uses in a way that achieves a reasonable return. The identification of bank fund sources and uses is necessary to understand the regulatory, managerial, and performance aspects of banks, discussed in the following chapters.

KEY TERMS

balloon payment	negotiable CD (NCD)
bullet loan	negotiable order of withdrawal
direct lease loan	(NOW) accounts
discount rate	protective covenants
Eurobanks	retail certificate of deposit
Eurodollars	revolving credit loan
federal funds rate	term loans
informal line of credit	usury laws
installment loans	working capital loan

QUESTIONS

15.1. Create a balance sheet for a typical bank, showing its main liabilities (sources of funds) and assets (uses of funds).

15.2. What are four major sources of funds for banks?

15.3. Name two examples of transaction deposits.

15.4. Briefly explain the automatic transfer service account (ATS).

15.5. Compare and contrast the retail CD and the negotiable CD.

15.6. How does the money market deposit account vary from other bank sources of funds?

15.7. Define federal funds, federal funds market, and federal funds rate.

15.8. Who sets the federal funds rate?

15.9. Why is the federal funds market more active on Wednesday?

15.10. Explain the use of the federal funds market in facilitating bank operations.

15.11. Describe the process of "borrowing at the discount window." What rate is charged, and who sets it?

15.12. Why do banks commonly borrow in the federal funds market rather than through the discount window?

15.13. How does the yield on a repurchase agreement differ from a loan in the federal funds market? Why?

15.14. What alternatives does a bank have if it needs temporary funds?

15.15. Why would banks most often issue bonds?

15.16. Explain the key differences between small and large banks with regard to the degree to which they rely on various fund sources.

15.17. Discuss the recent trends in the more important sources of funds.

15.18. What are the more common uses of funds by banks?

15.19. What is a bullet loan?

15.20. Why do banks invest in securities, when loans typically generate a higher return?

15.21. When reviewing the growth of bank assets, what trends are revealed for the loans and securities of all banks?

15.22. Is there a formula used to decide a bank's appropriate percentage of each source and use of funds? Explain.

15.23. Explain the dilemma faced by banks when determining the optimal amount of capital to hold.

15.24. Use recent issues of a business periodical to determine the federal funds rate and discount rate on a weekly basis over the last month. Compare the volatility of these rates, and explain the difference in degree of volatility.

15.25. Would you expect a bank to pay a lower rate on funds borrowed from repurchase agreements or the federal funds market? Why? Verify your answer by determining the federal funds rate on a weekly basis over the last month.

15.26. Why are NOW accounts popular? How would their popularity affect the bank's cost of funds? Explain.

15.27. Obtain recently quoted rates from a business periodical on the bank's main sources and uses of funds. Use these rates along with the average composition of liabilities and assets disclosed in this chapter to estimate the differential between the interest revenue percentage and the interest expense percentage.

15.28. The level of capital as a percentage of assets for commercial banks was disclosed in this chapter. How do you think this would compare to that of manufacturing corporations? How would you explain this difference?

PROJECT

1. EXAMINING CHANGES IN A BANK'S FINANCIAL STRUCTURE

Your professor will assign you (or your group) a bank, or allow you to choose your own bank. Use the most recent annual report of this bank to answer the following questions. (A more thorough analysis of the project can be conducted if the last 10 years are examined, which would require some older annual reports or financial statement data provided by investor's services such as *Moody's Banking and Finance Manual*.)

a. How has the bank's liability structure changed in recent years? Which major bank liabilities have increased as a percentage of total liabilities? Which major assets have increased as a percentage of total assets? How has the capital ratio changed over recent years?

b. Has this bank been a net borrower or lender in the federal funds market in recent years?

c. Based on changes in the bank's financial structure in recent years, do you think the bank's earnings per share will increase or decrease? Do you think the bank's performance will now be more or less sensitive to economic conditions?

The answers to this project can be used as a foundation for completing the projects in some of the following chapters if you are assigned the same bank.

REFERENCES

Becketti, Sean and Charles Morris. "Loan Sales: Another Step; in the Evolution of the Short-Term Credit Market." *Economic Review*, Federal Reserve Bank of Kansas City (November 1987): 22–31.

Booth, James R. "NOW Accounts: The Competitive Battle in the Western States." *Journal of Bank Research* (Winter 1983): 317–320.

Cosimano, Thomas, "Reserve Accounting and Variability in the Federal Funds Market." *Journal of Money, Credit, and Banking*, (May 1987): 199–209.

Cyrnak, Anthony. "Chain Banks and Competition: The Effectiveness of Federal Reserve Policy Since 1977." *Economic Review*, Federal Reserve Bank of San Francisco (Spring 1986): 5–16.

Flannery, Mark J. "Retail Bank Deposits as Quasi-Fixed Factors of Production." *American Economic Review* (June 1982): 527–536.

Garcia, Gillian. "The Garn–St Germain Depository Institutions Act of 1982." *Economic Perspectives*, Federal Reserve Bank of Chicago (March–April 1983): 1–31.

Kimball, R. C. "Variations in the New England NOW Account Experiment. *New England Economic Review*, Federal Reserve Bank of Boston (November–December 1980): 23–38.

Mingo, J. J. "The Microeconomics of Deposit Rate Ceilings: Inferences for NOW Accounts and Interest on Checking." *Journal of Banking and Finance* (December 1980): 387–396.

Morgan, George E. and S. E. Becker. "Environmental Factors in Pricing NOW Accounts in 1981." *Journal of Bank Research* (Autumn 1982): 168–178.

Rogowski, Robert J. "Pricing the Money Market Deposit and Super-NOW Accounts in 1983." *Journal of Bank Research* (Summer 1984): 72–81.

Wall, Larry D. "Affiliated Bank Capital." *Economic Review*, Federal Reserve Bank of Atlanta (April 1985): 12–19.

Electronic Funds Transfer

Electronic funds transfer has facilitated the flow of funds among businesses, households, governments, and financial institutions. The more common forms of electronic funds transfer include automated teller machine transfers, direct deposits or withdrawals of funds, and transfers initiated by telephone.

BANKING TRANSACTIONS

Electronic funds transfer has reduced the cost of accepting deposits. Shared automated teller machine networks have been developed to attract deposits without having to construct facilities or hire and train employees. Furthermore, economies of scale are achieved, as the main cost of the networks is fixed.

Another area of banking affected by electronic funds transfer is the *automated clearinghouse*, a payment mechanism by which institutions transfer funds electronically, substituting for payments by check. The automated clearinghouse not only reduces the costs related to the transportation of paper, but also reduces the float involved with check processing, thereby reducing delays in crediting and debiting accounts.

GOVERNMENT TRANSACTIONS

Because of electronic funds transfer, social security payments made by the government can be directly deposited to individuals' accounts. This eliminates much paperwork related to the processing and printing of each check. Government accounting procedures are also more efficient due to direct depositing.

HOUSEHOLD TRANSACTIONS

Electronic funds transfer offers convenience, security, and privacy. Consumers can avoid bank lines and the inconvenience of lost checks. They also have access to funds on days when the bank is closed. Furthermore, they can use the automated clearinghouse to receive direct deposit of social security checks and payroll checks. Electronic funds transfer can be used by consumers to make payments as well. For example, funds can be deducted directly from their bank accounts to make payments on automobile loans, home mortgages, or even insurance premiums.

Consumers have not yet fully capitalized on the benefits of the electronic funds transfer, as people are often reluctant to change their habits. Consequently, electronic funds transfer has been slow to develop for the household sector.

BUSINESS TRANSACTIONS

Electronic funds transfer has been very useful to businesses by providing point-of-sale transactions, in which instantaneous transfers of funds are made from the purchaser's account to the seller's account. This cuts down on the number of transactions by check, credit card, and cash, allowing each retail outlet to reduce its transaction costs. Moreover, the risks involved in accepting checks is eliminated. Because cash need not be handled inside the business, point-of-sale transactions protect against dishonest employees. In addition, the bookkeeping of a retail business with point-of-sale systems is simplified as well. Easier accountability of sales occurs when an exact record of the sale takes place on a point-of-sale terminal. Due to the lower costs associated with the handling sales and less risk of embezzlement, retail firms may pass part of their cost savings on to consumers. Therefore, electronic funds transfer can benefit various sectors at the same time.

Businesses that receive large volumes of cash receipts (such as utilities) use electronic funds transfer for collection in order to reduce the processing tasks. Another use of electronic funds transfer in other types of businesses is the arrangement of direct deposits of salaries and pension contributions into bank accounts. Once again, time and money are saved on the processing.

INTERNATIONAL TRANSACTIONS

International trade often requires payments to corresponding banks, and these payments are made more quickly and efficiently by using the electronic transfer system. It is likely that this system will also be more frequently applied to handle tourism and business travel transactions.

CLEARING AND SETTLEMENT OF TRANSFER PAYMENTS

During the course of a normal day, over $1 trillion in large-dollar (wholesale) wire transfer payments is exchanged among depository institutions. The electronic funds system allows for a more efficient transfer of these funds.

A typical transfer can be described as follows. A firm instructs its depository institution to make payment to another firm by wiring funds from its account to the other firm's account. The depository institution that wired the funds sends the relevant information (name of firms providing and receiving payment and name of depository institution where funds were wired) to the network clearinghouse. This clearinghouse debits the account of the institution that wired the funds and credits the account at the institution receiving the funds.

The *settlement* of the payment occurs when the clearinghouse notifies the receiving institution that the account is credited. The Federal Reserve System provides settlement services through what is referred to as *Fedwire*, in which fund transfers occur through reserve accounts of depository institutions at the twelve regional Federal Reserve banks.

An alternative settlement facility, known as the *Clearinghouse Interbank Payments System (CHIPS)*, is composed of a group of depository institutions that provide settlement services. Payment transfers served by CHIPS are confirmed at the end of the day, when the clearinghouse determines which account balances represent net credit and net debit positions for the day. At this time, funds are transferred among reserve accounts.

It is possible for a depository institution to have net debit obligations during the day that exceed its reserve balance. In this case, the institution must make up the deficiency. The clearinghouse incurs the risk that it will be unable to do so. In order to avoid excessive risk, banks were encouraged by the Fed in 1986 to voluntarily limit their net debit amount. Each depository institution's limit depends on its capital. The Federal Reserve later specified more restrictive limitations, which were implemented in 1988.

Bank Regulation

COMMERCIAL BANK REGULATION IN PERSPECTIVE

Numerous commercial banks have already begun to capitalize on recent regulatory changes in the banking industry. For example, many large and medium-sized banks now offer first and second mortgages, insurance, discount brokerage, trust services, and even some investment banking services. Their activities in insurance, brokerage, real estate, and investment banking have been somewhat limited by bank regulations. However, in recent years they have substantially increased their offerings of these types of activities and are requesting permission to offer services for which they have historically been banned.

In recent years, a wave of regulatory reform proposals have been discussed in the banking industry. Two prominent examples follow:

■ The Proxmire-Garn bill would expand the powers of bank holding companies in the securities industry. In addition, it would enable securities firms to own banks.

■ The Cranston-D'Amato bill would allow banks to engage in all types of financial services, including insurance, real estate, and brokerage.

■ How will the composition of sources and uses of funds change for commercial banks as regulations are modified?

■ Will the risk of commercial banks increase or decrease as regulatory reforms occur?

■ As commercial banks continue to offer insurance and brokerage services, will insurance and brokerage firms offer banking services?

These and other related questions are addressed in this chapter.

OUTLINE

Bank regulations are designed to prevent commercial banks from becoming too risky and thus maintain public confidence in the financial system. This chapter discusses the regulatory structure of the banking system, with an emphasis on the most critical regulations. It also describes the more significant deregulatory steps taken in recent years and their impact on the banking industry.

REGULATORY STRUCTURE OF THE BANKING SYSTEM

The regulatory structure of the banking system in the United States is dramatically different from that of other countries. There are more than 14,000 separately owned commercial banks in the United States, supervised by 3 federal agencies and 50 state agencies. The regulatory structure in other countries is much simpler.

The opening of a commercial bank in the United States requires a charter from either the state or federal government. A bank that obtains a state charter is referred to as a *state bank*, while a bank that obtains a federal charter is known as a *national bank*. The federal charter is issued by the Comptroller of the Currency. An application for a bank charter must be submitted to the proper supervisory agency, should provide evidence of the need for a new bank, and disclose how it will be operated. Regulators determine if the bank satisfies general guidelines to qualify for the charter.

State banks may decide whether they would like to be a member of the Federal Reserve System (the Fed). The Fed provides a variety of services for commercial banks and controls the amount of funds within the banking system. About 35 percent of all banks are members of the Federal Reserve. These banks are generally larger than the norm; their combined deposits make up about 70 percent of all bank deposits.

Before 1980 nonmember banks were subject to reserve requirements enforced by their respective states. Because the Fed's requirements were generally more restrictive than state requirements, Fed members were forced to hold a much greater percentage of their funds as noninterest-bearing reserves. Consequently, many member banks decided to withdraw their membership. Today, both member and nonmember banks can borrow from the Fed, but both are also subject to the Fed's reserve requirements. The advantages and disadvantages of being a Fed member bank are not as significant as they once were.

Commercial banks can obtain insurance from the *Federal Deposit Insurance Corporation (FDIC)*, or some private insurance agency. Presently, about 98 percent of all banks are insured by the FDIC.

National banks are regulated by the Comptroller of the Currency, while state banks are regulated by their respective state agency. Banks that are members of the Federal Reserve are regulated by the Fed. Banks that have FDIC insurance are regulated by the FDIC. Because all national banks must be members of the Federal Reserve, and all Fed member banks must hold FDIC insurance, national banks are regulated by the Comptroller of the Currency, the Fed, and the FDIC. State banks are regulated by their respective state agency, and the Fed (if they are a Fed member), and the FDIC (if they carry insurance from the FDIC).

To reduce the regulatory overlap, regulators have divided up common regulatory duties as follows. The Comptroller of the Currency regulates the national banks (there are over 4,000). The Federal Reserve regulates the state-chartered member banks (over 1,000). The FDIC works jointly with the states to regulate state-chartered nonmember banks insured by the FDIC (over 8,000). Commercial banks not insured by the FDIC are regulated by their respective states. For some special situations, two regulatory authorities are assigned the task of regulation. A more complete breakdown of regulators is shown in Exhibit 16.1.

Due to the regulatory overlap, it has often been argued that a single regulatory agency should be assigned the role of regulating the banking industry. A counterargument is that no single regulator would be able to satisfy the desires of the FDIC, the Fed, the Comptroller of the Currency, and the state agencies. Yet, all of these regulatory bodies share similar objectives of enhancing the efficiency and public confidence in the banking system. If a single regulatory agency could achieve these objectives, regulatory overlap could be reduced.

REGULATION OF BANK OWNERSHIP

Commercial banks can be independently owned by a holding company. While some multi-bank holding companies (owning more than one bank)

EXHIBIT 16.1   Regulators of Various Functions

	Type of Bank			
	National	*State Member*	*Insured State*	*Noninsured State*
Chartering and licensing	Comptroller	State authority	State authority	State authority
Intra-state branching	Comptroller	Fed. Reserve and state authority	FDIC and state authority	State authority
Intra-state mergers, acquisitions and consolidations	Comptroller	Fed. Reserve and state authority	FDIC and state authority	State authority
Reserve requirements	Fed. Reserve	Fed. Reserve	Fed. Reserve	Fed. Reserve
Access to the discount window	Fed. Reserve	Fed. Reserve	Fed. Reserve	Fed. Reserve
Deposit insurance	FDIC	FDIC	FDIC	None or State Insurance Fund
Supervision and examination	Comptroller	Fed. Reserve and state authority	FDIC and state authority	State authority
Prudential Limits: safety and soundness	Comptroller	Fed. Reserve and state authority	FDIC and state authority	State authority
Rulemaking: consumer protection	Fed. Reserve	Fed. Reserve and state authority	Fed. Reserve and state authority	Fed. Reserve and state authority
Enforcement: consumer protection	Comptroller	Fed. Reserve and state authority	FDIC and state authority	State authority

SOURCE: Public Information Department, Federal Reserve Bank of New York.

exist, **one-bank holding companies (BHCs)** are more common. More banks are owned by holding companies than are owned independently. Since 1970 more than 7,000 applications were filed with the Federal Reserve System to become BHCs. Approximately 98 percent of these applications were approved. The popularity of a holding company structure results from the following advantages. In 1970 amendments to the Bank Holding Company Act of 1956 were enacted, allowing BHCs to participate in various non-banking activities, such as leasing, mortgage banking, and data processing. The ability of BHCs to offer these products provides greater potential for product diversification.

Most states that permit BHC expansion allow BHCs to acquire financial institutions anywhere in the state, so BHCs can diversify geographically without establishing new branches. BHCs also have more flexibility in raising new capital and in repurchasing shares of stock.

There are also some disadvantages of a BHC structure, such as organizational costs (professional and staffing fees) and greater regulatory monitoring. However, the recent popularity in BHC organizations suggests that these disadvantages are usually more than offset by the advantages.

BALANCE SHEET REGULATIONS

In addition to maintaining required reserves, banks are subject to a variety of other regulations. They must maintain a minimum level of capital, which is used to cushion any operating losses they incur. They are restricted to a maximum loan amount of 15 percent of their capital to any single borrower (up to 25 percent if the loan is adequately collateralized). This forces them to diversify their loans to a degree. Banks are not allowed to use borrowed or deposited funds to purchase common stock, although they can manage stock portfolios through trust accounts that are owned by individuals. Banks can invest only in bonds that are investment-grade quality (as measured by a Baa rating or higher by Moody's or a BBB rating or higher by Standard & Poor's). These regulations are intended to prevent banks from taking excessive risk.

OFF-BALANCE-SHEET REGULATIONS

Banks offer a variety of *off-balance-sheet* commitments. For example, a **standby letter of credit** provides the bank's guarantee on the financial obligations of a borrower to a specific party. That is, if the borrower cannot pay, the bank will. Letters of credit are often used to back commercial paper issued by corporations. As another example, some banks commit to a specific exchange of currencies at a future point in time. A sudden change in exchange rates could cause a sizable loss to banks whose foreign exchange positions are not hedged. As a final example, banks act as the intermediary on interest rate **swaps** (typically a swap of fixed-rate interest payments for variable-rate payments between two parties). Banks usually guarantee payments over the specified period in the event that one of the parties defaults on its payments.

The various off-balance-sheet transactions discussed here have become popular because they provide fee income. That is, banks charge a fee for guaranteeing against default of another party and for facilitating transactions between parties. Yet, off-balance-sheet transactions also expose the banks to risk. If during a severe economic downturn, many corporations should default on their commercial paper or on payments specified by interest rate swap agreements, the banks that provided guarantees would incur large losses.

Bank exposure to off-balance-sheet activities has become a major concern to regulators. Banks could be riskier than their balance sheets indicate because of these transactions. Since this type of business is somewhat new, there is much disagreement on how to measure its risk. Nevertheless, regulators are likely to more closely monitor these activities over time and may even implement higher capital requirements for banks that conduct more off-balance-sheet activities.

INTEREST RATE REGULATIONS

Banks have historically been regulated as to the interest rates they can charge on some loans and offer on deposits. A brief discussion of these regulations follows.

Loan Rate Regulations

All consumer loans offered by banks were at one time subject to interest rate ceilings. Each state has the authority to impose *usury laws* in the effort to keep consumers from being overcharged on loans, although banks argue that competition should automatically prevent overcharging.

When the general level of interest rates exceeded the usury ceilings imposed by some states, banks could not charge a market-determined loan rate on consumer loans, so they began to provide less consumer loans. As a result, consumers had difficulty in obtaining loans from banks. Ironically, the ceiling rates imposed on bank loans that were intended to help consumers actually hurt them. Most usury laws have since been eliminated or amended.

Deposit Rate Regulations

After the Great Depression, during which the banking industry experienced deposit runs, bank regulators took several steps to renew public confidence in the banking system. One of the most significant and controversial steps was **Regulation Q,** which placed interest rate ceilings on savings deposits. This was expected to limit the competition for funds by banks and enhance the safety of the banking system.

If interest rate ceilings had not been imposed, efficient banks would have been able to offer more attractive interest rates on deposits (since their operating costs would be low), thereby obtaining the majority of funds. Less efficient banks would have been unable to survive. The absence of regulations would have allowed for the survival of only the more efficient banks. Regulators might argue that a more regulated (though less efficient) banking system was necessary to prevent excessive bank failures. However, some critics would contend that the number of failures in a less regulated environment would represent the number of inefficient banks that deserve to fail. Whatever that number is, it is not excessive if they are inefficient. Exhibit 16.2 illustrates the historical ceiling rate imposed on savings deposits. Until the 1960s, the ceiling was not thought to have a major impact, since market-determined rates were typically below it anyway. However, by 1969 market-determined rates were significantly higher. For example, Treasury bill rates were more than 3 percent above the ceiling rate that banks could offer on time deposits.

Even though the ceiling rate on deposits was periodically raised by bank regulators over time, the increase was not large enough to prevent the process of **disintermediation,** whereby savers transferred funds from rate-restricted deposits to alternative investments with market-determined rates. As shown in Exhibit 16.2, the ceiling was periodically raised by ¼ percent or ½ percent. This did not keep pace with market rates, which were as high as 15 percent by 1981, versus a 5.25 percent ceiling on passbook savings accounts at that time.

How Efficiency Is Affected by the Transition from Unit Banking to Limited Branching

To determine whether branch banking is better for consumers than unit banking, a state that had switched from unit banking to branch banking was examined. The prices charged by banks for services were measured before and after branching to determine whether branching caused too much control by a few banks (leading to higher prices). In addition, any changes in various operational costs were measured to determine if banks increased their efficiency by branching. In general, the results showed that consumers are offered more conveniences in branching states and that there is no adverse impact on prices charged in these states. Thus, the argument for intrastate branching has some support.

SOURCE: Stanley L. Graham, "Limited Branching in Minnesota: Its Impact on Banking Consumers," *Quarterly Review*, Federal Reserve Bank of Minneapolis (Winter 1981): 1–6.

Throughout the late 1960s and the 1970s, banks argued that they should be allowed to compete on an equal footing for any available funds. While regulators were not initially willing to remove the deposit rate ceiling on savings deposits, they did allow new financial instruments to be offered by banks in the late 1970s and early 1980s, with market-determined rates. As

EXHIBIT 16.2 Comparison of Market and Regulated Interest Rates

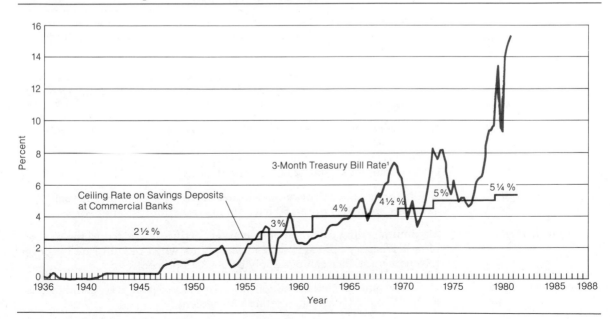

SOURCE: *Review*, Federal Reserve Bank of St. Louis (December 1981): 4.

a result of deregulated deposit rates, and the creation of new types of deposit accounts, disintermediation is no longer a serious problem for banks. Exhibit 16.3 summarizes the phase-out of Regulation Q. While banks now have flexibility on various types of time deposits, they cannot offer interest on conventional demand deposit accounts.

GEOGRAPHIC REGULATIONS

Banks have been subject to both intrastate and interstate restrictions that prevented them from entering particular geographic areas.

Intrastate Regulations

The geographic market in which a bank is allowed to establish branches varies among states. States implement one of three branching laws: (1) statewide branching, (2) limited branching, or (3) unit banking (which allows full banking services to be offered only at the home office). Even though they can provide loans in any geographic market they desire, banks subject to intrastate branching restrictions are more limited in their ability to grow, since their growth is determined by the deposits they can attract. Bank holding companies in these states are granted more branching freedom than banks not owned by a holding company. They can own a controlling interest in more than one bank, even if branching is not allowed by the state. They also have flexibility in pursuing non-banking activities, and can raise funds through sales of commercial paper (unlike an individual bank). Most large banks are owned by bank holding companies.

EXHIBIT 16.3   Summary of Phase-Out of Regulation Q

Effective Date of Change	Nature of Change
June 1978	Money market certificates established with minimum denomination of $10,000, 26-week maturity and ceiling rates based on the 6-month Treasury bill rate.
November 1978	Automatic transfer service (ATS) savings account created, allowing funds to be transferred automatically from savings to checking account when needed.
June 1979	Small saver certificates established with no minimum denomination, maturity of 30 months or more and ceiling rates based on the yield on 2½-year Treasury securities, with maximums of 11.75 percent at commercial banks and 12.00 percent at thrifts.
June 2, 1980	Ceiling rates on small saver certificates relative to yield on 2½-year Treasury securities raised 50 basis points (maximums retained).
June 5, 1980	Maximum ceiling rate on money market certificates raised to the 6-month Treasury bill rate plus 25 basis points when the bill rate is above 8.75 percent. Other ceilings apply below 8.75 percent.
January 1, 1981	NOW accounts permitted nationwide. On the previous day, ceiling rates on NOW and ATS accounts set at 5.25 percent.

EXHIBIT 16.3   Continued

Effective Date of Change	Nature of Change
August 1, 1981	Caps on small saver certificates of 11.75 percent at commercial banks and 12.00 percent at thrifts eliminated. Ceiling rates fluctuate with 2½-year Treasury security yields.
October 1, 1981	Adopted rules for the All Savers Certificates specified in the Economic Recovery Act of 1981.
December 1, 1981	New category of IRA/Keogh accounts created with minimum maturity of 1½ years, no regulated interest rate ceiling and no minimum denomination.
May 1, 1982	New time deposit created with no interest rate ceiling, a required denomination of $500 (but no specified minimum) and an initial minimum maturity of 3½ years.
	New short-term deposit instrument created with a $7,500 minimum denomination, 91-day maturity and a ceiling rate tied to the 91-day Treasury bill discount rate.
	Maturity range of small saver certificate adjusted to 30–42 months.
September 1, 1982	New deposit account (7- to 31-day account) created with ceiling rate based on 91-day Treasury bill discount rate, minimum daily balance of $20,000 and either a fixed term or a required notice period of 7 to 31 days.
December 14, 1982	Money market deposit account (MMDA) created with minimum balance of not less than $2,500, no interest ceiling, no minimum maturity, up to six transfers per month (no more than three by draft), and unlimited withdrawals by mail, messenger or in person.
January 5, 1983	Super NOW account created with same features as the MMDA, except that unlimited transfers are permitted. Interest rate ceiling eliminated and minimum denomination reduced to $2,500 on 7- to 31-day account. Minimum denomination reduced to $2,500 on 91-day accounts and money market certificates of less than $100,000.
April 1, 1983	Minimum maturity on small saver certificates reduced to 18 months.
October 1, 1983	All interest rate ceilings eliminated except those on passbook savings and regular NOW accounts. Minimum denomination of $2,500 established for time deposits with maturities of 31 days or less (below this minimum, passbook savings rates apply).
January 1, 1984	Rate differential between commercial banks and thrifts on passbook savings accounts and 7- to 31-day time deposits of less than $2,500 eliminated. All depository institutions may now pay a maximum of 5.50 percent.
January 1, 1985	Minimum denominations on MMDAs, Super NOWs and 7- to 31-day ceiling-free time deposits will be reduced to $1,000.
January 1, 1986	Minimum denominations on MMDAs. Super NOWs and 7- to 31-day ceiling-free time deposits will be eliminated.

SOURCE: *Review*, Federal Reserve Bank of St. Louis, March 31, 1986.

Banks began to set up *automatic teller machines (ATMs)* across geographic boundaries in the early 1980s. As a result, they can tap other markets for deposits even if they cannot legally establish branches there.

Banks in unit-banking states would argue that they can service consumers more conveniently by establishing branches throughout the state. Yet, the state may contend that their migration into new markets would cause excessive competition and therefore bank failures.

Interstate Regulations

The McFadden Act of 1927 forbade banks to establish branches across state lines. This restriction was imposed on all banks, regardless of their intrastate branching status. The Douglas Amendment to the Bank Holding Company Act of 1956 complemented the McFadden Act by preventing interstate acquisitions of banks by bank holding companies (unless the state where the acquired bank was located gave permission).

Because banks were historically restricted from crossing state lines, no single bank could control the entire market for bank deposits. Thus, geographic restrictions effectively limit the concentration of any bank in the lending business. No single bank can control the entire loan market if it has limited deposit-accepting capabilities. Furthermore, geographic restrictions discourage banks from offering consumer loans or small business loans outside their boundaries. The cost of providing such services long-distance would not allow these banks to be competitive with local banks. For large commercial loans, however, the amount of the loan transaction overshadows the cost of long-distance servicing. Thus, the market for large commercial loans is considered to be nationwide, even with geographic restrictions on branching.

Under a system of unrestricted interstate banking, the number of banks would decrease as some mergers and acquisitions would occur. The consumer might not notice the difference since there would still likely be as many branches as there are today. However, those branches would be owned by fewer banks.

The banking concentration levels of some non–U.S. industrialized countries that do not have branching restrictions are shown is Exhibit 16.4. For some of these countries, the majority of deposits are concentrated in five or less banks (although these banks have several branches scattered throughout the entire country). Compare this with more than 14,000 separately owned banks in the United States.

DEREGULATION OF GEOGRAPHIC BARRIERS

The migration of banks into new areas from which they were previously banned has become quite common in recent years. Some of the more common methods used to cross state lines are

- Qualify as a non-bank bank.
- Capitalize on reciprocal banking arrangements.
- Acquire a failing institution in another state.
- Capitalize on grandfather provisions.

EXHIBIT 16.4 Comparison of Banking Concentration among Countries

Country	Number of Commercial Banks	Number of Bank Offices	Population per Bank	Population per Bank Office	Share of Deposits at 5 Largest Banks
United States	14,451	54,235	15,676	4,177	19.2%
W. Germany[a]	243	41,000	254,156	1,506	61.8
Canada	11	7,425	2,221,636	3,296	77.7
United Kingdom[b]	35	14,000	1,601,914	4,004	56.8
Japan[c]	86	13,420	1,378,825	8,835	34.5
France	206	40,200	262,913	1,347	76.1
Italy	1,170	11,970	48,987	4,787	35.1
Switzerland	432	5,501	14,682	1,153	46.7

NOTE: The fact that institutions and banking laws vary greatly from one country to another makes comparisons difficult.

a Although West Germany has 243 commercial banks, six largely dominate the market. The remaining banks are 99 regional and 136 private institutions. West Germany also has many cooperative banks which provide credit to small industrial firms and the rural population; mortgage banks which provide credit to home and municipal development builders; and cooperative banks owned by trade unions which provide credit to their own members.

b The United Kingdom has 296 "recognized banks" though only 35 are commercial banks owned within the country. In addition to the 35 there are 12 discount houses, 25 consulting banks, and 224 branches of foreign banks.

c Japan's commercial banks are made up of 13 city banks, 63 regional, 7 trust and 3 long-term credit banks.

SOURCE: *New England Economic Review* (March–April 1984): 6.

While there have been other ways in which banks have crossed state lines, the four ways described here illustrate how a bank can enter markets that were previously prohibited. Full-scale interstate banking appears to be inevitable in the near future.

Qualify as a Non-bank Bank

A depository institution is considered to be a commercial bank if it both accepts demand deposits and provides commercial loans. Thus, a depository institution that provides commercial and consumer loans and offers all types of deposits except demand deposits is not legally defined as a commercial bank. Consequently, it is not subject to regulations enforced by the Bank Holding Company Act of 1956 or the 1970 amendment to it. As a second example, a depository institution that provides consumer loans but not commercial loans is also not legally defined as a commercial bank and could therefore escape the related regulations.

There is a fine line between commercial bank operations and the operations of these so-called *limited-service banks, consumer banks, loan offices,* and so forth, that avoid offering either demand deposits or commercial loans. All of these financial institutions are often classified as *non-bank banks.* Commercial banks have often created such non-bank banks in an effort to cross state lines and enter new markets.

There has been much discussion about plugging this non-bank loophole. Regulators have prevented some commercial banks from establishing various types of non-bank banks that, in aggregate, would offer the full services of a commercial bank in another state. At this point in time, the rules are not completely clear. Some commercial banks have recognized the possi-

Court Challenges to Non-bank Banks

Independent Bankers Association of America, Community Bankers of Florida, Inc., Florida Bankers Association, Barnett Bank of Jacksonville, Barnett Bank of Martin County vs. C. T. Conover, U.S. District Court, Jacksonville, Florida, No. 84-1403, February 15, 1985.

These groups of banks are challenging the Comptroller's authority to issue national bank charters for nonbank banks on the ground that these entities are not eligible for such charters. The district court issued a preliminary ruling which prohibited the Comptroller from issuing final charters to nonbank banks, although preliminary approvals were still permitted. As a result, within a month, the Federal Reserve Board announced it would suspend processing of applications that were pending from bank holding companies, citing the court's decision, which, "unless reversed or limited, eliminates the ability of banking holding companies to open nationally-chartered nonbank banks."

The court considered several factors in its preliminary ruling. One major issue is whether associations that do not have powers both to accept demand deposits and to make commercial loans are engaged in the "business of banking" within the meaning of the National Bank Act. Here the court found that demand deposits and commercial loans are core activities in the banking business; both powers are essential for a financial institution to receive a national bank charter. Another important argument that the court found persuasive bears on the two exceptions Congress has made in the chartering of national bank associations. These exceptions are trust companies, which manage and invest their clients' funds, and bankers' banks, which coordinate and buy and sell various banking services for their member banks. Congress, recognizing that both of these associations did not engage in the business of accepting demand deposits and making commercial loans, authorized specific amendments to the National Bank Act which allowed the Comptroller to charter these so-called "limited charter institutions." By analogy, the court argued that the Comptroller should seek Congressional authority to charter nonbank banks. Finally, the court disagreed with the Comptroller's contention that he really was issuing full charters to nonbank banks, and that such associations voluntarily agree to

---

bility that the loopholes will be plugged and have accelerated their efforts to capitalize on them beforehand. If interstate banking were fully legalized across all states, banks would not need to use such loopholes.

Capitalize on Reciprocal Banking Arrangements

In recent years, several states have allowed out-of-state banks to enter under a variety of conditions, most commonly the reciprocal banking arrangement, whereby two states agree that their respective banks can cross the state line. In this case, a bank can grow within the two states but is still restricted from entering any other state. An expanded version of this arrangement is a reciprocal agreement among several states. That is, banks in any one of a group of states are allowed to enter other states within that group. Such an arrangement exists in the southeast region of the United

limit the exercise of those powers. Instead, the court argued that when nonbank banks apply for final approval from the Comptroller, legally they have given up one of the two powers, resulting in substantially the same outcome as if the charters were limited.

Independent Bankers Association of America vs. Federal Reserve Board, U.S. District Court, Washington, D.C., No. 84-3201, February 27, 1985. This court ruled that the Comptroller does have legal authority to issue final charters for nonbank banks to Dimension Financial Corporation, a Denver subsidiary of Valley Federal Savings and Loan Association. Rather than address the National Bank Act issue, the court decided whether the BHCA applies to the Dimension charters. In this case, the court found that the Dimension charters for nonbank banks did not raise a substantive question under the BHCA, and therefore the proposal was not subject to Fed jurisdiction. Although this court ruled the Comptroller acted properly, the conflicting ruling of the Florida court appears to override it.

Florida Department of Banking and Finance and Florida Bankers Association vs. Federal Reserve Board, U.S. Court of Appeals, Eleventh Circuit, No. 84-3269, May 20, 1985. In this important ruling, the federal appeals court overturned the U.S. Trust case, in which the Fed approved, subject to several conditions, the conversion of a trust subsidiary into a nonbank bank that did not make commercial loans. The court relied upon Congressional intent, rather than a literal interpretation of the amendments to the BHCA, in its finding that a limited purpose bank is indeed a bank under the Douglas Amendment to the BHCA. Apparently, the ruling prohibits the Fed, and by extension the Comptroller, from approving such nonbank bank applications unless the state expressly permits such entities. In September, the U.S. Department of Justice filed a brief with the Supreme Court urging them to revise the appeals court ruling on U.S. Trust. The Solicitor General argued that Congress intended to include commercial loans as a necessary element in the two-part definition of a bank.

SOURCE: *Business Review*, Federal Reserve Bank of Philadelphia (November–December 1985): 15.

States. By January 1987, 34 states plus the District of Columbia had created legislation to allow entrance by out-of-state banks under specified conditions (some of the laws did not take effect immediately).

Each reciprocal arrangement has its own provisions. For example, a state may allow only specific types of depository institutions to enter. Some states may not even require that other states reciprocate with similar permission. The specifics of these arrangements can be quite detailed, and may change over time. The legality of reciprocal arrangements was challenged in 1985, but the Supreme Court ruled it constitutional.

In recent years, interstate banking laws have been relaxed considerably. Exhibit 16.5 provides details for those states that permit some form of interstate banking. The column to the right of each state listed discloses the states whose banks can participate in the arrangement. This exhibit does not indicate when there is permission to enter other states through

Chapter 16

Bank Regulation

EXHIBIT 16.5 Interstate Banking Provisions of Various States

State	Area Covered by Interstate Legislation[1]
Alabama	Reciprocal, 12 states (AR, FL, GA, KY, LA, MD, MS, NC, SC, TN, VA, WV) and DC
Alaska	National, no reciprocity
Arizona	National, no reciprocity
California	National, reciprocal as of 1991
Connecticut	Reciprocal, 5 states (MA, ME, NH, RI, VT)
District of Columbia	Reciprocal, 11 states (AL, FL, GA, LA, MD, MS, NC, SC, TN, VA, WV)
Florida	Reciprocal, 11 states (AL, AR, GA, LA, MD, MS, NC, SC, TN, VA, WV) and DC
Georgia	Reciprocal, 9 states (AL, FL, KY, LA, MS, NC, SC, TN, VA)
Idaho	Reciprocal, 6 states (MT, NV, OR, UT, WA, WY)
Illinois	Reciprocal, 6 states (IA, IN, KY, MI, MO, WI)
Indiana	Reciprocal, 4 states (IL, KY, MI, OH)
Kentucky	National, reciprocal
Louisiana	National, reciprocal
Maine	National, no reciprocity
Maryland	Reciprocal, 14 states (AL, AR, DE, FL, GA, KY, LA, MS, NC, PA, SC, TN, VA, WV) and DC
Massachusetts	Reciprocal, 5 states (CT, ME, NH, RI, VT)
Michigan	National, reciprocal
Minnesota	Reciprocal, 4 states (IA, ND, SD, WI)
Mississippi	Reciprocal, 13 states (AL, AR, FL, GA, KY, LA, MO, NC, SC, TN, TX, VA, WV) as of July 1, 1990
Missouri	Reciprocal, 8 states (AR, IA, IL, KS, KY, NE, OK, TN)
Nevada	National, no reciprocity
New Jersey	Reciprocal, 13 states (DE, IL IN, KY, MD, MI, MO, OH, PA, VA, TN, WI, WV) and DC National reciprocal
New York	National, reciprocal
North Carolina	Reciprocal, 12 states (AL, AR, FL, GA, KY, LA, MD, MS, SC, TN, VA, WV) and DC
Ohio	National, reciprocal

1 Several states prohibit acquisition of banks in operation for less than a specified number of years. Some allow out-of-state firms to acquire problem institutions.

EXHIBIT 16.5   Continued

State	Area Covered by Interstate Legislation[1]
Oklahoma	National. After initial entry, BHC must be from state offering reciprocity or wait 4 years to expand.
Oregon	8 states, no reciprocity (AK, AZ, CA, HI, ID, NV, UT, WA)
Pennsylvania	National, reciprocal as of March 4, 1990
Rhode Island	National, reciprocal
South Carolina	Reciprocal, 12 states (AL, AR, FL, GA, KY, LA, MD, MS, NC, TN, VA, WV) and DC
Tennessee	Reciprocal, 13 states (AL, AR, FL, GA, IN, KY, LA, MO, MS, NC, SC, VA, WV)
Texas	National, no reciprocity
Utah	National, no reciprocity
Virginia	Reciprocal, 12 states (AL, AR, FL, GA, KY, LA, MD, MS, NC, SC, TN, WV) and DC
Washington	National, reciprocal
West Virginia	National, reciprocal
Wisconsin	Reciprocal, 8 states (IA, IL, IN, KY, MI, MN, MO, OH)

NOTE: Provisions are as of January 1, 1987.

SOURCE: *Federal Reserve Bulletin* (February 1987): 82.

non-banking activities. Regional interstate banking has been most common in the southeastern states. Several are in the process of relaxing their restrictions further.

Acquire a Failing Institution in Another State

A provision of the Garn–St Germain Act of 1982 allows a depository institution to enter another state if it is acquiring a failing depository institution there (even if a reciprocal arrangement does not exist for that state). The intent is to encourage banks to acquire failing banks so that these failing banks can continue to exist (although under new ownership). In some cases, depository institutions within the state may not be willing to acquire a failing bank nearby , but other out-of-state institutions may. As a result of this law, Citicorp, the parent of Citibank in New York, has been able to acquire failing financial institutions in California, Florida, and Illinois. Several other interstate acquisitions have taken place as well.

Capitalize on Grandfather Provisions

In some cases, banks had previously established themselves in other states through some banking-law loophole or unusual circumstance. Because it

Litigation Highlights

The legal battles over securities underwriting are too numerous to document fully, but the trends in the arguments and in the courts' decisions can be seen from looking at a few of the highlights. In 1963, following a ruling by the Comptroller of the Currency, a number of banks began underwriting municipal revenue bonds (in addition to the permitted general obligation bonds). The major argument here was that municipal *revenue* bonds barely existed at the time of the Act's passage (only approximately 3 percent of all municipal bonds issued in 1933 were revenue bonds) so that the Act did not apply to these instruments. However, in the case of Baker, Watts and Co. vs. Saxon in 1966, this underwriting activity was expressly prohibited as being contrary to the intent of Glass-Steagall. Similarly, in 1962 Citibank began selling shares in an open-ended mutual fund managed by the bank. This was challenged by the securities industry, arguing that Citibank had a direct "salesman's stake" in such a fund and that this was contrary to the intent of Glass-Steagall. In 1971, in Investment Company Institute vs. Camp, this activity was also declared illegal. In more recent legal disputes, commercial banks have had greater success, especially where it has been easier to establish that the bank has been providing an "agency function," rather than dispensing advice in the activity concerned. Thus banks were allowed to establish *automatic* investment services in 1977 and banks and bank holding companies were authorized to acquire discount brokerage houses in 1984. Although commercial paper was ruled a security in 1983, the district court, in A. G. Becker and the Securities Industry Association vs. the Federal Reserve Board, asked the Fed to make an initial determination of whether certain commercial paper activities constitute underwriting or whether they are permissible for bank holding companies. In June 1985, the Board decided that Bankers Trust's assistance to commercial paper issuers in private placement did not constitute underwriting so long as the bank did not promote the issue widely, take an ownership interest in the issue, or extend credit directly or indirectly to the issuer to compensate for unsold amounts. The court will review the Fed's opinion.

SOURCE: *Business Review*, Federal Reserve Bank of Philadelphia (July–August 1985): 19.

might be difficult or unfair to order the bank to discontinue such activities, regulators may allow a *grandfather provision* permitting those banks to continue such activities, but forbidding future attempts by others. For example, 21 bank holding companies were allowed to retain ownership of out-of-state subsidiaries due to a grandfather clause of the Bank Holding Company Act.

REGULATION OF NON-BANKING ACTIVITIES

In recent years, banks have attempted to diversify their business beyond conventional banking services. The most widely considered services are related to the securities, insurance, and real estate industries. Banks argue that they can provide these services to consumers at a lower cost and that, by offering a more diversified set of products, they will be less exposed to recessionary business cycles. Thus, their chance of failure is reduced, and the soundness of the banking system would be improved.

Some argue, however, that certain characteristics of banks could give them an unfair advantage over other firms that provide these services. Because there are arguments for and against bank involvement in these services, bank regulators have had difficulty in deciding what services banks should be allowed to offer. They have permitted banks to provide some services in the securities, insurance, and real estate markets, as discussed next.

Bank Provision of Securities Services

The Banking Act of 1933 (better known as the Glass-Steagall Act) stated that banking and securities activities are to be separated. This act was prompted by problems during the 1929 period when some banks sold some of their poor-quality securities to their trust accounts established for individuals. Some banks were also involved in *insider trading*, as they used confidential information on firms that had requested loans to buy or sell corporate securities. The Glass-Steagall Act prevents any firm that accepts deposits from underwriting stocks and bonds of corporations. Banks can underwrite general obligation bonds of states and municipalities or purchase and sell securities for their trust accounts. In addition, they can hold investment-grade corporate bonds within their asset portfolio. Yet, they act as a creditor here and not a stockholder. Because state-chartered banks that are not members of the Federal Reserve are not subject to Glass-Steagall, they have been able to offer investment banking services. In addition, subsidiaries of U.S. bank holding companies are allowed to offer some investment banking services in offshore markets.

The separation of securities activities from banking activities is justified by the potential conflicts of interest that could result. For example, if a bank is allowed to underwrite securities, it could advise its corporate customers to purchase these securities and could threaten to cut off future loans if they did not oblige. Furthermore, it might provide loans to customers only if it is understood that a portion of the funds would be used to purchase securities underwritten by the bank.

Banks may suggest that any potential conflicts of interest can be prevented by regulators. Furthermore, banks may have easier access to marketing, technological, and managerial resources, and could reduce prices of securities-related services to consumers. In addition, banks could also serve as a financial supermarket where securities activities would be taken care of as well as the normal banking services. This would be an added convenience to customers. Finally, the increased competition could force all firms providing securities activities to be more efficient.

Ideally, banks would enter the securities industry to the extent that efficiency would be enhanced but would not use their unique characteristics to gain an unfair advantage over the competitors. Regulators have argued over how to achieve this objective. There appears to be no perfect solution that will satisfy both banks and the securities firms.

The separation between banking and securities activities has been blurred, as banks are now allowed to offer discount brokerage services in the securities industry. They can purchase or sell securities for their clients but historically were not allowed to advise them on which securities to buy or sell. Many banks would like to expand into full-service brokerage services, where advising could also be provided. Of course, this is where the conflict of interest becomes more obvious, as some critics fear that a bank's inside information obtained from corporations applying for loans would be communicated to its brokerage advisory department.

In June 1986, the Fed ruled that brokerage subsidiaries of bank holding companies can sell mutual funds. In addition, some banks have requested financial services firms to establish a mutual fund to be used almost exclusively by bank customers. In this arrangement, often referred to as *private label fund,* the bank cannot sell shares of the fund but can make its customers aware of it.

In July 1987 a federal appeals court ruled that bank holding companies can operate brokerage subsidiaries that offer investment advice and execute securities transactions. If the ruling is not overturned, many bank holding companies will increase their business in the securities markets.

Bank Provision of Insurance Services

As with securities services, banks have also been anxious to offer insurance services. The arguments for and against bank involvement in the insurance industry are quite similar to those regarding involvement in the securities industry. Banks would suggest that they could increase competition in the insurance industry, as they would be able to offer services at a lower cost. They already have facilities and office space, and could offer their customers the convenience of "one-stop shopping" (especially if securities services were also allowed there).

Attempts by banks to provide insurance services have been opposed by the insurance industry. There is concern that banks could pressure customers to accept their insurance services as a condition for obtaining loans or other services from the bank, rather than because they preferred the bank's insurance services. In this case, the bank holds an unfair advantage over insurance companies in attracting customers.

To a limited degree, banks have already participated in insurance activities. Banks involved in some insurance activities before 1971 have *grandfathered* in their rights to these activities. Exhibit 16.6 lists some examples of this involvement. In addition to these examples, some banks have entered into cooperative arrangements with insurance companies whereby they sometimes lease space in their buildings for a payment equal to a percentage of sales of the insurance company. Exhibit 16.7 provides some examples of this form of involvement. Regulatory provisions have become even more confusing as banks in some states have been permitted by state regulators to enter into insurance activities. As interstate banking continues to evolve, it will be interesting to see how regulators react to actions of banks that move into these states specifically for the purpose of offering insurance services.

When banks participate in insurance activities through leasing space to a company, they are approaching their goal of a one-stop financial services enterprise. At the same time, any unfair advantage they would have over insurance companies due to their unique banking characteristics would not

EXHIBIT 16.6 Examples of Bank Involvement in Insurance Activities[a]

Bank Holding Company	State	Insurance Activities[b]
Bank of Montana System	MT	Plans to expand into general lines of insurance in 15 bank offices.
Bank of Virginia Co.	VA	Received Reserve Bank approval on June 10, 1985 to engage in general agency activities in Virginia. Currently offers personal property and casualty lines, and plans to expand into life and some commercial lines.
Bank Shares, Inc.	MN	Active in general lines of insurance since the 1950s through the Marquette Holm Insurance Agencies.
Bremer Financial Corp.	MN	Active in general lines of insurance in three states through the 26 First American Agencies.
Central Banking System, Inc.	CA	Looking into possible expansion of insurance activities.
Citizens & Southern Georgia Corp.	GA	In the planning process of expanding its insurance activities.
Dacotah Bank Holding Co.	SD	Ten bank- or BHC-owned agencies offer primarily property and casualty lines.
First Bank System, Inc.	MN	Active in full personal and commercial lines in six states through 56 FBS Insurance Agencies.
First Oklahoma Bancorp.	OK	Spun off insurance agency to shareholders in 1976.
First Security Corp.	UT	Received Federal Reserve Board approval on March 11, 1985 for general agency activities in Utah and Reserve Bank approval on April 26, 1985 for nationwide agency activities. Plans to pursue this authority through First Security Insurance, Inc., a BHC subsidiary. Currently offers general lines through a state-chartered bank subsidiary.
First Virginia Banks, Inc.	VA	Received Reserve Bank approval on June 22, 1985 to engage in general agency activities in six states and the District of Columbia and plans to pursue this authority.
First Wisconsin Corp.	WI	Received Federal Reserve Board approval on January 1, 1985 to engage in general agency activities in six states and is in the process of finalizing its expansion plans. Currently offers director and officer liability and blanket bond insurance.
Norwest Corp.	MN	Active in a variety of personal and commercial lines in five states through Norwest Agencies, Inc.
St. Joseph Bancorp.	IN	St. Joseph Insurance Agency offers general personal and commercial lines through the Bruner Cassady Neeser Agency.

445

EXHIBIT 16.6   Continued

Bank Holding Company	State	Insurance Activities[b]
United Banks of Colorado	CO	Received Reserve Bank approval on May 29, 1985 to conduct general agency activities on a nationwide basis and plans to pursue this authority.
United Virginia Bankshares, Inc.	VA	Exploring options in moving into non-credit-related insurance.

a Exemption G of the Garn-St Germain Depository Institutions Act of 1982 allows bank holding companies engaged in insurance agency activities prior to January 1, 1971 to continue to engage in such activities. If the Exemption G BHC desires to expand the scope of its grandfathered insurance agency activities, Federal Reserve System approval is required. On March 13, 1985, the Board of Governors delegated its authority to approve general insurance agency activities on a nationwide basis to the 12 Federal Reserve Banks. The approval process now requires that the BHC file notification of its intention to expand its existing operations with its Federal Reserve Bank. Absent any objections by the Reserve Bank, the BHC may generally commence operations 30 days from the Reserve Bank's receipt of the notification.
b Insurance activities refers to non-credit-related insurance only. All 16 bank holding companies engage in credit-related insurance through agency and/or underwriting activities.

SOURCE: New England Economic *Review* (September–October 1985): 38.

have any effect here. Thus, an arrangement such as this seems like a reasonable compromise. Yet, the bank is not able to take full advantage of its facilities if it can only lease space to an insurance company rather than using the space to provide its own insurance services. In addition, it has no direct control over the performance of the insurance company to whom it leases space.

While real estate is another area that banks have attempted to enter, it will not be given special attention here since the same arguments can be drawn from the previous discussion to support or criticize bank involvement. The degree to which banks should enter into securities, insurance, real estate, or any other non-bank services depends upon one's perspective. Consumers could benefit from a one-stop servicing firm where all non-bank and bank services could be accommodated. In addition, if bank entrance into non-bank areas would increase efficiency and competition, consumers would benefit from lower prices. Future related regulations will likely aim to enhance consumer satisfaction and convenience without giving banks an unfair advantage.

Over time, the various financial service industries have become increasingly integrated. For example, in 1981 Bank America Corporation purchased Charles Schwab, a discount brokerage service (although Schwab was sold back to its founder in 1987). In addition, Bank America has leased space in its branch lobbies to an insurance company. As another example of a firm diversified into financial services, Sears is owner of a savings bank, Allstate Insurance Company, Allstate Life Insurance Company, Coldwell Banker (a real estate company), and Dean Witter (a brokerage firm).

Non-bank Provision of Banking Services

There is not only a question of what services banks should be allowed to provide, but what banking services should be allowed by financial institutions other than banks. Some non-bank banks offer banking services but

EXHIBIT 16.7 Common Methods of Bank Participation in Insurance Activities

Banking Organization	State	Insurance Company	Insurance Broker	Types of Insurance	Arrangement with Insurance Broker	Began Service
American National Bank of Bakersfield	CA	John Hancock Mutual Life Insurance Company	John Hancock	Full personal and commercial lines	Fixed lease in 2 bank lobbies. John Hancock does all marketing, including direct mail.	July 1985
Bank of America	CA	Capital Holding Corp. Government Employees Insurance Co.	Insure America Sales Agency[a]	Auto, homeowners, and life	Fixed lease in 18 bank lobbies. The program is aimed at the "mass market." Bank involvement in the marketing is minimal.	September 1984
		Equitable Life Assurance Society of the U.S.	Equitable	Life	Fixed lease in 20 bank offices. The program is targeted for the "upscale market." Bank involvement in the marketing is minimal.	June 1985
Bank One—Columbus	OH	Nationwide Insurance Company	Nationwide	Full personal and commercial lines	Fixed lease of space off 2 bank lobbies. Nationwide does all marketing, bank involvement is minimal.	January 1983
Citibank	NY	American International Group	American International Life Assurance Co. of New York[b]	Life	Fixed lease with a percentage of sales over a certain level. The 13 personal insurance centers are visible from the street. AIG does all marketing, including direct mail.	August 1984

EXHIBIT 16.7 Continued

Banking Organization	State	Insurance Company	Insurance Broker	Types of Insurance	Arrangement with Insurance Broker	Began Service
First Interstate Bank of California	CA	Safeco Insurance Company of America	CMC Agency[c]	Property and casualty lines	Fixed lease in 1 bank lobby. Some joint advertising. Agency trying different distribution methods including direct mail, telemarketing, and statement stuffers.	October 1984
First Tennessee Bank	TN	Aetna Life & Casualty Company	Craddock Insurance Agency[d]	Accident, auto, health, homeowners, and life	Percentage of sales lease in 7 bank lobbies. Craddock does all marketing, including direct mail, telemarketing, and statement stuffers.	August 1984
Hawkeye Bancorp.	IA	Cigna	Bank-owned agencies	Accident, auto, health, homeowners, life, and commercial lines	Hawkeye Insurance Services, Inc. manages the 28 agencies. Agents are available in the bank though not always in the lobby.	January 1984[e]
Marine Midland Bank	NY	A number of companies	Mariner Group, Inc.[f]	Plan to offer a variety of personal and commercial lines	Percentage of sales lease planned in 8 offices. Mariner Group does all the marketing, including direct mail, telemarketing, and statement stuffers.	May 1985

EXHIBIT 16.7 Continued

Banking Organization	State	Insurance Company	Insurance Broker	Types of Insurance	Arrangement with Insurance Broker	Began Service
Marshall & Ilsely Corp.	WI	A number of companies	M & I Insurance Services[g]	Full personal and commercial lines	Percentage of sales lease in 9 bank offices. Have 11 additional sales offices staffed by licensed bank employees. Engage in some joint advertising.	December 1983
Mercantile Bancorp.	MO	Metropolitan Life Insurance Company	Metropolitan	Accident, auto, health, homeowners, life, and a variety of commercial lines	Percentage of sales lease in 9 bank lobbies. Metropolitan does all the marketing and plans to expand into 31 more bank offices.	March 1985

a Insure America Sales Agency is a subsidiary of Capital Holding Corp.
b American International Life Assurance Co. is a member company of American International Group (AIG)
c CMC Agency markets insurance to First Interstate customers and is owned by a third party.
d Craddock Insurance Agency is an independent insurance agency located in Memphis, Tennessee.
e Hawkeye Bancorp has been involved in insurance for 11 years through a state-chartered bank, though the program with Cigna began in January 1984.
f Mariner Group, Inc. was created specifically to market insurance to Marine Midland customers and is owned by a third party.
g M & I Insurance Services is a subsidiary of M & I Bank of Madison, Wisconsin.

SOURCE: *New England Economic Review,* Federal Reserve Bank of Boston (September–October 1985): 42–43.

Impact of Non-banking Activities on Bank Risk

An argument in favor of allowing bank holding companies to own subsidiaries that provide brokerage services is that it enables them to diversify their businesses and reduce their risk. A counterargument is that they will therefore engage in riskier activities and increase their risk. A recent study by Boyd and Graham assessed the relationship between the bank holding company's degree of non-banking activities and its risk. Over the entire 13-year period (from 1971 to 1983) there was no relationship between the two variables, implying that these non-banking activities have no impact on a bank's risk. However, when the data set was segmented into two subperiods, a positive association was detected in the 1971–1977 subperiod (when bank holding companies' activities were less regulated). In the second subperiod, when Fed regulatory policy was more stringent, there was no relationship. Since this study implies that the risk of bank holding companies is not reduced by engaging in non-banking activities, and might even be increased, risk-reduction does not appear to be a valid reason for permitting such activities. Of course, one may argue that bank holding companies should nevertheless be allowed to participate in the same non-banking activities as other financial institutions.

SOURCE: John H. Boyd and Stanley L. Graham, "Risk Regulation and Bank Holding Company Expansion into Nonbanking," *Quarterly Review*, Federal Reserve Bank of Minneapolis (Spring 1986): 2–17.

do not obtain federal insurance on deposits. Consumers may presume that these institutions are federally insured commercial banks. Non-bank banks that recently failed include Delta Industrial Bank of Colorado, Republic Financial Corporation of Oklahoma, and Southern Industrial Banking Corporation of Tennessee. Even when private insurance is obtained by non-banks, depositors may have a prolonged delay before being reimbursed if the non-bank bank fails. When the non-bank bank of Western Community Money Center of California failed in 1984, depositors had to wait six months to get just one-fourth of their funds back from a private insurance company. Further reimbursement was to come from liquidation of assets, which was expected to take several years.

Some non-bank banks are eligible to obtain federal insurance if they are willing to accept supervision by the FDIC on how they invest their money. Such supervision could force these institutions to be more conservative, thereby foregoing investments with potentially higher returns. While their decision to avoid federal insurance can be beneficial to them, consumers bear the cost if they fail.

DEREGULATION ACT OF 1980

For many years, discussions by Congress, the regulatory agencies, and depository institutions focused on reducing bank regulations. In 1980 an act called The Depository Institutions Deregulation and Monetary Control Act (DIDMCA) was established to achieve these objectives. The act contained a wide variety of provisions, but the main ones can be categorized into two categories: (1) those intended to deregulate the banking (and other depository institutions) industry and (2) those intended to improve monetary control. Because this section focuses on deregulation, only the first category of provisions is discussed here.

DIDMCA was a major force in deregulating the banking industry and increasing competition among banks. Its main deregulatory provisions were

- Phase-out of deposit rate ceilings
- Allowance of checkable deposits for all depository institutions
- New lending flexibility of depository institutions
- Explicit pricing of Fed services

Each of these provisions is discussed in turn.

Phase-out of Deposit Rate Ceilings

The interest rate ceilings (enforced by Regulation Q) on time and savings deposits of depository institutions were scheduled to be phased out over time. By April 1986 these ceilings were completely eliminated, allowing banks to make their own decisions on what interest rates to offer for time and savings deposits.

Allowance of Checkable Deposits for All Depository Institutions

DIDMCA allowed NOW accounts for all depository institutions across all 50 states as of 1981. While only commercial banks are allowed to offer demand deposits, this advantage was diminished by the DIDMCA ruling. Because NOW accounts normally require a higher minimum balance, they are not suitable for all consumers; however, their ability to pay interest has attracted those that can afford the minimum balance.

New Lending Flexibility for Depository Institutions

DIDMCA allowed more flexibility for depository institutions to enter into various types of lending. For example, savings and loan associations were allowed to offer a limited amount of commercial and consumer loans. Consequently, competition among depository institutions for consumer and commercial loans increased, and the asset mix of different depository institutions has become more similar over time.

Explicit Pricing of Fed Services

The Federal Reserve had historically provided Fed members with services such as check-clearing at no charge. Nonmember banks obtained these services elsewhere. In an effort to improve efficiency in the banking system, DIDMCA required that the Fed explicitly charge for its services and offer them to any depository institutions that desired them. The reasoning was that if the Fed did not provide these services efficiently, new firms would enter the market and charge a lower price for the services. Thus, the Fed would continue to offer only those services that it could provide efficiently.

Of course, it would still retain its regulatory and monetary control powers, regardless of whichever other services it continued or eliminated.

Beyond these deregulatory provisions, DIDMCA called for an increase in the maximum deposit insurance level from $40,000 to $100,000 per depositor at each given bank to reduce the chances of deposit runs.

Impact of DIDMCA

Due to DIDMCA, there has been a shift from conventional demand deposits to NOW accounts. In addition, consumers have shifted funds from the conventional passbook savings accounts to various types of CDs that pay market interest rates. Consequently, banks now pay more for funds than what they would pay if DIDMCA had not occurred. Also, DIDMCA has increased competition between depository institutions.

GARN–ST GERMAIN ACT

Banks and other depository institutions were further deregulated in 1982 as a result of the Garn–St Germain Act. This act came at a time when some depository institutions (especially savings and loan associations) were experiencing severe financial problems. One of its more important provisions permitted depository institutions to offer money market deposit accounts (MMDAs), which have no minimum maturity and no interest ceiling. This account allows for a maximum of six transactions per month (three by check). It is very similar to the traditional accounts offered by **money market mutual funds** (whose main function is to sell shares, and pool the funds to purchase short-term securities that offer market-determined rates). Because the MMDA offers savers similar benefits, it allows depository institutions to compete against money market funds in attracting saver's funds.

A second key deregulatory provision of the Garn–St Germain Act permitted depository institutions to acquire failing institutions across geographic boundaries (as mentioned earlier). The intent was to reduce the number of failures that require liquidation, as the chances of finding a potential acquirer for a failing institution are improved when geographic barriers are removed. Also, competition was expected to increase, as depository institutions previously barred from entering specific geographic areas could do so by acquiring failing institutions.

While the proper degree of deregulation is disputed, consumers appear to have benefited from deregulatory trends in recent years. They now have a greater variety of financial services to choose from, and the pricing of services is controlled by intense competition. Recent research[1] supports these statements.

HOW REGULATORS MONITOR BANKS

Regulators monitor banks in order to detect any serious deficiencies that might develop, so that they can be corrected before the bank fails. The more

1 See the research by Evans, listed in the references.

failures they can prevent, the higher the public confidence will be in the banking industry. The evaluation approach used by the FDIC, applied to more than 8,000 state-chartered nonmember banks, is described here.

The single most common cause of bank failure is poor management. Unfortunately, no reliable measure of poor management exists. Therefore, the FDIC rates banks on the basis of five characteristics, together comprising the *CAMEL ratings* (so named for the acronym that identifies the five characteristics examined):

- Capital adequacy
- Asset quality
- Management
- Earnings
- Liquidity

A brief description of each characteristic follows.

Capital Adequacy

Because adequate bank capital is thought by regulators to reduce the risk of the bank, the **capital ratio** (typically defined as capital divided by assets) is determined. Regulators have become increasingly concerned that some banks do not hold enough capital, and have increased capital requirements. If banks hold more capital, they can more easily absorb potential losses and are more likely to survive. Banks with higher capital ratios are therefore assigned a higher capital adequacy rating. However, a bank with a relatively high level of capital could fail if the other components of its balance sheet were not properly managed. Thus, the FDIC must evaluate other characteristics of banks in addition to capital adequacy.

Asset Quality

Each bank makes its own decisions as to how deposited funds should be allocated, and these decisions determine its level of default risk. The FDIC therefore evaluates the quality of the bank's assets.

The difficulty in rating an asset portfolio can be illustrated with the following example. A bank currently has 1,000 loans outstanding to firms in a variety of industries, each loan with specific provisions as to how it is secured (if at all) by the borrower's assets. Some of the loans have short-term maturities, while others are for longer terms. Imagine the task of assigning a rating to this bank's asset quality. Even if all the bank's loan recipients are current on their loan repayment schedules, this does not guarantee that the bank's asset quality deserves a high rating. The economic conditions that have existed during the period of prompt loan repayment may not persist in the future. Thus, an appropriate examination of a bank's asset portfolio should incorporate the portfolio's exposure to potential events in the future (such as a recession). The reason for the regulatory examination is not to grade past performance, but to detect any problem that could cause the bank to fail in the future. Because of the difficulty involved in assigning a rating to a bank's asset portfolio, it is possible that some banks may be rated lower or higher than they deserve.

Management

Each of the characteristics examined relates to the bank's management. Yet, the FDIC specifically rates the bank's management according to administrative skills, the ability to comply with existing regulations, and the ability to cope with a changing environment. The evaluation of this characteristic is clearly subjective.

Earnings

While the CAMEL ratings are mostly concerned with risk, earnings are very important. Banks fail when their earnings become consistently negative. A commonly used profitability ratio to evaluate banks is **return on assets (ROA)**, defined as earnings after taxes divided by assets. In addition to assessing a bank's earnings over time, it is also useful to compare the bank's earnings with industry earnings. This allows for an evaluation of the bank relative to its competitors.

Liquidity

Some banks commonly obtain funds from some outside sources (such as the discount window or the federal funds market). Yet, regulators would prefer that banks do not consistently rely on these sources. Such banks are more likely to experience a liquidity crisis whereby they are forced to borrow excessive amounts of funds from outside sources. If existing depositors sense that the bank is experiencing a liquidity problem, they may withdraw their funds, compounding the problem.

Rating Bank Characteristics

Each of the CAMEL characteristics is rated on a 1-to-5 scale, with 1 representing an outstanding rating, and 5 a very poor rating. A composite rating is determined as the mean rating of the five characteristics. Banks with a composite rating of 4.0 or more are considered to be *problem banks*. They are closely monitored, since their risk level is perceived as very high.

Exhibit 16.8 discloses the number of problem banks in recent years. The number has consistently increased from year to year, with the largest net change occurring in 1986.

The rating system described here is essentially a screening device. Because there are so many banks, regulators do not have the resources to closely monitor each bank on a frequent basis. The rating system identifies what are believed to be problem banks. Over time, some problem banks improve and clear themselves from that "problem list," while others deteriorate further and ultimately fail. Still other banks become new additions on the problem list.

Although examinations by regulators may help detect problems experienced by some banks in time to save them, many problems still go unnoticed, and by the time they are detected, it may be too late to find a remedy. While an analysis of financial ratios can be useful, the task of assessing a bank is as much an art as it is a science. Subjective opinion must complement objective measurements in order to provide the best possible evaluation of a bank.

EXHIBIT 16.8   FDIC Number of Problem Banks

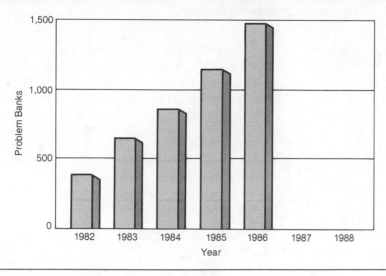

SOURCE: *1986 FDIC Annual Report* and *Economic Commentary*, October 1, 1987.

The Federal Reserve and Comptroller of the Currency also use systems for detecting bank problems. While the systems may vary, they all involve the examination of financial ratios that measure a bank's capital adequacy, asset quality, earnings, and liquidity. Because financial ratios measure current or past performance rather than future performance, they do not always detect problems in time to correct them. However, many banks experiencing problems deteriorate slowly over time. These banks may show signs of deterioration in time to search for a solution.

Any system used to detect financial problems may err in one of two ways. It may classify a bank as safe when in fact it is failing, or as very risky when in fact it is safe. The first type of mistake is more costly, since some failing banks are not identified in time to help them. To avoid this mistake, bank regulators could lower their benchmark composite rating. However, then there would now be many more banks on the problem list, requiring close supervision, and the FDIC would have to spread its limited resources too thin.

There is some evidence that shareholders perceive the FDIC assessment of banks to be effective. A study by Murphy[2] that assessed shareholder reaction to banks identified as problem banks found that these banks experienced abnormally low returns just after the problem list was leaked to the public. This suggests that either the regulators had information that shareholders did not, or that regulators assessed existing information differently than shareholders did. Regardless of the reason for the discrepancy, shareholders responded to it, which implies that this information was not fully embedded in share prices.

2 See the research by Murphy, listed in the references.

Performance of CAMEL Ratings versus Other Systems

Several banks that have failed in recent years were not even on the problem list until just before their failure. This suggests that the CAMEL rating system does not always detect banks that are in trouble. A recent study by Pettway and Sinkey combined a screening method that analyzed various accounting ratios with a second method that screened according to stock returns. This dual-screening method was found to outperform the regulatory screening system. Another recent study by Shick and Sherman found that the risk-adjusted stock returns of banks were reduced 15 months before the bank's ratings were lowered. Thus, stock prices may be reasonable indicators of deterioration in the bank's financial condition, implying that the market recognizes bank's problems before regulators do. However, this method is limited to those banks whose stocks are actively traded. Continued research may either enhance the regulatory screening method or replace it.

SOURCE: Richard H. Pettway and Joseph F. Sinkey, Jr., "Establishing On-Site Bank Examination Priorities: An Early Warning System Using Accounting and Market Information," *Journal of Finance* (March 1980): 137–150; and Richard A. Shick and Lawrence F. Sherman, Bank Stock Prices as an Early Warning System for Changes in Condition," *Journal of Bank Research* (Autumn 1980): 136–145.

Corrective Action by Regulators

When a bank is classified as a problem bank, regulators thoroughly investigate the cause of its deterioration. Corrective action is often necessary. Regulators may more frequently and thoroughly examine these banks and discuss with bank management possible remedies to cure the key problems. For example, regulators may request that the bank boost its capital level or delay its plans to expand. They can require that additional financial information be periodically updated to allow continued monitoring. They have the authority to remove particular officers and directors of a problem bank, if this would enhance the bank's performance. They even have the authority to take legal action against a problem bank if it does not comply with their suggested remedies. However, such a drastic measure is rare and would not solve the existing problems of the bank.

If regulatory corrective action does not improve problem banks, then further deterioration may lead to failure. If a failing bank has FDIC insurance, the FDIC must decide whether to liquidate the bank's assets or search for another bank that may be willing to take control of the failing bank. In the case of liquidation, the FDIC will reimburse insured depositors and allocate the remaining proceeds received from liquidation among uninsured depositors and creditors (such as bondholders who own bonds previously issued by the bank) and the FDIC.

Alternatively, the FDIC may approve of an acquisition by another bank of the failing bank and would likely contribute funds to the acquiring bank (since the FDIC would not have to reimburse depositors if the failing bank is acquired). Regardless of whether the failing bank is liquidated or is acquired by another bank, it loses its identity. A bank failure of either type is an expense to the FDIC. This explains why the FDIC devotes resources toward detecting a bank's problems in time to find a remedy.

Any success by the bank regulators in reducing bank failures could increase the public's confidence in the safety of the banking system. However, there is a possible trade-off involved. If banks reduce bank failures by imposing regulations that reduce competition, bank efficiency will be reduced. Perhaps the ideal compromise is for regulators to allow fierce competition but to detect financial problems of banks in time so that they can be cured. In this way, the number of failures within such a competitive environment would be minimized and efficiency achieved without reducing the public's confidence in the banking system.

Some critics may claim that the FDIC's role in detecting problems of banks is not necessary—that bank management should be just as capable of detecting its own problems as the FDIC. Furthermore, if a bank is inefficiently managed, perhaps no amount of help by the FDIC will be sufficient to cure the bank's problems. The FDIC intervention would only prolong the inevitable failure of this bank and increase costs to society.

SUMMARY

The main types of banking regulations can be classified as (1) balance sheet regulations, (2) interest rate regulations, and (3) geographic regulations. All three types have been deregulated to a degree in recent years. Much of banking deregulation is due to the Depository Institutions Deregulation and Monetary Control Act of 1980 and the Garn–St Germain Act of 1982. These acts allowed for more flexibility as to types of deposit accounts offered and the rates offered on these accounts.

Bank regulators are balancing the objective of promoting efficiency (through deregulation) with maintaining public confidence in the financial system (through regulation). The actual impact of deregulation will vary among banks. Those banks that are relatively more efficient should increase their market share and benefit, while less efficient banks will be driven out of the industry.

KEY TERMS

capital ratio	Regulation Q
disintermediation	return on assets (ROA)
money market mutual funds	standby letter of credit
one-bank holding companies	swaps

QUESTIONS

16.1. Why were member banks withdrawing their Federal Reserve membership in the 1970s? Why did this trend stop in the 1980s?

431 16.2. How are bank's balance sheet decisions regulated?

431 16.3. Provide examples of off-balance-sheet activities. Why are regulators concerned about them?

16.4. What are usury laws? How can they influence lending decisions of banks?

16.5. What is disintermediation? How does it relate to bank regulations?

16.6. Briefly describe the McFadden Act of 1927.

16.7. Briefly describe the Douglas Amendment to the Bank Holding Company Act of 1956.

436 16.8. Compare the degree of banking concentration in the United States to that of other major countries. Explain the differences.

16.9. Why would commercial banks try to establish non-bank banks?

452 16.10. How does the Garn–St Germain Act affect the potential degree of interstate banking?

443 16.11. Briefly describe the Glass-Steagall Act.

16.12. To what extent can banks offer brokerage services?

443 16.13. Why might there be a conflict of interests if banks offered brokerage services on a full-scale basis?

16.14. How have banks used leasing to participate in the insurance industry?

451 16.15. Describe the main provisions of DIDMCA that relate to deregulation.

16.16. How did the Garn–St Germain Act allow depository institutions greater flexibility to attract deposits?

PROJECT

1. ASSESSING HOW A BANK'S FINANCIAL STRUCTURE AND PERFORMANCE ARE AFFECTED BY DEREGULATION.

Your professor will assign you (or your group) a bank or allow you to choose one. Use the most recent annual report (along with earlier annual reports if they are available) of the bank to answer the following questions:

a. Identify any services that the bank now offers as a result of deregulatory provisions in the banking industry.

b. Identify any changes in the bank's sources and uses of funds that are the result of deregulation.

c. Identify any services that the bank plans to offer in the future as a result of deregulatory provisions in the banking industry.

d. Summarize the bank's current status and future regarding the geographic markets it serves.

e. Do you think the bank has increased its potential performance as a result of how it has reacted to deregulatory provisions? Explain.

f. Do you think the bank's risk has changed as a result of how it has reacted to deregulatory provisions? Explain.

g. Do you think this bank will benefit from deregulation? Explain.

REFERENCES

"A Financial Service Merger That Breaks the Mold." *Finance*, November 19, 1984, 147–151.

"A Look at the Economy and Some Banking Issues." *FRBNY Quarterly Review* (Spring 1985): 1–6.

"Bankers as Brokers." *Businessweek*, April 11, 1983, 70–74.

Beatty, Randolph P., John F. Reim, and Robert F. Schapperle. "The Effect of Barriers to Entry on Bank Shareholder Wealth: Implications for Interstate Banking." *Journal of Bank Research* (Spring 1985): 8–15.

Bennett, Barbara A. "Bank Regulation and Deposit Insurance: Controlling the FDIC's Losses." *Economic Review*, Federal Reserve Bank of San Francisco (Spring 1984): 16–30.

Benston, George J. "Federal Regulation of Banking: Analysis and Policy Recommendations." *Journal of Bank Research* (Winter 1983): 216–244.

Boyd, John H. and Stanley L. Graham. "Risk, Regulation, and Bank Holding Company Expansion into Nonbanking." *Quarterly Review*, Federal Reserve Bank of Minneapolis (Spring 1986): 2–17.

Brown, Donald M. "The Effect of State Banking Laws on Holding Company Banks." *Review* (August–September 1983): 26–35.

"Can Interstate Banking Increase Competitive Market Performance? An Empirical Test." *Economic Review*, Federal Reserve Bank of Atlanta (January 1984): 4–10.

Chase, Samuel B., Jr. and John J. Mingo. "Diversification of Commercial Bank and Nonbanking Activities." *The Journal of Finance* (May 1975): 281–292.

Collins, John T. "Congressional Update and Outlook on Interstate Banking." *Economic Review*, Federal Bank of Atlanta (March 1985): 23–27.

Cosimano, Thomas. "The Federal Funds Market Under Bank Deregulation." *Journal of Money, Credit, and Banking* (August 1987): 326–339.

Evans, John. "Commercial Banks and the Consumer Services Revolution." *Journal of Bank Research* (September 1986).

Elkins, James A. and Paul M. Horvitz. "Reorganization of the Financial Regulatory Agencies." *Journal of Bank Research* (Winter 1983): 245–263.

Felgran, Steven D. "Banks as Insurance Agencies: Legal Constraints and Competitive Advances." *New England Economic Review*, Federal Reserve Bank of Boston (September–October 1985): 34–49.

Felgran, Steven D. "Bank Entry into Securities Brokerage." *New England Economic Review*, Federal Reserve Bank of Boston (November–December 1984): 12–31.

"From Bad to Worse at Bank America." *Business Week*, February 3, 1986, 78.

Furlong, Frederick and Michael Keeley. "Bank Capital Regulation and Asset Risk." *Economic Review*, Federal Reserve Bank of San Francisco (Spring 1987): 20–40.

Gagnon, Joseph. "What Is a Commercial Loan?" *New England Economic Review* (July–August 1983): 36–41.

Goudreau, Robert E. "S&L Use of New Powers: Consumer and Commercial Loan Expansion." *Economic Review*, Federal Reserve Bank of Atlanta (December 1984): 15–35.

Graham, Stanley L. "Limited Branching in Minnesota: Its Impact on Banking Consumers." *Quarterly Review*, Federal Reserve Bank of Minneapolis (Winter 1981): 1–6.

Greenwald, Carol S. "Who's Regulating the Regulators?" *The Bankers Magazine* (March–April 1981): 39–43.

Guffey, Roger. "After Deregulation: The Regulatory Role of the Federal Reserve." *Economic Review*, Federal Reserve Bank of Atlanta (June 1983): 3–7.

Heggestead, Arnold A. "Riskiness of Investment in Nonbank Activities by Bank Holding Companies." *Journal of Economics and Business* (Spring 1975): 219–223.

"How Banks Cope with Glass-Steagall." *Bankers Magazine* (September–October 1986): 18–23.

Kareken, John. "The Emergence and Regulation of Contingent Commitment Banking." *Journal of Banking and Finance* (September 1987): 359–378.

Loy, Susan and Paul M. Mason. "Commercial Bank and Savings and Loan Competition: Two Industries or One?" *Journal of Business and Economic Perspectives* (1986): 79–88.

Lucas, Deborah and Robert McDonald. "Bank Portfolio Choice With Private Information About Loan Quality: Theory and Implications for Regulation." *Journal of Banking and Finance* (September 1987): 473–498.

Martin, John and Arthur Keown. "One-Bank Holding Company Formation and the 1970 Bank Holding Company Act Amendment:

An Empirical Examination Allowing for Industry Group Effects." *Journal of Banking and Finance* (June 1987): 213–222.

Moulton, Janice M. "Nonbank Banks: Catalyst for Interstate Banking." *Business Review*, Federal Reserve Bank of Philadelphia (November–December 1985): 3–18.

Murphy, Neil B. "Disclosure of the Problem Bank Lists: A Test of the Impact." *Journal of Bank Research* (Summer 1979): 88–96.

Pettway, Richard H. and Joseph F. Sinkey, Jr. "Establishing On-Site Bank Examination Priorities: An Early-Warning System Using Accounting and Market Information." *Journal of Finance*, 137–150.

Postlewaite, Andrew and Xavier Vives. "Bank Runs as an Equilibrium Phenomenon." *Journal of Political Economy* (June 1987): 485–491.

"Protecting Big Banks Against Themselves." *Business Week*, February 3, 1986, 80.

Pyle, David H. "Deregulation and Deposit Insurance Reform." *Economic Review*, Federal Reserve Bank of San Francisco (Spring 1984): 5–15.

Rogowski, Robert J. "The Small Players in the Financial Services Game." *The Bankers Magazine* (November–December 1984): 59–63.

Roth, Howard. "Effects of Financial Deregulation on Monetary Policy." *Economic Review*, Federal Reserve Bank of Kansas City (March 1980): 17–29.

Saunders, Anthony. "Securities Activities of Commercial Banks: The Problem of Conflicts of Interest." *Business Review*, Federal Reserve Bank of Philadelphia (July–August 1985): 17–27.

Savage, Donald T. "Interstate Banking Developments." *Federal Reserve Bulletin* (February 1987): 79–92.

Shick, Richard A. and Lawrence F. Sherman. "Bank Stock Prices as an Early Warning System for Changes in Condition." *Journal of Bank Research* (Autumn 1980): 136–145.

Simpson, Gary W. "Capital Market Prediction of Large Commercial Bank Failures: An Alternative Analysis." *Financial Review*, 33–53.

"The Regulatory Maze Is Part of Banking's Problem." *Business Week*, October 29, 1984, 110.

Whalen, Gary. "Operational Policies of Multibank Holding Companies." *Economic Review*, Federal Reserve Bank of Cleveland (Winter 1981–1982): 20–31.

Regulatory Issues in Banking

REGULATORY ISSUES IN PERSPECTIVE

A recent regulatory ruling related to an issue discussed in this chapter will help put bank regulatory issues in perspective. In August 1988, the Federal Reserve approved minimum capital guidelines for U.S. banks, allowing for an international accord with eleven other countries.

As a result of the Fed's ruling, capital requirements for bank holding companies and state-chartered banks that are members of the Federal Reserve System will be increased to 8 percent by the end of 1992. This ruling is closely related to a continued debate about how much capital banks should be required to maintain.

While the issue above differs distinctly from some of the other issues introduced in this chapter, all issues include an underlying debate about how much regula-

tion is enough. Commercial banks generally favor a less regulated environment, while regulators typically believe that a lack of regulations could increase the risk of commercial banks. Furthermore, the public's confidence in the banking system could be reduced if bank risk increases. For any bank regulatory issues, the following questions can be considered:

- Is regulation necessary?
- Should large and small banks be regulated in the same manner?
- What are the advantages and disadvantages of reduced regulation?

These and other questions related to four prominent regulatory issues are addressed in this chapter.

OUTLINE

The banking industry has received much attention over recent years due to several controversial regulatory issues, namely

- FDIC insurance pricing
- Capital adequacy
- Interstate banking
- Government rescue of failing banks

The international debt crisis also has important regulatory implications, and it is covered in detail in Chapter 20. Regardless of how the laws related to regulatory issues change over time, these controversies shall remain.

THE FDIC INSURANCE PRICING ISSUE

The Federal Deposit Insurance Corporation (FDIC) offers depositors at qualified banks insurance on their deposits. The annual fee is about .083 percent of total deposits (or $.83 per $1,000 of deposits), regardless of the bank's size or degree of risk. Part of the premium is rebatable, depending on the FDIC's expenses during the year. The rebate per dollar of deposits is similar for all banks.

Federal deposit insurance has existed since the creation of the FDIC in 1933 as a response to the bank runs that occurred in the late 1920s and early 1930s. During the 1930–1932 Depression period, about 5,100 banks failed, representing more than 20 percent of the existing banks at that time. The initial wave of failures caused depositors to withdraw their deposits from other banks, fearing that failures would spread. Their action actually forced bank failures to spread. If deposit insurance had been available, depositors might not have removed their deposits, and some bank failures might have been avoided.

The specified amount of deposits per person insured by the FDIC has increased from $2,500 in 1933 to $100,000 today. Approximately 98 percent of all commercial banks are now insured by the FDIC. The insured deposits make up 80 percent of all commercial bank balances, as the very large deposit accounts are insured only up to the $100,000 limit. Federal deposit insurance continues to be instrumental in preventing bank runs. Depositors are not so quick to remove their deposits due to a rumor about a bank or the banking system when they realize that their deposits are insured by the federal government.

FDIC insurance has received much attention lately, as many critics suggest that the insurance pricing policy is unfair. The more risky commercial banks benefit from the policy at the expense of conservative commercial banks. Unlike private insurance, no risk premium is charged for riskier policy holders. Consequently, the FDIC has been criticized for subsidizing risky banks at the expense of safe banks.

Banks are encouraged to become more risky when they know they will be charged the same insurance premium but will have an opportunity to achieve higher returns. The depositors who supply the funds to banks are not concerned about the risk, since their funds are backed by insurance. Therefore, the bank can attract deposit accounts of $100,000 or less just as easily as if it had a more conservative management style.

In the early 1900s, deposit insurance was offered to banks by some states. The percentage of insured banks that failed was significantly higher than uninsured ones, indicating that insured banks do take more risks.

Proposals to Reform Deposit Insurance

While deposit insurance has enhanced the safety of the banking system by preventing bank runs, it has also, as just explained, encouraged banks to take more risk. This is sometimes referred to as the **moral hazard** problem. Several proposals have been offered to resolve this problem:

- Charge a risk premium to riskier banks
- Let large depositors incur risk
- Improve control over banks
- Enforce greater disclosure by banks
- Reduce the insured amount per depositor
- Implement a private deposit insurance program

Each of these proposals is discussed in turn.

CHARGE A RISK PREMIUM TO RISKIER BANKS. Those commercial banks that use riskier bank management policies could be charged a risk premium on their deposit insurance. The size of the premium would depend on the bank's risk. This variable-rate insurance would discourage banks from implementing riskier strategies. Such a proposal has some support, since it would basically resemble the current practice of pricing other types of insurance. Yet, there is no consensus as to the pricing structure that should be used. A method for assessing bank risk and distinguishing among risk levels would have to be devised—a difficult task since there is disagreement on how to measure bank risk.

Banks are susceptible to the possibility of massive withdrawals, default risk on the loans they make, default risk on the securities they purchase, interest rate risk on their asset and liability structure, and capital risk (having insufficient capital to cover any losses). It is difficult for the FDIC to properly evaluate the level of each type of risk exhibited by a particular bank. Furthermore, it is also difficult to properly weigh the importance of each individual type of risk when estimating the bank's overall risk.

One possible method for measuring bank risk is to use the CAMEL ratings (explained in Chapter 16) assigned to banks by the FDIC. The FDIC periodically monitors banks according to five characteristics (capital adequacy, asset quality, management, earnings, and liquidity). Whenever a bank's CAMEL rating is poor (as determined by a rating of 4 to 5), it is identified as a *problem bank,* and is more closely monitored in the future. The problem banks could be forced to pay a risk premium on insurance since their risk is perceived as being higher.

Ideally, each bank would pay an insurance premium that reflects its unique level of risk. Classifying banks into one of two risk categories does not fully achieve this goal, since banks within either of the two categories may not exhibit the same exact risk. Yet, there is no obvious method for establishing several risk categories. The more risk categories used, the more likely would be the possibility of the FDIC classifying a bank in the wrong category and therefore charging an unfair premium on insurance.

While this risk-adjusted insurance premium proposal has its limitations, it could be an improvement over the current system, and it has been given serious consideration by bank regulators. Formal proposals have already been outlined on the use of CAMEL ratings to distinguish among risk categories and the insurance rates to charge banks in each category. However, the momentum of such proposals has been slowed due to some evidence that CAMEL ratings cannot correctly distinguish between safe and risky banks. Over the fiscal years of 1981 through 1983, 73 commercial banks failed. Thirty-four percent of these banks were assigned a CAMEL rating of 1 or 2 (the best two categories) a year before they failed. Fifty-seven percent of these banks were assigned a CAMEL rating of 1 or 2 as of two years before they failed. If the CAMEL ratings cannot adequately distinguish between safe and risky banks, some other method of assessing bank risk may be necessary to determine insurance premiums.

Another proposed solution for proper risk assessment is to use an *ex post* risk measurement. That is, regulators would use the recent performance of a bank to set deposit insurance premiums. A limitation of this approach is that risky banks could earn a superior rating and therefore be charged a low premium as long as their policies result in high performance. For example, banks that concentrate on oil loans and are highly exposed to default risk could perform favorably if the oil industry were thriving. Banks with high exposure to interest rate risk could perform well if they had correctly forecasted interest rate movements. Therefore, banks that take more risk could conceivably be charged lower insurance premiums.

Another limitation of assessing risk from the evaluation of ex post financial characteristics is that it is not designed to detect fraudulent activity. Many bank failures occur as a result of fraud. Thus, banks that are financially sound today may still possibly fail due to fraud in the near future. Because it may be difficult to correctly determine a bank's risk and therefore charge the appropriate insurance rate, other proposals to deal with the deposit insurance issue are discussed.

LET LARGE DEPOSITORS INCUR RISK.   It has sometimes been argued that because depositors with over $100,000 in banks are only partially insured, they will carefully evaluate the risk of banks where they consider placing their deposits. Depositors become general creditors of the failed bank for the amount by which their deposits exceed the insured limit. Consequently, banks should be encouraged to avoid excessive risk, because they will not be able to attract large deposits if they are too risky. Risk-adjusted insurance premiums would not be needed, as risky banks will be penalized by being unable to attract large deposits. Indeed, this entire argument is questionable, since depositors with over $100,000 will not necessarily avoid banks that take on excessive risk. If the failing bank is not liquidated, but instead purchased by another bank (often aided by FDIC funds), the depositors with over $100,000 do not lose anything. The transaction is referred to as a *purchase-and-assumption (P&A)*, where the failed bank's liabilities are assumed by another bank. The FDIC provides additional cash to the purchasing bank if the value of the failed bank's assets is less than the deposit liabilities to be assumed. Because a P&A transaction is a common solution to a failing bank, even large deposits have typically been fully covered. Thus, depositors with over $100,000 have little incentive to assess the risk of banks (as is also true for small depositors).

It has been proposed that depositors with over $100,000 should receive only a pro rata share of what the FDIC could have recovered from liquidation of a failing bank. This would hold even when the failing bank is purchased by another bank due to a P&A transaction. In this case, a P&A would not recover the entire amount of some depositor's funds and might therefore provide more of an incentive for such depositors to search for safer banks. If they did, banks might be encouraged to avoid excessive risk. However, a problem with this proposal is that these depositors may not be able to determine a bank's risk. Even the FDIC has difficulty in properly assessing a bank's risk.

Another limitation with this proposal is that depositors with more than $100,000 could simply break their savings up into $100,000 pieces and deposit only one piece per bank. In this way, the entire amount of funds would be insured, and these depositors would not have to assess the risk of banks. Because banks could then incur excessive risk without being penalized, this proposal does not resolve the moral hazard problem.

IMPROVE CONTROL OVER BANKS.   An alternative method for dealing with the moral hazard problem is to improve control over banks. That is, the FDIC could monitor banks more frequently and force them to assume less risk. It could require that banks with risky asset portfolios increase their capital or restructure their asset portfolio. While the insurance rates would remain the same across all banks, the restrictions enforced by the FDIC would vary from bank to bank, depending on their perceived risk. This idea is controversial because the FDIC has not shown that it can properly distinguish between safe and risky banks and might therefore impose restrictions wrongly.

ENFORCE GREATER DISCLOSURE BY BANKS.   If banks were required to disclose more information about their balance sheet and income statement data, their risk would be more easily identified. Perhaps this would signal to shareholders the existing risk, and would encourage banks to implement more conservative management (now that their risk would be more obvious). If so, the FDIC might not be as concerned about the moral hazard problem, since shareholders would penalize risky banks. However, shareholders might be attracted to banks with higher risk, since more risky investments by the bank allow for the opportunity of higher returns. Thus, more thorough disclosure will not necessarily resolve the moral hazard problem either.

REDUCE INSURED AMOUNT PER DEPOSITOR. If the maximum insured amount per depositor were much lower ($5,000 or so), depositors would be more concerned about a bank's risk. Banks might therefore be unable to attract funds if they incurred excessive risk. However, recall that the primary reason for deposit insurance is to prevent bank runs. Any rumors about a bank could easily cause many depositors to withdraw their funds if only $5,000 per account is insured. Furthermore, as mentioned before, depositors might not be capable of assessing a bank's risk.

A related proposal is to insure only a fraction of the deposit amount, such as 80 cents to the dollar. While this proposal would make banks more concerned about maintaining low risk, it is subject to the same criticism as lowering the insured amount to each depositor. The slightest rumor—even a false one—could scare depositors enough to cause a run on one or several banks.

At the other extreme, the FDIC could insure all deposits, even those that exceed $100,000. In this way, depositors with over $100,000 would not be so sensitive to rumors about banks. This proposal might discourage bank runs, but it would not resolve the issue of how to price insurance according to a bank's risk.

IMPLEMENT A PRIVATE DEPOSIT INSURANCE PROGRAM. If private insurance companies insured bank deposits, the insurance rates charged to banks would reflect the risk involved. Of course, these insurance companies would also face the problem of measuring the risk of each bank. In the long run, they might become adept at such measurement, since it would be critical to their survival; the insurance company would have to generate enough payments to cover the depositors of any failed banks. Competition within the insurance industry would probably force the rates charged to be reasonable. While there would be a period of transition for insurance companies to adequately price deposit insurance, this could be an efficient long-term solution. For private insurance to be effective, the public must perceive that it is safe. The FDIC may be perceived by some as a bottomless pit, since even if its insurance funds are depleted, it can be bailed out with other federal funding.

THE CAPITAL ADEQUACY ISSUE

A bank's capital level is closely monitored by regulators. The capital ratio, defined as capital divided by assets, is a commonly used measure for determining whether a bank is holding adequate capital. The average capital ratio for a sample of banks is illustrated in Exhibit 17.1 over time. It shows the capital ratio measured according to book value and market value. Normally, the book value measurement is used by regulators. Notice how it declined until 1981, and then began to reverse its trend. This reversal was partially due to regulatory pressure on banks to boost their capital ratio. Some regulators have proposed the need for still further increases in capital. In March 1985 a minimum capital ratio requirement of 6 percent (using a broadly defined measure of capital) was imposed, although federal bank regulators exempted some struggling banks.

Banks have a variety of methods to boost their capital ratio in order to satisfy regulators. One way is to cut their dividends and retain more future earnings, thereby increasing capital. Yet, because some shareholders may prefer the present dividend policy, banks should consider alternative methods, such as selling some of their investment securities and using the funds to pay off some outstanding liabilities. A given amount of capital would then represent a larger percentage of assets. However, banks may not desire to reduce the volume of their business just to increase the capital/asset ratio. As a final alternative, they could issue more common stock—a commonly used method in the mid 1980s.

While banks can boost their capital ratio by using one or more of the methods just described, they have argued that there is no reason why they should be forced to do so. Arguments for and against the enforcement of higher capital ratios follow.

Arguments for Higher Capital Ratios

Regulators claim that banks need a sufficient amount of capital to absorb potential operating losses. Otherwise, bank failures could become contagious and reduce public confidence in the banking system. At an extreme, this could lead to a massive run on bank deposits. Not only would a higher level of capital cushion against losses and prevent failures, it could reduce the FDIC's reimbursement expenses.

EXHIBIT 17.1   Average Capital-to-Asset Ratio for a Sample of Banks

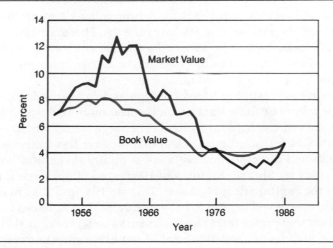

SOURCE: *FRBSF Weekly Letter*, July 3, 1987.

Arguments against Higher Capital Ratios

There is no clear-cut evidence of a relationship between the capital ratio and failure among banks. In fact, two recently troubled large banks (Continental Illinois and Seafirst) had a relatively high level of capital during their rough times. A low capital ratio has not provided an early warning signal that banks are about to experience problems.

There are periods when a bank may be expanding and desire to issue more stock to support new investment in fixed assets. Yet, to issue new shares simply because it needs to maintain an arbitrarily chosen capital ratio is a questionable practice. If the bank is forced to increase capital, it may actually increase its risk as it attempts to earn higher profit margins on riskier loans in order to prevent its return on equity from decreasing.

As a final argument against the enforcement of capital ratios, banks may suggest that the *market*, not regulators, should dictate the capital ratio. That is, if a bank's capital ratio were too low, the *market* would view the bank unfavorably, and the bank's stock price would be low. This would provide the bank with an incentive to revise its capital ratio.

Regulators contend that for many industries, the market may be appropriate for dictating corporate policy. Yet, the banking industry is a critical component of the financial system. If the market is allowed to determine a bank's capital ratio, there may be excessive risk, as the participants in the market find risk acceptable when the potential return is sufficient. The market does not consider the social consequences of a bank run that could occur if depositors lose confidence in the banking system.

Proposal for Setting the Appropriate Capital Ratio

While the capital ratio level has not yet been found to increase the possibility of a bank's failure, the evidence is not sufficiently clear to ignore it. The capital ratio is one of many variables that can affect a bank's risk. Perhaps a more equitable manner of setting the capital ratio would be to adjust it according to a bank's characteristics. Those banks that have made more risky loans could be considered more likely to incur losses and therefore be required to maintain higher capital ratios. As with setting deposit insurance premiums, setting a capital ratio according to a bank's risk is difficult because there is no standard procedure for measuring risk.

The Fed proposed new guidelines for setting a bank's minimum capital that depend on the riskiness of its investments. The plan identified four categories of assets, each to be assigned a specific risk rating. Those banks that held a greater percentage of assets in the riskier categories would be forced to maintain a higher level of capital.

An alternative suggestion is to enforce more stringent standards on larger banks, since failure of these banks would cause more widespread concern about the safety of the banking system. The large banks would obviously resent this proposal, since they may feel that they are less likely to fail than smaller banks and therefore deserve a lower minimum capital level.

A recent study by Shome, Smith, and Heggestad offers some interesting insight into the capital adequacy issue. This study found that market participants often perceived capital to be inadequate. That is, banks could have increased their share price (and therefore firm value) by raising their capital ratios. These findings suggest that capital requirements enforced by regulators do not necessarily conflict with managerial goals to maximize shareholder wealth.

THE INTERSTATE BANKING ISSUE

Consumers, regulators, and banks look at interstate banking from a different perspective. Even banks themselves do not fully agree on whether full-scale interstate banking should be allowed. The large banks generally favor laws that would permit interstate banking across all 50 states. Small banks are generally against it. Some medium-sized banks are in favor of it while others are not. Arguments for and against interstate banking follow.

Arguments for Interstate Banking

One of the most widely used arguments in favor of interstate banking is that it would allow banks to grow and more fully achieve a reduction in operating costs per unit of output as output increases. This is commonly referred to as *economies of scale*. If economies of scale could be fully achieved only when banks become very large (through entering new markets), interstate banking could lead to a more efficient banking industry. The strength of this argument depends on whether banks must expand across state lines for economies of scale to be fully realized.

A second argument for interstate banking is that it would allow banks in stagnant markets to penetrate growing markets where business would be better. Banks located in the stagnant areas would support this argument, while other banks initially established in the growing markets may not. Perhaps allowing banks in stagnant areas to enter growing areas would improve their performance and reduce the bank failure rate, thus increasing the public's confidence in the banking industry. In addition, banks would be pressured to become efficient as a result of the increased competition.

Arguments against Interstate Banking

An extreme argument against interstate banking is that the ultimate result will be the survival of only a small group of banks. In this event, competition could actually subside, reducing efficiency and consumer satisfaction. It is hard to imagine an industry with over 14,000 banks converging into just a few banks over time. Furthermore, the Sherman Act and Clayton Act could be enforced to prohibit such a high degree of concentration within the industry. Yet, even with these laws, there is still a possibility that the banking industry could become so heavily concentrated that savers and borrowers would have only a very limited set of alternative banks to choose from.

A second argument against full-scale interstate banking is that even if interstate banking increased efficiency in the banking industry, its means to this end could be harmful. That is, a high bank failure rate could reduce the public's confidence in the banking industry. This could increase the likelihood of a run on deposits (although it might be argued that deposit insurance would prevent such a run).

A third argument against full-scale interstate banking is that the small banks might not survive it. If they fail, small consumers and businesses

Would Full-scale Interstate Banking Generate Economies of Scale?

Research on economies or diseconomies of scale in the banking industry could offer insight into the interstate banking issue. The typical method of testing for economies of scale is to first define a proxy for a bank's output, such as volume of loans, or average number of bank accounts serviced by a bank. Next, data are collected on whatever proxy is used to measure output and on average cost per unit (defined as the bank's total operating costs/output) for each bank included in the study. Then the relationship between output and average cost per unit among all the banks can be assessed.

Several studies have measured economies of scale in banking. One of the most widely referenced studies found the following:

■ In unit-banking states, banks with less than $25 million experienced economies of scale.

Banks with $75 million to $300 million in deposits experienced significant diseconomies of scale. Banks with more than $300 million in deposits experienced slight diseconomies of scale.

■ In branching states, banks with more than $25 million in deposits experienced significant diseconomies of scale, when the number of accounts was used as a measure of output. The average cost per unit to smaller banks was insensitive to the number of accounts.

These results do not necessarily suggest that larger banks would improve their performance by reducing their size, but that banks should not use potential economies of scale to justify plans for growth. Banks may still improve their overall performance if growth causes a significant improvement in revenues.

SOURCE: George G. Benston, Gerald A. Hanweck, and David B. Humphrey, "Operating Costs in Commercial Banks," *Economic Review*, Federal Reserve Bank of Atlanta (November 1982): 6–21.

might not be served as well by the larger banks. This concern was announced by the Small Business Administration when interstate banking legislation was proposed in 1982. As regionalized interstate banking has become a reality, the concern continues.[1] There is no evidence that large banks would fail to serve small consumers or small businesses well, however. Because small consumers and small businesses save or borrow in smaller amounts, they would not be treated the same as large corporations—they would typically receive lower rates on deposits and pay higher rates on loans— yet, this is the current situation as well.

A related argument is that interstate banking would integrate the local and national financial flows and transfer funds out of the local communities to large corporations. To a certain extent, this transfer process already exists. But, since interest rates are market-determined, an excessive outflow

1 See, for example, Constance Dunham, "Interstate Banking and the Outflow of Local Funds," *New England Economic Review*, Federal Reserve Bank of Boston (March–April 1986): 7–19.

of funds from small communities could place upward pressure on interest rates there, causing a flow of funds back to those communities.

Recent research[2] found that larger banks are sometimes at a competitive disadvantage to smaller banks for some product lines. Thus, smaller banks may be able to retain particular market segments, regardless of the degree of interstate expansion by large and medium-sized banks. Therefore, interstate banking would not likely eliminate existing products and services offered to small consumers and small businesses.

A final argument against interstate banking is that it might cause *diseconomies of scale* (increased cost per unit of output as output increases) as the expanding banks grew to a size that created managerial overlap. The result would be reduced efficiency in the banking system, perhaps not realized until several years after attempts by several large banks to expand. Should the diseconomies of scale be significant enough, they might lead to increased bank failures. The news of financial deterioration of large banks could reduce consumer confidence in the banking system and prompt a run on bank deposits.

Potential Solution for Interstate Banking

Any proposed solution for the interstate banking issue will have its critics, since everyone will not benefit from any single solution. The ideal solution to interstate banking would somehow capitalize on its advantages and prevent its potential disadvantages from occurring. This is easier said than done. Recall that a potential advantage of full-scale interstate banking is increased competition, but a major concern is excessive concentration (a few banks controlling much of the industry) and ultimately reduced competition. Bank regulators could allow interstate banking but prevent any bank from capturing too much of the market. For example, they could limit any single bank's assets to be no greater than, say, 15 percent of all bank assets. This proposal would allow for intense competition, and thus promote efficiency, but would limit the degree of concentration. While this proposal is highly simplified, it illustrates the potential for regulators to devise laws enabling consumers to benefit from interstate banking.

THE GOVERNMENT RESCUE ISSUE

Some troubled banks have received preferential treatment by bank regulators. The most obvious example is Continental Illinois Bank, which was rescued by the federal government in 1984. Continental Illinois Bank had experienced serious loan default problems in 1983 and 1984. As of May 1984, its depositors with more than the $100,000 insurable limit began to withdraw their funds. Roughly 75 percent of the time deposits at Continental were in accounts of over $100,000. Its concentration of large accounts was primarily due to its limited ability to obtain additional deposit funds by expanding geographically (since it was subject to unit-banking restrictions). Thus, Continental emphasized large CDs, which were marketed

2 See B. Frank King, "Changes in Large Banks' Shares," *Economic Review*, Federal Reserve Bank of Atlanta (November 1982): 35–40.

worldwide. Continental normally relied on new deposits to cover any with-drawal requests by old depositors. In May of 1984, though, large deposits were being placed elsewhere. This caused a liquidity crisis for the bank, as cash inflows (new deposits) were not sufficient to cover cash outflows (de-posit withdrawals). To temporarily correct the cash deficiency, Continental borrowed heavily through the discount window from the Federal Reserve System.

Shareholders also recognized Continental's financial problems. Exhibit 17.2 compares the stock price index movements of Continental to those of other money center banks and the S&P 500. The indexes were designed to be equal as of October 1983. In less than a year, Continental's index declined by more than 80 percent, versus minor declines in the money center bank index and S&P 500 index.

Continental's problems intensified as the remaining depositors began to withdraw their funds. This is a common occurrence for banks that fail. However, unlike most other situations, the bank regulators intervened. Dur-ing the massive deposit withdrawals in May 1984, the FDIC announced that it would guarantee *all* deposits (and nondeposit liabilities) of Continental, even those beyond the normal $100,000 limit. This was an attempt to pre-vent further deposit withdrawals until some arrangements could be made to rescue Continental. In July of 1984, the FDIC arranged for a rescue plan where it would support Continental through purchasing some of its existing loan commitments and providing capital, with the total support amounting to over $5 billion.

During this same time period, other troubled banks were failing without receiving any rescue attempt from the federal government. The reason for the Continental rescue plan was that, as one of the largest banks in the country, Continental's failure could have reduced public confidence in the

EXHIBIT 17.2   **Impact of Continental's Liquidity Crisis on its Stock Price**

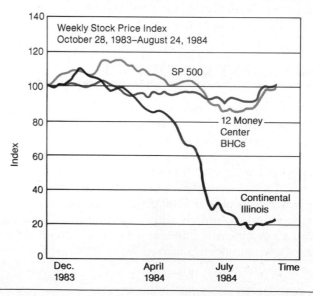

SOURCE: *FRBSF Weekly Letter*, August 31, 1984.

banking system. Also, the rescue effort was less expensive to the FDIC than dealing with Continental's failure. But even if its direct costs to the FDIC had been higher, the potential indirect costs (such as the possible chain reaction of deposit withdrawals at other large banks) of letting the bank fail could have been too great to risk. Regardless of the reason for the FDIC's rescue, the fact remains that Continental Illinois Bank was rescued while troubled smaller banks were not. This has important implications to the banking industry, identified in the following arguments for and against a government rescue.

Argument for Government Rescue

If the federal government had not intervened and Continental had failed and been liquidated, only the depositors with less than $100,000 would have been assured a full reimbursement. Then depositors with over $100,000 at other banks could have become more concerned about their risk, and other large banks that were also experiencing serious loan default problems would have been likely candidates for runs on their deposit accounts. Even if other large banks were financially sound, a false rumor could have heightened depositors' worries and caused a run on deposits. If by chance, a run did occur due to even a false rumor, another large bank could fail—only the beginning of the domino effect that could occur. Because the insurance fund of the FDIC represents about 1 percent of total domestic insured deposits at insured banks, it cannot afford to bail out several large banks.

To examine whether depositors may become more concerned about large banks due to one large bank's problems, review Exhibit 17.3, which shows the spread between the rates on large three-month CDs versus three-month Treasury bills. The larger the spread, the larger is the risk premium required by depositors. Notice that the risk premium hovered around 40 to 60 basis points in 1983 and early 1984. In May of 1984, when Continental's problems became widely publicized, the risk premiums of CDs of other large banks increased to over 100 basis points (1 percent), reaching about 190 basis points (1.90 percent) by July. The jump in the spread was likely due to the rumors about Continental. This illustrates how problems at a single large bank could reduce depositors' confidence in all large banks. Therefore, the possibility of a domino effect due to a single large bank's failure seems realistic and supports the FDIC's move to rescue Continental.

As expected, the spread on Continental's large CD premium also rose to levels similar to Exhibit 17.3. Yet, the spread remained high even after the FDIC guaranteed the full amount of all Continental deposits, implying that an investor could have earned 1 to 2 percent (annually) more on a Continental CD than a Treasury bill, while both securities would be risk-free. Perhaps the continued spread was due to the lack of a documented guarantee on the full deposit amount.

Another argument for rescuing a large bank is its potential adverse effect on smaller banks that maintain interbank deposits. Deposits are maintained at large banks by smaller banks in return for various services that a larger bank can provide for them. Yet, Congressional staff has determined that even if Continental's losses absorbed 60 percent of its assets, only 27 smaller banks would have failed if Continental had been allowed to fail.[3] If Conti-

3 See *Economic Commentary*, Federal Reserve Bank of Cleveland, August 1, 1987.

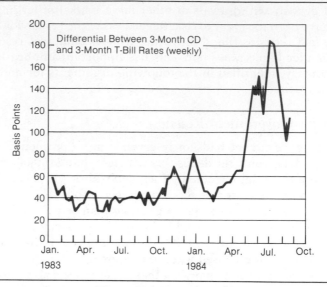

SOURCE: *FRBSF Weekly Letter,* August 31, 1984.

nental's losses absorbed 30 percent of its assets, only six banks would have failed.

Recent research by Lamy and Thompson examined the impact of the Penn Square Bank failure on other banks. This research found that the variability of bank stock returns (a commonly used measure of bank risk) increased significantly after the closing of Penn Square Bank. While Penn Square was not nearly as large as Continental, it had various dealings with other banks. Thus, the market perceived that these banks and perhaps others could be affected by the closing of Penn Square. This information may support the effort to prevent particular banks from failing.

Argument against Government Rescue

A federal government bail-out can be expensive. In January 1987 Continental Illinois Bank stated that the FDIC would recover as little as $1.1 billion of the $2.81 billion of troubled loans that it assumed in 1984, depleting the FDIC's reserve fund.

If the federal government rescues a large bank, it sends a message to the banking industry that large banks will not be allowed to fail. Consequently, large banks may take excessive risks without concern about failure. If risky ventures of a large bank (such as loans to very risky borrowers) pay off, the return will be high. If they do not pay off, the federal government will bail these large banks out. This argument has also been used as a result of the international debt crisis, where large banks with risky loans to less developed countries (LDCs) were aided by U.S. government financial support of the LDCs (increasing the chance that the LDCs would pay the U.S. banks back). If large banks can be assured that they will be rescued, their shareholders will benefit, since there is limited downside risk. The value of the

FDIC Bail-out of First Republic

In February 1988 First Republic Bank of Dallas sought help from the federal government in order to restructure its operations and rebuild its reserves. First Republic was the thirteenth largest bank in the United States at the time of this request. It incurred losses of about $657 million in 1987, mostly as a result of defaulted real estate loans.

As depositors became concerned with First Republic's situation, they began to withdraw their deposits. During a five-day period in February 1988, $600 million in deposits was withdrawn. In March 1988 the FDIC pro-

vided a $1 billion loan to First Republic, and the deposit run stopped. The loan was a temporary solution until a complete bail-out could be provided.

It has been estimated that the FDIC may spend as much as $5 billion on a complete bail-out. As with the Continental Illinois bail-out, the FDIC imposed restrictions on various policies of First Republic as a condition of the loan. The arguments for and against bailing out Continental Illinois Bank as discussed in this chapter also apply to First Republic.

stock can decline only so far due to a crisis before government intervention will cause investors to have a favorable opinion of the bank and push the stock price back up. Yet, all of the smaller banks are at a disadvantage, since the downside risk to their shareholders is much greater. The federal government is unlikely to rescue them should they fail.

Just as deregulation can enhance efficiency, government intervention could reduce efficiency. Large banks would not need to improve their operations in order to survive, since they could count on the government to bail them out. If medium-sized banks felt that they were treated unfairly relative to large banks, they might establish the long-term goal of becoming large enough so that they would also be classified by the FDIC as "a bank so big that it cannot be allowed to fail." With the loosening of restrictions on interstate banking, banks have a greater potential for growth. Yet, an objective to grow just to be backed by the federal government may conflict with the optimal size to maximize efficiency. Of course, efficiency would no longer be as critical for banks that have the support of the federal government.

Proposals for Government Rescue

There may never be full agreement as to whether the federal government should have bailed out Continental. The critical question is how the federal government should react in the future if another large bank is failing. An ideal solution would prevent a run on deposits of other large banks, yet not reward a poorly performing bank with a bail-out. One possible solution would be for regulators such as the Federal Reserve and the FDIC to play a greater role in assessing bank financial conditions over time. In this way, they might be able to recognize problems before they become too severe.

Chapter 17

Regulatory Issues in Banking

475

But there is no guarantee that increased regulatory reviews would have prevented Continental's financial problems. Bankers might suggest that regulators cannot contribute anything beyond what they already know. Thus, the role of a regulator should be more of a policeman (watching for illegal operations) than a consultant. In addition, increased regulatory reviews would be an additional cost to the federal government.

An alternative proposal is for the Federal Reserve to use its power as lender of last resort. If the financial problems of a large bank cause withdrawals of other banks, the Fed could make its discount window accessible to these banks. However, if numerous banks experienced illiquidity simultaneously, the Fed might be forced to provide a substantial amount of funds to the banking system.

SUMMARY

Controversy surrounds four regulatory issues in the banking industry: the premium to be charged on deposit insurance, the minimum level of capital that banks should maintain, the geographic boundaries where banks can establish branches, and the degree to which failing banks should be rescued. Decisions on these issues are challenging and cannot please everyone. Yet, they can be clearly stated and set for a lengthy period of time so that banks can implement policies without concern about changing regulations. Even as these issues are handled by regulators, the controversies resulting from the issues are likely to remain.

QUESTIONS

17.1. Explain some advantages and disadvantages of the variable-rate insurance proposal.

17.2. What led to the establishment of FDIC insurance?

17.3. Explain the "moral hazard" problem as related to deposit insurance.

17.4. Explain the ex post measurement of risk that the FDIC could use to set deposit insurance premiums.

17.5. How does the purchase-and-assumption transaction affect depositors of a failing bank?

17.6. Explain how a bank's level of capital could affect the probability of a run on deposits.

17.7. Explain the potential impact of a bank's efforts to maintain a high level of capital on its return on equity.

17.8. Explain how banks could achieve a higher capital ratio without issuing new stock.

17.9. What does this chapter suggest about the relationship between the capital ratio and failure among banks (based on past research)? Does this evidence support the minimum capital ratios imposed by regulators? Explain.

17.10. How do economies of scale in banking relate to the issue of interstate banking?

17.11. What does the past evidence on economies of scale suggest about the idea of allowing interstate banking in order to achieve maximum efficiency?

17.12. Why did Continental Bank obtain such a high proportion of its funds from large CD accounts?

17.13. How can the financial problems of one large bank affect the market's risk evaluation of other large banks?

17.14. How might the FDIC's rescue of Continental affect the long-term growth objectives of medium-sized banks?

17.15. Why are bank regulators more concerned with a large bank failure than a small bank failure, besides the difference in direct cost to the FDIC?

PROJECTS

1. ASSESSMENT OF THE INSURANCE PRICING ISSUE.

Provide a proposal for pricing deposit insurance. Explain why your proposal would be preferable to other alternatives. Cite any sources of information used to develop your proposal.

2. ASSESSMENT OF THE CAPITAL ADEQUACY ISSUE.

Should regulators require minimum capital ratios? If so, should all banks be subject to the same requirements? Is there an appropriate method by which riskier banks could be required to maintain higher capital ratios? Defend your opinions, and cite any sources of information used to develop them.

3. ASSESSMENT OF THE INTERSTATE BANKING ISSUE.

a. Obtain the annual report of a commercial bank of your choice or assigned by your professor. From this report, how has the bank operated across state lines? Also, summarize the bank's future planning for growth. Does the bank plan to grow within its headquarters state, in adjacent states, or nationally? How does it plan to enter other states? How do you expect this growth to affect its performance? Why?

b. Use any related literature from the library to propose a policy for interstate banking. Explain why your policy would be better than alternative policies. (Cite all of your information sources.)

4. ASSESSMENT OF GOVERNMENT RESCUES OF FAILING BANKS.

Use any related literature from the library along with your own ideas to propose a policy for handling bank failures? That is, should banks be rescued? What characteristics (if any) must a bank have in order to be rescued by the FDIC? Explain why your policy would be better than alternative policies. (Cite all of your sources of information.)

REFERENCES

References Related to Deposit Insurance Pricing

"Bennett, Barbara and David Pyle. "Risk-Adjusted Deposit Insurance Premiums." FRBSF Weekly Letter, August 10, 1984.

Bennett, Barbara. "Bank Regulation and Deposit Insurance." FRBSF Weekly Letter, August 17, 1984.

Bennett, Barbara A. "Bank Regulation and Deposit Insurance Controlling the FDIC's

Losses," *Economic Review*, Federal Reserve Bank of San Francisco (Spring 1984): 16–30.

Benston, George J. "Deposit Insurance and Bank Failures." *Economic Review*, Federal Reserve Bank of Atlanta (March 1983): 4–17.

Flannery, Mark J. "Deposit Insurance Creates a Need for Bank Regulation." *Business Review*, Federal Reserve Bank of Philadelphia (January–February 1982): 17–27.

Flannery, Mark J. and Aris A. Protopapadakis. "Risk-Sensitive Deposit Insurance Premia: Some Practical Issues." *Business Review*, Federal Reserve Bank of Philadelphia (September–October 1984): 3–10.

Furlong, Frederick T. "FDIC's Modified Payout Plan." *FRBSF Weekly Letter*, May 18, 1984.

Furlong, Frederick T. "A View on Deposit Insurance Coverage." *Economic Review*, Federal Reserve Bank of San Francisco (Spring 1984): 31–38.

Kareken, John H. "Deposit Insurance Reform or Deregulation Is the Cart, Not the Horse." *Quarterly Review*, Federal Reserve Bank of Minneapolis (Spring 1983): 1–9.

Keeton, William R. "Deposit Insurance and the Deregulation of Deposit Rates." *Economic Review*, Federal Reserve Bank of San Francisco (April 1984): 28–45.

Pennacchi, George. "A Re-examination of the Over- (or Under-) Pricing of Deposit Insurance." *Journal of Money, Credit, and Banking* (August 1987): 340–360.

Pennacchi, George. "Alternative Forms of Deposit Insurance: Pricing and Bank Incentive Issues." *Journal of Banking and Finance* (June 1987): 291–312.

Pyle, David H. "Deregulation and Deposit Insurance Reform." *Economic Review*, Federal Reserve Bank of San Francisco (Spring 1984): 5–15.

Scadding John L. "Insurance and Managing Bank Risk-Taking." *FRBSF Weekly Letter*, October 19, 1984.

Thomson, James. "The Use of Market Information in Pricing Deposit Insurance." *Journal of Money, Credit, and Banking* (November 1987): 528–537.

Wall, Larry D. "Deposit Insurance Reform: The Insuring Agencies Proposals." *Economic Review*, Federal Reserve Bank of Atlanta (January 1984): 43–57.

Wall, Larry D. "The Future of Deposit Insurance: An Analysis of the Insuring Agencies' Proposals." *Economic Review*, Federal Reserve Bank of Atlanta (March 1984): 26–39.

"When Some Banks Are More Equal Than Others." *Business Week*, October 8, 1984, 43.

"Why Some Banks May Pay More for Deposit Insurance." *Business Week*, January 9, 1984, 28.

References Related to Bank Capital

Ehlen, James G., Jr. "A Review of Bank Capital and Its Adequacy." *Economic Review*, Federal Reserve Bank of Atlanta (November 1983): 54–61.

"Fed Proposes Guidelines Based on Risk to Set Minimum Bank Capital Reserves." *The Wall Street Journal*, January 16, 1986, 3.

Gilbert, R. Alton, Courtenay C. Stone, and Michael E. Trebing. "The New Bank Capital Adequacy Standards." *Review*, Federal Reserve Bank of St. Louis (May 1985): 12–20.

Heggestad, Arnold A. and B. Frank King. "Regulation of Bank Capital: An Evaluation." *Economic Review*, Federal Reserve Bank of Atlanta (March 1982): 35–43.

Mitchell, Karlyn. "Capital Adequacy at Commercial Banks." *Economic Review*, Federal Reserve Bank of Kansas City (September–October 1984): 17–30.

"More Capital Won't Cure What Ails Banks." *Fortune*, January 7, 1985, 80–86.

Noonan, John H. and Susan Kay Fetner. "The Role of Capital and Capital Standards." *Economic Review*, Federal Reserve Bank of Atlanta (November 1983): 50–53.

Shome, Dilip, Stephen D. Smith, and Arnold A. Heggestad. "Capital Adequacy and the Valuation of Large Commercial Banking Organizations." *Journal of Financial Research* (Winter 1986): 331–341.

Vokey, Richard S. and Kevin L. Kearns. "Issues in Capital Adequacy Regulation." *The Bankers Magazine* (September–October 1985): 35–43.

Wall, Larry D. "Regulation of Banks' Equity Capital." *Economic Review*, Federal Reserve Bank of Atlanta (November 1985): 4–18.

Wall, Larry D. "Affiliated Bank Capital." *Economic Review*, Federal Reserve Bank of Atlanta (April 1985): 12–19.

References Related to Interstate Banking

Beatty, Randolph P., John Reim, and Robert F. Schapperle. "The Effect of Barriers to Entry on Bank Shareholder Wealth: Implications for Interstate Banking." *Journal of Bank Research* (Spring 1985): 8–15.

Benston, George G., Gerald A. Hanweck, and David B. Humphrey. "Operating Costs in Commercial Banks." *Economic Review*, Federal Reserve Bank of Atlanta (November 1982): 6–21.

Benson, John N. "Will Bank Capital Adequacy Restrictions Slow the Development of Interstate Banking?" *Economic Review*, Federal Reserve Bank of Atlanta (May 1983): 46–65.

Collins, John T. "Congressional Update and Outlook on Interstate Banking." *Economic Review*, Federal Reserve Bank of Atlanta (March 1985): 23–27.

Duncan, F. H. "Intermarket Bank Expansions: Implications for Interstate Banking." *Journal of Bank Research* (Spring 1985): 16–21.

Dunham, Constance. "Interstate Banking and the Outflow of Local Funds." *New England Economic Review*, Federal Reserve Bank of Boston (March–April 1986): 7–19.

Eisenbeis, Robert A. "Regional Forces for Interstate Banking." *Economic Review*, Federal Reserve Bank of Atlanta (May 1983): 24–31.

Gilbert, Alton R. "Recent Changes in Handling Bank Failures and Their Effects on the Banking Industry." *Review*, Federal Reserve Bank of St. Louis (June–July 1985): 21–28.

Horvitz, Paul. "Alternative Avenues to Interstate Banking." *Economic Review*, Federal Reserve Bank of Atlanta (May 1983): 32–39.

King, B. Frank. "Interstate Expansion and Bank Costs." *Economic Review*, Federal Reserve Bank of Atlanta (May 1983): 40–45.

King, B. Frank. "Changes in Large Banks' Shares." *Economic Review*, Federal Reserve Bank of Atlanta (November 1982): 35–40.

McCall, Alan S. "Economies of Scale, Operating Efficiencies, and the Organizational Structure of Commercial Banks." *Journal of Bank Research* (Summer 1980): 95–100.

References Related to Government Rescue of Banks

"A Well-Timed Purge at Continental Illinois." *Business Week*, December 17, 1984, 83–84.

Benston, George J. "Financial Disclosure and Bank Failure." *Economic Review* (March 1984): 5–12.

"Can Continental Illinois Still Find a Rescuer?" *Business Week*, July 23, 1984, 69–70.

"Continental Illinois: Salvaged but Not Really Saved." *Business Week*, August 6, 1984, 20.

"Could the Continental Crisis Happen Again?" *Business Week*, August 13, 1984, 60.

FRBSF Weekly Letter, several issues.

Furlong, Frederick T. "Market Responses to Continental Illinois." *FRBSF Weekly Letter*, August 31, 1984.

Gray, Andres. "In the Wake of Continental." *The Bankers Magazine* (November–December 1984): 83–84.

Keran, Michael W. and Frederick T. Furlong. "The Federal Safety Net for Commercial Banks: Part I." *FRBSF Weekly Letter*, July 17, 1984.

Knapp, Michael C. "Penn Square Revisited." *The Bankers Magazine* (January–February 1984): 75–79.

Lamy, Robert and Rodney Thompson. "Penn Square, Problem Loans, and Insolvency Risk." *Journal of Financial Research* (Summer 1986).

Longstreth, Bevis. "In Search of a Safety Net for the Financial Services Industry." *Banker's Magazine* (July–August 1983): 27–34.

Mayer, Thomas. "Should Large Banks Be Allowed to Fail?" *Journal of Financial and Quantitative Analysis* (November 1975): 603–610.

Pettway, Richard H. and Joseph F. Sinkey, Jr. "Establishing On-Site Bank Examination

Priorities: An Early-Warning System using Accounting and Market Information." *Journal of Finance* (March 1980): 137–150.

Shick, Richard A. and Lawrence F. Sherman. "Bank Stock Prices as an Early Warning System for Changes in Condition." *Journal of Bank Research* (Autumn 1980): 136–145.

"The Federal Safety Net for Commercial Banks: Part II." *FRBSF Weekly Letter*, August 3, 1984.

"The Problems Continental Illinois' Rescue Is Creating." *Business Week*, June 4, 1984, 108–112.

"What Will the Finance World Look Like?" *Institutional Investor* (December 1982): 185–193.

"When Banks Can't Afford to Fail." *Business Week*, June 4, 1984, 136.

"Will Megabucks Solve the Problems at Continental Illinois?" *Business Week*, May 28, 1984, 31.

Part Five

Commercial Banking

Bank Management

BANK MANAGEMENT IN PERSPECTIVE

Wells Fargo & Company has used a unique management style throughout the 1980s. When deposit rates were increased in the early 1980s, Wells Fargo closed many of its foreign branches in Europe and Africa and focused on its home market, California. In addition, it cut its staff by 30 percent. Its banking operations are focused on local retail markets, with a special emphasis on trust accounts and real estate lending. It substantially reduced its international corporate and government loans, and increased consumer loans.

Wells Fargo acquired Crocker Bank in 1986, which enabled it to strengthen its position in various California markets and to assume Crocker's large trust business. Yet, some of Crocker's operations were not compatible with Wells Fargo's objectives. Most of Crocker's senior executives were fired and $6 billion of Crocker Bank's assets were sold. Even though Wells Fargo is one of the largest banks in the U.S., its operations are similar to mid-sized banks. The managerial decisions made by Wells Fargo require some general risk-return principles applied to obtaining and using funds.

The restructured operations at Wells Fargo were closely evaluated by stockholders and investment analysts. Many large and medium-sized banks have restructured their operations during the late 1980s in order to focus on new businesses and/or geographic markets. Some of the changes have resulted from deregulation in the banking industry. These changes usually affect the bank's potential performance and its risk.

■ What types of risk does Wells Fargo face?
■ How has Wells Fargo's risk been affected by its restructured operations?
■ In what ways would Wells Fargo incur less risk than other large banks?

These and other questions related to bank management decisions are addressed in this chapter.

OUTLINE

The performance of any commercial bank depends on the management of its assets, liabilities, and capital. And increased competition has made efficient management necessary for survival. Most managerial decisions involve a risk-return trade-off. Commercial banks that structure their asset and liability portfolios according to interest rate or economic growth projections are in a position to generate high returns. However, they are more exposed to risk if their projections are wrong. A conservative management approach reduces risk but also reduces potential return. Bank managers search for a trade-off that will satisfy shareholder preferences.

Bank management of assets, liabilities, and capital is integrated. A bank's asset growth can be achieved only if it obtains the necessary funds. Furthermore, growth may require an investment in fixed assets (such as additional offices) that will require an accumulation of bank capital. Integration of asset, liability, and capital management assures that all policies will be consistent with a cohesive set of economic forecasts. An integrated balance sheet approach is necessary to manage liquidity risk, interest rate risk, and default risk. The management of each type of risk is described in turn.

MANAGING LIQUIDITY

Banks can experience illiquidity when cash outflows (due to deposit withdrawals, loans, etc.) exceed cash inflows (new deposits, loan repayments, etc.). They can resolve any cash deficiency by either creating additional liabilities or by selling assets. Banks have access to various forms of borrowing, such as the federal funds market or the discount window. They also maintain some assets that can be readily sold in the secondary market. The decision on how to obtain funds depends on the situation. If the need for funds is temporary, an increase in short-term liabilities (from the federal funds market or the discount window) may be more appropriate. However, if the need is permanent, a policy for increasing deposits or selling liquid assets may be more appropriate.

Since some assets are more marketable than others in the secondary market, the bank's asset composition can affect its degree of liquidity. At an extreme, banks could assure sufficient liquidity by using most of their funds to purchase Treasury securities. However, they must also be concerned with achieving a reasonable return on their assets, which often conflicts with the liquidity objective. While Treasury securities are liquid, their yield is low relative to bank loans and other investment securities. Recent research has shown that high-performance banks are able to maintain relatively low (but sufficient) liquidity. Banks should maintain the level of liquid assets that would satisfy their liquidity needs but use their remaining funds to satisfy their other objectives. As the secondary market for loans has become active, banks are more able to satisfy their liquidity needs with a higher proportion of loans while striving for higher profitability.

MANAGING INTEREST RATE RISK

The composition of a bank's balance sheet will determine how its profitability is influenced by interest rate fluctuations. If a bank expects interest rates to consistently decrease over time, it will consider allocating most of its funds to rate-insensitive assets, such as long-term and medium-term loans (all with fixed rates), as well as long-term securities. These assets will continue to provide the same periodic yield. As interest rates decline, the bank's cost of funds will decrease, and its overall return will increase.

If a bank expects interest rates to consistently increase over time, it will consider allocating most of its funds to rate-sensitive assets such as short-term commercial and consumer loans, long-term loans with floating interest rates, and short-term securities. The short-term instruments will mature soon so reinvestment will be at a higher rate if interest rates increase. The longer-term instruments will continue to exist, so the bank will benefit from increasing interest rates only if they have floating rates.

While banks can construct an asset portfolio that will benefit from a given interest rate movement in the future, there is no guarantee about the direction in which interest rates will move. The chance that rates will move in the opposite direction to that anticipated represents the bank's exposure to interest rate risk.

A major concern of banks is how interest rate movements will affect performance, particularly earnings. If their liability portfolio and asset portfolio were equally sensitive to interest rate movements, they could maintain a stable **spread** over time, meaning the difference between the bank's average rate earned on assets minus its average rate paid on liabilities. A more formalized comparison of the bank's interest revenues and expenses is provided by the **net interest margin,** computed as

$$\frac{\text{Net}}{\text{interest}} = \frac{\text{Interest revenues} - \text{Interest expenses}}{\text{Assets}}$$

In some cases, net interest margin is defined to include only the earning assets, excluding any assets that are not generating a return to the bank (such as required reserves). Because the rate sensitivity of a bank's liabilities normally does not perfectly match that of the assets, the net interest margin changes over time. The change depends on whether bank assets are more or less rate-sensitive than bank liabilities, the degree of difference in rate-sensitivity, and the direction of interest rate movements.

During a period of rising interest rates, a bank's net interest margin will likely decrease if its liabilities are more rate-sensitive than its assets, as illustrated in Exhibit 18.1. Under the opposite scenario where market interest rates are declining over time, rates offered on new bank deposits, as well as those earned on new bank loans, would be affected by the decline in interest rates. Yet, the deposit rates would typically be more sensitive if their turnover is quicker, as illustrated in Exhibit 18.2.

Methods to Assess Interest Rate Risk

Commercial banks that assess their exposure to interest rate movements use the following methods:

- Gap measurement
- Duration measurement
- Sensitivity of performance to interest rate movements

GAP MEASUREMENT. Banks can attempt to determine their interest rate risk by monitoring their **gap** over time, defined here as

$$\text{gap} = (\text{rate-sensitive assets}) - (\text{rate-sensitive liabilities})$$

An alternative formula is the **gap ratio,** which is measured as volume of rate-sensitive assets divided by rate-sensitive liabilities. A gap of zero (or gap ratio of 1.00) suggests that rate-sensitive assets equal rate-sensitive liabilities, so that net interest margin should not be significantly influenced

---

EXHIBIT 18.1   **Impact of Increasing Interest Rates on a Bank's Net Interest Margin (If the Bank's Liabilities Are More Rate-Sensitive Than Its Assets)**

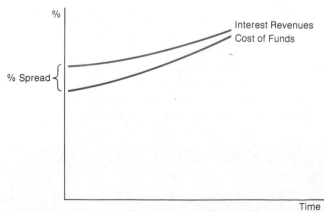

EXHIBIT 18.2 **Impact of Decreasing Interest Rates on a Bank's Net Interest Margin (If the Bank's Liabilities Are More Rate-Sensitive Than Its Assets)**

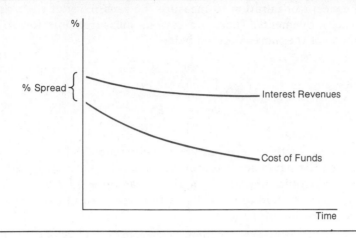

by interest rate fluctuations. A negative gap (or gap ratio of less than 1.00) suggests that rate-sensitive liabilities exceed rate-sensitive assets. Banks with a negative gap are typically concerned about a potential increase in interest rates, which could reduce their net interest margin.

While the gap as described here is an easy method for measuring a bank's interest rate risk, it has limitations. Banks must decide how to classify their liabilities and assets as rate-sensitive versus rate-insensitive. For example, should a Treasury security with a year to maturity be classified as rate-sensitive or rate-insensitive? How short must a maturity be to qualify for the rate-sensitive classification?

Each bank may have its own classification system, since there is no perfect measurement of their gap. Whatever system is used, there is a possibility of misinterpreting the gap measurement. Consider a bank that obtains much of its funds by issuing CDs with seven-day and one-month maturities, as well as money market deposit accounts (MMDAs). Also assume that the bank typically uses these funds to provide loans with a floating rate, adjusted once per year. These sources of funds and uses of funds will likely be classified as rate-sensitive. Thus, the gap will be close to zero, implying that the bank is not exposed to interest rate risk. Yet, there is a difference in the *degree* of rate sensitivity between the bank's sources and uses of funds. The rates paid by the bank on its sources of funds would change more frequently than rates earned on its uses of funds. Thus, the bank's net interest margin would likely be reduced during periods of rising interest rates. This reduction would not be detected by the gap measurement.

DURATION MEASUREMENT. An alternative approach to assess interest rate risk is to measure duration. Some assets or liabilities are more rate-sensitive than others, even if the frequency of adjustment and maturity are equal. The value of a ten-year zero coupon bond is more sensitive to interest rate fluctuations than a ten-year bond that pays coupon payments (as was

Chapter 18

Bank Management

demonstrated in Chapter 3). Thus, the market value of assets in a bank that invested in zero-coupon bonds would be very susceptible to interest rate movements. The duration measurement can capture these different degrees of sensitivity. In recent years, banks and other financial institutions have used the concept of **duration** to measure the sensitivity of their assets to interest rate movements. There are various measurements for an asset's duration, one of the more common being

$$D = \frac{\sum_{t=1}^{n} \dfrac{P_t(t)}{(1+i)^t}}{\sum_{t=1}^{n} \dfrac{P_t}{(1+i)^t}}$$

where P_t represents the interest or principal payments of the asset, t is the time at which the payments are provided, and i is the asset's yield to maturity. As an example, a bond with a $1,000 par value offering an 8 percent coupon rate with a yield to maturity of 14 percent and three years to maturity has a duration of

$$D = \frac{\dfrac{\$80(1)}{(1+.14)^1} + \dfrac{\$80(2)}{(1+.14)^2} + \dfrac{\$80(3)}{(1+.14)^3} + \dfrac{\$1,000(3)}{(1+.14)^3}}{\dfrac{\$80}{(1+.14)^1} + \dfrac{\$80}{(1+.14)^2} + \dfrac{\$80}{(1+.14)^3} + \dfrac{\$1,000}{(1+.14)^3}}$$

$$= \frac{\$70.18 + \$123.11 + \$161.99 + \$2,024.91}{\$70.18 + \$61.55 + \$54.00 + \$674.97}$$

$$= \frac{\$2,380.19}{\$860.70}$$

$$= 2.76$$

For comparison, the duration of a zero-coupon bond with the same 14 percent yield to maturity and three years to maturity has a duration of

$$D = \frac{\dfrac{\$0(1)}{(1+.14)^1} + \dfrac{\$0(2)}{(1+.14)^2} + \dfrac{\$0(3)}{(1+.14)^3} + \dfrac{\$1,000(3)}{(1+.14)^3}}{\dfrac{\$0}{(1+.14)^1} + \dfrac{\$0}{(1+.14)^2} + \dfrac{\$0}{(1+.14)^3} + \dfrac{\$1,000}{(1+.14)^3}}$$

$$= \frac{\$2,024.91}{\$674.97}$$

$$= 3.0$$

The duration of the zero-coupon bond is always equal to its maturity, whereas that of a coupon bond is always less than its maturity. Duration essentially converts the coupon bond into a measure that can be compared to the zero-coupon bond. In the preceding example, the zero-coupon bond's duration is 1.087 times the coupon bond's duration (computed as 3.00 divided by 2.76). This implies that the zero-coupon bond is 1.087 times as interest rate-sensitive as the coupon bond.

Other things equal, assets with shorter maturities have shorter durations; also, assets that generate more frequent coupon payments have shorter durations than those that generate less frequent payments. The duration of an asset portfolio is equal to the weighted average of the duration of individual components (the weights measure the proportional market value of each component). Banks and other financial institutions concerned with interest rate risk use duration to compare the rate-sensitivity of their entire asset and liability portfolios. They can attempt to create liability durations that conform to their asset duration. Because duration is especially critical for savings and loan associations (S&Ls), a numerical example of measuring the duration of an S&L's entire asset and liability portfolio is provided in Chapter 21.

While duration is a valuable technique for comparing the rate-sensitivity of various securities, its capabilities are limited when applied to assets that can be terminated on a moment's notice. For example, consider a bank that offers a fixed-rate five-year loan that can be paid off early without penalty. If the loan is not paid off early, it is perceived as rate-insensitive. Yet, there is the possibility that the loan will be terminated anytime over the five-year period. In this case, the bank would reinvest the funds at a rate dependent on market rates at that time. Thus, the funds used to provide the loan *can be* sensitive to interest rate movements, but the degree of sensitivity depends on when the loan is paid off. In general, loan prepayments are more common when market rates decline, since borrowers refinance by obtaining lower rate loans to pay off existing loans. The point here is that the possibility of prepayment makes it impossible to perfectly match the rate sensitivity of assets and liabilities.

SENSITIVITY OF PERFORMANCE TO INTEREST RATE MOVEMENTS. The two methods described for assessing interest rate risk are based on the bank's balance sheet composition. An alternative method would be to simply determine how performance has historically been influenced by interest rate movements. To do this, a proxy must be identified for bank performance and for prevailing interest rates, and a model that can estimate the relationship between the proxies must be chosen. A common proxy for performance is return on assets, return on equity, or the percentage change in stock price. A common proxy for interest rates is any market-determined rate, such as the Treasury bill yield. To determine how performance is affected by interest rates, *regression analysis* can be applied to historical data. For example, using Treasury bill yields (Y_T) as the interest rate proxy, the S&P 500 stock index as the market return (R_M), and the bank's stock return *(R)* as the performance proxy, the following regression model could be used:

$$R = b_0 + b_1 R_M + b_2 Y_T + u$$

where R_M is the return on the market, b_0, b_1, and b_2 are regression coefficients, and u is an error term. An additional independent variable representing the industry (such as the return on a banking stock index) may also be included in the model. The regression coefficient b_2 in this model would suggest how the return is affected by interest rate movements. A positive (negative) coefficient would suggest that performance is favorably (adversely) affected by rising interest rates. If the coefficient is not significantly different from

Chapter 18

Bank Management

zero, this would suggest that the bank's stock returns are insulated from interest rate movements.

Because a bank's assets and liabilities are replaced over time, exposure to interest rate risk must be continually reassessed. As exposure changes, the reaction of bank performance to a particular interest rate pattern will change.

Methods to Reduce Interest Rate Risk

Interest rate risk was closely monitored by banks during the late 1970s and the 1980s, as interest rate movements were very volatile. Interest rate risk can be reduced by

- Maturity matching
- Using floating-rate loans
- Using financial futures contracts
- Using interest rate swaps

MATURITY MATCHING.   One obvious method of reducing interest rate risk is to match each deposit's maturity with an asset of the same maturity. For example, if the bank receives funds for a one-year CD, it could provide a one-year loan or invest in a security with a one-year maturity. While this strategy would avoid interest rate risk, it could not be effectively implemented. Banks receive a large volume of short-term deposits and would not be able to match up maturities on deposits with the longer loan maturities. Borrowers rarely request funds for a period as short as one month, or even six months. In addition, the deposit amounts are typically small relative to the loan amounts. A bank would have difficulty in combining deposits with a particular maturity to accommodate a loan request with the same maturity.

USING FLOATING-RATE LOANS.   An alternative solution is the use of the floating-rate loan, which allows banks to support long-term assets with short-term deposits without overly exposing themselves to interest rate risk. Floating-rate loans cannot, however, completely eliminate the risk. If the cost of funds is changing on a more frequent basis than the rate on assets, the bank's net interest margin is still affected by interest rate fluctuations.

When banks reduce their exposure to interest rate risk by replacing long-term securities with more floating-rate commercial loans, they increase their exposure to default risk, since the commercial loans provided by banks typically have a higher frequency of default than securities held by banks. In addition, bank liquidity risk would increase, since loans are not as marketable as securities.

USING FINANCIAL FUTURES CONTRACTS.   Another method of reducing interest rate risk is to use financial futures contracts, which lock in the price at which specified financial instruments can be purchased or sold on a specified future settlement date. For example, there are futures contracts available on CDs. When banks lock in the price at which they can sell CDs for a particular settlement date, this effectively locks in their cost of obtaining these funds. Consequently, their overall cost of future funds is somewhat insulated from interest rate movements.

Exhibit 18.3 illustrates how the use of financial futures contracts can reduce the uncertainty about a bank's net interest margin. The sale of CD futures, for example, reduces the potential adverse effect of rising interest rates on its interest expenses. Yet, it also reduces the potential favorable effect of declining interest rates on its interest expenses. Assuming that the bank initially had more rate-sensitive liabilities, its use of futures would reduce its gap and therefore reduce the impact of interest rates on its net interest margin. More details on how financial futures can be used to hedge interest rate risk are provided in Chapter 21.

A recent study by Koppenhaver found evidence that banks whose liabilities are more rate-sensitive can benefit considerably from hedging with financial futures contracts. This study found that financial futures can reduce the variability of profits by as much as 80 percent.

USING INTEREST RATE SWAPS. A popular technique to hedge interest rate risk, the interest rate swap, has been especially useful for savings institutions whose liabilities are more rate-sensitive than their assets. It is thoroughly discussed in Chapter 21, but since some commercial banks engage in interest rate swaps, a brief description is also provided here.

A bank whose liabilities are more rate-sensitive than its assets can swap payments with a fixed interest rate in exchange for payments with a variable-interest rate over a specified period of time. If interest rates rise, the bank benefits because the payments to be received will increase while its outflow payments are fixed. This can offset the adverse impact of rising interest rates on the bank's net interest margin.

An interest rate swap requires another party that is willing to provide variable-rate payments in exchange for fixed-rate payments. Financial institutions that have more rate-sensitive assets than liabilities may be willing to assume such a position, since they could reduce their exposure to interest rate movements in this manner. A financial intermediary is typically needed to match up the two parties that desire an interest rate swap. Some investment banking firms and large banks serve in this role.

EXHIBIT 18.3   **Effect of Financial Futures on the Expected Spread of Banks that Have More Rate-sensitive Liabilities than Assets**

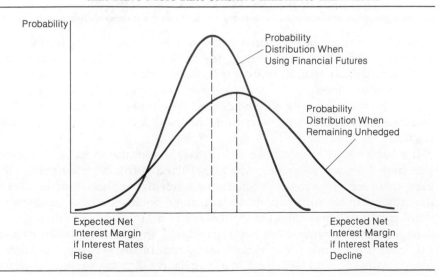

Accounting Rules and Futures Contracts

Current accounting procedures for futures contracts are set out in a uniform policy on bank contract activity issued by the Federal Reserve Board, the Federal Deposit Insurance Corporation, and the Comptroller of the Currency on November 15, 1979, revised March 12, 1980. Federal regulations give banks the option of carrying futures contracts on a mark-to-market or lower-of-cost-or-market basis. Other rules require all open contract positions be reviewed at least monthly, at which time market values are determined. Futures contracts are valued on either the market or lower-of-cost and market method, at the option of the bank, except that the accounting for trading account contracts and cash positions should be consistent. Underlying securities commitments relating to open futures contracts are not reported on the balance sheet; the only entries are for margin deposits, unrealized losses and, in certain instances, unrealized gains related to the contracts. In addition, banks must maintain general ledger memorandum accounts or commitment registers to identify and control all commitments to make or take delivery of securities. Following monthly contract valuation, unrealized losses would be recognized as a current expense item, and banks that value contracts on a market basis would also recognize unrealized gains as current income. Acquisition of securities under futures contracts are recorded on a basis consistent with that applied to the contracts, either market or lower-of-cost-or-market.

The Financial Accounting Standards Board (FASB), in its ruling effective December 31, 1984, introduced new guidelines for futures contracts. The new rules allow firms to use hedge accounting for future transactions.[1] In hedge accounting, a futures position is defined as a hedging transaction if it can be linked directly with an underlying asset or liability and if the price of the futures contracts is highly correlated with the price of the underlying cash position. If these conditions are met, and if the underlying cash position is not carried at market, futures gains

MANAGING EXPOSURE TO DEFAULT RISK

Most of a bank's funds are used either to make loans or to purchase debt securities. For either use of funds, the bank is acting as a creditor and is subject to default risk. In this context, default risk refers to the possibility that loans provided by the bank will not be repaid or that securities purchased by the bank will not be honored. The types of loans provided and securities purchased will determine the overall default risk of the asset portfolio.

If a bank wants to minimize default risk, it can use most of its funds to purchase Treasury securities, which are virtually free of default risk. However, these securities may not generate a much higher yield than the average overall cost of obtaining funds. In fact, some bank sources of funds can be more costly to banks than the yield earned on Treasury securities.

At the other extreme, a bank concerned with maximizing its return could use most of its funds for consumer and small business loans. Yet such an asset portfolio would be subject to a high degree of default risk. If economic

or losses can be *deferred* until the position is closed out. The gains or losses can then become part of the accounting basis of the underlying cash position to be *amortized* over the remaining life of the asset or liability, and therefore taken into income gradually.

The FASB standards require that banks and other firms formulate their hedged positions in light of their entire mix of assets and liabilities so that macro interest rate exposure is reduced by micro hedges. By insisting that all futures hedges be linked to an identifiable instrument "or group of instruments, such as loans that have similar terms" to qualify for hedge accounting, the FASB is encouraging banks to analyze thoroughly their overall exposure to interest rate risk as well as the components that make up that risk. The FASB standards, however, do not allow hedge accounting for the macro hedging of an overall gap on a bank's balance sheet that cannot be identified with a specific item.

The FASB statements call for the classification of deferred gains and losses as an adjustment to the carrying amount of the hedged items. Bankers should be aware that if such an adjustment is made to appropriate general ledger accounts, the computation of average daily balances for the purpose of determining average yields will be distorted unless special provisions are made. In addition, other FASB statements require that the amortization of the deferred futures gains or losses to interest income or expense start no later than the date that a particular contract is closed out. Profits or losses from the futures position must be taken into the income stream over that time period when the bank expected an adverse impact from interest rates.

1 Bank regulators reactions to FASB statement, if any, are yet to be determined. As a result, bank futures transactions are still governed by federal banking regulations.

SOURCE: This information was published in an article by Elijah Brewer, "Bank Gap Management and the Use of Financial Futures," *Economic Perspectives*, Federal Reserve Bank of Chicago, p. 21.

conditions deteriorate, a relatively large amount of high-risk loans may default.

The ideal objective for managing assets is to simultaneously maximize return on assets and minimize default risk. But, obviously, both objectives cannot be achieved simultaneously. The return on any bank asset depends on the risk involved. Because riskier assets offer higher returns, a bank's strategy to increase its return on assets will typically entail an increase in the overall default risk of its asset portfolio.

Because a bank cannot simultaneously maximize return and minimize default risk, it must compromise. That is, it will select some assets that generate high returns but are subject to a relatively high degree of default risk and also some assets that are very safe but offer a lower rate of return. This way the bank attempts to earn a *reasonable* return on its overall asset portfolio and maintain default risk at a *tolerable* level. What return level is reasonable? What level of default risk is tolerable? There is no consensus on these answers. The actual degree of importance attached to a high return versus low default risk is dependent on the risk-return preferences of a bank's shareholders and managers.

Chapter 18

Bank Management

As economic conditions change, so does the overall default risk of a bank's asset portfolio. Exhibit 18.4, which shows the delinquency rate on bank credit cards, provides a measure of default risk on consumer loans. The delinquency rates were relatively high during the recessionary period in the early 1980s. The credit card business has increased significantly in recent years. Because banks charge higher rates on financing credit card accounts than on most other loans, they can boost their expected return by increasing their credit card business. This is a typical example of increasing default risk in the attempt to increase return. Many banks have become more lenient in their credit standards in order to generate a greater amount of credit card business. Consequently, more undeserving consumers have obtained credit cards, and the delinquency rate has increased. For those banks that were too lenient, the wide spread between the return on credit card loans and the cost of funds has been offset by a high level of bad debt (default) expenses.

The relative default risk incurred by banks can be assessed by comparing the respective compositions of their asset portfolios. However, publicly available information does not provide a complete breakdown on asset composition. We can determine from financial statements the bank's securities as the percentage of total assets, and loans as a percentage of total assets. But we are not provided information about the risk levels of loans offered by the bank, or of securities purchased. Normally, a higher percentage of loans is perceived as more risky. Nevertheless, a bank with a greater percentage of loans could exhibit less default risk than a bank more heavily concentrated in securities if the former bank's loans are directed to very creditworthy firms while the latter bank's security holdings are somewhat risky.

Over time, economic conditions change and can cause banks to adjust their asset portfolios accordingly. For example, banks generally reduce loans and increase their purchases of low-risk securities during recessionary pe-

EXHIBIT 18.4 Delinquency Rate on Credit Cards

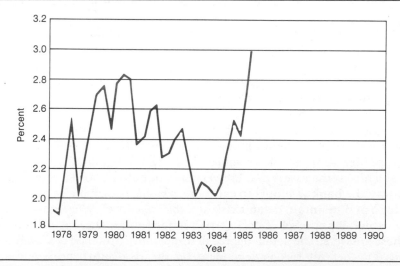

SOURCE: Federal Reserve Bank of New York, Annual Report, 1985, 7.

riods. In addition, they tend to provide a larger than normal volume of loans during an economic upswing.

Diversifying Default Risk

While all consumer and commercial loans exhibit some default risk, there are methods by which this risk can be managed. Banks should diversify their loans to assure that their customers are not dependent on a common source of income. For example, a bank in a small farming town that provides consumer loans to farmers and commercial loans to farm equipment manufacturers is highly susceptible to default risk. If the farmers experience a bad growing season due to poor weather conditions, they may be unable to repay their consumer loans. Furthermore, the farm equipment manufacturers would simultaneously experience a drop in sales and may be unable to repay their commercial loans.

This example is one of obvious mismanagement of the loan portfolio. In some cases, the mismanagement may not be so obvious. For example, consider a bank within a city that provides most of its commercial loans to firms in that city and has diversified its loans across various industries to avoid the problem just described. Assume that this city is the home of a large naval base. If for some reason, the servicemen employed at that base are sent out to sea, the city's firms may not be able to generate sufficient business to repay their loans. This example illustrates how corporate borrowers from different industries but the same geographic region can be similarly affected by a particular event.

To properly avoid excessive exposure to default risk, a bank should diversify its loans among various industries as well as geographic regions. But even a well-diversified loan portfolio can be highly exposed to default risk. A recession may have a systematic impact on all industries and geographic regions.

It has sometimes been suggested that a bank can reduce its loan exposure to a recessionary economy by diversifying its loans among countries. For example, a U.S. bank could lend some of its funds to firms or governments in other countries. Therefore, only part of its loan portfolio would be exposed to a U.S. recession. While this strategy deserves consideration, the international debt crisis in the early 1980s has dampened the desire by banks to implement it. During this crisis, several less developed countries (LDCs) could not repay the loans that were provided to them by U.S. banks. Many of these countries were simultaneously experiencing severe economic problems, that were due in part to a worldwide recession in 1982. During this recession, the global demand for LDC exports was substantially reduced. Consequently, the LDC income was not sufficient to repay loans.

The international debt crisis suggests that international diversification of loans among countries does not always prevent the possibility of several simultaneous defaulted loans. The crisis was largely attributed to the similar economic cycles of these countries. If all borrowers around the world are similarly affected by specific events, then international diversification of loans is not a viable solution.

In reality, diversifying loans across countries can often reduce the loan portfolio's exposure to any single economy or event. However, if the urge to diversify into geographic regions requires the acceptance of loan applicants with very high risk, the bank is defeating its purpose. The international debt crisis is discussed in greater detail in Chapter 20.

Credit Analysis

An important part of managing default risk is the credit assessment of loan applicants. A bank employs a staff of credit analysts to review the financial information of corporations applying for loans. From their review, they prepare an evaluation of the firm's creditworthiness. The evaluation should indicate the probability that the firm can meet its loan payments, so that a decision can be made as to whether the firm should be granted the loan. If a loan is to be granted, the evaluation can be used to determine the appropriate interest rate. Banks have historically provided loans at the so-called **prime rate** to the most creditworthy corporations. The loan applicants deserving of a loan may be rated on a basis of 1 to 5 (1 being the highest quality). The rating will dictate the premium to be added to the base rate. For example, a rating of 5 may dictate a 2 percent premium above the prime rate, while a rating of 3 may dictate a 1 percent premium. Given the current prime rate along with a rating of the potential borrower, the loan rate can be determined.

The prime rate charged by most banks is shown in Exhibit 18.5. Its movement is not continuous like the commercial paper rate (also shown in Exhibit 18.5), since it is set by banks and adjusted only periodically to keep it in line with market rates (and therefore consistently above the bank's cost of funds). During late 1981 and 1982, as rates decreased significantly, the prime rate was frequently revised. During 1983 market rates were less volatile, and the prime rate was less volatile as well. A higher prime rate in the early 1980s does not imply a higher profit margin to the bank, but rather a higher cost of obtaining funds.

Some loans to high-quality (low-risk) customers are commonly offered at rates below the prime rate. This does not necessarily imply that banks have reduced their spread. It may instead imply that the banks have redefined the prime rate to represent the appropriate loan rate for borrowers with a moderate risk rating. Thus, a discount would be attached to the prime rate when determining the loan rate for borrowers with a superior rating.

Each bank has its own formula for setting loan rates. Some banks may use their cost of funds rather than the prime rate as a base. They would

EXHIBIT 18.5 Prime Rate Offered by Commercial Banks

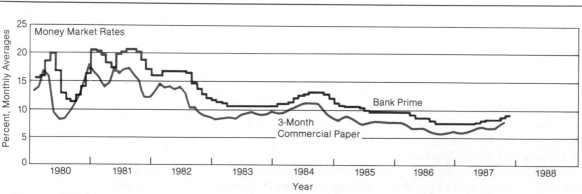

SOURCE: *Economic Trends*, Federal Reserve Bank of Cleveland (December 1987): 19.

attach larger premiums to their base, since the cost of funds will typically be at least 2 percent below the prime rate. Thus, a rating of 3 may translate to a loan rate of "cost of funds + 3 percent" (rather than the 1 percent premium if the prime rate is used as the base).

For each type of borrower, a separate formula may be used for attaching a premium to some base rate. This is necessary since a specific rating has a different interpretation for different loan types. For example, a corporation that receives a rating of 1 will likely receive a lower loan rate than an individual with a rating of 1, since consumer loans are generally perceived to be riskier on average than corporate loans. Whatever formula is used for each type of loan should account for the prevailing cost of funds and the borrower's risk.

From time to time, the competition among banks for the provision of loans will change, causing banks to disregard or revise their loan rate formula. For example, if competition intensifies and a particular bank realizes that it may lose a customer by charging a loan rate according to its conventional formula, it may decide to adjust that rate downward in order to maintain its relationship with that customer.

All banks will inevitably provide some loans that are nonperforming and eventually may be written off. In recent years, banks have often sold such loans at a discount in the secondary market. In this way, they can improve the market perception of their respective balance sheets. Financial institutions that can afford more risk and have a good reputation for dealing with troubled borrowers may consider purchasing these loans. While the large money center banks are the major participants in the secondary market for loans, smaller banks, savings and loan associations, insurance companies, and pension funds have acted as common purchasers of these loans.

BANK CAPITAL MANAGEMENT

To please shareholders, banks typically attempt to maintain only the amount of capital that is sufficient to support bank operations. If they have too much capital as a result of issuing excessive amounts of stock, each shareholder will receive a smaller proportion of any distributed earnings.

A common measure of the return to the shareholders is the *return on equity* (ROE), measured as

$$ROE = \frac{\text{net profit after taxes}}{\text{equity}}$$

The term *equity* represents the bank's capital. The return on equity can be broken down as follows:

$$ROE = \text{return on assets (ROA)} \times \text{leverage measure}$$

$$\frac{\text{net profit after taxes}}{\text{equity}} = \frac{\text{net profit after taxes}}{\text{assets}} \times \frac{\text{assets}}{\text{equity}}$$

The ratio (assets/equity) is sometimes called the *leverage measure*. Leverage reflects the volume of assets a firm supports with equity. The greater the leverage measure is, the greater the amount of assets per dollar's worth of equity. The above breakdown of ROE is useful because it can demonstrate how excessive capital can lower a bank's ROE. Consider two banks called Hilev and Lolev that each have a return on assets (ROA) of 1 percent. Hilev

Bank has a leverage measure of 15, while Lolev Bank has a leverage measure of 10. The ROE for each bank is determined:

ROE	=	ROA	× leverage measure
ROE for Hilev Bank	=	1%	× 15
	=	15%	
ROE for Lolev Bank	=	1%	× 10
	=	10%	

Even though each bank's assets are generating a 1 percent ROA, the ROE of Hilev Bank is much higher, because Hilev Bank is supporting its assets with a smaller proportion of capital. Bank regulators require banks to hold a minimum amount of capital, since capital can be used to absorb losses. Banks, however, generally prefer to hold a relatively low amount of capital for the reasons just expressed.

If banks are holding an excessive amount of capital, they can reduce it by distributing a high percentage of their earnings to shareholders (as dividends). Thus, capital management is related to the bank's dividend policy.

A growing bank may need more capital to support construction of new buildings, purchases of office equipment, and so forth. It would therefore need to retain a larger proportion of its earnings than a bank that has no plans for future growth. If the growing bank preferred to provide existing shareholders with a sizable dividend, it would then have to obtain the necessary capital through issuing new stock. This strategy allows the bank to distribute dividends but dilutes proportional ownership of the bank. An obvious trade-off exists here. The solution is not so obvious. A bank in need of capital must assess the trade-off involved and enact a policy that it believes will maximize the wealth of shareholders.

MANAGEMENT BASED ON FORECASTS

Some banks will position themselves to significantly benefit from an expected change in the economy. Exhibit 18.6 provides possible policy decisions for four different forecasts and suggests how a bank might react to each. This exhibit is simplified in that it does not consider future economic growth and interest rate movements simultaneously. Furthermore, it does not consider other economic forecasts that would also be considered by banks. However, it illustrates the type of risk-return trade-off constantly faced by bank managers. For example, if managers expected a strong economy, they could boost earnings by shifting into relatively risky loans and securities that pay a high return. If a strong economy does occur as expected, only a small percentage of the loans and securities will default, and the bank's strategy will result in improved earnings. However, if the bank's forecast turns out to be wrong, its revised asset portfolio will be more susceptible to a weak economy. The bank could be severely damaged during a weak economy, since several borrowers are likely to default on their loans and securities.

Other, more conservative banks could not have been as influenced by an inaccurate forecast of the economy if they maintained a sizable portion of very safe loans and securities. However, if the economy had strengthened as predicted, these banks would not have benefited. The degree to which a bank is willing to revise its balance sheet structure in accordance with economic forecasts depends on the confidence in those forecasts and its willingness to incur risk.

Because the first two forecasts shown in Exhibit 18.6 are on economic growth, they relate to default risk. The last two forecasts are on interest rates and therefore relate to interest rate risk. Banks cannot completely adjust their balance sheet structure in accordance with economic forecasts. For example, they cannot implement a policy of accepting only long-term CDs just because they believe interest rates will rise. Yet, they could attract

EXHIBIT 18.6 Bank Management of Liabilities and Assets Due to Economic Forecasts

Economic Forecast by the Banks	Appropriate Adjustment to Liability Structure Based on the Forecast	Appropriate Adjustment to Asset Structure Based on the Forecast	General Assessment of Bank's Adjusted Balance Sheet Structure
1. Strong economy		Concentrate more heavily on loans; reduce holdings of low-risk securities	Increased potential for stronger earnings; increased exposure of bank earnings to default risk
2. Weak economy		Concentrate more heavily on risk-free securities and low-risk loans; reduce holdings of risky loans	Reduced default risk; reduced potential for stronger earnings if the economy does not weaken
3. Increasing interest rates	Attempt to attract CDs with long-term maturities	Apply floating-interest rates to loans whenever possible; avoid long-term securities	Reduced interest rate risk; reduced potential for stronger earnings if interest rates decrease
4. Decreasing interest rates	Attempt to attract CDs with short-term maturities	Apply fixed-interest rates to loans whenever possible; concentrate on long-term securities or loans	Increased potential for stronger earnings; increased interest rate risk

a greater than normal amount of long-term CDs by offering an attractive interest rate on long-term CDs and advertising this rate to consumers.

The bank's balance sheet management will affect its performance (as measured from its income statement) in the following ways. First, its liability structure will influence its interest and non-interest expenses on the income statement. If it obtains a relatively large portion of its funds from conventional demand deposits, interest expenses should be relatively low, while its noninterest expenses (due to check-clearing, processing, etc.) should be relatively high. A bank's asset structure can also affect expenses. If it maintains a relatively large portion of commercial loans, its noninterest expenses should be high due to the labor cost of assessing the borrower's credit, along with loan-processing costs. Yet, banks with the heaviest concentration in commercial loans expect their additional interest revenues to more than offset the additional noninterest expenses incurred. Their strategy would pay off only if they can avoid a sizable number of defaulted loans. Of course, this is the risk they must take in striving for a high return.

Ideally, banks would use an aggressive approach when they can capitalize on favorable economic conditions but insulate themselves during adverse economic conditions. Because economic conditions cannot always be accurately forecasted for several years in advance, there will continue to be defaults on loans by even the well-managed banks. This is a cost of doing business. Banks attempt to use proper diversification so that a domino effect of defaulted loans will not occur within their loan portfolio. Similarly, interest rate movements can not always be accurately forecasted. Thus, banks should not be overly aggressive in attempting to capitalize on interest rate forecasts. They should assess the sensitivity of their future performance to each possible interest rate scenario that could occur, to assure that their balance sheet is structured to survive any possible scenario.

INTEGRATED BANK MANAGEMENT: AN EXAMPLE

In an attempt to consolidate some of the key concepts of this chapter, consider the following example. Assume that you are hired as a consultant by Atlanta Bank to evaluate its favorable and unfavorable aspects. Atlanta Bank's balance sheet is disclosed in Exhibit 18.7.

A bank's balance sheet can best be evaluated by adjusting the actual dollar amounts of balance sheet components to a percentage of assets. This conversion allows for a comparison of the bank with its competitors. Exhibit 18.8 shows each balance sheet component as a percentage of total assets for Atlanta Bank (derived from Exhibit 18.7). To the right of each bank percentage is the assumed industry average percentage for a sample of banks with a similar amount of assets. For example, the bank's required reserves are 4 percent of assets (same as the industry average), its floating-rate commercial loans are 30 percent of assets (versus an industry average of 20 percent), and so on. The same type of comparison is provided for liabilities and capital on the right side of the exhibit. A comparative analysis relative to the industry can indicate the management style of Atlanta Bank.

It is possible to evaluate the potential level of interest revenues, interest expenses, noninterest revenues, and noninterest expenses for Atlanta Bank relative to the industry. Furthermore, it is possible to assess the bank's exposure to default risk and interest rate risk as compared to the industry.

EXHIBIT 18.7 Balance Sheet of Atlanta Bank (in Millions of Dollars)

Assets			Liabilities and Capital		
Required reserves		$ 400	Demand deposits		$ 500
Commercial loans			NOW accounts		1,200
Floating-rate	3,000		MMDAs		2,000
Fixed-rate	1,100				
Total		4,100	CDs		
Consumer loans		2,500	Short-term	1,500	
			From 1 to 5 yrs	4,000	
Mortgages			Total		5,500
Floating-rate	500				
Fixed-rate	None		Long-term bonds		200
Total		500	CAPITAL		600
Treasury securities					
Short-term	1,000				
Long-term	None				
Total		1,000			
Corporate securities					
High-rated	None				
Moderate-rated	1,000				
Total		1,000			
Municipal securities					
High-rated	None				
Moderate-rated	None				
Total		None			
Fixed assets		500			
TOTAL ASSETS		**$10,000**	**TOTAL LIABILITIES and CAPITAL**		**$10,000**

A summary of Atlanta Bank based on the information in Exhibit 18.8 is provided in Exhibit 18.9. While its interest expenses are expected to be above the industry average, so are its interest revenues. Thus, it is difficult to determine whether Atlanta Bank's net interest margin will be above or below the industry average. Because it is more heavily concentrated in risky loans and securities, its default risk is higher than the average bank. Yet, its interest rate risk is less due to its relatively high concentration of medium-term CDs and floating-rate loans. A gap measurement of Atlanta Bank can be conducted by first identifying the rate-sensitive liabilities and assets, as follows:

Rate-Sensitive Assets	Amount (in Millions)	Rate-Sensitive Liabilities	Amount (in Millions)
Floating-rate loans	$3,000	NOW accounts	1,200
Floating-rate mortgages	500	MMDAs	2,000
Short-term Treasury securities	1,000	Short-term CDs	1,500
	4,500		4,700

EXHIBIT 18.8 Comparative Balance Sheet of Atlanta Bank

Assets	Percent of Assets for Atlanta Bank	Average Percent for Industry	Liabilities and Capital	Percent of Total for Atlanta Bank	Average Percent for Industry
Required reserves	4%	4%	Demand deposits	5%	17%
Commercial loans			NOW accounts	12	10
Floating-rate	30	20	MMDAs	20	20
Fixed-rate	11	11			
Total	41	31	CDs		
Consumer loans	25	20	Short-term	15	35
			From 1 to 5 yrs	40	10
Mortgages			Total	55	45
Floating-rate	5	7			
Fixed-rate	0	3	Long-term bonds	2	2
Total	5	10	CAPITAL	6	6
Treasury securities					
Short-term	10	7			
Long-term	0	8			
Total	10	15			
Corporate securities					
High-rated	0	5			
Moderate-rated	10	5			
Total	10	10			
Municipal securities					
High-rated	0	3			
Moderate-rated	0	2			
Total	0	5			
Fixed Assets	5	5		—	—
TOTAL ASSETS	100%	100%	TOTAL LIABILITIES and CAPITAL	100%	100%

$$\text{Gap} = \$4,500 \text{ million} - \$4,700 \text{ million}$$
$$= -\$200 \text{ million}$$

$$\text{Gap ratio} = \frac{\$4,500 \text{ million}}{\$4,700 \text{ million}}$$
$$= \text{approx. } .957$$

The gap measurements suggest somewhat similar rate-sensitivity on both sides of the balance sheet.

The future performance of Atlanta Bank relative to the industry depends on future economic conditions. If interest rates rise, it will be more insulated than other banks. If interest rates fall, other banks will likely benefit to a greater degree. Under conditions of a strong economy, Atlanta Bank would likely benefit more than other banks, due to its aggressive lending approach. Conversely, an economic slowdown could cause more loan defaults, and Atlanta Bank would be more susceptible to possible defaults than other banks. This could be confirmed only if more details were provided (such as

EXHIBIT 18.9 Evaluation of Atlanta Bank Based on its Balance Sheet

Expenses	Main Influential Components	Evaluation of Atlanta Bank Relative to Industry
Interest expenses	All liabilities except demand deposits	Higher than industry average since it concentrates more on high-rate deposits than the norm.
Noninterest expenses	Loan volume and checkable deposit volume	Questionable; its checkable deposit volume is less than the norm, but its loan volume is greater than the norm.
Interest revenues	Volume and composition of loans and securities	Potentially higher than industry average because its assets are generally riskier than the norm.
Exposure to default risk	Volume and composition of loans and securities	Higher concentration of loans than industry average; it has a greater percentage of risky assets than the norm.
Exposure to interest rate risk	Maturities on liabilities and assets; use of floating-rate loans	Lower than the industry average; it has more medium-term liabilities, less assets with very long maturities, and more floating-rate loans

a more comprehensive breakdown of the balance sheet). Of course, a realistic evaluation would involve additional details.

EXAMPLES OF BANK MISMANAGEMENT

Poor bank management will lead to subpar performance or possibly even failure. To illustrate the financial problems that can result, the actual situations for four large well-known banks are summarized below.

Franklin National Bank

Franklin National Bank used an aggressive management approach during the late 1960s and early 1970s. It provided fixed-rate long-term loans to customers with a questionable credit standing. The funds obtained to support these loans were of a short-term nature and therefore were rate-sensitive. Overall, the bank had a high exposure to default risk and interest rate risk. As interest rates began to increase, the rate-sensitive liabilities became more expensive while the interest payments received on long-term fixed rate assets were unaffected. In addition, a substantial amount of the risky loans defaulted.

In 1973 a deposit run on the bank occurred as the bank's financial problems were realized by the public, subjecting the bank to high liquidity risk. Meanwhile, the bank took speculative positions in foreign exchange in an effort to offset its other losses. Again, the aggressive action backfired as the values of its foreign exchange positions declined, and Franklin National Bank failed in 1974. It has often been suggested that this bank failed because of its foreign exchange dealings. While this was the final nail in the coffin, other managerial decisions related to default risk and interest rate risk led to its initial problems.

First Pennsylvania Bank

First Pennsylvania Bank used an aggressive management approach over the 1970s. It provided a substantial volume of loans in the early 1970s to customers whose creditworthiness was questionable. The 1974–1975 recession caused massive business failures and led to a high default percentage on its loans. In addition, First Pennsylvania implemented a balance sheet management approach in the mid 1970s that concentrated on rate-sensitive liabilities (short-term deposits) and rate-insensitive assets. Because interest rates increased substantially, the cost of the rate-sensitive liabilities increased, while the interest revenues on rate-insensitive assets were generally unaffected. Financial problems due to these management errors led to a run on deposits, (causing high liquidity risk), and the FDIC subsequently intervened to remedy the financial problems and reorganize the bank.

Penn Square Bank

Penn Square Bank used an aggressive lending approach of heavily concentrating on energy-related loans in the late 1970s and early 1980s. These loans were used by corporations to explore for and produce various forms of energy. Due to the decline in energy prices in 1981 and 1982, many energy-related ventures no longer appeared feasible. The initially forecasted return on such ventures was based on overly optimistic market prices of energy. In addition, the collateral on these loans was deficient. When borrowers were unable to repay loans, Penn Square commonly "rolled" interest into their existing loans. That is, it would provide a new loan to borrowers that would be used to pay principal and interest on prevailing loans. Then these prevailing loans were recorded as "paid" rather than "overdue" (this strategy has also been used by large banks on loans to less developed countries). Penn Square could not afford to roll interest into the growing number of nonperforming loans, and it failed in 1982.

Continental Illinois Bank

Continental Illinois Bank experienced sizable defaults on its loans in the early 1980s. A portion of these defaults were due to loan participations whereby Continental provided loans for energy-related ventures originated by Penn Square Bank. Like the loans made by Penn Square, the loans by Continental in which Penn Square acted as the agent also defaulted. While Penn Square originated the loans, Continental was held responsible for assuring that the loan customers were creditworthy. As news of Continental's financial problems became widespread in 1983, those depositors with deposit amounts exceeding the $100,000 insurable limit began to withdraw their funds. Because Continental heavily relied on large depositors for its funds, its deposit level declined dramatically. This liquidity risk compounded Continental's problems, and the FDIC subsequently intervened to rescue the troubled bank.

Implications of Bank Mismanagement

The preceding examples are not meant to imply that banks should always implement ultra-conservative strategies. In such a competitive environment, conservative management can cause a bank to fall behind its competitors. However, a proper balance should be maintained. The aggressive lending approaches used by the banks described left them severely exposed to default risk. Furthermore, a wide gap between the amount of rate-sensitive liabilities versus assets is extremely risky, especially given the volatility of interest rates over time. Banks can provide a moderate amount of high-yielding loans and maintain a moderate gap based on their interest rate forecast without overexposing themselves to the possibility of failure. These examples of bank mismanagement demonstrate the consequences of being overexposed to an inaccurate forecast. Obviously, a correct forecast may have allowed these banks to experience very high performance levels. Yet, the most successful banks over the last several years have not been overly aggressive.

SUMMARY

Due to the reduction of regulatory barriers, competition in the banking industry has increased and will continue to do so. Only the well-managed banks will survive. Thus, bank management has become much more important in recent years.

Bank management should be implemented in a manner that meets overall objectives. Because the individual objectives of maximizing return and minimizing the risk cannot be simultaneously achieved, each bank must strike a balance between its risk and return objectives. Banks that are more willing to accept risk will structure their balance sheets to take full advantage of economic forecasts. Banks with a more conservative philosophy will structure their balance sheet to better defend against adverse conditions, although they will forego potential benefits if conditions are more favorable.

Bank management, along with the prevailing economic environment, will dictate bank performance. To assess the efficiency of previous managerial decisions, bank performance should be examined over time. During some periods, severe economic conditions may cause most banks to experience poor performance. Alternatively, favorable economic conditions may cause most banks to perform very well. Because the economy can have a systematic impact on all banks, the managerial efficiency of an individual bank can best be assessed by comparing its performance to that of competitors within the industry. An assessment of bank performance is presented in the following chapter.

KEY TERMS

duration	net interest margin
gap	prime rate
gap ratio	spread

QUESTIONS

18.1. What is accomplished when a bank integrates its liability management with its asset management?

18.2. Given the liquidity advantage of holding Treasury bills, why do banks hold only a relatively small portion of their assets as Treasury bills?

18.3. How do banks resolve illiquidity problems?

18.4. If a bank expects interest rates to decrease over time, how might it alter the degree of rate-sensitivity on its assets and liabilities?

18.5. List some rate-sensitive assets and some rate-insensitive assets of banks.

18.6. If a bank is very uncertain about future interest rates, how might it insulate its future performance from future interest rate movements?

18.7. Define the formula for the net interest margin, and explain why it is closely monitored by banks.

18.8. Assume that a bank expects to attract most of its funds through short-term CDs and would prefer to use most of its funds to provide long-term loans. How could it achieve this and still reduce interest rate risk?

18.9. According to this chapter, have banks been able to insulate themselves against interest rate movements? Explain.

18.10 Define a bank's gap and what it attempts to determine. Interpret a negative gap.

18.11. What are some limitations of measuring a bank's gap?

18.12. How do banks use the duration measurement?

18.13. Why do loans that can be prepaid on a moment's notice complicate the bank's assessment of interest rate risk?

18.14. Can a bank simultaneously maximize return and minimize default risk? If not, what can be done instead?

18.15. As economic conditions change, how do banks adjust their asset portfolio?

18.16. What two ways should a bank properly diversify its loans? Why?

18.17. Is international diversification of loans a viable solution to default risk? Defend your answer.

18.18. Do all commercial borrowers receive the same interest rate on loans? Explain.

18.19. Why might a bank retain some excess earnings rather than distribute them as dividends?

18.20. If a bank has more rate-sensitive liabilities than rate-sensitive assets, what will happen to its net interest margin during a period of rising interest rates? During a period of declining interest rates?

18.21. Does the use of floating-rate loans eliminate interest rate risk? Explain.

18.22. Explain the reasons for Franklin National Bank's failure.

PROBLEMS

18.1. Suppose a bank earns $201 million in interest revenue but pays $156 million in interest expense. It also has $800 million in earning assets. What is its net interest margin?

18.2. If a bank earns $169 million net profit after tax and has $17 billion invested in assets, what is its return on assets?

18.3. If a bank earns $75 million net profits after tax and has $7.5 billion invested in assets and $600 million equity investment, what is its return on equity?

18.4. Use the balance sheet for San Diego Bank in Exhibit A and the industry norms in Exhibit B to answer the following questions:

a. Estimate the gap and the gap ratio and determine how San Diego Bank would be affected by an increase in interest rates over time.

b. Assess San Diego Bank's default risk. Does it appear high or low relative to the industry? Would San Diego Bank perform better or worse than other banks during a recession?

c. For any type of bank risk that appears to be higher than the industry, explain how the balance sheet could be restructured to reduce the risk.

EXHIBIT A Balance Sheet for San Diego Bank (in Millions of Dollars)

Assets			Liabilities and Capital	
Required reserves		$ 800	Demand deposits	$ 800
Commercial loans			NOW Accounts	2,500
Floating-rate	None		MMDAs	6,000
Fixed-rate	7,000			
Total		7,000	CDs	
Consumer loans		5,000	Short-term	9,000
			From 1 to 5 yrs.	None
Mortgages			Total	9,000
Floating-rate	None			
Fixed-rate	2,000		Federal funds	500
Total		2,000	Long-term bonds	400
Treasury securities			CAPITAL	800
Short-term	None			
Long-term	1,000			
Total		1,000		
Long-term corporate securities				
High-rated	None			
Moderate-rated	2,000			
Total		2,000		
Long-term municipal securities				
High-rated	None			
Moderate-rated	1,700			
Total		1,700		
Fixed Assets		500		
TOTAL ASSETS		20,000	TOTAL LIABILITIES AND CAPITAL	20,000

EXHIBIT B Industry Norms in Percentage Terms

Assets		Liabilities and Capital	
Required reserves	4%	Demand deposits	17%
Commercial loans		NOW accounts	10
Floating-rate	20		
Fixed-rate	11	MMDAs	20
Total	31		
		CDs	
Consumer loans	20	Short-term	35
		From 1 to 5 yrs.	10
Mortgages		Total	45
Floating-rate	7		
Fixed-rate	3	Long-term bonds	2
Total	10		
		CAPITAL	6
Treasury securities			
Short-term	7		
Long-term	8		
Total	15		
Long-term corporate securities			
High-rated	5		
Moderate-rated	5		
Total	10		
Long-term municipal securities			
High-rated	3		
Moderate-rated	2		
Total	5		
Fixed Assets	5		
TOTAL ASSETS	100%	TOTAL LIABILITIES AND CAPITAL	100%

PROJECT

1. ASSESSING A BANK'S MANAGERIAL POLICIES.

Your professor will assign you (or your group) a bank or allow you to choose one. Use the most recent annual report of the bank to answer the following questions. (A more thorough analysis of the project can be conducted if the last ten years are examined, which would require some previous annual reports or financial statement data provided by investor's services, such as *Moody's Banking and Finance Manual*.)

a. Summarize how the bank manages its liquidity risk (if explained in the annual report).

b. Determine the bank's gap and its gap ratio over recent years. How would the bank's net interest margin be affected if interest rates increase in the future? Explain?

c. If a software regression package is available, determine how the bank's stock returns have been affected by interest rates over time using the model described in the chapter. Interpret the regression results. Based on this regression analysis, how would the bank's net interest margin be affected if interest rates increase in the future? Do these implications coincide with those of part b?

d. Summarize the bank's use of floating-rate loans, financial futures contracts, or interest rate swaps to manage its interest rate risk.

e. Describe the bank's present status regarding loans to less developed countries. Is it highly exposed? What has it done (if anything) to reduce its exposure to LDC loans?

f. How has the bank's capital ratio changed over time? How will this change affect its risk? How does it affect existing and potential profitability?

g. How will the bank perform if economic conditions are very favorable? Would it be severely affected by a recession? Explain. Based on your projections of interest rates and economic conditions, provide your assessment of the bank. Would you recommend buying or selling stock of this bank? Explain.

REFERENCES

Andrews, Suzanna. "Can Banks Succeed in Futures?" *Institutional Investor* (February 1984): 173–186.

Blackwell, James M. and George M. McCabe. "The Hedging Strategy." *Journal of Bank Research* (Summer 1981): 114–118.

Booth, Geoffrey and Peter Koveos. "A Programming Model for Bank Hedging Decisions." *Journal of Financial Research* (Fall 1986): 271–279.

Booth, James R. Richard L. Smith, and Richard W. Stolz. "Use of Interest Rate Futures by Financial Institutions." *Journal of Bank Research* (Spring 1984): 15–20.

Booth, James and Dennis Officer. "Expectations, Interest Rates, and Commercial Bank Stocks." *Journal of Financial Research* (Spring 1985): 51–57.

Chance, Don M. and William R. Lane. "A Reexamination of Interest Rate Sensitivity in the Common Stocks of Financial Institutions." *Journal of Financial Research* (Spring 1980): 49–55.

Cothren, Richard. "Asymmetric Information and Optimal Bank Reserves." *Journal of Money, Credit, and Banking* (February 1987): 68–77.

Crane, Dwight B. and Robert Eccles. "Commercial Banks: Taking Shape for Turbulent Times." *Harvard Business Review* (November–December 1987): 94–109.

Dermine, Jean. "The Measurement of Interest Rate Risk by Financial Intermediaries." *Journal of Bank Research* (Summer 1985): 86–90.

Flannery, Mark J. "How Do Changes in Market Interest Rates Affect Bank Profits?" *Business Review*, Federal Reserve Bank of Philadelphia (September–October 1980): 13–22.

Gardener, E. P. M. "Balance Sheet Management—New Tool for an Old Problem." *Banker's Magazine* (July–August 1983): 58–62.

Gendreau, Brian. "When Is the Prime Rate Second Choice?" *Business Review*, Federal Reserve Bank of Philadelphia (May–June 1983): 13–21.

Giroux, Gary A. "A Survey of Forecasting Techniques Used by Commercial Banks." *Journal of Bank Research* (Spring 1980): 51–53.

Greenbaum, Stuart and Anjan Thakor. "Bank Funding Modes: Securitization versus Deposits." *Journal of Banking and Finance* (September 1987); 379–401.

Haslem, John A., James P. Bedingfield, and A. J. Stagliano. "An Analysis of Liquidity Measures and Relative Bank Profitability." *Akron Business and Economic Review* (Winter 1985): 37–43.

Jain, Arvind and Satyadev Gupta. "Some Evidence of "Herding" Behavior by U.S. Banks."

Journal of Money, Credit, and Banking (February 1987): 78–89.

James, Christopher. "Off-Balance Sheet Banking." Economic Review, Federal Reserve Bank of San Francisco (Fall 1987): 21–36.

James, Christopher. "Some Evidence on the Uniqueness of Bank Loans." Journal of Financial Economics, (December 1987): 217–236.

Kanatas, George. "Commercial Paper, Bank Reserve Requirements, and the Informational Role of Loan Commitments." Journal of Banking and Finance (September 1987): 425–448.

Keen, Howard Jr. "The Impact of a Dividend Cut Announcement on Bank Share Prices." Journal of Bank Research (Winter 1983): 274–281.

Koppenhaver, G. D. "Selective Hedging of Bank Assets with Treasury Bill Futures Contracts." Journal of Financial Research (Summer 1984): 105–119.

Mitchell, Karlyn. "Interest Rate Risk Management at Tenth District Banks." Economic Review, Federal Reserve Bank of Kansas City (May 1985): 3–19.

Pavel, Christine and Paula Binkley. "Costs and Competition in Bank Credit Cards" Economic Perspectives, Federal Reserve Bank of Chicago (March–April 1987): 3–13.

Pavel, Christine and David Phillis. "Why Commercial Banks Sell Loans: An Empirical Analysis." Economic Perspectives, Federal Reserve Bank of Chicago (May–June 1987): 3–14.

Picou, Glenn. "Managing Interest Rate Risk with Interest Rate Futures." The Bankers Magazine, 76–86.

Rosenberg, Joel L. "The Joys of Duration." Bankers Magazine, (March–April 1986): 62–67.

Simmons, Richard. "Would Banks Buy Daytime Fed Funds?" Economic Perspectives, Federal Reserve Bank of Chicago (May–June 1987): 36–43.

Sprenkle, Case. "Liability and Asset Uncertainty for Banks." Journal of Banking and Finance (March 1987): 147–160.

Thakor, Anjan and Gregory Udell. "An Economic Rationale for the Pricing Structure of Bank Loan Commitments." Journal of Banking and Finance (June 1987): 271–289.

Whittaker, J. Gregg. "Interest Rate Swaps: Risk and Regulation." Economic Review, Federal Reserve Bank of Kansas City (March 1987): 3–13.

Market Reaction to Policies

Bank managers attempt to implement policies that enhance the bank's stock performance. They can assess the market's reaction to previous policies implemented by various banks by performing an event study. If the market reacts favorably, this suggests that the policy is anticipated to improve the bank's performance over time. If the market reacts unfavorably, this implies that the policy is expected to reduce the bank's performance. When there is no market reaction, the policy is expected to have no impact on the bank's performance. To assess market reaction, the cumulative average residual (CAR) analysis is often utilized. A brief explanation of CAR analysis follows. For a more thorough explanation, see the article by Fama, Fisher, Jensen and Roll listed at the end of the appendix.

Consider the bank policy to cut dividends. One may hypothesize that a dividend cut could be favorably received by the market if the amount representing the reduced dividends is expected to be reinvested by the bank in a manner that will generate high returns in the future. However, an alternative hypothesis is that a dividend cut signals that the bank is expecting poor performance in the future and cannot afford its present dividend payment schedule. To determine how bank share prices are affected, a sample of banks that cut dividends must first be identified. Then the announcement date of each bank's dividend cut must be determined. The announcement date is more important than the actual date in which the dividends are cut, because investors would likely react immediately to the announcement if they are to react at all.

Daily stock returns for each bank in the sample are compiled for a period prior to their respective announcement dates (sometimes weekly observations are used instead). This so-called *estimation period* is used to estimate the bank's beta with the following model:

$$R_{j,t} = b_0 + b_1 R_{m,t} + u_t$$
where $R_{j,t}$ = the bank's return over day t
$R_{m,t}$ = the market return over day t

$$b_0 = \text{intercept}$$
$$b_1 = \text{estimated beta of the bank}$$
$$u_t = \text{error term}$$

The length of the estimation period is somewhat subjective, but for our example, assume that it begins 120 days before the announcement date and ends 20 days before the announcement date. Then the expected return of each bank is determined over the so-called examination period, based on the regression coefficients and the actual values of the market return.

For our example, assume that the examination period extended from 19 days before the announcement date until 40 days after the announcement date. The expected return for each observation over this period represents the return on the bank's stock that should have occurred in the absence of any abnormal reaction by the market. By comparing the actual return to the bank's expected return, we can determine whether any abnormal return $(AR_{j,t})$ occurred for the bank during the observation t:

$$AR_{j,t} = R_{j,t} - E(R_{j,t})$$
$$= R_{j,t} - (b_0 + b_1 R_{m,t})$$

The abnormal returns (sometimes called *residuals*) are estimated for each observation over the examination period. Positive abnormal returns suggest that the actual return is more than it would have been in the absence of any market reaction and therefore that the market reacted favorably. A negative abnormal return implies that the actual return was less than it would have been in the absence of any market reaction and therefore that the market reacted unfavorably.

In some cases, an abnormal return will occur before the announcement date, which suggests that the market anticipated the news before it was officially announced. Since the examination period usually contains some observations prior to the announcement date, it is possible to detect such an anticipated reaction.

The market reaction to a single bank's policy is not normally considered to be sufficient for making implications about the industry as a whole. For this reason, the procedure described here is replicated for each bank that had a similar announcement. For each observation within the examination period, the abnormal returns (or residuals) are consolidated among all banks to estimate an average residual for the portfolio

$$(AR_{p,t}):$$

$$AR_{p,t} = \sum_{j=1}^{n} AR_{j,t} / n$$

for all n banks that were examined. The average residual is estimated over each day of the examination period, with specific emphasis around the announcement date. The average residuals, starting on the first day of the examination period, are accumulated over each successive day to determine cumulative average residuals. Because the average residuals for any given observation could differ from zero by chance, they are tested to determine whether they are statistically significant (different from zero). This test provides greater reliability about any implications that are drawn from the analysis.

The analysis described here (or some derivative of it) has been used to assess the market reaction to a variety of bank managerial policies, such as bank recapitalization plans and the formation of holding companies. It has also been used to assess market reaction to regulatory events, such as the elimination of deposit rate ceilings and intrastate banking regulations. It has even been used to assess market reaction to the international debt crisis. The analysis has also been applied to events affecting other financial institutions, such as brokerage firms, savings institutions, and insurance companies.

SOURCE: Eugene Fama, Lawrence Fisher, Michael Jensen and Richard Roll, "The Adjustment of Stock Prices to New Information," *International Economic Review* (February 1969): 1–21.

Bank Performance

BANK PERFORMANCE IN PERSPECTIVE

The performance of some major commercial banks in the first quarter of 1988 is summarized below:

■ Chase Manhattan Corporation experienced a high increase in profit as it recovered from large foreign loan losses in the previous year. Its profits were also enhanced by the sales of various divisions.

■ First Bank System Incorporated experienced a decrease in profit because of the poor performance of its bond portfolio as interest rates increased.

■ Continental Illinois experienced a high increase in profit partially because the volume of nonperforming loans declined. In addition, it exchanged much of its Mexican loans and increased the spread between the average rate earned on assets versus the average rate paid on deposits.

■ Bank America's net income was $109 million or 56 cents per share over the quarter. This reflected an improvement, as Bank America experienced losses during the previous three years. The improvement was attributed to its reduced loan losses and a reduction in noninterest expenses.

■ Wells Fargo experienced high earnings partially because of its increase in noninterest income and reductions in noninterest expenses.

■ Mellon Bank improved its earnings primarily because of its reduction in loan losses.

───────

■ What other factors affect bank performance?

■ How can bank performance be quantitatively measured?

■ Do large banks typically outperform small banks?

These and other related questions are addressed in this chapter.

OUTLINE

A commercial bank's performance is examined for various reasons. Bank regulators identify banks that are experiencing severe problems so that they can remedy them. Shareholders need to determine whether they should buy or sell their bank's stock. Investment analysts must be able to advise prospective investors on which banks to invest in. Furthermore, commercial banks evaluate their own performance over time to determine the outcomes of previous management decisions so that changes can be made where appropriate. Without persistent monitoring of performance, existing problems can remain unnoticed and lead to financial failure in the future.

This chapter discusses the overall performance of banks in recent years, including comparisons by size classification, and identifies the characteristics that have the most influence on performance.

PERFORMANCE EVALUATION OF BANKS

Exhibit 19.1 summarizes the performance of all U.S.–chartered insured commercial banks. The characteristics identified in the first column are discussed in order from the top down. Each characteristic is measured as a percentage of assets, in order to control for growth when assessing the changes in each characteristic over time.

Gross interest income represents interest income generated from all assets. It is affected by market rates and the composition of assets held by banks. As a percentage of assets for all banks in aggregate, it was highest in 1981, since interest rates were at their peak then.

Exhibit 19.2 shows that in 1985 and 1986, the gross interest income of money center banks was significantly lower than that of small and medium-sized banks. This was partially due to the concessions money center banks granted to borrowers from less developed countries that were unable to meet their loan repayment schedule.

Gross interest expense (in Row 2 of Exhibit 19.1) represents interest paid on deposits and on other borrowed funds (from the federal funds market, discount window, etc.). It is affected by market rates and the composition of liabilities. Since NOW accounts and money market deposit accounts (MMDAs) have become popular, banks have recently attracted a smaller percentage of funds through traditional noninterest-bearing demand deposit accounts. In addition, low interest rate passbook savings accounts have not drawn as much funds because of the alternative CDs available. Due to deregulation, a greater percentage of the bank's sources of funds have market-determined interest rates. However, gross interest expenses have decreased during the 1980s for all banks in general because of the decline in market interest rates.

A comparison of gross interest expense among the four bank size classes is presented in Exhibit 19.3. The interest expense of money center banks is consistently above that of other banks, as money center banks obtain a greater percentage of their deposits on a wholesale (large-denomination) basis. In contrast, small banks attract significantly more small-denomination deposits from consumers at the passbook savings rate.

The **net interest margin** (in Row 3 of Exhibit 19.1) represents the difference between gross interest income and gross interest expenses (as a percentage of assets). Exhibit 19.1 shows that gross interest income and gross interest expenses have been similarly affected by interest rate movements; therefore, the net interest margin of all banks in aggregate has remained somewhat stable.

While the performance of banks in aggregate has changed from year to year, it is generally more stable than that of other financial institutions over time. This may be surprising in light of the banking industry's regulatory evolution. A major reason for the relatively stable bank performance

EXHIBIT 19.1 Performance Summary of all Insured Commercial Banks, 1981–1987

Item	1981	1982	1983	1984	1985	1986[1]	1987
1. Gross interest income	11.93%	11.36%	9.63%	10.23%	9.44%	8.38%	8.21%
2. Gross interest expenses	8.77	8.07	6.38	6.97	6.06	5.10	4.94
3. Net interest margin	3.17	3.28	3.25	3.26	3.38	3.28	3.27
4. Noninterest income	.90	.96	1.03	1.19	1.32	1.40	1.55
5. Loan loss provision	.26	.40	.47	.57	.67	.77	1.26
6. Noninterest expenses	2.77	2.93	2.96	3.05	3.19	3.22	3.31
7. Securities gains (losses)	−.08	−.06	.00	−.01	.06	.14	.05
8. Income before tax	.96	.85	.85	.83	.90	.82	.30
9. Taxes[2]	.20	.14	.18	.19	.21	.19	.18
10. Net income	.76	.71	.67	.64	.70	.64	.12
11. Cash dividends declared	.30	.31	.33	.32	.33	.33	.36
12. Net retained earnings	.46	.40	.34	.33	.37	.31	−.24
13. Net interest margin, taxable equivalent[3]	3.53	3.66	3.60	3.73	3.77	3.68	3.50

1 Before 1984, data are based on averages for call dates in December of the preceding year and in June and December of the current year. In 1984, data are based on averages for call dates at the beginning and end of the year only. After 1984, data are based on averages of the call date in December of the preceding year and all four call dates in the current year.
2 Includes all taxes estimated to be due on income, extraordinary gains, and securities gains.
3 For each bank with profits before tax greater than zero, income from state and local obligations was increased by $[t/(1 - t)]$ times the lesser of profits before tax or interest earned on state and local obligations (t is the marginal federal income tax rate). This adjustment approximates the equivalent pretax return on state and local obligations.

SOURCE: *Federal Reserve Bulletin* (July 1987): 538, and (July 1988): 404.

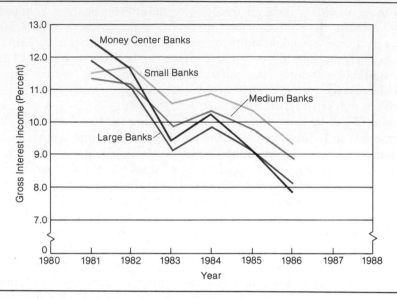

SOURCE: *Federal Reserve Bulletin* (July 1987): 537–551.

in aggregate is that some banks have effectively insulated against market interest rate movements.[1]

Exhibit 19.4 shows that the net interest margin is consistently highest for the small banks, and lowest for the money center banks. These results are expected, given the differences in gross interest income and gross interest expense illustrated in Exhibits 19.2 and 19.3.

Noninterest income (in Row 4 of Exhibit 19.1) results from fees charged on services provided, such as lockbox services, banker's acceptances, cashier's checks, and foreign exchange transactions. It has consistently risen over time for all banks in aggregate, as banks are offering more fee-based services than in the past. However, this income is not as significant as net interest income. If banks are successful in entering related industries (such as insurance or real estate), noninterest income will increase over time.

Exhibit 19.5 shows that noninterest income is consistently highest for money center banks and lowest for the smallest banks. These differences occur because money center banks provide more services for which they can charge fees. Small banks provide few services that generate noninterest income.

The **loan loss provision** (in Row 5 in Exhibit 19.1) is an account established by the bank in anticipation of loan losses in the future. It should increase during periods when loan losses are more likely such as during a recessionary period. In many cases, there is a lagged impact as some borrowers survive the recessionary period but never fully recover from it and subsequently fail. As shown in Exhibit 19.1, the provision for loan losses for all banks in aggregate was much lower in 1981 relative to the other years. The

Part Five

Commercial Banking

1 See the research by Flannery, listed in the references.

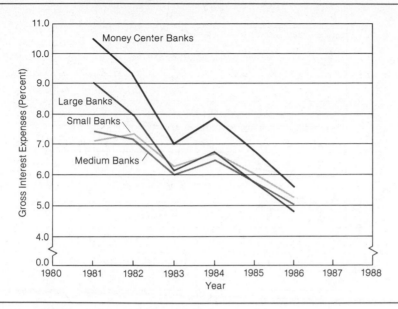

SOURCE: *Federal Reserve Bulletin* (July 1987): 537–551.

1982 recession combined with the international debt crisis had a long-lasting impact on loan losses, which steadily increased through 1987.

Exhibit 19.6 shows that the loan loss provision was lower for the money center banks in the early 1980s. However, the international debt crisis caused some money center banks to boost their loan loss reserves in the mid 1980s. Many small banks have boosted their loan loss reserves in reaction to their

**EXHIBIT 19.4   Comparison of Net Interest Margin
among Bank Classes**

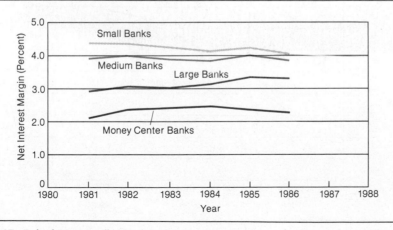

SOURCE: *Federal Reserve Bulletin* (July 1987): 537–551.

EXHIBIT 19.5   Comparison of Noninterest Income (as a Percent of Assets) among Bank Classes

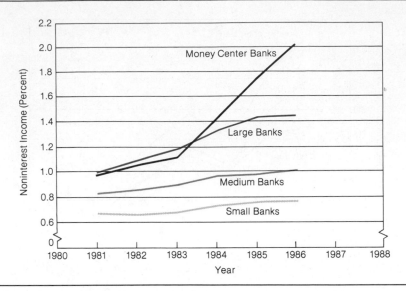

SOURCE: *Federal Reserve Bulletin* (July 1987): 537–551.

high concentration of agricultural loans, which have had a high default rate in recent years.

Noninterest expenses (in Row 6 of Exhibit 19.1) include salaries, office equipment, and other expenses not related to the payment of interest on

EXHIBIT 19.6   Comparison of Loan Loss Provision (as a Percent of Assets) among Bank Classes

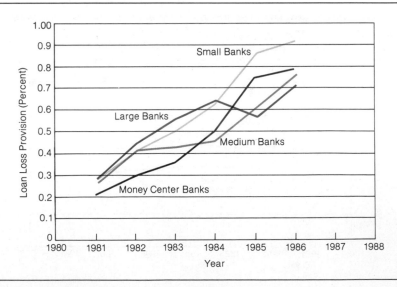

SOURCE: *Federal Reserve Bulletin* (July 1987): 537–551.

deposits. These expenses have averaged about 3 percent of total assets for all banks in aggregate, but have increased over time.

Securities gains and losses (in Row 7 of Exhibit 19.1) result from the bank's sale of securities, and as shown, have been negligible. Yet, this is partially because all banks in aggregate are considered here. An individual bank's gains and losses might be more significant.

When summing net interest income, noninterest income, and securities gains, and subtracting from this sum the provision for loan losses and noninterest expenses, the result is *income before tax*. This income figure consistently decreased over the early 1980s, primarily due to an increase in noninterest expenses and provision for loan losses. Yet, in 1985 the increase in net interest margin and noninterest income offset the increase in noninterest expenses, causing an increase in net income before tax. In 1986 and 1987, net income before tax declined, mainly because of higher loan loss provisions.

The key income statement item, according to many analysts is *net income*, which accounts for any taxes paid. The net income figure disclosed near the bottom of Exhibit 19.1 is measured as a percentage of assets and therefore represents the *return on assets (ROA)*. Fluctuations in ROA for banks in aggregate can be explained by assessing changes in its components, as shown in Exhibit 19.7. While the net interest margin has been somewhat stable, the noninterest income has risen over time. However, this has been roughly offset by the combined increase in noninterest expenses and the loan loss provision.

Exhibit 19.8 shows that the ROA for small banks more than doubled that of money center banks in the early 1980s, partially because of the higher net interest margin. Even though small banks continued to have a higher net interest margin in the mid 1980s, their loan loss provision increased at a higher rate. Consequently, their ROA declined significantly. The medium-sized banks have consistently had an ROA that exceeds that of the money center banks by .3 percent on average.

Any individual bank's performance depends on its policy decisions as well as uncontrollable factors relating to the economy and government regulations (Exhibit 19.9). Gross interest income and expenses are affected by the sources and uses of bank funds and the movements in market interest rates.

Noninterest income is earned on a variety of services, including many new services being offered by banks as some regulatory provisions have been eliminated. Noninterest expenses are partially dependent on personnel costs associated with the credit assessment of loan applications, which in turn are affected by the bank's asset composition (proportion of funds allocated to loans). Noninterest expenses also depend on the liability composition, since the handling of small deposits is more time-consuming than that of large deposits. Banks offering more nontraditional services will incur higher noninterest expenses, although they expect to offset the higher costs with higher noninterest income. Loan losses depend on the composition of assets (proportion of loans versus securities), the quality of these assets, and the economy. The return on assets is influenced by all previously mentioned income statement items and therefore by all policies and other factors that affect those items.

The performance characteristics of money center banks differ from small banks because of the differences in their balance sheet composition. For

Impact of the Tax Reform Act of 1986 on Commercial Banks

Bank performance can be so strongly affected by revisions in tax laws. The table below summarizes the major provisions of the Tax Reform Act of 1986 as related to commercial banks.

	Previous Law	Tax Reform Act of 1986
Deductibility of interest on funds used to purchase tax-exempt bonds	Banks were allowed to deduct 80 percent of the interest paid on funds used to purchase tax-exempt bonds.	Deductibility is eliminated for interest paid on funds used to purchase tax-exempt bonds after August 7, 1986. There is an exception for bonds of small issuers.
Deductions for bad debts	Banks could use either the experience method or the percentage-of-eligible-loans method to establish allowable targets for loan-loss reserves. The addition to reserves necessary to raise reserves to the target level was deductible.	Banking organizations with assets over $500 million must use the specific charge-off approach rather than the reserve approach, and the balance on existing reserves must be recaptured by 1990. There is an exception to the recapture rule for financially troubled banks.
Corporate tax rates	The top corporate tax rate was 46 percent, and there was a graduated structure for small companies.	For taxable years beginning on or after July 1, 1987, the top corporate rate is 34 percent. The graduated rate structure for small companies is also modified. Prior to July 1, 1987, the rates are a blend from previous law and the revised law.

instance, small banks obtain a greater percentage of their funds from traditional demand deposits (at zero percent interest) and small savings accounts (at a relatively low interest rate), while money center banks attract much of their funds through large deposits at a market-determined interest rate. Thus, the net interest margin for money center banks is typically lower than for smaller banks. Consequently, their return on assets (ROA) would likely be lower, unless their noninterest income as a percentage of assets is significantly higher.

An alternative measure of overall bank performance is **return on equity (ROE).** A bank's ROE is affected by the same income statement items that

	Previous Law	**Tax Reform Act of 1986**
Foreign tax credit	Businesses received a credit for foreign taxes paid up to the amount of tax that would have been paid on foreign earnings if they were taxed at the U.S. rate.	Formulas for computing foreign tax credits use separate baskets of income rather than averaging together many types of income. Banks are affected by the separate basket for interest income. Substantial transition rules apply.
Investment tax credit	A 10 percent credit applied to most purchases of equipment and machinery. Banks earned investment tax credits primarily through their leasing activities.	The investment tax credit is eliminated as of January 1, 1986.
Minimum tax	Corporations were subject to an add-on tax, equal to 15 percent of certain preferences minus regular tax paid.	The structure of the minimum tax is changed from an add-on tax to an alternative tax. Corporations must pay a 20 percent tax on taxable income plus tax-preference items if this would exceed their regular tax. Banks are affected by the book income preference. Foreign tax credits will be allowed to offset no more than 90 percent of corporations' liability under the alternative minimum tax.

SOURCE: *New England Economic Review*, Federal Reserve Bank of Boston (May–June 1987): 13.

affect ROA and, in addition, by the bank's degree of financial leverage, as follows:

$$\text{ROE} = \text{ROA} \times \frac{\text{leverage}}{\text{multiplier}}$$

$$\frac{\text{net income}}{\text{equity capital}} = \frac{\text{net income}}{\text{total assets}} \times \frac{\text{total assets}}{\text{equity capital}}$$

Chapter 19

Bank Performance

EXHIBIT 19.7 Overview of the Key Components Affecting Return on Assets
(for Banks in Aggregate)

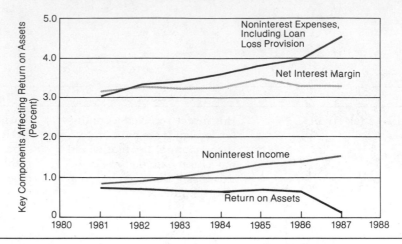

SOURCE: *Federal Reserve Bulletin* (July 1987): 537–551, and (July 1988): 404.

The leverage multiplier is simply the inverse of the capital ratio (when only equity counts as capital). The higher the capital ratio is, the lower the leverage multiplier and the lower the degree of financial leverage.

Exhibit 19.10 shows that in the early 1980s, the ROE was somewhat similar among banks of all classes. Although banks with a greater amount of assets generally experienced a lower ROA during this period (refer to

EXHIBIT 19.8 Comparison of Return on Assets
among Bank Classes

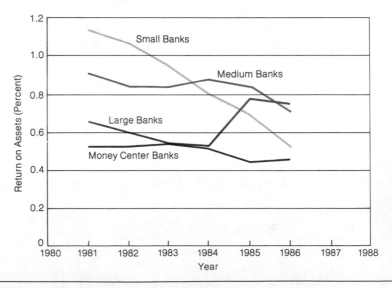

SOURCE: *Federal Reserve Bulletin* (July 1987): 537–551.

EXHIBIT 19.9 Influence of Bank Policies and Other Factors on a Bank's Income Statement

Income Statement Item as a Percentage of Assets	Bank Policy Decisions Affecting the Income Statement Item	Uncontrollable Factors Affecting the Income Statement Item
(1) Gross interest income	■ Composition of assets ■ Quality of assets ■ Maturity and rate-sensitivity of assets ■ Loan pricing policy	■ Economic conditions ■ Market interest rate movements
(2) Gross interest expenses	■ Composition of liabilities ■ Maturities and rate sensitivity of liabilities	■ Market interest rate movements
(3) Net interest margin = (1) − (2)		
(4) Noninterest income	■ Service charges ■ Nontraditional activities	■ Regulatory provisions
(5) Noninterest expenses	■ Composition of assets ■ Composition of liabilities ■ Nontraditional activities ■ Efficiency of personnel ■ Costs of office space and equipment ■ Marketing costs ■ Other costs	■ Inflation
(6) Loan losses	■ Composition of assets ■ Quality of assets ■ Collection dept. capabilities	■ Economic conditions ■ Market interest rate movements
(7) Pre-tax return on assets = (3) + (4) − (5) − (6)		
(8) Taxes	■ Tax planning	■ Tax laws
(9) After-tax return on assets = (7) − (8)		
(10) Financial leverage, measured here as (assets/equity)	■ Capital structure policies	■ Capital structure regulations
(11) Return on equity = (9) × (10)		

Exhibit 19.8), they had a lower capital ratio (implying a higher degree of financial leverage) offsetting the relatively low ROA.

In the mid 1980s, the ROA of small banks declined. While it still exceeded that of money center banks, the small banks' relatively high level of equity investment caused their ROE to be significantly lower than that of money center banks, and other banks as well. In the mid 1980s, the large banks (except money center banks) experienced the highest ROE, because they improved their ROA and also used a relatively low level of equity capital.

EXHIBIT 19.10   Comparison of Return on Equity among Bank Classes

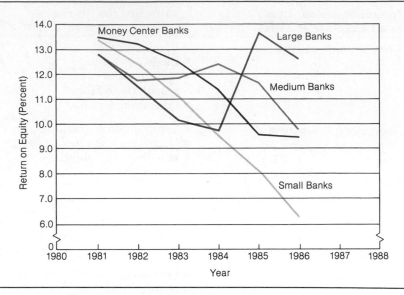

SOURCE: *Federal Reserve Bulletin* (July 1987): 537–551.

USING STOCK PRICES TO ASSESS PERFORMANCE POTENTIAL

When assessing the bank's performance, income statements do not always tell the whole story. For example, new risky loans do not affect a bank's past performance, but may affect the bank's future performance. To assess a bank's performance potential, bank stock price movements can be analyzed. Exhibit 19.11 illustrates the stock price trends of two samples of banks, of medium-sized banks with asset levels of between $1 billion and $10 billion and the other of larger banks with an asset level exceeding $10 billion. As a basis of comparison, the Standard and Poor's (S&P) 500 Stock Index is also included. Exhibit 19.11 shows that bank stocks closely follow the movements of other stocks (represented by the S&P 500). That is not surprising since the expected performance of banks is significantly influenced by the expected performance of the firms to which they lend.

Exhibit 19.11 also illustrates how the bank stocks in both samples were adversely affected during recessionary periods (such as 1974, 1980, and 1982). During the 1974 and 1980 recessions, stock prices of medium-sized banks were more severely affected than large banks. Yet during the 1982 recession, stocks of the larger banks were damaged to a greater degree, primarily because of the international debt crisis. Many money center banks had a high concentration of loans to governments of less developed countries that were unable to repay their loans on time. Although the loans were rescheduled in order to avoid default, the depressed stock prices of banks reflected the market's anticipation that some of those loans might never be

EXHIBIT 19.11   Stock Performance of Banks

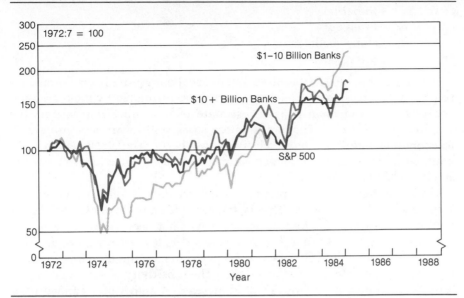

SOURCE: *FRBSF Weekly Letter*, July 12, 1985.

NOTE: Month-end closing price levels calculated from returns, excluding dividends. The bank stock indices are based on equally weighted average returns for the population of all 22 bank holding companies in the $10+ billion size group, excluding Seafirst and Continental Illinois, and a sample of 55 bank holding companies in the $1–10 billion size group. Had Seafirst and Continental Illinois been included in the $10+ billion index, the level of that index in 1985 would have been slightly lower.

repaid. In fact, research by Cornell and Shapiro has shown that the market clearly differentiated between banks according to their outstanding loans to less developed countries.

The medium-sized banks have been evaluated quite favorably in the stock market since 1982. This is partially due to their low level of exposure in international lending and their potential for interstate mergers. Medium-sized banks also benefited from the creation of money market deposit accounts (MMDAs) in December 1982. They used this innovative account as a key source of funds, and it provided them with greater access to medium and large depositors.

RISK EVALUATION OF BANKS

In assessing bank performance, risk should not be ignored. However, no consensus measurement exists that would allow for comparison among all banks of various types of risk (such as loan default risk and liquidity risk).

Some analysts measure a firm's risk by its **beta,** which represents the degree of sensitivity of its stock returns to the returns of the stock market as a whole. It is normally measured by the following regression model:

$$R_{j,t} = b_0 + b_1 R_{m,t} + u_t$$

where $R_{j,t}$ = the stock return for the firm of concern in period t

$R_{m,t}$ = the return on a stock market index (such as the S&P 500 index) in period t

b_0 = intercept

b_1 = slope coefficient

u_t = error term

The regression model is applied to historical data (usually on a quarterly basis). The regression coefficients b_0 and b_1 are estimated by the regression analysis. The coefficient b_1 is an estimate of beta since it measures the sensitivity of R_j to R_m. The banks whose stock returns are less vulnerable to economic conditions have relatively low betas. The stock returns of a bank with very conservative management are likely to be less sensitive to stock market movements.

While the beta reflects sensitivity to market conditions, it ignores any firm-specific characteristics. That is, the beta measures **systematic risk,** but ignores unsystematic risk. A bank's beta will not necessarily remain constant from one period to another. If the bank decides to use more aggressive policies, its beta will likely increase. Its performance and therefore its stock price would become more volatile, since the sensitivity of the bank's stock returns to economic conditions would increase. A higher beta can work for or against the bank, depending on future economic conditions.

An evaluation of bank betas, shown in Exhibit 19.12, can indicate which banks are more likely to benefit (or deteriorate) from future economic conditions. A beta of 1.00 suggests that a firm's stock fluctuates by about the same degree as the stock market. Betas above and below 1.00 suggest changes greater and smaller (respectively) than the market. The exhibit shows that the smallest banks had the lowest betas, implying that they generally are not as risky as the larger banks. Perhaps the lower betas for small banks can be attributed to their operating characteristics. Their loan default rate may not be as sensitive to market conditions as the larger banks that heavily concentrate on commercial loans.

Because betas can change over time, we might learn more about the risk of banks in different size classes by segmenting the data into subperiods (Exhibit 19.13). Notice in the exhibit that in all subperiods except 1979–1981, the largest banks generally had the highest betas while the small banks had the lowest betas. While bank betas have changed over time, there appears to be no clear pattern as to whether banks are in general becoming more or less sensitive to economic conditions over time.

EXHIBIT 19.12   Betas for Banks in Different Size Classifications (August 1972 to September 1984)

Classification Group	Mean Beta
All banks	.93
Banks with assets greater than $10 billion	1.06
Banks with assets between $5 billion and $10 billion	1.03
Banks with assets between $1 billion and $5 billion	.83

NOTE: The results shown are based on a study of bank holding companies.

SOURCE: *Economic Review*, Federal Reserve Bank of San Francisco (Winter 1985): 11.

Exhibit 19.14, which lists the betas of several banks as reported by Value Line Investment Service, confirms that the larger banks (such as Bank America Corp., Banker's Trust N.Y. Corp., and Chase Manhattan) tend to have higher betas.

HOW TO EVALUATE A BANK'S PERFORMANCE

Up to this point, the discussion of bank performance has mostly focused on the overall industry and different size classifications. While this information can be beneficial, analysts often need to evaluate an individual bank's performance, in which case financial statements are used. The income and expenses disclosed earlier in Exhibit 19.1 serve as an industry benchmark for evaluating a bank's performance.

Examination of Return on Assets (ROA)

The ROA will usually reveal when a bank's performance is not up to par, but it does not indicate the reason for poor performance. Its components must be evaluated separately. Exhibit 19.15 identifies the factors that affect bank performance as measured by the ROA and ROE. If a bank's ROA is less than desired, it is possibly incurring excessive interest expenses. Banks typically know about what deposit rate is necessary to attract deposits and therefore are not likely to pay excessive interest. Yet, if all their sources of funds require a market-determined rate, that will force relatively high interest expenses. A relatively low ROA could also be due to low interest received on loans and securities due to a bank being overly conservative with its funds or being locked into fixed rates prior to an increase in market interest rates. High interest expenses and/or low interest revenues (on a

EXHIBIT 19.13 Betas for Banks Over Various Subperiods

	Beta During the Subperiod:			
Classification Group	*Aug. 1972 to Dec. 1975*	*Jan. 1976 to Dec. 1978*	*Jan. 1979 to Dec. 1981ᵃ*	*Jan. 1982 to Sept. 1984*
All banks	1.00	.88	1.13	.98
Banks with assets greater than $10 billion	1.19	1.07	1.00	1.23
Banks with assets between $5 billion and $10 billion	1.06	1.01	1.22	1.14
Banks with assets between $1 billion and $5 billion	.87	.73	1.16	.78

a Betas for this subperiod were computed after excluding a portion of the data, since this portion could have caused misleading estimates of beta. For a more complete explanation of the beta estimation process, see the *Economic Review*, Federal Reserve Bank of San Francisco (Winter 1985): 5–16.

SOURCE: *Economic Review*, Federal Reserve Bank of San Francisco (Winter 1985): 11.

EXHIBIT 19.14   Betas of Various Banks as Reported by Value Line Investment Service

Bank	Beta
Bank America Corp.	1.20
Bankers Trust N.Y. Corp.	1.25
Barnett Banks of Florida	.95
Chase Manhattan	1.20
Chemical N.Y.	1.15
First Wachovia	.85
First Union	.90
Irving Bank	.90
J.P. Morgan & Co.	1.20
Marine Midland Banks	.90
Manufacturers Hanover	1.20
Mellon Bank Corp.	.95
Midatlantic Banks	.70
NCNB Corp.	1.15
Rainer Bancorp	.85
Security Pacific Corp.	1.15
State Street Boston	.90
Sterling Bancorp	.75
Suntrust Banks	.90
U.S. Bancorp	.90
Valley National Corp.	.85
Wells Fargo & Co.	1.05

SOURCE: *Value Line* (December 1987).

relative basis) will reduce the net interest margin and therefore reduce the ROA.

A relatively low ROA may also result from insufficient noninterest income. Some banks have made a much greater effort than others to offer services that generate fee (noninterest) income. Since a bank's net interest margin is somewhat dictated by interest rate trends and balance sheet composition, many banks attempt to focus on noninterest income in order to boost their ROA.

A bank's ROA can also be damaged by heavy loan losses. Yet, if the bank is too conservative in its attempt to avoid loan losses, its net interest margin will be low (due to the low interest rates received from very safe loans and investments). Because of the obvious trade-off here, banks generally attempt to shift their risk-return preferences according to economic conditions. They may increase their concentration of relatively risky loans during periods of prosperity when they might improve their net interest margin without incurring excessive loan losses. Conversely, they may increase their concen-

EXHIBIT 19.15   Breakdown of Performance Measures

Measures of Bank Performance	Financial Characteristics Influencing Performance Measure	Bank Decisions Affecting Financial Characteristic
1) Return on assets (ROA)	Net interest margin	Deposit rate decisions Loan rate decisions Loan losses
	Noninterest revenues	Bank services offered
	Noninterest expenses	Overhead requirements Efficiency Advertising
	Loan losses	Risk level of loans provided
2) Return on equity (ROE)	ROA	See above
	Leverage multiplier	Capital structure decision

tration of relatively low-risk (and low-return) investments when economic conditions are less favorable.

Banks with relatively low ROAs often incur excessive noninterest expenses, such as overhead and advertising expenses. Any waste of resources due to inefficiencies can lead to relatively high noninterest expenses.

A recent study by Wall attempted to identify the characteristics of more profitable banks and found that they generally had a relatively low level of noninterest expenses. Profitability was not related to bank size or market concentration. Another study, by Watro, found that banks with a relatively high concentration of securities had significantly higher earnings. This may seem surprising since securities are usually expected to generate lower revenues than loans. However, banks with relatively high security holdings normally experience less defaults and incur less noninterest expenses, and these advantages can offset the lower expected interest income.

Examination of Income Statement

The income statement of an individual bank also helps reveal its performance, especially when compared to industry averages. Consider the information disclosed in Exhibit 19.16 for Bank America and the industry over recent years. Because of differences in accounting procedures, the information may not be perfectly comparable. In addition, industry data on money center banks rather than all banks may be a more appropriate benchmark. Nevertheless, the comparison in Exhibit 19.16 can at least identify some general reasons for the financial problems experienced by Bank America.

Bank America's performance has declined since 1982. Its net income before tax as a percentage of assets decreased consistently from a high of .86 percent in 1981. A comparison with the industry figures suggests that its net interest margin and noninterest income have been higher than the norm.

Bank Performance

Impact of Barriers to Entry on Bank Performance

Several studies have analyzed the impact of market concentration or regulatory barriers to entry on performance. One study by Hannon found that bank profitability is negatively related to the threat of entry. A study by McCall suggested that more liberal branching laws would increase competition and reduce the profitability of banks presently operating in these areas. A study by Watro found that bank earnings were negatively related to the number of competitors within the local community. A study by Whitehead and Lujytes found that the geographic expansion by banks into new markets tends to increase competition. A higher degree of competition usually results in lower prices to consumers. These studies had somewhat similar implications for regulatory barriers such as intrastate and interstate branching restrictions, namely that a loosening of such barriers would create a more competitive and efficient banking environment.

There is some concern that the banking industry could become highly concentrated if barriers to entry were eliminated. One recent study by Smirlock concluded that market concentration would not affect bank profitability if barriers to entry were removed, and that high concentration would not result in collusive behavior. A related study by Whalen also found no relationship between market concentration and bank profitability in recent years and concluded that geographic expansion by banks will not bring them unfair advantages. Overall, the research suggests that efficiency will be maximized and consumers will be best served if all geographic barriers to entry are removed.

Impact of Bank Size on Performance

The effect of bank size on performance depends on how revenues per unit of output and costs per unit of output change as bank size increases. Several studies have assessed whether economies of scale exist (whether costs per unit of output are lower for larger banks). These studies carry important implications as to whether banks can improve their performance by expanding. To assess whether economies of scale exist, proxies are needed to measure units of output and cost per unit of output. Most studies, including that of Benston, Hanweck, and Humphrey have found that larger banks generally do not have lower costs per unit of output.

Some studies have focused specifically on the relationship between bank size and performance. One recent study by Schuster that used market share as a proxy for bank size found no relationship between performance and size. Other studies have found that smaller banks tend to perform better (see the article by King).

Impact of Interest Rate Movements on Bank Performance

Among studies that have examined whether bank performance is affected significantly by interest rate movements, a recent study by Flannery found the answer to be no. The implication was that banks can effectively insulate themselves against interest rate movements, and these results applied to the entire sample. Of course any bank that did not effectively match the rate-sensitivity on both sides of the balance sheet would be affected by interest rate movements.

Another recent study, by Booth and Officer, found a significant negative relationship between anticipated (and unanticipated) interest rate movements and bank stock returns, implying that stocks are adversely affected by the market's expectations of rising interest rates. The market apparently believes that commercial bank performance is susceptible to interest rate movements.

A recent study by Scott and Peterson that also assessed the sensitivity of commercial bank stock returns to interest rate movements focused on the 1977–1984 period and used the following regression model:

$$r_p = B_0 + B_1 MI + B_2 r + e$$

where r_p = stock returns of a portfolio of commercial banks

MI = percentage change in the market index (the S&P 500 Index was used as a proxy)

r = a measure of unexpected interest rate changes (see the article by Scott and Peterson for an explanation of the proxy used for this variable)

B_0 = intercept

B_1 = regression coefficient that measures the sensitivity of stock returns to the market index returns

B_2 = regression coefficient that measures the sensitivity of stock returns to the interest rate movements

e = error term

The coefficient B_1 was estimated to be .673 by the regression analysis, suggesting that a 1 percent change in the market is associated with a .673 percent change in the portfolio returns. Thus, the commercial bank stocks were positively correlated with the market.

The coefficient B_2 was estimated to be $-.401$ by the regression analysis, suggesting that an unexpected 1 percent increase in interest rates is associated with a .401 percent decrease in stock returns of commercial banks. This coefficient was found to be statistically significant. Thus, stock returns on commercial banks were adversely affected by an unexpected increase in interest rates. These results are relevant to managers and investors of commercial banks. Even if interest rates cannot be forecasted with perfect accuracy, investors can use the regression coefficient B_2 to estimate how a company's stock returns will be affected by a variety of possible interest rate outcomes.

Impact of Mergers on Bank Performance

Banks have frequently pursued mergers in recent years in an effort to improve their performance. A bank merger may be beneficial for the following reasons. First, the bank's larger size allows for increased lending capacity to any individual corporation. This can make the bank more attractive to large corporations that need substantial financing. Second, the bank may be able to spread technology and advertising costs over a greater volume and reduce its per-unit costs. Third, a merger may better enable the bank to prevent hostile takeovers. Fourth, a merger can increase a bank's access to depositors, especially when the merger partner is established in a different location.

There are also some possible disadvantages. First, a merger may create conflicts among the personnel. Managers of the two

continued

531

RELATED RESEARCH

continued from p. 531
merged banks may have different role perceptions and objectives. Second, it is difficult to merge information (data processing) systems of two banks. Third, it is difficult to merge documentation procedures of two banks. Fourth, mergers that result in excessive growth may deplete the bank's capital. While this last reason deserves consideration, it should be noted that recent research by Amel has shown that banks with high relative growth do not experience capital depletion, or any other extraordinary financial problems. The severity of problems associated with bank mergers depends on the ability of management to establish clear and cohesive personnel structure and procedures for all types of tasks.

It is too early to determine whether the recent mergers are beneficial to banks. A recent study by James and Wier found that the shareholders of acquired financial institutions have benefited from a merger while shareholders of the acquiring financial institutions have been unfavorably affected. Over the period from 1974 through 1985, Wier and James determined that the average return for shareholders of acquired banks around the announcement date of the acquisition was 15 percent. In contrast, the average return for shareholders of the acquiring banks around the announcement date was − 1 percent.

A recent study by Pettway and Trifts analyzed banks that acquired failing banks and found that shareholders anticipated the announcement during the ten days prior to the acquisition date and reacted favorably to this anticipated event. The favorable reaction was detected by abnormally high risk-adjusted returns on the acquiring bank's shares prior to the acquisition. However, the risk-adjusted returns were abnormally low shortly after the acquisition date, lasting for about 50 days. This implies that acquiring banks may be overbidding for failing banks.

SOURCES: Timothy Hannon, "Bank Profitability and the Threat of Entry," *Journal of Bank Research* (Summer 1983): 157–163; Alan S. McCall, "Economies of Scale, Operating Efficiencies and the Organizational Structure of Commercial Banks," *Journal of Bank Research* (Summer 1980); 95–100; Paul R. Watro, "Closely Watched Banks," *Economic Commentary*, Federal Reserve Bank of Cleveland (January 30, 1984); David D. Whitehead and Jan Lujytes, "An Alternative View of Bank Competition: Profit or Share Maximization," *Economic Review*, Federal Reserve Bank of Atlanta (November 1982): 48–57; Michael Smirlock, "Evidence on the (Non) Relationship Between Concentration and Profitability in Banking," *Journal of Money, Credit, and Banking* (February 1985): 69–83; and Gary Whalen, "Competition and Bank Profitability: Recent Evidence," *Economic Commentary*, Federal Reserve Bank of Cleveland (November 1, 1986).

George J. Benston, Gerald A. Hanweck, and David B. Humphrey, "Operating Costs in Commercial Banking," *Economic Review*, Federal Reserve Bank of Atlanta (November 1982): 6–21; Leo Schuster, "Profitability and the Market Share of Banks," *Journal of Bank Research* (Spring 1984): 56–61; and Frank B. King, "Changes in Large Bank's Market Shares," *Economic Review*, Federal Reserve Bank of Atlanta (November 1982): 35–40.

Mark J. Flannery, "Interest Rates and Bank Profitability: Additional Evidence," *Journal of Money, Credit, and Banking* (August 1983): 355–362; James R. Booth and Dennis T. Officer, "Expectations, Interest Rates, and Commercial Bank Stock," *Journal of Financial Research* (Spring 1985): 51–58; and William L. Scott and Richard L. Peterson, "Interest Rate Risk and Equity Values of Hedged and Unhedged Financial Intermediaries," *Journal of Financial Research* (Winter 1986): 325–329.

Dean F. Amel, "Effects of Rapid Growth in Large Banks," *Bankers Magazine* (November–December 1986): 5–9; Christopher James and Peggy Wier, "Returns to Acquirers and Competition in the Acquisition Market: The Case of Banking," *Journal of Political Economy* (April 1987): 335–370 Richard H. Pettway and Jack W. Trifts, "Do Banks Overbid When Acquiring Failed Banks?" *Financial Management* (Summer 1985): 5–15.

EXHIBIT 19.16   Evaluation of Bank America (all variables are measured as a percentage of assets)[a]

	1981		1982		1983	
	BA	*Industry*	*BA*	*Industry*	*BA*	*Industry*
Net interest margin	2.99%	3.17%	2.98%	3.28%	3.30%	3.25%
Noninterest income	1.04	.90	1.15	.96	1.27	1.03
Loan loss provisions	.34	.26	.49	.40	.62	.47
Noninterest expenses	2.83	2.77	2.96	2.93	3.35	2.96
Net income before tax[a]	.86	.96	.68	.85	.60	.85

	1984		1985		1986		1987	
	BA	*Industry*	*BA*	*Industry*	*BA*	*Industry*	*BA*	*Industry*
Net interest margin	3.89%	3.26%	3.94%	3.38%	3.32%	3.28%	3.28%	3.27%
Noninterest income	1.54	1.19	2.06	1.32	2.04	1.40	2.04	1.55
Loan loss provisions	.83	.57	2.09	.67	1.76	.77	1.97	1.26
Noninterest expenses	4.05	3.05	4.24	3.19	3.91	3.22	4.24	3.31
Net income before tax[a]	.55	.83	(0.33)	.90	(0.31)	.82	(0.89)	.30

a The industry net income before tax also accounts for securities gains and losses.

SOURCE: Bank of America's 1985 and 1987 Annual Report; and *Federal Reserve Bulletin* (September 1986): 618, and (July 1988): 404.

Yet, its loan loss provision has also been higher, even exceeding 2 percent of total assets in 1985. In addition, its noninterest expenses have been consistently higher than the norm. Exhibit 19.17 gives a separate comparison of each variable to the industry norm over time to confirm the conclusions drawn.

Any particular bank will perform a more thorough evaluation of itself than that shown here. For example, the recent annual reports provided by Bank America provide a comprehensive explanation for its subpar performance in recent years, along with a discussion of how it plans to improve its performance over time.

A troubled bank's dividend payout policy should always be examined. Many banks that experience a sharp drop in earnings continue to pay out the same amount of dividends to shareholders as before, perhaps believing that their drop in earnings is just a one-time occurrence. If earnings remain low, though, and dividends are not reduced, the bank's capital will be reduced. However, some banks prefer not to reduce their dividend if possible, since they worry that it might signal to investors (correctly or not) that future earnings will not be sufficient to maintain current dividends. The result would be a sell-off of stock. Recent research by Keen supports this fear.

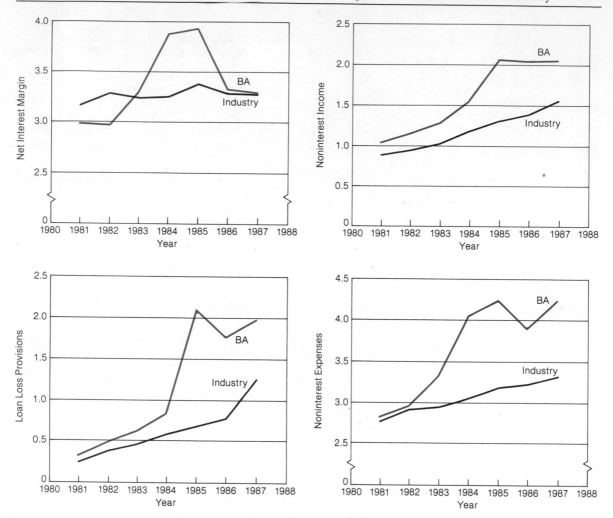

Sources of Information Used in Evaluating Bank Performance

Various investment services can enhance the analysis of a bank's financial statements. Exhibit 19.18 provides an example of an analysis by one well-known service (Value Line) of Citicorp, the holding company of Citibank, the largest bank in the United States. Some of the key performance characteristics discussed in this chapter are included here. The beta of Citicorp is 1.2. The spreadsheet of financial data includes total assets, net interest income, loan loss provisions, noninterest income, noninterest expenses, and ROA (referred to as "% Earned Total Assets"). Because Citicorp's size has consistently increased (review total assets over time), the components that make up ROA should be measured as a percent of assets. This would help to explain any movements in Citicorp's ROA over time.

EXHIBIT 19.18.   An Analysis of Citicorp's Performance

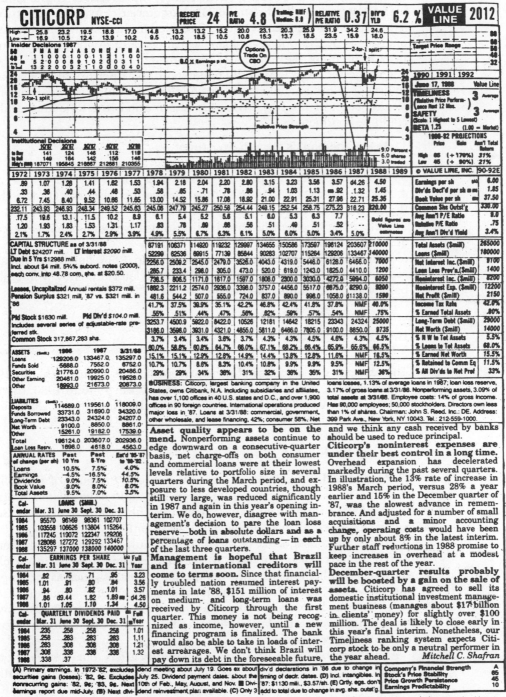

NOTE: Copyright 1988, Value Line Inc. Reprinted by permission.

535

The Value Line analysis also measures return on equity (referred to as "% Earned Net Worth") and the dividend payout ratio (referred to as "% All Dividends to Net Prof."). Furthermore, it provides forecasts of financial ratios along with all other financial characteristics over the next two years.

In addition to the yearly figures disclosed in the spreadsheet, Value Line's analysis provides quarterly loans, earnings, and dividend data. Finally, a brief write-up of the company is presented.

A suggested exercise to fully understand bank performance evaluation is to first obtain financial statements and/or the Value Line analysis of a particular bank of interest. With this information, the following evaluation could be conducted:

1. Assess the bank's growth over time.
2. Assess the bank's risk, using the beta as a measure.
3. Assess the bank's earnings per share over time.
4. Assess the bank's ROA over time; determine why its ROA has changed (by breaking down ROA into its components).
5. Determine whether the bank is allocating a greater or smaller percentage of its funds toward loans.
6. Assess the bank's loan loss provision and ROA during and just after recessionary periods (such as 1982–1983) to determine how vulnerable the bank was to economic conditions.

BANK FAILURES

The extreme consequence of poor performance is failure. Exhibit 19.19 illustrates bank failure frequency over time. From 1940 to 1980, there were usually less than 20 bank failures per year. But there were 138 failures in 1986 and 184 in 1987.

Reasons for Bank Failure

The cause of failure is often attributed to one or more of the following characteristics. First, fraud within the bank could have existed. Fraud represents a wide range of activities, including embezzlement of funds. Second, a high loan default percentage can lead to failure. While banks recognize the potential consequence of a high loan default percentage, some continue to fail for this reason anyway. A thorough examination of any bank may show a general emphasis toward a specific industry—such as oil, shipbuilding, aerospace, agriculture, or national defense systems—that makes it vulnerable to a slowdown in that industry (or a related one). Moreover, no matter how well a bank diversifies its loans, its loan portfolio is still susceptible to a recessionary cycle.

A third reason for bank failure is a liquidity crisis. If a rumor of potential failure for a particular bank circulates, depositors may begin to withdraw funds from that bank, even though the bank is insured by the FDIC. The panic can even occur when the rumor is not justified. Under these conditions, a bank may be unable to attract a sufficient amount of new deposits, and its existing deposit accounts will subside. Once deposit withdrawals begin, it is difficult to stop the momentum. Some depositors who might not have worried about the rumor itself may worry that massive withdrawals re-

EXHIBIT 19.19   Frequency of Bank Failures Over Time

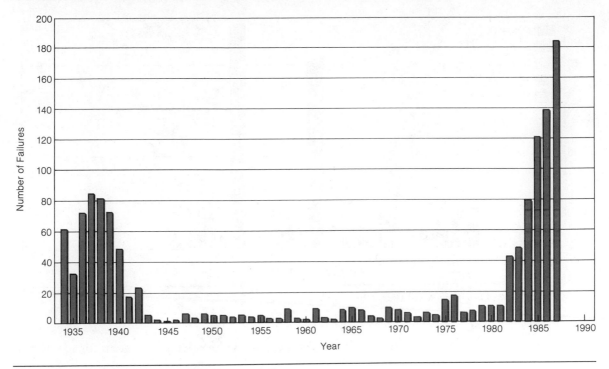

SOURCE: *New England Economic Review* (July–August 1987): 38.

sulting from the rumor will create a problem for the bank and for this reason withdraw their funds as well.

A fourth reason for bank failures is increased competition. Deregulation has made the banking industry more competitive. When banks offer more competitive rates on deposits and loans the result is a reduced net interest margin—and possibly failure if the margin is not large enough to cover other noninterest expenses and loan losses.

Some geographic markets have experienced more failures than others as shown in Exhibit 19.20. More failures were experienced in the Midwest than any other region, mostly as a result of bad agricultural loans. The southwest region was a distant second in failure frequency. Yet, on a percentage basis (failures divided by total existing banks) the southwest and northwest regions experienced a higher failure rate than the midwest region. This is verified by Exhibit 19.21, which shows the failure rate per region in recent years. In 1986 more than 1.5 percent of banks in these regions failed, primarily due to defaults on energy and real estate–related loans. Of the 184 banks that failed in 1987, 50 were located in Texas and 31 were located in Oklahoma.

The Office of the Comptroller of the Currency reviewed 162 national banks that failed since 1979 and found the following common characteristics among many of these banks:

■ 81 percent of the banks did not have a loan policy or did not closely follow their loan policy.

EXHIBIT 19.20   Comparison of Failure Frequency among Regions

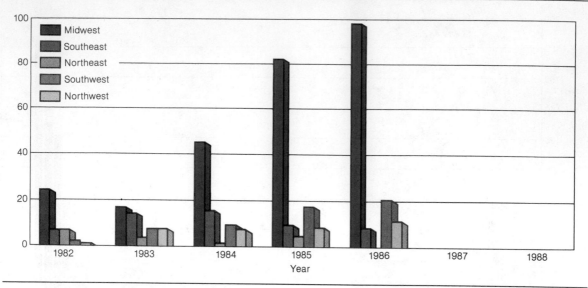

SOURCE: *New England Economic Review* (July–August 1987): 40.

■ 59 percent of the banks did not use an adequate system for identifying problem loans.

■ 63 percent did not adequately monitor key bank officers or departments.

■ At 57 percent of the banks, major corporate decisions were made by one individual.

EXHIBIT 19.21   Comparison of the Failure Rate among Regions

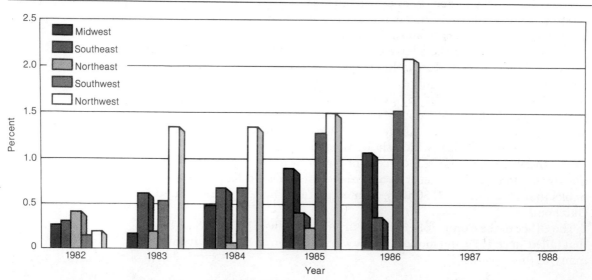

SOURCE: *New England Economic Review* (July–August 1987) 40.

Because all of these characteristics are controllable at banks, it appears that many banks failed not because of the environment but because of inadequate management.

SUMMARY

Bank performance changes over time due to changes in regulations, economic conditions, and management strategies. While banks do not have control over regulations and economic conditions, they control their managerial policies. When banks experience poor performance, they must conduct a thorough investigation to determine the cause, and then develop a remedy. Performance evaluation can often identify previous policies that were not effective and may help determine appropriate policies for the future.

KEY TERMS

beta	noninterest expenses
gross interest expense	noninterest income
gross interest income	return on equity (ROE)
loan loss provision	securities gains and losses
net interest margin	systematic risk

QUESTIONS

19.1. How can gross interest income rise while the net interest margin remains somewhat stable for a particular bank?

19.2. How did deregulation affect gross interest expenses (as a percentage of assets)?

19.3. What has been the trend in noninterest income in recent years? Explain.

19.4. How would a bank generate a higher income before tax (as a percentage of assets) when its net interest margin decreased?

19.5. Suppose a bank generates net interest margin of 1.50 percent. Based on past experience, would the bank experience a loss or a gain? Explain.

19.6. Why are large money center banks' net interest margins typically lower than those of smaller banks?

19.7. What does the beta of a bank indicate?

19.8. What are some of the more common reasons for a bank to experience a low ROA?

19.9. Why is it important for banks to have a consistent dividend payout policy, even if they are in trouble?

19.10. When evaluating a bank, what are some of the key aspects to review?

19.11. Why do banks consider mergers?

19.12. What are some potential disadvantages of bank mergers?

19.13. What are some reasons for bank failures identified in this chapter?

19.14. Assume that SUNY bank plans to liquidate Treasury security holdings and use the proceeds for small business loans. Explain how the different income statement items would be affected over time as a result of this strategy. Also identify any income statement items that are more difficult to estimate as a result of this strategy.

PROBLEM

19.1. Hawaii Bank anticipates the following:

- Loan loss reserves at end of year = 1 percent of assets
- Gross interest income over the next year = 9 percent of assets
- Noninterest expenses over the next year = 3 percent of assets
- Noninterest income over the next year = 1 percent of assets
- Gross interest expenses over the next year = 5 percent of assets
- Tax rate on income = 30 percent
- Capital ratio (defined as capital/assets) at end of year = 5 percent

    a. Forecast Hawaii Bank's net interest margin.
    b. Forecast Hawaii Bank's earnings before taxes as a percent of assets.
    c. Forecast Hawaii Bank's earnings after taxes as a percent of assets.
    d. Forecast Hawaii Bank's return on equity.
    e. Hawaii Bank is considering a shift in its asset structure to reduce its concentration of Treasury bonds and increase its volume of loans to small businesses. Identify each income statement item that would be affected by this strategy, and explain whether the forecast for that item would increase or decrease.

PROJECTS

1. ASSESSMENT OF BANK PERFORMANCE.

Obtain an investment advisory report (such as Value Line) or annual reports on a commercial bank of your or your group's choice (or one assigned by your professor). Use this information to determine the following:

    a. Is the bank's noninterest income becoming more important over time? Why?
    b. How have the bank's noninterest expenses as a percentage of assets changed over time? Explain why any changes may have occurred.
    c. How have the bank's provision for loan losses as a percentage of assets changed over recent years? If any significant change occurred, explain why.
    d. Compare the bank's net interest margin to the general level of interest rates over recent years. Explain the relationship you find. The net interest margin is also affected by the bank's sources and uses of funds. Did the bank's net interest margin appear to be affected by any recent changes in sources or uses of funds? Explain.

2. IMPACT OF INTEREST RATES ON BANK EARNINGS.

a. Develop a model that could be used to determine how the return on assets for a particular bank (chosen by you or your professor) is affected by interest rate movements. Include all relevant variables for which data are available.

b. Test your model to determine how the return on assets was affected by interest rate movements. Do the results support the type of relationship you hypothesized? Explain.

c. Identify any limitations of your model.

d. Suggest how you could use your model to forecast a bank's return on assets (ROA) based on projections of any variables that affect ROA.

3. ESTIMATION OF BANK RISK.

Use historical data to estimate the bank's beta. Does this bank appear to have a relatively high or low level or risk relative to other banks? Explain.

4. IMPACT OF INTEREST RATES ON BANK STOCK PRICES.

a. Develop a model that could be used to determine how the bank's stock returns are affected by interest rate movements. Include all relevant variables for which data are available.

b. Assume that the bank's returns are thought to be significantly influenced by characteristics that are particularly relevant to the banking industry. Specify a model that could capture this influence.

c. Apply your model to historical data to determine how the bank's stock returns have been affected by interest rate movements. Do the results support the type of relationship you hypothesized? Explain.

d. Identify any limitations of your model.

REFERENCES

Amel, Dean F. "Effects of Rapid Growth in Large Banks." *Bankers Magazine* (November–December 1986): 5–9.

Arshadi, Nasser and Edward Lawrence. "An Empirical Investigation of New Bank Performance." *Journal of Banking and Finance* (March 1987): 33–48.

Beatty, Randolph P. "The Effect of Barriers to Entry on Bank Shareholder Wealth: Implications for Interstate Banking." *Journal of Bank Research* (Spring 1985): 8–15.

Beebe, Jack. "Bank Stock Performance Since the 1970s." *Economic Review*, Federal Reserve Bank of San Francisco (Winter 1985): 5–18.

"Behind the Banking Turmoil." *Business Week*, October 29, 1984, 100–107.

Benston, George J., Gerald A. Hanweck, and David B. Humphrey. "Operating Costs in Commercial Banking." *Economic Review*, Federal Reserve Bank of Atlanta (November 1982): 6–21.

Blair, Dudley W. and Dennis L. Placone. "The New Market Structure of the Banking Industry." *Journal of Business and Economic Perspectives* (1986): 9–16.

Booker, Irene O. "Tracking Banks from Afar: A Risk-Monitoring System." *Economic Review*, Federal Reserve Bank of Atlanta (November 1983): 36–41.

Booth, James R. and Dennis T. Officer. "Expectations, Interest Rates, and Commercial Bank Stocks." *Journal of Financial Research* (Spring 1985): 51–58.

Bovenzi, John F., James A. Marino, and Frank E. McFadden. "Commercial Bank Failure Prediction Models." *Economic Review*, Federal Reserve Bank of Atlanta (November 1983): 14–26.

"Can Interstate Banking Increase Competitive Market Performance? An Empirical Test." *Economic Review*, Federal Reserve Bank of Atlanta (January 1984): 4–10.

Chance, Don M. and William R. Lane. "A Re-Examination of Interest Rate Sensitivity in the Common Stocks of Financial Institutions." *The Journal of Financial Research* (Spring 1980): 59–55.

Clark, Jeffrey. "The Efficient Structure Hypothesis: More Evidence From Banking." *Quarterly Review of Economics and Business* (Autumn 1987): 25–39.

Cornell, Bradford and Alan C. Shapiro. "The Reaction of Bank Stock Prices to the International Debt Crisis." *Journal of Banking and Finance* (March 1986): 55–73.

Desai, Anand and Roger Stover. "Bank Holding Company Acquisitions, Stockholder Returns, and Regulatory Uncertainty." *Journal of Financial Research* (Summer 1985): 145–155.

Drabenstott, Mark and Anne O'Mara McDonley. "The Effect of Financial Futures on Small Bank Performance." *Economic Review*, Federal Reserve Bank of Kansas City (November 1982): 15–31.

Flannery, Mark J. "Interest Rates and Bank Profitability: Additional Evidence." *Journal of Money, Credit, and Banking* (August 1983): 355–362.

Flannery, Mark J. "How Do Changes in Market Interest Rates Affect Bank Profits?" *Business Review*, Federal Reserve Bank of Philadelphia (September–October 1980): 13–22.

"Following Bank Performance." *Bankers Magazine* (July–August 1986): 29–35.

Forrestal, Robert P. "Bank Safety: Risks and Responsibilities." *Economic Review* (August 1985): 4–12.

Frieder, Larry A. and Vincent P. Apilado. "Bank Holding Company Research: Classification, Synthesis, and New Directions." *Journal of Bank Research* (Summer 1982): 80–95.

Frieder, Larry A. and Vincent P. Apilado. "Bank Holding Company Expansion: A Refocus on Its Financial Rationale." *Journal of Financial Research* (Spring 1983): 67–81.

Gregorash, George, Eileen Maloney and Don Wilson. "Crosscurrents in 1986 Bank Performance." *Economic Perspectives*, Federal Reserve Bank of Chicago (May–June 1987): 23–35.

Hannan, Timothy. "Bank Profitability and the Threat of Entry." *Journal of Bank Research* (Summer 1983): 157–163.

Jahankhani, Ali and Morgan J. Lynge, Jr. "Commercial Bank Financial Policies and Their Impact on Market-Determined Measures of Risk." *Journal of Bank Research* (Autumn 1980): 169–178.

Keen, Jr., Howard. "The Impact of a Dividend Cut Announcement on Bank Share Prices." *Journal of Bank Research* (Winter 1983): 274–281.

Keeton, William and Katherine Hecht. "Banking Performance in Tenth District States." *Economic Review*, Federal Reserve Bank of Kansas City (July–August 1987): 3–23.

Keeton, William and Charles Morris. "Why Do Banks' Loan Losses Differ?" *Economic Review*, Federal Reserve Bank of Kansas City (May 1987): 3–21.

King, Frank B. "Changes in Large Bank's Market Shares." *Economic Review*, Federal Reserve Bank of Atlanta (November 1982): 35–40.

McCall, Alan S. "Economies of Scale, Operating Efficiencies, and the Organizational Structure of Commercial Banks." *Journal of Bank Research* (Summer 1980): 95–100.

McCall, Alan S. and John T. Lane. "Multi-Office Banking and the Safety and Soundness of Commercial Banks." *Journal of Bank Research* (Summer 1980): 87–94.

McNulty, James E. "Economies of Scale: A Case Study of the Florida Savings and Loan Industry." *Economic Review*, Federal Reserve Bank of Atlanta (November 1982): 22–30.

Meeker, Larry and Laura Gray. "A Note on Non-Performing Loans as an Indicator of Asset Quality." *Journal of Banking and Finance* (March 1987): 161–168.

Morris, Charles S. and Katherine M. Hecht. "Do Multibank Holding Companies Affect Banking Market Concentration?" *Economic Review*, Federal Reserve Bank of Kansas City (April 1986): 19–30.

"Multibank Holding Companies: Recent Evidence on Competition and Performance in Banking Markets." *Journal of Bank Research* (Autumn 1983): 212–220.

Pamy, Kurt and Lawrence Sherman. "Information Analysis of Several Large Failed Banks." *Journal of Bank Research* (Autumn 1979): 145–150.

Peavy, John W. "Financial Determinants of Commercial Bank Bond Ratings." *The Bankers Magazine* (November–December 1981): 87–92.

Pettway, Richard H. and Joseph F. Sinkey, Jr. "Establishing On-Site Bank Examination Priorities: An Early-Warning System Using Accounting and Market Information." *Journal of Finance* (March 1980): 137–150.

Pettway, Richard H. and Jack W. Trifts. "Do Banks Overbid When Acquiring Failed

Banks?" *Financial Management* (Summer 1985): 5–15.

Putnam, Barron H. "Early Warning Systems and Financial Analysis in Bank Monitoring." *Economic Review*, Federal Reserve Bank of Atlanta (November 1983): 6–13.

Rose, Peter. "The Impact of Mergers in Banking: Evidence From a Nationwide Sample of Federally Chartered Banks." *Journal of Economics and Business* (November 1987): 289–312.

Santoni, G. J. "The Effects of Inflation on Commercial Banks." *Review*, Federal Reserve Bank of St. Louis (March 1986): 15–26.

Schuster, Leo. "Profitability and the Market Share of Banks." *Journal of Bank Research* (Spring 1984): 56–61.

Shick, Richard A. and Lawrence F. Sherman. "Bank Stock Prices as an Early Warning System for Changes in Condition." *Journal of Bank Research* (Autumn 1980): 136–145.

Simpson, Gary W. "Capital Market Prediction of Large Commercial Bank Failures: An Alternative Analysis." *Financial Review* (February 1983): 33–53.

Sinkey, Joseph F. "The Performance of First Pennsylvania Bank Prior to Its Bail Out." *Journal of Bank Research* (Summer 1983): 119–133.

Sinkey, Joseph F., Jr. "The Problem with Problem and Failed Banks." *The Bankers Magazine*, (May–June 1980): 31–35.

Smirlock, Michael. "Evidence on the (Non) Relationship between Concentration and Profitability in Banking." *Journal of Money, Credit, and Banking* (February 1985): 69–83.

Trifts, Jack and Kevin Scanlon. "Interstate Bank Mergers: The Early Evidence." *Journal of Financial Research* (Winter 1987): 305–311.

Wall, Larry. "Has Bank Holding Companies' Diversification Affected Their Risk of Failure." *Journal of Economics and Business* (November 1987): 313–326.

Wall, Larry D. "Why Some Banks Are More Profitable Than Others?" *Economic Review*, Federal Reserve Bank of Atlanta (September 1983): 42–48.

Whalen, Gary. "The Impact of Bank Holding Company Consolidation: Evidence from Shareholder Returns." *Economic Review*, Federal Reserve Bank of Cleveland (IIIQ:1985): 2–10.

Watro, Paul R. "Bank Earnings: Comparing the Extremes." *Economic Commentary*, Federal Reserve Bank of Cleveland, November 15, 1985.

Watro, Paul R. "Closely Watched Banks." *Economic Commentary*, Federal Reserve Bank of Cleveland, January 30, 1984.

Whalen, Gary. "Concentration and Profitability in Non-MSA Banking Markets." *Economic Review*, Federal Reserve Bank of Cleveland (1987 Quarter 1).

Whalen, Gary. "Competition and Bank Profitability: Recent Evidence." *Economic Commentary*, Federal Reserve Bank of Cleveland, November 1, 1986.

Whitehead, David D., and Jan Lujytes. "An Alternative View of Bank Competition: Profit or Share Maximization." *Economic Review*, Federal Reserve Bank of Atlanta (November 1982): 48–57.

International Banking

INTERNATIONAL BANKING IN PERSPECTIVE

Throughout the 1980s several U.S. banks reduced their volume of international loans. Yet this does not necessarily imply that international banking is becoming less important. The composition of international banking services has been restructured. For example, several banks have expanded their business with importers and exporters. Even regional banks such as Barnett Bank and Sun Bank are heavily involved in this activity. Several banks, including State Street Boston, Bankers Trust, and J.P. Morgan & Company, have expanded their foreign exchange operations over time. State Street Boston now has foreign exchange divisions in London, Zurich, and Hong Kong, which allows it to provide around-the-clock currency services for customers.

Regulatory differences among countries has encouraged U.S. banks to enter those foreign markets that are less regulated. In this way, commercial banks in the United States (such as Citicorp, Chase Manhattan, Chemical Bank, and Bank America) provided some investment banking services in foreign markets that they have been restricted from offering in the United States.

While international lending to less developed countries has declined, the management of existing loans to these countries is still a major issue. In addition, loans to corporations and governments of major countries will persist. Thus, international lending will continue to be an important function of many commercial banks.

- What types of services are offered by international bank divisions?
- What risks do banks with international loans face?
- What options are available to banks that have provided loans to less developed countries?
- Why are banks affected by fluctuations in exchange rates?

These and other related questions are addressed in this chapter.

OUTLINE

International banking has received more attention in recent years for three reasons. First, banks are increasingly establishing subsidiaries and branches in foreign countries. Second, banking regulations in many countries have loosened, allowing easier entry or access to banking markets. Third, international lending has become a major issue as a result of the international debt crisis that continues to plague many large banks.

This chapter first discusses migration by banks into foreign countries. It then describes the risks of a Eurobank. Next, it describes the cause and ongoing issues of the international debt crisis. Finally, it explains how banks assess the risk of countries to whom they consider lending.

MIGRATION BY BANKS TO FOREIGN COUNTRIES

Due to historical barriers against interstate banking, some U.S. commercial banks were better able to achieve growth by penetrating foreign markets. It is somewhat ironic that the New York banks historically had branches in Taiwan and Hong Kong but not in New Jersey or Connecticut. If full-fledged interstate banking had been allowed throughout the years, large U.S. commercial banks would probably have concentrated more on the U.S. markets. As it was, international markets were their primary sources of growth. Their international business is normally corporate-oriented rather than consumer-oriented.

The most common method for U.S. commercial banks to expand is through establishing *branches*, which are full-service banking offices that can compete directly with other banks located in that area. Commercial banks may also consider establishing *agencies*, which can provide loans but cannot accept deposits or provide trust services.

Exhibit 20.1 shows that the growth in international banking by U.S. banks was somewhat consistent throughout the 1970s but has subsided since 1981. Attempts by U.S. banks to establish foreign branches are subject to Federal Reserve Board approval. Among the factors considered by the Board are the bank's financial condition and experience in international business. The U.S. bank presence is larger in the United Kingdom than any other foreign country. Deposits in foreign branches of U.S. banks are not insured by the FDIC.

Since 1913 Edge Act corporations have been established by banks to specialize in international banking and foreign financial transactions. These corporations are not constrained by existing regulations against interstate banking. They can accept deposits and provide loans, as long as these functions are specifically related to international transactions.

International business allows firms to diversify among various economies so that their performance is less dependent on economic conditions of any single country. This is the motive for many U.S. commercial banks establishing branches across the world. Such international diversification of loans is thought to reduce the impact of a U.S. recession on the risk of U.S. bank loan portfolios. Furthermore, the establishment of branches allows a bank to do business face to face with subsidiaries of U.S.–based multinational corporations. The global expertise of some of the larger U.S. banks distinguishes them from the small and medium banks and enables them to dominate business by attracting the large corporations.

While U.S. banks have entered non–U.S. markets, non–U.S. banks have also entered U.S. markets. Initially, they entered primarily to serve the non–U.S. corporations that set up subsidiaries in the United States. Because this still serves as their primary function, they concentrate on corporate rather than consumer services.

EXHIBIT 20.1 Growth in International Banking by U.S. Banks

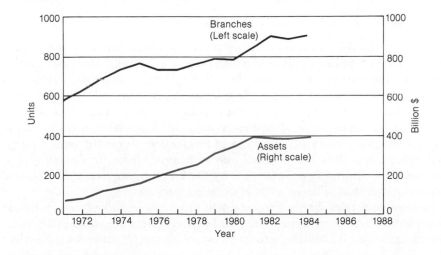

SOURCE: Board of Governors of the Federal Reserve System; *U.S. Industrial Outlook 1986;* and International Trade Administration.

Chapter 20

International Banking

The number of foreign bank offices in the United States has consistently increased throughout the 1970s and 1980s. Exhibit 20.2 identifies where headquarters of these offices are. More than one-third of all foreign bank offices in the United States are from Japan, Canada, the United Kingdom, and France. Almost half of these offices are located in New York, where many of the foreign-owned corporations conduct business. As an example of non–U.S. bank involvement in the U.S., Japanese banks use the U.S. market as a source of funds during periods of tight credit in Japan. Japanese banks also increase their business in the United States when Japanese–U.S. trade increases, which suggests how international banking is dependent on international trade activity.[1]

The International Banking Act of 1978

In 1978 the International Banking Act (IBA) was passed to restrict foreign-owned banks from accepting deposits across state lines. They were only allowed to accept deposits in other states by establishing Edge Act corporations. U.S.–owned banks were subject to similar restrictions at the time the IBA was passed.

The IBA also required that foreign-owned banks in the United States obtain deposit insurance and adhere to product and service restrictions enforced by the Bank Holding Company Act. In general, the IBA eliminated some comparative advantages of these foreign-owned banks. Recent research by Aharony, Saunders, and Swary has shown that the act had a strong positive effect on stock returns of the money center banks that were competing with foreign banks on an unequal basis before the act was passed.

INTERNATIONAL BANKING REGULATIONS

Bank regulations often differ distinctly among countries or continents. A brief overview of European bank regulations, then of Japanese bank regulations, follows.

European Bank Regulations

The central banks retain supervisory power over the banks in most European countries, unlike the United States, where other regulatory authorities share a large portion of responsibility. In the Nordic countries, authorities other than the central bank have the primary supervisory role. They conduct on-site examinations to monitor credit policies, foreign activities, and internal control. They also periodically monitor financial reports to assess capital adequacy and risk. The Bank of England analyzes the bank's financial reports but does not conduct on-site examinations. In Germany and Switzerland, auditors are appointed by bank regulators to conduct on-site examinations that address a list of detailed questions.

In most countries, banks can establish branches or subsidiaries without approval of their home supervisory authorities. There are some exceptions. Dutch banks must obtain approval to establish foreign branches. Swedish

1 For additional information, see the research by Poulson, listed in the references.

EXHIBIT 20.2 Foreign Bank Offices in the United States (as of December 31, 1986)

Country	U.S. Offices	Country	U.S. Offices
Japan	96	Mexico	11
Canada	50	Philippines	11
United Kingdom	44	Columbia	9
France	42	India	9
Hong Kong	31	Thailand	9
Brazil	28	Singapore	8
Spain	27	Argentina	7
Italy	26	Denmark	6
Israel	25	Indonesia	6
Germany	21	Luxemburg	6
South Korea	21	Pakistan	6
Switzerland	18	Belgium	5
Netherlands	17	Ireland	5
Australia	15	Other	69
Venezuela	15	Total	643

SOURCE: Board of Governors of the Federal Reserve System, and *U.S. Industrial Outlook 1988.*

banks are not allowed to establish foreign branches. Italian banks must abide by some restrictions.

European banks are generally allowed to offer investment banking services. Since U.S. banks have historically been restricted from some investment banking activities, they have established subsidiaries that offer these services in Europe.

European countries historically had diverse regulations on capital adequacy. However, there has been much progress recently to develop a uniform method of monitoring capital ratios in the industrialized countries.

European countries also have different lending limits. The United Kingdom restricts a bank's loan to an individual borrower to be no more than 10 percent of the bank's capital. Italy allows the loan amount to an individual borrower to be as much as 100 percent of the bank's capital.

Most industrialized European countries have some form of deposit insurance. Italy and Sweden are the only industrialized European countries that do not. Deposit insurance is required in the United Kingdom but optional elsewhere.

Japanese Bank Regulations

Most countries have loosened regulations in recent years. The Japanese government's deregulatory stages serve as an example. It has deregulated interest rates and allowed foreign investors to purchase capital market instruments. It also allowed some foreign financial institutions to establish subsidiaries there. There were 79 foreign-owned banks in Japan in 1986, 19 from the United States. In addition, there were 36 foreign securities firms in Japan, (18 from the United States) versus only 8 in 1983.

In April 1984 the Japanese government allowed foreign-owned banks to deal in Japanese public securities and to underwrite government bonds. In

June 1985 it allowed foreign banks to manage Japanese trust and pension funds.

Even with the loosened regulations, foreign banks accounted for only 4 percent of all banking assets in Japan. One of the main reasons is that foreign banks have only a limited access to some popular deposit accounts.

While U.S. banking deregulation has received much attention, the entire international banking system has been deregulated in recent years. Many provisions have been relaxed, including those relating to interest rate ceilings, foreign exchange controls, and lending activities. The result is reduced barriers, and a more competitive international banking system. During this deregulatory cycle, regulators have paid more attention to the capital adequacy of banks. As the capital requirements have been increased, banks have increased their provision of off-balance sheet products.

INTERNATIONAL REGULATORY CONCERNS

Gerald Corrigan, president of the Federal Reserve Bank of New York, mentioned some major concerns for international banking in the future:

■ Regulations of banks among countries are inconsistent. Greater harmony is needed between bank regulations across countries; in this way, banks from all countries would be competing under a similar set of guidelines.
■ International payments between banks are increasing at a rapid pace; the efficiency of the payments system is achieved through oral agreements; however, there is more risk of defaulted payments when using such informal negotiations.
■ The substantial increase in takeovers has occurred with a corresponding increase in financial debt; the amount of outstanding debt could become excessive.

In general, international banking regulations need to promote efficiency without increasing the public's risk perception of banks. This objective is also commonly stated on the domestic level as well.

RISKS OF A EUROBANK

Eurobanks, like other commercial banks, must manage their exposure to various types of risk. However, their degree of exposure can differ because of their unique characteristics. The most common types of risk to which Eurobanks are exposed are default, exchange rate, and interest rate risk.

Default Risk

When U.S. banks provide foreign loans, they must often work with less information than they usually have for domestic loans. This is true even when they have branches in the countries where the loans are provided. Regulations in foreign countries pertaining to the method and amount of information disclosure are typically not as strict as in the United States. Even if the bank requests additional information, the industry norms on financial ratios will vary significantly among countries. Thus, banks may be unsure of the proper benchmarks to use when assessing a loan applicant. To deal with this problem, some banks attempt to lend only to the very large corporations that have a global household name. Alternatively, they may concentrate on loans to national governments, who theoretically can use their taxing or money-printing powers to guarantee loan repayment. However, the international debt crisis in the early 1980s proved that loans to national governments are not automatically safe.

The loan portfolio of any given foreign branch of a large U.S. bank is likely to be heavily concentrated in the country where it is located. Yet, the consolidation of all branches may show a widely diversified loan portfolio. If a branch attempts to diversify across countries, it is unable to concentrate on the local area that it knows best. Because loans by each branch are narrowly focused on a particular economy, the performance of each branch can be highly susceptible to that economy. In general, the loan policy of the branch is to diversify loans across industries within the economy, while the overall loan policy of the entire commercial bank is to diversify loans across countries. Both objectives may be achieved if the commercial bank has established branches in various countries.

Exchange Rate Risk

When a bank providing a loan requires that the borrower repay in the currency denominating the loan, it may be able to avoid exchange rate risk. However, some international loans contain a clause that allows repayment in a foreign currency, thus allowing the borrower to avoid exchange rate risk instead. A commercial bank may have to approve this clause in order to secure the borrower's business.

In many cases, banks will convert available funds (from recent deposits) to whatever currency corporations want to borrow. Thus, they create an asset denominated in that currency, while the liability (deposits) is denominated in a different currency. If the liability currency appreciates against the asset currency, the bank's profit margin is reduced.

All large banks are exposed to exchange rate risk to some degree. They can attempt to hedge this risk in various ways. For example, consider a U.S. bank that converted dollar deposits into a British pound loan for a British corporation. Assume that the British firm will pay 50,000 pounds interest per year. The U.S. bank may attempt to engage in forward contracts to sell 50,000 pounds forward for each date in which it will receive those interest payments. That is, it could search for corporations that may wish to purchase 50,000 pounds on the dates of concern.

In reality, a large bank will not hedge every individual transaction but will instead *net out* the exposure and be concerned only with *net exposure*. Large banks enter into several international transactions on any given day. Some reflect future cash inflows in a particular currency while others reflect cash outflows in that currency. The bank's exposure to exchange rate risk is determined by the net cash flow in each currency.

Interest Rate Risk

The performance of commercial banks can be susceptible to interest rate fluctuations, regardless of their degree of international business. Yet, the existence of foreign currency balances makes management of interest rate risk even more challenging. The strategy of matching the overall interest rate–sensitivity of assets to that of liabilities will not automatically achieve a low degree of interest rate risk. For example, consider a Eurobank that has deposits denominated mostly in marks, while its floating-rate loans are denominated mostly in dollars. Even if the bank matches the average deposit maturity with the average loan maturity, the difference in currency denominations creates interest rate risk. The deposit and loan rates on various currencies depend on the interest rates in those respective countries. Thus, the performance of a bank concentrated in mark deposits and dollar loans will be adversely affected if German interest rates increase and U.S. rates decrease.

Even if the currency mix of a bank's assets is similar to that of its liabilities, and overall rate-sensitivity of assets and liabilities is similar, interest rate risk may still exist. Consider a bank that has short-term dollar deposits and medium- or long-term fixed-rate mark deposits. Assume that it provides short-term (or adjustable-rate) mark loans and long-term dollar loans. An increase in U.S. rates would reduce the spread on U.S. dollar loans versus deposits, since the dollar liabilities are more rate-sensitive than the dollar assets. In addition, an increase in German rates would increase the spread on the mark loans versus deposits, since the mark assets are more rate-sensitive than the mark liabilities. This example illustrates that exposure to interest rate risk can be minimized only if the rate-sensitivities of assets and liabilities are matched for each currency.

Combining All Types of Risk

When default risk, exchange rate risk, and interest rate risk are considered simultaneously, asset and liability management of a Eurobank becomes very complex. The management of one type of risk can affect exposure to another type. For example, a Eurobank that receives a large amount of French franc deposits may attempt to minimize its exchange rate exposure by calling on those local firms that would most likely need to borrow French francs. The bank is simply attempting to maintain the same currency concentration on both sides of the balance sheet. Yet, those particular firms may presently be close to their debt capacity. The bank would therefore need to decide whether to accept a high degree of default risk in order to minimize exchange rate risk. If it decided against channeling these funds to those firms with already high debt, it might be forced to provide loans in some other currency, thereby increasing its exchange rate exposure.

The Eurobank's exposure to various risks can best be understood by considering the typical daily transactions. During any given day, Eurobanks receive deposits in a variety of different currencies, amounts, and maturities and provide loans in various currencies, amounts, and maturities. It is unlikely that even a single deposit will perfectly match a loan request in terms of currency, amount, and maturity. Thus, the bank is constantly converting currencies received as deposits to the type of loans desired, thereby creating a short position in one currency and long position in another. It may also involve the use of short-term deposits to make medium-term loans, exposing the bank to interest rate risk. The Eurobank's exposure to the various forms of risk occurs as it accommodates the precise desires of savers and borrowers. If it is not willing to provide a deposit or loan with the specific currency, amount, and maturity desired by corporations or governments, some other Eurobank will.

INTERNATIONAL DEBT CRISIS

At any given point in time, some countries may be experiencing strong economic growth while others are stagnant. This is a primary reason for limiting the total percentage of loans to any one country. Yet, the 1980 and 1982 recessions affected all countries. To the extent that countries trade with each other, economies are integrated. The stagnant economies in Europe and the United States adversely affected each other in the early 1980s, and exporting volume declined. Furthermore, their demand for exports from less developed countries (LDCs) decreased. Because many LDC economies are highly dependent on their export business, the recession in the United States and Europe had a dramatic impact. In addition, the market price of oil was reduced due to the oil glut at that time. Consequently, the oil-exporting LDCs were generating less revenue than anticipated. As a result of the recession and declining oil prices, borrowers residing in many LDCs (governments and corporations) were not generating enough cash to repay their loans.

The debt problems of the LDCs were adversely affected by the strengthening dollar during the 1980s. Many of the loans provided to LDCs were denominated in U.S. dollars. As the dollar strengthened, more of the LDC's currency was needed to make payments. In addition, the interest rates in the early 1980s were at their peak, exceeding 20 percent in 1981. The high market interest rates combined with the strengthening U.S. dollar, caused the effective (exchange rate–adjusted) interest rate on previous loans to be 30 percent or more.

Commercial banks recognize that some borrowers will experience problems that may delay payments or even cause default. Yet, the banks were not expecting several borrowers to simultaneously announce their inability to repay loans. The situation was intensified by a plea of some of the borrowers for additional funds to rescue them from economic disaster. This put the bankers on the spot. They were already being criticized for being too aggressive with their lending. Now they were forced to decide among two alternative actions: (1) provide additional loans and incur the risk that these loans as well as previous loans would never be paid back or (2) reject the LDC's request for additional funds, realizing that the LDCs would then likely be more willing to first repay older loans from the banks that rescued them, should their economies improve.

The negotiating power of LDCs was enhanced because they, as a group, announced their inability to repay loans. If a single LDC had defaulted, the lending commercial banks would not have been as concerned. However, when several LDCs simultaneously are unable to repay loans, banks are not as willing to write off all loans at once. They instead search for a long-term economic rescue plan that may someday allow for repayment.

The commercial banks also had more negotiating power as a group. The LDCs may not be as concerned with threats of a single commercial bank (if certain conditions of the loan agreement are not met), since there are other banks with which the LDCs could do business in the future. But if all lending banks as a group require the LDCs to meet certain conditions, the consequences of not following through are more severe. Also, any LDCs could be black-balled in the international lending arena.

Negotiations between the commercial banks, LDCs, and the International Monetary Fund (IMF) were held in 1983. The IMF participated since one of its main functions is to promote international business. If negotiations between commercial banks and the LDCs had broken down, international trade between the developed countries and the LDCs would have been significantly reduced. In November 1983 the IMF Funding Bill was passed to provide additional funding to those LDCs that could meet specified economic goals. The goals differed for each LDC.

During the international debt crisis, several banks were attempting to reduce their foreign loan exposure and thus satisfy existing and potential shareholders. Some banks were willing to swap foreign loans to achieve a more diversified mix and therefore be less exposed to events in any single country. Foreign loans were sold at sizable discounts. Some Middle Eastern and European banks attempted to sell their entire Latin American loan portfolio. The banks attempting to sell their loans were essentially unwilling to restructure the loan terms and allow time for the LDCs to recuperate. They instead desired to sell the loans cheap and incur the loss immediately. The perceived probability of loan repayment can be assessed by reviewing the discounts on LDC loans sold in the secondary market. Exhibit 20.3 shows the market price for which loans to various countries were selling in the secondary loan market as of June 1986. This exhibit suggests little market confidence that loans to Bolivia and Peru will be repaid. The other LDC loans were selling for between 60 cents and 85 cents to the dollar, representing discounts from 15 to 40 percent. Recent research by Bruner and Simms has found that news on the international debt crisis caused abnormally low returns for the large commercial banks that were heavily exposed.

Historically, loan rescheduling allowed for a short-term delay of loan repayments, such as one or two years. This had only a slight impact on the cash flows of lending banks. However, it does not allow the borrowers much time to cure their financial problems. The IDC required banks to offer mul-

---

EXHIBIT 20.3 Secondary Market Price of Loans to Less Developed Countries (as of June 1986)

Country	Loan Price (Cents per Dollar)
Argentina	63
Bolivia	7
Brazil	76
Chili	68
Columbia	85
Ecuador	64
Mexico	60
Peru	20
Uruguay	64
Venezuela	77

SOURCE: *Economic Review*, Federal Reserve Bank of Kansas City (January 1987): 25.

tiyear rescheduling, giving borrowers a long-term approach for curing their financial problems, but also requiring the banks to be more patient in receiving their loan repayments. Multiyear rescheduling was offered to several of the LDCs.

The international debt crisis affected the risk distribution of new international financing provided by lenders and investors, as shown in Exhibit 20.4. The term "new financing arranged" is defined here to include loans provided, debt securities purchased, standby loan facilities offered, and banker's acceptances. The amount of financing arranged initially decreased or stabilized for each of the three markets shown in this exhibit. As international economic conditions began to improve in the mid 1980s, new financing increased for the industrialized countries (G-10 and Switzerland), increased slightly for the middle market borrowers, and decreased for LDCs.

Many LDCs still continue to experience economic problems. Exhibit 20.5 shows the amount of total debt for various LDCs and the amount of debt owed to U.S. banks as of 1986. The exhibit shows that U.S. banks are highly exposed to Brazil, Mexico, and Venezuela. The debt owed to the United States relative to total debt is highest for Venezuela.

The ability of debtor nations to cover their debt depends on their ability to export and to attract foreign investment. Since they are unable to attract foreign investment when their existing debt level is perceived to be high, they must rely on exports. Given that many countries have this same goal in mind, they cannot all attain it. Some countries can be net exporters only if others are willing to be net importers.

To achieve a more favorable balance of trade, governments of LDCs may consider imposing barriers on imports or intervening in the foreign exchange market to reduce their home currency value. The former solution commonly causes inefficiencies in local production and retaliation by other

EXHIBIT 20.4   New Financing Arranged for Three Groups of Countries

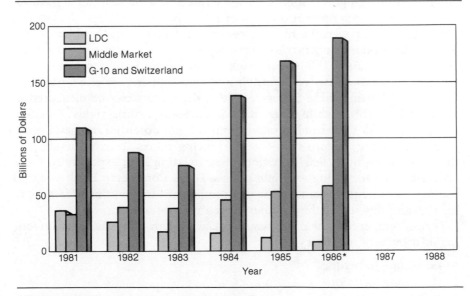

SOURCE: *FRBNY Quarterly Review* (Winter 1987): 47.

EXHIBIT 20.5 Total and U.S.–Owed Debt of Less Developed Countries (in Billions of Dollars)

	Total Debt	Debt Owed to the U.S.
Argentina	49.6	8.50
Bolivia	4.2	.14
Brazil	104.5	23.90
Chili	21.5	5.90
Columbia	13.6	2.60
Ecuador	7.7	2.10
Mexico	97.3	24.80
Peru	14.2	1.65
Uruguay	4.7	.89
Venezuela	36.5	20.40

SOURCE: *Economic Review*, Federal Reserve Bank of Kansas City (January 1987): 25.

country governments. While the latter solution may generate a more favorable trade balance, foreign loan repayments are more expensive when loans are denominated in a foreign currency.

While the impact of the international debt crisis is not over, commercial banks are more prepared to deal with it than they were in the early 1980s. The crisis has demonstrated that diversifying loans among foreign countries does not guarantee low risk, and that loans for foreign governments are not risk-free. These lessons have changed the long-term planning of commercial banks.

COUNTRY RISK ASSESSMENT

Banks have historically used country risk analysis for measuring the risk of loans to foreign governments. Country risk assessment systems have recently received more attention as a result of the international debt crisis. Those banks that were highly exposed to the loans of the problem LDCs either had a poor country risk assessment system or did not take their assessment seriously. While each bank has its own unique assessment system, most systems involve identifying factors that influence country risk and then weighting these factors. Some of the factors can be measured in an objective fashion while others must be measured subjectively. An effective country risk assessment system would signal potential financial problems of a country before they occur, allowing banks to avoid lending to those countries, or at least to reduce their existing loan exposure to those countries. The following example of how Texas Commerce Bank assessed country risk identifies some of the more important factors that affect country risk and illustrates the complexity of a risk assessment.

Texas Commerce Bank used a country risk system that was based on four major aspects of a country:

1. Economic indicators
2. Debt management
3. Political factors
4. Structural factors

Discriminant Analysis for Identifying Characteristics That Affect Country Risk

Discriminant analysis is useful for identifying factors that are distinctly different between two groups. It has historically been used to identify factors that distinguish (or discriminate) between successful and failing firms. It could even be used to distinguish between good and bad sports teams, or between successful and unsuccessful employees of a firm.

As a popular technique for country risk assessment, it attempts to identify factors that distinguish between countries experiencing debt-repayment problems and countries not experiencing problems. Once these factors are known, they can be closely monitored in the future.

The factors hypothesized to discriminate between two groups must first be identified and must be numerically measurable. Then, the factors are measured by historical data. One group (such as the successful group) is assigned a value of 1 while the other group is assigned a value of zero. Discriminant analysis generates a discriminant function that determines not only which factors distinguish between the two groups, but the type of influence each factor has.

Recent research by Morgan used discriminant analysis to assess the influence of variables on the likelihood that a country would need to reschedule its loan repayments. Morgan found the following characteristics of countries whose loan payments were rescheduled:

■ Their total debt to exports ratio was relatively high.
■ Their proportion of floating-rate loans (relative to total loans) was relatively high.
■ Their real growth rate in gross domestic product (GDP) was relatively low.

Additional results are provided in the article itself.

While discriminant analysis is useful for identifying characteristics that distinguish countries that rescheduled loans versus those that did not, its accuracy in predicting reschedulings depends on whether those characteristics continue to have a similar impact on reschedulings. For example, using Morgan's results, one would expect that a country with a greater proportion of floating-rate loans would have a higher probability of experiencing loan-repayment problems. However, if interest rates decreased in the future, countries with a greater proportion of floating-rate loans might be favorably affected.

SOURCE: John B. Morgan, "A New Look at Debt Rescheduling Indicators and Models," *Journal of International Business Studies* (Summer 1986): 37–54.

Short-term and medium-term models of these four aspects were developed in order to determine an overall short-term rating for a country and an overall medium-term rating. Two time horizons were used because a country's economic outlook may vary with the time horizon used. The measurement of each major aspect is described in turn.

Economic Indicators

The economic indicator model evaluates the country's economic environment. Some of the more relevant factors for this model are

Chapter 20

International Banking

The Debate over Product Convergence

Multinational theory suggests that in the past a country's banks followed its companies overseas. The new multinationals turned to the familiar home banks for financial advice in the new lands and later included foreign banks in relationships as they became familiar with the terrain or when foreign expertise was recognized as being roughly equivalent to what was available from home country banks. More recently, however, a blurring of differences between foreign and domestic banks and the growing universality of these institutions has caused events to unfold in other ways. More significantly, the geographical merging does not represent an increase in market efficiency but introduces attitudinal discontinuities that present new opportunities for selective exploitation by companies. Consider the evolution of this trend.

Emerging U.S. multinationals are providing their primary banks with the same reasons for expanding overseas. The requests for assistance are urgent since the international arena is increasingly turbulent. For these companies, the rewards and the risk of damaging losses are greater, and judgment, particularly in foreign exchange, is often swift. But the experience of the last decade has confirmed that the primary banks, often large regionals, are not following their clients overseas. Today, the reasons for the hesitation are clear. Regionals must gear up for domestic deregulation, which is expected to require the full application of their skills and resources. Furthermore, regionals have not been encouraged by the sobering experiences of predecessors, many of whom are presently retrenching or leveling their foreign operations.

In addition, a global bank transformation is changing the attitude of domestic companies toward their primary banks. The change stems from the growing universality of banks. Take the United States, for example, into which several large foreign banks have expanded, some having acquired domestic entities to complete their assimilation. Through frequent contact, the overseas capabilities of the foreign parent are well-known to emerging multinationals even before they venture overseas. A similar trans-

- Changes in the consumer price index
- Real growth in gross domestic product
- Current account balance divided by exports

A statistical technique called *discriminant analysis* was applied to these and other economic indicators in order to determine how they influence debt-repayment problems. This analysis creates a function that can be used to assign an overall rating to the country's economic indicators.

Debt Management

The debt management model evaluates the country's ability to manage debt. The more relevant variables for rating debt management include

formation is occurring abroad, with U.S. banks resembling and competing with the domestic institutions of those countries.

INTERCHANGEABLE

These universal banks, operating in many geographic markets as domestic entities, have seemingly converged in the eyes of the buyer. But are the products and services of these universal banks really interchangeable? Will they ever fully converge so that the products and services are truly interchangeable?

The answer to both questions is no—not as long as the banks are impelled by different motivations. The differences will necessarily remain since they are reflective of national traits. Motivations arise from policies set at senior levels and represent the social and cultural orientation of management. The resulting attitudes percolate to the lower levels of the institutions, where daily interaction in the marketplace occurs.

Consider one example to which so many business differences can be pegged—bank management's perception of timing. Compared to U.S. banks, the thinking of foreign institutions is less dominated by the necessity for a quick payback and early returns on products. Foreign institutions have the same eagerness for returns, but their planning period is longer. In contrast, the U.S. banks' shorter time period is often related to the greater resources invested in developing a product or a relationship. Senior management would like its laden launch boats to return sooner to harbor with the most treasured riches, as analytically described in the product life-cycle theory.

It is necessary, therefore, to recognize that despite increasing outward similarities in bank products and services, significant underlying differences will remain. By understanding the various motivations of the banks from various countries, managers of companies will have the opportunity for enlightened selection and profit-taking.

SOURCE: Reprinted with permission from: BANKERS MAGAZINE, MAY/JUNE 1986, Copyright © 1986, Warren, Gorham, & Lamont, Inc., 210 South Street, Boston MA, 02111. All Rights Reserved.

- Debt service and short-term debt divided by total exports
- Ratio of total debt to gross domestic product
- Short-term debt divided by total debt

Other things being equal, the higher the debt service and short-term debt are relative to exports or to gross domestic product, the higher the probability that a country would experience debt-repayment problems. The ratio of short-term debt to total debt indicates the percentage of debt principal that must be repaid in the near future. A high percentage could cause cash flow problems in the near future. In addition, countries with a high percentage are usually more vulnerable to interest rate movements. Discriminant analysis was used to determine how these factors can distinguish between countries that do and do not experience debt-repayment problems.

Chapter 20

International Banking

The discriminant function is generated from the analysis and can use current data on any given country to assign a debt management rating.

Political Factors

The political rating model is used to measure governmental characteristics and political stability. The political factors (some of which follow) are generally measured subjectively.

- Probability of destabilizing riots or civil arrest
- Probability of increased terrorist activities
- Probability of civil war
- Probability of foreign war
- Probability of government overthrow, coup d'etat

Each factor was assigned a probability ranging from 1 (extremely likely) to 5 (extremely unlikely). Ten factors were used for this model.

Structural Factors

The structural rating model measures socioeconomic conditions. Some of the more important structural factors are

- Natural resource base
- Human resource base
- Leadership

These factors are also subjectively rated.

Overall Rating

Each of the four models assigns a score between zero and 100, and the overall rating is determined by weighing the importance of the models. An example of how the overall rating is determined is shown in Exhibit 20.6. Notice that a grade is assigned for both the short- and medium-term horizons. The grades for this hypothetical example were higher for the short-term. Economic indicators were thought to be more important in the short-term horizon while the political rating was more important for the medium-term horizon.

The overall numerical grade for each horizon can be converted into a rating based on Standard and Poor's rating system on securities. Our example country's short-term horizon received a rating of A while its medium-term horizon received a grade of BBB (see Exhibit 20.7).

Country Risk Ratings

Institutional Investor magazine surveys international bankers in March and September of each year to obtain country credit ratings. It discloses the average rating for each country in its March and September issues. As shown in Exhibit 20.8, some countries, such as the United States, Japan, and West Germany have stable country risk ratings. Ratings for other countries, such as Mexico, Brazil, Israel, Libya, and Argentina have declined considerably.

EXHIBIT 20.6 Example of Determining Country Risk Ratings

	Short-term Horizon			Medium-term Horizon		
	Weight	Grade	Weighted Grade	Weight	Grade	Weighted Grade
Debt management model	.3	80	24	.3	70	21
Economic indicator model	.3	90	27	.2	70	14
Political rating model	.2	60	12	.3	50	15
Structural rating model	.2	75	15	.2	60	12
			78			62

EXHIBIT 20.7 Conversion of a Country's Grade into a Rating

Overall Grade Rating	Rating	
91–100	AAA	Excellent
81–90	AA	
71–80	A	
61–70	BBB	Satisfactory quality, average risk
51–60	BB	
41–50	B	
31–40	CCC	Low quality, high risk
21–30	CC	
11–20	C	
0–10	D	Excessive risk

SUMMARY

With the growth and deregulation of international banking, the markets for banking are becoming more integrated. This is likely to improve efficiency but has also created regulatory concerns. Banking regulations differ among countries, and sometimes between home-owned and foreign-owned banks within a country. Consequently, the performance of a bank's international operations can be highly dependent on how it is regulated, relative to its competitors. If banking regulations were uniform across countries, all banks could compete on the same level.

The international debt crisis has changed the international strategies of banks. While risky loans to foreign countries have been reduced, many banks have increased their degree of international involvement in nonlending services and in lending to middle-market and industrialized countries.

QUESTIONS

20.1. Explain the difference between branches and agencies of U.S. banks.

20.2. What are Edge Act corporations?

20.3. What was the purpose of the International Banking Act (IBA)?

EXHIBIT 20.8 Country Risk Ratings

Country	3/80	3/81	3/82	3/83	3/84	3/85	3/86	3/87	3/88
U.S.	98.2	98.1	97.5	96.1	96.0	95.6	96.3	94.1	91.0
Switzerland	98.5	97.0	95.9	95.4	95.4	94.7	95.3	94.2	94.1
Japan	95.4	95.2	95.8	95.1	95.1	95.1	95.5	96.0	94.6
W. Germany	98.4	96.3	93.9	93.0	92.7	93.1	94.2	94.2	93.1
U.K.	91.3	89.9	88.3	88.9	88.6	88.8	88.7	86.7	86.7
Canada	93.2	92.0	92.5	87.0	86.7	87.1	88.1	86.5	85.9
Norway	88.2	89.5	87.8	86.5	85.7	86.2	87.2	82.2	80.3
Netherlands	89.9	89.6	87.2	86.6	85.6	86.3	87.6	87.0	87.0
Australia	88.2	90.0	90.2	87.6	83.9	83.9	81.3	76.3	70.7
Austria	86.3	85.9	83.9	81.0	81.3	82.5	83.5	83.2	84.1
France	92.3	90.2	84.6	80.5	78.8	80.4	82.7	84.1	84.9
Singapore	78.6	78.6	78.5	77.6	78.0	79.3	76.7	74.8	75.4
Sweden	85.0	83.5	79.8	76.7	76.4	78.7	79.3	79.7	80.8
Finland	74.4	77.5	75.1	74.7	74.5	77.2	78.7	77.9	78.5
Belgium	87.4	84.4	77.3	72.3	72.3	74.4	75.8	76.7	77.4
Saudi Arabia	78.6	73.6	72.9	72.7	72.2	69.6	68.3	60.6	60.3
Italy	74.7	74.7	72.4	70.6	71.1	73.5	76.2	79.6	77.6
New Zealand	77.2	78.0	75.5	73.0	70.1	70.7	69.1	64.1	65.2
Denmark	73.3	73.0	71.7	68.7	69.6	72.2	74.1	72.9	73.0
USSR	71.5	69.6	65.5	59.7	61.5	64.5	68.0	65.5	65.4
Czechoslovakia	60.7	57.6	51.6	43.1	43.6	46.8	51.8	53.0	54.3
East Germany	61.4	58.4	51.9	41.3	43.0	47.6	53.9	56.3	58.4
Venezuela	71.2	69.3	63.3	57.4	37.7	36.9	39.7	36.9	35.8
Mexico	71.8	71.4	62.8	36.9	36.2	39.1	36.4	28.7	28.0
Libya	58.2	51.8	42.8	37.0	33.4	31.4	30.1	29.5	23.2
Brazil	58.0	49.7	56.3	48.1	30.0	31.7	31.9	35.5	29.4
Israel	47.7	41.4	35.7	32.4	28.3	28.9	28.8	33.0	34.6
Chile	52.9	54.4	52.1	44.0	27.3	25.0	24.6	26.0	27.2
Turkey	11.4	13.7	17.4	21.9	27.3	34.3	37.3	39.7	40.5
Argentina	62.6	63.4	50.5	30.2	25.0	22.0	22.7	24.8	24.8
Iran	15.8	13.7	11.3	13.8	18.4	18.9	18.1	19.5	18.3
Poland	41.6	32.9	13.0	8.3	10.2	14.1	14.7	16.4	17.8

NOTE: On a rating scale of 0 to 100, where 0 represents the lowest level of creditworthiness, and 100 represents the highest level of creditworthiness.

SOURCE: *Institutional Investor*, several issues, reprinted with permission of Institutional Investor Magazine.

20.4. In what ways has the Japanese government deregulated its financial markets recently?

20.5. Explain how banks become exposed to exchange rate risk.

20.6. Oregon Bank has branches overseas that concentrate in short-term deposits in dollars and floating-rate loans in British pounds. Because it maintains rate-sensitive assets and liabilities of equal amounts, it believes it has essentially eliminated its interest rate risk. Do you agree? Explain.

20.7. Dakota Bank has a branch overseas with the following balance sheet characteristics: 50 percent of the liabilities are rate-sensitive and denominated in Swiss francs; the remaining 50 percent of liabilities are rate-insensitive and are denominated in dollars. With regard to assets, 50 percent of assets are rate-sensitive and are denominated in dollars; the remaining 50 percent of assets are rate-insensitive and are denominated in Swiss francs. Is the performance of this branch susceptible to interest rate movements? Explain.

20.8. Why were many LDCs generating less cash flows than they anticipated prior to the international debt crisis?

20.9. How did the strengthening dollar during the 1980s affect the ability of LDCs to repay the loans to U.S. banks?

20.10. Explain why LDCs increased their negotiating power when they joined together to announce their inability to repay loans.

20.11. Theory suggests that diversification of loans among countries can insulate a bank's loan portfolio from any single event. Yet, the international debt crisis devastated the market value of loan portfolios of some large U.S. banks. Does this mean that diversification cannot sufficiently reduce risk? Explain.

20.12. Identify the four major aspects of a country that are commonly analyzed by country risk assessment systems. How can evaluations of these aspects be used to determine an overall rating for the country?

PROJECT

1. Obtain the annual report of a large commercial bank of your choice or assigned by your professor. From the report, how has the bank been involved in international business? Has the bank's involvement in international business improved its overall performance? Explain. Does the bank plan to reduce any of its international operations? (Identify them.) Why? Does it plan to increase any of its international operations? (Identify them.) Why? How should its planned adjustments in international business affect its risk and potential earnings.

REFERENCES

Aharony, Joseph, Anthony Saunders, and Itzhak Swary. "The Effects of the International Banking Act on Domestic Bank Profitability." *Journal of Money, Credit, and Banking* (November 1986): 493–506.

Aliber, Robert Z. "International Banking: A Survey." *Journal of Money, Credit, and Banking* (November 1984): 661–712.

Aliber, Robert Z. "International Banking: Growth and Regulation." *Columbia Journal of World Business* (Winter 1975): 9–15.

Bruner, Robert F. and John M. Simms, Jr. "The International Debt Crisis and Bank Security Returns in 1982." *Journal of Money, Credit, and Banking* (February 1987): 46–55.

Chrystal, K. Alec. "International Banking Facilities." *Review*, Federal Reserve Bank of St. Louis (April 1984): 5–11.

Cooke, W. P. "A Supervisory Perspective of Risks in Banking." *The World of Banking* (November–December 1986): 18–24.

Crane, Dwight B. and Samuel L. Hayes, III. "The Evolution of International Banking Competition and Its Implications for Regulation." *Journal of Bank Research* (Spring 1983): 39–53.

Danielsson, Stig. "Key Elements in Bank Supervision Systems in Europe. *The World of Banking* (May–June 1986): 17–20.

De Lattre, Andre. "Innovative Approaches to the Debt Crisis." *Banker's Magazine* (May–June 1985): 30–37.

Dornbusch, Rudiger. "International Debt and Economic Instability." *Economic Review*, Federal Reserve Bank of Kansas City (January 1987): 15–32.

Fieleke, Norman S. "International Lending on Trial." *New England Economic Review*, Federal Reserve Bank of Boston (May–June 1983): 5–13.

"Foreign Financial Institutions in Japan." *FRBSF Weekly Letter*, April 24, 1987.

Gilbert, Nick. "Foreign Banks in America: They're Still Coming." *Euromoney* (August 1985): 150–155.

Gluck, Jeremy. "International Middle-Market Borrowing." *Quarterly Review*, Federal Reserve Bank of New York (Winter 1987): 46–52.

Johnson, Manuel H. "Reflections on the Current International Debt Situation." *Economic Review* (June 1987): 3–8.

Laney, Leroy O. "The Secondary Market in Developing Country Debt." *Economic Review*, Federal Reserve Bank of Dallas (July 1987): 1–12.

Morgan, John B. "Assessing Country Risk at Texas Commerce." *Banker's Magazine* (May–June 1985): 23–29.

Ogilvie, Nigel R. "Foreign Banks in the U.S. and Geographic Restrictions on Banking." *Journal of Bank Research* (Summer 1980): 73–79.

Poulsen, Annette B. "Japanese Bank Regulation and the Activities of U.S. Offices of Japanese Banks." *Journal of Money, Credit, and Banking* (August 1986): 366–373.

"Recent Innovations in International Banking: The Policy Implications." *The World of Banking* (July–August 1986): 4–7.

Ricks, David and Jeffrey S. Arpan. "Foreign Banking in the United States." *Business Horizons* (February 1976): 84–87.

"The Bank's Latest Game: Loan Swapping." *Fortune*, December 12, 1983, 111–112.

Accounting for Troubled Foreign Loans*

The increase in loan loss provisions at major banks had a pronounced effect on reported 1987 bank profitability. Banks with more than $1 billion in assets accounted for 82 percent of the assets and 78 percent of the loan losses of the banks in the 1986 sample. These very large banks accounted for 83 percent of the assets and 92 percent of the loan losses in 1987. Another way of gauging the effect of loan loss provisions is to examine the ratio of net income before loan loss provisions, extraordinary items, and taxes to the banks' total assets in 1986 and 1987.[1] This ratio improved from 1986's 1.52 percent for the largest banks to 1.55 percent in 1987. However, loan loss expense as a percentage of total assets also more than doubled from 0.71 percent in 1986 to 1.53 percent, in 1987. As a consequence, net income before taxes and extraordinary items fell from 0.81 percent in 1986 to 0.02 percent in 1987.

This box seeks to address two issues: why did the large banks not provide substantial increases in their loan loss allowances prior to 1987, and what is the effect of the increase in allowances? An understanding of how banks account for loan losses would be helpful before addressing these questions.

ACCOUNTING PROCEDURES

After every period a bank examines its existing loan portfolio and estimates the expected losses on outstanding loans. The loan loss allowance (on the bank's balance sheet) is then increased to match expected losses, with the amount of the increase charged against income as a provision for possible loan losses. Losses on individual loans during the next accounting period

*This appendix is a reprint from the *Economic Review*, Federal Reserve Bank of Atlanta, contained within the article "Commercial Bank Profitability Still Weak in 1987," by Larry Wall, August 1988, p. 28–41.

1 A before-tax ratio is used to avoid potential differences in the tax treatment of loan loss provisions at different banks.

are charged against the loan loss allowance but are not immediately reflected in the bank's income accounts. Similarly, if the bank recovers more than expected on loans that were previously charged off, the bank's accountants add the amount of the recovery back to the loan loss allowance. At the end of the period, the amount in the loan loss allowance is equal to its beginning-of-period value, less any charge-offs and plus any recoveries. The bank then begins the cycle again by determining expected losses on loans and comparing that with its loan loss allowance.

This procedure may seem needlessly complicated; a far simpler approach would be to recognize loan losses when the loan is written off.[2] One reason for following the more complicated procedure, though, is that it accords with the important accounting principal of conservatism, that when "reasonable support exists for alternative methods ... the accountant should select the accounting option with the least favorable effect on net income and financial position in the current period."[3] Recognizing expected loan losses before they occur is more conservative than waiting until the loan is written off. The more complicated procedure is also required to meet the needs of the accrual method of accounting, which is used by all large banks. Banks following the accrual method recognize revenue in the period when the payment is earned, regardless of when it is received.[4] The accrual method also requires that after revenue associated with a period is determined, the costs associated with that income must also be recognized. For institutions in the business of making loans, one of the expenses stems from the fact that some of their loans will not be fully repaid. Therefore, accrual accounting requires that the bank anticipate suffering some losses in the loan portfolio.

The responsibility for a bank's loan loss allowances rests with its management. The managers of an organization are in the best position to evaluate its financial condition, which is typically communicated to existing and potential shareholders in its annual financial statements. A bank's auditors may suggest increases in the allowance, but they cannot force management to follow such suggestions. Bank regulators may compel managers to increase their loan loss allowances if, in the regulators' opinion, the allowance is inadequate. Thus far, federal bank regulators have encouraged banks to review carefully their allowance for losses but have not ordered large increases in loan loss allowances.

WHY ARE THE 1987 WRITEOFFS SO LARGE?

The problems that at least some Latin American countries would have in repaying their debt have been obvious since the problems with Mexican debt emerged in August 1982. Yet until 1987, most major banks did not significantly increase their loan loss allowances to account for their exposure to Latin American debt. Why did many large banks take so long to increase their loan loss allowances?

2 The new tax law requires the simpler treatment of losses for tax purposes.
3 See Meigs, Mosich, Johnson, and Keller (1974): 22.
4 For example, suppose a bank makes a three-month loan on November 1, 1987, with no interest payment due until February 1, 1988. The bank would recognize two months of interest revenue (from November 1 through December 31) in its 1987 income and one month of interest revenue in its 1988 income.

The banks' reluctance to increase their allowances could be justified on the grounds that the losses might not occur. The troubled foreign borrowers were seeking to extend the term of their repayments but none had repudiated its outstanding debt. Thus, the banks could still receive repayment in full. The problem with this explanation for the failure to increase allowances is that it mistakes the purpose of the loan loss allowance. The loan loss allowance exists to account for losses that may be reasonably expected on a bank's existing loan portfolio; those portions of loans that have incurred actual losses should be written off.

The expected amount of losses is open to some question, but the market clearly expected banks to absorb some losses on their Latin American debt. The secondary market in Latin American debt has priced the debt of individual countries at a discount to their face values. In some cases these discounts have been substantial. The secondary market may be criticized as being too thin to provide reliable prices, but the general conclusion that some losses are expected on loans to some Latin American countries is supported by the bank equity markets. Informal examination of bank stock prices suggests that banks with substantial exposure to Latin American countries have traded at a large discount to their book values for several years. On a more formal level, Robert F. Bruner and John M. Simms, Jr. (1987) show that within six days of the 1982 announcement that Mexico would suspend principal repayments, the market was discounting bank stock prices based on each bank's loans to Mexico.

Another explanation for the delay in increasing allowances is that many banks could not afford to increase their provision because their exposure to Latin American debt exceeded their capital. Some banks would have been left with no capital had they increased their loan loss allowances. One response to this explanation is that banks need not and should not have increased their provisions to cover *all* of their troubled Latin American debt. The financial markets have not been indicating that the troubled loans were worthless, merely that the face value of the loans overstated their economic value. Most banks could have afforded some increase in their allowances.

Perhaps the best justification for the delay is that increasing provisions may have had an adverse effect on the negotiations with troubled Latin American borrowers. An increase in loan loss allowances may have encouraged some countries to seek better terms than the banks were prepared to offer. An increase in allowances may also have discouraged certain banks from participating in the restructuring of outstanding debt. Some banks with relatively small exposure may have been unwilling to provide additional loans at a time when they were increasing their allowances on existing loans. This justification raises a troubling question: is the purpose of accounting statements to provide an unbiased "scorecard," or is it one more tool to be manipulated?

WHAT IS THE SIGNIFICANCE OF THE INCREASED ALLOWANCE?

The increase in loan loss allowances has very little direct effect on banks or borrowers. In some sense this increase was merely a set of accounting entries, but these entries potentially have significant indirect effects. The market clearly attached significance to the action. James J. Musumeci and Joseph F. Sinkey, Jr. (1988) report significant abnormal returns to a portfolio of ten money-center banks the day after Citicorp announced it increased loan loss allowance.

Loan loss allowances are sometimes referred to as *loan loss reserves*. Unfortunately the term *loan loss reserves* may create the mistaken impression that a bank sets aside funds (cash) in reserve to cover its loan losses. An increase in the loan loss account, however, does not directly cause any change in the allocation of a bank's assets. Loan loss allowances merely reduce the net value of the bank's loans on its accounting records.

An increase in the loan loss allowance may indirectly cause a bank to reduce its dividends or seek additional equity. The federal government and many state governments restrict bank dividends based on the bank's current earnings and recent retained earnings as reported on their financial statements.[5] An increase in loan loss provisions reduces a bank's income and hence its ability to pay a dividend. Large increases in allowances will also decrease a bank's equity capital as reported in its accounting records and possibly trigger regulatory demands for additional equity. However, the regulators can already demand additional equity for organizations with a substantial volume of troubled loans, regardless of the reported value of the bank's equity.

The increase in banks' loan loss allowances has no direct effect on the Latin American debtors. The banks did not waive their right to repayment on any loans, and they still hope to be repaid in full. Bank managers may be psychologically more prepared to make concessions on the loans since the losses were acknowledged in an earlier period (in part because additional concessions would have less of an impact on their bonuses). However, the provisions could have the opposite effect if they made the banks feel less financially vulnerable to pressure from the Latin American borrowers.

Though they increased their loan loss provisions, banks were not able to deduct from taxable income an amount equivalent to the increased provision. The Tax Reform Act of 1986 changed the rules on the accounting for loan losses. Banks with assets in excess of $500 million may reduce their taxable income only by the amount of loan losses they actually incur in a year. Thus, a large bank can recognize losses on Latin American debt for tax purposes only when it either writes off part of the loans or sells some of its loans at a loss.

In summary, many U.S. banks, particularly larger banks outside the Southeast, waited until last year to increase substantially their loan loss allowances on foreign, especially Latin American, loans. Though this increase is primarily an accounting adjustment with little direct effect on banks or borrowers, indirect effects may result. The impact of these adjustments on bank profitability will likely be lessened in 1988, unless the country's larger banks continue increasing loan loss allowances on troubled foreign debt.

5 National banks are prohibited from making dividend payments in excess of the current year's income plus the sum of the prior two years' retained earnings. State chartered banks face limitations imposed by state law and may also be limited by the actions of their federal bank supervisor.

Joint United States-United Kingdom Proposed Risk-Based Capital Standard

FEBRUARY 1987

In February 1987, the Federal Reserve published for comment a proposed framework for evaluating the adequacy of commercial bank and holding company capital with regard to both on- and off-balance sheet risk.[1] It was jointly developed with the Bank of England, the Office of the Comptroller of the Currency and the FDIC. This summary is presented because the framework is a more informative structure than the simpler standard now in use by U.S. bank regulators that uses a ratio of primary capital to total assets. The proposal is still under development as part of a multinational effort to bring consistency to the evaluation of capital at major banks in all international financial centers.[2]

CAPITAL-TO-RISK RATIO

The proposal would create a capital-to-risk ratio to relate a banking institution's adjusted primary capital to its weighted risk assets. Primary capital should be freely available to absorb current losses while permitting an organization to function as a going concern. Under the proposal, it would consist of two classes of capital funds: base primary capital and limited primary capital. The latter would be limited to a specified percentage of base primary capital.

PRIMARY CAPITAL

The February 1987 proposal defined base primary capital funds to include common stockholders' equity, general reserves for unidentified losses, and

1 *Federal Register*, vol. 52, no. 33, p. 5119, February 19, 1987.
2 On December 10, 1987, banking authorities released the next version of this capital proposal.

minority interests in the equity accounts of consolidated subsidiaries. Other capital instruments would be qualified as limited primary capital to the extent the total does not exceed 50 percent of tangible base primary capital, that is, base primary capital reduced by intangible assets. Limited primary capital funds would include perpetual preferred stock, limited-life preferred stock with an original maturity of at least 25 years, and certain debt that is subordinated to deposits. To qualify, subordinated debt must be unsecured, repayable only with equity or similar debt, and convertible to equity if other capital is depleted. It must also permit deferral of interest payments during periods of financial distress.

PROPOSED CAPITAL STANDARD

Risk ratio is compared to a requirement

$$\text{Risk ratio} = \frac{\text{Adjusted primary capital}}{\text{Weighted risk assets}}$$

Adjusted primary capital = Base primary capital
+ Limited primary capital
− Deductions

Weighted risk assets = Sum (risk weights × assets)
+ Sum (risk weights × conversion factors × off-balance sheet exposures)

DEDUCTIONS FROM PRIMARY CAPITAL

The February 1987 proposal would calculate adjusted primary capital by adding base and limited primary capital and deducting intangible assets and equity investments in unconsolidated affiliates. When deducted from capital, an equity investment in an affiliate would also be deducted from the risk-weighted asset base.

PROPOSED RISK WEIGHTS

Each of a banking organization's assets would be assigned to one of five risk categories and weighted according to the relative risk of that category. The determination of asset groupings and the assignment of weights primarily would reflect credit risk considerations, with some sensitivity to liquidity and interest rate risk. The categories would distinguish among broad classes of obligors and, to a lesser extent, among maturities and types of collaterization. A credit equivalent approach would be used in weighting the risks of off-balance sheet activities. Under this approach, the face amount of an off-balance sheet exposure would be multiplied by a credit conversion factor, and the resulting credit equivalent amount would be assigned to the appropriate risk category as if it were a balance sheet item. Assets collateralized by cash or U.S. government securities would be accorded a lower risk weight, but the proposal would not explicitly recognize other forms of collateral or guarantees in weighting asset risk. However, examiners would continue to consider all forms of collateral and guarantees in evaluating asset quality and making an overall assessment of capital adequacy.

The following tables provide a summary of major asset and off-balance sheet weightings contained in the February 1987 U.S.-U.K. proposal.

EXHIBIT 20B.1 Summary of Risk Weights for On-Balance Sheet Assets

0 percent
Cash—domestic and foreign

10 percent
Short-term (one year or less) claims on U.S. government and its agencies.

25 percent
Cash items in process of collection
Short-term claims on domestic and foreign banks
Long-term claims on and guarantees of the U.S. government
Claims (including repurchase agreements) collateralized by cash or U.S. government or agency debt
Local currency claims on foreign governments to the extent that bank has local currency liabilities

50 percent
Claims on or collateralized by U.S. government-sponsored agencies
Municipal general obligations

100 percent
Claims on private entities and individuals
Claims on foreign governments that involve transfer risk

EXHIBIT 20B.2 Conversion Factors for Off-Balance Sheet Exposures

100 Percent
Direct credit substitutes including financial guarantees and standby letters of credit
Repurchase agreements and other asset sales with· recourse, if not already included on the balance sheet

50 Percent
Trade-related contingencies including commercial letters of credit and performance bonds
Other commitments with original maturity over five years, including revolving underwriting facilities

25 Percent
Other commitments with original maturity of one to five years

10 Percent
Other commitments with original maturities of one year or less

NOTE: Swaps, over-the-counter options, and other difference contracts would be treated separately

SOURCE: FRBNY Quarterly Review (Autumn 1987): 9–10.

Nonbank Financial Institutions

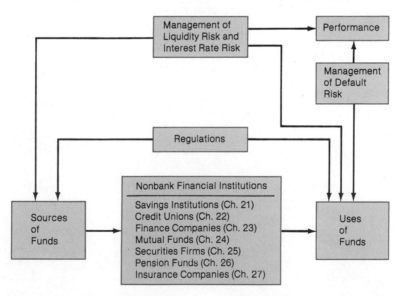

The chapters in Part Six cover the key nonbank financial institutions. Each of these chapters is devoted to a particular type of financial institution, with a focus on sources of funds, uses of funds, regulations, management, and recent performance. Each financial institution's interaction with other institutions and participation in financial markets is also emphasized in these chapters.

Savings Institutions

SAVINGS INSTITUTIONS IN PERSPECTIVE

In recent years, the financial problems of savings institutions have received much attention. Yet there are some exceptions. Franklin Savings Corporation of Ottawa, Kansas has grown from about $200 million in assets in 1981 to about $10 billion recently. Some of the main reasons for its success are listed below:

■ It offers attractive rates on deposits in order to attract large amounts of savings from investors

■ It attracts deposits from firms with large amounts of short-term funds

■ It offers adjustable-rate mortgages and avoids fixed-rate mortgages in order to reduce interest rate risk

■ It uses much of its funds to purchase mortgage-backed securities

■ It uses financial futures and options on futures to reduce any interest rate risk to which it is exposed

The strategies described above represent high volume, an acceptable margin, and low risk. Some other savings institutions use distinctly different strategies, such as offering relatively low deposit rates and the provision of fixed-rate mortgages. In addition, some savings institutions have preferred not to hedge their interest rate risk.

■ Are there any possible disadvantages of Franklin's strategy?

■ Why don't all other savings institutions copy Franklin's strategy?

■ How can financial futures reduce interest rate risk?

■ Would you expect Franklin's spread (net interest margin) to be larger or smaller than other savings institutions, ignoring possible loan losses?

This chapter discusses these and other questions related to the management and performance of savings institutions.

SOURCE: USA Today, June 29, 1988, P. B1–B2.

OUTLINE

The term *savings institutions* refers to savings and loan associations and savings banks. These institutions are somewhat similar in that they obtain most of their funds from consumers and use most of their funds to provide mortgages for consumers. Their operations differ from commercial banks, which use most of their funds for business loans and commercial real estate loans. This chapter explains the background, operations, regulation, managerial strategies, and recent performance of savings institutions.

BACKGROUND ON SAVINGS INSTITUTIONS

Savings and loan associations (sometimes called S&Ls or savings associations) are the most dominant form of savings institutions, holding in aggregate more than $700 billion of consumer savings. The distribution of S&Ls by size is shown in Exhibit 21.1. Roughly 85 percent of them have assets between $25 million and $5 billion. Less than 1 percent of these associations have assets of over $5 billion.

S&Ls can be either state- or federal-chartered. The deposits of federal-chartered S&Ls are insured up to $100,000 per depositor by the Federal Savings and Loan Insurance Corporation (FSLIC). The FSLIC charges S&Ls an annual insurance premium of one-twelfth of 1 percent on their deposits. It can also charge a supplemental premium if necessary. The FSLIC charges similar premiums for all participating institutions, regardless of their risk.

The Federal Home Loan Bank Board (FHLBB), created in 1932, regulates all federally chartered S&Ls. Its headquarters is in Washington D.C., and its 12 district banks are spread across the United States (although not perfectly overlapping the 12 district bank locations of the Federal Reserve System). The FHLBB can approve or disapprove federal charter requests by S&Ls and provides loans to S&Ls for liquidity purposes. It obtains most of its funds by issuing debt securities.

S&Ls can be either mutual- or stock-owned. Because mutual S&Ls do not have stockholders, they are technically owned by their depositors. The majority of S&Ls are mutual.

Savings banks have similar characteristics to those of S&Ls. They can be state- or federal-chartered, although most are state-chartered. In addition, they have access to Federal Home Loan Bank funding. They can also be mutual or stock-owned. While most savings banks are mutual, there has been an increasing tendency in recent years to convert to stock ownership in order to have greater access to capital. If a stock-owned savings bank desires to boost capital, it can simply issue more stock.

Savings banks differ from S&Ls in the following ways. While S&Ls are spread across the entire country, savings banks are mainly concentrated along the northeastern portion of the United States. Savings banks have the choice of insuring their deposits with either the state or with the Federal Deposit Insurance Corporation (FDIC). They are not as heavily concentrated in mortgages and have more diversified uses of funds. While savings banks have had more flexibility in their investing practices than S&Ls, the difference has narrowed over time. In those states where the state regulations imposed on savings banks are very flexible, savings banks will likely continue to offer more diversified services to customers.

While the differences between savings banks and S&Ls are important, these two types of savings institutions are similar in many respects. The remainder of this chapter discusses savings institutions in general, with a specific focus on savings banks or S&Ls only when necessary.

SOURCES OF FUNDS

The main sources of funds for savings institutions are deposits, borrowed funds, and capital. Each of these sources is discussed in turn.

Deposits

Savings institutions obtain most of their funds from a variety of savings and time deposits, including passbook savings, retail CDs, and money market deposit accounts (MMDAs). Before 1978 savings institutions focused primarily on passbook savings accounts. During the early and mid 1970s, *disintermediation* (explained earlier) was common, since market interest

EXHIBIT 21.1 Distribution of Savings and Loan Associations by Size

Asset Size (in Millions of Dollars)	Number of Savings and Loan Associations	Percentage of Total
Under $25	457	14.1%
Between $25 and $50	554	17.1
Between $50 and $100	714	22.0
Between $100 and $250	779	24.0
Between $250 and $500	343	10.6
Between $500 and $1,000	193	5.9
Between $1,000 and $5,000	176	5.4
$5,000 and over	30	.9
Total	3,246	100.0%

SOURCE: *Savings Institution Sourcebook*, United States League of Savings Institutions (1986): 45.

rates exceeded the passbook savings rate. Because disintermediation reduced the volume of savings at S&Ls, it reduced the amount of mortgage financing available. Recent research by Throop has determined that residential investment may have been reduced by as much as 12 percent during some periods as a result of disintermediation.

In 1981 savings institutions across the country were allowed to offer NOW accounts as a result of the Deregulation Act of 1980 (DIDMCA). This was a major event, since they were previously unable to offer checking services. Suddenly, the differences between commercial banks and savings institutions was not so obvious to savers. NOW accounts enabled savings institutions to be perceived as full-service financial institutions.

The creation of MMDAs in 1982 (as a result of the Garn–St Germain Act) allowed savings institutions to offer limited checking combined with a market-determined interest rate, and therefore compete against money market funds. Because these new accounts offered close-to-market interest rates, they were a more expensive source of funds than passbook savings. The new types of deposit accounts have increased the rate-sensitivity of savings institution liabilities to interest rate movements.

Like commercial banks, savings institutions were historically unable to offer a rate above a regulatory ceiling on deposits. In 1978 a loosening of regulations allowed them to offer limited types of retail CDs with rates tied to Treasury bills. As a wider variety of retail CDs were allowed in the late 1970s and early 1980s, and MMDAs were introduced in 1982, the ceiling rate on passbook savings was no longer as relevant. As of March 31, 1986, all deposits were free from ceiling rates.

Borrowed Funds

When savings institutions are unable to attract sufficient deposits, they can borrow from their district Federal Home Loan Bank (FHLB), and they also have access to the Federal Reserve discount window. The Fed's discount window is generally used only for very short-term funding such as a few days, whereas the FHLB advances can be provided for a period of several years (although they generally have maturities of less than two years). FHLB loans are typically backed by mortgages owned by the savings institutions that are requesting funds. Exhibit 21.2 shows that FHLB advances have become a popular source of funds.

In addition to the FHLB advances and the Fed's discount window, savings institutions can also obtain funds through repurchase agreements and in the federal funds market.

Capital

The **capital** (or net worth) of a savings institution is primarily composed of retained earnings and funds obtained from issuing stock. During periods when savings institutions are performing well, capital is boosted by additional retained earnings. Capital is commonly used to support ongoing or expanding operations.

Savings institutions are required to maintain a minimum level of capital in order to cushion against potential losses that could occur and thus help to avoid possible failure. During the early 1980s losses were common among savings institutions, and the capital levels were reduced. Concerned with the erosion of capital, the FHLBB has recently attempted to tighten its requirements. All FSLIC-insured institutions must maintain a net worth level of 3 percent of liabilities. For newly formed institutions, the minimum is 7 percent over the first fiscal year, subsequently declining to 5 percent and possibly 3 percent if proper approval is given.

In August 1986 the FHLBB adopted regulations that would phase in higher capital requirements for existing savings institutions. The minimum ratio of book value net worth to liabilities was to be increased to 6 percent over a phase-in period of between 6 and 12 years.

EXHIBIT 21.2   Trend of FHLB Advances Over Time

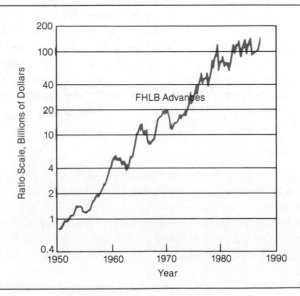

SOURCE: *Federal Reserve Chart Book.*

USES OF FUNDS

The main uses of funds for savings institutions are

- Cash
- Mortgages
- Mortgage-backed securities
- Investment securities
- Consumer and commercial loans
- Other uses

Each of these uses is discussed in turn.

Cash

Savings institutions maintain cash to satisfy reserve requirements enforced by the Federal Reserve System and to accommodate withdrawal requests of depositors. In addition, some savings institutions hold correspondent cash balances at other financial institutions in return for various services.

Mortgages

Mortgages are the primary asset of savings institutions. They typically have long-term maturities and can usually be prepaid by borrowers. Mortgages can be sold in the secondary market, although their market value changes in response to interest rate movements, so they are subject to interest rate risk as well as default risk. To protect against interest rate risk, savings institutions use a variety of techniques discussed later in this chapter. To protect against default risk, the real estate represented by the mortgage serves as collateral.

Mortgage-backed Securities

Savings institutions commonly issue securities that are backed by mortgages in order to obtain funds. Other savings institutions with available funds can purchase these securities. The seller may continue to service the mortgages, but it passes on the periodic payments to the purchaser, retaining a small amount as a service fee. The cash flows to these holders of mortgage-backed securities will not necessarily be even over time, since the mortgages can be prepaid before their stated maturity.

Investment Securities

All savings institutions invest in securities such as Treasury bonds and corporate bonds. Because savings banks are not as heavily concentrated in mortgage loans and mortgage-backed securities, they hold a greater percentage of investment securities than S&Ls. These securities provide liquidity, as they can quickly be sold in the secondary market if funds are needed. Savings banks are also able to invest in corporate stocks, while S&Ls are not.

Exhibit 21.3 shows how the level of mortgages and securities has changed over time for S&Ls. While residential mortgages still dominate their asset

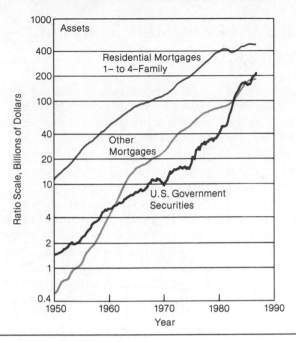

SOURCE: *Federal Reserve Chart Book.*

portfolio, S&Ls have significantly increased their proportional investment in other mortgages and U.S. government securities.

Consumer and Commercial Loans

Many savings institutions are attempting to increase their consumer loans and commercial loans. As a result of DIDMCA and the Garn–St Germain Act, the lending guidelines for federally chartered savings institutions were loosened. Subsequent to these acts, many state-chartered savings institutions were also granted more lending flexibility by their respective states. Specifically, the acts allowed federally chartered savings institutions to invest up to 30 percent of their assets in non-mortgage loans and securities. A maximum 10 percent of assets can be used to provide non-real estate commercial loans.

Savings institutions have taken advantage of the deregulatory acts by providing corporate and consumer loans with maturities typically ranging between one and four years. Because consumer and corporate loan maturities closely match their liability maturities, savings institutions that reduce their mortgage loan concentration in favor of more corporate and consumer loans will reduce their exposure to interest rate risk. However, their willingness to offer these loans results in some noninterest costs. They must advertise to corporations and consumers that they have now entered this new business, and they must also hire personnel with expertise in these

Chapter 21

Savings Institutions

581

Deposit Runs on Ohio and Maryland Savings Institutions

On March 6, 1985, $55 million of depositor withdrawals occurred at Home State Savings Bank of Cincinnati, Ohio. During the next two days, an additional $100 million was withdrawn. The runs on the institutions were triggered by unique events growing out of Home State Savings Bank's investments with ESM Government Securities, Inc., a government securities dealer based in Fort Lauderdale, Florida. ESM had made large repurchase agreements with Home State totaling approximately $145 million. Alleged fraudulent dealings of ESM caused their failure, which in turn caused difficulties for Home State.

Deposits at Home State Savings Bank were insured by the Ohio Deposit Guarantee Fund (ODGF), a private fund that insured about 70 state-chartered savings institutions in Ohio. Savings and loan leaders in Ohio originally organized ODGF to provide insurance for institutions considered too small to require or qualify for federal deposit insurance. ODGF was less expensive than federal deposit insurance and enforced less restrictions, which led to its popularity. Yet, it could not cover the losses of Home State.

Runs at other Ohio S&Ls insured by ODGF occurred when the Home State closing was announced. Daily deposit withdrawals at seven Cincinnati area institutions ranged from $6 million to $60 million in only four days. These runs occurred only at ODGF-insured institutions.

Several steps were taken to resolve these problems. First, a bill was passed to form a new Savings Association Guarantee Fund, ODGF-II, that was to raise $40 million. A state emergency loan of $50 million was to be combined with this $40 million. As a second step, Ohio's governor, F. Celeste, declared a bank holiday and on March 15, 1985, closed down the savings institutions insured by ODGF.

Another step was a meeting between Ohio bankers and state officials at the Federal Reserve Bank of Cleveland to discuss purchases of ODGF-insured institutions. Due to lack of information, especially about the quality of assets, proposals for the purchase of any of these institutions could not be completed. Because they were insured by private insurance, they were not required to file financial reports. Forty-four ODGF-insured institutions eventually received full or conditional approval for federal deposit insurance. Twenty-five institutions, including Home State, were merged into or acquired by other institutions.

This same scenario occurred in Maryland in May 1985. Once again, an S&L insured only by private insurance was involved. A run on Maryland S&Ls occurred as a result of news that one of the S&Ls was in financial trouble. Maryland state officials ordered a grand jury to investigate the transactions of alleged fraudulent real estate dealings by the principal owners of the Old Court Savings and Loan Association. In addition, Merrit Commercial Savings and Loan Association was ordered by State regulators to discontinue some of its riskier investment practices.

To circumvent these events in Maryland, Governor Harry Hughes appointed court conservators to run both Old Court and Merritt. He also ordered 100 other privately insured S&Ls in Maryland to limit withdrawals to $1,000 per month per depositor. Legislatures ordered privately insured S&Ls to obtain federal deposit insurance. These events changed deposit insurance regulations in other states. Many states began to require any privately insured S&L to obtain federal insurance.

fields. The increased emphasis on corporate and consumer loans can increase their overall degree of default risk. The loss rate on mortgage loans has been significantly less than the loss rate on credit card loans.

While savings institutions are now more able to enter the corporate and consumer lending fields, their participation in these fields is still limited by regulators. Thus, mortgages and mortgage-backed securities will continue to be their primary assets.

Other Uses of Funds

Savings institutions can provide temporary financing to other institutions through the use of *repurchase agreements*. In addition, they can lend funds on a short-term basis through the *federal funds market*. Both methods allow them to efficiently use funds that they will have available for only a short period of time.

ALLOCATION OF SOURCES AND USES OF FUNDS

Exhibit 21.4 shows balance sheet information for all FSLIC insured institutions (mainly S&Ls). Mortgages dominate the assets, while savings deposits dominate the liability items. S&Ls have been increasing their borrowing of funds from sources other than the FHLB and have also increased their investment in assets other than mortgages. This reflects their effort to depend less on savings deposits as a source of funds and mortgages as a use of funds. Nevertheless, their asset portfolios are not nearly as diversified as those of commercial banks.

Exhibit 21.5 shows balance sheet information for savings banks. As is true for S&Ls, mortgages dominate the asset portfolio of savings banks. Yet, the more diversified asset structure of savings banks is evident. The liability structure of savings banks is quite similar to that of S&Ls.

EXHIBIT 21.4 Balance Sheet Information for Savings and Loan Associations

	1987	
Assets	*Amount in Millions of $*	*Percentage of Total Assets*
Mortgages	$383,840	39%
Mortgage-backed securities	151,986	16
Cash and other investment securities	135,297	14
Other	304,686	31
Total assets	$975,809	100
Liabilities and Net Worth		
Savings deposits	$730,324	75%
Borrowed funds from FHLBB	84,421	9
Borrowed funds from other sources	104,357	11
Other liabilities	21,587	2
Net worth	35,106	3
Total liabilities and net worth	$975,809	100

SOURCE: *Federal Reserve Bulletin* (November 1987). The dollar value of mortgages was estimated by the author.

EXHIBIT 21.5   Balance Sheet Information for Savings Banks

Assets	1987 Amount in Millions of $	1987 Percentage of Total Assets
Loans		
Mortgages	$137,044	53%
Other	37,189	14
Securities		
U.S. government	15,694	6
Mortgage-backed securities	31,144	12
State and local government	2,046	1
Corporate and other	17,583	7
Cash	5,063	2
Other assets	14,837	5
Total assets	$260,600	100%
Liabilities and Net Worth		
Deposits	$202,030	78%
Other liabilities	36,167	14
Net worth	21,133	8
	$260,600	100%

SOURCE: *Federal Reserve Bulletin* (November 1987). The dollar value of mortgages was estimated by the author.

REGULATION OF SAVINGS INSTITUTIONS

Like other financial institutions, savings institutions have been closely regulated over the years. Exhibit 21.6 discloses the regulators of various savings institution activities. The specific regulator varies with the activity of interest and the type of savings institution involved. For example, the state has some input on various activities of state-chartered savings institutions, but not on federally chartered institutions. Supervision and examination powers vary according to whether the savings institution is mutual or stock-owned. As is true for the commercial banking industry, the savings institution industry's regulatory structure suffers from overlap. Over time, there may be some consolidation among regulators, or even consolidation with the commercial banking regulators.

Savings institutions have historically been regulated according to their sources and uses of funds, the locations where they could establish branches (geographic regulations), and the products or services offered. Regulations on sources and uses of funds were already described in this chapter. Now the geographic and product regulations will be described.

Geographic Regulations

Savings institutions are generally allowed to branch throughout the state, although interstate movement is more restricted. Federally chartered savings institutions are typically prohibited from crossing state lines. State-

EXHIBIT 21.6   Regulators of Various Savings Institutions' Activities

	Type of Savings Institution:			
	Savings and Loan Associations		Mutual Savings Banks	
	Federal	State	Federal	State
Chartering and licensing	FHLBB	State authority	FHLBB	State authority
Intrastate branching	FHLBB	FHLBB and state authority	FHLBB	FDIC and state authority
Intrastate	FHLBB	FDIC and state authority	FHLBB	FDIC and state authority
Intrastate mergers, acquisitions and consolidations	FHLBB	FDIC and state authority	FHLBB	FDIC and state authority
Reserve requirements	Fed. Reserve	Fed. Reserve	Fed. Reserve	Fed. Reserve
Access to discount window	Fed.Home Loan Bank and Fed. Reserve	Fed.Home Loan Bank and Fed. Reserve	Fed. Reserve	Fed. Reserve
Deposit insurance	FSLIC	FDIC or state ins. fund	FSLIC or FDIC	FDIC or state ins. fund
Supervision and examination	FHLBB	FSLIC or state authority	FHLBB	FDIC and state authority
Safety and soundness	FHLBB	FHLBB or state authority	FHLBB	FDIC and state authority
Rulemaking, consumer protection	Fed. Reserve and FHLBB	Fed. Reserve, FHLBB and state authority	Fed. Reserve and FHLBB	Fed. Reserve, FHLBB and state authority
Enforcement, consumer protection	FHLBB	FHLBB, FSLIC, or state authority	FHLBB	FDIC, state authority, or FHLBB

SOURCE: Public Information Department, Federal Reserve Bank of New York.

chartered savings institutions may enter certain states. Interstate mergers involving savings institutions have been allowed when the intent is to save a failing depository institution, as stipulated by the Garn–St Germain Act. Attempts by savings institutions or other financial institutions to enter other states are evaluated on a case-by-case basis. As an example, Citicorp, the largest bank in the United States, was able to acquire failing savings in-

Chapter 21

Savings Institutions

stitutions in California, Florida, and Illinois. Even when savings institutions are prohibited from establishing branches in other states, they are allowed to operate automatic teller machines (ATMs) across state lines.

Product Regulations

Savings institutions have not only diversified their asset portfolio in recent years, but also the products and services they provide. They have attempted to offer products that were historically offered only by real estate, insurance, or brokerage firms. For example, some savings institutions serve as limited agents for registered brokerage firms and are therefore able to offer their customers access to discount brokerage services. They can introduce the service and provide a toll-free number where trades can be ordered. Some joint ventures also exist, whereby the savings institution will allow a registered broker to offer services on its grounds. The offering of a discount brokerage service and other nontraditional services by savings institutions can attract customers searching for a one-stop shop. Yet, there is still some uncertainty as to whether investors will be comfortable ordering their investment transactions from the place where they make their savings deposits. Even though the discount brokerage business simply executes trades requested and does not provide advice, some investors may still prefer to obtain discount brokerage services elsewhere. For this reason, many savings institutions still do not offer this service.

EXPOSURE TO RISK

Like commercial banks, savings institutions are exposed to liquidity risk, default risk, and interest rate risk. Each type of risk as related to savings institutions is described in turn.

Liquidity Risk

Because savings institutions commonly use short-term liabilities to finance long-term assets, they depend on additional deposits to accommodate withdrawal requests. If new deposits are not sufficient to cover withdrawal requests, these institutions could experience liquidity problems. To remedy this situation, they could obtain funds through repurchase agreements or borrow funds in the federal funds market. Yet, these sources of funds will resolve only a short-term shortage of funds. Federal Home Loan Bank borrowings may be more appropriate if a longer-term liquidity problem exists.

An alternative remedy to insufficient liquidity is to sell assets in exchange for cash. Savings institutions can sell their Treasury securities or even some of their mortgages in the secondary market. However, while the sale of assets can boost liquidity, it also reduces the size and possibly earnings of S&Ls. Therefore, minor liquidity deficiencies are typically resolved by increasing liabilities rather than selling assets.

Default Risk

Because mortgages represent the primary asset, they are the main reason for default risk at savings institutions. While Federal Housing Authority (FHA) and Veterans Administration (VA) mortgages originated by savings institutions are insured against default risk, conventional mortgages are not. Private insurance can normally be obtained for conventional mortgages, but savings institutions often incur the risk themselves rather than pay for the insurance. If they perform adequate credit analysis on their potential borrowers, and geographically diversify their mortgage loans, they should be able to maintain a low degree of default risk.

Interest Rate Risk

The exposure of savings institutions to interest rate risk has received much attention over the last 15 years, especially during the 1970s and early 1980s, when interest rates increased substantially. Since their assets were mostly rate–insensitive, while their liabilities were mostly rate–sensitive, their spread between interest earnings and interest expenses narrowed when interest rates increased, as shown in Exhibit 21.7. The spread even became negative in the early 1980s.

MEASUREMENT OF INTEREST RATE RISK

Because their performance is susceptible to interest rate movements, savings institutions commonly attempt to measure the duration of their assets and liabilities and then implement policy decisions that will reduce the difference between asset and liability duration. Recall that a popular equation for duration was provided in Chapter 18. The following example illustrates how a savings institution could measure the duration of its liabilities and assets.

Assume that Tucson Savings Institution (TSI) desires to measure the duration of its assets and liabilities. It first needs to classify each balance sheet component into various maturity categories, as shown in Exhibit 21.8. The

---

EXHIBIT 21.7   Spread between the Mortgage Yield and Cost of Funds

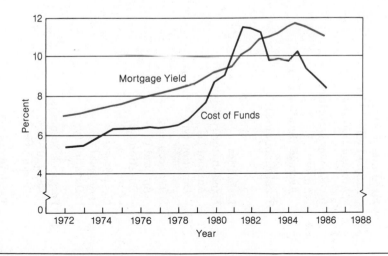

SOURCE: FSLIC; FHLBB; and *U.S. Industrial Outlook 1987*, 49–2.

EXHIBIT 21.8 Duration Schedule for Tucson Savings Institution (Dollar Amounts are in Thousands)

				Rate Readjustment Period				
	Less Than 6 Months	6 Months to 1 Year	1–3 Years	3–5 Years	5–10 Years	10–20 Years	Over 20 Years	Total
Assets								
Adjustable-rate mortgages								
Amount ($)	$ 7,000	$15,000	$ 4,000	$1,000	$ 0	$ 0	$ 0	$27,000
Average Duration (yr)	.30	.80	1.90	2.90	0	0	0	.91
Fixed-rate mortgages								
Amount ($)	500	500	1,000	1,000	2,000	10,000	5,000	$20,000
Average Duration (yr)	.25	.60	1.80	2.60	4.30	5.50	7.60	5.32
Investment securities								
Amount ($)	2,000	3,000	4,000	2,000	1,000	0	2,000	$14,000
Average Duration (yr)	.20	.70	1.70	3.20	5.30	0	8.05	2.65
Total Amount ($)	$ 9,500	$18,500	$ 9,000	$4,000	$3,000	$10,000	$7,000	$61,000
								Asset duration = 2.76
Liabilities								
Fixed-maturity deposits								
Amount ($)	$14,000	$ 9,000	$ 2,000	$1,000	$ 0	$ 0	$ 0	$26,000
Duration (yr)	.30	.60	1.80	2.80	0	0	0	.62
NOW accounts								
Amount ($)	4,000	0	0	0	0	0	0	$ 4,000
Duration (yr)	.40	0	0	0	0	0	0	.40
MMDAs								
Amount ($)	15,000	0	0	0	0	0	0	$15,000
Duration (yr)	.20	0	0	0	0	0	0	.20
Passbook accounts								
Amount ($)	13,000	0	0	0	0	0	0	$13,000
Duration (yr)	.40	0	0	0	0	0	0	.40
Total Amount ($)	$46,000	$ 9,000	$ 2,000	$1,000	$ 0	$ 0	$ 0	$58,000
Duration (yr)								Liability duration = .45

rates on most adjustable-rate mortgages are adjusted every year, which is why the amounts under the longer-term categories show zero. The average duration for each category is provided below the dollar amount. Some fixed-rate mortgages are classified in the earlier term categories since they are maturing or will be sold soon. The duration of .91 for adjustable-rate mortgages is a weighted average of their durations, computed as (7,000/27,000).30 + (15,000/27,000).80 + (4,000/27,000)1.9 + (1,000/27,000)2.9.

The durations for fixed rate mortgages and investment securities were computed in a similar manner. The duration for total assets of 2.76 years was computed as a weighted average of the individual assets: (27,000/61,000).91 + (20,000/61,000)5.32 + (14,000/61,000)2.65 = 2.76.

A similar procedure was used to estimate the duration of liabilities. NOW accounts and passbook savings have no specified maturity, but their rate is adjusted less frequently than the rate on MMDAs, which is why MMDAs have a shorter duration. The total liability duration is about .45 years. TSI's total asset duration is more than six times its liability duration. Its future performance is highly exposed to interest rate movements. Real net worth (as measured by market value) would decrease substantially in response to an increase in interest rates. TSI can reduce its exposure to interest rate risk by reducing its proportion of assets in the long-duration categories.

The impact of change in interest rates on the market value of net worth can be estimated as follows. First, the *net adjusted duration* (NAD) must be estimated:

$$NAD = \frac{D_A - D_L}{1 + k}$$

where D_A = asset duration
D_L = liability duration
k = current market yield

In our example, if current market yields were 8 percent, TSI's net adjusted duration would be

$$NAD = \frac{2.76 - .45}{1.08}$$

$$= 2.14$$

This implies that if all market interest rates rise by 1 percent, TSI's real net worth would decline by 2.14 percent.

Computer programs are used by financial institutions to estimate their asset and liability duration and apply sensitivity analysis to proposed balance sheet adjustments. For example, TSI could determine how the asset and liability duration would change if it plans a promotional effort to issue five-year deposits and uses the funds to offer adjustable-rate mortgages.

Application of Interest Rate Risk Measurement to Industry Data

Exhibit 21.9 compares the balance sheet allocation for savings institutions as of December 1981 and as of June 1987. The deposit data in 1981 was not segmented by maturity, but most deposits were interest rate–sensitive. The mismatch in interest rate–sensitivity between assets and liabilities is obvious. By 1987 savings institutions reduced the mismatch by using adjustable-

EXHIBIT 21.9   Evaluation of Interest Rate Risk in 1981 and 1987

Assets	Percentage of Total Assets as of:	
	December 1981	June 1987
Mortgage loans		
Adjustable-rate	0	31
Fixed-rate	78	38
Total	78	69
Nonmortgage loans	3	7
Liquidity portfolio	10	14
Fixed assets	2	1
Other assets	8	10
Total	100	100
Liabilities and Capital		
Deposits and savings accounts		
NOW accounts, MMDAs, and passbook saving accounts		23
Fixed-maturity (1 year or less)		29
Fixed-maturity (1 to 3 years)		15
Fixed-maturity (over 3 years)		8
Total	78	75
Borrowed money		9
FHLB advances		10
Other borrowed	14	19
Other liabilities	4	2
Net worth (capital)	5	4
Total	100	100

SOURCE: *Economic Review*, Federal Reserve Bank of Kansas City (March 1988): 8–9; *Quarterly Thrift Financial Aggregates;* and Federal Home Loan Bank Board.

rate mortgages and attracting more long-term deposits. However, the interest rate–sensitivity on liabilities is still much greater than on assets.

MANAGEMENT OF INTEREST RATE RISK

Savings institutions have a variety of methods that can be used to manage their interest rate risk, including the use of

- Adjustable-rate mortgages
- Financial futures contracts
- Interest rate swaps
- Interest rate caps

Each of these techniques is discussed in turn.

Adjustable-Rate Mortgages (ARMs)

The interest rates on **adjustable-rate mortgages (ARMs)** are tied to market-determined rates such as the one-year Treasury bill rate and are periodically adjusted in accordance with the formula stated in the ARM contract. A

Impact of Unexpected Interest Rate Movements on Stock Returns of S&Ls

A recent study by Scott and Peterson assessed the sensitivity of savings and loan associations (S&Ls) to interest rate movements during the 1977–1984 period, using the following regression model:

$$r_p = B_0 + B_1 MI + B_2 r + e$$

where r_p = stock returns of a portfolio of savings and loan associations

MI = percentage change in the market index (the S&P 500 Index was used as a proxy)

r = a measure of unexpected interest rate changes (see the article for an explanation of the proxy used for this variable)

B_0 = intercept

B_1 = regression coefficient that measures the sensitivity of stock returns to the market index returns

B_2 = regression coefficient that measures the sensitivity of stock returns to the interest rate movements

e = error term

The coefficient B_1 was estimated to be 1.353 by the regression analysis, suggesting that a 1 percent change in the market is associated with a 1.353 percent change in the portfolio returns. Thus, the S&L stocks are positively correlated with the market. The coefficient B_2 was estimated to be -3.61, suggesting that an unexpected 1 percent increase in interest rates is associated with a 3.61 percent decrease in stock returns of S&Ls. This coefficient was found to be statistically significant. Thus, stock returns on S&Ls are adversely affected by an unexpected increase in interest rates. The negative coefficient is not surprising, but the magnitude of the coefficient illustrates how highly sensitive the stock returns of S&Ls are to interest rate movements.

SOURCE: William L. Scott and Richard L. Peterson, "Interest Rate Risk and Equity Values of Hedged and Unhedged Financial Intermediaries," *Journal of Financial Research* (Winter 1986): 325–329.

variety of formulas have been used. ARMs enable savings institutions to maintain a more stable spread between interest earnings and interest expenses.

While ARMs reduce the adverse impact of rising interest rates, they also reduce the favorable impact of declining interest rates. Suppose a savings institution that obtained most of its funds from short-term deposits used the funds to provide fixed-rate mortgages. If interest rates decline, and the savings institution does not hedge its exposure to interest rate risk, the spread will increase. However, if ARMs are used as a hedging strategy, the interest on loans would decrease during a period of declining rates, so the spread would not widen. Of course, ARMs also prevent the spread from

Chapter 21

Savings Institutions

decreasing during a period of rising interest rates. The use of ARMs increasing during the 1980s, accounting for more than 60 percent of single-family conventional mortgages by 1984. Their popularity diminished in the mid 1980s when interest rates declined but increased again in 1988.

ARMs used during the 1970s helped savings institutions perform better but exposed consumers to interest rate risk. While ARMs typically have a maximum cap limiting the increase in interest rates (such as 2 percent per year and 5 percent over the loan life), the impact on consumer mortgage payments is still significant. Because some consumers may prefer fixed-rate mortgages, most savings institutions will continue to offer them and will therefore incur interest rate risk. Thus, additional strategies besides the use of ARMs are necessary to reduce this risk.

Financial Futures Contracts

A **financial futures contract** allows for the purchase of a specified amount of a particular financial security for a specified price at a future point in time. Sellers of futures contracts are obligated to sell the securities for the contract price at the stated future point in time.

Treasury bond financial futures contracts are used by some savings institutions because the cash flow characteristics of Treasury bonds resemble fixed-rate mortgages. Like mortgages, Treasury bonds offer fixed periodic payments, so their market value moves inversely to interest rate fluctuations. Savings institutions that sell futures contracts on these securities can effectively hedge their fixed-rate mortgages. If interest rates rise, the market value of the securities represented by the futures contract will decrease. Savings institutions would benefit from the difference between the market value at which they can purchase these securities in the future and the futures price at which they will sell the securities. This could offset the reduced spread between their interest revenues and interest expenses during the period of rising interest rates.

While the concept of using financial futures to guard against interest rate risk is simple, the actual application is more complex. It is difficult to perfectly offset the potential reduction in the spread with a futures position.

Interest Rate Swaps

Another strategy for reducing interest rate risk is the **interest rate swap,** which allows savings institutions to swap fixed-rate payments (an outflow) in exchange for variable-rate payments (an inflow). The fixed-rate outflow payments can be matched against the fixed-rate mortgages held so that a certain spread can be achieved. In addition, the variable-rate inflows due to the swap can be matched against its variable cost of funds. In a rising rate environment, the institution's fixed-rate outflow payments for the swap agreement remain fixed, while its variable-rate inflow payments due to the swap increase. This favorable result can partially offset the normally unfavorable impact of rising interest rates on a savings institutions's spread. However, an interest rate swap also reduces the favorable impact of declining interest rates. Inflow interest payments decrease while the outflow interest payments remain the same during a period of declining rates.

Assume that Denver Savings Institution (DSI) has large holdings of 11 percent fixed-rate mortgages. Because its sources of funds are mostly interest rate-sensitive, it desires to swap fixed-rate payments in exchange for variable-rate payments. It informs Colorado Bank of its situation, since it knows that this bank commonly engages in swap transactions. Colorado Bank searches for a client and finds that Brit Eurobank desires to swap variable-rate dollar payments in exchange for fixed dollar payments. Colorado Bank then develops the swap arrangement illustrated in Exhibit 21.10. DSI will receive variable-rate payments based on the London Interbank Offer Rate (LIBOR), the rate charged on loans between Eurobanks, and, in exchange, will provide fixed payments. Because the variable-rate payments fluctuate with market conditions, DSI's payments received will vary over time. The length of the swap period and the *notional* amount (the amount to which the interest rates are applied to determine the payments) can be structured to the participant's desires. The financial intermediary conducting the swap charges a fee, such as .1 percent of the notional amount per year. Some financial intermediaries for swaps may act as the counterparty and exchange the payments desired, rather than just match up two parties.

Now assume that the fixed payments to be paid were based on a fixed rate of 9 percent, and LIBOR is initially 6 percent. Exhibit 21.11 shows how DSI's spread is affected by various possible interest rates when unhedged versus when hedging with an interest rate swap. This exhibit assumes that DSI's cost of funds is 1 percent below LIBOR. If rates remain at their present level of 6 percent, DSI's spread would be 5 percent if unhedged and only 3 percent when using a swap. However, if rates increase beyond 8 percent, the spread on the swap exceeds the unhedged spread because the higher cost of funds causes a lower unhedged spread. The swap arrangement would provide DSI with increased payments that offset the higher cost of funds. The advantage of a swap is that it can lock in the spread to be earned on existing assets—or at least reduce the possible variability of the spread.

When interest rates decrease, a savings institution's outflow payments would exceed inflow payments on a swap. However, the spread between the interest rates received on existing mortgages and those paid on deposits should increase, offsetting the net outflow from the swap. During periods of declining interest rates, mortgages are often prepaid, which could result in a net outflow from the swap without any offsetting effect. Under these conditions, a savings institution may be able to create an opposite swap to mitigate the impact of the existing swap. Yet, the terms of a new swap will be different because of the change in interest rates.

EXHIBIT 21.10   Illustration of an Interest Rate Swap.

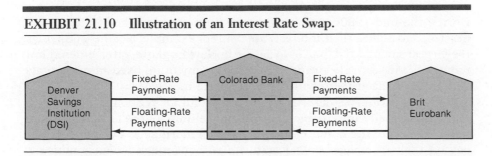

EXHIBIT 21.11 Comparison of DSI's Spread: Unhedged versus Hedged

Unhedged Strategy	6%	7%	8%	9%	10%	11%
Average rate on existing mortgages	11%	11%	11%	11%	11%	11%
Average cost of deposits	6	7	8	9	10	11
Spread	5	4	3	2	1	0
Hedging with an Interest Rate Swap						
Fixed interest rate earned on fixed-rate mortgages	11	11	11	11	11	11
Fixed interest rate owed on swap arrangement	9	9	9	9	9	9
Spread on fixed-rate payments	2	2	2	2	2	2
Variable interest rate earned on swap arrangement	7	8	9	10	11	12
Variable interest rate owed on deposits	6	7	8	9	10	11
Spread on variable-rate payments	1	1	1	1	1	1
Combined total spread when using the swap	3	3	3	3	3	3

Interest Rate Caps

An alternative method of hedging interest rate risk is an **interest rate cap**, which is an agreement (for a fee) to receive payments when the interest rate of a particular security or index rises above a specified level during a specified time period. Some commercial banks and brokerage firms offer interest rate caps. The maturity can be tailored to the savings institution's desires. The cap provides compensation during periods of rising interest rates, which can offset the reduction in the spread during such periods.

The fee paid for the caps depends on the terms. The lower the specified ceiling level of an interest rate cap at a given point in time, the higher would be the fee (since the probability of receiving compensation is higher). The longer the maturity of an interest rate cap, the higher would be the fee (for the same reason).

Concluding Comments About Interest Rate Risk Management

During the mid 1980s many savings institutions used the strategies just described to reduce their interest rate risk. For example, Northeast Savings, the largest savings and loan association in New England, often entered into numerous interest rate swaps. It also sold many of its fixed-rate mortgage loans and replaced them with adjustable-rate mortgages.

While the strategies described here are useful for reducing interest rate risk, it is virtually impossible to completely eliminate the risk. This is partially because of the potential prepayment on mortgages. Consumers often pay off their mortgages before maturity without much advance notice to

Are There Economies of Scale in the Savings and Loan Industry?

In recent years there have been several mergers of savings and loan associations. The extent to which the increased size will benefit S&Ls depends partially on whether economies of scale exist. A recent study by Goldstein, McNulty, and Verbrugge measured the sensitivity of operating costs to output. *Operating costs* were defined to include salaries and all other operating expenses except interest expenses. The proxy used to measure output was total assets. (See the article for more specific details about the model used.) The analysis found that economies of scale exist and are more pronounced in the smaller size class, but also exist in the medium and larger classes as well. The results suggest that savings and loan associations may achieve greater efficiency through growth, regardless of their present size. Because the characteristics of the industry are changing, the impact of growth on efficiency may change over time. Savings and loan associations have attempted to diversify in recent years in order to behave as full-service financial institutions. While diversification could reduce their risk, it may also limit their ability to benefit from economies of scale. Perhaps future research will reassess economies of scale in a more recent time period to determine whether today's more diversified S&Ls can increase efficiency through growth.

SOURCE: Steven J. Goldstein, James E. McNulty, and James A. Verbrugge, "Scale Economies in the Savings and Loan Industry Before Diversification," *Journal of Economics and Business* (August 1987): 199–208.

the savings institutions. Consequently, savings institutions do not really know the actual maturity of the mortgages they hold, and cannot perfectly match the interest rate sensitivity of their assets and liabilities.

PERFORMANCE OF SAVINGS INSTITUTIONS

Exhibit 21.12 shows the return on average assets (ROA) of federally insured savings institutions over time. The ROA of the savings institutions was relatively stable up to the mid 1970s, as interest rates were somewhat stable during that period. Once interest rates began to fluctuate to a greater degree, so did the ROA of savings institutions. The adverse impact of increasing interest rates on ROA in the late 1970s and early 1980s is evident. Unprepared for those large increases, these institutions experienced substantial losses in 1981 and 1982. Commercial banks were not as exposed because their assets and liabilities share a somewhat similar sensitivity to interest rate movements.

The ROA of savings institutions improved in 1983 as market interest rates began to decline, thereby reducing their cost of funds. The improved performance continued throughout the mid 1980s as interest rates remained low. The high correlation between ROA and the spread between mortgage yield and cost of funds is verified by comparing Exhibit 21.12 with Exhibit

Chapter 21

Savings Institutions

EXHIBIT 21.12 Return on Average Assets for Federally Insured Savings Institutions

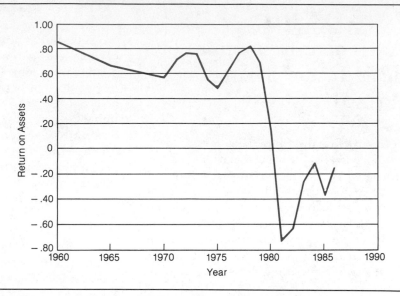

SOURCE: *Savings Institution's Sourcebook,* United States League of Savings Institutions (1986): 53; 1986 figure estimated by author.

21.7 and explains why savings institutions are most concerned with their exposure to interest rate risk.

MUTUAL-TO-STOCK CONVERSIONS

A **mutual-to-stock conversion** by savings institutions simply shifts the ownership structure from depositors to investors who purchase the institution's stock. This has been a popular method to boost capital. Savings institutions owned by depositors are less able to increase capital. Because regulators now monitor capital levels more closely, many savings institutions have converted to stock-ownership so that they can more easily meet capital requirements. Before the mid 1970s, mutual-to-stock conversions were rare, due to a host of potential court- and tax-related barriers. Since 1980, however, over 200 conversions have taken place, and in 1983 the dollar value of conversions exceeded $2.5 billion. This record level was partially due to conversions by some very large savings institutions. After 1983 the dollar value of conversions declined, but the number of conversions increased, indicating continued interest in this trend.

Beyond the capability to boost capital, stock-owned institutions also provide their owners with greater potential to benefit from their performance. The dividends and/or stock price of a high-performance institution can grow, thereby providing direct benefits to the shareholders. Conversely, the owners (depositors) of a mutual institution do not directly benefit from high performance. Although they have a pro rata claim to the mutual savings institution's net worth while they maintain deposits there, their claim is eliminated once they close their account. They can exercise their claim on the net worth only if the mutual institution is liquidated. However, regulations prohibit liquidation of savings institutions unless they are insolvent.

Another difference between stock-owned and mutual institutions is that a stock-owned institution's management is under the control of the shareholders, who elect the board of directors, while mutual institution owners typically sign over their voting rights to management. Because of the difference in owner control, stock-owned institutions are more susceptible to unfriendly takeovers. It is virtually impossible for another firm to take control of a mutual institution's management, since management generally holds all voting rights. From the owners' perspectives, the stock-owned institution may seem more desirable, since the owners may have more influence on managerial decisions. Recent research by Bulmash has found that medium and large mutual S&Ls were less risky than stock-owned S&Ls but also incurred higher operating expenses and generated less profits. Among very small S&Ls, stock-owned S&Ls had higher operating expenses, lower profits, and greater risk.

The Conversion Process

The process of mutual-to-stock conversion varies; however, a general description of a typical conversion follows. First, a plan of conversion by management must be approved by the board of directors, and then approved by regulators. Owners of the institution are then notified of a meeting, where they vote on the conversion. If the vote favors conversion, the institution proceeds with the accounting and legal work necessary to prepare the application.

Once the institution is ready to issue stock, its situation is assessed by an independent appraisal to determine the price at which the stock will be sold. Priority for purchasing the stock is generally given to the institution's owners, managers, and others (the specific priority schedule is somewhat complex and varies considerably). Any remaining stock not purchased by those receiving priority is then offered publicly.

Because existing depositors are given priority over the public, investors have become increasingly interested in establishing deposits in mutual institutions that are likely to enact a conversion in the future. This way they acquire priority rights to the initial stock issue, provided that they become eligible at least 90 days prior to the date the plan is adopted.

A recent study by Hadaway and Hadaway found that savings institutions converting from mutual- to stock ownership used a more aggressive management approach after the conversion and experienced a higher rate of growth and operating efficiency.

SAVINGS INSTITUTION MERGERS

In recent years, merger and acquisition activity within the savings institution industry has increased, partially because, for the many institutions experiencing financial problems, a merger or acquisition may be the only salvation. Yet, some high-performance savings institutions have also been involved in this activity, since it can broaden their markets and possibly enhance their efficiency. Some functions, such as advertising and accounting, are much more cost effective for larger institutions. In addition, the combining of two operations can also increase efficiency. Consider one savings institution that has a well-developed computer system for servicing mortgages, while a second institution has traditionally dominated the local mortgage origination. A combination of the two institutions could multiply the respective advantages. However, some mergers and acquisitions also can have unfavorable effects. The personnel of two institutions may clash due to a difference in managerial philosophies or because of a modified management structure.

Merger-Conversions

When a mutual S&L is involved in an acquisition, it first converts to a stock-owned S&L. If it is the acquiring firm, it will then arrange to purchase the existing stock of the institution to be acquired. Conversely, if it is to be acquired, its stock will be purchased by the acquiring institution. This process is often referred to as a **merger-conversion.** While merger-conversions are relatively new to the industry, they are becoming popular.

INTERACTION OF SAVINGS INSTITUTIONS WITH OTHER FINANCIAL INSTITUTIONS

Savings institutions interact with various types of financial institutions, as summarized in Exhibit 21.13. They compete with commercial banks and money market mutual funds to obtain funds, and also with commercial banks and finance companies in lending funds. Their hedging of interest rate risk is facilitated by investment companies that act as financial intermediaries for interest rate swaps and caps. Their ability to sell mortgages in the secondary market is enhanced by insurance companies that purchase them.

Many savings institutions have other financial institutions as subsidiaries. For example, Cal Fed Inc., which owns California Federal Savings and Loan, has consumer finance, trust company, mortgage banking, and property/casualty insurance subsidiaries. Great Western Financial Corporation has consumer finance, securities brokerage, and retail brokerage subsidiaries. Glen Fed Inc., which owns Glendale Federal Savings and Loan Association, has insurance, mortgage banking, real estate, and discount securities brokerage.

PARTICIPATION OF SAVINGS INSTITUTIONS IN FINANCIAL MARKETS

Savings institutions commonly participate in various financial markets, as summarized in Exhibit 21.14. They compete against money market mutual funds in the money markets. In addition, mortgage markets provide a source of funds to savings institutions that desire to issue mortgage-backed securities or sell their mortgages in the secondary market. Bond markets serve as a use of funds to savings institutions with excess funds and as a source of funds to savings institutions that issue new bonds in the primary market

EXHIBIT 21.13 Interaction between Savings Institutions and Other Financial Institutions

Type of Financial Institution	Interaction with Savings Institutions
Commercial banks	■ Savings institutions compete with commercial banks in attracting deposits, providing consumer loans, and providing commercial loans. ■ Some savings institutions and commercial banks have merged in recent years. ■ Some savings institutions sell mortgages to commercial banks.
Finance companies	■ Savings institutions compete with finance companies in providing consumer and commercial loans.
Money market mutual funds	■ Savings institutions compete with money market mutual funds in attracting short-term deposits of investors.
Investment companies and brokerage firms	■ Savings institutions often contact investment companies to engage in interest rate swaps and interest rate caps. ■ Savings institutions have made agreements with brokerage services for their customers in order to indirectly offer brokerage services.
Insurance companies	■ Mortgages sold by savings institutions in the secondary market are sometimes purchased by insurance companies.

or sell bond holdings in the secondary market. Futures markets and options markets have enabled savings institutions to reduce interest rate risk that results from their investment in mortgages and bonds.

FUTURE OUTLOOK FOR SAVINGS INSTITUTIONS

Savings institutions will likely continue to diversify their mix of investments and services over time and therefore reduce their exposure to interest rate risk. However, they must also become accustomed to some new product offerings, thereby increasing their exposure to some other risks. For example, the savings institution's entrance into commercial lending will result in more noninterest expenses and will increase their exposure to default risk.

A conflict between diversification and specialization may ensue. An attempt to provide every possible service provides consumers with a one-stop shop and reduces the institution's dependency on the performance of any

EXHIBIT 21.14 Participation of Savings Institutions in Financial Markets

Financial Market	Participation by Savings Institutions
Money markets	■ Savings institutions compete with other depository institutions for short-term deposits. ■ Some savings institutions issue commercial paper.
Mortgage markets	■ Savings institutions sell mortgages in the secondary market and issue mortgage-backed securities.
Bond markets	■ Savings institutions purchase bonds for their investment portfolios. ■ Savings institutions issue bonds to obtain long-term funds.
Futures markets	■ Some savings institutions hedge against interest rate movements by taking positions in financial futures.
Options markets	■ Some savings institutions hedge against interest rate movements by taking positions in options on futures contracts.

single service. Yet, a high degree of diversification prevents savings institutions from specializing in the services they do best. Because of deregulation, some services that were previously prohibited are now allowed. As savings institutions experiment with these services over time, they will have to strike a balance between specialization and diversification. That is, they will diversify to a degree but will not offer all possible products at any cost just because they are now allowed to do so.

Since the characteristics vary among savings institutions, what works for one institution may not work for another. Thus, each must choose its own product offerings, geographic markets, and principal customers. The marketing function of savings institutions is likely to become more important in the future, as they enter new geographic markets and offer new products—a clear departure from their traditional business of offering more limited products and serving only the local market.

Because savings institutions recognize the up-front costs of offering new products, they may search for ways to participate in some product offerings through an agent. For example, an attempt to enter the corporate lending business requires an experienced credit analysis department. Due to the significant cost of creating such a department, some savings institutions may consider channeling funds through another institution that has a credit analysis department. The institution acting as an agent would likely service the loan and receive a fee for its contribution. This type of **loan participation** is common in the commercial banking industry. Recent research by Goudreau and Ford has found that large S&Ls will more likely enter the commercial lending business. They can absorb the start-up costs (including marketing and credit analysis expenses) associated with offering new products.

SUMMARY

Savings institutions are similar to commercial banks in that they attract funds through various deposits. They now even have the authority to offer checkable (NOW) accounts, which makes them more similar to commercial banks than before. However, their uses of funds differ distinctly. Because of their heavy concentration of mortgages, savings institutions are much more exposed to interest rate risk. Their performance over time has been highly dependent on interest rate movements and on their ability to deal with these movements. As time passes, savings institutions are becoming more adept at hedging this risk. Yet, interest rate risk still remains the most critical issue to contend with.

KEY TERMS

adjustable-rate mortgages	interest rate swap
capital	loan participation
financial futures contract	merger-conversion
interest rate cap	mutual-to-stock conversion

QUESTIONS

21.1. Explain, in general terms, how savings institutions vary from commercial banks with respect to their sources of funds and uses of funds.

21.2. Discuss how a savings and loan association may be chartered and the insurance associated with each type.

21.3. Identify and discuss the regulatory agency for savings institutions.

21.4. Who are the owners of mutual savings and loan associations?

21.5. What are the alternative forms of ownership of a savings institution?

21.6. What are some differences between savings banks and savings and loan associations?

21.7. What are the major sources of funds for savings institutions? Discuss each.

21.8. Identify and discuss the main uses of funds for savings institutions.

21.9. How did the creation of money market deposit accounts influence the savings institution's overall cost of funds?

21.10. The allowance of NOW accounts for savings institutions across the nation in 1981 was thought to be a major historical event. Why was this so critical to savings institutions?

21.11. Identify nondepository sources of funds (other than capital) of savings institutions.

21.12. Discuss the entrance of savings institutions into consumer and commercial lending. What are the potential risks and rewards of this strategy?

21.13. Describe the liquidity and default risk of savings institutions, and discuss how each is managed.

21.14. What is an adjustable-rate mortgage? Discuss potential advantages they offer a savings institution.

21.15. Explain how savings institutions could use financial futures to reduce interest rate risk.

21.16. Explain how savings institutions could use interest rate swaps to reduce interest rate risk. Would savings institutions that used swaps perform better or worse than those that were unhedged during a period of declining interest rates? Explain.

21.17. What effect did the Depository Institution Deregulation and Monetary Control Act (DIDMCA) of 1980 and the Garn–St Germain Act of 1982 have on savings institutions?

21.18. What is a mutual-to-stock conversion? What are some of the potential advantages of the conversion?

21.19. Describe a merger-conversion.

21.20. Discuss the conflict between diversification and specialization of savings institutions.

21.21. If market interest rates were expected to decline over time, would an S&L with rate-sensitive liabilities and with a large amount of fixed-rate mortgages perform best by (1) using an interest rate cap, (2) using an interest rate swap, (3) selling financial futures, or (4) remaining unhedged? Explain.

21.22. Boca Savings & Loan Association has a large portion of 10-year fixed-rate mortgages that it originated in 1980 and has financed with funds from short-term deposits. It uses the yield curve to assess the market's anticipation of future interest rates. It believes that expectations of future interest rates are the major force in affecting the yield curve. Assume that a downward-sloping yield curve exists. Based on this information, should Boca consider engaging in interest rate swaps to hedge its spread? Explain.

PROBLEM

1. Stetson Savings and Loan Association has forecasted its cost of funds as follows:

Year	Cost of Funds
1	6%
2	5%
3	7%
4	9%
5	7%

It expects to earn an average rate of 11 percent on its assets over the next five years. It considers engaging in an interest rate swap in which it would swap fixed payments of 10 percent in exchange for variable-rate payments of LIBOR + 1 percent. Assume LIBOR is expected to consistently be 1 percent above Stetson's cost of funds. Determine the spread to be earned in each year if Stetson uses the interest rate swap.

PROJECTS

1. FINANCIAL ANALYSIS OF SAVINGS AND LOAN ASSOCIATIONS.

Obtain annual reports or investment survey summaries (such as *Value Line*) for a savings and loan association assigned by your professor or one of your choice, and answer the following questions.

a. How has its asset portfolio composition changed in recent years?

b. How has its liability portfolio composition changed in recent years?

c. How have the recent changes in asset and liability composition affected the S&L's risk and potential return?

d. How do you think its performance would be affected by an increase in interest rates? Explain.

e. Based on the annual report, does the savings and loan association appear to be increasing its nontraditional services? Elaborate.

f. Has the savings and loan association migrated into other states? If so, how? Is it planning interstate expansion? If so, how?

g. Has the savings and loan association's performance been better or worse than in previous years? Why?

h. Has the savings and loan association's noninterest income as a percentage of total assets increased or decreased in recent years? Elaborate.

i. How has the savings and loan association's net interest margin changed in recent years? Does its net interest margin appear highly influenced by interest rate movements? If so, in what way?

2. IMPACT OF INTEREST RATE MOVEMENTS ON AN S&L'S ROA.

a. Develop a model that could be used to determine how the savings and loan association's return on assets (ROA) is affected by interest rate movements. Include all relevant variables for which data are available.

b. Apply your model to historical data to determine how its return on assets was affected by interest rate movements. Do the results support the type of relationship you hypothesized? Explain.

c. Identify any limitations of your model.

d. Suggest how you could use your model to forecast a savings and loan association's return on assets based on projections of any variables that affect ROA.

3. IMPACT OF INTEREST RATE MOVEMENTS ON AN S&L'S STOCK RETURNS.

a. Develop a model that could be used to determine how the savings and loan association's stock returns are affected by interest rate movements. Include all relevant variables for which data are available.

b. Assume that the savings and loan association's returns are thought to be significantly influenced by characteristics particularly relevant to the savings and loan association industry. Specify a model that would capture this influence.

c. Apply your model to historical data to determine how the savings and loan association's stock returns are affected by interest rate movements. Do the results support the type of relationship you hypothesized? Explain.

d. Identify any other variables that should be included in the model if the data were available.

REFERENCES

Allen, Pat. "Commercial Loans Transform a Traditional Portfolio." *Savings Institutions* (October 1985): 20–126.

"Bankers Debate Key Thrift Institution Issues." *ABA Banking Journal* (July 1985): 40–42.

Bartlett, Sarah, Vicky Cahan, and Teresa Carson. "Thrifts, the Rich Get Richer, the Poor May Die." *Businessweek*, April 28, 1980, 80–81.

Bartlett, Sarah. "When an S&L Buyout Isn't Good

News." *Businessweek,* June 9, 1986, p. 86.

Basch, Donald. "Rivalry and Expense-Preference Behavior Among Savings Banks: The Role of Deposit Rate Ceilings." *Journal of Economics and Business* (August 1987): pp. 225–238.

Benston, George J. "Thrift Failures and Direct Investment." *Bankers Magazine* (May–June 1985): 55–61.

Brooks, Harry F. "Agency Valuers Apply Techniques and Sound Judgement." *Savings Institutions* (May 1986): 58–60.

Bulmash, Samuel, B. "Loan Default Risk, Return on Equity and Size Effects and Ownership Control—Empirical Evidence on Savings and Loan Associations in the USA." *Journal of Business, Finance, and Accounting* (Summer 1985): 313–326.

Buynak, Thomas M. "The Thrift Industry: Reconstruction in Progress." *Federal Reserve Bank of Cleveland,* June 1, 1986.

"Commercial Loans Transform a 'Traditional' Portfolio." *Savings Institutions* (October 1985): 120–126.

Dunham, R. Constance. "Mutual-to-Stock Conversion by Thrifts: Implications for Soundness." *New England Economic Review,* Federal Reserve Bank of Boston (January–February): 31–45.

Dunham, R. Constance. "Recent Developments in Thrift Commercial Lending." *New England Economic Review,* Federal Reserve Bank of Boston (November–December 1985): 41–48.

Dunham, R. Constance and Margaret Guerin-Calvert. "How Quickly Can Thrifts Move into Commercial Lending?" *New England Economic Review,* Federal Reserve Bank of Boston (November–December 1983): 42–53.

Flannery, Mark J. and Christopher M. James. "The Effect of Interest Rate Changes on the Common Stock Returns of Financial Institutions." *Journal of Finance* (September 1984): 1141–1153.

Ford, John K. and Thomas O. Stanley. "Consumer Lending Alters the Risk and Return of Loan Portfolios." *Savings Institutions* (November 1985): 52–55.

Furlong, Frederick T. "Savings and Loan Asset Composition and the Mortgage Market." *Economic Review,* Federal Reserve Bank of San Francisco (Summer 1985): 14–24.

Goldstein, Steven, James McNulty, and James Verbrugge. "Scale Economies in the Savings and Loan Industry before Diversification." *Journal of Economics and Business* (August 1987): 199–208.

Gooptu, Sudarshan and Raymond Lombra. "Aggregation Across Heterogeneous Depository Institutions." *Financial Review* (November 1987): 369–378.

Goudreau, Robert E. and Harold D. Ford. "Changing Thrifts: What Makes Them Choose Commercial Lending?" *Economic Review,* Federal Reserve Bank of Atlanta (June–July 1986): 24–39.

Goudreau, Robert E. "S&L Use of New Powers: A Comparative Study of State- and Federal-Chartered Associations." *Economic Review,* Federal Reserve Bank of Atlanta (October 1984): 18–33.

Goudreau, Robert E. "S&L Use of New Powers: Consumer and Commercial Loan Expansion." *Economic Review,* Federal Reserve Bank of Atlanta (December 1984): 15–35.

Gray, Edwin J. "Savings Institutions Must Restructure for Survival, New FHLBB Chairman Urges." *Savings Institutions* (September 1983); 58–61.

Hadaway, Beverly and Samuel Hadaway. "Implications of Savings and Loan Conversions in a Deregulated World." *Journal of Bank Research* (Spring 1984): 44–55.

Handorf, William C., Robert L. Losey, and Michael P. McCarthy. "The Thrifts Tomorrow." *The Bankers Magazine* (July–August 1983): 36–42.

Hilliard, Jimmy E. and James A. Verbrugge. "Savings Institutions Must Manage Rate Risk." *Savings Institutions* (September 1983): 68–72.

Horvitz, Paul M. "Reorganization of the Financial Regulatory Agencies." *Journal of Bank Research* (Winter 1983): 245–263.

"Institutions Trim Costs For Bigger Profits." *Savings Institutions* (September 1985): 47–53.

Kohers, Theodore and W. Gary Simpson. "Ownership Form, Regulatory Status, and Performance in the Savings and Loan Industry." *Review of Business and Economic Research* (Fall 1984): 63–71.

Kulczycky, Maria. "Institutions Trim Costs for

Bigger Profits." *Savings Institutions* (September 1985): 47–53.

Kulczycky, Maria. "Merger Loan Sales Provide Chances to Alter Portfolio Mix." *Savings Institutions* (March 1985): 58–64.

Loy, Susan and Paul M. Mason. "Commercial Bank and Savings and Loan Competition: Two Industries or One?" *Journal of Business and Economic Perspectives* (1986): 79–88.

Madura, Jeff and William C. Weaver. "Hedging Mortgages with Interest Rate Swaps versus Caps: How to Choose." *Real Estate Finance Journal* (Summer 1987): 90–96.

Masulis, Ronald. "Changes in Ownership Structure: Conversions of Mutual Savings and Loans to Stock Charter." *Journal of Financial Economies* (March 1987): 29–54.

McNulty, James E. "Economies of Scale: A Case Study of the Florida S&L Industry." *Economic Review*, Federal Reserve Bank of Atlanta (November 1982): 22–30.

"Merger, Loan Sales Provide Chances to Alter Portfolio Mix." *Savings Institutions* (March 1985): 58–64.

Mester, Loretta. "A Multiproduct Cost Study of Savings and Loans." *Journal of Finance* (June 1987); 423–445.

Moulton, Janice M. "Antitrust Implications of Thrifts' Expanded Commercial Loan Powers." *Business Review*, Federal Reserve Bank of Philadelphia (September–October 1984): 11–21.

Neely, Walter and David Rochester. "Operating Performance and Merger Benefits: the Savings and Loan Experience." *Financial Review* (February 1987): 111–130.

Nowesnick, Mary. "Savings Institutions Must Restructure for Survival, New FHLBB Chairman Urges." *Savings Institutions*, (September 1983): 58–61.

Peabody, Betty Sue. "The Turnaround at Citi-corp Savings." *The Bankers Magazine* (September–October 1984): 5–8.

Rhoades, Stephen. "The Effect of Nonbank Thrift Institutions on Commercial Bank Profit Performance in Local Markets." *Quarterly Review of Economics and Business* (Spring 1987): 16–28.

Rosenberg, Joel L. "The Joys of Duration." *Banker's Magazine* (March–April 1986): 62–67.

Scott, William L. and Richard L. Peterson "Interest Rate Risk and Equity Values of Hedged and Unhedged Financial Intermediaries." *Journal of Financial Research* (Winter 1986): 325–329.

Serrantino, Savatore. "Those Incredible New Savings and Loans." *The Bankers Magazine* (March–April 1983): 74–77.

"The Thrift Industry: Reconstruction in Progress." Federal Reserve Bank of Cleveland: Economic Commentary, June 1, 1986.

Throop, Adrian W. "Financial Deregulation, Interest Rates, and the Housing Cycle." *Economic Review*, Federal Reserve Bank of San Francisco (Summer 1986); 63–78.

Vrabac, Daniel J. "Savings and Loan Associations: An Analysis of the Recent Decline in Profitability." *Economic Review*, Federal Reserve Bank of Kansas City (July–August 1982): 3–19.

Walker, David A. "Effects of Deregulation on the Savings and Loan Industry." *Financial Review* (April 1982): 94–110.

Weaver, William C., and Jeff Madura. "Contending with Interest Rate Risks for Mortgage Lenders." *Real Estate Finance Journal* (Winter 1987): 7–12.

"When an S&L Buyout Isn't Good News." *Business Week* June 9, 1986, 86.

Williams, Jo Monci. "Uncle Sam Enters the S&L Business." *Fortune*, November 25, 1985, 67–79.

Credit Unions

CREDIT UNIONS IN PERSPECTIVE*

About ten years ago students approached the National Credit Union Administration wanting to charter their own credit union. Now there are nearly 20 campuses that have started student owned and operated credit unions. An example of the experiences these students have endured is the story of the Washington Square Federal Credit Union (WSFCU), serving alumni and students of San Jose State University. Start-up funds had to be solicited from area credit unions, alumni and potential student members and the students needed to negotiate appropriate interest rates to fund the organization.

Once the initial deposits were obtained, the students had to create and market products desirable to their members. Funds were tight and the capital needed to create and implement new programs and products had to be generated out of retained earnings. This led to slow growth. Also, the National Credit Union Administration (NCUA) examiners were watching the progress closely. If WSFCU failed, the NCUA would be obligated to pay depositors up to $100,000 out of the (NCUA) insurance fund.

Significant progress has been made since WSFCU gained its charter. Growth has allowed the students to add desirable products and expand operating hours, and the NCUA seems satisfied with the stability of the organization. Despite a high-risk membership, the credit union has made over $70,000 of loans to students without having a single loan default. Yet the credit union still faces challenges in the areas of accounting, deposit growth, marketing and the continuity of volunteers.

■ How do credit unions differ from other depository institutions with respect to sources of funds?
■ How sensitive is credit union performance to interest rate movements?
■ How are credit unions regulated?

These and other related questions are addressed in this chapter.

*Written by Lawrence C. Rose, Associate Professor of Finance, San Jose State University.

OUTLINE

The characteristics of credit unions vary distinctly from those of the other financial institutions discussed so far. This chapter describes the background, objectives, operations, regulations, risks, and performance of credit unions.

BACKGROUND OF CREDIT UNIONS

Credit unions (CUs) are nonprofit organizations composed of members with a common bond—an affiliation with a particular labor union, church, university, or even residential area. Qualified persons can typically become a member of a CU by depositing $5 or more into an account. Because CUs do not issue stock, they are technically owned by the depositors. The deposits are called *shares*, and interest paid on the deposits is called *dividends*. Since CUs are nonprofit organizations, their income is not taxed. Like savings institutions and commercial banks, CUs can be federal- or state-chartered. If the state does not offer a charter, a federal charter is necessary.

While a few CUs (such as the Navy Federal CU) have assets of over $1 billion, most are very small. In aggregate, their assets are much smaller than aggregate assets of the commercial bank or savings institution industries. They are growing at a faster rate, however. Exhibit 22.1 displays the total asset size of CUs over the last several years, distinguishing between federal and state-chartered CUs. In the late 1970s federal-chartered CUs were just slightly ahead of state-chartered ones but later grew at a much higher rate and are now significantly larger than the aggregate size of state-chartered CUs.

A distribution of federally chartered CUs by size is shown in Exhibit 22.2. More than half of them have assets of less than $5 million, and more than 80 percent have assets less than $10 million. The large number and small average size of CUs is due to the common bond requirement.

OBJECTIVES OF CREDIT UNIONS

Because CUs are owned by members, their objective is to satisfy those members. CUs offer interest on share deposits to members who invest funds. In addition, they provide loans to members who are in need of funds. They are simply acting as an intermediary for the members by repackaging deposits from member savers and providing them to member borrowers. If

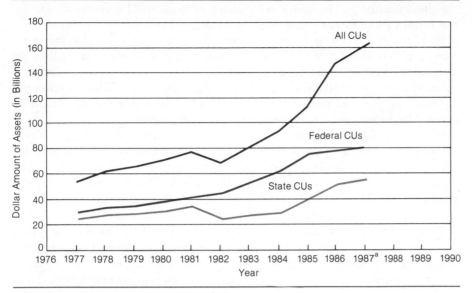

a June data were used for 1987.

SOURCE: *Federal Reserve Bulletin*, various issues.

CUs accumulate earnings, they can use the earnings to either offer higher
rates on deposits or reduce rates on loans. Either choice would benefit some
members but not others. In many cases, CUs instead use excess earnings
for advertising to attract more potential members who qualify for the common bond. Growth can allow CUs to be more diversified and more efficient
if economies of scale exist.

SOURCES AND USES OF CREDIT UNION FUNDS

CUs obtain most of their funds from share deposits by members. The typical
deposit is similar to a passbook savings account deposit at commercial

EXHIBIT 22.2   Distribution of Federally Chartered Credit Unions (FCUs)
            by Size

Asset Size	Number of FCUs	Percentage of Total
Less than $500,000	2,130	22.6%
$500,000 to $1 million	1,223	13.0
$1 million to $5 million	3,143	33.5
$5 million to $10 million	1,078	11.5
$10 million to $100 million	1,643	17.5
More than $100 million	184	2.0
	9,401	100.0%

SOURCE: 1987 Annual Report of the NCUA.

Chapter 22

Credit Unions

banks or savings institutions, as it has no specified maturity and is insured up to $100,000. CUs also offer share certificates, which provide higher rates than share deposits but require a minimum amount (such as $500) and a specified maturity. The share certificates offered by CUs compete against the retail CDs offered by commercial banks and savings institutions.

In addition to these savings accounts, most CUs also offer checkable accounts called *share drafts*. These accounts can pay interest and allow an unlimited amount of checks to be written. They normally require a minimum balance to be maintained. Share drafts offered by CUs can compare against the NOW accounts and money market deposit accounts (MMDAs) offered by commercial banks and savings institutions.

If CUs need funds temporarily, they can borrow from other credit unions, or from the Central Liquidity Facility (CLF). The CLF acts as a lender for CUs in a manner similar to the Federal Reserve's discount window. The loans are commonly used to accommodate seasonal funding and specialized needs, or to boost the liquidity of troubled CUs. Any funds held by the CLF are invested in short-term securities until CUs request additional loans.

Exhibit 22.3 shows the percentage distribution of CU sources of funds. Share drafts have become more popular over time. The proportion of regular share deposits and share certificates has been somewhat stable in recent years. The proportion of funds obtained through regular share deposits is relatively large compared to the counterpart passbook accounts offered by other depository institutions—a favorable characteristic, since it allows CUs to obtain much of their funds at a relatively low cost.

Exhibit 22.4 shows the average cost to federal-chartered CUs of obtaining funds over time. Considering how volatile market interest rates have been, the average cost of funds to CUs has been relatively stable over time. The sensitivity of the cost of funds to interest rate movements has been signif-

EXHIBIT 22.3 Percentage Distribution of Federal Credit Union Sources of Funds

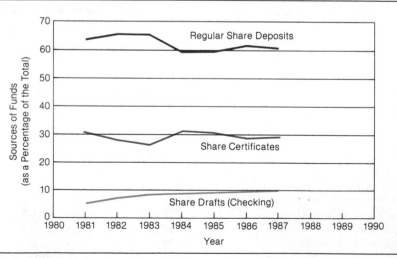

SOURCE: 1987 Annual Report of the NCUA.

EXHIBIT 22.4   Average Cost of Funds for Federal Credit Unions (Percent)

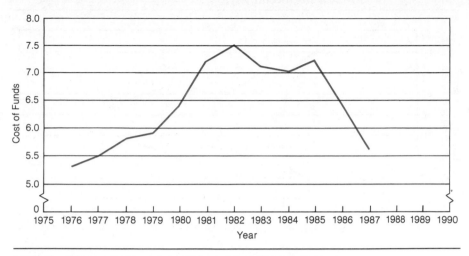

SOURCE: 1985 Annual Report and 1987 Annual Report of the NCUA.

icantly lower for CUs than for savings institutions or commercial banks, resulting from the greater proportion of passbook deposits at CUs. The rates offered on these accounts have remained somewhat stable, while rates on CDs and other accounts commonly used by savings institutions and commercial banks move with the market interest rates.

CUs use the majority of their funds for loans to members. These loans finance automobile, home improvement, or other personal expenses. They are typically secured and carry maturities of five years or less. Some CUs offer long-term mortgage loans, but many prefer to avoid assets with long maturities. In addition to loans, CUs purchase government and agency securities to maintain adequate liquidity.

Until recently, rates charged by CUs on loans were constrained by a regulatory ceiling. In the late 1970s and early 1980s, market rates on securities reached the ceiling rates on loans, and the return on relatively risky loans was no higher than the return on high-grade securities. Consequently, CUs restructured their asset portfolio to concentrate on securities in favor of loans. Exhibit 22.5 illustrates the change in CU asset composition over time. While the ceiling rates were imposed on loans to benefit the borrower, they adversely affected those who were unable to obtain funds because of the CU's shift from loans to securities.

Exhibit 22.6 shows the average yield earned by CUs on loans and investments over time. The yield on loans is generally above that of investments, since their investments usually have a relatively low degree of default risk. Because loans dominate the asset portfolio, the overall average yield on assets is more closely tied to the average loan yield. The difference between the average yield on loans versus investments has been more pronounced in recent years.

EXHIBIT 22.5   Distribution of Federal Credit Union Loans versus Investments (Securities)

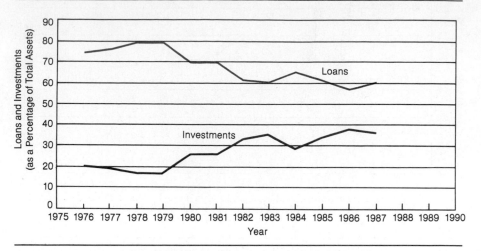

SOURCE: 1985 Annual Report and 1987 Annual Report of the NCUA.

REGULATION OF CREDIT UNIONS

CUs are supervised and regulated by the National Credit Union Administration (NCUA), which is composed of three board members, one of which is distinguished as chairman. The board members are appointed by the

EXHIBIT 22.6   Average Yields on Loans and Investments by Federal Credit Unions

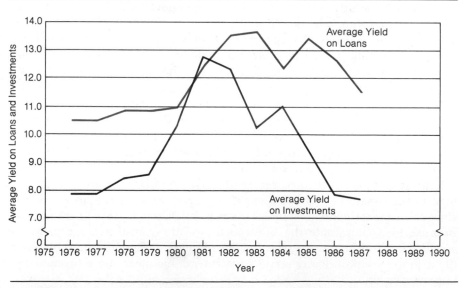

SOURCE: 1985 Annual Report and 1987 Annual Report of the NCUA.

president of the United States and confirmed by the Senate. They serve staggered six-year terms. The NCUA participates in the creation of new CUs, since it has the power to grant or revoke charters. It also examines the financial condition of CUs, and supervises any liquidations or mergers.

The NCUA has divided the United States into six regions, where its regional offices are responsible for monitoring operations of local CUs. In order to examine the CUs, the NCUA employs a staff of 360 examiners. All federal-chartered CUs as well as those state-chartered CUs applying for federal insurance are examined by the staff. Each CU completes a semiannual call report that provides financial information. This information is first input into a computer by the NCUA examiners to derive financial ratios that measure the financial condition of CUs. The ratios are then compared to an industry norm in order to detect any significant deviations. Then a summary of the CU, called a Financial Performance Report, is completed to identify any potential problems that deserve special attention in the future.

As part of the assessment of financial condition, examiners of the NCUA classify each CU into a specific risk category, ranging from Code 1 (low risk) to Code 5 (high risk). This is intended to serve as an early warning system so that those CUs that are experiencing problems or are in potential danger can be closely monitored in the future. The idea is very similar to that of the Federal Deposit Insurance Corporation (FDIC) system for tracking the commercial banks it insures. Exhibit 22.7 provides a breakdown of assigned risk ratings among CUs in recent years. Less than 10 percent have been assigned the more risky (4 and 5) ratings in any given year. While this system will not always correctly classify CUs in their proper risk category, it can at least alert the examiners as to which CUs are experiencing financial problems.

CUs are regulated as to the types of services they offer. At one time they were regulated as to the rates they could offer on share deposits or charge

EXHIBIT 22.7 Distribution of Risk Ratings among Federal Credit Unions

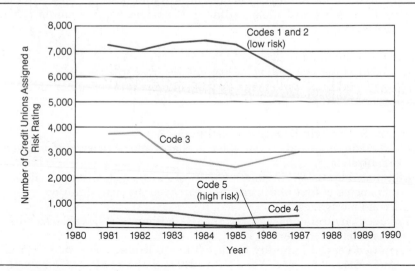

SOURCE: 1987 Report of the NCUA.

EXHIBIT 22.8 Regulatory Changes for Credit Unions

1977 Amendments to Federal Credit Union Act
    Increased loan maturities on nonresidential loans to 12 years.
    Allowed 30-year residential mortgage loans and 15-year mobile home and
        home-improvement loans.
    Permitted self-replenishing lines of credit.
    Permitted participation loans with other financial institutions.
    Permitted government-insured or guaranteed loans.
    Lowered reserve formula for larger credit unions.
    Allowed different types of share accounts, including share certificates.

1978 Financial Institutions Regulatory and Interest Rate Control Act
    Restructured NCUA into three-member board.
    Established Central Liquidity Facility under NCUA.
    NCUA regulations
    Permitted sale of mortgages to FNMA, FHLMC, or GNMA.
    Set maximum rate on small share certificates at 8 percent.
    Permitted market rates on large share certificates ($100,000 or more).
    Permitted six-month, $10,000 certificates paying ¼ percent above the six-
        month Treasury bill rate.

1979 Congress
    Gave 90-day authorization (starting December 28) for credit unions to
        offer share drafts.
    NCUA regulations required credit unions with over $2 million in assets or
        offering share drafts to hold 5 percent of member accounts plus notes
        payable in liquid assets.

1980 Depository Institutions Deregulation and Monetary Control Act
    Classified credit unions as depository institutions.
    Gave permanent authority for share drafts.
    Set required reserves on share drafts.
    Established timetable for phasing out interest ceilings.
    Raised loan rate ceiling to 15 percent and authorized NCUA to increase
        this ceiling.
    Required Federal Reserve System to price its services.
    NCUA regulations raised loan ceiling to 21 percent for nine-month period
        (starting December 3).

1981 NCUA regulations
    Extended 21 percent ceiling on loan interest rate to June 1982.
    Allowed credit unions to make variable interest rate consumer and
        mortgage loans.

1982 Garn–St Germain Depository Institutions Act
    Freed credit unions to set par value of shares and to determine internal
        organization.
    Eliminated limits on size and maturity of mortgage loans, allowed
        refinancing of first mortgages, and extended maturity limit on
        second mortgages.
    Excluded credit unions with less than $2 million in reservable accounts
        from reserve requirements.
    Permitted Central Liquidity Facility (CLF) to lend to the National Credit
        Union Share Insurance Fund (NCUSIF) and also made CLF an agent
        of the Federal Reserve System.

EXHIBIT 22.8   Continued

NCUA regulations
Allowed credit unions to determine the kinds of shares offered and the
   dividend rates paid.
Repealed fixed liquidity requirement on federally insured credit unions.
Permitted credit unions greater flexibility in the kinds of services they
   can offer and the joint sharing of activities with other credit unions.

1983 NCUA regulations expanded definition of "family member" in common
   bond requirement.

SOURCE: *Economic Review*, Federal Reserve Bank of Kansas City, (June 1984): 9.

on loans, but the Deregulation Act of 1980 led to a phasing out of deposit
ceiling rates. While some states still enforce ceilings, they are usually maintained above market levels and therefore do not interfere with normal operations. In addition, CUs are now able to offer residential loans of any size
or maturity and can sell the mortgages they originate.

A more detailed breakdown of regulatory changes is presented in Exhibit
22.8. Many of the changes were the result of the Deregulation Act (DIDMCA)
of 1980 and the Garn–St Germain Act of 1982.

Exhibit 22.9 compares some of the regulations on deposits and loans for
federal CUs to those of state-chartered CUs in six different states. Note how
the regulations of federal CUs can differ from state-chartered CUs and those
of the various states differ. Thus, the degree to which CUs can offer various
products and services is influenced by type of charter and by location. In
addition to services and rates, loans offered by CUs to officers and directors
of CUs also carry certain limitations.

INSURANCE FOR CREDIT UNIONS

About 90 percent of CUs are insured by the National Credit Union Share
Insurance Fund (NCUSIF). They pay an annual insurance premium of one-
twelfth of 1 percent of share deposits. A supplemental premium is added if
necessary. Some states require their CUs to be federally insured; others
allow insurance to be offered by alternative insurance agencies.

NCUSIF was created in 1970, without any contributing start-up capital
from the U.S. Treasury and Federal Reserve. All federal-chartered CUs are
required to obtain insurance from NCUSIF. State-chartered CUs are eligible
for NCUSIF insurance only if they meet various guidelines. The maximum
insurance per depositor is $100,000. As of January 1, 1986, the fund insured
15,058 CUs, 4,933 of which were state-chartered.

During the 1970s NCUSIF's main source of funds was insurance premiums. Because economic conditions were generally favorable, the aggregate
insurance premiums received from CUs outweighed payouts to depositors
of failing CUs. In the early 1980s, NCUSIF expenses increased, causing the
NCUA Board to impose a supplemental insurance premium equal to two-
thirds of the normal $\frac{1}{12}$ of 1 percent premium. In 1983 another supplemental
premium, equal to the normal premium, was assessed. In 1985 NCUSIF
obtained legislation that allowed for capitalized deposits for the fund. Be-

EXHIBIT 22.9 Comparison of Deposit and Loan Regulations for Federal Credit Unions (CUs) and State-Chartered CUs in Six Different States (as of January 1, 1985)

Type of Charter	Unsecured Loan Limit to One Member	Secured Loan Limit to One Member	Limit on Amount of Mortgages Held	Maximum Dividend Rate[a]	Maximum Participation Loan
Federal Credit Unions	10% of unimpaired capital and surplus	10% of unimpaired capital and surplus	None[b]	None	10% of unimpaired capital and surplus; must retain at least 10% interest in any loan participated out
State-chartered Credit Unions					
Connecticut	2½% of unimpaired capital and surplus or $15,000, whichever is less	10% of unimpaired capital and surplus or $200, whichever is greater	60% of unimpaired capital and surplus	None	10% of unimpaired capital and surplus
Maine	10% of total assets	10% of total assets	35% of total shares, capital and surplus	None	10% of total shares, capital and surplus
Massachusetts	$7,500 for credit unions under $4 million in assets, $10,000 for those over $4 million	Varies by loan category and by asset size of credit union[c]	80% of assets	8% for regular share accounts, unless undivided earnings, reserves and surplus exceed 15% of assets	Credit unions with over $4 million in assets can participate in first mortgages up to 10% of shares and surplus

New Hampshire	Credit union bylaws[a]	Credit union bylaws[a]	None	None, but only credit unions with $3 million in assets allowed to buy participation
Rhode Island	e	None	None	None
Vermont	10% of total assets or $200, whichever is greater	5% of assets for fixed-rate mortgages with maturities over 15 years; 10% of assets for all mortgages	None	Law is silent

a Maximum statutory rate; in some cases, states impose other limitations on dividend rates such as a maximum percentage of surplus which may be paid out in a given year.

b Before September 1, 1984 federal credit unions were limited to a maximum of 25 percent of assets in fixed rate mortgages.

c Massachusetts recently revised its state credit union laws, with changes effective in September and October 1984. State credit unions are now allowed to make home improvement loans up to $20,000; mobile home loans up to $35,000; recreational vehicle loans up to $30,000; auto loans up to $25,000; and second mortgages up to $25,000. For first mortgage loans of no more than 80 percent of the value of the mortgaged property, credit unions with under $4 million in assets may loan up to $75,000 per parcel and $120,000 per member. Credit unions with assets over $4 million may loan up to $110,000 per parcel and $145,000 per member.

d Loan limits and services to be offered must be stated in the credit union's bylaws, which must be approved by the state banking commissioner.

e The loan limit to one member is set by vote of the credit union membership at each annual meeting.

SOURCE: For federal credit unions, The Federal Credit Union Act, National Credit Union Administration Rules and Regulations. For state credit unions: State of Connecticut Office of the Banking Commissioner, Maine Bureau of Banking, Massachusetts Division of Banks, New Hampshire Banking Department, Rhode Island Banking Division, Vermont Department of Banking and Insurance. Table from: *New England Economic Review*, Federal Reserve Bank of Boston, (May–June 1985): 32.

cause it had use of these deposits, NCUSIF waived the normal annual insurance premium in 1985.

The NCUA has proposed that private insurance be allowed for credit unions and that all credit unions be allowed to choose their source of insurance. The NCUA has also proposed an additional one-time charge on credit unions in order to beef up the existing insurance fund. In recent years, the idea of consolidating federal insurance agencies of all depository institutions has been considered. Yet, the NCUA opposes such an idea since it believes the interests of credit unions would be overshadowed by those of commercial banks and savings institutions.

CREDIT UNION EXPOSURE TO RISK

Like other depository institutions, CUs are exposed to liquidity risk, default risk, and interest rate risk. Yet, because their balance sheet structure differs from other institutions, their exposure to each type of risk also differs.

Liquidity Risk

If CUs experience an unanticipated wave of withdrawals without an offsetting amount of new deposits, they could become illiquid. They can borrow from the Central Liquidity Facility in order to resolve temporary liquidity problems. However, if the shortage of funds is expected to continue, they need to search for a more permanent cure. Other depository institutions have greater ability to boost deposit levels because they can tap various markets. While some depository institutions attract deposits from international investors, the potential market for a CU's depositors is much more localized. Because the market is restricted to those consumers who qualify as members, CUs are less capable of quickly generating additional deposits.

Default Risk

Because CUs concentrate on personal loans to their members, their exposure to default risk is primarily derived from those loans. Most of their loans are secured, which reduces the loss to CUs in the event of default. Poor economic conditions can have a significant impact on loan defaults. Some CUs will perform much better than others due to more favorable economic conditions around their area. However, even during favorable economic periods, CUs with very lenient loan policies could experience losses. A common concern of CUs is that their credit analysis on loan applicants might be inadequately conducted by the volunteers they employ. Yet, the loans provided by CUs do not require elaborate credit analysis, since they are consumer-oriented.

The performance of CUs is highly dependent on the timeliness of loan repayments. Exhibit 22.10 shows that the delinquency rate was highest during the 1982 recession but has diminished since then. Loan defaults have increased since 1984 but have consistently been less than 1 percent of total assets.

EXHIBIT 22.10   Loan Delinquency and Default Rates of Federal Credit
Unions

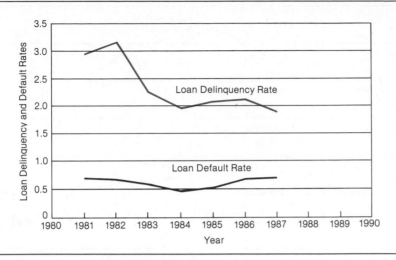

NOTE: Each variable was measured as a percentage of total assets.

SOURCE: 1985 Annual Report and 1987 Annual Report of the NCUA.

Interest Rate Risk

The majority of maturities on consumer loans offered by CUs are short-term, causing their asset portfolio to be rate–sensitive. Because their sources of funds are also generally rate–sensitive, movements in interest revenues and interest expenses of CUs are highly correlated. Therefore, the spread between interest revenues and interest expenses remains somewhat stable over time, regardless of how interest rates change. CUs are much more insulated from interest rate risk than those savings institutions that are heavily concentrated in fixed-rate mortgages.

PERFORMANCE OF CREDIT UNIONS

As with all depository institutions, the performance of CUs depends largely on the difference between their interest revenues and expenses. Exhibit 22.11 compares the average yield on assets to the average cost of funds. The difference represents the average interest rate spread of CUs, which has consistently been maintained between 4.1 percent and 5.3 percent. The spread has been quite stable over time because the interest rate–sensitivity of CU assets is somewhat similar to that of CU liabilities.

Exhibit 22.12 discloses the number of federal-chartered credit unions with negative earnings (losses) over recent years. The high correlation between the delinquent or defaulted loans in Exhibit 22.10 and the CU earnings losses in Exhibit 22.12 shows how dependent a CU's overall performance is on its loan portfolio.

Chapter 22

Credit Unions

EXHIBIT 22.11 Interest Rate Spread Generated by Federal Credit Unions

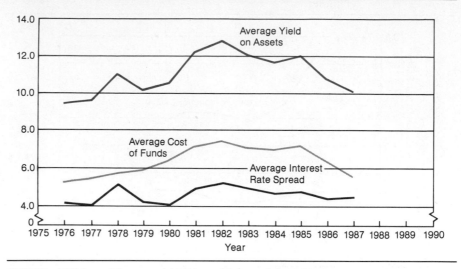

SOURCE: 1985 Annual Report and 1987 Annual Report of the NCUA.

If CUs experience economies of scale, growth should be a major objective. A study by Kim found that moderate economies of scale exist for mortgage lending and investment activities of CUs, but diseconomies of scale exist for nonmortgage lending.

ADVANTAGES AND DISADVANTAGES OF CREDIT UNION OPERATIONS

CUs can offer attractive rates to their member savers and borrowers because they are nonprofit and therefore not taxed. In addition, their noninterest expenses are relatively low, since their labor, office, furniture, and so forth are often donated or provided at a very low cost through the affiliation that all members have in common.

Some characteristics of CUs can be unfavorable. Their volunteer labor may not have the incentive to manage operations efficiently. In addition, the common bond requirement for membership restricts a given CU from growing beyond the potential size of that particular affiliation. The common bond also limits the ability of CUs to diversify. This is especially true when all members are employees of a particular institution. If that institution imposes labor layoffs, many members may simultaneously experience financial problems and withdraw their share deposits or default on their loans. This could cause the CU to become illiquid at a time when more members need loans to survive the layoff.

Even when the common bond does not represent a particular employer, many CUs are unable to diversify geographically, since all members live in the same area. Thus, an economic slowdown in this area would have an adverse impact on most members. Furthermore, CUs cannot diversify among various products the way that commercial banks and savings institutions do. They are created to serve the members and therefore concentrate heavily on providing loans to members. Finally, in the event that CUs do need funds,

EXHIBIT 22.12 Number of Federal-Chartered Credit Unions (FCUs) That Experienced Losses

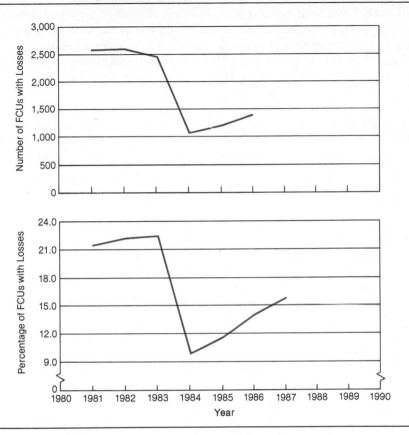

SOURCE: 1985 Annual Report and 1987 Annual Report of the NCUA.

they are unable to issue stock, since they are owned by depositors rather than shareholders.

Because the disadvantages named outnumber the advantages, it may seem as if CUs are doomed to fail. In reality, they have performed quite well, in spite of their inability to diversify. Their loans to members have historically shown a relatively low delinquency rate compared to consumer loans provided by other financial institutions.

In order to better diversify their services and take greater advantage of economies of scale, there has been an increasing tendency for CUs to merge. Thus, some CUs now allow a person to be from any one of a list of employers, organizations, and so on, in order to qualify as a member. CUs are now also trying to diversify their products by offering traveler's checks, money orders, and sometimes life insurance to their members.

SUMMARY

CUs are created to satisfy the needs of their members. The composition of liabilities and assets differ from other financial institutions because they do business almost exclusively with their members. Their interest rate risk has been limited because of their concentration in short- and medium-term loans. Their default risk is largely tied to the members who borrow funds. While other financial institutions are often restricted by regulators from offering specific services, CUs are restricted to even a greater degree. Because their members are consumers, they tend to focus on consumer-oriented services. Yet, this is not necessarily a disadvantage to CUs since they are in business to satisfy their members, who are their shareholders.

QUESTIONS

22.1. Who are the owners of credit unions?

22.2. Explain the tax status of credit unions and the reason for that status.

22.3. What is the typical size range of credit unions? Give reasons for that range.

22.4. Describe the main sources of funds for credit unions.

22.5. The average cost of funds to credit unions has been relatively stable even though market interest rates have been volatile. Explain.

22.6. Why did credit unions increase their emphasis on securities while reducing loans in the early 1980s?

22.7. Who regulates credit unions? What are their powers?

22.8. Where do credit unions obtain deposit insurance?

22.9. Explain how credit union exposure to liquidity risk differs from that of other financial institutions.

22.10. Explain why credit unions are more insulated from interest rate risk than some other financial institutions.

22.11. Identify some advantages of credit unions.

22.12. Identify disadvantages of credit unions that relate to their common bond requirement.

22.13. How are credit unions diversifying and achieving economies of scale? Explain.

REFERENCES

"Credit Unions May Have a Better Idea." *Savings Institutions* (March 1985): 132–133.

Davids, Lewis E. "Comparing Bank, Savings and Loan, and Credit Union Installment Loan Costs." *The Bankers Magazine* (July–August 1982): 35–37.

Dunham, Constance and Gary G. Heaton. "The Growing Competitiveness of Credit Unions." *New England Economic Review*, Federal Reserve Bank of Boston (May–June 1985): 19–33.

Heaton, Gary G. and Constance R. Dunham. "The Growing Competitiveness of Credit Unions." *New England Economic Review*, Federal Reserve Bank of Boston (May–June 1985): 19–34.

Kim, H. Youn. "Economies of Scale and Economies of Scope in Multiproduct Financial Institutions: Further Evidence from Credit Unions." *Journal of Money, Credit, and Banking* (May 1986): 220–226.

Pearce, Douglas K. "Recent Developments in the Credit Union Industry." *Economic Review*, Federal Reserve Bank of Kansas City (June 1984): 3–19.

Welsh, Harold T. "Credit Unions: The Quiet Competitor." *The Bankers Magazine* (January–February 1985): 28–30.

Finance Companies

FINANCE COMPANIES IN PERSPECTIVE

During the early 1980s, the performance of Commercial Credit had been declining. In 1985 it incurred negative earnings and had a below-investment-grade credit rating. However, in the mid-1980s, Commercial Credit restructured its asset and financial structure in order to improve performance. In 1985 it sold about $2 billion of its assets and streamlined operations. In early 1986 it sold its vehicle-leasing operations. Its credit rating improved, allowing it to raise about $500 million during 1987 at a low cost.

Less than $30 million of Commercial Credit's $1 billion of net worth represents fixed assets, which suggests that it has efficiently used its fixed assets to build net worth over time. While Commercial Credit presently has operations in 28 states, it expects to establish branch offices in most other states as well. In addition, it plans to build a financial services empire by expanding its insurance business and other financial services.

■ How would Commercial Credit Company, or any other consumer finance company, achieve a high return on equity?
■ What types of risks are Commercial Credit Company and other finance companies exposed to?
■ What other types of financial services could be offered by Commercial Credit Company and other finance companies?

These and other related questions are addressed in this chapter.

OUTLINE

All of the financial institutions discussed so far can be classified as *depository institutions* because they attract most of their funds from depositors. *Finance companies* differ from these institutions in that their funds obtained are of a nondepository nature. Their main purpose is to provide short- and intermediate-term credit to consumers and businesses. Although other financial institutions provide this service, only the finance company specializes in it. Many finance companies operate with a single office, while others have hundreds of offices across the country, and even in foreign countries. Some finance companies are subsidiaries of bank holding companies, insurance companies, and manufacturing firms. There are even finance companies whose subsidiaries offer insurance or commercial banking services. This chapter discusses the main characteristics of finance companies, including the different types, their sources and uses of funds, risks, and regulations.

TYPES OF FINANCE COMPANIES

Until recently, most finance companies could be classified into one of two types. The so-called **consumer finance companies** concentrated on direct loans to consumers, while so-called **sales finance companies** concentrated on purchasing credit contracts from retailers and dealers. The differences in business caused a distinct difference in balance sheet structure. Consumer finance companies provided smaller loans and operated with more offices. Their main source of funds was long-term loans. Sales finance companies provided larger loans and obtained most of their funds by selling commercial paper.

In recent years, both types of finance companies have diversified their sources and uses of funds. Thus, it is difficult to classify most finance companies as a particular type today.

SOURCES OF FINANCE COMPANY FUNDS

The main sources of funds for finance companies are

- Bank loans
- Commercial paper issues
- Deposits
- Bonds
- Capital

Each source is discussed in turn.

Bank Loans

Finance companies commonly borrow from commercial banks and can consistently renew the loans over time. For this reason, bank loans can provide a continual source of funds, although some finance companies use bank loans mainly to accommodate seasonal swings in their business.

Commercial Paper Issues

While commercial paper is available only for short-term financing, finance companies can continually roll over their issues to create a permanent source of funds. Only the most well-known finance companies, however, have traditionally been able to issue commercial paper in order to attract funds, because unsecured commercial paper exposes investors to the risk of default. In the past, small or medium-sized finance companies would have had difficulty in placing unsecured commercial paper. In recent years, secured commercial paper has become popular, so more finance companies might have access to funds through this market.

The most well-known finance companies can issue commercial paper through direct placement and thus avoid a transaction fee, lowering their cost of funds. Most companies, however, utilize the services of a commercial paper dealer.

Deposits

Under certain conditions, some states allow finance companies to attract funds by offering customer deposits similar to those of the depository institutions discussed in previous chapters. While deposits have not been a major source of funds for finance companies, they may become more widely used where legal.

Bonds

Finance companies in need of long-term funds can issue bonds. The choice to attract funds through issuing bonds versus some alternative short-term financing depends on the company's balance sheet structure and its expectations about future interest rates. When the company's assets are less interest rate–sensitive than its liabilities, and when interest rates are expected to increase, bonds could provide long-term financing at a rate that is completely insulated from rising market rates. If the finance company is confident about projections of rising interest rates, it might consider using the funds obtained from bonds to offer loans with variable interest rates.

Capital

Finance companies can build their capital base by retaining earnings or by issuing stock. As with other financial institutions, capital as a percent of total assets is maintained at a low level.

Relative Importance of Fund Sources

Exhibit 23.1 shows how the major sources of funds of finance companies have changed over time. Commercial paper and long-term debt, the two most popular sources of funds, have almost doubled over the last five years. The increase in long-term debt was most pronounced in the mid 1980s when interest rates had declined and finance companies attempted to lock in these rates over an extended period of time.

USES OF FINANCE COMPANY FUNDS

Finance companies use funds for

- Consumer loans
- Business loans
- Leasing
- Real estate loans

Each use of funds is described in turn.

Consumer Loans

Consumer loans are extended by finance companies in the form of personal loans. One of the most popular types is the automobile loan offered by a finance company that is owned by a car manufacturer. For example, General Motors Acceptance Corporation (GMAC) finances purchases of automobiles built by General Motors. Ford Motor Company, and Chrysler Corporation also have their own finance companies. In recent years, the interest rate offered on such loans has been lower than market rates. Subsidiaries of automobile manufacturers may use unusually low rates to increase automobile sales.

The aggregate volume of loans by finance companies for financing automobiles depends on their competitors. During the recessions in 1980 and 1982, credit unions and commercial banks reduced their activity in this area, allowing finance companies to increase their market share. These competitors returned to the market during the economic expansion in 1983 and 1984, causing a reduction in the finance companies' market share. However, in 1985 finance companies regained market share as a result of offering incentive programs in association with automobile dealerships.

EXHIBIT 23.1   Sources of Funds by Domestic Finance Companies (in Billions of Dollars)

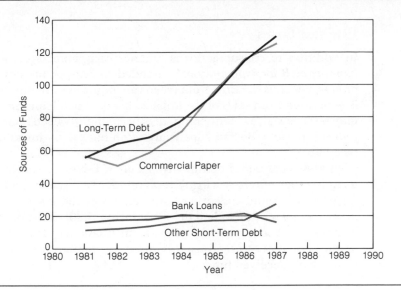

SOURCE: *Federal Reserve Bulletin*, various issues.

In addition to automobile purchases, finance companies offer personal loans for home improvement, mobile homes, and a variety of other personal expenses. Personal loans are often secured by a co-signer or by real property. The maturities on personal loans are typically less than five years.

Some finance companies also offer credit card loans through a particular retailer. For example, a retail store may sell products to customers on credit and then sell the credit contract to a finance company. Customers make payments to the finance company under the terms negotiated with the retail store. The finance company is responsible for the initial credit approval and for processing of credit card payments. The retailer can benefit from the finance company's credit allowance through increased sales, while the finance company benefits from the arrangement due to increased business. Finance companies increase their customer base in this way and are accessible for additional financing for those customers who proved to be creditworthy. The specific arrangement between a finance company and retailer can vary.

As a related form of consumer credit, some finance companies offer consumers a credit card that can be used at a variety of retail stores. For example, Beneficial Corporation offers the Bencharge card, which is acceptable at more than 25,000 small stores. In addition, Beneficial has become a large issuer of the premier MasterCards and Visas that offer a credit line of $7,500 to consumers. Their entrance into the credit card business is a useful method for attracting consumer loan applicants. In addition, borrowers with charge cards tend to meet their loan payments so that they can retain the use of their cards.

The main competition in the consumer loan market comes from commercial banks and credit unions. Finance companies have consistently provided more credit to consumers than credit unions have, but they are a distant second to commercial banks. Savings institutions have recently entered this market and are now also considered a major competitor.

Business Loans

In addition to consumer loans, finance companies also provide *business (commercial) loans*, commonly intended to finance the *cash cycle* of companies, which is the time from when raw materials are purchased until cash is generated from sales of the finished goods. Such loans are short-term but may be renewed, as many companies permanently need financing to support their cash cycle. Business loans are often backed by inventory or accounts receivable.

Finance companies commonly act as a **factor** for accounts receivable, meaning they purchase a firm's receivables at a discount and are responsible for processing and collecting the balances of these accounts. They would incur any losses due to bad debt. Factoring reduces the processing costs of businesses. It also provides short-term financing, as cash is sent by the finance company to the business prior to the point at which the business would have received funds.

Leasing

Another way finance companies provide financing is by *leasing*. They purchase machinery or equipment for the purpose of leasing it to businesses that prefer to avoid the additional debt on their balance sheet that purchases would require. This can be important to a business that is already close to debt capacity and is concerned about additional debt adversely affecting its credit rating.

Real Estate Loans

Finance companies offer *real estate loans* in the form of mortgages on commercial real estate and second mortgages on residential real estate. The offering of second mortgages has become increasingly popular over time. These mortgages are typically secured and historically have a relatively low default rate.

Relative Importance of Uses of Funds

Exhibit 23.2 shows how the volume of consumer, business, and real estate credit provided by finance companies has changed over time. While the volume of business credit had consistently dominated since the mid 1970s, it was matched by the volume of consumer credit in the late 1980s. Allocation of funds to mortgages is substantially smaller.

REGULATION OF FINANCE COMPANIES

When finance companies are acting as bank holding companies, or are subsidiaries of bank holding companies, they are federally regulated. Otherwise they are regulated by the state. They are subject to a loan ceiling, which

EXHIBIT 23.2 Finance Company Allocation of Funds Over Time

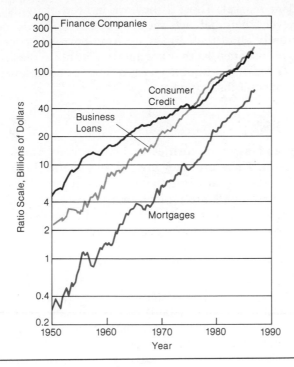

SOURCE: 1987 Federal Reserve Chart Book.

places a maximum limit on the loan size. They are also subject to ceiling interest rates on loans provided and to a maximum length on the loan maturity. These regulations are imposed by states, and they vary among states. Because ceiling rates are now sufficiently above market rates, they do not normally interfere with the rate-setting decisions by finance companies.

Finance companies are subject to state regulations on intrastate business. If they plan to set up a new branch, they must convince regulators that it would serve the needs of the people based in that location.

RISKS FACED BY FINANCE COMPANIES

Finance companies, like other financial institutions, are exposed to three types of risks:

- Liquidity risk
- Interest rate risk
- Default risk

Yet, because their characteristics differ from those of other financial institutions, their degree of exposure to each type of risk differs as well.

Liquidity Risk

Finance companies generally do not hold assets that could be easily sold in the secondary market. Thus, if they are in need of funds, they have to borrow. However, their balance sheet structure does not call for much liquidity. Virtually all of their funds are from borrowings rather than deposits anyway. Consequently, they are not susceptible to unexpected deposit withdrawals. Overall, the liquidity risk of finance companies is less than that of other financial institutions.

Interest Rate Risk

Both liability and asset maturities of finance companies are short- or intermediate-term. Therefore, they are not as susceptible to increasing interest rates as are savings institutions. However, they can still be adversely affected, since their assets are typically not as rate–sensitive as their liabilities. They can shorten their average asset life or make greater use of adjustable rates if they wish to reduce their interest rate risk.

Default Risk

Because the majority of a finance company's funds are allocated as loans to consumers and businesses, default risk is a major concern. Customers that borrow from finance companies usually exhibit a moderate degree of risk. The loan delinquency rate of finance companies is typically higher than that of other lending financial institutions. However, their higher average rate charged on loans can possibly more than offset a higher default level. The relative high-return and high-risk loan characteristics of finance companies can make their performance quite sensitive to prevailing economic conditions.

PERFORMANCE OF FINANCE COMPANIES

The recent performance of finance companies varies with their operating characteristics. Those companies that focus on the core business of consumer lending will normally be more sensitive to general economic conditions. Finance companies that offer more diversified financial services are more sensitive to industry-specific conditions, such as insurance-related events.

Investment services such as Value Line report a finance company's revenues over the last several years, which can be reviewed to assess growth. Profitability can be measured by the dollar amount of net profit, and a ratio of net profit to net worth (referred to in the publication, *Value line*, as "% Earned Net Worth)."

CAPTIVE FINANCE SUBSIDIARIES

A **captive finance subsidiary (CFS)** is a wholly owned subsidiary whose primary purpose is to finance sales of the parent company's products and services, provide wholesale financing to distributors of the parent compa-

Market Reaction to Establishment of Captive Finance Subsidiaries

Two possible benefits of a captive finance subsidiary are (1) separating accounts receivable into a subsidiary would increase efficiency, and (2) a captive subsidiary can increase a firm's debt capacity. One might argue that in terms of cash flow, liquidity, and profitability, the combined perception of a separated parent and subsidiary should be the same as if there has been no separation. However, the tendency of some firms, such as General Motors Corporation, Ford Motor Company, Sears Roebuck Corporation, and several other corporations, to establish captive finance subsidiaries suggests that there is a perceived advantage to such a strategy.

A recent study by Kim, McConnell, and Greenwood assessed the market reaction to the formation of captive finance subsidiaries by using cumulative average residual (CAR) analysis. Stock returns were abnormally high shortly before the formation, while bond returns were abnormally low. This implies that stockholders benefited at the expense of bondholders as a result of the anticipated formation of a captive finance company. The reason is that creditors of the newly formed captive finance company will have first claim (ahead of existing bondholders) on the cash flows generated by receivables.

SOURCE: E. H. Kim, John J. McConnell, and Paul R. Greenwood, "Capital Structure Rearrangement and Me-First Rules in an Efficient Capital Market," *Journal of Finance*, (June 1977): 789–810. For a review of research on captive finance subsidiaries, see Iraj Fooladi, Gordon Roberts, and Jerry Viscione, "Captive Finance Subsidiaries, Overview, and Synthesis," *Financial Review* (May 1986); 259–275.

ny's products, and purchase receivables of the parent company. The actual business practices of a CFS typically include various types of financing apart from just the parent company business. When a captive is formed, an operating agreement is made between the captive and the parent company that includes specific stipulations, such as the type of receivables that qualify for sale to the captive and specific services to be provided by the parent.

The motive to create a CFS can be easily understood by evaluating the automobile industry. Automobile manufacturers were unable to finance dealers' inventories, so had to demand cash from each dealer. Many dealers were unable to sell cars on an installment basis, since they needed cash immediately. Banks were the primary source of capital to dealers. However, banks viewed automobiles as luxury items not suitable for bank financing and were not willing to buy the installment plans created from automobile sales. For this reason, the automobile manufacturers became involved in financing.

The most substantial growth in captive finance companies occurred between 1946 and 1960, due to liberalized credit policies and a need to finance growing inventories. By 1960 more than 100 captive finance subsidiaries existed.

There are several advantages of maintaining a CFS. It can be used to finance distributor or dealer inventories until a sale occurs, making production less cyclical for the manufacturer. It can serve as an effective mar-

Chapter 23

Finance Companies

keting tool by providing retail financing. It can also be used to finance products leased to others.

A CFS is a profitable operation in itself. Most well-managed finance companies earn 12 to 15 percent on their equity capital. A CFS allows a corporation to clearly separate its manufacturing and retailing activities from its financing activities. Therefore, it is less expensive and easier to analyze each segment of the parent company. Also, when lending to a captive rather than a division of the parent company, the lender need be less concerned with the claims of others. Unlike commercial banks, a CFS has no reserve requirements and no legal prohibitions on how to obtain funds or use funds.

Furthermore, a competitive advantage can be gained by a firm with a captive finance company, since sale items such as automobiles and housing may depend on the financing arrangements available.

Captive finance subsidiaries have diversified their financing activities away from just the parent company's product installment plans. General Electric Credit Corporation (GECC) has been the most innovative of all the captive finance companies. Its financing includes industrial and equipment sales, consumer installment credit, and second mortgage loans on private residences.

The creation of a captive finance subsidiary can affect the debt capacity of the parent company as a whole. Roberts and Viscione evaluated 21 Canadian captive finance companies, 9 merchandising, and 12 manufacturing companies. The average debt-to-total-assets ratios for these firms increased more than the ratios of firms without captives over the time frame of three years prior and three years after the formation of the captive. Next, 45 U.S. firms, representing five industries, that formed captive finance subsidiaries were assessed. In each industry, there was a significant increase in the average debt ratios for the three-year period after the captive was formed as compared with the prior three-year period. Both evaluations concluded that a captive finance subsidiary allows more debt. Therefore, firms with captive finance subsidiaries experience increased debt-capacity. The credit ratings of bonds issued by the firms that formed captives were unaffected when the firms increased their debt usage.

INTERACTION OF FINANCE COMPANIES WITH OTHER FINANCIAL INSTITUTIONS

Finance companies and their subsidiaries often interact with other financial institutions, as summarized in Exhibit 23.3. They are more closely related to commercial banks, savings and loan associations, and credit unions because of their concentration in consumer lending. However, those finance companies with subsidiaries that specialize in other financial services compete with insurance companies and pension plans.

PARTICIPATION OF FINANCE COMPANIES IN FINANCIAL MARKETS

Finance companies utilize various financial markets to manage their operations, as summarized in Exhibit 23.4. The use of financial markets by finance companies for the core business is mainly to obtain funds. However,

EXHIBIT 23.3   Interaction between Finance Companies and Other Financial Institutions

Type of Financial Institution	Interaction with Finance Companies
Commercial banks and savings and loan associations (S&Ls)	■ Finance companies compete with banks and S&Ls for consumer loan business (including credit cards), commercial loans, and leasing. ■ Finance companies obtain loans from commercial banks. ■ Finance companies have acquired some commercial banks. ■ Some finance companies are subsidiaries of commercial banks.
Credit unions	■ Finance companies compete with credit unions for consumer loan business.
Investment banking firms	■ Finance companies issue bonds that are underwritten by investment banking firms.
Pension funds	■ Insurance subsidiaries of finance companies manage pension plans of corporations and therefore compete with pension funds.
Insurance companies	■ Insurance subsidiaries of finance companies compete directly with other insurance companies.

the subsidiaries of finance companies often utilize financial markets as a method for investing funds or to hedge investment portfolios against interest rate risk or market risk. They may even diversify their financial services in foreign countries. As large finance companies such as Beneficial Corporation expand internationally, they will be better able to use the international bond and commercial paper markets as a source of funds.

RECENT DEVELOPMENTS IN FINANCE COMPANIES

Some finance companies are entering new industries in an attempt to diversify their product offerings. For example, they have acquired insurance companies to enter the insurance business. They now offer traditional banking-related services such as credit cards and even commercial loans. Some have acquired commercial banks located in various states. In addition, they have recently concentrated on large loans secured by real property, and some of the larger finance companies have diversified into a variety of nonfinancial businesses as well.

While some finance companies are becoming more diversified, others, such as Beneficial Corporation, are now concentrating on the consumer lending business. Beneficial Corporation suffered large losses from its insurance subsidiary, which may have been a major reason for its desire to refocus on its core business.

EXHIBIT 23.4   Participation of Finance Companies in Financial Markets

Type of Financial Market	Participation by Finance Companies
Money markets	■ Finance companies obtain funds by issuing commercial paper.
Bond markets	■ Finance companies issue bonds as a method of obtaining long-term funds. ■ Subsidiaries of finance companies commonly purchase corporate and Treasury bonds.
Mortgage markets	■ Finance companies purchase real estate and also provide loans to real estate investors. ■ Subsidiaries of finance companies commonly purchase mortgages.
Stock markets	■ Finance companies issue stock to establish a capital base. ■ Subsidiaries of finance companies commonly purchase stocks.
Futures markets	■ Subsidiaries of finance companies that offer insurance-related services sometimes use futures contracts to reduce the sensitivity of their bond portfolio to interest rate movements, and also may trade stock index futures to reduce the sensitivity on their stock portfolio to stock market movements.
Options markets	■ Subsidiaries of finance companies that offer insurance-related services sometimes use options contracts to protect against temporary declines in particular stock holdings.

MULTINATIONAL FINANCE COMPANIES

INTERNATIONAL

ASPECTS

Some finance companies are large multinational corporations with subsidiaries in several countries. For example, the consumer finance division of Beneficial Corporation has over 1,000 offices in the United States, Canada, West Germany, and in the United Kingdom. U.S–based finance companies penetrate foreign countries to enter new markets and to reduce their exposure to U.S. economic conditions.

SUMMARY

Finance companies differ from other financial institutions because of their composition of fund sources and uses. They obtain much of their funds by issuing commercial paper and long-term bonds. Their main uses of funds are consumer and business credit. Because their balance sheet composition differs from other financial institutions, their exposure to risk differs as well. They have a relatively low degree of liquidity risk, since their sources of funds generally have predictable maturities. In addition, they have sufficient flexibility to match the interest rate–sensitivity on sources and uses of funds. Thus, they can maintain interest rate risk at a low level. Their primary concern is default risk, since their loan portfolios are normally more risky than those of other financial institutions.

KEY TERMS

captive finance subsidiary (CFS)
consumer finance companies

factor
sales finance companies

QUESTIONS

23.1. Are the sources of funds for finance companies generally short-term or long-term? Explain.

23.2. Is the cost of funds obtained by finance companies very sensitive to market interest rate movements? Explain.

23.3. How are small and medium-sized finance companies able to issue commercial paper?

23.4. Why do some well-known finance companies directly place their commercial paper?

23.5. Describe the trends in the major sources of funds for finance companies in recent years.

23.6. Explain why some finance companies are associated with automobile manufacturers. Why do some of these finance companies offer below-market rates on loans?

23.7. Describe the major uses of funds by finance companies.

23.8. Explain how finance companies benefit from offering consumers a credit card.

23.9. Explain how finance companies provide financing through leasing.

23.10. What was the historical difference between so-called consumer finance companies and sales finance companies?

23.11. Explain how the liquidity position of finance companies differs from that of depository institutions such as commercial banks.

23.12. Explain how the interest rate risk of finance companies differs from that of savings institutions.

23.13. Explain how the default risk of finance companies differs from that of other lending financial institutions.

23.14. Explain how finance companies are regulated.

PROJECT

1. FINANCIAL ANALYSIS OF A FINANCE COMPANY.

Obtain an annual report of a finance company assigned by your professor or one of your choice. Based on this report, answer the following questions:

 a. How has its asset portfolio composition changed in recent years?

 b. Have the recent changes in asset composition affected the company's risk and potential return?

c. How do you think the company would be affected by an increase in interest rates? Explain.

d. Based on its annual report, does the company appear to be increasing its nontraditional services? Elaborate.

REFERENCES

Andrews, Victor L. "Captive Finance Companies." *Harvard Business Review* (July–August 1964): 80–92.

Jensen, Michael and William Meckling. "Theory of the Firm: Managerial Behavior, Agency Costs, and Ownership Structure." *Journal of Financial Economics* (October 1976): 305–360.

Lewellen, Wilbur G. "Finance Subsidiaries and Corporate Borrowing Capacity." *Financial Management* (Spring 1972): 21–32.

Roberts, Gordon S. and Jerry A. Viscione. "The Captive Finance Company: Solution or Straw Man?" *Credit and Financial Management* (December 1979): 34–35.

Roberts, Gordon S. and Jerry A. Viscione. "Captive Finance Subsidiaries: The Manager's View." *Financial Management* (Spring 1981): 36–42.

CHAPTER 24

Mutual Funds

MUTUAL FUNDS IN PERSPECTIVE

Over the last decade, mutual funds have grown rapidly in response to their advantages to individual and institutional investors. To illustrate the types of mutual funds available, the following list represents some of the funds offered by Vanguard:

Equity Funds

- Explorer II
- Naess & Thomas Special Fund
- Vanguard World Fund
- PRIMECAP Fund
- Windsor II
- Vanguard Index Trust

Income Funds

- Vanguard Municipal Bond Fund
- Vanguard Fixed Income Securities Fund
- Vanguard Money Market Reserves
- Vanguard Bond Market Fund

Balanced Funds

- Wellington Fund
- Wellesby Income Fund
- Vanguard STAR Fund
- Vanguard Convertible Securities Fund

In addition to these funds, Vanguard offers funds that specialize in the following industries:

- energy
- health care
- gold and precious metals
- technology

Vanguard also offers funds containing foreign securities, such as its international growth fund. Furthermore, it provides a simplified retirement plan, and even offers discount brokerage services for investors who wish to purchase or sell particular stocks. Numerous other mutual funds also provide these types of services.

- Which types of mutual funds are most susceptible to the economy and to interest rate movements?
- Which types of mutual funds have the highest potential return?
- What types of financial institutions invest in mutual funds?

These and other related questions are addressed in this chapter.

OUTLINE

Mutual funds have become a very popular type of financial institution for individual and institutional investors. This chapter first provides a background on mutual funds and describes how mutual funds are managed and the risk-return tradeoff involved. It also identifies the types of mutual funds and summarizes their recent performance. Money market funds are described, followed by a discussion of real estate investment trusts.

BACKGROUND ON MUTUAL FUNDS

Small investors who purchase securities individually are often unable to diversify due to their limited investment. Mutual funds offer a way by which these investors can diversify. Some mutual funds contain 50 or more securities, and the minimum investment typically ranges between $250 and $2,500. Small investors could not afford to create such a diversified portfolio on their own. Moreover, the mutual fund uses experienced portfolio managers, so investors do not have to manage the portfolio themselves. Finally, mutual funds offer the investor liquidity, through their willingness to repurchase the investor's shares upon request.

Because of their diversification, management expertise, and liquidity, mutual funds have grown at a rapid pace. More than 2,000 different mutual funds exist today, with total assets having increased from about $293 billion at the beginning of 1984 to about $450 billion in 1988. The number of mutual fund shareholder accounts grew from 9.8 million in 1979 to over 54 million in 1988. The percent of households holding mutual funds increased from about 6 percent to more than 20 percent over this same period.

Some financial intermediaries such as savings banks and pension funds also invest in mutual funds and have recently increased their holdings in them. Many investment companies offer a family of mutual funds—as many as 30 different funds—so that they can accommodate the diverse preferences of investors. An investor can transfer from one fund to another within the same family.

LOAD VERSUS NO-LOAD MUTUAL FUNDS

Mutual funds can be classified as either **load,** meaning there is a sales charge, or **no-load,** meaning funds are promoted strictly by the mutual fund of concern. Load funds are promoted by registered representatives of brokerage firms, who earn a sales charge typically ranging between 3 percent and 8 percent. Investors in a load fund pay this charge, through the difference between the bid and ask prices of the load funds. Some investors may feel that the sales charge is worthwhile, since a brokerage firm helps determine the type of fund that is appropriate for them. Other investors who feel capable of making their own investment decisions often prefer to invest in no-load funds. Some no-load mutual funds can be purchased through a discount broker for a relatively low fee (such as 1 to 2 percent), although they receive no advice from the discount broker. In recent years, some small no-load funds have become load funds, since they could not attract investors without a large budget to advertise nationally. As a load fund, they will be recommended by various brokers and financial planners, who will earn a commission on any shares sold. Some other no-load funds now charge a 2 or 3 percent fee, even though they are not offered through brokers. The fee supports any advertising by the fund.

MANAGEMENT OF MUTUAL FUNDS

The primary responsibility of the portfolio managers hired by the mutual fund is to invest in a portfolio of securities that satisfies the desires of investors. A successful portfolio will become attractive to other investors and thus grow over time. To cover managerial expenses, mutual funds charge management fees of typically less than 1 percent of the total assets per year.

Besides the compensation to portfolio managers, management expenses of a mutual fund include record-keeping and clerical fees. These expenses can be significant, as any given fund may represent ownership by several thousand investors.

Like other portfolio managers, the managers of mutual funds analyze economic and industry trends and forecasts, and assess the potential impact of various conditions on companies. They adjust the composition of their portfolio in response to changing economic conditions. Securities of some industries (such as auto and financial) have become more popular among mutual funds over time, at the expense of others (such as agricultural equipment, mining, and oil).

OPEN-END VERSUS CLOSED-END FUNDS

Open-end mutual funds are willing to repurchase their shares from investors at any time. This is an attractive characteristic since it offers liquidity to investors. **Closed-end mutual funds** also sell shares to investors but do not repurchase the shares they sell. Instead, the shares are sold on a stock exchange. The number of shares sold by a closed-end investment company usually remains fixed, equal to the initial amount issued. When the demand for a particular closed-end mutual fund is strong, the market price may be higher than its net asset value. However, closed-end funds commonly have a market value less than the net asset value. The initial offering of a closed-end fund is normally sold above its net asset value to cover the underwriting commissions earned by investment banking firms. Because many closed-end funds are initially priced above the net asset value and then decline over time, some traders in these funds sell them *short* (agree to sell the funds at a future point in time at a specified price). If the market price decreases, they are able to purchase the fund for a price lower than they agreed to sell it for.

Stock and bond mutual funds normally invest in stocks and bonds, while money market mutual funds invest in money market securities. All mutual funds serve as financial intermediaries because they accept investor's funds and repackage them to make investments. This differs from a depository institution's role only in that most of the accounts offered by depository institutions guarantee a specific rate of return. Conversely, the investors' return on a mutual fund or money market mutual fund depends on the fund's performance. Thus, investors are usually more concerned with *potential* performance when considering which fund to invest in, whereas their choice of a depository institution is often based on *guaranteed* performance (quoted deposit rates) or on convenience.

RETURNS AND RISKS OF MUTUAL FUNDS

Mutual funds can generate returns to their shareholders in three ways. First, they can pass on any earned income (from dividends or coupon payments) as dividend payments to the shareholders. Second, they can pass on capital gains through the sale of securities within the fund. Shareholders can choose either to accept any dividend payments and capital gains distributions or to request that the distributions be reinvested into the fund, thereby representing a purchase of additional shares. A third type of return to shareholders is through mutual fund *share price appreciation*. As the market value of security holdings increases, the net asset value of the fund increases, and the shareholders benefit when they sell their mutual fund shares.

While investors in a mutual fund directly benefit from any returns generated by the fund, they are also directly affected if the portfolio generates losses. Because they own the shares of the fund, there is no other group of shareholders to which the fund must be accountable. This differs from commercial banks and stock-owned savings associations, which obtain their deposits from one group of investors and sell shares of stock to another.

TYPES OF MUTUAL FUNDS

Because investors have various objectives, no single portfolio could satisfy everyone. Consequently, a variety of mutual funds have been created. The more popular types include

- Growth funds
- Capital appreciation funds
- Income funds
- Growth and income funds
- Tax-free funds
- International funds
- Specialty funds

Each type is described in turn.

Growth Funds

For investors who desire a high return and are willing to accept a moderate degree of risk, **growth funds** are appropriate. These funds are typically composed of stocks of companies that have not fully matured and are expected to grow at a higher than average rate in the future. The primary objective of a growth fund is to generate an increase in investment value, with less concern about the generation of steady income. All growth funds do not necessarily share the same degree of risk. Some concentrate on companies that have existed for several years but are still experiencing growth, while others concentrate on relatively young companies.

Capital Appreciation Funds

Also known as *aggressive growth funds*, **capital appreciation funds** are composed of stocks that have potential for very high growth but may also be unproven. These funds are suited for investors who are more willing to risk a possible loss in value. In response to the rapid changes in the economy, portfolio managers of capital appreciation funds constantly revise the portfolio composition to take full advantage of their expectations. They sometimes even use borrowed money to support their portfolios, thereby using leverage to increase their potential return and risk.

Income Funds

For investors who are mainly concerned with stability of income rather than capital appreciation, **income funds** are appropriate. They are usually composed of bonds that offer periodic coupon payments, and vary in exposure to risk. Some income funds composed of only corporate bonds are susceptible to default risk, while those composed of only Treasury bonds are not. A third type of income fund contains bonds backed by government agencies, such as the Government National Mortgage Association (called (GNMA, or Ginnie Mae). These funds are normally perceived to be less risky than a fund containing corporate bonds. Those income funds exhibiting more default risk will offer a higher potential return, other things being equal.

In addition to default risk, income funds are exposed to interest rate risk. Those with a longer average time to maturity are more exposed. Treasury bonds are just as susceptible to interest rate risk as other bonds with similar maturity and coupon characteristics. Some income funds commonly adjust their average maturity in anticipation of market conditions and interest rate movements.

While stability of income can be achieved from owning income funds, that market values of even the medium-term income funds are quite volatile over time due to their sensitivity to interest rate movements. Thus, income funds are best suited for investors that rely on the fund for periodic income and plan to maintain the fund over a long period of time.

Some income mutual funds use a covered call strategy on a portion of the portfolio. These so-called option income mutual funds invest in stocks and sell call options on those stocks. The premiums received from selling the call options increase the income generated by the mutual funds. However, during bull markets the stocks on which call options were written must be sold as the options are exercised. Thus, the mutual funds forego the potential return which could have been achieved if they were able to retain the shares. Some option-income mutual funds write options on only 35 to 50 percent of their stock portfolio. This strategy generates less option premium income but reduces the potential amount of stocks which the fund would have to sell if the options are exercised.

Growth and Income Funds

For investors that prefer potential for capital appreciation along with some stability in income a *growth and income* fund, which contains a unique combination of growth stocks and fixed-income bonds, may be most appropriate. For those funds that emphasize greater investment in growth stocks rather than bonds, there is greater potential for capital appreciation but a lower amount of fixed income generated from the fund.

Tax-free Funds

High tax-bracket investors have historically purchased municipal bonds as a method to avoid taxes. Because these bonds are susceptible to default, a diversified portfolio is desirable. Mutual funds containing municipal bonds allow high tax-bracket investors with even small amounts of funds to avoid taxes while maintaining a low degree of default risk. Since municipal bonds typically have long maturities, the market values of tax-free mutual funds are usually exposed to a high degree of interest rate risk. Some of these funds, however, reduce their exposure to interest rate fluctuations by holding only municipal bonds that will mature in the near future.

International Funds

In recent years, there has been increasing awareness of foreign securities. Investors historically avoided foreign securities because of the high information costs and transaction costs associated with purchasing them and monitoring their performance. International mutual funds were created to allow foreign investment in securities without incurring these excessive costs.

The returns on international stock mutual funds are affected not only by foreign companies' stock prices but also by the movements of currencies that denominate these stocks. As a foreign currency's value strengthens against the U.S. dollar, the value of the foreign stock as measured in U.S. dollars increases. Thus, U.S. investors can benefit not only from higher stock prices, but also from a strengthened foreign currency (against the dollar). Of course, they can also be adversely affected if the foreign currencies denominating the stocks depreciate. The strong U.S. dollar during the early 1980s dampened investor interest in international mutual funds. Then, as a result of the weak dollar from 1985 to 1988, investment in these funds increased substantially.

International mutual funds can be classified as **global** or **foreign.** Global funds include some U.S. stocks within their portfolio, while foreign funds typically exclude U.S. stocks. International mutual funds have historically comprised stocks from several different countries in order to limit exposure of the portfolio to economic conditions in any single foreign economy. Yet, in recent years some new international mutual funds have been designed to fully benefit from a particular emerging country or continent. While there is greater potential return from such strategy, there is also greater risk, since the entire portfolio value is sensitive to a single economy. International funds are discussed further at the end of this chapter.

Specialty Funds

Some mutual funds called specialty funds, represent a group of companies sharing a particular characteristic. For example, there are industry-specific funds such as energy, banking, or high-tech funds. In addition, some funds include only stocks of firms that are likely takeover targets. There are even mutual funds that specialize in options or other commodities, such as precious metals. The risk of specialty funds varies with the particular characteristics of each.

GROWTH AND SIZE COMPARISON OF MUTUAL FUNDS

Exhibit 24.1 shows the growth in the number of mutual funds over time. The increasing popularity of bond funds is partially attributed to declining interest rates during the early and mid 1980s, making these funds more attractive than alternative short-term securities. The popularity of stock funds is mainly due to stock market boom periods that occurred over time, along with the relatively low returns offered by alternative short-term securities in some periods. While net sales (sales minus redemptions) has grown for both types of funds, the growth in bond funds has been much more pronounced.

Exhibit 24.2 shows the distribution of mutual funds according to investment objective. There are more long-term municipal bond funds and growth funds than any other type. While mutual funds were originally targeted for the more common conservative investors, a variety of funds has recently been created to accommodate all types of investors.

EXHIBIT 24.1 Number of Stock and Bond Funds Over Time

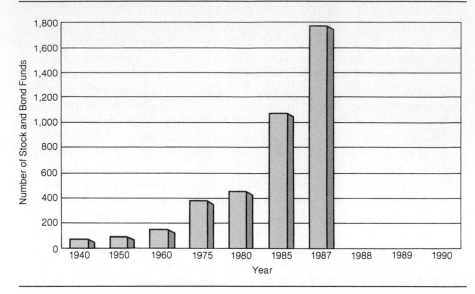

SOURCE: *1988 Mutual Fund Fact Book*, Investment Company Institute.

The breakdown of mutual funds into load versus no-load is provided in Exhibit 24.3. Almost all option/income and government income funds have a load. The only type of mutual funds in which no-loads dominate are the aggressive growth funds and international funds. While load funds are more common, no-load funds are available for investors who do not need the advice of a broker, regardless of the type of fund desired.

EXHIBIT 24.2 Sales Distribution of Mutual Funds (Excluding Money Market Mutual Funds)

Type of Mutual Fund	1980	1987
Aggressive growth	53	186
Growth	137	308
Growth and income	77	188
Precious metals		22
International		81
Balanced	21	31
Income	56	219
Option/income	10	19
U.S. government income		148
Ginnie Mae		55
Corporate bond		42
Long-term municipal bond	42	368
Other		145
Total	458	1,781

SOURCE: *1986 Mutual Fund Fact Book;* and *1988 Mutual Fund Fact Book*, Investment Company Institute.

Part Six

Nonbank Financial
Institutions

644

EXHIBIT 24.3 Classification of Mutual Fund Assets by Investment Objective and Load Status

Investment Objective	Aggregate Assets (in Millions of Dollars)	
	Load Funds	No-Load Funds
Aggressive growth	$ 10,088.6	$ 16,527.7
Growth	30,940.1	12,604.7
Growth and income	38,985.8	19,810.6
Precious metals	2,415.7	1,632.3
International	2,608.0	4,355.5
Balanced	6,136.0	2,780.2
Income	24,133.9	13,489.0
Option/income	4,863.3	226.2
U.S. government income	86,069.3	2,242.6
Ginnie Mae	27,490.3	6,044.3
Corporate Bond	8,055.6	951.0
Long-term municipal bond	32,782.7	16,392.0
Other	57,184.1	10,440.0
Total	331,752.8	107,496.1

SOURCE: *1988 Mutual Fund Fact Book*, Investment Company Institute.

Exhibit 24.4 shows the composition of all mutual fund assets in aggregate. Common stocks dominate, followed by U.S. government bonds and then municipal bonds. Common stocks comprised over 80 percent of the aggregate asset value of mutual funds in the early 1970s. Its percentage has steadily declined, as investment by mutual funds into bonds has increased by a much higher proportion over time.

REGULATION AND TAXATION OF MUTUAL FUNDS

Mutual funds must adhere to a variety of federal regulations. They must register with the Securities and Exchange Commission (SEC) and also provide a prospectus to interested investors that discloses details about the components of the fund and the risks involved. Mutual funds are also reg-

EXHIBIT 24.4 Distribution of Aggregate Mutual Fund Assets

Asset	Asset Value (in Billions of $)	Percentage of Total
Corporate bonds	$ 41.6	9.2%
Preferred stock	5.6	1.2
Common stock	176.4	38.9
Municipal bonds (long-term)	68.6	15.1
U.S. government securities	134.0	29.5
Other	27.6	6.1
Total	453.8	100.0

SOURCE: *1988 Mutual Fund Fact Book*, Investment Company Institute.

RELATED RESEARCH

Performance of Mutual Funds

A variety of studies (listed in the references for this chapter) have attempted to assess mutual fund performance over time. To measure mutual fund performance solely by return is not a valid test, since it will likely be highly dependent on the performance of the stock and bond markets during the period of concern. An alternative measure of performance is a comparison of the mutual fund return to the return of some index of the market (such as the Dow Jones Industrial Average or Standard and Poor's 500 Index).

A study by Jensen found that mutual funds did not outperform the market in general. Another study by Carlson found that mutual funds did not outperform the S&P 500 or NYSE Composite. Carlson also found no relationship between the performance and size of mutual funds, and no relationship between the performance and expense ratio of mutual funds. Furthermore, he found that no-load funds outperformed load funds. A study by Klemkosky found that the rank-ordering of mutual fund performance over two-year periods was unstable. Thus, the past performance of mutual funds is not necessarily an appropriate indicator of future per-

formance. While the studies mentioned here are only a small portion of the research on mutual funds, they are somewhat representative.

To appropriately evaluate a mutual fund's performance, risk should also be considered. Even when returns are adjusted to account for risk, mutual funds have, on average, failed to outperform the market. These results may seem surprising, since the funds are managed by experienced portfolio managers. Yet, many individual stock purchase decisions are also ultimately derived from the so-called expert advice of investment companies that instruct their brokers on what securities to recommend. In addition, advocates of market efficiency would suggest that beyond insider information, market prices should already reflect any good or bad characteristics of each stock, making it difficult to construct a portfolio whose risk-adjusted returns will consistently outperform the market. Even if mutual funds do not outperform the market, they can still be attractive to investors who wish to diversify and who prefer that a portfolio manager make their investment decisions.

SOURCE: Robert S. Carlson, "Aggregate Performance of Mutual Funds 1948–1967," *Journal of Financial and Quantitative Analysis* (March 1970): 1–32; Michael C. Jensen, "The Performance of Mutual Funds in the Period 1945–1964," *Journal of Finance* (May 1968): 389–416; and Robert C. Klemkosky, "The Bias in Composite Performance Measures," *Journal of Financial and Quantitative Analysis* (June 1973): 505–514.

ulated by state laws, many of which attempt to assure that investors fully understand the fund.

If a mutual fund distributes at least 90 percent of its taxable income to shareholders, it is exempt from taxes on dividends, interest, and capital gains distributed to shareholders. The shareholders are, of course, subject to taxation on these forms of income.

BACKGROUND ON MONEY MARKET FUNDS

Money market mutual funds, sometimes called *money market funds (MMFs),* are portfolios of money market (short-term) instruments constructed and managed by investment companies. The portfolio is divided into shares that are sold to individual investors. Because investors can participate in some MMFs with as little as $1,000, they are able to invest in money market instruments that they could not afford on their own. Most MMFs allow check-writing privileges, although there may be restrictions on the number of checks written per month, or on the minimum size of the check amount.

MMFs send periodic account statements to their shareholders to update them on any changes in their balance. They also send shareholders periodic updates on any changes in the asset portfolio composition, providing a breakdown of the names of securities and amounts held within the MMF portfolio.

Because the sponsoring investment company is willing to purchase MMFs back at any point in time, investors can liquidate their investment whenever they desire. Exhibit 24.5 compares the sales of MMFs by the sponsoring companies to redemptions (repurchases of shares). In most years, additional sales exceed redemptions, allowing the companies to build their MMF portfolios by purchasing more securities. When redemptions exceed sales, the

EXHIBIT 24.5 Comparison of Aggregate Sales to Redemptions for Money Market Funds (in Billions of Dollars)

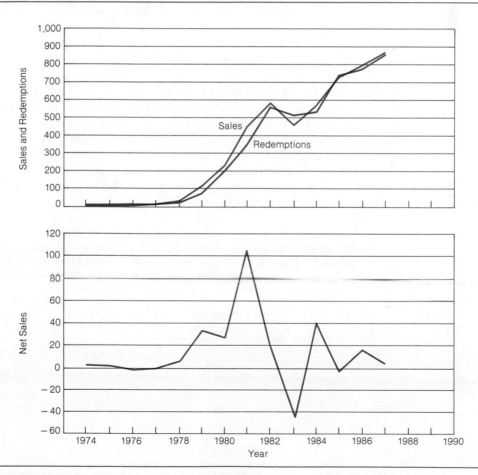

SOURCE: *1988 Mutual Fund Fact Book*, Investment Company Institute.

company accommodates the amount of excessive redemptions by selling some of the assets contained in the MMF portfolios. Thus, the dollar value of the asset portfolio will change in response to the popularity of the MMF. The value of MMFs with redemptions equal to sales (zero net sales) will still increase as their returns are reinvested.

The growth of MMFs as measured by number of funds and aggregate assets is illustrated in Exhibit 24.6. When interest rates reached their peak in 1981, 63 new money market funds were created, accommodating the increased demand by both individuals and institutions. In 1982, 122 new money market funds were created as short-term interest rates were still attractive. Some of these new accounts resulted from investors withdrawing deposits from savings accounts at depository institutions that were subject to interest rate ceilings. In 1983 more MMFs were created, but total MMF assets declined. This was primarily due to the introduction of money market deposit accounts by depository institutions. From 1983 on, money market funds experienced steady growth in terms of both number of funds and aggregate assets.

CHARACTERISTICS OF MONEY MARKET FUNDS

The main characteristics distinguishing MMFs from each other are the composition and maturity of their assets. Each of these characteristics is described here.

Asset Composition

Exhibit 24.7 shows the composition of money market fund assets in aggregate. Commercial paper dominates and is followed by repurchase agreements. This composition represents the importance of each type of asset for money market funds overall and does not represent the typical composition of any particular MMF. Each MMF is usually more concentrated in whatever assets reflect its objective. During recessionary periods, the proportion of Treasury bills in MMFs normally increases, while the proportion of the more risky money market securities decreases.

EXHIBIT 24.6   Growth of Money Market Funds (Including Short-Term Municipal Bond Funds)

Year	Number of MMFs	Total Dollar Value (in Millions) of MMF Net Assets
1980	96	74,447.7
1981	159	181,910.4
1982	281	206,607.5
1983	307	162,549.5
1984	329	209,731.9
1985	348	207,535.3
1986	360	228,345.8
1987	389	254,676.4

SOURCE: *1988 Mutual Fund Fact Book*, Investment Company Institute.

EXHIBIT 24.7 Composition of Money Market Fund Assets in Aggregate

Asset	Dollar Amount (in Billions)	Percentage of Total
U.S. Treasury bills	4.9	1.9%
Other Treasury securities	9.4	3.7
Other U.S. securities	27.0	10.6
Repurchase agreements	39.3	15.4
Commercial bank CDs	24.2	9.5
Other domestic CDs	9.3	3.6
Eurodollar CDs	21.6	8.5
Commercial paper	100.5	39.5
Banker's acceptances	10.7	4.2
Other	7.6	3.0
Total assets	254.6	100.0

NOTE: Estimates are rounded.

SOURCE: *1988 Mutual Fund Fact Book*, Investment Company Institute.

Maturity

Exhibit 24.8 shows the average maturity of MMFs over time. The average maturity is determined by individual asset maturities, weighted according to their relative value. In the mid 1970s, the average maturity was relatively long. As interest rates increased, yields of MMFs were slower to adjust, as the rates on existing assets were fixed. Those MMFs with shorter asset maturities were able to more quickly capitalize on higher interest rates. By the late 1970s the average maturity on MMFs declined to less than half of what it was during the mid 1970s. Thus, most MMFs were in a position to fully benefit from the peak interest rates in 1981. The average maturity of

EXHIBIT 24.8 Weighted Average Maturity of Money Market Fund Assets

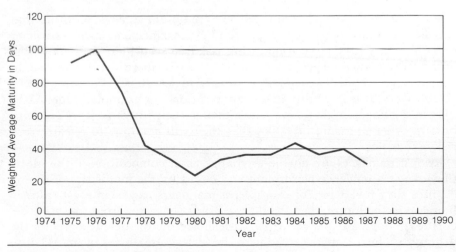

SOURCE: *1988 Mutual Fund Fact Book*, Investment Company Institute.

money market funds has been less volatile during the 1980s as compared to the 1970s.

RISK OF MONEY MARKET FUNDS

From an investor's perspective, MMFs usually have a low level of default risk. There may be some concern that an economic down turn could cause frequent defaults on commercial paper, or that several banking failures could cause defaults on Eurodollar certificates of deposit and banker's acceptances. Yet, these instruments subject to default risk have short-term maturities. Thus, MMFs can quickly shift away from securities issued by any particular corporations that may fail in the near future.

Because MMFs contain instruments with short-term maturities, their market values are not too sensitive to movements in market interest rates (as are mutual funds containing long-term bonds). While the short-maturity characteristic is sometimes perceived as an advantage, it also causes the returns on money market funds to decline in response to decreasing market interest rates. It is for this reason that some investors choose to invest in a money market fund offered by an investment company that also offers a bond mutual fund. During periods when interest rates are expected to decline, a portion of the investor's funds can be transferred from the money market fund to the bond mutual fund upon the investor's request.

The expected returns on MMFs are low relative to bonds or stocks due to the following factors. First, their default risk is normally perceived to be lower than that of corporate bonds. Second, they have less interest rate risk than bond funds. Third, they consistently generate positive returns over time, whereas bond and stock funds can experience negative returns. Because MMFs are normally characterized as having relatively low risk and low expected return, they are popular among investors who need a conservative investment medium. Furthermore, they provide liquidity with their check-writing privileges.

MANAGEMENT OF MONEY MARKET FUNDS

The role of MMF portfolio managers is to maintain an asset portfolio that satisfies the underlying objective of a fund. If the managers expect a stronger economy, they may replace maturing risk-free securities (Treasury bills) with more commercial paper or CDs. The return on these instruments would be higher yet would not overexpose the fund to default risk. For some MMFs there is very little flexibility in the composition. For example, some MMFs may as a rule maintain a high percentage of their investment in Treasury bills in order to assure investors that they will continue to refrain from risky securities.

Even if managers are unable to change asset composition of the MMF, they can still influence performance by changing the maturities of the securities they invest in. For example, if managers expect interest rates to increase in the future, they should use funds generated from maturing securities to purchase new securities with shorter maturities. The greater the degree to which a manager adjusts the average maturity of an MMF to capitalize on interest rate expectations, the greater will be the reward or penalty. If the expectation turns out to be correct, the MMF will yield relatively high returns, and vice versa.

While investing individuals and institutions do not manage the portfolio composition or maturity of an MMF, they have a variety of MMFs to choose from. If they expect a strong economy, they may prefer an MMF that contains securities with some risk that offer higher returns than Treasury bills. If they expect interest rates to increase, they could invest in MMFs with a short average maturity. They are in a sense managing their investment by choosing an MMF with the characteristics they prefer. Some investment companies offer several MMFs, allowing investors to switch from one fund to another based on their expectations of economic conditions.

A recent study by Shawky, Forbes, and Frankle examined money market fund management and performance and found no relationship between the asset size and performance of money market funds. That is, size did not appear to influence performance. This study also found that money market funds that spent more on the management of portfolio tended to have higher performance.

REGULATION AND TAXATION OF MONEY MARKET FUNDS

As a result of the Securities Act of 1933, sponsoring companies must provide full information on any MMFs they offer. In addition, they must provide potential investors with a current prospectus that describes the fund's investment policies and objectives. The Investment Company Act of 1940 contains numerous restrictions that prevent conflict of interests by the fund's managers.

Earnings generated by MMFs are generally passed on to the fund's shareholders in the form of interest payments, or converted into additional shares. If the fund distributes at least 90 percent of its income to its shareholders, the fund itself is exempt from federal taxation. This tax rule is designed to avoid double taxation. While the fund can avoid federal taxes on its income, shareholders are subject to taxes on the income they receive, regardless of whether it is in the form of interest payments or additional shares.

REAL ESTATE INVESTMENT TRUSTS

A **real estate investment trust (REIT)** (pronounced "reet") is a closed-end mutual fund that invests in real estate or mortgages. Like other mutual funds, they allow small investors to participate with a low minimum investment. The funds are pooled to invest in mortgages and in commercial real estate. REITs generate income for shareholders by passing through rents on real estate or interest payments on mortgages. Most existing REITs can be sold on stock exchanges, which allows investors to sell them at any time. The composition of a REIT is determined by its portfolio manager, who is presumed to have expertise in real estate investments. In the early and mid 1970s, many of the mortgages held by REITs defaulted. Consequently, investors' interest in REITs declined. While the price of a REIT is somewhat influenced by its portfolio composition, it is basically determined by supply and demand. Even if the portfolio has performed well in the past, the REIT's share value may be low if investors are unwilling to invest in it. In 1986, 21 new REITs were created, resulting in a total of 143 REITs. By August 1987 another 14 REITs were created.

REITs can be classified as **equity REITs,** which invest directly in properties, or **mortgage REITs,** which invest in mortgage and construction loans. A third type of REIT, called a **hybrid,** invests in both properties and mortgages.

Equity REITs are sometimes purchased to hedge against inflation, since rents tend to rise and property values rise with inflation. Their performance varies according to the perceived future value of the real estate held in each portfolio. REITs that have concentrated in potential high-growth properties are expected to generate a higher return than those with a more nationally diversified portfolio. However, they are also susceptible to more risk if the specific locations experience slow growth. For example, Houston was at one time considered to be a high-growth area, but then the decline in oil prices adversely affected its economy.

Because mortgage REITs essentially represent a fixed-income portfolio, their market value will be influenced by interest rate movements. As interest rates rise, the market value of mortgages declines, and therefore the demand for mortgage REITs declines. If interest rates are expected to decrease, mortgage REITs become more attractive.

In 1986 equity REITs generated a return of 21.6 percent, 13.9 percent from share price appreciation and 7.7 percent from dividends. Mortgage REITs generated a return of 10.5 percent in 1986, .6 percent from price appreciation and 9.9 percent from dividends. Hybrid REITs generated a return of 13.1 percent in 1986, 4.4 percent from price appreciation, and 8.7 percent from dividends.

INTERACTION BETWEEN MUTUAL FUNDS AND OTHER FINANCIAL INSTITUTIONS

Mutual funds interact with various financial institutions, as described in Exhibit 24.9. They serve as an investment alternative for portfolio managers of financial institutions such as insurance companies and pension funds. In addition, they are offered by subsidiaries of financial institutions such as commercial banks and insurance companies. They can provide financing to all financial institutions by purchasing securities issued by these institutions.

USE OF FINANCIAL MARKETS BY MUTUAL FUNDS

Each type of mutual fund uses a particular financial market as described in Exhibit 24.10. Since the main function of mutual funds is to invest, all securities markets are commonly used. The futures and options markets are also utilized to hedge against interest rate risk or market risk.

EXHIBIT 24.9 Interaction between Mutual Funds and Other Financial
Institutions

Type of Financial Institution	Interaction with Mutual Funds
Commercial banks and savings and loan associations (S&Ls)	■ Money market mutual funds invest in certificates of deposit at banks and S&Ls, and in commercial paper issued by bank holding companies. ■ Some commercial banks (such as Security Pacific and Chase Manhattan) have investment company subsidiaries that offer mutual funds. ■ Some stock and bond mutual funds invest in securities issued by banks and S&Ls.
Finance companies	■ Some money market mutual funds invest in commercial paper issued by finance companies. ■ Some stock and bond mutual funds invest in stocks and bonds issued by finance companies.
Insurance companies	■ Some stock mutual funds invest in stocks issued by insurance companies. ■ Some insurance companies (such as Kemper) have investment company subsidiaries that offer mutual funds. ■ Some insurance companies market particular mutual funds.
Pension funds	■ Pension fund portfolio managers invest in mutual funds.

INTERNATIONAL MUTUAL FUNDS

As discussed earlier, under "Types of Mutual Funds," international mutual funds have facilitated international capital flows. They can reduce the excessive transaction costs that might be incurred by small investors who attempt to invest in foreign securities on their own. They also increase the degree of integration among stock markets. Investors are now more capable of shifting their funds from one country to another. Consequently, international stock markets will likely become more integrated over time. As international markets become more accessible, the volume of U.S. investment in foreign securities will become more sensitive to events and financial market conditions in those countries.

INTERNATIONAL

ASPECTS

SUMMARY

Mutual funds allow investors with small amounts of funds to invest in all types of securities. In addition, they offer diversification advantages. Their

EXHIBIT 24.10 How Mutual Funds Utilize Financial Markets

Type of Market	How Mutual Funds Use That Market
Money market	■ Money market mutual funds invest in various money market instruments, such as Treasury bills, commercial paper, banker's acceptances, and certificates of deposit.
Bond market	■ Some bond mutual funds invest mostly in bonds issued by the U.S. Treasury or a government agency. Others invest in bonds issued by municipalities or firms. ■ Foreign bonds are sometimes included in a bond mutual fund portfolio.
Mortgage market	■ Some bond mutual funds invest in bonds issued by the Government National Mortgage Association (GNMA or "Ginnie Mae"), who uses the proceeds to purchase mortgages that were originated by some financial institutions.
Stock market	■ Numerous stock mutual funds include stocks with various degrees of risk and potential return.
Futures market	■ Some bond mutual funds may periodically attempt to hedge against interest rate risk by taking positions in financial futures contracts.
Options market	■ Some stock mutual funds may periodically hedge specific stocks by taking positions in stock options. ■ Some specialty mutual funds take positions in stock options for speculative purposes.

popularity has encouraged the creation of special mutual funds that are designed to focus on a particular type of investment, such as gold, Japanese stocks, or even Australian bonds. The popularity of any type of mutual fund will change with changes in investor preferences for stocks, bonds, or money market securities. However, the general popularity of mutual funds will likely continue. New types of mutual funds will be created as market conditions and investor preferences change.

KEY TERMS

capital appreciation funds	income funds
closed-end mutual funds	load
equity REIT	money market mutual funds
foreign funds	mortgage REIT
global funds	no-load
growth funds	open-end mutual funds
hybrid REIT	real estate investment trust

QUESTIONS

24.1. How do open-end mutual funds differ from closed-end mutual funds?

24.2. Explain why mutual funds are attractive to small investors.

24.3. Explain the difference between load and no-load mutual funds.

24.4. How can mutual funds generate returns to their shareholders?

24.5. Like the mutual funds, commercial banks and stock-owned savings institutions sell shares. Yet, proceeds received by mutual funds are used in a different way. Explain.

24.6. Support or refute the following statement: Investors can avoid all types of risk by purchasing a mutual fund that contains only Treasury bonds.

24.7. Describe the ideal mutual fund for investors that wish to generate tax-free income and also maintain a low degree of interest rate risk.

24.8. Explain how changing foreign currency values can affect the performance of international mutual funds.

24.9. What type of security is dominant when reviewing all stock and bond mutual funds in aggregate?

24.10. Explain how the income generated by a mutual fund is taxed when it distributes at least 90 percent of its taxable income to shareholders.

24.11. Have mutual funds outperformed the market, according to recent research? Explain.

24.12. Would mutual funds be attractive to some investors even if they are not expected to outperform the market? Explain.

24.13. How do money market funds (MMFs) differ from other types of mutual funds?

24.14. How can a money market fund accommodate shareholders who wish to sell their shares when the amount of proceeds received from selling new shares is less than the amount needed?

24.15. Explain the relative risk of the various types of securities that a money market fund may invest in.

24.16. Is the value of a money market fund or bond fund more susceptible to increasing interest rates? Explain.

24.17. Which security is dominant when assessing the portfolio of money market funds in aggregate?

24.18. Has the average maturity of money market fund assets increased or decreased over time? Is this a favorable strategy if interest rates are expected to decline over the next several years? Explain.

24.19. Explain how the income generated by a money market fund is taxed if it distributes at least 90 percent of its income to shareholders.

24.20. Explain the difference between equity REITs and mortgage REITs. Which type would likely be a better hedge against high inflation? Why?

PROJECTS

24.1. Obtain a prospectus for a money market fund of your choice. Identify the allocation toward commercial paper, Treasury bills, CDs, banker's acceptances, etc. Is this fund generally more risky or less risky than a fund with all domestic CDs? Explain.

24.2. Compare historical returns on a particular growth stock fund against the returns of the S&P 500 Stock Index. Are the fund's returns more or less volatile than that index? Explain why the fund has or has not outperformed the index lately.

24.3. Evaluate the historical returns on a particular income fund. Determine how the returns are affected by interest rate movements.

24.4. Evaluate the historical returns on a particular international fund. Explain why that fund has been performing better or worse than most U.S. stocks in recent years.

24.5. Obtain the prospectus for two international funds of your choice. Identify the countries (or continents) that each fund invests in. Which fund is likely to generate more volatile returns? Explain.

REFERENCES

"A Deluge of Data from Discount Brokers." *Fortune*, July 8, 1985, 125–126.

Ang, James S. and Jess H. Chua. "Mutual Funds: Different Strokes for Different Folks?" *Journal of Portfolio Management* (Winter 1982): 43–47.

Carlson, Robert S. "Aggregate Performance of Mutual Funds 1948–1967." *Journal of Financial and Quantitative Analysis* (March 1970): 1–32.

Chang, Eric C. and Wilbur G. Lewellen. "An Arbitrage Pricing Approach to Evaluating Mutual Fund Performance." *Journal of Financial Research* (Spring 1985): 15–30.

Chang, Eric C. and Wilbur G. Lewellen. "Market Timing and Mutual Fund Investment Performance." *Journal of Business* (January 1984): 57–72.

Elton, Edwin, Martin Gruber and Joel Rentzler. "Professionally Managed, Publicly Traded Commodity Funds." *Journal of Business* (April 1987): 175–199.

Grant, Dwight. "Portfolio Performance and the 'Cost' of Timing Decisions." *Journal of Finance* (June 1977): 837–838.

"Hanging Out a Financial Planning Shingle." *Institutional Investor* (September 1983): 215–220.

Henriksson, Roy D. "Market Timing and Mutual Fund Performance: An Empirical Investigation." *Journal of Business 57* (January 1984): 75–96.

Jensen, Michael C. "The Performance of Mutual Funds in the Period 1945–1964." *Journal of Finance* (May 1968): 389–416.

Jensen, Michael C. "Risk, the Pricing of Capital Assets, and the Evaluation of Investment Portfolios." *Journal of Business* (April 1969): 167–247.

Klemkosky, Robert C. "How Consistently Do Managers Manage?" *Journal of Portfolio Management* (Winter 1977): 11–15.

Klemkosky, Robert C. "The Bias in Composite Performance Measures." *Journal of Financial and Quantitative Analysis* (June 1973): 505–514.

Lehmann, Bruce and David Modest. "Mutual Fund Performance Evaluation: A Comparison of Benchmarks and Benchmark Comparisons." *Journal of Finance* (June 1987): 233–265.

Mains, Norman E. "Risk, the Pricing of Capital Assets, and the Evaluation of Investment Portfolios: Comment." *Journal of Business* (July 1977): 371–384.

Malkiel, Burton. "The Valuation of Closed-End Investment Company Shares." *Journal of Finance* (June 1977): 847–886.

Martin, John D., Arthur J. Keown, Jr., and James L. Farrell. "Do Fund Objectives Affect Diversification Policies?" *Journal of Portfolio Management* (Winter 1982): 19–28.

McDonald, John G. "Objectives and Performance of Mutual Funds, 1960–1969." *Jour-*

nal of Financial and Quantitative Analysis (June 1974): 311–333.

"Mutual Funds Make Some Inroads." *Institutional Investor* (July 1983): 123–126.

Shawky, Hany A. "An Update on Mutual Funds: Better Grades." *Journal of Portfolio Management* (Winter 1982): 29–34.

Shawky, Hany A., Ronald Forbes, and Alan Frankle. "Liquidity Services and Capital Market Equilibrium: The Case for Money Market Mutual Funds." *Journal of Financial Research* (Summer 1983): 141–152.

"Should Retail Brokers Double as Investment Bankers?" *Institutional Investor* (February 1983): 141–143.

Veit, E. Theodore and John M. Cheney. "Are Mutual Funds Market Timers?" *Journal of Portfolio Management* (Winter 1982): 35–42.

CHAPTER 25

Securities Firms

SECURITIES FIRMS IN PERSPECTIVE

During the late 1980s, securities firms were frequently the center of attention in financial markets:

■ After the crash of 1987, several securities firms experienced a decline in their brokerage business, and scaled down their business. Shearson Lehman Brothers merged with E. F. Hutton and restructured operations.

■ During the crash of 1987, some stock portfolios of financial institutions which were hedged against downside risk experienced sizable declines in value. Securities firms that developed these hedging techniques were under fire.

■ Securities firms that used various forms of "index arbitrage" in the financial markets for their own accounts were criticized for causing more volatile security prices. In 1988, some securities firms suspended "index arbitrage" for their own accounts, including Morgan Stanley & Company, Salomon Brothers and Paine Webber Group Incorporated.

■ Some securities firms were aggressively pursuing the mergers and acquisitions business, in which they often finance one firm's acquisition of another. However, recent legislative and court developments on hostile takeovers have discouraged securities firms from participating. Some securities firms, such as Drexel Burnham Lambert, have responded by focusing on leveraged buyouts and friendly takeovers.

■ In the first quarter of 1988, securities firms such as Morgan Stanley Group Inc. and First Boston began to recover from the impact of the crash, as their earnings improved substantially.

■ What businesses have the most impact on the performance of securities firms?

■ How do securities firms participate in the flow of funds between financial institutions?

■ How are securities firms regulated?

These and other questions related to securities firms are addressed in this chapter.

OUTLINE

Securities firms offer a variety of services, most of which can be classified as investment banking or brokerage. The well-known securities firms such as Merrill Lynch, Salomon Brothers, and Shearson Lehman Hutton have investment banking and brokerage divisions, although their allocation of resources to these divisions may differ. Investment banking focuses on primary market services, such as advising clients about issuing securities and underwriting the securities. Brokerage focuses on secondary market services, such as advising clients on which securities to buy or sell and executing security transactions. This chapter describes securities firms in detail, with an emphasis on how they serve clients and participate in financial markets.

BACKGROUND ON SECURITIES FIRMS

Securities firms were originally created as small private partnerships with a single office and a small staff. Most have remained as partnerships or have become incorporated but do not have public shareholders. The growth of any securities firm is likely to result in a greater degree of efficiency, since the cost of compiling and assessing information can be spread among a larger customer base.

The securities industry is regulated by the National Association of Securities Dealers (NASD) and existing securities exchanges. Regulations are imposed to prevent unfair or illegal practices, assure orderly trading, and address customer complaints. The Securities and Exchange Commission (SEC) regulates the issuance of securities and specifies disclosure rules for the issuers. It also regulates the exchanges and the participating brokerage firms. Whereas the SEC's involvement is based on the establishment of general guidelines, day-to-day regulatory duties are the responsibility of the exchanges or the NASD.

In addition to the SEC, NASD, and exchanges, the Federal Reserve Board has some regulatory influence because it determines the credit limits *(margin requirements)* on securities purchased. The Securities Investor Protection Corporation (SIPC) offers insurance on cash and securities deposited at brokerage firms and also can liquidate failing brokerage firms. The insurance limit is $500,000, including $100,000 against claims on cash. All brokers that are registered with the SEC are assessed premiums by the SIPC, which are used to maintain its insurance fund. In addition to its insurance fund, the SIPC has a $500 million revolving line of credit with a group of banks and can borrow up to $1 billion from the SEC. Because the SIPC boosts investor confidence in the securities industry, economic efficiency is increased, and market concerns are less likely to cause a run on deposits of cash and securities at securities firms.

FUNCTIONS OF THE SECURITIES INDUSTRY

There are three major functions of the securities industry:

- Maintaining orderly markets
- Raising new capital
- Managing investment capital

Each is discussed in turn.

Maintaining Orderly Markets

In the 1800s taverns were often used as a site for securities transactions. As organized *exchanges* were established, the securities transaction process was standardized as to the method of payment, process of transferring securities, and specification of practices considered to be fraudulent. For the typical security transaction on an exchange, brokerage firms represent both the buyer and seller.

Raising New Capital

Investment banking firms (IBFs) play a major role in helping corporations and governments raise capital. They place bonds of corporations and governments and stocks of corporations with investors. Because they specialize in the placement of securities, they can more effectively distribute securities than the governments or corporations that are attempting to raise capital. The participation of IBFs in placing securities is more thoroughly discussed later in this chapter.

Managing Investment Capital

Brokerage firms and investment banking firms commonly offer advice on investments. They compile and assess information that can affect future security prices, then identify the types of investments that are suitable for a particular investor. Or they may help an investor achieve higher risk-adjusted returns. To achieve such objectives, of course, investment advisors must have access to more useful information than others or be more capable of assessing this information. In general, the information used to assess securities is related to either the original issuer of the securities or economic variables that can affect the security's market price.

INVESTMENT BANKING SERVICES

One of the main functions of investment banking firms is raising capital for corporations. They originate, structure, and place securities in the capital markets to raise funds for corporations. Their role is primarily as an intermediary rather than as a lender or investor. Therefore, the compensation for raising funds is typically in the form of fees rather than interest income.

Another critical function of investment banking firms is providing advice on mergers and acquisitions. This function is related to raising funds since many mergers and acquisitions require outside financing, and investment banking firms that are able to raise large amounts of funds in the capital markets are more likely to be chosen as advisors for mergers and acquisitions. A key component of the advisory function is the valuation of a business. Investment banking firms assess the potential value of target firms so that they can advise corporations on whether to merge and on the appropriate price to offer. The valuation process also is used for advising on potential divestitures and on leveraged buyouts. Investment banking firms not only focus on valuation aspects, but also help firms with procedural matters regarding the implementation of a merger, acquisition, or divestiture.

In recent years, investment banking firms have loaned their own funds to companies involved in a merger or acquisition. They have even provided equity financing in some cases, whereby they became part-owner of the acquired firms.

How Investment Banks Facilitate Leveraged Buyouts

Investment banking firms facilitate *leveraged buyouts (LBOs)* in three ways. First, they assess the market value of the firm (or division) of concern, so that the participants planning to purchase it do not pay more than its value. Second, they arrange financing, which involves raising borrowed funds and purchasing any common stock outstanding that is held by the public. Finally, they may be retained in an advisory capacity.

A group may not be able to afford an LBO because of constraints on the amount of funds it can borrow. The IBF may therefore consider purchasing a portion of the firm's assets, which provides the group with some financial support. It will either search for an immediate buyer of these assets or maintain them over a period of time. If it chooses the latter alternative, it may finance the purchase by issuing bonds. Its return on this deal is based on the difference between the net cash inflows generated by the assets and the cash outflows resulting from the bond issue. Some IBFs have generated substantial returns on these deals, as the assets were later sold at a much higher price than the purchase price. Yet, the transaction may pose a significant risk to IBFs. First, there is no guarantee that the assets will sell at a premium. Second, their financing with bonds normally occurs with a lag. They initially borrow short-term until bonds are issued. If interest rates rise prior to the issue date, their cost of long-term financing may be much higher than they anticipated. If IBFs engage in more LBO financing activity, their holdings of other assets will increase, and their overall performance will be more susceptible to economic downturns. However, the potential fee-income and returns on asset holdings may more than offset this risk.

Merrill Lynch has designed a mutual fund that finances LBOs. The investment in the mutual fund is used mostly to purchase *junk bonds* of firms that went private. In addition to purchasing junk bonds, the mutual fund also provides **bridge loans** for firms until junk bonds can be issued. The fund also invests in the equity of some firms.

How Investment Banks Facilitate New Stock Issues

An IBF acts as an intermediary between a corporation issuing securities and investors by providing the following services:

- Origination
- Underwriting
- Distribution
- Advising

ORIGINATION. When a corporation decides to publicly issue additional stock, it may contact an IBF. The IBF can recommend the appropriate amount of stock to issue, since it can anticipate the amount of stock the market can likely absorb without causing a reduction in the stock price. Once the IBF and the corporation have determined the amount of stock to be issued, the corporation must specify whether the stock to be issued should be preferred or common along with other provisions.

Next, the IBF will evaluate the corporation's financial condition to determine the appropriate price for the newly issued stock. If the firm has issued stock to the public before, the price should be the same as the market price on its outstanding stock. If not, the firm's financial characteristics will be compared with other similar firms in the same industry that have stock outstanding to help determine the price at which the stock should be sold.

The issuing corporation then registers with the SEC. All information relevant to the security, as well as the agreement between itself and the IBF, must be provided within the **registration statement,** which is intended to assure that accurate information is disclosed by the issuing corporation. Some publicly placed securities do not require registration if the issue is very small or sold entirely within a particular state. SEC approval does not guarantee the quality or safety of the securities to be issued; it simply acknowledges that a firm is disclosing accurate information about itself. Included within the required registration information is the **prospectus,** which discloses relevant financial data on the firm and provisions applicable to the security. The prospectus can be issued only after the registration is approved, which typically takes 20 to 40 days.

UNDERWRITING STOCK. As a result of negotiations between the IBF and an issuing corporation, an **underwriting spread** is determined—the difference between the price the IBF is willing to pay for stock and the price at which it expects to sell the securities. In essence, the underwriting spread represents a commission to the IBF for selling the stock. The actual commission earned by the IBF depends upon the price at which the stock is sold. The issuing firm is not directly affected by the actual selling price of the stock, if it was guaranteed a certain price by the IBF.

Suppose that Panther Corporation planned to issue 4 million shares of new stock, and an IBF guaranteed a selling price of $19 per share, then sold the stock for $20 per share. The underwriting spread earned by the IBF is $1 for every share sold at $20, or 5 percent. The underwriting spread on a percentage basis will average around 3 percent for large issues of stocks and as high as 10 percent or more on small issues.

The original IBF may form an **underwriting syndicate** of IBFs, which are requested to underwrite a portion of the stock. Each participating IBF earns the underwriting spread and assumes the risk for the portion of securities it is assigned. Thus, the risk to the original IBF is reduced to only the stock it is responsible for selling. If the stock sells for a price lower than expected, the original IBF will not be affected as much, since it has allocated much of the responsibility to other IBFs in the syndicate. The original IBF hopes that the other IBFs invited into the syndicate will someday return the favor when they are the original underwriters and need participation from other IBFs. A syndicate may be composed of just a few IBFs, for a relatively small stock issue, or as many as 50 or more for a large issue.

IBFs may not be willing to act as underwriters for securities issued by relatively risky corporations. Instead, they may offer their best efforts in selling the stock. This results in a **best-efforts agreement,** whereby the IBF does not guarantee a price to the issuing corporation. While an issuing corporation would normally prefer to have its stock underwritten, it may have to accept a best-efforts agreement if its financial performance is questionable or unproven. In this case, the issuing corporation bears the risk because it does not receive a guaranteed price from the IBF on the stock to be issued.

DISTRIBUTION OF STOCK.   Once all agreements between the issuing firm, the originating IBF, and other participating IBFs are complete, and the registration is approved by the SEC, the stock may be sold. The prospectus is distributed to all potential purchasers of the stock, and the issue is advertised to the public. In some cases, the issue sells within hours. However, if the issue does not sell as expected, the underwriting syndicate will likely have to reduce the price to complete the sale. The demand for the stock is somewhat influenced by the sales force involved in selling the stock. Some IBFs participating in a syndicate have brokerage subsidiaries that can sell stock on a retail level. Others may specialize in underwriting but still utilize a group of brokerage firms to sell the newly issued stock. The brokers earn a commission on the amount they sell but do not guarantee a specific amount of sales.

When a corporation publicly places stock, it incurs two types of **flotation costs,** or costs of placing the securities. First, the underwriting spread is paid to the underwriters, who guarantee the issuing firm a set price for the stock. Second, **issue costs** from issuing stock include printing, legal, registration, and accounting expenses. Because these issue costs are not significantly affected by the size of the issue, flotation costs as a percentage of the value of securities issued is lower for larger issues.

ADVISING. The IBF acts as an advisor throughout the origination stage as to the various terms of the stock. Even after the stock is issued, the IBF may continue to provide advice on the timing, amount, and terms of future financing. Included within this advice would be recommendations on the appropriate type of financing (bonds, stocks, or long-term commercial loans).

How Investment Banks Facilitate New Bond Issues

The IBF's role for placing bonds is somewhat similar to the placement of stock. The four main services of the IBF as related to the placement of bonds are explained in turn.

ORIGINATION. The IBF may suggest a maximum amount of bonds that should be issued, based on the issuer's characteristics. If the issuer already has a high level of outstanding debt, the issuance of bonds may not be well received by the market, because the issuer's ability to meet the debt payments would be questionable. Consequently, the bonds would need to offer a relatively high yield, which reflects a high cost of borrowing to the issuer.

Next, the coupon rate, the maturity, and other provisions are decided, based on the characteristics of the issuing firm. The asking price on the bonds will be influenced by evaluating market prices of existing bonds that are similar in their degree of risk, term to maturity, and other provisions.

Issuers of bonds must register with the SEC. The registration statement contains information about the bonds to be issued, states the agreement between the IBF and the issuer, and also contains a prospectus with financial information about the issuer.

UNDERWRITING BONDS. Some issuers of bonds, particularly public utilities, may solicit competitive bids from various IBFs on the price of bonds so as to select the IBF with the highest bid. However, IBFs provide several services to the issuer, so price is not the only consideration. Corporations typically select an IBF based on reputation rather than competitive bids.

Underwriting spreads on newly issued bonds are normally lower than on newly issued stock, because bonds can often be placed in large blocks to financial institutions. Conversely, a stock issue must be segmented into smaller pieces, and is more difficult to sell.

As with stocks, the IBF may organize an underwriting syndicate of IBFs to participate in the placement of the bonds. Each IBF assumes a portion of the risk. Of course, the potential income earned by the original IBF is reduced, too. If the IBF is uncomfortable in guaranteeing a price to the issuer, it may offer only a best-efforts agreement rather than underwriting the bonds.

DISTRIBUTION OF BONDS. Upon SEC approval of registration, a prospectus is distributed to all potential purchasers of the bonds, and the issue is advertised to the public. If demand is sufficient, the asking price may be reduced to assure a sale of the entire issue. The flotation costs generally range from .5 to 3 percent of the value of bonds issued, which can be significantly lower than the flotation costs of issuing common or preferred stock.

ADVISING. As with the placement of stock, IBFs that place bonds for issuers may serve as an advisor to the issuer even after placement is completed. Most issuers of bonds will need to raise long-term funds in the future and will consider the IBF's advice on the type of securities to issue at that time.

How Investment Banks Facilitate Private Placements

If an issuing corporation knows of a potential purchaser for its entire issue, it might be able to sell its securities directly without offering the bonds to the general public (or using the underwriting services of the IBF). This so-called **private placement** (or *direct placement*) avoids the underwriting fee. Corporations have been increasingly using private placements. Potential purchasers of securities that are large enough to buy an entire issue include insurance companies, commercial banks, pension funds, and mutual funds. Securities could even be privately placed with two or more of these institutions. A private placement is more common for the issuance of bonds than for stocks.

The price paid for privately placed securities is determined by negotiations between the issuing corporation and purchaser. While the IBF is not needed here for underwriting, it may advise the issuing corporation on the appropriate terms of the securities and identify potential purchasers.

The provisions within a privately placed issue can be tailored to the desires of the purchaser, unlike the standardized provisions of a publicly placed issue. A possible disadvantage of a private placement is that the demand may not be as strong as for a publicly placed issue, since only a fraction of the market is targeted. This could force a lower price for the bonds, resulting in a higher cost of financing for the issuing firm.

BROKERAGE SERVICES

Customer requests for brokerage firms to execute securities transactions can usually be classified as one of the following:

- Market orders
- Limit orders
- Short-selling

Each is discussed in turn.

Market Orders

Requests by customers to purchase or sell securities at the market price existing when the order reaches the exchange floor are called **market orders.** In most cases, the actual transaction will occur within an hour from the time of request by the customer, assuming that the request was made while the markets are open.

Performance of Brokerage Firm Portfolios

Brokerage firms not only advise clients on which stocks to buy or sell but also manage their own portfolios of funds. A study by CDA Investment Technologies Inc. evaluated the three-year performance of these portfolios and found that the brokerage-affiliated money managers were generally outperformed by the average money manager and the Standard and Poor's 500 Index. A related study conducted by Mercer-Meidinger-Hansen Inc. over a five-year period found that the brokerage-affiliated money managers slightly outperformed the average money manager but, again, were outperformed by the Standard and Poor's 500 Index. The brokerage firms may suggest that these results are not conclusive because the money portfolios they manage are not necessarily composed of the securities that they recommend to their clients. In fact, money managers of brokerage firms often subscribe to a variety of outside research publications, suggesting that they do not make portfolio decisions solely on the basis of in-house recommendations.

SOURCE: John R. Dorfman, "Issues Brokers Buy Often Don't Do Well," *The Wall Street Journal*, April 24, 1987, 13.

Limit Orders

Requests by customers to purchase or sell securities at a specified price or better are called **limit orders.** Specialists of an exchange are responsible for monitoring limit orders and executing the transactions in accordance with the limits specified. Some limit orders are cancelled if they are not executed within one day. Other limit orders will remain until they are executed or cancelled by the customer. Some investors order a sale of securities when the price reaches a specified minimum. This is referred to as a **stop-loss order.** If the price were to remain above the specified minimum, the securities would not be sold.

Short Selling

Investors can speculate on expectations of a decline in securities prices by **short selling,** or selling securities that they do not own. For example, an investor who anticipated that the price of Exxon stock would decline could request a short sale of Exxon stock from a broker. The broker would borrow the stock from an inventory of stocks held on margin (from other accounts) and sell it for the investor. The investor is required to deposit funds that reflect the market value of the stock. At some point in the future, the investor would request a purchase of the stock and repays the broker for the stock borrowed. If the stock price declined by the time the investor requested the purchase, the short-sale strategy would generate a positive return. Short-sellers are required to reimburse the owners of the stock for any missed dividends.

Full-Service versus Discount Brokerage Services

The brokerage business can be classified as either **full-service,** in which information and advice is provided, or discount, in which securities transactions are executed upon request. Discount brokerage firms have about 20 percent of retail brokerage business. They are often unable to maintain a long-term relationship with clients because they provide a service difficult to differentiate from competitors. Full-service brokerage firms provide a more personalized advisory service.

While discount brokers still concentrate on executing stock transactions, they recently expanded their services to include precious metals, options, and municipal bonds. Some also offer credit cards, cash management accounts, twenty-four-hour phone service, and research reports.

Many discount brokerage firms are owned by large commercial banks, which have historically been prohibited from offering full-service brokerage services. For example, Security Pacific offers a large discount brokerage service and has even set up brokerage branches in some J.C. Penney stores. Since 1983 Chase Manhattan Corporation has owned Rose & Company, a large discount brokerage firm. Bank America owned Charles Schwab & Company until Schwab bought his company back.

Brokerage Firm Dilemma: Diversity versus Concentration of Services

Over the last several years, brokerage firms have diversified into a variety of businesses. In 1973, 55 percent of brokerage firm revenues were attributed to commissions. Over time, they have relied less on commission income and more on their own investment portfolios. January 1987 commissions represented less than 21 percent of revenues.

As various financial institutions have begun to offer new services, many brokerage firms have considered reducing their diversity of businesses. For example, Salomon Brothers announced its intentions to discontinue its business of placing municipal bonds and commercial paper prior to the stock market crash. Shearson Lehman Brothers, E. F. Hutton, Morgan Stanley, Goldman Sachs, and Drexel Burnham Lambert announced plans to lay off employees before the crash. Subsequent to the crash, Shearson Lehman merged with E. F. Hutton, and their combined workforce was reduced significantly in an attempt to increase efficiency.

INTERACTION OF SECURITIES FIRMS WITH OTHER FINANCIAL INSTITUTIONS

Securities firms commonly interact with various types of financial institutions as summarized in Exhibit 25.1. They offer investment advice and execute security transactions for financial institutions that maintain security portfolios. They also compete against those financial institutions with brokerage subsidiaries. The following examples illustrate how brokerage firms and other types of financial institutions interact:

■ In 1987 Shearson Lehman sold a 13 percent interest to Nippon Life Insurance Company of Japan.

EXHIBIT 25.1 Interaction between Securities Firms and Other Financial Institutions

Type of Financial Institution	Interaction with Securities Firms
Commercial banks and savings institutions	■ Securities firms compete with those commercial banks and savings institutions that provide brokerage services. ■ Those commercial banks that underwrite commercial paper or provide advice on mergers and acquisitions compete directly with securities firms. ■ In countries other than the U.S., commercial banks and brokerage firms commonly compete, since regulations do not attempt to separate banking and securities activities. ■ In 1988 securities firms acquired some financially troubled savings institutions.
Mutual funds	■ Securities firms execute trades for mutual funds. ■ Some mutual funds were organized by securities firms.
Insurance companies	■ Securities firms advise portfolio managers of insurance companies on what securities to buy or sell. ■ Securities firms execute securities transactions for insurance companies. ■ Securities firms advise portfolio managers of insurance companies on how to hedge against interest rate risk and stock-market risk. ■ Securities firms underwrite stocks and bonds that are purchased by insurance companies. ■ Securities firms compete with some insurance companies in the sales of some mutual funds to investors. ■ Securities firms obtain financing on LBOs from insurance companies. ■ Securities firms compete with some insurance companies that have developed their own mutual funds. ■ Some securities firms have acquired, or have merged with insurance companies in order to offer more diversified services (Prudential-Bache is an example).
Pension funds	■ Securities firms advise pension fund portfolio managers on securities to purchase or sell. ■ Securities firms execute securities transactions for pension funds. ■ Securities firms advise pension fund portfolio managers on how to hedge against interest rate risk and stock-market risk.

■ In 1987 Home-Group, an insurance company, acquired Gruntal Financial Corporation, a brokerage firm.

■ In 1987 Paine Webber sold an 18 percent equity interest to Yasuda Mutual Life Insurance Company.

■ In 1987 Primerica Corporation, a financial services firm, acquired Smith Barney, Harris Upham & Company.

Because securities firms commonly offer banking and insurance services, while many insurance companies and commercial banks offer securities services, it is sometimes difficult to distinguish among financial institutions.

Competition between Securities Firms and Commercial Banks

Commercial banks can compete against securities firms by offering discount brokerage services—for fees typically from 40 to 70 percent less than full-service fees. Of course, they still must compete with discount brokerage firms. They can offer such discount services by either acquiring a discount brokerage firm or creating a subsidiary to perform the services. If they opt for the latter course, they face the up-front costs of organizing the operations and training new personnel. In addition, an initial promotional effort is necessary, whereas in an acquisition, the bank could continue to use the acquired firm's name and reputation for the brokerage business.

Still another method is to purchase brokerage services from a registered brokerage firm. In this case, the bank simply acts as an intermediary between customers and the brokerage firm. It normally receives the transactions and communicates the information to the brokerage firm, which executes the transaction. It may even provide customers with a toll-free number that is answered with the name of the bank, so that customers will believe the brokerage operation is run by the bank. In this arrangement, the bank promotes the service and receives a portion of the commissions generated—the portion being determined by the degree of work (regarding custodial services, mailing periodic statements, etc.) the bank is responsible for.

The Glass-Steagall Act of 1933 separated the functions of commercial banks and investment banking firms, allowing commercial banks to underwrite general obligation municipal bonds but generally prohibiting them from other securities activities. However, in recent years commercial banks have acquired brokerage subsidiaries and have served in an advisory capacity for mergers and acquisitions. As of 1987 commercial banks were allowed to underwrite commercial paper. Since then, they have not only offered advice on mergers and acquisitions and on private placements of securities, but have also served as an intermediary for interest rate swaps and currency swaps. In these ways, they compete directly with securities firms.

PARTICIPATION OF SECURITIES FIRMS IN FINANCIAL MARKETS

Securities firms participate in all types of financial markets as summarized in Exhibit 25.2. Their investment banking divisions participate in the primary markets by placing newly issued securities, while the brokerage divisions concentrate mostly on executing secondary market transactions for investors. Both the investment banking and brokerage divisions serve as advisors to financial market participants.

EXHIBIT 25.2 Participation of Securities Firms in Financial Markets

Type of Financial Market	Participation by Securities Firms
Money markets	■ Some securities firms, such as Merrill Lynch, have created money market mutual funds, which invest in money market securities. ■ Securities firms underwrite commercial paper and purchase short-term securities for their own investment portfolios.
Bond markets	■ Securities firms underwrite bonds in the primary market, advise clients on bonds to purchase or sell, and serve as brokers for bond transactions in the secondary market. ■ Some bond mutual funds have been created by securities firms. ■ Securities firms facilitate mergers, acquisitions, and LBOs by placing bonds for their clients. ■ Securities firms purchase bonds for their own investment portfolios.
Mortgage markets	■ Securities firms place securities that are backed by mortgages for various financial institutions.
Stock markets	■ Securities firms underwrite stocks in the primary market, advise clients on what stocks to purchase or sell, and serve as brokers for stock transactions in the secondary market. ■ Securities firms purchase stocks for their own investment portfolios.
Futures markets	■ Securities firms advise large financial institutions on how to hedge their portfolios with financial futures contracts. ■ Securities firms serve as brokers for financial futures transactions.
Options markets	■ Securities firms advise large financial institutions on how to hedge portfolios with options contracts. ■ Securities firms serve as brokers for options transactions.

INTERNATIONALIZATION OF THE BROKERAGE BUSINESS

INTERNATIONAL

ASPECTS

Since 1986 many securities firms have increased their presence in foreign countries. In October 1986 the so-called Big Bang allowed for deregulation in the United Kingdom. With the commission structure competitive instead of fixed, British securities firms recognized that they would have to rely more on other services, as commission income would be reduced by competitive forces. Commercial banks from the United States have established investment banking subsidiaries overseas, where regulations do not attempt to separate banking and securities activities.

Most large securities firms have established a presence in foreign markets. For example, Morgan Stanley has offices in Frankfurt, London, Melbourne, Sydney, Tokyo, and Zurich. Merrill Lynch has 523 offices spread across the United States and numerous other countries. The effort of securities firms to become internationalized is due to the following possible advantages. First, their international presence allows them to place securities in various markets for corporations or governments. Second, some corporations that are heavily involved with international mergers and acquisitions prefer advice from securities firms that have subsidiaries in all potential markets. Third, institutional investors that invest in foreign securities prefer securities firms that can easily handle such transactions.

The Japanese government recently allowed foreign securities firms to enter its markets. Merrill Lynch, Morgan Stanley, Goldman Sachs, and other non-Japanese securities firms from other countries acquired seats on the Tokyo Stock Exchange. As of December 1987 the Tokyo Stock Exchange announced that it would allow 16 other firms to acquire a seat, including First Boston, Prudential-Bache, and Shearson Lehman. Yet, there are still explicit and implicit barriers to entry or at least limits on the degree of penetration by non-Japanese firms. Some securities firms complain that restrictions are excessive or vague. While Japanese securities firms enter other financial markets, non-Japanese securities firms account for less than 3 percent of transactions in the Tokyo Stock Exchange. Certainly many Japanese securities firms have entered U.S. markets. For example, Nomura Securities and Daiwa Securities have become primary dealers of U.S. government securities. In addition, other Japanese financial institutions have made large equity investments in U.S. securities firms such as Goldman Sachs, Paine Webber, and Shearson Lehman.

SUMMARY

Securities firms offer investment banking services to facilitate primary market transactions and brokerage services to facilitate secondary market transactions. They play a critical role in transferring funds from firms and individuals with excess funds to those with deficient funds. U.S. regulations have historically separated securities activities from activities offered by other financial institutions. However, various financial institutions now offer services that compete directly with securities firms. As regulations are either eliminated or reduced, the securities industry will become even more competitive.

KEY TERMS

best-efforts agreement	**full-service**
bridge loans	**issue costs**
flotation costs	**limit orders**

market orders
private placement
prospectus
registration statement

short selling
stop-loss order
underwriting spread
underwriting syndicate

QUESTIONS

25.1. Explain the role of the SEC, NASD, and security exchanges in regulating the securities industry.

25.2. What is the purpose of the SIPC?

25.3. Why are investment banks that are more capable of raising funds in the capital markets preferred by corporations that need advising on a proposed acquisition?

25.4. How do investment banks facilitate leveraged buyouts?

25.5. Describe the origination process for corporations that are about to issue new stock.

25.6. Describe the underwriting function of an investment bank.

25.7. What is the best-efforts agreement?

25.8. Describe the flotation costs incurred by a corporation that issues stock.

25.9. Compare flotation costs of issuing bonds versus stock. Which are higher?

25.10. Describe a direct placement of bonds. What is an advantage of a private placement? What is a disadvantage?

25.11. Describe new services recently offered by discount brokers.

25.12. Explain why securities firms from the United States have expanded into foreign markets.

PROJECT

1. ASSESSING A SECURITIES FIRM'S OPERATIONS.

Obtain a recent annual report of a securities firm of your choice or one assigned by your professor, and answer the following questions:

a. Describe the securities firm's operations. Does it appear to focus on investment banking activities or brokerage activities?

b. Describe the securities firm's performance in recent years. Offer possible reasons for the change in performance over the last few years.

c. Has the securities firm expanded into new foreign markets in recent years? If so, why?

d. Summarize any information offered on the impact of the stock market crash of 1987 on this securities firm.

e. Does the securities firm plan to diversify into more services in the future or to concentrate on a few key services? Elaborate.

REFERENCES

Chu, Franklin J., "The Myth of Global Investment Banking" *Bankers Magazine* (January–February 1988): 58–61.

Conner, Daryl R. and Byron G. Fiman, "Making the Cultural Transition to Investment Banking," *Bankers Magazine* (January–

February 1988): 31–35.

Dyche, David. "Investment Banking: What Do Banks Need to Compete?," *Bankers Magazine* (March–April 1988): 42–46.

Saunders, Anthony and Michael Smirlock. "Intra- and Inter Industry Effects of Bank Securities Market Activities: The Case of Discount Brokerage." *Journal of Financial and Quantitative Analysis.* (December 1987): 467–482.

Shapiro, Harvey D. "The New Look in Private Placements." *Institutional Investor* (May 1983): 145–149.

Pension Funds

PENSION FUNDS IN PERSPECTIVE

Newbold Asset Management of Philadelphia serves corporations and governments by managing their pension funds. As of 1988, it was managing more than $3 billion in pension fund assets. Its management of pension fund assets has been ranked highly in 1987 and 1988 by *Institutional Investor Magazine*. Newbold has twelve portfolio manager-analysts who search for stocks which have low price-earnings (P/E) ratios. Their portfolio composed for any corporate or government pension fund will usually contain 20 to 35 stocks. For the 1983–1987 period, Newbold generated an average annual return of 19.6 percent. Its performance is even more favorable when considering that the stocks it chooses exhibit relatively low risk.

Newbold's management fee is one half of 1 percent of the first $20 million and is scaled down for amounts exceeding $20 million. Its clients include the State of Illinois, Philadelphia Electric Company and Syntex Corporation. It has recently added Cooper Tire & Rubber, Farmland Industries, Louisville Gas & Electric, Sterling Drug, Chicago Transit, the city of Gainesville, Florida, and Pennsylvania Municipal Employees as clients. With the large amount of funds managed, Newbold is a major participant in the financial markets. Some other well-known and high-performing managers of pension fund assets include J. P. Morgan Investment Management, Mellon Capital Management Corporation, Wells Fargo Investment Advisers, and Sun Bank Investment Management Group.

■ What types of securities are usually purchased with pension funds?
■ What types of risk is a typical pension fund portfolio exposed to?
■ How have pension regulations affected the size and management of pension funds?

These and other related questions are addressed in this chapter.

The information on Newbold was drawn from *Institutional Investor*, February 1988, pp. 75–79.

OUTLINE

Pension funds provide a savings plan for employees that can be used for retirement. They serve a critical function in the United States, where the residents save a smaller percentage of their disposable income than residents of most other developed countries. In fact, there is evidence that increases in social security benefits and private pension benefits reduce the saving tendencies of consumers. This tendency, combined with the trend of longer lives, necessitates an organized plan for pre-retirement saving. There is considerable uncertainty as to whether the Social Security System will adequately support future needs, or even continue in the future, so employees are likely to become more dependent on their pensions over time. This chapter gives the background of government and private pension funds and explains their management and regulation.

BACKGROUND ON PENSION FUNDS

Pension plans were used in the late 1800s by the large, regulated transportation companies. By the early 1900s, they were commonly offered by commercial banks, utility companies, mining companies, government agencies, and unions. However, they were severely affected by the Great Depression, as many companies were unable to provide the benefits they promised. Due to substantial layoffs, contributions were low. Consequently, companies tightened their requirements for employees to qualify for a pension and reduced pension benefits. Some even abolished them.

The credibility of pension plans began to develop slowly after the Great Depression. They became especially important during World War II, as the Wage Stabilization Program prevented firms from offering high salaries in the tight labor market, so fringe benefits such as a good pension plan were necessary to attract labor. Then, during the Korean War in the early 1950s, wage and price controls were imposed, again enhancing the appeal of a good pension plan. In the 1960s and 1970s, a broader variety of such plans were created.

All pension funds receive premiums from the employer and/or the employee. In aggregate, most of the contributions come from the employer. Public pension funds can be either state and local, or federal. The most well-known government pension fund is social security. In addition to that system, all government employees and almost half of all non-government employees participate in other pension funds.

Many public pension plans are funded on a pay-as-you-go basis. At some point, the strategy could cause the future benefits owed to outweigh contributions to an extent that either prevents the pension funds from fulfilling their promises or requires more contributions. This underfunding is potentially dangerous over the long run, as existing employee and employer contributors are essentially supporting previous employees. Some public pension plans have recently attempted to reduce their degree of underfunding.

Private pension plans are created by private agencies, including industrial, labor, service, nonprofit, charitable, and educational organizations. Because some pension funds are so large, they represent major investors in corporate securities. For example, the pension funds of some major corporations were valued as of July 1987 as follows:

Firm	Value of Pension Fund
Lockheed	$ 7.0 billion
Xerox	2.7 billion
Bell Atlantic	11.0 billion
General Motors	32.0 billion
Honeywell	1.8 billion
International Paper	1.7 billion

The total value of private pension fund assets is $916 billion, matching the combined asset value of all finance companies, mutual savings banks, and credit unions. According to a recent survey,[1] U.S. corporations spend an average of almost 40 percent of their payroll on benefits. Another recent survey[2] found that more than two-thirds of large corporations have overseas pension plans. Sixty percent of the corporations that responded to the survey now give more attention to management of these plans.

Exhibit 26.1 shows that in recent years, private pension plan benefits have exceeded contributions, as assets continued to grow because of the large capital gains earned during the stock market boom of the 1980s. The market value of many pension fund portfolios experienced an abrupt decline during the stock market crash in October 1987.

TYPES OF PRIVATE PENSION PLANS

Private pension funds can be classified by the manner in which contributions are received and benefits are paid. For a **defined-benefit plan,** contributions

1 See Solveigh Jansson, "Why Talk is No Longer Cheap," *Institutional Investor* (October 1986): 255–262.
2 See "A New Focus on Overseas Plans," *Institutional Investor* (July 1986): 109–112.

EXHIBIT 26.1   Comparison of Pension Fund Contributions and Benefits

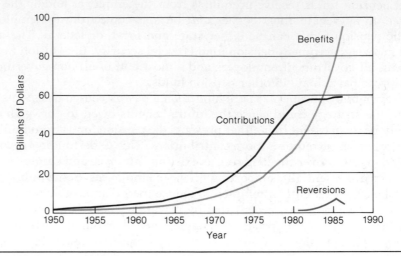

SOURCE: *New England Economic Review*, Federal Reserve Bank of Boston (November–December 1987): 5.

are dictated by the benefits that will eventually be provided. When the value of pension assets exceeds the current and future benefits owed to employees, companies respond by reducing future contributions. Alternatively, they may distribute the surplus amount to the firm's shareholders rather than the employees. Thus, the management of the pension fund can have a direct impact on shareholders. Over the early and mid 1980s the asset values of the most defined-benefit pension funds have increased substantially more than the required benefit payment.

As an alternative to the defined benefit plan, a **defined-contribution plan** provides benefits that are determined by the accumulated contributions and return on the fund's investment performance. This type of plan allows a firm to know with certainty the amount of funds to contribute, whereas that amount is undetermined in the defined-benefit plan until the return is known. However, the defined-contribution plan provides uncertain benefits to the participants.

As shown in Exhibit 26.2, there are more defined-contribution plans than defined-benefit plans. However, there are more participants in defined-benefit plans, and the aggregate value of assets of defined-benefit plans is greater. New plans allow employees more flexibility to choose what they want. In recent years, the defined-benefit plan has been commonly replaced by the defined-contribution plan. Employees can often decide the pace of their contributions and how their contributions should be invested. Communications from the benefits coordinator to the employees has become much more important, since employees now have more influence on their pension plan contributions and the investment approach used to invest the premiums.

EXHIBIT 26.2 Participation in Private Pension Plans

	Defined-Benefit	Defined-Contribution	Total
Number of plans	223,200	551,800	775,000
Percentage of total plans	28.8%	71.2%	100%
Participants	41,000,000	32,900,000	73,900,000
Percentage of total participants	55.5%	44.5%	100%
Total assets	$836.8 billion	$458 billion	$1,295.1 billion
Percentage of total assets	64.6%	35.4%	100%

SOURCE: Board of Governors of the Federal Reserve System; Flow of Funds Accounts; U.S. Department of Labor; and *New England Economic Review*, Federal Reserve Bank of Boston (November–December 1987): 4. The estimate of participants is based on 1984 data.

PENSION FUND MANAGEMENT

Regardless of the manner in which premiums are contributed, the premiums received must be managed (invested) until needed to pay benefits. Some pension funds attempt to use a **matched funding** strategy in which investment decisions are made with the objective of generating cash flows that match planned outflow payments. An alternative strategy is **projective funding,** which offers managers more flexibility in constructing a pension portfolio that can benefit from expected market and interest rate movements. Some pension fund portfolios may be segmented to satisfy some matched funding, leaving the rest of the portfolio for projective funding.

An informal method of matched funding is to invest in long-term bonds to fund long-term liabilities, and intermediate bonds to fund intermediate liabilities. The appeal of matching is the assurance that the future liabilities are covered regardless of market movements. However, it limits the manager's discretion, allowing only investments that match future payouts. For example, portfolio managers required to use matched funding would need to avoid callable bonds, since these bonds could potentially be retired before maturity. This precludes consideration of many high-yield bonds. In addition, each liability payout may require a separate investment to which it can be perfectly matched, which requires several small investments and increases the pension's transaction costs.

Management of Insured versus Trust Portfolios

The management of some pensions is performed by life insurance companies. Contributions for these plans, called **insured plans,** are often used to purchase annuity policies, so that the life insurance companies can provide benefits to employees upon retirement.

As an alternative, some pension funds are managed by the trust departments of financial institutions. Contributions are invested by the trust, and benefits are paid to employees upon retirement. While the day-to-day investment decisions of a trust are controlled by the managing institution, the corporation owning the pension normally specifies general guidelines that the institution should follow. These guidelines might include the percentage of the portfolio that should be used for stocks or bonds, a desired minimum rate of return on the overall portfolio, the maximum amount to be invested in real estate, the minimum acceptable quality ratings for bonds, the maximum amount to be invested in any one industry, the average maturity of bonds held in the portfolio, the maximum amount to be invested in options, and minimum size of companies to invest in.

Corporations may be willing to pay commercial banks to manage their funds because they have trust departments that specialize in the management of pension portfolios. Some corporations prefer to split their pension portfolio among the trusts of several different commercial banks. In this way, the overall portfolio is less sensitive to the investment performance of a single trust department. Such an allocation system also allows the corporation to monitor each trust department performance by comparison to the other trust departments.

There is a significant difference between the asset composition of pension portfolios managed by life insurance companies versus trusts. Assets managed by insurance companies are designed to create annuities, whereas the assets managed by the trust departments still belong to the corporation. The insurance company becomes legal owner of the assets and is allowed to maintain only a small portion of its assets as equities. Therefore insurance companies concentrate on bonds and mortgages. Conversely, the pension portfolios managed by trusts concentrate on corporate stock.

Pension portfolios managed by trusts offer potentially higher returns than the insured plans and also have a higher degree of risk. The average return of trust plans is much more volatile over time, as illustrated in Exhibit 26.3. The return trend is patterned after the stock market.

EXHIBIT 26.3 Returns of Pension Plans Managed by Life Insurance Companies versus Trusts

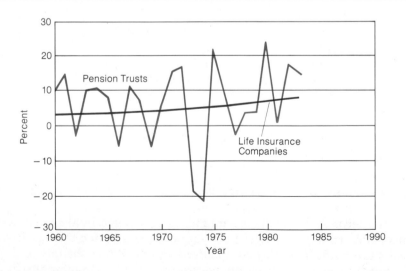

SOURCE: Board of Governors of the Federal Reserve System; U.S. Department of Commerce; Bureau of Economic Analysis; American Life Insurance Corporation; and *Economic Commentary*, Federal Reserve Bank of Cleveland, February 16, 1986.

Pension Fund Reaction to the Situation in South Africa

A recent survey by *Institutional Investor* of pension fund managers was conducted to determine the reaction to the situation in South Africa. Some of the more relevant results are as follows:

■ Only 2.7 percent of the respondents believed that they were under pressure by shareholders, employees, or other groups to sell securities of South African companies.

■ 11.6 percent of the respondents have given serious consideration to selling these security holdings.

■ 5.5 percent of the respondents expected that they would sell some of these security holdings.

■ 62.7 percent of the respondents believe that the avoidance of the securities issued by South African companies would impair the pension fund's performance.

Pension fund managers that have not considered selling these security holdings were asked to explain why (more than one explanation was sometimes offered by each respondent):

■ 32.5 percent of the respondents said that they are unwilling to jeopardize performance

■ 16.7 percent of the respondents said that costs of managerial turnover and portfolio revision would be too high.

■ 42.9 percent of the respondents believe that ethical considerations should not be a part of the investment decision.

■ 49.2 percent of the respondents believe that the involvement of U.S. companies in South Africa will be beneficial in the long run.

SOURCE: *Institutional Investor* (March 1986): 101–102.

Only a small fraction of pension trust funds is used to purchase mortgages. Commercial bank trust departments that manage these trusts are much more acclamated to the trading of stocks and bonds and are not as comfortable with mortgages or mortgage-backed securities. The risk-return characteristics of mortgages and mortgage-backed securities are quite similar to those of Treasury or high-grade corporate bonds. Since trust portfolios already contain these bonds, additional investment in mortgages and mortgage-backed securities may not necessarily reduce the portfolio's interest rate risk.

Some pension funds have begun to invest in leveraged buyouts (LBOs). Because an LBO is mostly financed with borrowed funds, the returns to the business are distributed among a relatively small group of shareholders. While the potential returns from such an investment are much higher than conventional pension fund investments, the risk is also much higher. There is some question as to whether pension fund portfolio managers should be investing funds in such a risky manner, given that some employees rely on these funds for retirement income. Yet, pension fund managers could counter that the conventional investment in stocks is also subject to considerable downside risk.

Chapter 26

Pension Funds

681

Management of Private versus State and Local Government Portfolios

Exhibit 26.4 shows the changing composition of private pension portfolios over time. Common stock has consistently dominated. Since the late 1970s, credit market instruments other than bonds (such as mortgages) have consistently represented the second largest component, followed by corporate bonds.

Exhibit 26.5 shows the changing composition of state and local government pension funds over time. While all components have grown, credit market instruments have increased most rapidly, surpassing corporate stock holdings in 1978 and corporate bond holdings in 1984. In comparison to private pension funds, the state and local government pension funds tend to concentrate more on credit market instruments and less on corporate stock.

Management of Defined-Benefit versus Defined-Contribution Portfolios

Exhibit 26.6 compares the asset composition of defined-benefit plans versus defined-contribution plans. The latter contain a greater percentage of bonds than the former. Both types of plans allocate the majority of their funds to stocks and bonds.

EXHIBIT 26.4   Trends in Key Assets of Private Pension Funds

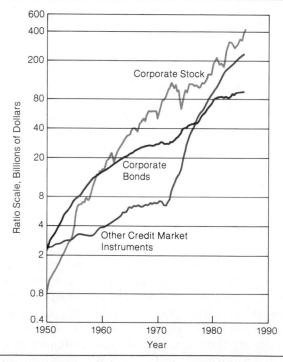

SOURCE: *1987 Federal Reserve Chart Book.*

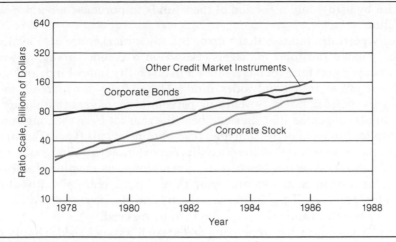

SOURCE: *1987 Federal Reserve Chart Book.*

EXPOSURE OF PENSION FUND PORTFOLIOS TO RISK

Pension fund portfolio managers are very concerned about interest rate risk. If they hold long-term, fixed-rate bonds, the market value of their portfolio will decrease during periods when interest rates increase. To reduce interest rate risk, pension portfolio managers have recently reduced their average maturity on fixed-rate bonds.

Pension funds that are willing to accept "market" returns on bonds can purchase bond index portfolios that have been created by investment companies. The bond index portfolio may include investment-grade corporate bonds, Treasury bonds, and U.S. government agency bonds. It does not include the entire set of these bonds, but enough (200 or so) of them to

EXHIBIT 26.6   Composition of Assets in Defined-Benefit and
Defined-Contribution Plans

	Percentage of Assets in:	
	Defined-Contribution Plans	*Defined-Benefit Plans*
Stocks	37.2%	40.5%
Bonds	38.2	31.1
Cash	6.9	7.3
Mortgages and other	17.7	21.1
	100.0%	100.0%

SOURCE: Board of Governors of the Federal Reserve System; Flow of Fund Accounts; U.S. Bureau of the Census; U.S. Department of Labor; and *England Economic Review,* Federal Reserve Bank of Boston (November–December 1987): 4.

mirror market performance. Investing in a market portfolio is a passive approach that does not require any analysis of individual bonds. Some pension funds are not willing to accept a totally passive approach, so compromise by using only a portion of their funds to purchase a bond market portfolio.

Equity portfolio indexes that mirror the stock market are also available for the passive portfolio managers. Based on a recent survey, about 18 percent of pension fund managers invest in an equity index fund, and about 4 percent invest in a bond index fund.[3] This reflects an increase in the popularity of index funds. Seventy-six percent of managers that do not use index funds suggested that they can beat the market over the long run.

Portfolio managers of pension funds can obtain various types of insurance to limit the downside risk of the portfolio. For example, a policy could insure beyond a specified decline (such as 10 percent) in the asset value of a pension fund. This insurance allows managers to use more aggressive investment strategies. The cost of the insurance depends on the provisions of the contract and length of time the portfolio is to be insured.

The pension funds for some companies, such as Lockheed, simply concentrate investment in stocks and bonds and do not employ immunization techniques (to hedge the portfolio against risk). Lockheed has generally focused on highly liquid investments so that the proportion of stocks and bonds within the portfolio can be revised in response to market conditions.

Other pension funds use a more aggressive approach. For example, Eastman Kodak's pension fund portfolio includes real estate, oil and gas, and leveraged buyouts. General Motors' pension fund portfolio includes venture capital, and international securities. The pension fund portfolio of Xerox Corporation includes venture capital and junk bonds.

PENSION PORTFOLIO EVALUATION

Pension portfolio performance is generally very susceptible to market conditions. Thus, the difference in returns over time is more likely to result from changes in market conditions than from a change in managerial expertise. To assess performance over a particular period, a benchmark is needed, as shown in the following example.

Assume that a manager of Spartan Pension Fund was required to maintain a portfolio of 60 percent bonds and 40 percent stocks. The performance of this portfolio may be compared to a benchmark portfolio composed of 60 percent times a quoted bond index plus 40 percent times a quoted stock index. The risk-adjusted returns of the portfolio can be compared to the risk-adjusted returns of the benchmark portfolio. Methods used to measure risk-adjusted returns were described in Chapter 8. As an example, the Sharpe Index of a Pension portfolio could be measured as

$$\text{Sharpe Index} = \frac{R_p - R_f}{SD_p}$$

3 See "The Abiding Faith in Active Management," *Institutional Investor* (May 1986): 97–100.

Life of a Pension Fund Portfolio Manager

Managers of pension funds determine the portfolio composition of available funds. They must remain within any guidelines imposed by the sponsoring corporation on a private pension fund or by the government agency of concern on a public pension fund. In some cases, a pension fund is managed by various portfolio managers, each assigned a subset of a portfolio (such as stocks of small companies, long-term bonds, etc.).

Managers use a variety of information to make their portfolio decisions. They are overloaded with free, sometimes daily, information from all the major securities firms, which hope that the managers will use their brokerage services when the pension fund portfolio is to be restructured. Given the relatively large trade orders by pension funds, a single trade will normally generate thousands of dollars in commissions to the investment company. While managers could reduce transaction costs by using a discount brokerage service, they would not receive advice. The advice from full-service securities firms may be in the form of mailed information or even through personal meetings with head advisors of these companies.

Portfolio managers have access to computers to use their time efficiently. Computer terminals show current stock prices of any selected stocks, as well as all news issues and articles that relate to any selected companies. Other terminals are available for screening the entire population of available stocks (to aid selection of those that satisfy a variety of requirements). For example, the portfolio manager may presently wish to consider investment in companies that can meet specific guidelines on the price/earnings ratio, liquidity ratio, and so on. The terminal can, within seconds, identify the list of companies that meet these requirements.

The performance of pension fund managers is sometimes assessed on a short-term basis. This creates a dilemma for them, since the nature of the portfolio is to provide long-run benefits to the employees. Consequently, the risk-return preferences of a pension fund's portfolio managers can differ from those of the employees that the pension fund represents, and this may explain the frequent shifting in the portfolio composition of pension funds. Some pension fund managers may be mostly concerned with short-term goals that would enhance their employment marketability rather than long-run goals suited toward the employees that contribute to the pension funds.

where R_p = average return of pension portfolio over all periods,
R_f = average risk-free rate over all periods
SD_p = standard deviation of pension portfolio returns

If a portfolio beta is thought to be a more appropriate risk proxy than the standard deviation, the Treynor Index would be a more acceptable measure of risk-adjusted returns (see Chapter 8).

If a manager has the flexibility to adjust the relative proportion of stocks versus bonds, the portfolio performance should be compared to a benchmark that would likely have represented a passive strategy. For example,

Chapter 26

Pension Funds

assume that the general long-run plan is a balance of 60 percent bonds and 40 percent stocks. Also assume that management decided to create a more bond-intensive portfolio in anticipation of lower interest rates. The risk-adjusted returns on this actively managed portfolio could be compared to a benchmark portfolio composed of 60 percent times a bond index plus 40 percent times a stock index.

Any difference between the performance of the pension portfolio and the benchmark portfolio would result from (1) the manager's shift in relative proportion of bonds versus stocks and (2) the composition of bonds and stocks within their respective portfolios. A pension portfolio could conceivably have stocks that outperform the stock index and bonds that outperform the bond index, yet be outperformed by the benchmark portfolio when the shift in the relative bond/stock proportion backfires. In this example, a period of rising interest rates could have caused the pension portfolio to be outperformed by the benchmark portfolio.

In many cases, the performance of stocks and bonds in a pension fund are evaluated separately. Stock portfolio risk is usually measured by the portfolio's beta, or the sensitivity to movements in a stock index (such as the S&P 500). Bond portfolio risk can be measured by the bond portfolio's sensitivity to a bond index or to a particular proxy for interest rates.

PENSION REGULATIONS

The regulations of pension funds vary with the type of plan. For defined-contribution plans, the sponsoring firm's only responsibility is its contributions to the fund. The primary government regulation is the set of Internal Revenue Service tax rules that apply to pension fund income. Regulations on defined-benefit plans, however, require the sponsoring firm to provide the benefits specified.

Before 1974 private pension funds were criticized for unfair treatment of participants. For example, some pension plans required 25 straight years of continuous service in order to be vested and therefore qualify for their pension. Any time short of the specified number of years resulted in no pension at all. Another criticism was that some companies were under-funded and consequently unable to provide the benefits promised to employees at the time of retirement.

A third criticism was that most pension plans had committed to a fixed amount of benefits, so that above average growth of the portfolio value offered no additional pension benefits to employees, while very poor performance could cause benefits to fall short of what was originally promised. Under these conditions, employees would naturally prefer more conservative investment decisions by the portfolio managers.

To resolve these problems, the Employee Retirement Income Security Act (ERISA) of 1974 (also called the **Pension Reform Act**) was enacted. It requires three vesting schedule options from which a pension fund could choose:

1. One hundred percent vesting after 10 years of service.
2. Graded vesting, with 25 percent vesting after 5 years of service, increasing 5 percent per year over the next 5 years, and then 10 percent vesting over the following 5 years, reaching 100 percent vesting after 15 years.

3. Fifty percent vesting when a participant's age and years of service sum to 45, increasing by 10 percent per year to 100 percent vesting 5 years later.

These options applied to all employees that worked at least 1,000 hours over the previous year and were at least 25 years of age.

The options were revised as of 1989, to shorten the time necessary to become vested. Corporations were required to choose between these vesting options:

1. One hundred percent vesting after 5 years of service.
2. Graded vesting, with 20 percent vesting in the third year, 40 percent in the fourth, 60 percent in the fifth, 80 percent in the sixth, and 100 percent in the seventh year.

While ERISA's vesting options were revised as shown here, ERISA was responsible for originally specifying the vesting options available to pension funds.

An additional stipulation of ERISA is that any contributions be invested in a "prudent" manner, meaning that pension funds should concentrate their investments in high-grade securities. While this was implicitly expected before, ERISA explicitly acknowledges this so-called *fiduciary responsibility* (monitored by the U.S. Department of Labor) to encourage portfolio managers to serve the interests of the employees rather than themselves. Pension plans can face legal ramifications if they do not oblige.

ERISA also allows employees changing employers to transfer any vested amount into the pension plan of their new employer or to invest it into an *individual retirement account (IRA)*. With either alternative, taxes on the vested amount are still deferred until retirement when the funds become available.

The Pension Benefit Guarantee Corporation

A final result of ERISA was the establishment of the **Pension Benefit Guarantee Corporation (PBGC),** intended to provide insurance on pension plans. This federally chartered agency guarantees participants of defined-benefit pension plans that they will receive their benefits upon retirement. If the pension fund is incapable of fully providing the benefits promised, the PBGC makes up the difference. The PBGC does not receive government support. It is financed by annual premiums, income from assets acquired from terminated plans, and income generated by investments. During 1987 and 1988, it charged participants of defined-benefit plans a premium of $8.50 per year, (increased from $2.60 in April 1986). As of January 1989, it charged participants of private defined-benefit plans a premium of $16. It also receives employer-liability payments when an employer terminates its pension plan.

About 40 million Americans, or one-third of the work force, have pension plans insured by the PBGC. As a wholly owned independent government agency, it differs from other federal regulatory agencies in that it has no regulatory powers. Although it has had negative net worth since its creation in 1974, its cash flow has been sufficient to cover current expenses. By the beginning of 1987, the PBGC's accumulated deficit plus impending terminations was almost $4 billion.

The PBGC monitors pension plans periodically to determine whether they can adequately provide the benefits they have guaranteed. If the plan is judged inadequate, it is terminated and the PBGC (or a PBGC appointee) takes control as the funds manager. The PBGC has a claim on up to 30 percent of a firm's net worth, if needed to support the underfunded pension assets.

While the establishment of PBGC was necessary, there is some concern that its continual intervention may cause it to become underfunded. The value of claims paid out by the PBGC over fiscal years 1975 through 1979 averaged $37.3 million per year. In the following five-year period, the value of claims averaged $129.8 million per year.

The PBGC's funding requirements depend on all the pension funds it monitors. Because the market values of these funds are similarly susceptible to economic conditions, funding requirements are volatile over time. A poor economic environment will force depressed stock prices and simultaneously reduce the asset values of most pension funds. While the Federal Deposit Insurance Corporation (FDIC) and Federal Savings and Loan Insurance Corporation (FSLIC) are in a somewhat similar predicament, these insurance agencies are backed by the full faith and credit of the federal government. The PBGC is not federally backed.

When companies experience problems, they often cut their pension contributions to the minimum funding level established by ERISA. In a sense, the funding of pensions becomes a financing source for firms experiencing cash flow problems. Nevertheless, the obligated benefits to be paid out continue to accumulate (on defined-benefit plans). As an example, in 1981 Allis-Chalmers pension plans were over 60 percent funded. However, the company used minimum funding during the early 1980s, and pension assets declined due to payments to the large retired work force. In 1985, when the PBGC took over, the plan was just 3 percent funded.

The financial burden placed on the PBGC escalated in September 1986, when LTV Corporation terminated one of its pension plans. In January 1987, the PBGC assumed three other LTV pension plans as a result of a federal court ruling. Not only did this substantially increase the PBGC's accumulated deficit, but it also strained cash flow. Consequently, the PBGC has had to liquidate some of its investments to cover current cash outflows.

To resolve the potential problems faced by PBGC, various remedies have been considered to provide additional funding. The increased premiums will beef up the PBGC's pool of available funds. In addition, proposals are being considered to increase the employer's liability if it terminates its pension fund. Laws have been imposed to prevent the dumping of unfunded liabilities on the PBGC. Thus, the amount of support provided by the PBGC may be reduced in the future.

Other Regulatory Aspects

Contributions to pension plans that comply with ERISA are exempt from income taxes until the benefits are paid out. This allows employees to defer income taxes until after retirement when their tax bracket will likely be lower. Any employer contributions are accounted for as a current business expense.

Regulation of public pension plans varies among states. State pension plans must usually adhere to specific state rules and requirements. Some states allow their state pension funds to engage in any "prudent investment," while other states provide an authorized list of approved investments. There has been a general tendency for state pension funds to loosen their investment guidelines. For example, many state pension funds are now authorized to trade options contracts.

Self-employed individuals are unable to utilize pension plans offered by other companies, but they can establish their own pension plan, called a *Keogh plan*. Contributions of a maximum specified amount can be deposited with a depository institution, life insurance company, or securities firm. These institutions manage Keogh plans, but allow the contributor some discretion as to how the funds should be invested.

An additional individual pension plan, mentioned earlier, is the individual retirement account (IRA). A maximum of $2,000 of income per employee ($2,250 if the spouse is unemployed) can be contributed to the IRA per year. As with other pension contributions, this contributed income into an IRA is not taxed until the funds become available after retirement. Any contributions to a Keogh plan or IRA that are withdrawn before age 59½ are subject to a penalty.

IMPACT OF ACCOUNTING AND TAX REVISIONS ON PENSION FUNDS

Recent accounting rule revisions have allowed companies to more quickly recognize gains and losses. These revisions prevent companies from using interest rate assumptions for pension earnings in order to stabilize the reported level of pension fund earnings over time. Consequently, the volatility of pension fund returns may increase. While a thorough discussion of the new rules is beyond the scope of this discussion, it should be noted that the rules could have a significant impact on the portfolio composition of pension funds. Those managers concerned about return volatility may take a more conservative approach to offset the impact of the accounting rule revisions.

The new rules require underfunded pension plans to claim their degree of underfunding as a liability on their balance sheets. This rule is especially relevant to unionized industries that have accommodated collective bargaining requests with the use of pension funds, thereby increasing the degree by which they are underfunded.

Because values of stocks are more volatile than bonds, the asset value of a pension fund composed of stocks is more susceptible to a market downturn. Such a decline could cause underfunding, and the subsequent reporting of it on the balance sheet. Consequently, pension funds may attempt to avoid such a possibility by reducing their proportion of stocks.

Tax reform has had a significant impact on pension plans, as it affects a variety of pension-related tax laws. Income invested into IRAs is tax-deferred only for employees not covered by pension plans. In addition, employees are no longer allowed to withdraw nontaxable (after-tax) contributions made to the IRA before withdrawing taxable (before-tax) contributions. Both types must be simultaneously withdrawn.

Bank Management of Pension Funds

Many commercial banks manage pension funds for corporations and other institutions. However, some banks have begun to divest the investment units that manage pension funds. For example, Manufacturers Hanover Corporation recently sold its investment unit to Paine Webber Inc. In addition, Bank America sold its investment unit, Citicorp has attempted to sell its unit, and some analysts anticipate that Chase Manhattan Corporation and Chemical New York Corporation might also consider selling their units. One of the more common reasons for big banks to sell these units is the need to create additional bank reserves for loan losses. The investment units may be appropriate assets to sell since they generally have not performed as well as expected. The competition in pension fund management is fierce, and banks have been forced to cut their fees. In addition, the salaries of employees who manage the funds are very high. Turnover of employees is also high, since managers often leave banks for higher salaries at securities firms.

The fees for managing individual pensions are usually about 1 percent of the assets managed. Fees for managing institutional pension funds are commonly between .3 percent and .7 percent.

SOURCE: "Some Big Banks Bail Out of Managing Pension Funds as Profits Are Squeezed," *The Wall Street Journal*, January 19, 1988, 10.

INTERACTION OF PENSION FUNDS WITH OTHER FINANCIAL INSTITUTIONS

Exhibit 26.7 illustrates the participation of various financial institutions and markets for managing a pension fund. First, the sponsor corporation decides on a trust pension fund through a commercial bank's trust department or an insured pension fund through an insurance company. The financial institution that is delegated the task of managing the pension fund then receives periodic contributions and invests them. Many investments into the stock, bond, or mortgage markets require the brokerage services of securities firms. Managers of pensions instruct securities firms on the type and amount of investment instruments to purchase. In some cases, the financial institutions may bypass securities firms by purchasing a directly placed new issue of bonds or stocks by a corporation. The premiums contributed to pension funds are ultimately used to provide financing for corporations and governments that issue securities. Exhibit 26.8 summarizes the interaction between pension funds and other financial institutions.

PARTICIPATION OF PENSION FUNDS IN FINANCIAL MARKETS

Because pension fund portfolios are normally dominated by stocks and bonds, the participation of pension fund managers in the stock and bond markets is obvious. Pension fund managers also participate in money and

EXHIBIT 26.7 Use of Financial Institutions and Markets for Managing a Pension Fund

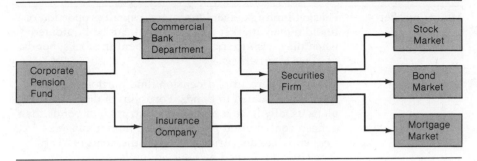

mortgage markets to fill out the remainder of their respective portfolios. They sometimes utilize the futures and options markets as well in order to partially insulate their portfolio performance from interest rate and/or stock market movements. Exhibit 26.9 summarizes how pension fund managers participate in various financial markets.

FOREIGN INVESTMENT BY PENSION FUNDS

Several pension funds allocate a portion of their investment to foreign stocks and bonds. Since they are consequently exposed to exchange rate risk, they sometimes use forward contracts, currency futures contracts, and currency options contracts to hedge their exposure. Some pension funds have taken

INTERNATIONAL

ASPECTS

EXHIBIT 26.8 Interaction between Pension Funds and Other Financial Institutions

Type of Financial Institution	Interaction With Pension Funds
Commercial banks	▪ Commercial banks sometimes manage pension funds.
Insurance companies	▪ Insurance companies sometimes create annuities for pension funds.
Mutual funds	▪ Some pension funds invest in various mutual funds.
Brokerage firms and investment banking firms	▪ Brokerage firms normally execute securities transactions for pension funds. ▪ Brokerage firms offer investment advice to pension portfolio managers. ▪ Investment banking firms commonly act as advisers on leveraged buyouts in which pension funds participate. ▪ Investment banking firms underwrite newly issued stocks and bonds that are purchased by pension funds.

EXHIBIT 26.9 Participation of Pension Funds in Financial Markets

Financial Market	Participation by Pension Funds
Money market	Pension fund managers maintain a small proportion of liquid money market securities that can be liquidated when they wish to increase investment in stocks, bonds, or other alternatives.
Bond market	At least 25 percent of a pension fund portfolio is typically allocated to bonds. Portfolios of defined-benefit plans usually have a higher concentration of bonds than defined-contribution plans. Pension fund managers frequently conduct transactions in the bond market. Since income earned by pension funds is tax-exempt, bond portfolio managers of pension funds usually avoid tax-free municipal bonds.
Mortgage market	Pension portfolios frequently contain some mortgages, although the relative proportion is low compared with bonds and stocks.
Stock market	At least 30 percent of a pension fund portfolio is typically allocated to stocks. In general, defined-contribution plans usually have a higher concentration of stocks than defined-benefit plans.
Futures market	Some pension funds use futures contracts on debt securities and on bond indexes to hedge the exposure of their bond holdings to interest rate risk. In addition, some pension funds use futures on stock indexes to hedge against market risk.
Options market	Some pension funds use stock options to hedge against movements of particular stocks. They may also use options on futures contracts to secure downside protection against stock and/or bond price movements.

positions in currency futures and options for speculative reasons rather than to hedge exposure. The level of pension fund interest in international investing grew during the mid 1980s when the U.S. dollar weakened against major currencies. The exchange rate-adjusted returns on foreign stocks and bonds generally exceeded returns on U.S. securities during this period.

SUMMARY

Pension funds serve as an important source of funds to corporations and governments. Their specific allocation of investment funds is influenced by the type of managing institution (insured plan versus a trust) and the characteristics of the individual portfolio managers. Regulatory reform resulting from ERISA has had significant implications for employers offering pension plans. Many of the ERISA provisions have a favorable impact on employees. A key provision created the Pension Benefit Guarantee Corporation, which guarantees that participants of pension plans will receive benefits.

KEY TERMS

defined-benefit plan
defined-contribution plan
insured plans
matched funding

Pension Benefit Guarantee
   Corporation (PBGC)
Pension Reform Act
projective funding

QUESTIONS

26.1. Compare the amount of saving as a percentage of disposable income in the United States to that of other countries. What does this comparison suggest about the importance of pension funds in the U.S.?

26.2. Why were pension plans adversely affected during the Great Depression?

26.3. What was the main reason for the growth of pension plans during World War II and during the Korean War?

26.4. What is the danger of an underfunded pension plan?

26.5. Describe a defined-benefit pension plan.

26.6. Describe a defined-contribution plan, and explain how it differs from a defined-benefit plan.

26.7. What type of general guidelines may be specified for a trust that is managing a pension fund?

26.8. Why do some corporations allocate portions of their pension fund to be managed by different trusts (rather than using a single trust)?

26.9. Explain the general difference in the composition of pension portfolios managed by trusts versus insurance companies. Explain why this difference occurs.

26.10. Explain the risk-return characteristics of a leveraged buyout as a potential investment by pension portfolio managers.

26.11. Explain a general difference between the portfolio composition of private pension funds versus public pension funds.

26.12. How can pension funds reduce their exposure to interest rate risk?

26.13. What are bond index portfolios, and how are they useful to pension fund managers?

26.14. How can portfolio managers limit the downside risk of the pension portfolio, even when they make risky investments?

26.15. Explain why the objective of the pension fund manager may not necessarily be similar to the objective of employees participating in the pension plan.

26.16. Identify some common criticisms of private pension plans before 1974 that led to ERISA.

26.17. Explain how ERISA affected employees that frequently change employers.

26.18. How have some corporations used their pension plans as a source of funds to finance corporate operations?

26.19. What is the main purpose of the Pension Benefit Guarantee Corporation (PBGC)?

26.20. Describe possible remedies to potential funding problems of the PBGC.

693

REFERENCES

"A New Focus on Overseas Plans." *Institutional Investor* (July 1986): 109–112.

Antler, Jacob and Yehuda Kahane. "The Gross and Net Replacement Ratios in Designing Pension Schemes and In Financial Planning: The Israeli Experience." *Journal of Risk and Insurance* (June 1987): 283–297.

Arnott, Robert and Peter L. Bernstein. "The Right Way to Manage Your Pension Fund." *Harvard Business Review* (January–February 1988): 95–102.

"Beneficial: New Ways to Mass-Market Loans." *Fortune*, October 28, 1985, 41.

Cooper, Wendy. "Trying to Bridge the Pension Gap." *Institutional Investor* (May 1983): 115–122.

DeMagistris, Robin C. and Carl J. Palash. "Impact of IRAs on Saving." *Quarterly Review*, Federal Reserve Bank of New York (Winter 1982–83): 24–32.

Donnelly, Barbara. "Is Portfolio Insurance All It's Cracked Up to Be?" *Institutional Investor* (November 1986): 124–139.

Ehrlich, Edna E. "Foreign Pension Fund Investments in the United States." *Quarterly Review*, Federal Reserve Bank of New York (Spring 1983): 1–12.

Estrella, Arturo. "Corporate Use of Pension Overfunding." *Quarterly Review*, Federal Reserve Bank of New York (Spring 1984): 17–25.

Gropper, Diane Mal. "Are Leveraged Buy-outs Really for Pension Funds?" *Institutional Investor* (April 1983): 11–116.

Gropper, Diane Mal. "How Public Funds Are Waking Up." *Institutional Investor* (October 1983): 227–236.

Hubbard, R. Glenn. "Pension Wealth and Individual Saving." *Journal of Money, Credit, and Banking* (May 1986): 167–178.

Ippolito, Richard A. "The Economic Burden of Corporate Pension Liabilities." *Financial Analysts Journal* (January–February 1986): 22–34.

"Is There Life After Tax Reform?" *Institutional Investor* (December 1986): 142–155.

Jansson, Solveigh. "The Private Life of Public Funds." *Institutional Investor* (July 1984): 89–96.

Jansson, Solveigh. "Why Talk Is No Longer Cheap." *Institutional Investor* (October 1986): 255–262.

Laderman, Jeffrey. "Protecting Stock Profits If the Bear Attacks." *Businessweek*, March 31, 1986, 62.

Leibowitz, Martin L. "The Dedicated Bond Portfolio in Pension Funds—Part 1: Motivations and Basics." *Financial Analysts Journal* (January–February 1986): 68–75.

Leibowitz, Martin L. "Total Portfolio Duration: A New Perspective on Asset Allocation." *Financial Analysts Journal* (September–October 1986): 18–29.

Munnell, Alicia M. "Employee Benefits and the Tax Base." *New England Economic Review*, Federal Reserve Bank of Boston (January–February 1984): 39–55.

Munnell, Alicia M. "The Current Status of Social Security Financing." *New England Economic Review*, Federal Reserve Bank of Boston (May–June 1983): 46–62.

Munnell, Alicia H. "ERISA—The First Decade: Was the Legislation Consistent with Other National Goals?" *New England Economic Review*, Federal Reserve Bank of Boston (November–December 1984): 44–64.

Munnell, Alicia H. "Who Should Manage the Assets of Collectively Bargained Pension Plans?" *New England Economic Review* (July–August 1983): 18–30.

"Propping Up the PBGC." *Institutional Investor* (September 1986): 157–170.

Rohrer, July. "The Pension Management Party Is Over." *Institutional Investor* (November 1984): 61–68.

Rowland, Mary. "The Furor Over Workers' Compensation." *Institutional Investor* (May 1983): 231–240.

"The Abiding Faith in Active Management." *Institutional Investor* (May 1986): 97–100.

Insurance Companies

INSURANCE COMPANIES IN PERSPECTIVE

A review of Transamerica Corporation's financial status exemplifies how insurance companies are restructuring their operations:

■ Over the last two years, Transamerica has divested $1.1 billion of nonfinancial operations, including some group life and health operations of its life insurance companies. This allows Transamerica to focus its business on other financial services.

■ Transamerica has also acquired $1.1 billion of financial services businesses, which reflects a shift in diversification strategies. The diversification *within* the financial services area offers more opportunities of capitalizing on the firm's image and expertise.

■ In 1987, Transamerica acquired Borg-Warner Acceptance Corporation and changed its name to Transamerica Commercial Finance Corporation. This acquisition allowed Transamerica to enter the commercial lending market.

■ Transamerica has increased its leasing business. In 1987, operating earnings from leasing were $28 million, more than 150 percent above the previous year.

■ As Transamerica focused on specialized insurance businesses, its life insurance earnings stabilized somewhat, while its property and casualty insurance earnings increased substantially.

■ Transamerica's 1987 annual report states that only about 50 percent of its future earnings will result from its insurance businesses. The related financial services now offered by Transamerica will make up the remaining earnings.

■ What types of insurance are offered by insurance companies?
■ What risks do insurance companies face?
■ How do insurance companies participate in financial markets?
■ How do insurance companies interact with other financial institutions?
■ Why are insurance companies diversifying their services?

These and other related questions are addressed in this chapter.

OUTLINE

Insurance companies play a major role in financial markets by supplying funds to a variety of financial and nonfinancial corporations, as well as government agencies. This chapter first describes their role and then examines the various types of life insurance offered. Next, it identifies the main sources and uses of funds by life insurance companies and explains their asset management approach. It also describes the role of property and casualty insurance companies and explains how their characteristics differ from those of life insurance companies. Finally, it provides an overview of the regulatory aspects and performance in the insurance industry.

ROLE OF LIFE INSURANCE COMPANIES

Life insurance companies compensate (provide benefits to) the beneficiary of a policy upon the policyholder's death. They charge policyholders a premium that should reflect the probability of making a payment to the beneficiary as well as the size and timing of the payment. Despite the difficulty of forecasting the life expectancy of a given individual, life insurance companies have historically forecasted the benefits they would have to provide beneficiaries with reasonable accuracy. Since they hold a large portfolio of policies, they use actuarial tables and mortality figures to forecast the percent of policies that will require compensation over a given period, based on characteristics that would affect this percentage (such as the age distribution of policyholders).

OWNERSHIP OF LIFE INSURANCE COMPANIES

In 1987 there were 2,321 life insurance companies, classified by either stock or mutual ownership. A stock-owned company is owned by its stockholders, while a mutual life insurance company is owned by its policyholders. About 94 percent of U.S. life insurance companies are stock-owned, and in recent years some of the mutual life insurance companies converted to become stock-owned. As with the savings institutions industry, a primary reason for the conversions was to gain access to capital through the issuance of stock.

TYPES OF LIFE INSURANCE POLICIES

The face value of life insurance in the United States was $6.7 trillion as of 1987, covering about two-thirds of the U.S. population. In recent years, a variety of life insurance policies have been offered. Some of the more common types of policies are described here.

Whole-Life Insurance

From the perspective of the insured policyholders, **whole-life insurance** protects them until death or as long as premiums are promptly paid. In addition, whole-life policies provide a form of savings to policyholders. They build a *cash value* that the policyholder is entitled to even if the policy is cancelled.

From the perspective of the life insurance company, whole-life policies generate periodic (typically quarterly or semiannual) premiums that can be invested until the policyholder's death, at which time benefits are paid to the beneficiary. The amount of benefits is typically fixed.

Term Insurance

Term insurance is temporary, providing insurance only over a specified term, and does not build a cash value for policyholders. The premiums paid represent only insurance, not savings. It is, however, significantly less expensive than whole-life insurance. Policyholders must compare the cash value of whole-life insurance to their additional costs to determine whether it is preferable to term insurance. Those that prefer to invest their savings themselves would likely opt for term insurance.

To accommodate people who need more insurance now than later, decreasing term insurance is available in which the benefits paid to a beneficiary decrease over time. This form of insurance is common for a family with a mortgage. As time passes, the mortgage balance decreases, and the family is more capable of surviving without the breadwinner's earnings. Thus, less compensation would be needed in later years.

Variable Life Insurance

Under **variable life insurance,** the benefits awarded by the life insurance company to a beneficiary vary with the assets backing the policy. Until

1984, the premium payments on variable life insurance were constant over time. However, *flexible-premium* variable life insurance has been available since 1984, allowing flexibility on the size and timing of payments.

Universal Life Insurance

Universal life insurance combines the features of term and whole-life insurance. It specifies a period of time over which the policy will exist but also builds a cash value for policyholders over time. Interest is accumulated from the cash value until the policyholder uses those funds. Universal life insurance allows flexibility on the size and timing of the premiums, too. The growth in a policy's cash value is dependent on this pace. The premium payment is divided into two portions. The first is used to pay the death benefit identified in the policy and to cover any administrative expenses. The second is used for investments and reflects savings for the policyholder. The Internal Revenue Service forbids the value of these savings from exceeding the policy's death benefits.

Group Plans

Life insurance companies also commonly offer employees of a corporation a **group life policy.** This service has become quite popular and has generated a large volume of business in recent years. It can be distributed at a low cost because of its high volume. Group life coverage amounted to $2.8 trillion in 1987, or 42 percent of total life coverage, compared to only 26 percent of total life insurance coverage in 1974.

In recent years, group life insurance has often covered not only the group members but their respective dependents as well. Group policies are most popular for employers and employees. In addition, some unions and professional associations participate in these plans.

PROVISION OF HEALTH CARE INSURANCE

In recent years, insurance companies such as Cigna and Travelers Insurance have begun to operate **health maintenance organizations** (HMOs), which are intermediaries between purchasers and providers of health care. Employers of a company covered by an HMO are charged an annual fee or premium in return for provision of all medical expenses by a medical staff designated by the HMO. Because health care costs have been frequently underestimated, many HMOs experienced losses in recent years, and some insurance companies have sold their HMOs as a result.

SOURCES AND USES OF INSURANCE COMPANY FUNDS

Life insurance companies obtain much of their funds from premiums, as shown in Exhibit 27.1. Total premiums (life plus health insurance) represent about 39 percent of total income. The next most important source of funds is through provision of **annuity plans,** which offer a predetermined amount of retirement income to individuals. The annuity plans have become very

EXHIBIT 27.1 Distribution of U.S. Life Insurance Company Income

Source of Income	Amount (in Millions of Dollars)	Percentage of Total Income
Life insurance premiums	66,213	23.5%
Health insurance premiums	44,153	15.6
Annuity plans	83,712	29.7
Investment income	75,435	26.7
Other income	12,744	4.5
Total income	282,257	100.0%

SOURCE: American Council of Life Insurance, 1986 data.

popular, and now generate proportionately more income to insurance companies than in previous years. The third largest source of funds is *investment income,* which results from the investment of funds received from premium payments into securities.

The uses of funds by life insurance companies strongly influence their performance. Exhibit 27.2, which displays the assets of life insurance companies, indicates how funds have been used. Their main assets will be described.

Government Securities

Life insurance companies invest in U.S. Treasury securities, state and local government bonds, and foreign bonds. Exhibit 27.3 shows a consistent increased investment in each type of security over all years. The U.S. Treasury

EXHIBIT 27.2 Assets of U.S. Life Insurance Companies (in Millions of Dollars)

Dollar Assets	1987 Value	Percentage of Total Assets
Government securities		
U.S.	$ 65,186	6.4%
State and local	11,539	1.1
Foreign	14,502	1.4
Total	91,227	8.9
Corporate securities		
Bonds	459,537	44.8
Stocks	89,230	8.7
Total	548,767	53.5
Mortgages	208,839	20.4
Real estate	33,538	3.3
Policy loans	53,334	5.2
Other assets	88,755	8.7
Total assets	$1,024,460	100.0%

SOURCE: *Federal Reserve Bulletin* (November 1987).

EXHIBIT 27.3 Dollar Value of Government Security Holdings by Life Insurance Companies Over Time (in Millions of Dollars, End of Period)

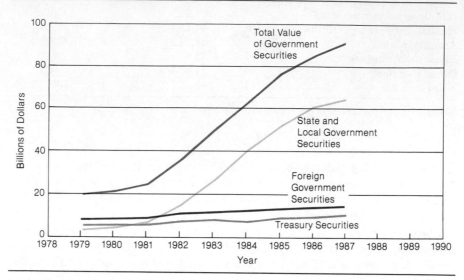

SOURCE: *Federal Reserve Bulletin*, various issues. November data were used for 1987.

securities are risk-free but generally offer a lower after-tax return than any other investments. Because of their active secondary market, they can accommodate any liquidity needs.

Corporate Securities

Corporate bonds represent the most popular asset of life insurance companies. There is usually a mix between short-, medium-, and long-term bonds for cash management and liquidity needs. Short-term rates are usually lower. While corporate bonds provide a higher yield than government securities, they have a higher degree of default risk.

Since life insurance companies expect to maintain a portion of their long-term securities until maturity, this portion can be somewhat illiquid. Thus, they have the flexibility to obtain some high-yielding, directly placed securities whereby they can directly negotiate the provisions. Because such non-standardized securities are less liquid, life insurance companies balance their asset portfolio with other more liquid securities. A minor portion of corporate securities are foreign. The foreign bond holdings typically represent industrialized countries and are therefore considered to have low default risk. Of course, the market values of these foreign bonds would still be susceptible to interest rate and currency fluctuations.

Insurance companies also invest in corporate stocks, although their holdings in stocks are significantly less than their bond holdings. Exhibit 27.4 illustrates the dollar value of bond and stock holdings over time. The dollar value of stock holdings has consistently increased, but not by as much as bond holdings.

EXHIBIT 27.4 **Dollar Value of Corporate Security Holdings by Life Insurance Companies Over Time (in Billions of Dollars, End of Period)**

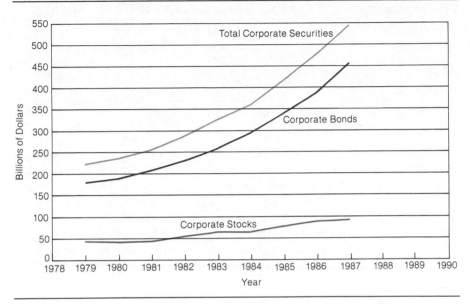

SOURCE: *Federal Reserve Bulletin,* various issues.

The stock market crash of October 1987 affected life insurance companies differently because of differences in the proportion of funds they allocated to stocks. For example, Prudential-Bache Securities Inc. had only about 3 percent of its funds invested in stocks at the time of the crash, lower than most other insurance companies. However, some of its other investments, such as junk bonds (used to finance leveraged buyouts) were adversely affected because the risk perception of investors increased in response to the crash.

Mortgages

Life insurance companies hold all types of mortgages, including one- to four-family, multifamily, commercial, and farm-related. These mortgages are typically originated by another financial institution and then sold to insurance companies in the secondary market. Yet, they are still serviced by the originating financial institution. As shown in Exhibit 27.5, commercial mortgages make up over 70 percent of total mortgages. They help to finance shopping centers and office buildings.

Real Estate

While life insurance companies finance real estate by purchasing mortgages, their return is limited to the mortgage payments, as they are simply acting as a creditor. In an attempt to achieve higher returns, they sometimes

Chapter 27

Insurance Companies

701

EXHIBIT 27.5   Breakdown of Mortgages Held by Insurance Companies

Type of Mortgage	Dollar Amount of Holdings (in Millions of Dollars)	Percent of Total Mortgage Holdings
1- to 4-family	$ 13,142	6.2%
Multifamily	22,168	10.5
Commercial	165,364	78.5
Farm	9,889	4.7
Total	$210,563	100.0%

SOURCE: *Federal Reserve Bulletin* (May 1988).

purchase the real estate themselves and lease it out for commercial purposes. The ownership of the real estate offers them the opportunity to generate very high returns but also exposes them to greater risk. Real estate values can be volatile over time and can have a significant effect on the market value of a life insurance company's asset portfolio.

Exhibit 27.6 illustrates the dollar value of mortgage and real estate holdings over time. While investment in both types of assets has grown over time, the mortgage holdings have been much larger.

Policy Loans

Life insurance companies lend a small portion of their funds to whole-life policyholders (called *policy loans*). Whole-life policyholders can borrow up to their cash value, at a guaranteed rate of interest as stated in their policy over a specified period of time. Other sources of funds for individuals typ-

EXHIBIT 27.6   Dollar Value of Mortgages and Real Estate Held by Life Insurance Companies Over Time (in Billions of Dollars, End of Period)

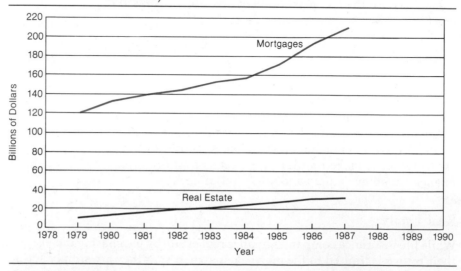

SOURCE: *Federal Reserve Bulletin*, various issues. November data were used for 1987.

ically do not guarantee an interest rate at which they can borrow. For this reason, policyholders tend to borrow more from life insurance companies during periods of rising interest rates, when other alternative forms of borrowing would be more expensive.

An additional use of funds is for *loss reserves*, which can be used to offset poor performance. Insurance companies must price their product (in terms of premiums) before they know the cost of goods sold (benefit payments). They establish loss reserves in order to absorb losses in rough periods. However, every dollar allocated as loss reserves is a dollar reduction in operating income.

Insurance actuaries normally forecast a range of losses for each class of business. A conservative approach would set the reserves according to the upper end of the loss range. Yet, because of the pressure to report positive income, many insurers have set abnormally low reserves. State regulators discourage abnormally low loss reserves but do not have the resources to monitor each company's reserve position.

Exhibit 27.7 compares the asset composition of life insurance companies at two points in time. The dominance of corporate securities is evident. The most pronounced increase in use of funds is in U.S. government securities, followed by bonds.

INSURANCE COMPANY EXPOSURE TO RISK

The three major types of risk faced by life insurance companies are interest rate risk, default risk, and liquidity risk. Each type is discussed in turn.

Interest Rate Risk

Because life insurance companies carry a large amount of fixed-rate long-term securities, the market value of their asset portfolio can be very sensitive

EXHIBIT 27.7 Change in Asset Composition of Life Insurance Companies Over Time

Assets	1980	1987
Government securities		
United States	1.1%	6.4%
State & local	1.4	1.1
Foreign	1.9	1.4
Total government securities	4.4	8.9
Corporate securities		
Bonds	39.8	44.8
Stocks	9.9	8.7
Total corporate securities	49.7	53.5
Mortgages	27.3	20.4
Real estate	3.2	3.3
Policy loans	8.7	5.2
Other assets	6.6	8.7
Total assets	100.0%	100.0%

Chapter 27

Insurance Companies

to interest rate fluctuations. As an example, as interest rates rose during the 1970s, life insurance companies were unable to fully capitalize on these rates, because much of their funds were tied up in long-term bonds. Exhibit 27.8 compares the yield on life insurer's invested assets to the yield on newly issued corporate bonds at various points in time. The yields to life insurers are significantly lower than the newly issued corporate bonds in all periods shown since 1970.

Life insurance companies have been reducing their average maturity on securities. In addition, they have been investing in long-term assets that offer floating rates, such as commercial mortgages. Both strategies reduce the impact of interest rate movements on the market value of their assets.

Default Risk

The corporate bonds, mortgages, and state and local government securities contained in the asset portfolio are subject to default risk. To deal with this risk, life insurance companies typically invest only in securities assigned a high credit rating. They also diversify among security issuers so that the repayment problems experienced by any single issuer will have only a minor impact on the overall portfolio.

A related risk to life insurance companies is *market risk*. Their real estate and corporate stock holdings may be adversely affected by an economic downturn. The values of these assets are determined by market conditions, which in turn depend on the state of the economy. To the extent that market conditions can cause a higher default rate, market risk and default risk overlap to a degree. A good example of market risk is the October 1987 stock market crash, which significantly reduced the market value of stock holdings of life insurance companies.

EXHIBIT 27.8   Yield Comparison of Life Insurer's Assets to Newly Issued Corporate Bonds

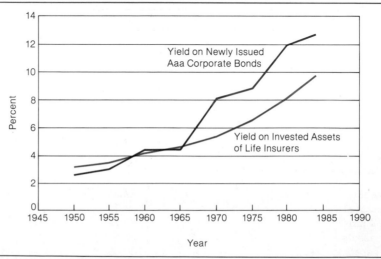

SOURCE: *Federal Reserve Bulletin* (July 1986): 451.

Impact of Unexpected Interest Rate Movements on Stock Returns of Life Insurance Companies

A recent study by Scott and Peterson assessed the sensitivity of life insurance companies to interest rate movements during the 1977–1984 period, using the following regression model:

$$r_p = B_0 + B_1 MI + B_2 r + e$$

where r_p = stock returns of a portfolio of life insurance companies

MI = percentage change in the market index (the S&P 500 Index was used as a proxy)

r = a measure of unexpected interest rate changes (see the article for an explanation of the proxy used for this variable)

B_0 = intercept

B_1 = regression coefficient that measures the sensitivity of stock returns to the market index returns

B_2 = regression coefficient that measures the sensitivity of stock returns to the interest rate movements

e = error term

The coefficient B_1 was estimated to be .793 by the regression analysis, suggesting that a 1 percent change in the market is associated with a .793 percent change in the portfolio returns. Thus, the life insurance stocks are positively correlated with the market. The coefficient B_2 was estimated to be $-.437$ by the regression analysis, suggesting that an unexpected 1 percent increase in interest rates is associated with a .437 percent decrease in stock returns of life insurance companies. This coefficient was found to be statistically significant. Thus, stock returns on life insurance companies are adversely affected by an unexpected increase in interest rates. These results are relevant to managers of life insurance companies and investors that consider purchasing stocks of such companies. Even if interest rates cannot be forecasted with perfect accuracy, investors would like to know how a company's stock returns will be affected by a variety of possible interest rate outcomes.

SOURCE: William L. Scott and Richard L. Peterson, "Interest Rate Risk and Equity Values of Hedged and Unhedged Financial Intermediaries," *Journal of Financial Research* (Winter 1986): 325–329.

Liquidity Risk

An additional risk to life insurance companies is liquidity risk. A high frequency of claims at a single point in time could force liquidation of assets at a time when the market value is low, thereby depressing performance. Yet, claims due to death are not likely to occur simultaneously. Life insurance companies can therefore reduce their exposure to this risk by diversifying the age distribution of their customer base. If the customer base becomes unbalanced and is heavily concentrated at the older age group, life insurance companies should increase their proportion of liquid assets in order to prepare for a higher frequency of claims.

Chapter 27

Insurance Companies

Even though life insurance companies can attempt to balance their age distribution, they are still susceptible to a liquidity deficiency. As interest rates rise, consumers tend to accelerate their voluntary terminations of life insurance and use the funds to make their own investments. Consequently, the cash inflows to life insurance companies are reduced, endangering their liquidity position.

Another liquidity concern results from the historical regulations on the interest rate at which life insurance companies can lend to their customers. In the past, when market interest rates exceeded these limits, customers often borrowed simply for the purpose of reinvesting the funds in assets earning higher returns. This type of arbitrage activity sometimes resulted in an annual return of 8 percent or more above the interest rate at which the funds were borrowed. Exhibit 27.9 compares loan activity and interest rates over time. When interest rates are high, loan activity is high, and the potential for deficient liquidity increases. In recent years, changes in state regulations have allowed life insurance companies more freedom to charge loan rates that more closely reflect the market. This will likely stabilize the volume of policy loans provided and reduce the liquidity risk experienced by life insurance companies.

ASSET MANAGEMENT

Because life insurance companies tend to receive premiums from policy-holders for several years before paying out benefits to a beneficiary, their performance can be significantly affected by asset portfolio management. Like other financial institutions, they adjust their asset portfolio to counter changes in the factors that affect their risk. If they expect a downturn in the economy, they may reduce their holdings of corporate stocks and real estate. If they expect higher interest rates, they may reduce their holdings of fixed-rate bonds and mortgages. As an example, the portfolio of Travelers Insurance Corporation generated large capital gains due to lower interest rates over the mid 1980s. In addition, it has attempted to diversify into

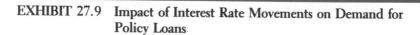

EXHIBIT 27.9 Impact of Interest Rate Movements on Demand for Policy Loans

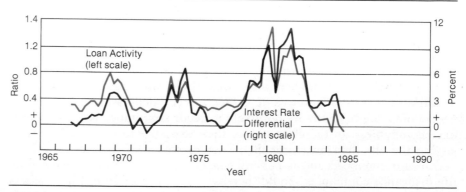

SOURCE: *Federal Reserve Bulletin* (July 1986): 452.

higher-yielding real estate and has paid more attention to global investments.

To cope with the existing forms of risk, life insurance companies attempt to balance their portfolio so that any adverse movements in the market value of some assets will be offset by favorable movements in others. For example, under the presumption that interest rates will move in tandem with inflation, life insurance companies can use real estate holdings to partially offset the potential adverse effect of inflation on bonds. When higher inflation causes higher interest rates, the market value of existing bonds decreases. However, the market values of real estate holdings tend to increase with inflation. Conversely, an environment of low or decreasing inflation may cause real estate values to stagnate but nevertheless have a favorable impact on the market value of bonds and mortgages (since interest rates would also likely be low). While such a strategy may be useful, it is much easier to implement on paper than in practice. Because real estate values can fluctuate to a great degree, life insurance companies allocate only a limited amount of funds to real estate. In addition, real estate is less liquid than most other assets.

Many insurance companies are diversifying into other businesses. For example, Traveler's Insurance Corporation and Prudential Bache provide a wide variety of financial products. Such a strategy not only provides diversification but enables these companies to package products when policyholders desire to cover all these needs at once.

Overall, life insurance companies want to earn a reasonable return while maintaining their risk at a tolerable level. The degree to which they avoid or accept the various forms of risk depends on their degree of risk aversion. Those companies that accept a greater amount of risk in the asset portfolio are likely to generate a higher return. However, if market conditions move in an unexpected manner, they will be more severely damaged than companies that employed a more conservative approach.

PROPERTY AND CASUALTY INSURANCE COMPANIES

Property and casualty (PC) insurance protects against fire, theft, liability, and other events that result in economic or noneconomic damage. Property insurance protects businesses and individuals from the impact of financial risks associated with the ownership of property, such as buildings, automobiles, and other assets. Casualty insurance insures potential liabilities for harm to others as a result of product failure or accidents. PC insurance companies charge policyholders a premium that should reflect the probability of providing indemnification. The possible degree of indemnification and the timing also affect the size of the premium. In 1987 there were more than 3,500 individual PC companies. No single company controls more than 10 percent of the property/casualty insurance market share.

The characteristics of PC insurance are much different from life insurance. First, the policies often last one year or less, as opposed to the long-term or even permanent life insurance policies. Second, PC insurance encompasses a wide variety of activities, ranging from auto insurance to business liability insurance. Life insurance is more focused. Third, future compensation amounts paid on PC insurance are more difficult to forecast than on life insurance. PC compensation depends on a variety of factors, including inflation, trends in terrorism, and the generosity of courts on lawsuits. These factors are difficult to forecast and can vary by areas of the country. Because of the greater uncertainty, PC insurance companies need to maintain a more liquid asset portfolio. Earnings can be quite volatile over time, as the premiums charged may be based on highly overestimated or underestimated compensation.

A unique aspect of the property and casualty insurance industry is its cyclical nature. As interest rates rise, companies tend to lower their rates to acquire more premium dollars to invest. They are hoping losses will hold off long enough to make the cheaper premium profitable through increased investment income. As interest rates decline, the price of insurance will rise to offset decreased investment income. If the timing of the cycle is not predicted well, a company can experience inadequate reserves and a drain on cash. This method of adapting prices to interest rates is called *cash flow underwriting*. It can backfire for companies that focus on what they can earn in the short run and ignore what they will pay out later.

The primary uses of funds for non-life (such as PC) insurance companies are illustrated in Exhibit 27.10. State and local government securities dominate and are followed by other debt instruments, then by corporate stock. The growth of the corporate stock holdings has been more volatile than that of the other two asset components. The most obvious difference in the asset structure of non-life insurance companies relative to life insurance companies is the much higher concentration of state and local government securities.

Impact of the Tax Reform Act

The Tax Reform Act of 1986 affected PC insurance companies in the following ways. It required that loss reserves, or funds reserved to pay future claims, be discounted. Prior to the act, loss reserves were tax-deductible in the year they were set aside, even if they were not used to cover future claims until a future point in time. The discounting of loss reserves enforced by the Tax Reform Act of 1986 essentially accounted for the interest income

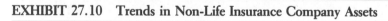

EXHIBIT 27.10   Trends in Non-Life Insurance Company Assets

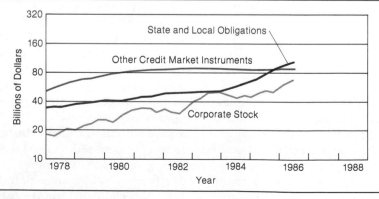

SOURCE: *Federal Reserve Chart Book.*

that could be earned by insurance companies that invest their loss reserves until they needed to cover claims.

A second provision of the Tax Reform Act affecting insurance companies is that 20 percent of unearned premium reserves (funds collected from premiums and set aside until the policy expires) must be included as taxable income. It also enforced an alternative minimum tax, requiring the company to pay the greater of this tax or the regular tax.

Third, the act requires that PC companies must convert 15 percent of their tax-exempt income into taxable income. Fourth, it requires that dividends received by the insurance companies from stock holdings are 80 percent tax-deductible (versus 85 percent before the act).

Overall, the Tax Reform Act causes more revenues to be taxable and reduces the tax-deductibility of some expenses. However, it adjusted the tax rate on corporate taxable income to 34 percent from 46 percent, which may offset the other tax changes.

REINSURANCE

Insurance companies commonly obtain **reinsurance,** which effectively allocates a portion of their return and risk to other insurance companies. It is similar to a commercial bank acting as the lending agent by allowing other banks to participate in the loan. A particular PC insurance company may agree to insure a corporation but spread the risk by inviting other insurance companies to participate. Reinsurance allows a company to write larger policies, since a portion of the risk involved will be assumed by other companies.

The estimated number of companies willing to offer reinsurance has declined significantly, due to generous court awards and the difficulty in assessing the amount of potential claims. For example, Centennial Insurance Company recently experienced losses of over $200 million in the reinsurance business as a result of underestimating the amount of potential claims. Reinsurance policies are often described in the insurance industry as "having long tails," which implies that the probability distribution of possible returns on reinsurance is widely dispersed. While many companies still offer reinsurance, their premiums have substantially increased in recent years. If the desire to offer reinsurance continues to decline, the primary insurers will be less able to "sell off" a portion of the risk they assume when writing policies. Consequently, they will be pressured to more closely evaluate the risk of the policies they write.

REGULATION OF INSURANCE COMPANIES

The insurance industry has been highly regulated, entirely by state agencies (called *commissioners* in some states). Each state attempts to make sure that insurance companies are providing adequate services and also approves the rates insurers may charge. Insurance company agents must be licensed. In addition, the forms used for policies are state-approved to avoid misinterpretation of wording.

State regulators also evaluate the asset portfolio of insurance companies to assure that reasonably safe investments are undertaken and that adequate reserves are maintained to protect policyholders. For example, some states have limited investment in junk bonds to no more than 20 percent of total assets.

The National Association of Insurance Commissioners (NAIC) facilitates cooperation among the various state agencies where an insurance issue is a national concern. It is involved in common reporting issues where it attempts to maintain a degree of uniformity. It also conducts research on insurance issues and participates in legislative discussions.

The Insurance Regulatory Information System (IRIS) has been developed by a committee of state insurance agencies to assist each state's regulatory duties. IRIS compiles financial statements, lists of insurers, and other relevant information pertaining to the insurance industry. In addition, it assesses the companies' respective financial statements by calculating 11 ratios that are then evaluated by NAIC regulators in order to monitor the financial health of a company. NAIC provides IRIS assessment results to all state insurance departments that can be used as a basis for comparison when evaluating the financial health of any company. The regulatory duties of state agencies often require a comparison of a particular insurance company to the industry norm. The comparison is conducted to assess one or more financial ratios of a company. Use of the industry norm facilitates the evaluation.

A regulatory system is designed to detect any problems of a company in time to search for a remedy before it deteriorates further. The more commonly used financial ratios assess a variety of relevant characteristics, including

- The ability of the company to absorb either losses or a decline in the market value of its investments
- Return on investment
- Relative size of operating expenses
- Liquidity of the asset portfolio

The objective of monitoring these characteristics is to assure that insurance companies do not become overly exposed to default risk, interest rate risk, and liquidity risk.

In June 1986 the New York state legislature adopted a *flex rating* regulation, whereby companies could adjust their rates only within limits. To change rates beyond these limits requires approval from the state insurance department. Other states have also begun to set limits on rates. In addition, several states now require that insurance companies provide advance notice of premium changes. Regulators also are requiring full company disclosure of financial information, so that they can determine whether premium adjustments are justified.

The regulation of rates is intended to help consumers. Yet, there is some concern that it will reduce competition and may force insurers to abandon insurance activities that are no longer profitable.

The flex rating system may reduce the degree of price cutting, since there would be a limit to percentage price increases later on. This could be beneficial, as price cutting was so severe in the mid 1980s that it devastated the performance of many insurers.

PERFORMANCE EVALUATION OF INSURANCE COMPANIES

Some of the more common indicators of an insurance company's performance are quoted in investment service publications such as *Value Line*. A time series assessment of the dollar amount of life insurance and/or property-casualty insurance premiums indicates the growth in the company's insurance business. A time series analysis of investment income can be used to assess the performance of the company's portfolio managers. However, the dollar amount of investment income is affected by several factors that are not under the control of portfolio managers, such as the amount of funds received as premiums that can be invested in securities, and market interest rates. In addition, a relatively low investment income may result from high concentration in stocks that pay low or no dividends rather than from poor performance.

Because insurance companies have unique characteristics, the financial ratios of other financial institutions are generally not applicable. Liquidity of an insurance company can be measured using the following ratio:

$$\text{liquidity ratio} = \frac{\text{invested assets}}{\text{loss reserves and unearned premium reserves}}$$

The higher the ratio is, the more liquid the company. This ratio can be evaluated by comparing it to the industry average.

The profitability of insurance companies is often assessed using the return on net worth (or policyholder's surplus) as a ratio, follows:

$$\text{return on net worth} = \frac{\text{net profit}}{\text{policyholder's surplus}}$$

Value Line refers to this ratio as "% earned net worth." *Net profit* consists of underwriting profits, investment income, and realized capital gains. Changes in this ratio over time should be compared to changes in the industry norms, since the norm is quite volatile over time.

The net profit encompasses all income sources and therefore provides only a general measure of profitability. Various financial ratios could be used to focus on a specific source of income. For example, underwriting gains or losses are measured by the net underwriting margin:

$$\text{net underwriting margin} = \frac{\text{premium income} - \text{policy expenses}}{\text{total assets}}$$

When policy expenses exceed premium income, the net underwriting margin is negative. Yet, as long as other sources of income can offset such a loss, net profit will still be positive.

INTERACTION OF INSURANCE COMPANIES WITH OTHER FINANCIAL INSTITUTIONS

Insurance companies interact with financial institutions in several ways, as summarized in Exhibit 27.11. They compete in one form or another with all types of financial institutions. As time passes, their penetration in these nontraditional markets will likely increase. In addition, other financial institutions will continue to increase their offerings of insurance-related services, so that differences between insurance companies and other financial institutions are diminished.

EXHIBIT 27.11 Interaction between Insurance Companies and Other Financial Institutions

Type of Financial Institution	Interaction with Insurance Companies
Commercial banks and savings and loan associations (S&Ls)	■ Insurance companies compete with banks and S&Ls for financing leveraged buyouts. ■ Insurance companies sometimes compete with banks and S&Ls by offering CDs. ■ Insurance companies sometimes compete with banks by offering an account from which checks can be written. ■ Insurance companies merge with banks in order to offer various banking services. ■ Insurance companies may face more competition for insurance-related services as banks and S&Ls attempt to offer such services.
Finance companies	■ Insurance companies are sometimes acquired by finance companies and maintained as subsidiaries.
Securities firms	■ Insurance companies compete directly with securities firms by offering mutual funds.
Brokerage firms	■ Insurance companies compete directly with brokerage firms by offering securities-related services. ■ Insurance companies compete directly with brokerage firms that offer insurance-related services; many brokerage firms, such as Merrill Lynch now offer a wide variety of insurance-related services and plan to increase their offerings in the future.
Investment banking firms	■ Insurance companies compete with investment companies for financing leveraged buyouts. ■ Insurance companies commonly purchase stocks and bonds issued by corporations that were underwritten by investment banking firms. ■ Insurance companies issue stock that is underwritten by investment banking firms.
Pension funds	■ Insurance companies offer to manage pension plans for corporations.

PARTICIPATION BY INSURANCE COMPANIES IN FINANCIAL MARKETS

The manner by which insurance companies use their funds indicates their form of participation in the various financial markets. They are common participants in the stock, bond, and mortgage markets because their asset portfolio is concentrated in these securities. They also use the money markets to purchase short-term securities for liquidity purposes. While their participation in money markets is less than in capital markets, they have recently increased their holdings of money market instruments such as Treasury bills and commercial paper. Some insurance companies use futures and options markets to hedge the impact of interest rates on bonds and mortgages and to hedge against anticipated movements in stock prices. The participation by insurance companies in the futures and options markets is generally for risk-reduction rather than speculation. Exhibit 27.12 summarizes the manner by which life insurance companies participate in financial markets.

MULTINATIONAL INSURANCE COMPANIES

INTERNATIONAL

ASPECTS

Some life insurance companies are multinational corporations with subsidiaries and joint ventures in several countries. They became internationalized as a result of their efforts to penetrate new markets and to serve firms that operate overseas. In 1988, Prudential-Bache Securities Inc. announced its intentions to increase its offerings of global financial services. Insurance companies with some international business may have reduced their exposure to the U.S. economy. However, they must comply with foreign regulations regarding services offered in foreign countries. While differences in regulations among countries increases the information costs of entering foreign markets, it may enable U.S. insurance companies to offer products or services that they could not offer in the United States.

The reinsurance business is enhanced by international participation. U.S. insurance companies earn premiums when assuming specified risks from foreign insurance companies.

Many insurance companies use a portion of their funds to purchase foreign stocks and bonds. This investment strategy became more popular during the 1985–1988 period, when non–U.S. securities generated high returns to U.S. investors as a result of the weak dollar. The investment in foreign securities was just one more way in which insurance companies could diversify their assets. Some of the foreign bonds purchased were issued by corporations, while others were issued by governments and international agencies. Because insurance companies have increased their investment in foreign securities, they more closely monitor the factors that influence foreign security returns, such as foreign stock market movements, foreign interest rates, and exchange rates.

Insurance companies have not only invested in foreign securities but also in foreign real estate as well. The majority of foreign real estate purchased by U.S. insurance companies is in Canada.

EXHIBIT 27.12   Participation of Insurance Companies in Financial Markets

Financial Market	Participation by Insurance Companies
Money markets	■ Insurance companies maintain a portion of their funds in money market securities, such as Treasury bills and commercial paper, in order to maintain adequate liquidity.
Bond markets	■ About 36 percent of life insurance company assets and 9 percent of PC insurance company assets are allocated to corporate bond portfolios. ■ Insurance companies frequently purchase bonds that are "directly placed," and they are less likely to liquidate these bonds before maturity. ■ Insurance companies also purchase Treasury bonds for their safety and liquidity. ■ Some U.S. insurance companies purchase foreign bonds, primarily issued by Canadian firms.
Mortgage markets	■ Life insurance companies have, in aggregate, allocated about 20 percent of their assets to a mortgage portfolio. They hold mostly conventional mortgages, as only a small percentage of their mortgages are federally insured. While PC companies also hold mortgages, their mortgage portfolio represents a smaller percentage of total assets.
Stock markets	■ Life insurance companies have, in aggregate, allocated about 9 percent of their assets to a stock portfolio, while PC companies have allocated about 17 percent of their assets to a stock portfolio. Foreign stocks are often included in their stock portfolios.
Futures markets	■ Some insurance companies sell futures contracts on bonds or a bond market index to hedge their bond and mortgage portfolios against interest rate risk. ■ Some insurance companies take positions in stock market index futures to hedge their stock portfolios against market risk.
Options markets	■ Some insurance companies purchase call options on particular stocks that they plan to purchase in the near future. ■ Some insurance companies also purchase put options or write call options on stocks they own that may experience a temporary decline in price.

While insurance companies have increased their holdings of foreign assets, they have been targeted by foreign companies as takeover candidates. The foreign interest in U.S. insurance companies grew as a result of the potential loosening of regulations in the insurance industry. In addition, the weak dollar in 1988 was another incentive, since foreign companies could acquire U.S. insurance companies at a low price. At least 20 insurance companies in the United States are owned by firms from Europe or Japan.

While foreign markets offer insurance companies the opportunity for growth and geographic diversification, they also have some disadvantages. The governments in some countries may block entry, impose unfavorable tax rates on foreign insurance companies, or discourage the public from purchasing insurance from such companies. Exchange rate movements may adversely affect the value of cash flows remitted by the foreign insurance subsidiaries to the parent. The host government may impose restrictions on exchange rate convertibility in order to prevent the remittance of cash flows. Finally, the host government may acquire corporations, providing whatever compensation it believes is reasonable. While all of these types of risk must be assessed, they are much more likely to occur in some countries than in others.

RECENT DEVELOPMENTS IN INSURANCE COMPANIES

The business characteristics of insurance companies are rapidly changing in terms of the services offered and investment strategies. With regard to services, life insurance companies have created new types of insurance such as the **universal-variable policy,** which allows flexible premium payments (similar to a universal life insurance policy), and investment alternatives (similar to a variable policy).

Like all other types of financial institutions, insurance companies have attempted to enter new product and service markets as a means of diversification. For example, some insurance companies offer certificates of deposit to investors, thereby competing directly with commercial banks for these offerings. In addition, Metropolitan Life Insurance Company recently began to offer a cash management account from which checks can be written. Those insurance companies that have merged with brokerage firms (Prudential-Bache Securities Inc. is a prominent example) offer a wide variety of securities-related services. Several insurance companies offer mutual funds to investors.

In recent years, insurance companies have used aggressive investment policies, investing in oil and gas drilling partnerships and financing leveraged buyouts. These forms of investments offer a higher expected return than more traditional investment instruments but also have a higher degree of default risk. Much of the investment in leveraged buyouts has been through the purchase of junk bonds. While junk bonds have had a low default rate in recent years, a recession could cause an abrupt increase in defaults.

Insurance companies have become more aware of their exposure to interest rate risk and more knowledgable about techniques to hedge the risk, increasingly utilizing futures contracts and interest rate swaps to manage their exposure.

SUMMARY

Insurance companies not only provide financial services to consumers, but also facilitate the flow of funds by investing funds in stocks and debt instruments. They provide financing to the Treasury, state and local governments, and corporations. They also help to create an active secondary mortgage market by serving as a common purchaser of existing mortgages. The asset management of insurance companies, as with other financial institutions, balances the desire for high return with exposure to risk.

The unique characteristics of insurance companies require a greater degree of regulation than many other industries. Some of the more important regulatory functions aim to prevent unfair practices and enhance overall performance. To achieve this objective, the balance sheet components and activities of insurance companies are closely monitored.

Fierce competition has encouraged insurance companies to search for new products and services. Like commercial banks, they are striving to become the consumer's one-stop shop for financial services. The future asset composition and performance of insurance companies depend largely on the services and products that regulators allow them to offer.

KEY TERMS

annuity plans
group life policy
health maintenance organizations
reinsurance
term insurance

universal life insurance
universal-variable policy
variable life insurance
whole-life insurance

QUESTIONS

27.1. How is whole-life insurance a form of savings to policyholders?

27.2. How do whole-life and term insurance differ from the perspective of insurance companies? From the perspective of the policyholders?

27.3. Identify the characteristics of universal life insurance.

27.4. Explain group life insurance.

27.5. What are the main assets of life insurance companies? Identify the main categories.

27.6. How do insurance companies finance real estate?

27.7. What is a policy loan? When are they popular? Why?

27.8. What is the main use of funds by life insurance companies?

27.9. What are two strategies that reduce the impact of changing interest rates on the market value of life insurance companies' assets?

27.10. What has recent research found with respect to the sensitivity of life insurance equity values to interest rate movements?

27.11. How do insurance companies manage default risk and liquidity risk?

27.12. Discuss the liquidity risk experienced by life insurance companies concerning policy loans. Be sure to identify any changes that may have occurred.

27.13. What purpose do property and casualty (PC) insurance companies serve?

27.14. Identify the different characteristics of PC insurance as compared to life insurance.

27.15. Explain the concept of cash flow underwriting.

27.16. Explain how a life insurance company's asset portfolio may be affected by inflation.

27.17. What is reinsurance?

27.18. What is NAIC, and what is its purpose?

PROJECT

1. FINANCIAL ASSESSMENT OF AN INSURANCE COMPANY.

Obtain annual reports and an investment survey summary (such as *Value Line*) for a particular life insurance company of your choice or one assigned by your professor, and answer the following questions:

a. How has its asset portfolio composition changed in recent years?

b. Have the recent changes in asset composition affected the company's risk and potential return?

c. How do you think the company would be affected by an increase in interest rates? Explain.

d. Based on its recent annual report, does the company appear to be increasing its nontraditional services? Elaborate.

REFERENCES

Cross, Mark, Wallace Davidson III and John Thornton. "The Impact of a Captive Insurance Company's Formation on a Firm's Value After the Carnation Case." *Journal of Business Research* (August 1987): 329–338.

Mayers, David and Clifford W. Smith. "Ownership Structure and Control: The Mutualization of Stock Life Insurance Companies." *Journal of Financial Economics* (May 1986): 73–98.

Milligan, John W. "Can Hank Greenberg Keep the Magic Alive at AIG?" *Institutional Investor* (January 1986): 288–290.

Milligan, John W. "Second Thoughts About Loss Reserves." *Institutional Investor* (May 1986): 295–302.

Rosenberg, Hilary. "Can Insurers Live with Rate Regulation?" *Institutional Investor* (October 1986): 329–332.

Samson, Dannys and Howard Thomas. "Linear Models as Aids in Insurance Decision-Making: The Estimation of Automobile Insurance Claims." *Journal of Business Research* (June 1987): 247–256.

Scott, William L. and Richard L. Peterson. "Interest Rate Risk and Equity Values of Hedged and Unhedged Financial Intermediaries." *Journal of Financial Research* (Winter 1986): 325–329.

Glossary

Adjustable-rate mortgage (ARM) Allows the mortgage interest rate to adjust to market conditions.

American depository receipts (ADRs) Certificates that represent ownership of a foreign stock.

Amortization schedule Schedule of monthly payments of principal and interest for a mortgage, based on the maturity and interest rate of the mortgage.

Annuity An even stream of payments over a given period of time.

Annuity plans Offer a predetermined amount of retirement income to individuals.

Appreciate An increase in the value of a currency.

Ask quote Price at which one (usually a broker or dealer) is willing to sell a security (or commodity).

Balloon-payment mortgage Mortgage requiring interest payments for a specified period and full payment of principal (a balloon payment) at the end of the period.

Banker's acceptance Represents a bank accepting responsibility for a future payment.

Best-efforts agreement Placement of securities by an investment banking firm (IBF) in which the IBF does not guarantee a price to the issuing corporation.

Beta Measurement of the sensitivity of an individual asset's return to the market return.

Bid quote Price at which one (usually a broker or dealer) is willing to purchase a security (or commodity).

Blanket mortgage A bond issue that is backed by all of the firm's real property.

Bond price elasticity Measurement of the sensitivity of bond prices to interest rate movements; specifically, it measures the percentage change in bond prices in response to a percentage change in interest rates.

Bridge loans Loans provided to firms involved in mergers or leveraged buyouts until bonds can be issued.

Call feature Provision that allows the issuer of bonds to buy them back before maturity at a specific price.

Call premium (on bonds) Difference between the bond's par value and call price.

Capital Primarily consists of retained earnings and funds obtained from issuing stock.

Capital appreciation funds Mutual funds consisting of stocks that have the potential for very high growth, but may also be unproven.

Capital asset pricing model (CAPM) Valuation model used to estimate the return of an asset, given a measurement of the asset's beta, the risk-free rate, and the market return.

Capital market instruments Securities that have a maturity of more than one year.

Capital markets Markets where long-term (capital market) securities and stocks are traded.

Capital ratio Ratio of capital to assets.

Captive finance subsidiary A wholly owned subsidiary whose primary purpose is to finance sales of the parent company's products and services, provide wholesale financing to distributors of the parent company's products, and purchase receivables of the parent company.

Chattel mortgage Mortgage secured by personal property.

Closed-end mortgage bond Debt security with provisions which prohibit the firm from issuing additional bonds with the priority of claim against assets.

Closed-end mutual funds Mutual funds that do not repurchase their shares from investors; the shares are sold in a secondary market, such as on a stock exchange.

Collateral trust bonds Type of chattel mortgages that are normally secured by common stock and/or bonds issued by subsidiaries of the issuing firm.

Collateralized mortgage obligations (CMOs) Mortgage-backed securities, segmented into tranches, so that investors can choose a tranche that fits their desired timing of payments.

Commission brokers Execute orders for their customers.

Consumer finance companies Concentrate on direct loans to consumers.

Convertibility clause Allows investors to convert bonds into a specified number of common stock shares.

Corporate bonds Debt securities issued by corporations, typically having a maturity of ten years or longer.

Cross-hedging The use of a futures contract on one financial instrument to hedge a position in a different financial instrument.

Crowding-out effect Effect of excessive government borrowing, which can place upward pressure on interest rates and crowd out private borrowers (such as firms and individuals).

Currency futures contracts Futures contracts that allow one to purchase or sell a specified currency at a specified price on a specified settlement date.

Dealers Make a market in specific securities by adjusting their inventory of securities.

Debentures Long-term debt securities unsecured by specific property.

Debt management Decisions by the Treasury to finance the deficit.

Debt securities Represent IOUs; the purchasers of debt securities are creditors.

Deficit units Financial market participants that obtain funds from the markets.

Defined-benefit plan Pension plan that provides benefits as specified by the plan.

Defined-contribution plan Pension plan that provides benefits as determined by the accumulated contributions and the return on the fund's investment performance; the contributions are specified, but the benefits are not.

Demand-pull inflation Inflation resulting from excessive demand.

Depreciate A decrease in the value of a currency.

Dirty float System whereby exchange rates are market determined, without boundaries, but subject to government intervention.

Discount broker Executes transactions, but is not allowed to offer advice.

Discount rate Interest rate which the Federal Reserve charges for loans provided to depository institutions through the discount window.

Duration Method of measuring the sensitivity of particular bonds or a bond portfolio to interest rate movements; the longer a bond's duration, the greater is its sensitivity to interest rates.

Edge Act corporations Established by commercial banks to specialize in international banking and foreign transactions.

Equity REIT A closed-end mutual fund that invests directly in properties.

Equity securities Refer to common stock or preferred stock, and represent ownership in a business.

Eurobanks Banks that participate in the Eurocurrency market by accepting deposits and providing loans in foreign currencies.

Euro-commercial paper Short-term securities issued by corporations in foreign markets without the backing of a banking syndicate.

Eurocredit market Market in which banks provide Eurocredit loans, which usually have medium-term maturities and are denominated in various foreign currencies.

Eurocurrency market Market in which banks accept deposits and provide loans in foreign currencies.

Eurodollar certificate of deposit Large U.S. dollar deposits placed in non-U.S. banks.

Eurodollar floating-rate CDs Eurodollar CDs that have floating interest rates over time; the rates are tied to LIBOR or some other market-determined interest rate.

Eurodollar market Market in which banks outside the U.S. accept dollar deposits and provide dollar loans.

European Currency Unit (ECU) Unit of account that represents a weighted average of European exchange rates; the ECU is the base unit of account to which various European currency values are pegged.

Factor A firm (typically a finance company) that purchases a firm's receivables at a discount and is responsible for processing and collecting the balances of these accounts.

Federal funds rate Interest rate at which depository institutions lend funds to each other in the federal funds market.

First mortgage bond Long-term security that has first claim on specified assets.

Fisher effect Relationship between interest rates and expected inflation; the nominal interest rate is thought to equal a real interest rate plus the expected inflation rate.

Fixed-rate mortgage Specifies an interest rate that remains fixed for the life of the mortgage regardless of market conditions.

Floor traders Trade contracts for their own account.

Flotation costs Costs of placing securities.

Forward exchange rate Exchange rate at which one currency can be converted into another currency for a specified future date.

Forward rate Represents the market's forecast of the future interest rate (under specified conditions).

Freely floating system System in which exchange rates are determined entirely by market forces, without any government intervention.

Full-service broker Provides information and advice, in addition to executing transactions.

Gap Difference between interest rate-sensitive assets and interest rate-sensitive liabilities.

General obligation bonds Debt securities issued by municipalities in which the payments are supported by their ability to tax.

Graduated-payment mortgage Mortgage that allows payments to rise on a graduated basis over the first five to ten years, and level off from then on.

Group life policy Insurance policy covering a group of policyholders who share a similar affiliation such as an employer or union.

Growing-equity mortgage Mortgage that allows payments to rise on a graduated basis throughout the life of the mortgage.

Growth funds Mutual funds that are composed of stocks of companies that are still experiencing growth; the objective is to generate an increase in investment value, with less concern about the provision of steady income.

Health maintenance organizations (HMOs) Intermediaries between purchasers and providers of health care.

Immunize To insulate a portfolio of securities from the effect of interest rate movements.

Income funds Mutual funds consisting of securities that provide periodic dividends or coupon payments; they usually consist of coupon bonds; they are designed to provide investors with a stable income.

Insured plans Pension plans that are managed by life insurance companies.

Interest rate cap Agreement (for a fee) to receive payments when the interest rate of a particular security or index rises above a specified level during a specified time period.

Interest rate parity Relationship between the interest rate differential and a forward premium (or discount).

Interest rate risk Risk that the market value of assets will decline in response to interest rate movements.

Interest rate swaps A swap of fixed-rate payments for variable-rate payments.

Interest-inelastic Reference to a demand for (or supply of) funds schedule that reflects insensitivity of the quantity demanded (or supplied) to interest rate levels.

International Banking Act (IBA) Key banking law that restricted foreign-owned banks from accepting deposits across state lines.

Investment-grade bonds Bonds that are rated as Baa or better by Moody's and BBB or better by Standard and Poor's.

Issue costs Costs of issuing securities, including printing, legal, registration, and accounting expenses.

Junk bonds Low-grade long-term debt securities.

Limit orders Requests by customers to purchase or sell securities at the market price existing when the order reaches the exchange floor.

Limited open-end mortgage Debt security that allows a firm to issue a specified amount of additional debt with the same priority of claim against the assets.

Liquidity premium theory Theory suggesting that investors prefer securities that are more liquid; to the extent that long-term securities are less liquid, investors require a premium to invest in these securities, other things being equal; this can affect the shape of a yield curve.

Load mutual fund A mutual fund that charges a fee (load) to investors who purchase shares.

Loan participation Loan provided by a group of lenders to a single borrower, which spreads the default risk of the loan among all lenders in the group.

Loanable funds theory Theory of interest rate determination based on the demand and supply of loanable funds.

Locational arbitrage The act of purchasing a currency at one bank (location) and selling at another, to capitalize on a discrepancy in exchange rates.

M₁ A measure of money, consisting of currency held by the public and checkable deposits at depository institutions.

M₂ A measure of money, consisting of M_1, plus savings accounts, small time deposits, money market deposit accounts, money market funds, and some other items.

Major Market Index (MMI) Represents 20 stocks; its movements are very similar to that of the Dow Jones Industrial Average.

Margin call Call from a broker that requires additional margin money.

Market orders Requests by customers to purchase or sell securities at the market price existing when the order reaches the exchange floor.

Matched funding Investment strategy used by some pension funds to generate cash flows that will match planned outflow payments.

Merger-conversion An arrangement for a mutual savings and loan association (S&L) to convert to stock ownership prior to merging with another S&L.

Money market deposit accounts (MMDAs) Accounts offered by depository institutions from which a limited number of checks can be written and an interest rate is offered.

Money market instruments Securities that have a maturity of one year or less.

Money market mutual funds Portfolios that are created by selling shares to investors; proceeds are used to invest in money market securities.

Money markets Markets where short-term (money market) securities are traded.

Moral hazard Refers to banks being encouraged to take risk when deposit insurance pricing does not penalize risk-taking.

Mortgage pass-through securities Debt securities that offer payments that are passed through the issuer (as mortgage payments) to investors.

Mortgage REIT A closed-end mutual fund that invests in mortgage and construction loans.

Municipal Bond Index (MBI) futures A futures contract on an index based on the Bond Buyer Index of 40 actively traded general obligation and revenue bonds.

Municipal bonds Debt securities issued by municipalities.

Negotiable certificate of deposit (CD) Security issued by large commercial banks and other depository institutions as a short-term source of funds; it typically specifies a fixed interest rate and has a maturity of one year or less.

No-load mutual fund A fund that does not charge a fee (load) to investors who purchase shares.

One-bank holding companies Company that owns a commercial bank.

Open-end mortgage bond Long-term debt security with provisions in which the firm can issue additional debt in the future using the same assets as collateral and giving the same priority of claim against those assets.

Open-end mutual funds Mutual funds that are willing to repurchase their shares from investors at any time.

Organized exchange Visible marketplace for secondary market transactions (examples are the New York Stock Exchange and the American Stock Exchange).

Participation certificates Debt securities issued by the Federal Home Loan Mortgage Association, in which the proceeds are used to finance the origination of conventional mortgages at financial institutions.

Portfolio insurance Insulating a portfolio's market value against interest rate movements and market movements.

Preemptive rights Priority rights granted to a group of people (such as existing shareholders) to purchase new stock.

Preferred habitat theory Theory suggesting that while investors and borrowers may normally concentrate on a particular natural maturity market, certain events may cause them to wander from their natural maturity habitat.

Primary markets Markets that facilitate the placement of newly issued securities.

Private placement Placement of securities directly to investors.

Projective funding Investment strategy that allows pension portfolio managers flexibility in constructing the portfolio to benefit from expected market and interest rate movements.

Publicly issued pass-through securities (PIPs) Securities backed by conventional mortgages (which are insured by private insurance companies).

Purchasing power parity (PPP) Theory suggesting that the exchange rate will, on average, change by a percentage that reflects the inflation differential between two countries.

Real estate investment trust (REIT) A closed-end mutual fund that invests in real estate or mortgages.

Registration statement Statement that assures that accurate information is disclosed by the issuing corporation about the securities to be issued, and its agreement with the investment banking firm that will place the securities.

Regulation Q Placed interest rate ceilings on savings deposits.

Repurchase agreement Represents the sale of securities by one party to another with an agreement to repurchase the securities at a specified date and price.

Return on assets (ROA) Ratio of net income to total assets.

Return on equity (ROE) Ratio of net income to equity.

Revenue bonds Debt securities issued by municipalities in which the payments must be generated by the project supported by the proceeds from the bonds issued.

Riding the yield curve Represents the purchasing of securities with longer term maturities than the planned investment horizon during periods in which the yield curve is upward-sloping.

Sales finance companies Concentrate on purchasing credit contracts from retailers and dealers.

Secondary markets Markets that facilitate the transfer of existing securities among financial market participants.

Segmented markets theory Theory suggesting that investors and borrowers choose securities that satisfy their forecasted cash needs; such needs can influence the demand for short-term versus long-term securities, the supply of short-term versus long-term securities for sale, and therefore, the shape of the yield curve.

Shared appreciation mortgage Mortgage that specifies a below-market interest rate; the lender is compensated for offering such attractive rates by sharing in the appreciation of the home upon the sale of the home.

Sharpe Index Measurement of a security's performance, which reflects the average excess return of the security (above the risk-free rate) relative to the security's standard deviation (a measure of risk).

Shelf-registration Registering to issue new securities prior to actual issuance; this process allows firms to issue securities when desired without a registration delay (assuming registration was completed earlier).

Short selling Selling securities that are borrowed, and later repaying the broker (who lent the stock) for the stock borrowed.

Special drawing rights (SDRs) Unit of account that represents a weighted average of exchange rates of major currencies; SDRs represent an international reserve asset created by the International Monetary Fund.

Spot exchange rate Exchange rate at which one currency can be converted into another currency for immediate delivery.

Standby letter of credit Provides a bank's guarantee on the financial obligations of a borrower to a specific party.

Stop-loss order The order of a sale of securities when the price reaches a specified minimum.

Strike price Price at which an option is exercised.

Subordinated debentures Long-term debt securities that are junior to the claims of both mortgage bonds and regular debentures.

Surplus units Financial market participants that provide funds to the markets.

Systematic risk Variability of a security that is due to market movements; this type of risk is also referred to as nondiversifiable risk.

Term insurance Insurance that is effective only over a specified term, and does not build a cash value for policyholders.

Term structure of interest rates Relationship between term to maturity and annualized yield for securities whose other characteristics are similar.

Treynor Index Measurement of a security's performance, which reflects the average excess return of the security (above the risk-free rate) relative to the security's beta (a measure of systematic risk).

Underwrite To guarantee the issuer of securities a specific price.

Underwriting spread Difference between the price an investment banking firm is willing to pay for stock and the price at which it expects to sell the securities.

Underwriting syndicate Group of IBFs which participate in underwriting securities.

Universal life insurance Insurance over a specified period of time, which builds a cash value for policyholders over time.

Universal-variable policy Allows flexible premium payments and investment alternatives for policyholders.

Variable life insurance Insurance that offers benefits which vary with the assets backing the policy.

Whole-life insurance Insurance that protects policyholders until death, and builds a cash value that the policyholder is entitled to, even if the policy is cancelled.

Yield curve The connection of points representing each security's term to maturity and annualized yield; the slope of the yield curve indicates how the annualized yield is influenced by the term to maturity.

Yield surface Graphic illustration of how a yield curve shifts over time.

Yield to maturity The return to investors in bonds; it represents the discount rate at which the future payments to be generated by the bonds equals the purchase price of the bonds.

Zero-coupon bond Bond that pays no coupon payments.

Index